PENGUIN REFERENCE

Citizens Advice Guide to Your Rights

From its origins as an emergency service during the Second World War, the Citizens Advice Bureau service has evolved into a network of charities that offers free, confidential, impartial and independent advice, helping to resolve five and a half million new problems every year.

D0784997

The Citizens Advice Guide to Your Rights

Practical, independent advice

Citizens Advice

PENGUIN BOOKS

PENGUIN BOOKS

Published by the Penguin Group

Penguin Books Ltd, 80 Strand, London WC2R ORL, England

Penguin Group (USA) Inc., 375 Hudson Street, New York, New York 10014, USA

Penguin Group (Canada), 90 Eglinton Avenue East, Suite 700, Toronto, Ontario, Canada M4P 2Y3
(a division of Pearson Penguin Canada Inc.)

Penguin Ireland, 25 St Stephen's Green, Dublin 2, Ireland
(a division of Penguin Books Ltd)

Penguin Group (Australia), 250 Camberwell Road, Camberwell, Victoria 3124, Australia
(a division of Pearson Australia Group Pty Ltd)

Penguin Books India Pvt Ltd, 11 Community Centre, Panchsheel Park, New Delhi – 110 017, India

Penguin Group (NZ), 67 Apollo Drive, Rosedale, North Shore 0632, New Zealand
(a division of Pearson New Zealand Ltd)

Penguin Books (South Africa) (Pty) Ltd, 24 Sturdee Avenue, Rosebank 2196, South Africa

Penguin Books Ltd, Registered Offices: 80 Strand, London WC2R ORL, England

www.penguin.com

First published 2008

4

Set in 9.5/12pt PostScript Minion with TheSans display

Typeset by Data Standards Ltd, Frome, Somerset

Printed in England by Clays Ltd, St Ives plc

Contents

Acknowledgements

This edition would not have been possible without the enthusiasm and skills of Helen Brown and her colleagues in the Information Department at Citizens Advice.

Introduction

We might like to think that there was a time when our lives weren't ruled by the millions of laws, regulations, codes of practice, guidelines and procedures that surround us today. The reality is that the freedoms we hold dear are all exercised within a delicately balanced framework of rights and responsibilities, enshrined in all of that legislation. We need those laws but, for most people, finding your way around the systems and structures that hold them, especially if it's urgent and you've got a crisis on your hands, can be a nightmare.

The *Citizens Advice Guide to Your Rights* is designed to give you the basic information you need to get your head around a problem that needs solving, quickly and easily, whenever you need it. It gives advice about how to tackle the issue you face and where to look for further professional assistance and support.

In buying this book, you have bought into almost 70 years of Citizens Advice Bureau expertise in giving information and advice to the public. Citizens Advice Bureaux know from experience that what people want is independent, reliable and jargon-free information about their rights and responsibilities. They want to know where they stand, what they can do about the problems they face and who can help them. This is what this book will tell you.

The advice and information in these pages is based on AdviserNet, the Citizens Advice electronic information system, continuously updated and used by all CAB advisers – mostly trained volunteers – to help people with five and a half million problems each year. No other information database can rival it for breadth and accuracy. Although you may be able to find all of this information elsewhere – in a thousand libraries and a million websites – the *Citizens Advice Guide to Your Rights* is the only place you'll find it *all in one place* on your bookshelf.

Each chapter will give you:

- a practical understanding of a particular topic area

- snapshot answers to some of the most common queries that Citizens Advice Bureaux get asked
- *Who Can Help?* pointing you in the direction of further help and advice.

Some chapters also include a Jargon Buster to help you make sense of the relevant lingo.

Citizens Advice Bureaux give free, confidential, impartial and independent advice on a limitless range of subjects, including all of the ones in this book. If you can't find the answer you're looking for here, make an appointment at your local CAB. Just visit www.adviceguide.org.uk or look in your local telephone directory under 'C'.

About the Citizens Advice service

Citizens Advice Bureaux – all independent charities – have been a key part of local communities for nearly 70 years. Set up in 1939, to help people deal with problems at the outbreak of the Second World War, they now provide free information and advice from over 3,000 locations – in bureaux, from a variety of community venues, in people's homes, by e-mail, on the telephone and via a regularly updated and award-winning website at www.adviceguide.org.uk.

Because the CAB service is so firmly rooted in the community, it also sees at first hand the immediate effects of the laws that govern our daily lives. This means it is able to campaign, locally and nationally, for improvements in policies and services that benefit us all. So CAB advice helps solve problems for individuals and the wider community:

- for online CAB advice and to contact a Citizens Advice Bureau, go to www.adviceguide.org.uk
- to volunteer at your local Citizens Advice Bureau, call 08451 264 264 or go to www.citizensadvice.org.uk/join-us
- to find out more about the campaigning work of the Citizens Advice service or to support its work, go to www.citizensadvice.org.uk.

The factual information in this book relates to England and Wales only and should be used as general guidance only, not legal advice. We have made every effort to provide information that is as accurate and up to date as possible but laws are constantly changing, and much depends on individual circumstances. Specific advice should be sought for specific situations, where necessary from a CAB adviser or a solicitor.

Since the first edition of the *Citizens Advice Guide to Your Rights* was published in 2005, there have been a number of changes in the law, many of which will have a positive impact on the lives of individuals, families and communities. All of the following are covered in this second edition.

Families with children may now benefit from the introduction of childcare vouchers, while women are eligible for longer maternity leave and more maternity pay. The right to request flexible working has been extended to those caring for adult dependants.

Equality issues have been pushed up the agenda with the introduction of civil partnerships giving equal rights to same-sex couples; a ban on age discrimination at work; new rules outlawing discrimination in the provision of goods or services due to sexuality or religion; and improved rights for disabled people in transport services and housing law. The establishment of the Equality and Human Rights Commission brings together the functions of the Equal Opportunities Commission, Commission for Racial Equality and the Disability Rights Commission in one place for the first time. The organization will also deal with discrimination because of sexuality, age and religion and with human rights law.

Efforts to make our world a healthier place have included England and Wales joining Scotland by banning smoking in public places and the introduction of new rules about healthy food in schools. And in Wales free NHS prescriptions have been introduced.

Family

1
Family

CONTENTS

INTRODUCTION

Families are central to our lives and are the social units in which most of us live. They are tiny microcosms of our wider societies and life within the family, for better or worse, teaches children how to live in the world.

These days, the 'traditional' family unit – if there ever really was such a thing – is changing. Lesbians and gay people can now enter into a civil partnership which gives them most, if not all, of the same rights that married couples have. With separation and divorce on the increase, many children now live in single-parent families, or are not living with their birth parents at all but living in foster homes or permanently adopted. Step-families and families with same-sex parents are more common. At the same time, extended families, which provided a vital support network of aunts, uncles and cousins in the past, are now much more scattered.

Families, whatever their make-up, are where we live out every aspect of our lives and every family faces problems and challenges at one time or another. This section takes a 'cradle-to-grave' look at rights within the family, from how to get a birth certificate for a newborn and the vital difference between cohabitation and marriage to drawing up a will and how to have your ashes scattered where you want. It includes an A–Z of young people's rights and responsibilities and also looks at how the wider community can help families who are tackling problems like domestic violence.

BIRTH

Registering a birth

Births must usually be registered within 42 days. A 'stillbirth' should also normally be registered within 42 days.

A birth must be registered with the Registrar of Births and Deaths in the district in which the birth occurred. The address is in the telephone directory. There is no fee for registering a birth but there is a fee for an extra copy of the certificate.

What to do if a birth has not been registered

It is possible to apply to register a birth years after it occurred. You will need to give as many details as possible, such as the exact date and place of birth and including your or the child's full name and address. You should write to the General Register Office (GRO: www.gro.gov.uk) at GRO Corrections, PO Box 476, Southport, PR8 2WJ.

Birth certificates

There are two types of birth certificates:

- the full certificate. This is a copy of the entry in the birth register, giving all the recorded details
- the short certificate. This only gives the child's full name, sex, date and place of birth. It does not give the name and particulars of the mother or father. A short certificate is issued free of charge when a birth is first registered and is sufficient for most official purposes.

Obtaining copies of birth certificates

You can get a copy of a birth certificate in one of the following ways and a fee will be charged:

- by post or personal visit to the local register office where the birth was registered, or the local register office in the district where the birth took place
- by a personal visit to the Family Records Centre (0845 6037788; www.familyrecords.gov.uk). The address is: 1 Myddelton Street, London EC1R 1UW
- by post from the General Register Office. The address is: PO Box 2, Southport, Merseyside PR8 2JD
- by telephone/fax from the General Register Office (0845 6037788; fax 01704 550013), but this service is only available to credit card holders
- online from the General Register Office at www.gro.gov.uk.

You should provide as much information about the birth as possible. If you supply the index reference number of the entry, the fee will be lower than if you do not. The index reference number can be found by searching the indexes at the Family Records Centre or those larger libraries and public record offices that hold the indexes.

If you do not know your exact date of birth, a search will be made for one year either side of the year you give. If an entry cannot be traced, part of the fee paid will be kept and the balance returned, provided the balance is at least £2.

You can get a certificate, for social security purposes only, from the local registrar where the birth was registered. If you obtain the copy soon after the birth is registered, you will be charged a lower fee. Once the register has been passed to the Superintendent Registrar, the full fee is charged. The certificate will be kept by the Department for Work and Pensions (DWP).

Certificates after adoption

If you are aged 18 or over and have been adopted in England or Wales, you can apply for a copy of your original birth certificate.

If all the birth details are known, you should apply to the Superintendent Registrar in the district where your birth was registered. There is a fee for this. If you were adopted before 12 November 1975, you will have to see an experienced counsellor before you can get information from the original birth certificate.

If you were adopted on or after 12 November 1975, you can choose whether or not you would like to see a counsellor before getting information about your birth certificate.

You can also obtain a copy of the adoption certificate issued after the adoption order was granted.

Certificates from abroad

If you were born abroad, the birth may also have been registered in the UK. If so, a copy of the certificate can be obtained in the usual way – see above.

If the birth has not been registered in the UK, you may be able to get a copy of the birth certificate from the country where you were born. This can be done by contacting the relevant embassy in the UK. Alternatively, the Overseas Section at the General Register Office can help with enquiries. Their number is 0151 471 4801.

If you are unable to obtain a copy of your birth certificate from abroad, the Consular Division of the Foreign and Commonwealth Office (020 7008 1500) may be able to help. A fee is charged.

Transsexual people

If you are a transsexual person whose birth was registered in the UK and you have been granted a full gender recognition certificate by the Gender

Recognition Panel, you can get a new birth certificate reflecting your acquired gender. You will be able to get a short certificate free of charge. This will include the details of the date, place of birth and parentage on your original birth certificate, together with your acquired gender and new name. Someone looking at this certificate will not be able to tell that you have legally acquired a different gender.

There is also the option for the new birth certificate to show your birth surname, if this is different from the surname on your gender recognition certificate. You will also be able to buy an additional full birth certificate, if you want to.

Your original birth certificate will remain in existence, but will not be available for the public to see.

CHANGING A NAME

How to change your name

If you wish to be known by a different name, you can change your name at any time, provided you do not intend to deceive or defraud another person. There is no legal procedure to follow in order to change a name. You simply start using the new name. You can change your forename or surname, add names or rearrange your existing names.

Although there is no legal way to change a name, you may want evidence that you have done so (see *Evidence of change of name*, p. 9). However, you cannot usually change details on your birth certificate, except in limited circumstances – for example, if you have changed gender since birth (see *Transsexual people*, p. 7). Changing details on your birth certificate is complicated and, if you wish to do this, you should consult an experienced adviser.

Once you have decided to change your name, you can use the new name for all purposes: for example, publishing marriage banns, legal proceedings and obtaining or changing details on a driving licence or passport.

Changing a child's name

In the same way, a child's name can be changed at any time, provided it is not to deceive or defraud another person. There is no legal procedure that must be followed in order to change a child's name, providing all the people who need to give their consent have done so. The parent simply starts using the new name. A child's forename or surname can be changed, and names can be added or rearranged.

Again, the details on a child's birth certificate cannot be changed, except in limited circumstances, so if you wish to do so you should consult an experienced adviser.

If you are a child or young person under 16, your consent does not have to be given for your name to be changed. However, if you object to your name being changed you can apply for a court order to prevent the change, provided the court is satisfied that you have sufficient understanding of what is involved.

As a child or young person under 16, you cannot change your surname without your parent's consent.

Once a child's name has been changed, it can be used for all purposes, such as starting school and registering with a GP. However, evidence may be required.

Who can change a child's name?

You must have parental responsibility to change a child's name. A birth mother will always have parental responsibility for the child, but other people may have parental responsibility too. For example, married parents each have parental responsibility. An unmarried father may have acquired parental responsibility. Or if the mother is in a civil partnership, the other civil partner may have acquired parental responsibility.

When only one person has parental responsibility for a child, that person can change the child's name. When two or more people have parental responsibility for the child, one of them can lawfully change the child's name if all the others agree. Such agreements do not need to be in writing.

If there is a residence order in force, a child's name cannot be changed without the written agreement of anyone else who has parental responsibility or the permission of the court.

Evidence of change of name

You do not need legal proof that you have changed your name, provided that you can be identified by your new chosen name. However, there are some circumstances – for example, applying for a passport – when additional evidence of the change of name is required.

If you change your name when you get married or when you register a civil partnership, a copy of the marriage certificate or civil partnership certificate will usually be enough evidence that you have changed your name.

If you get divorced or dissolve your civil partnership, you may wish to go back to using the name you had before. A copy of the divorce certificate or dissolution certificate will usually be enough evidence that you have changed your name. If you want to go back to the name you were born with, you might need to provide a birth certificate.

Otherwise, the evidence required varies depending on the purpose for which it is needed and can include:

- a letter from a responsible person
- a public announcement
- a statutory declaration
- a deed poll.

Letter

A letter from a responsible person, such as a GP, solicitor, minister, priest or MP, will often be enough evidence that you have changed your name. The letter should state that the person has known you in both names and that the change of name is to be used for all purposes. A letter is not enough evidence if you are applying for a UK passport.

Public announcement

You may want to record your name change by placing an advertisement in a local or national newspaper. This should state that you have stopped using your previous name and have assumed a new one. A copy of the advertisement can then be used as evidence that you have changed your name.

Statutory declaration

For most purposes, a statutory declaration is generally accepted as evidence of your change of name.

A statutory declaration is a statement recording your intention to abandon your old name and adopt a new one. Preparing a statutory declaration can be complicated. If you want to prove your change of name by making a statutory declaration you should consult an experienced adviser.

Deed poll

A deed poll is a formal statement to prove that your name has been changed. For most people it will not be necessary to prepare a deed poll as evidence that they have changed their name. However, there may be cases when a deed poll is required. For example, some professional bodies require members to produce a deed poll as proof of any name change.

As a child or young person under 18 you can only have your change of name recorded by deed poll by a person who has parental responsibility for you. However, if you are over 16, this can only be done with your consent.

Changing your name by deed poll can be complicated so, if you want to use a deed poll as evidence of change of name, you may want to seek the advice of an experienced adviser.

LIVING TOGETHER

This section is about the rights of couples who live together without getting married or entering into a civil partnership. This is known as cohabitation. In different areas of the law, you may have fewer rights than married couples or civil partners. Unless it says otherwise, the information below refers both to same-sex and opposite-sex partners.

If you want to set down your legal rights in certain areas of your relationship with your partner, you can make a series of agreements that will be recognized by the courts. These agreements can be about, for example, shared responsibility for your children, ownership of property that you live in, and ownership of jointly owned possessions. You will need the help of an experienced solicitor to do this.

Responsibility for children

A male partner is not necessarily assumed to be the father of his child. An unmarried mother will have sole responsibility for her child unless:

- the birth of the child is jointly registered with the child's father *or*
- a formal agreement (this is called a parental responsibility agreement) is made with the father of the child *or*
- a court order is made in favour of the father *or*
- the father becomes the child's guardian (the father would only have responsibility if the mother died) *or*
- the father marries the mother.

However, both parents are responsible for supporting a child financially. If you are the father, you are financially responsible even if you are neither living with the mother nor named on the child's birth certificate. The Child Support Agency can contact you for maintenance if you no longer live with the child's mother.

If you separate, you and your partner may make an informal arrangement for contact with your child. If this is not possible, a court can be asked to intervene. The court order will usually allow contact between the child and the parent with whom the child is not living, unless there are exceptional circumstances.

Same-sex partners do not have automatic parental responsibility for their partner's children and you do not automatically become the step-parent of your partner's children when you start living with your partner. However, as a lesbian or gay partner, you can apply for a court order for parental responsibility for your partner's children.

Adoption

If you are living together, you can apply to adopt a child jointly.

Death and inheritance

If your partner dies without leaving a will, you will not automatically inherit anything unless you and your partner owned property jointly. You both need to make wills if you want to make sure that the other partner inherits. However, unlike married couples or civil partners, you will not be exempt from paying inheritance tax.

Debts

You and your partner are legally responsible for your own debts, for the whole of debts in joint names and for debts for which you have 'joint and several' legal responsibility. For example, you are responsible for paying all of a council tax bill, whether your partner contributes or not. If you have acted as guarantor for your partner, you will be legally responsible for the debt.

Money and possessions

The ownership of possessions can be complicated, but in general the rules are as follows:

- property you owned before you started living with your partner remains yours
- if you bought an item, generally you will own it
- property will be owned jointly if you bought it from a joint account
- if you give property to your partner, it will belong to your partner, though this can be difficult to prove
- if you give your partner housekeeping money, any property bought with savings from it will probably belong to you.

Bank accounts

If you are living with your partner and you have separate bank accounts, neither of you will have access to money held in the other partner's account. If one partner dies, any balance in the account will be the property of the estate and cannot be used until the estate is settled.

If you have a joint account, both partners will have access to the money in the account. If the account is in joint names, on the death of one partner, the whole account immediately becomes the property of the other.

Financial support

Neither partner has a legal duty to support the other financially.

If you and your partner live together and are claiming Income Support or income-based Jobseeker's Allowance, Working Tax Credit or Housing Benefit, you will be treated as a couple and your income assessed jointly.

Voluntary agreements to pay maintenance to each other may be difficult to enforce.

Pensions

The rules of pension schemes vary. Whether or not you can benefit from a scheme to which your partner belongs will depend on the scheme. Most schemes offer benefits to dependent children and some will offer benefits to a dependent partner. If your scheme offers benefits to a dependent opposite-sex partner, it should also offer benefits to your dependent same-sex partner. If this is not the case, there may be unlawful discrimination. You can arrange a personal pension to give cover to whoever the scheme member wants, but you will probably have to pay large contributions to the pension fund.

Student grants and loans

If you are a student living with your partner, your partner's income will be taken into account when deciding if you are entitled to a student grant. This does not apply if you depend on your parents financially.

Your partner's income is ignored when deciding whether you are eligible for a student loan for tuition fees.

A percentage of a student loan for living expenses may depend on your partner's income.

Housing

Tenants

If your partner is the sole tenant, you will usually have no rights to stay in the accommodation if your partner asks you to leave. This applies whether you live in private or public-sector accommodation. If you are in this situation, you should get help from an experienced solicitor.

It is advisable for partners who live together to be joint tenants as this gives them equal rights and responsibilities. It is possible to convert a sole tenancy to a joint tenancy if you and your partner and the landlord agree.

If you are a joint tenant and your partner leaves, seek legal advice.

If your partner is the sole tenant and leaves, you will be in a very vulnerable position. If you are in this position, you should get legal advice. A court can transfer a tenancy, whether it is a sole or joint tenancy.

Owner-occupiers

A property may be owned in the sole name of one partner or jointly.

If your partner is the sole owner-occupier, you may have no rights to remain in the home if your partner asks you to leave, although you may be able to protect your position. You will need to get legal advice on this.

If your relationship ends, and there are children, courts can include property as part of an overall settlement to protect the children.

If you and your partner own your property jointly you can be either 'joint tenants' or 'tenants in common'. (This is different from being a tenant where you rent property from a landlord.)

If you are 'joint tenants', your property cannot be sold without the agreement of both of you. If one of you dies, their share of the property passes automatically to the other.

If you own your property as 'tenants in common', each of you will have a share of your home that you can dispose of as you like. It is up to you to decide how much each share will be. If one of you dies, you can leave your share to whoever you like.

Next of kin and medical consent

Some organizations – for example, hospitals and prisons – will usually accept the name of an unmarried partner who lives with you as the next of kin. If you want to name your partner as next of kin, you should insist on this. However, there is little you can do if the organization still refuses to accept it.

If your partner is to have an operation and the consent of the nearest relative is needed, you may be able to give this, although, strictly speaking, if there is a husband or wife, they will be the nearest relative. An NHS Trust will allow you to nominate your next of kin formally when you are admitted to hospital and most hospitals recognize that a client's partner is probably the closest person, whatever their gender.

Who can help?

The website of the **Law Society** (www.lawsociety.org.uk) can help you find a solicitor who is an expert in the area of law you need.
You can also check on the **Community Legal Service** website (www.clsdirect.org.uk).

MARRIAGE

Who can get married?

According to UK law, a man and a woman may marry if they are both 16 years or over and free to marry – that is, single, widowed, divorced or if they were in a civil partnership which has been dissolved. The following people cannot marry:

- people aged 16 or 17 who do not have parental consent;
- certain close relatives;
- people of the same sex (although they can enter into a civil partnership which gives them many, if not all, of the rights of married couples – see p. 20). For

transsexual people, the relevant gender is the one on their current birth certificate – see p. 7.

Young people

If you are 16 or 17 you cannot marry without parental consent. Each parent with parental responsibility is entitled to give parental consent. In some circumstances, other people may give parental consent.

Transsexual people

A transsexual person who has been granted a full gender recognition certificate by the Gender Recognition Panel can get a new birth certificate which reflects their acquired gender. They will then be able to marry someone of the opposite gender. However, if you do not have a gender recognition certificate, you are legally considered to be the gender that is on your original birth certificate and you will not be able to marry someone of the opposite sex.

Getting engaged

Engagements are mainly for cultural reasons and have limited status. However, they can be used – for example, in immigration law – as evidence of intention to marry.

One of the parties can decide to end an engagement, as an agreement to marry cannot be legally enforced.

> ### My fiancé and I have decided not to go through with the wedding. Can I keep the ring?
>
> If an engagement is broken, a woman can keep the engagement ring unless, at the time she was given it, the man specifically said that it should be returned if the engagement were to be broken. Any other property belonging to the couple should be divided between them in the same way as property would be divided if the couple divorced. If the couple cannot agree about entitlement to property, either person can apply to a court to decide the issue, provided this is done within three years of the end of the engagement. Legal advice will be needed in these circumstances.

Where you can get married

You can get married in a register office. Or you could get married in a church, synagogue or Friends Meeting House, all of which are automatically approved for marriages.

Local authorities can approve other premises where marriages may take place and this could include other religious buildings. Applications for approval of premises can be made by the owner or trustee of a building but not by a couple who are marrying.

The premises must be regularly open to members of the public, so private homes are unlikely to be approved since they are not normally open to the public. Stately homes, hotels and civic buildings are likely to be thought suitable. Approval will not be given for open-air venues, such as beaches or golf courses. Generally, the premises will need to be permanent built structures, although it may be possible for approval to be given to a permanently moored, publicly open boat. Hot-air balloons or aeroplanes will not be approved.

If you want to get married in premises that a local authority has approved, you can obtain a list of premises from the local town hall. Or you can search for approved premises on the General Register Office's website (www.gro.gov.uk).

In some circumstances, you could get married somewhere else – for example, the home of one of the partners if the partner is housebound or in prison if one of the partners is a prisoner.

How to marry

You can get married by a civil ceremony or a religious ceremony.

In both cases, the following legal requirements must be met:

- the marriage must be conducted by a person or in the presence of a person authorized to register marriages in the district *and*
- the marriage must be entered in the marriage register and signed by both parties, two witnesses, the person who conducted the ceremony and, if that person is not authorized to register marriages, the person who is registering the marriage.

Civil marriage ceremonies

You and your partner must give notice of marriage in your local register office, whether or not you wish to marry in that district. The Registrar then issues authority for the marriage and you may marry in any register office or premises approved by the local authority in any district.

In the period between the notice of intention to marry and the ceremony, anyone with strong grounds for objecting to the marriage can do so. Making a false statement is a criminal offence.

Both partners must be resident in England or Wales for seven days before notice is given (on the eighth day). A notice must state where the marriage is to take place. The marriage can then take place after 15 days have elapsed from the date on which notice of the marriage is entered in the marriage notice book. There is a fee for giving notice of the marriage.

If either you or your partner is from overseas, special rules may apply when giving notice to marry. If you are in this situation, you should consult an experienced adviser.

The marriage must usually take place within twelve months from the date of entry of the notice. If the marriage does not take place within that time, the process must be repeated.

Religious marriage ceremonies

The Church of England and the Church in Wales are allowed to register a marriage at the same time as performing the religious ceremony.

Ministers and priests of all other religions can be authorized to register marriages and must have a certificate or licence to do so from the local Superintendent Registrar. For Jewish and Quaker marriages, the authorization is automatic. For all other religions, if the official performing the ceremony is not authorized, either a Registrar must attend the religious ceremony or the partners will need to have separate religious and civil ceremonies.

Religious ceremonies and civil ceremonies

If a couple has been married in a register office, the partners can have a religious marriage ceremony afterwards. The partners are likely to be asked for their marriage certificate. A religious ceremony that does not comply with the conditions stated above, and which takes place before a civil wedding, is not a valid marriage under UK law and the couple's status will be that of cohabitees.

Do I have to fill in any forms to change my name when I get married?

No, you do not have to fill in any forms or get permission legally to change your name. You just start using your changed name instead of your old one. However, you may find that some organizations want to see written evidence of your name change. This could be a letter from a doctor, minister or solicitor, or an announcement in the press. You may prefer to make a statutory declaration or change your name by deed poll.

Anyone who is 16 or over can change their name at any time. You can change your forename, your surname or both. You can add new names or drop a name you do not want. You can use your new name for all purposes, including getting married or applying for a passport. However, you cannot change your name for purposes of fraud.

Remarriage/second marriage

As long as the legal requirements described earlier are met, there is nothing to prevent you from marrying again in a civil ceremony in the UK if you are widowed or divorced, or if you were in a civil partnership that has been dissolved.

Religions and denominations have different rules about whether someone can remarry in a religious ceremony. If you or your partner has been married before or in a civil partnership, and you now want a religious ceremony, you will need to check with an official of the relevant religion.

Blessing ceremonies

Even if you are not allowed to marry in a religious ceremony – for example, because you belong to a religion that does not permit marriage of people who are divorced – it may be possible to arrange for your relationship to be blessed in a religious ceremony. This is at the discretion of the religious official concerned.

Forced marriages

It is a criminal offence to force a person to marry. If you are afraid that you may be forced into a marriage in this country, the police should be contacted. This is also the case where there is concern that another person may be forced into a marriage.

If you are afraid that you may be forced into marriage overseas, you should, before travelling, contact the Forced Marriage Unit at the Foreign and Commonwealth Office (020 7008 0151; www.fco.gov.uk) for advice. If you are concerned about someone else who has travelled overseas, you should also contact the Forced Marriage Unit.

CIVIL PARTNERSHIPS

What is a civil partnership?

A civil partnership is a legal relationship which can be registered by two people of the same sex. If you are in a gay or lesbian relationship, registering a civil partnership will give your relationship legal recognition. This will give you added legal rights, as well as responsibilities.

Once you have registered a civil partnership, it can only be ended if one of you dies, or if you apply to court to bring the partnership legally to an end.

In some situations, a same-sex couple who have not registered a civil partnership will have the same legal rights and responsibilities as a couple who have registered a civil partnership. This will be the case, for example, when working out your entitlement to welfare benefits and tax credits.

Who can register a civil partnership?

You and your lesbian or gay partner can register a civil partnership as long as all the following circumstances apply:

- you are both 16 or over. If you are 16 or 17, you will usually have to get written consent from your parents or guardians
- you have lived in the same area in England or Wales for at least seven days
- neither of you is already a civil partner or married
- you are not close relatives.

People aged 16 or 17 and parental consent

If you are 16 or 17, you will need the consent of each parent with parental responsibility to register a civil partnership.

You may not be able to get the consent of your parents, perhaps because you do not know where they are. Or your parents may refuse to give their consent for you to register a civil partnership. If this is the case, you can apply to a court for permission to register your civil partnership. You will need to get legal advice to do this.

How to register a civil partnership

There are two steps needed to register a civil partnership. The first step is to give notice of your intention to register and the second is to actually register the civil partnership.

Step one: giving notice

You and your partner will each need to give notice of your intention to register a civil partnership to the local register office where you live. You will need to do this even if you are going to register your civil partnership somewhere else. You must have lived in an area for at least seven days before you can give notice there.

When you give notice, you will be asked to give details of the date and place where the civil partnership is to be registered, so you must have agreed this with the venue where you are going to register first.

You will also have to give the register office certain personal details. These are your name, your address, your occupation, your nationality and whether you have been in a civil partnership or married before.

You each have to pay a fee to give notice of your intention to register a civil partnership.

If you are from overseas, or your partner is, special rules may apply when giving notice to enter into a civil partnership. If you are in this situation, you should consult an experienced adviser.

Once you have given notice of your intention to register a civil partnership, details from the notice will be made available in a register office for people to see. This will be in the area in which both of you live and the area where you are going to register, if this is different.

The details must be made available for people to see for 15 days before you can register your civil partnership. This is to give an opportunity for objections to be made.

After 15 days, you will be free to register your partnership within the next twelve months. If you do not register your civil partnership within this period, you will not be able to register unless you start the whole process again.

In some exceptional circumstances – for example, if one of you is terminally ill – you can ask for the 15-day waiting period to be waived.

Step two: registration

You can register your civil partnership in any register office or at any venue that has been approved to register civil partnerships. Anywhere that has been approved to hold civil marriages automatically has approval to register civil partnerships. Non-religious venues cannot choose whether to hold civil partnerships or not, if they hold weddings. This would be unlawful discrimination. However, religious organizations can refuse to hold civil partnerships in venues they run, such as a church hall, even if weddings are held there. A civil partnership cannot be registered on religious premises.

You can search for approved premises on the General Register Office's website (www.gro.gov.uk). You should check the venue is available before giving notice to register.

You and your partner have legally registered your civil partnership when you have signed a legal document, known as the civil partnership schedule. This must be done in front of a registrar and two witnesses. There is a fee for this.

There are no further legal requirements and you do not have to have a ceremony, although you can choose to have one if you want. Many local authorities will arrange for a ceremony in addition to the signing of the civil partnership document but they do not have to. No religious service is allowed at the signing of the civil partnership schedule. If you want a ceremony and the local authority refuses to carry one out, you could:

- find a register office in another local authority where you can sign the civil partnership schedule and have a ceremony
- find other approved premises where you can sign the civil partnership schedule and have a ceremony
- arrange a ceremony somewhere else after signing of the civil partnership schedule has taken place at the register office.

You can get a civil partnership certificate when you register. There is a fee for this.

Recognition for partnerships of same-sex couples formed overseas

Some same-sex couples may already have formed a civil union, registered partnership, domestic partnership or a same-sex marriage abroad.

If you are in one of these relationships, you can get automatic recognition in the UK as civil partners and will not need to register in the UK as well. However, you, your partner and your overseas relationship must meet certain conditions – get legal advice about this.

ENDING A RELATIONSHIP

Whatever your status was before you separated, when your relationship ends you may need to inform:

- your landlord or local authority rent office
- your mortgage lender
- the land registry
- water, gas, electricity and telephone companies
- your children's schools
- your bank or any other financial institution if you have a joint account – it may be advisable for one of the account holders to freeze the account to prevent the other withdrawing some or all of the money
- hire purchase or credit companies
- insurance companies, particularly if you have joint policies
- the post office, if it is necessary to have mail redirected
- your doctor, dentist and child health clinic.

You have a legal responsibility to inform your local Jobcentre Plus office, local authority Council Tax Benefit and Housing Benefit office, and HM Revenue and Customs (if you are getting Working Tax Credit or Child Tax Credit).

Ending the relationship if you were not married or in a civil partnership

If you are living with your partner but you are not married or in a civil partnership and your relationship ends, there is no need for you to take any legal action to formalize the separation. However, there may be issues concerning children, property and money to sort out. This can be done either by informal agreement or by a written separation agreement between you (see *Financial arrangements at the end of a relationship*, p. 30) If you and your partner cannot agree, a court can order who should stay in the home in the short term and can also transfer a tenancy.

Marriage or civil partnership: separating informally

If you and your partner are married or in a civil partnership, you can separate by an informal arrangement.

If there is agreement between you and your partner, you can make arrangements about children, money, housing and other property without going to court. However, any informal arrangement made when separating may affect future decisions if you do ever go to court. A court may overturn an arrangement made by a couple that it considers to be unreasonable or, in the case of a child, not in the child's best interests.

Separation agreements

A separation agreement is a written agreement between a couple who intend to stop living together, setting out how they wish to resolve the issues of money, property and children. Any couple can draw up an agreement as a way of resolving and confirming the arrangements they have come to.

Examples of the agreements you may want to make include:

- to live separately. If one of you does not agree on separation, the agreement should not be included, as it will prevent any future right to sue for desertion in divorce or civil partnership dissolution proceedings
- not to molest, annoy or disturb the other partner
- to provide maintenance for the other partner. This would normally say that maintenance will stop if the partner starts to live with someone else. Any agreement not to apply to a court for maintenance is invalid
- to provide maintenance for any children of the relationship. Any agreement not to apply to a court or to the Child Support Agency is invalid
- with whom the children should live and have contact.

The advantage of a written agreement is that it is easier to ensure that you both understand what has been agreed. It also means that either partner can go to court to vary the order at a future date. It is advisable to consult a solicitor when drawing up a separation agreement, but you should work out in advance the general areas you want to cover. This will reduce the legal costs. Assistance may be available under the legal help scheme.

Judicial separation (married couples)

A judicial separation is a court order which releases the partners of a marriage from the obligation to live together in the same way as a divorce. It is comparatively rare but can be used by couples who have a conscientious objection to divorce. The order does not dissolve the marriage so neither partner is free to remarry or enter into a civil partnership.

Separation orders (civil partners)

If you want to separate from your civil partner but you do not want to dissolve the civil partnership (or if it has been less than a year since you registered your civil partnership), you can apply to court for a separation order.

You do not have to wait for a year after registering your civil partnership before you can apply for a separation order and you do not have to have been living apart from your partner first. However, neither of you will be free to register another civil partnership or to marry unless you get a dissolution order.

Divorce (married couples)

You cannot apply for a divorce until you have been married for at least one year. There are no exceptions to this rule. To get divorced in England or Wales, the marriage must be recognized as valid by UK law and you must meet the residence rules.

If neither partner objects to the divorce it is called an *undefended* divorce. This is dealt with by a straightforward procedure, which does not necessarily require the use of a solicitor. If one of the partners does not agree to the divorce, it is called a *defended* divorce and will require the help of a solicitor.

Irretrievable breakdown

A divorce will be granted by the county court if you or your partner can show that the marriage no longer exists. Legally, this is known as the irretrievable breakdown of the marriage. For a marriage to have irretrievably broken down, one of the following must be proved:

- adultery
- unreasonable behaviour
- desertion
- two years' separation with consent
- five years' separation.

Adultery

A court may grant a divorce if one of you has had a sexual relationship with someone else (committed adultery) and your partner finds it intolerable to continue living together. The decision that it is intolerable must be made within six months of the adultery taking place. A woman who is raped has not committed adultery but a man who commits rape has.

The court will need evidence of the adultery – for example, dates – and will only grant the divorce if it is satisfied that adultery has occurred and that the other partner could no longer live with the partner who has committed adultery.

If the divorce is undefended, the court will usually only need statements and details. If the divorce is defended, then proof will be necessary and this may be difficult and expensive.

Unreasonable behaviour

A court may grant a divorce if you or your partner has behaved so badly that the other can no longer tolerate living together. Unreasonable behaviour can include mental or physical cruelty, including violence or abuse, and less obvious things like dominating a partner and not letting the other leave the house or speak to neighbours and friends, or refusing to pay for housekeeping.

If your partner has been violent to you, you can get specialist help – see p. 35.

If the divorce is defended, a great deal of evidence and detail will be needed – for example, evidence from witnesses such as friends or medical evidence.

Desertion

Desertion means that your partner left home against your wishes with no good reason. If your partner was away continuously for two out of the last two and a half years, you can apply for a divorce without the agreement of your partner. Even if you live together for a total of up to six months during this period, this does not stop the desertion being continuous. A court will want proof of the desertion and, if the divorce is contested, there may be disputes over who deserted whom.

Separation for two years

If you have lived apart for two years continuously and you both agree to a divorce, a court will accept this as proof of irretrievable breakdown. The two years apart will still be continuous even if you have actually lived together for up to six months in between.

Separation for five years

If you have lived apart for five years, either you or your partner can apply for a divorce without the other's agreement. The other partner can defend the divorce on the grounds that it would cause unreasonable hardship but a court will usually agree to a divorce where you have been separated for five years.

Applying for a divorce

The partner who is applying for the divorce is known as the petitioner. The other partner is the respondent.

If you want to start divorce proceedings, you will need to obtain the necessary forms from the court. The court office will tell you which forms you need, but court staff are not allowed to give legal advice to either partner or help complete forms. You can also get the forms from Her Majesty's Courts Service website at www.hmcourts-service.gov.uk.

If you are applying for a divorce and want help in completing the forms, you should consult an experienced adviser.

Undefended divorce

An undefended divorce is dealt with in the county court or the divorce registry in London. The partner who is applying for the divorce can go to any divorce county court. The address can be found in the local telephone directory (or look on Her Majesty's Courts Service website at www.hmcourts-service.gov.uk). In an undefended divorce, the use of a solicitor is not usually necessary for the divorce procedure itself. However, it may be advisable to consult a solicitor for general advice prior to starting divorce proceedings. A solicitor can be useful for advice on whether there are sufficient grounds, which grounds are appropriate, and what evidence may be needed. If there are disputes over children, property or money which you and your partner cannot resolve, it is usually advisable to consult a solicitor.

Defended divorce

A defended divorce will normally be heard in the High Court, although proceedings can be transferred to the divorce county court. In most cases, a defended divorce will be resolved before a court hearing. This is because in the course of the proceedings, the parties will usually accept that the marriage has indeed broken down irretrievably, even if the facts alleged in the petition are not accepted.

In a defended divorce, both partners should always consult a solicitor. When the case is heard, barristers will usually need to be employed as well. Solicitors' fees can become very high if there are lengthy disputes. It is advisable wherever possible for both partners to try to come to an agreement before going to court.

Undefended divorce: what the court will do

If the respondent does not intend to defend the divorce, the court will examine the petition and grant a decree nisi. No court hearing is needed. The marriage still exists at this stage.

The court may, however, want to discuss arrangements about any children of the relationship and possibly meet the children if they are old enough (nine years and over). An undefended divorce can take up to six months if there are no children or money issues involved. It can take longer if children are involved and the court is not satisfied with arrangements being made for them.

Six weeks after the court grants the decree nisi, the partner who applied for the divorce can apply to the court for a decree absolute. The decree absolute is the final stage and will confirm the divorce. It will be granted provided that the court has approved the arrangements for any children.

Dissolving a civil partnership

If you want to dissolve your civil partnership, you will need to apply to a court for a dissolution order. Your civil partnership must have lasted at least one year before you can apply for a dissolution. You must prove to the court that the civil partnership has 'irretrievably' broken down – that is, broken down on a permanent basis. You must be able to prove at least one of the following things:

- your partner has behaved unreasonably
- you and your partner have lived apart for two years and you both agreed to the dissolution
- you and your partner have lived apart for at least five years, if only one of you agrees to the dissolution
- your partner deserted you at least two years ago.

These rules are the same as those for people who are getting divorced – see above.

How to apply for a dissolution order

To apply for a dissolution order, you will need to get the necessary forms. You can get these by going to Her Majesty's Courts Service website at www.hmcourts-service.gov.uk. You can also get the forms from the nearest court that deals with civil partnership dissolutions. To find your nearest court, look up 'courts' in your telephone directory or go to Her Majesty's Courts Service website at www.hmcourts-service.gov.uk.

If your partner agrees to the dissolution of your civil partnership, the court will look at the forms and make a conditional order of dissolution. The dissolution will be made final six weeks from the date of the conditional order.

If your partner does not agree to the dissolution, you should consult a solicitor. Legal fees can be very high so it is best to try to come to an agreement before going to court.

Help with the legal costs of a divorce or dissolution – legal aid

Legal aid for an undefended divorce or dissolution is not usually available but it is available for matters concerning children, money and property connected with the dissolution. You may be able to get legal aid for a defended divorce or dissolution.

If you do get legal aid, in some cases you might have to pay some of the legal costs back out of money or property you are given when the divorce or dissolution order is made. This is called the statutory charge. Make sure your solicitor explains the statutory charge to you before you start the case.

For more information about help with legal costs, see p. 520.

Financial arrangements at the end of a relationship

At the end of a relationship, both parents are responsible for supporting their children financially.

Neither partner has a duty to maintain the other at the end of a relationship if they were just living together. However, if you were married or if you were in a civil partnership, either partner can apply for maintenance from the other. You can do this regardless of whether you have children, and whether or not you are divorcing or getting a dissolution.

There are three possible ways to arrange financial support:

- by voluntary agreement
- through the Child Support Agency (CSA) or
- through the courts.

Voluntary agreements

A voluntary agreement between a couple whose relationship has ended can be formal or informal, verbal or written. You can agree, for example, that one of you will make weekly payments to the other for the support of children, or will meet rent or mortgage payments or household bills, or pay for the children's clothing and holidays.

Before you decide on the terms of a voluntary agreement, it may be useful to consult a solicitor for advice on what would be an appropriate arrangement. It may also be useful to have an agreement drawn up by a solicitor in case of future dispute. It may be possible to obtain help with the costs of advice on and the drawing up of an agreement under the legal help scheme.

An informal voluntary agreement avoids the need for, and the costs of, solicitors. However, there is no guarantee that a partner will keep to its terms.

Child Support Agency (CSA)

The Child Support Agency (CSA) assesses and collects maintenance payments in respect of children who are under 16 (under 19 if they are in full-time non-advanced education). If the children of a relationship are living with you and the relationship has ended and you claim Income Support or income-based Jobseeker's Allowance, you will normally have to use the CSA to obtain maintenance for the children. If you claim Working Tax Credit or Child Tax Credit, you do not have to use the CSA.

Through the courts

If you have been married or in a civil partnership and your relationship is ending, or has ended, you can apply to a court to order your partner or former partner to pay maintenance. The court will consider all the financial resources and assets of both partners, including pension arrangements.

In some circumstances, the court can also make an order for child maintenance to be paid.

A court can make an order for periodical maintenance payments to be made – that is, a specific sum at regular intervals – or for a specified lump sum. It can also make an order about pension arrangements.

If you want to apply to a court for maintenance for yourself or a child you should obtain the help of a solicitor. You might get help with legal costs when you make an application to court for financial support. However, you might have to pay some of these costs back out of the money or property you are given by the court order. This is called the statutory charge. Make sure your solicitor explains the statutory charge properly to you before you start court action. Where pension arrangements are involved, you should also consider obtaining specialist financial advice.

Relationship breakdown and housing

Courts can give one of the partners short-term rights to the home – for example, the right to stay, to have access to the home or to exclude the other person.

Courts can make long-term arrangements about the home in certain cases where there are children or in the case of a judicial separation, divorce, separation order or dissolution of a civil partnership. In the case of a divorce or dissolution of a civil partnership, where there is a dispute about the home, the court will deal with the dispute as part of the divorce or dissolution.

Rights of married partners and civil partners to occupy the home

If you and your married partner or civil partner are owner-occupiers, it is often the case that only one of you is the actual owner. If this is the case, and you are the partner who is not the owner, you will need to ensure that you keep your right to live in the property and to prevent the owner selling it without your knowledge. Even if you actually move out when the relationship ends, you may want to move back in again with the children. To retain your right, you must register your 'right of occupation' by completing a form and sending it to either the District Land Registry or the Land Charges Department in Plymouth, depending on where the title of the property is registered.

This procedure is not complicated and it is not necessary to consult a solicitor, but you may want to consult an experienced adviser.

Relationship breakdown and children

Once a marriage or civil partnership ends, decisions have to be made about who will care for any children of the relationship. Many parents are able to make arrangements amicably between themselves about where the children live and about visits by the other parent. However, if this is not possible, decisions can be made by the courts, including the transfer of property and tenancies.

Many couples split up but never get divorced or get a dissolution order. If you separate informally (or if you have never been married or in a civil partnership), you may not ever need to go to court. You can make arrangements for the children that may last indefinitely. But if you are unable to resolve a disagreement over the care of or contact with the children, you may need to ask the court to resolve the dispute.

If you are getting a divorce, judicial separation, separation order or dissolution of a civil partnership, the court will not grant the order until it has looked at the arrangements for the children. If they are acceptable to both parents, the court will not make an order in relation to the child. It will only make a court order where it is necessary to do so to resolve a dispute.

Parental responsibility

The term *parental responsibility* covers all rights, duties, powers and responsibilities that a parent has for a child. This includes providing a home, feeding and clothing, providing protection and security, and ensuring that the child receives a satisfactory education.

Opposite-sex couples

If you were married at the time of your child's birth, or married each other since the birth, both partners will automatically have parental responsibility and continue to have it after divorce or separation. Each parent can exercise their parental responsibility independently of the other.

If you were not married, and do not subsequently marry each other, the mother automatically has parental responsibility. However, the father will have parental responsibility if he registers (or re-registers) the birth of his child with the child's mother. If he has not registered and wants parental responsibility, he has to apply to a court for this to be granted.

Same-sex couples

When a same-sex relationship ends, only the people with parental responsibility have a legal right to take part in decisions about who will care for the children on a day-to-day basis.

The mother automatically has parental responsibility. If you are in a same-sex relationship, you have no automatic parental responsibility for your partner's children. However, if you are in a civil partnership, you may have acquired parental responsibility by becoming a step-parent or by getting a court order. If you are not in a civil partnership, you cannot get parental responsibility as a step-parent but you may be able to acquire parental responsibility by applying to court.

What decisions can a court make?

A court will only make an order concerning a child if it feels it is in the best interests of the child to do so. The main orders that may be made by a court are for:

- a residence order to determine who the child should live with
- a contact order to determine who the child should have contact with and the form of contact.

Residence order

The court can make a residence order in favour of:

- one parent. This means that the child must live with that parent
- both parents. One residence order can be made in favour of both parents,

even if they are not living together. The order will specify how much time the child will live with each parent

- each parent. Each parent will have a separate order specifying how much time the child will live with them.

Contact order

The court will normally expect the parents to make their own arrangements to ensure that each of them maintains contact with the children. The court will only make a court order if they cannot agree.

The contact order may include conditions specifying where and how often contact should take place. It may also specify the type of contact – for example, visiting, telephoning or writing letters. Orders can also be made to allow contact between the child and, for example, other relatives or friends.

Family mediation

Family mediation is a way of assisting separating couples to resolve disputes and reach agreed decisions on specific issues arising from the breakdown of a relationship. It involves both partners and aims to clarify the issues between them and to help them make decisions.

Two main types of family mediation are available:

- *out-of-court mediation*, to which people can refer themselves or be referred by, for example, a solicitor or adviser, *and*
- *court-based dispute resolution*, to which people are referred by the court when children are involved.

Out-of-court family mediation

A couple can use out-of-court family mediation services as soon as possible after they have decided their relationship is ending and they feel able to discuss any disagreements. Mediation can be helpful before legal proceedings begin, to encourage co-operation between the couple and to prevent disputes from getting worse and agreement becoming harder to reach in the future. Family mediation can also be used after a judicial separation, divorce, separation or dissolution of a civil partnership if new issues arise or there are outstanding issues to be resolved.

If you have been referred to mediation by a solicitor, you may get financial help with the costs.

Out-of-court family mediation can be provided by a number of organizations. However, all family mediators should be members of the United Kingdom College of Family Mediators (0117 904 7223; www.ukcfm.co.uk).

You should check that any mediator is a member of this body to ensure that they are properly trained and supervised. The College has a directory that can be used to check whether a particular mediator is a member or to find a mediator to use.

Court-based dispute resolution

If you ask a court to make decisions about arrangements for your children at the end of your civil partnership, a Children and Family Reporter will usually be asked to get involved.

Children and Family Reporters work for the Children and Family Court Advisory Service (CAFCASS: 020 7510 7000; www.cafcass.gov.uk). In Wales, it is called CAFCASS Cymru and is the responsibility of the National Assembly of Wales; the contact details are the same as in England. Children and Family Reporters are independent of the courts and other agencies such as social services, education and health authorities. They are qualified in social work and experienced in working with children and families.

The Children and Family Reporter will try to help you and your partner work out the best possible arrangements for your children.

Sometimes the court will ask you and your partner, and any other parents involved, to meet with the Children and Family Reporter to see if you can sort things out without having to go on with the court case. If you can come to an agreement at this stage, the judge can make an order to confirm what was agreed.

If you cannot come to an agreement, the judge can order that a report is produced before the case goes any further.

Court-based dispute resolution schemes are free.

DOMESTIC VIOLENCE

Domestic violence covers a range of situations where one person in some way harms another person with whom they have some pre-existing relationship. It can therefore be one person physically attacking another or it may be another form of abuse such as pestering with phone calls, installing a lover in the family home, or putting superglue in the locks of the victim's car doors. For the above actions to be counted as domestic violence, the victim and the perpetrator must have had some form of relationship, but they do not need to be heterosexual partners and they need not live in the same property.

If you are the victim of a violent relationship, get immediate practical advice on the options available, which may be to:

- attempt to stop the violence and stay with the perpetrator of the violence
- leave home temporarily
- leave home permanently
- stay in the present home and get the perpetrator of the violence to leave
- take legal action.

Finding somewhere safe to stay

If you are a victim of a violent relationship, you may need somewhere safe to stay, either alone or with your children. The options are:

- stay at home if you think this is safe
- stay with relatives or friends
- if you are a woman, stay in a women's refuge. Your children could stay there with you
- get emergency accommodation from the local authority under homeless persons law – this will usually mean a bed and breakfast hostel
- get privately rented accommodation.

Women's Aid Refuges

Women's Aid Refuges are safe houses for women suffering domestic violence. Refuges provide somewhere safe for women and their children to stay and allow some time and space for the women to think about what to do next.

Staff at refuges are specialists in dealing with domestic violence, and so can give a lot of emotional and practical support – for example, advice on benefit claims, which solicitors to use and, if necessary, how to contact the police.

To find out your nearest refuge with spaces available, you should contact the National Domestic Violence helpline (0808 200 0247). Helpline staff will do their best to find you somewhere safe to stay that night even if the local refuge is full. They are also happy to talk to women about any questions they have about refuges.

Going to the local authority

Your local authority may have a duty to re-house you if it is not reasonable for you to occupy your home because of the risk or fear of domestic violence. Local authorities should deal sympathetically with applications from people who are in fear of violence. You can ask for a private interview, with someone of the same sex, and can take a friend with you for support.

The local authority may have a duty to provide temporary accommodation for you while it decides whether it has to re-house you on a permanent basis.

Going to privately rented accommodation

If you decide to go into privately rented accommodation you will be unlikely to be able to arrange it quickly. This is really only an option for people who have time to plan their departure and can afford this accommodation.

Longer-term solutions

Once you have found a safe place to stay for the short term, you will need to think about what to do in the longer term. You will need to consider:

- whether you wish to separate permanently from your partner – you should seek legal advice: see *Legal remedies and procedures* below
- whether you want to take action to keep the violent partner away from you – you should seek legal advice: see *Legal remedies and procedures* below
- housing. Your legal rights to the family home will depend upon the type of housing you are leaving, the legal status of your relationship and whether or not you have children. You should get legal advice to ensure that you do everything possible to protect rights to the family home. Seek advice about the family home even if you are leaving permanently because, if your partner sells the home, you may lose money and possessions
- children. If you have children, you will need to decide if you are taking the children with you. It may be safer for them if you take them with you. You may need to use the courts to resolve who the children should live with and with whom they should have contact. You should seek legal advice: see *Legal remedies and procedures* below
- money. You will need to sort out your benefit entitlement and tax arrangements and whether or not to apply to court for maintenance for yourself. You may also want to apply to the Child Support Agency (CSA) for a maintenance assessment for your children. If you claim certain benefits, you will auto-

matically be contacted by the CSA. However, you may be able to opt out if there is a risk to you or a child living with you because your partner is violent.

Legal remedies and procedures

If you want to discuss legal protection for yourself and your children, consult a solicitor who is experienced in family law work. Local Women's Aid groups, the police, rape crisis groups, or women's centres usually know of local solicitors who are both experienced and sympathetic. A local advice agency such as a law centre or Citizens Advice Bureau should be able to help you find a local solicitor who is experienced in this area of the law. Or you could look on the Community Legal Service website (www.clsdirect.org. uk).

You should make an appointment as soon as you feel ready, and you could take someone with you for support the first time you go to the solicitor. The initial interview will probably last quite a long time, during which the solicitor should discuss with you what courses of legal action are open to you and whether you are entitled to legal aid.

If you take legal action to protect yourself or your family from domestic violence, you may qualify for legal aid without having to meet the normal financial conditions.

Who can help?

The **National Domestic Violence helpline** (0808 200 0247) is a 24-hour helpline providing access to advice and support to women experiencing domestic violence. The helpline is provided jointly by Women's Aid and Refuge.

Women's Aid (helpline: 0808 200 0247; www.womensaid.org.uk) can also give details of refuges and the availability of refuge places for women throughout the UK.

Welsh Women's Aid (helpline: 0808 801 0800) provides confidential information in English and Welsh.

Refuge (helpline: 0808 200 0247; www.refuge.org.uk) provides safe emergency accommodation for women through a network of refuges throughout the UK. It also offers a children's programme, individual and group counselling for women who have suffered abuse, help with resettlement and an outreach project for women from ethnic minority communities.

Police domestic violence units There are a number of police domestic violence units that have staff specially trained to help people experiencing domestic violence. They work closely with other organizations such as local solicitors and Women's Aid groups. Your local police station, in the phone book under 'Police', will be able to tell you if they have a domestic violence unit, or where the nearest one is.

Survivors UK Ltd (helpline 0845 122 1201; www.survivorsuk.org) is a national helpline for men who have been victims of violence, sexual assault and rape. The helpline may be able to arrange counselling or a support group if you live in the London area. If you live outside London, Survivors UK may be able to provide details of an appropriate service outside the London area.

Everyman (helpline 020 7263 8884; www.everymanproject.co.uk) is a national helpline for men who are concerned about their violence and the consequences of it. The helpline can provide telephone counselling and advice about local services. A face-to-face counselling service is also available but only in the London area.

M-Power (0808 808 4321; www.male-rape.org.uk) is a national helpline for men who have been raped, assaulted or abused in childhood or adult life. The helpline also supports partners (male and female) and family members of abused men.

Perpetrators of violence

There are several specialist organizations that can help violent people who want to stop being violent. Some are self-help groups run by others who have had experience of violent behaviour, others may be run by trained counsellors. It may also be possible for you to get help through your GP.

COMMUNITY CARE

Community care services are care services that are arranged or provided by the local authority social services department, mainly to adults who have care needs. Community care services include a place in a care home or services to help you carry on living in your home and keep as much independence as possible. You may need community care services because of your age or because you are disabled or physically or mentally ill.

Services that are available

There is a wide range of services that may be available under the heading of community care. The following list gives only the main examples:

- a place in a care home
- home care services
- home helps
- adaptations to the home
- meals
- recreational and occupational activities.

Care homes

If you need long-term care, and you can no longer manage in your own home, one option may be moving into a care home.

All care homes can provide personal care if you need it. This could include help with washing, dressing or going to the toilet. Some care homes can also provide nursing care. You may need this if you are frail or have a medical condition.

Care homes must make it very clear what level of care they are offering. They are inspected twice a year. Local authorities run some care homes and others are run by charities or private companies.

Remember that you may have other options – for example, getting more help to live at home or moving into sheltered housing. You may want to consider a trial period in a care home to see how you get on.

To find out more about these options, go to your local Citizens Advice Bureau or contact Help the Aged (020 7278 1114; www.helptheaged.org.uk) or Age Concern (0800 00 99 66; www.ageconcern.org.uk).

If you think that living in a care home is the best option for you, first of all get in touch with your local authority's social services department. They will assess what your needs are. They may meet with you or discuss your needs over the phone. If the local authority agrees that a care home is the best choice, they have to arrange a place for you. How much you will have to pay depends on your savings and income and social services will pay the rest. The rules about payment for care homes are different to the rules about paying for other community care services.

If you do not like the care home that the local authority offers, you do not have to move in. You can ask for a place you like better and you may be allowed to move there.

If you can afford to pay for a place in a care home yourself, you do not have to go through the local authority. You can approach the care home directly and sort out the payments with them. But if there is any chance you might need help with fees in the future, it is best if you have your needs assessed by the local authority before you make other arrangements.

To find out more about paying for a place in a care home, contact Help the Aged (020 7278 1114; www.helptheaged.org.uk) or Age Concern (0800 00 99 66; www.ageconcern.org.uk).

If there is a problem when you are living in the care home, it is best to try to talk about it with the manager. But if the problem cannot be resolved in this way, you could make a formal complaint to the Commission for Social Care Inspection (CSCI: 0845 015 0120; www.csci.org.uk). This is the body which inspects care homes.

Home care services

Home care services generally mean help with personal tasks – for example, bathing and washing, getting up and going to bed, shopping, managing finances. Providing home care involves someone coming to your home at agreed times. This could be two or three times a day or even 24-hour care where necessary.

Home helps

Home helps can provide assistance with general domestic tasks, including cleaning and cooking, and may be particularly important in maintaining hygiene in the home.

Adaptations to the home

Adaptations to the home could be major or minor and can be particularly important in allowing you to remain at home. Major adaptations would include, for example, the installation of a stair lift or downstairs lavatory or the lowering of worktops in the kitchen. Minor adaptations would include, for example, hand rails in the bathroom.

Meals

The provision of meals as a community care service could mean a daily delivery of a meal or, in some areas, the delivery of a weekly or monthly supply of frozen food. It could also mean providing meals at a day centre or lunch club.

Recreational and occupational activities

A local authority can provide a range of recreational, occupational, educational and cultural activities, together with the necessary facilities – for example, at day centres. The activities could include lectures, games, outings, and help with living skills and budgeting. The local authority may also provide transport to enable you to make use of the facilities.

A local authority may also be able to provide radios, televisions and/or visiting library services.

How to get community care services

Unless you urgently need services, you will have to have your needs assessed by the local authority social services department before they will provide services for you. This is called a community care assessment. The local authority social services department must carry out an assessment for anyone who appears to need a community care service because they are, for example, elderly, disabled or suffering from a physical or mental illness.

If you think that you need community care services, you should contact your local authority social services department and ask for an assessment. A carer, friend or relative can also ask for an assessment on your behalf.

How an assessment is carried out

More than one person could be involved in carrying out the assessment, including a social worker, a physiotherapist and an occupational therapist. The assessment procedure may involve filling in a form but this will vary from area to area.

The assessment should take into account:

- your wishes as the person being assessed
- whether you have any particular physical difficulties – for example, problems with walking or climbing stairs
- whether you have any particular health or housing needs
- what sources of help you have access to, such as carers, family or nearby friends, and their willingness to continue providing care
- what needs these people who provide care may have.

What happens once the assessment has been carried out

Once an assessment has been carried out, the local authority has to decide whether or not to provide services to meet needs that have been identified. If the local authority is going to provide services these must be set out in a care plan. This should be given in writing if requested. The care plan will set out:

- the services which are to be provided, by whom, when and what will be achieved by providing them
- a contact point to deal with problems over services
- information on how to ask for a review of the services being provided if circumstances change.

Assessment for a carer

A carer is someone, often a relative or friend, who takes responsibility for looking after a disabled, ill or elderly person, and who does not provide the care as part of a job or as a volunteer with a voluntary organization. Some carers provide care for a few hours a week, others for 24 hours a day, every day. A carer does not have to be living with the person being cared for.

If you are a carer, you are entitled to ask for your needs to be assessed when an assessment is being carried out for the person you care for. You can ask to be assessed even if the person you care for is entitled to an assessment but does not want one. Some carers of disabled children can also have an assessment.

Local authorities can provide services direct to carers and offer you direct payments for your own needs. However, the results of the carer's assessment must be taken into account when the local authority decides what community care services the person being cared for will receive.

Paying for community care services

A local authority can charge for providing some community care services.

Some local authorities only charge for some services – for example, meals on wheels or home helps – while others charge for all services for which they are allowed to charge. Carers who are provided with services for their needs can be charged for those services.

The information below does **not** cover charges for care homes. For more information about how charges are made for care homes, contact Help the Aged (020 7278 1114; www.helptheaged.org.uk) or Age Concern (0800 00 99 66; www.ageconcern.org.uk).

A local authority must make information about charges generally available. If you are having your community care needs assessed by the local authority, you must also be given full information on charges for any services provided.

Some local authorities make a flat-rate charge for a service – for example, meals on wheels. Other local authorities may want to know how much income – for example, social security benefits – and savings you have and then charge according to a sliding scale. Local authorities in England and Wales must comply with the following government guidance when assessing how much you can pay for services:

- they must not charge you if you get Income Support, income-based Job-seeker's Allowance or Pension Credit (guarantee credit only) and your overall income is less than a certain amount
- in England they must not take your earnings or the earnings of your partner into account; in Wales, your partner's income can be taken into account
- the local authority should only take your savings and capital into account if they are above a set limit. Your home is not taken into account when it assesses your capital
- in England only, if the local authority takes into account your disability-related social security benefit (for example, Attendance Allowance or Disability Living Allowance), it must assess any extra expenses you have as a result of your disability (for example, extra heating or laundry costs)
- in Wales, some disability-related expenditure must be ignored when they assess how much you can pay for services
- the local authority should offer you advice on social security benefits.

If you have been asked to pay for services and you think the charges are unreasonable or you cannot afford to pay them, you can ask for the charges to be reviewed.

Direct payments
Direct payments are payments of money a local authority social services department makes to people to arrange their own community care services, instead of the local authority arranging the services.

In England, if you are entitled to receive community care services, your local authority social services department must give you the option of getting direct payments, as long as you are able to manage a direct payment.

In Wales, a local authority social services department must offer direct payments to:

- a disabled person of 16 or over
- the carer of a disabled person or child for whom the carer has parental responsibility
- a disabled person with parental responsibility for a child

- a carer aged 16 or over
- someone aged 65 or over
- someone who receives community care services and is aged 18 or over.

If you are offered a direct payment, you do not have to accept it if you would rather have services arranged by the local authority social services department.

The amount of direct payments you get should cover the cost of buying services to meet your needs. This includes any extra costs you have to pay in order to get the service. For example, if you employ your own carer, you will have to pay recruitment costs, holiday and sick pay, and insurance.

In the same way that you may have to pay for services arranged by the local authority social services department, you may have to make a contribution towards the cost of services you are buying with direct payments. The local authority social services department will work this out in the same way it works out how much you have to pay towards services it arranges itself. They will either deduct your contribution before paying you the direct payment or pay the direct payment in full and you will have to pay your contribution back.

If you do get direct payments, you will have to arrange your own services. Local support organizations may be able to help you with these arrangements and the National Centre for Independent Living (020 7587 1663; www.ncil.org.uk) can tell you which those organizations are.

MANAGING FINANCIAL AFFAIRS FOR SOMEONE ELSE

There may be times in life when you want to ask other people to manage your financial affairs for you. You might choose a close relative or friend. This might be because you think you may lose your mental capacity, or because you have had a physical illness or an accident resulting in physical injury. Ways of doing this are explored here.

Asking someone else to manage your financial affairs temporarily

Social security benefits

If you are temporarily unable to collect your benefit and it is normally paid into your bank or building society account, you should write to the bank or building society, asking them to give temporary power to someone else to operate your account (see below). If your benefit is normally paid by cheque, you can fill in the back of the cheque to allow someone else to cash it for you. If you want someone else to cash your benefit cheque for you on a regular basis, you should contact your Jobcentre Plus office to let them know.

Bank accounts

If the only temporary power you want to give someone is the power to operate a bank account on your behalf, you should just write to your bank. Many banks have their own form, called a form for third-party mandate, which they will ask you to complete and return to them.

General financial affairs

If you want someone to handle your financial affairs for a temporary period – for example while you are on holiday or while you can supervise what they do – you need an ordinary power of attorney. A power of attorney is a legal document that authorizes one or more people to handle your financial affairs, including property, shares and money, either generally or in relation to specific items.

Powers of attorney

Ordinary power of attorney

If you want someone to look after your financial affairs for a longer period of time, you can grant an *ordinary power of attorney*, which can relate to all your affairs or only to specific matters. You should not use an ordinary power of attorney if you have been diagnosed as having, or if you think that you may develop, any mental illness or degenerative disease that can lead to mental incapacity. This is because an ordinary power of attorney automatically comes to an end if you lose your mental capacity. On the other hand, if, for example, you have a physical illness or an accident resulting in physical injury, and you want someone else to look after your affairs for this period, you could create an ordinary power of attorney.

Lasting power of attorney

Your financial affairs

You may want to make arrangements so that someone else can look after your financial affairs if you lose your mental ability to do so yourself. This could be, for example, because you have been diagnosed as having a degenerative brain disease leading to mental incapacity, such as Alzheimer's disease. The way to make these arrangements is to draw up a lasting power of attorney. Unlike an ordinary power of attorney, a lasting power of attorney can come into effect and continue in force after you lose your mental capacity. It has to be registered and then it will come into effect immediately, unless you specify in it that it should not take effect until you lose your mental capacity. It must include your authority for the attorney to make decisions once you lose your mental capacity. If it doesn't include this, it will take effect as an ordinary power of attorney.

Your personal welfare and health

You can also draw up a lasting power of attorney to make decisions about your health and welfare in the event that you lose your mental capacity to take these decisions yourself. For example, this power of attorney could cover health issues such as whether you want to give your consent for medical treatment in the future, or housing issues, such as what sort of housing you might want to move to in the event of your losing mental capacity. You will need to draw up two separate documents if you want to cover both personal welfare and financial matters. A lasting power of attorney which covers personal welfare **cannot** come into effect before you lose your mental capacity.

Enduring power of attorney

Before 1 October 2007, there were powers of attorney called *enduring powers of attorney*. These dealt solely with financial matters. If you have already written and registered an enduring power of attorney, it will still be valid on or after 1 October 2007. If you have created an enduring power of attorney but not yet registered it, it can still be registered on or after 1 October 2007. However, you cannot create a new enduring power of attorney on or after 1 October 2007.

You can revoke a registered enduring power of attorney on or after 1 October 2007 and replace it with a lasting power of attorney, as long as you still have mental capacity. An enduring power of attorney could not cover decisions about health and welfare so even if you have a valid enduring power of attorney, you could, in addition, create a new lasting power of attorney to cover health and welfare, as long as you still have mental capacity.

Who can grant a power of attorney?

Someone who grants a power of attorney is called a donor. In order to be a donor, you must have mental capacity and you can only grant the power of attorney to do things that you have the right and capacity to do yourself. Only the donor can make the decision to create a power of attorney. If you instruct a solicitor or advice worker to draft one for you, the solicitor or advice worker should only accept instructions or authorization from you, whether in person or in writing, and not, for example, from the person who is to become your attorney.

Children

A child under 18 can be a donor of an ordinary power of attorney, but a child can only give an attorney the power to do things that they can legally do as a child.

Who can be an attorney?

Anyone who has mental capacity can be an attorney. If an attorney becomes bankrupt, this ends a lasting power of attorney which deals with financial matters and an enduring power of attorney. However, bankruptcy does not end a power of attorney which deals with personal welfare.

Trust corporations such as banks can be an attorney and professional attorneys can charge for their services.

Responsibilities of an attorney

When you are appointed as an attorney you are placed in a position of trust and you must act in the best interests of the donor. As an attorney, you can only do the things the donor has authorized you to do, and you cannot delegate any duties unless the donor has authorized delegation.

Who can help?

The **Office of the Public Guardian** (0845 330 2963; www.publicguardian.gov.uk) can give information about lasting and enduring powers of attorney. It also supplies some forms and can advise on current fees. Its staff cannot give legal advice or help people complete the forms.

DEATHS

Registering the death

The registration of the death is the formal record of the death.

When someone dies at home, the death should be registered at the register office for the district where they lived. If the death took place in hospital or in a nursing home, it must be registered at the register office for the district in which the hospital or home is situated. If it is more convenient, you can go to a different office to register the death and the details will be passed on to the correct office.

A death should be registered within five days but registration can be delayed for another nine days if the Registrar is told that a medical certificate has been issued. If the death has been reported to the coroner, you cannot register it until the coroner's investigations are finished.

It is a criminal offence not to register a death.

When you have registered the death, the Registrar will give you a green certificate (for which there is no charge) to give to the funeral director. This allows either burial or cremation to go ahead. Occasionally a Registrar may be able to issue a certificate for burial only (but never cremation) if no one has yet been able to register the death.

The Registrar will also give you a form to send to the Department for Work and Pensions (DWP). This allows it to deal with the pension and other benefits of the person who has died.

Death certificate

The death certificate is a copy of the entry made by the Registrar in the death register. This certificate is needed to deal with money or property left by the person who has died, including dealing with the will. You will need several copies of the certificate, for which there will be a charge.

Coroners

A coroner is a doctor or lawyer appointed by a local authority to investigate certain deaths. A coroner is completely independent of the local authority and has a separate office and staff.

Anyone who is unhappy about the cause of a death can inform a coroner about it, but in most cases a death will be reported to a coroner by a doctor or the police.

A death cannot be registered until the coroner's investigations are complete and a certificate has been issued allowing registration to take place. This means that the funeral will usually also be delayed. Where a post-mortem has taken place, the coroner must give permission for cremation.

Inquests

An inquest is a legal inquiry into a death. It is held in public (sometimes with a jury) by a coroner in cases where the death was violent or unnatural or took place in prison or police custody or where the cause of death is still uncertain after a post-mortem. The inquest should provide more information about how and why the death took place and whether anyone else was responsible. In some cases, a criminal prosecution may take place later.

Deaths abroad

If a death takes place abroad, it must be registered according to the law of that country. The death should also be reported to the British Consulate, which may be able to arrange for the death to be registered in the UK as well.

Returning a body to the UK is expensive but the cost may be covered by any travel insurance taken out by the person. If the death was on a package holiday the tour operator should be able to help with arrangements.

When a body is returned to the UK, the Registrar of Births, Deaths and Marriages for the district where the funeral is to take place must be told and will need to issue a certificate before burial can take place. If cremation is to take place, the Home Office also needs to give permission.

If the death was not due to natural causes, the coroner for the district will also need to be told and an inquest may need to take place.

Donation of organs for transplant or the body for medical research

Donation of organs

The person who died may have wanted to donate organs for transplant. This will be easier if they were on the NHS Organ Donor Register (0845 60 60 400; www.uktransplant.org.uk), carried a donor card and had discussed the donation plans with their family. Relatives will still be asked to give their consent before donation. Most organ donations come from people who have died while on a ventilator in a hospital intensive care unit.

Donation of the body for medical education or research

Some people wish to leave their bodies for medical education or research and anyone wanting to do this will need to make arrangements before they die and tell their relatives. When the person dies, relatives should contact the Human Tissue Authority (020 7211 3400; www.hta.gov.uk). They will advise on what should be done. If a body is accepted (and many bodies are not suitable), the medical school will arrange for eventual cremation or burial.

FUNERALS

A funeral can take place any time after death. Most funerals are arranged by the nearest relatives. However, if there are no relatives, anyone close to the person can arrange the funeral instead.

The person who has died may have left instructions (in their will or somewhere else) about the type of funeral they wanted and whether they wanted to be buried or cremated. There is no legal obligation for relatives to follow these instructions. In some cases, relatives may want burial or cremation to take place abroad. The rules about this are very complex and the help of a specialist funeral director will be needed. Permission from a coroner is always needed before a body can be sent abroad.

If there are no relatives or friends to arrange a funeral, the local authority or health authority will arrange a simple funeral. The public authority that arranges the funeral will then try to recover the cost from any money left by the person who died.

Funeral arrangements

Funeral directors

Most funerals are arranged through a funeral director (who used to be known as an undertaker). It is important to find a funeral director who belongs to one of the professional associations, such as the National Association of Funeral Directors (NAFD) or the Society of Allied and Independent Funeral Directors (SAIF), since these associations have codes of practice and complaints procedures. Some local authorities also run their own funeral services by arrangement with a local firm of funeral directors. If a funeral director is not a member of a professional association and a complaint is not dealt with satisfactorily, you may need to take legal action against the funeral director.

Funeral costs

The person who arranges the funeral is responsible for paying the final bill and it is important to know where the money for the funeral will come from.

The person who died may have taken out a pre-paid funeral plan, paying for their funeral in advance. It is important to check their personal papers to see if they had a plan. If they did, this should cover the whole cost of the funeral.

If there is no funeral plan, the cost of the funeral will normally be met out of any money left by the person who has died and, where money has been left, the funeral bill should be paid before any other bills or debts. Even if the person's bank account has been frozen following the death, it may be possible to have funds released from a building society or National Savings account on presentation of the death certificate. The person may also have had an insurance policy that will cover funeral costs. In other cases, relatives may need to borrow money until the person's money and property are sorted out. Some funeral directors will allow payment to be delayed until this has happened.

Some people do not leave enough money to pay for even a simple funeral. If this happens, the person arranging the funeral will have to pay for it, although other relatives or friends may be willing to contribute. There is no general death grant, but if you are in this situation and you receive a means-tested social security benefit (such as Income Support or Pension Credit), you may be able to get a payment from the Social Fund (known as a funeral payment) to cover the cost of a simple funeral. Even where a funeral payment is made, it may not cover the full cost of the funeral and you may still have to pay the difference.

The funeral director should always give a written estimate of the cost of the funeral, but the final bill may be higher. The bill will cover the costs of burial or cremation, the fees for the funeral service and the professional services of the funeral director. There will also be charges for extras, such as flowers, cars, service sheets and newspaper notices.

Other costs

Anyone who receives a means-tested benefit (such as Income Support) may be able to receive help from the DWP's Social Fund through a budgeting loan towards the cost of travelling to the funeral of a close relative.

If the person who is paying for the funeral is receiving a means-tested benefit, it may be possible to receive help from the Social Fund through a funeral payment towards the cost of travelling to the funeral.

Burial or cremation

A burial can take place in a churchyard, a local authority cemetery or a private cemetery. Burials can also take place on private land, or in a woodland site. Anyone living within the parish has the right to be buried in the parish churchyard, if there is space, or in any adjoining burial ground. The person's religion is not relevant. Some churches may allow others to be buried there as well (for example, ex-parishioners or those with family graves). There is no right to be buried in any particular part of a churchyard or burial ground. Burials inside a church are not allowed in urban areas and are very rarely allowed elsewhere.

Most cemeteries are owned by local authorities or private companies and are non-denominational, although some have space dedicated to particular religious groups. In the case of a local authority cemetery, anyone living in the authority's area has the right to burial in the cemetery. Others may also be allowed burial, but for a higher burial fee.

In most cemeteries there are various categories of graves. Some graves do not give exclusive rights to burial while others give the right of exclusive burial for a set period of time. It is important to check the papers of the person who has died to find out if they have already purchased a grave space in a churchyard, cemetery or woodland burial ground. Although there is no law preventing burials on private land (including a garden), anyone wishing to do this should contact their local authority, who may issue a certificate confirming that the burial is lawful. The Natural Death Centre (0871 288 2098; www.naturaldeath.org.uk) can give advice on environmentally friendly burials, as well as on inexpensive funerals that do not need the services of a funeral director.

Most crematoria are run by local authorities. Five forms are needed before cremation can take place, including a certificate from the person's GP, countersigned by another GP, and an application form completed by a relative. These forms are available from the funeral director. The costs of cremation are usually considerably less than the costs of a burial.

Funeral service

The person arranging the service may choose any form of service. If you do not want any form of religious ceremony, the British Humanist Association (helpline 020 7079 3580; www.humanism.org.uk) can give advice on a non-religious (secular) service.

If you do not want a service of any kind, the funeral director can arrange for burial or cremation without any form of service.

If, for any reason, there is no body, a memorial service can be arranged instead of a funeral service.

Disposal of ashes

Ashes may be scattered or buried at the crematorium, either by crematorium staff or by relatives and friends. Ashes can also be buried in a churchyard or cemetery, often with a short service.

Ashes can generally be scattered anywhere, but if you wish to scatter ashes on private land, you should get consent from the landowner.

Although UK law allows ashes to be taken abroad, many countries have strict rules on the importation of ashes and it is important to check before travelling.

Memorials

Churchyards and cemeteries have firm rules about the size and type of memorials that are allowed and it is important to check on these rules before ordering anything. Church of England churchyards usually have more rules than local authority cemeteries. Some woodland cemeteries permit wooden plaques, but most will only allow the planting of a tree. The design of the memorial may be subject to approval.

The funeral director will usually apply to the church or cemetery authority for permission to erect a memorial. The authority will normally charge for giving its permission. Names of local monumental masons can be obtained from the National Association of Memorial Masons (01788 542264; www.namm.org.uk).

The person erecting a memorial is responsible for maintaining it.

At a crematorium there will often be a Book of Remembrance and relatives may pay for an entry. It may also be possible to buy a memorial bush with a plaque.

If those attending a funeral have been asked to make donations to a charity, the funeral director will normally collect these and send them on to the charity. Relatives will be given a list of donations received.

Miscarriages, stillbirths and perinatal deaths

A miscarriage is the loss of a baby before the 24th week of pregnancy. No registration is needed.

A stillbirth is a birth after the 24th week of pregnancy where the child is not born alive. A doctor or midwife will issue a medical certificate of stillbirth, giving the cause. The parents must present the certificate to the Registrar of Births and Deaths within 42 days of the baby's delivery. If the parents are married, the Registrar will need details of both parents. If the parents are not married, only the details of the mother are required but the father can give his details. Many funeral directors make no charge for arranging the funeral of a stillborn baby and many cemeteries and crematoria also make no charge for burial or cremation.

If a baby lives for even a short time after being born and then dies, this is called a perinatal death. In a perinatal death, both the birth and death must be registered. When a baby has died within a month of being born, the birth and death can be registered at the same time.

The birth is registered in the normal way. The death is registered by taking the medical certificate of death to the Registrar of Births and Deaths within five days of the death. If this is not possible, the hospital or parent should telephone the Registrar and explain the situation, for example, that the mother is too ill to attend.

If the parents are married, the Registrar will need details of both parents. If the parents are not married, only the details of the mother are required but the father can give his details.

Bereavement benefits

Bereavement benefits are payments made by the Department for Work and Pensions (DWP) to married or civil partners – see p. 649.

Counselling and support

There are a number of organizations that can provide help and support if you have been bereaved.

For general counselling and support, contact **Cruse-Bereavement Care** (in England, 0844 477 9400; www.crusebereavementcare.org.uk; in Wales, 029 2088 6913; crusecymru@gmail.com).

For support following the death of a child, contact **Compassionate Friends** (0845 123 2304; www.tcf.org.uk).

For support following the sudden death of a baby (cot death), contact the **Foundation for the Study of Infant Deaths** (020 7233 2090; www.sids.org.uk).

For support following the death of a same-sex partner, contact the **Lesbian and Gay Bereavement Project** (020 7403 5969; www.stjohnshospice.org.uk).

For support following a stillbirth, contact the **Stillbirth and Neonatal Death Society** (SANDS: 020 7436 5881; www.uk-sands.org).

For support following a miscarriage, contact the **Miscarriage Association** (01924 200 799; www.miscarriageassociation.org.uk).

WILLS

It is important for you to make a will, whether or not you consider you have many possessions or much money. It is important to make a will because:

- if you die without a will, there are certain rules that dictate how your money, property or possessions should be allocated (this may not be the way that you would have wished your money and possessions to be distributed)
- unmarried partners and partners who have not registered a civil partnership cannot inherit from each other unless there is a will, so the death of one partner may create serious financial problems for the remaining partner
- couples with children under 18 should consider what arrangements they want to make if either one or both of them die – you can appoint one or more individuals to act as guardian(s) for your children
- it may be possible to reduce the amount of tax payable on the inheritance if advice is taken in advance and a will is made
- if your circumstances have changed, it is important that you make a will to ensure that your money and possessions are distributed according to your wishes. For example, if you have separated and your ex-partner now lives with someone else, you may want to change your will. If you get married or enter into a registered civil partnership, this will invalidate any previous will you have made.

Solicitors and other help with writing a will

There is no need for a will to be drawn up or witnessed by a solicitor. If you wish to make a will yourself, you can do so. However, you should only consider doing this if the will is going to be straightforward.

It is generally advisable to use a solicitor or to have a solicitor check a will you have drawn up to make sure it will have the effect you want. This is because it is easy to make mistakes and, if there are errors in the will, this can cause problems after your death. Sorting out misunderstandings and disputes may result in considerable legal costs, which will reduce the amount of money in the estate.

Some common mistakes in making a will are:

- not being aware of the formal requirements needed to make a will legally valid
- failing to take account of all the money and property available
- failing to take account of the possibility that a beneficiary may die before the person making the will
- changing the will (if alterations are not signed and witnessed, they are invalid)
- being unaware of the effect of marriage, divorce, a civil partnership or the dissolution of a civil partnership on a will
- being unaware of the rules that exist to enable dependants to claim from the estate if they believe they are not adequately provided for. These rules mean that the provisions in the will could be overturned.

There are some circumstances when it is particularly advisable to use a solicitor. These are where:

- you share a property with someone who is not your husband, wife or civil partner
- you wish to make provision for a dependant who is unable to care for themselves
- there are several family members who may make a claim on the will – for example, a second wife or children from a first marriage
- your permanent home is not in the United Kingdom
- you are not a British citizen
- you are resident in the UK but there is overseas property involved
- there is a business involved.

If you are a member of a trade union, you may find that the union offers a free will-writing service. A union will often use its own solicitors to undertake this work.

There are books that provide guidance on how to draw up a will. These can help you decide if you should draw up your own will and also help you decide if any of the pre-printed will forms available from stationers and charities are suitable. It is also possible to find help on the internet.

Will-writing services are available. However, will-writing firms are not regulated by the Law Society so there are few safeguards if things go wrong.

How much does a solicitor cost?

The charges for drawing up a will vary between solicitors and also depend on the complexity of the will. Before making a decision on who to use, it is always advisable to check with a few local solicitors to find out how much they charge. You may have access to legal advice through an addition to an insurance policy which might cover the costs of a solicitor preparing or checking a will. If you are a member of a trade union, you may find that the union offers a free wills service to members.

It is also worth giving some thought to what you want to say in the will before seeing a solicitor. This should help reduce the costs involved.

You may be able to get legal aid to help with the costs but only if you are eligible on financial grounds and are:

- 70 or over; *and/or*
- disabled; *and/or*
- a parent of a disabled person and wish to provide for that person in the will; *and/or*
- a single parent who wishes to appoint a guardian in your will.

What to put in your will

To save time and reduce costs when going to a solicitor, you should give some thought to the major points you want included in your will. You should consider such things as:

- how much money and what property and possessions you have – for example, property, savings, occupational and personal pensions, insurance policies, bank and building society accounts, shares
- who you want to benefit from your will. You should make a list of all the people to whom you wish to leave money or possessions. These people are known as beneficiaries. You also need to consider whether you wish to leave any money to charity
- who should look after any children under 18

- who is going to sort out the estate and carry out your wishes as set out in the will. These people are known as the executors.

Executors

Executors are the people who will be responsible for carrying out your wishes and for sorting out the estate. They will have to collect together all the assets of the estate, deal with all the paperwork and pay all the debts, taxes, funeral and administration costs out of money in the estate. They will need to pay out the gifts and transfer any property to beneficiaries.

It is not necessary to appoint more than one executor, although it is advisable to do so – for example, in case one of them dies. It is common to appoint two, but up to four executors can take on responsibility for administering the will after a death. The people most commonly appointed as executors are:

- relatives or friends
- solicitors or accountants
- banks
- the Public Trustee or in some cases the Official Solicitor if there is no one else willing and able to act.

It is important to choose executors with considerable care since their job involves a great deal of work and responsibility. You should always approach anyone you are thinking of appointing as an executor to see if they will agree to take on the responsibility. If someone is appointed who is not willing to be an executor, they have a right to refuse.

If an executor dies, any other surviving executor(s) can deal with the estate. If there are no surviving executors, legal advice should be sought.

Requirements for a valid will

In order for a will to be valid, it must be:

- made by a person who is 18 years old or over; *and*
- made voluntarily and without pressure from any other person; *and*
- made by a person who is of sound mind – this means the person must be fully aware of the nature of the document being written or signed and aware of the property and of the identity of the people who may inherit; *and*
- in writing; *and*
- signed by the person making the will in the presence of two witnesses; *and*

- signed by the two witnesses, in the presence of the person making the will, after it has been signed by that person. A witness or the married partner or civil partner of a witness cannot benefit from a will. If a witness is a beneficiary (or the married partner or civil partner of a beneficiary), the will is still valid but the beneficiary will not be able to inherit under the will.

Although it will be legally valid even if it is not dated, it is advisable to ensure that the will also includes the date on which it is signed.

As soon as the will is signed and witnessed, it is complete.

Once a will has been made, it should be kept in a safe place and other documents should not be attached to it. There are a number of places where you can keep a will:

- at home
- with a solicitor
- at a bank
- at the Principal Registry of the Family Division of the High Court, a District Registry or Probate Sub-Registry for safe keeping. If you wish to deposit a will in this way, you should visit the District Registry or Probate Sub-Registry or contact the Probate Department at the Principal Registry of the Family Division (020 7947 6000).

Searching for copies of a will

Postal application

When writing to request a copy of a will by post, the forename(s), surname, date of death and last known address of the person who has died must be provided to the York Probate Sub-Registry (01904 666777). They will pass requests to the probate registry keeping the will and grant of probate, which will in turn send the required copies direct to the individual. There is a fee for this service.

You can make a personal search free of charge by going to the Principal Registry of the Family Division – see above. If you want to inspect or take a copy of the will, there is a fee.

Or you could order a copy of a will or grant of probate at any District Probate Registry. You will need to give the full name of the person who died, the date probate was granted and the name of the registry office where it was issued. There is a fee. To find a District Probate Registry, go to Her Majesty's Courts Service website at www.hmcourts-service.gov.uk.

How to change a will

When a will has been made, it is important to keep it up to date to take account of changes in circumstances. It is advisable for you to reconsider the contents of a will regularly to make sure that it still reflects your wishes. The most common changes of circumstances which affect a will are:

- marriage and civil partnerships
- the end of a relationship
- the birth or adoption of children, if you wish to add these as beneficiaries in a will.

You may want to change your will because there has been a change of circumstances. You must not do this by amending the original will after it has been signed and witnessed. Any obvious alterations on the face of the will are assumed to have been made at a later date and so do not form part of the original legally valid will.

The only ways you can change a will are by making:

- a codicil to the will; *or*
- a new will.

Codicils

A codicil is a supplement to a will that makes some alterations but leaves the rest of it intact. This might be done, for example, to increase a cash legacy, change an executor or guardian named in a will, or to add beneficiaries. A codicil must be signed by the person who made the will and be witnessed in the same way. However, the witnesses do not have to be the same as for the original will.

There is no limit on how many codicils can be added to a will, but they are only suitable for very straightforward changes. If a complicated change is involved, it is usually advisable to make a new will.

Making a new will

If you wish to make major changes to a will, it is advisable to make a new one. The new will should begin with a clause stating that it revokes all previous wills and codicils. The old will should be destroyed. Revoking a will means that the will is no longer legally valid.

Destroying a will

If you want to destroy a will, you must burn it, tear it up or otherwise destroy it with the clear intention that it is revoked. There is a risk that if a copy subsequently reappears (or bits of the will are reassembled), it might be thought that the destruction was accidental. You must destroy the will yourself or it must be destroyed in your presence. A simple instruction alone to an executor to destroy a will has no effect. If the will is destroyed accidentally, it is not revoked and can still be declared valid.

Although a will can be revoked by destruction, it is always advisable that a new will should contain a clause revoking all previous wills and codicils. Revoking a will means that the will is no longer legally valid.

Challenging a will

A person may want to challenge a will because:

- they believe that the will is invalid; *or*
- they believe that they have not been adequately provided for in the will.

There are strict time limits for challenging a will. If you want to challenge a will you should seek legal advice as soon as possible.

If a person who makes a will commits suicide, the will is still valid.

A–Z OF YOUNG PEOPLE'S RIGHTS

In this information, 'child' means someone aged under 14 and 'young person' means someone aged 14 or over but under 18. 'Parent' means someone with parental responsibility.

Abortion

Whatever age you are, you are entitled to a confidential consultation with a doctor, provided you make it clear that you do not want a parent to be told. If you are under 16, the doctor will only tell your parents or another adult that you have been to see them in very exceptional circumstances. An example of exceptional circumstances is when a doctor believes you are at risk of serious harm. They would always discuss this with you first, before telling anyone else.

If you do not want to go to your family doctor, you should seek help from another agency, such as a Brook Centre (0800 0185 023; www.brook.org.uk) or a local family planning centre.

Women over 16 years do not need their parents' consent to have an abortion. If you are under 16, you normally need your parents' consent. However, the law does say that a girl under 16 can give consent to her own treatment if her doctor considers her to be mature enough to make the decision. In practice, very few doctors are prepared to give medical treatment under these circumstances. If you are under 16 and want an abortion, get advice from a Brook Centre or local family planning centre.

Adoption

If you are under the age of 18 you can be adopted if you are not married or in a civil partnership. As a child, you will have little say over who adopts you, but you should be consulted by the adoption agency or social services department involved in the adoption.

If you are under 18, you have no legal right to know the identity of your birth parents. Once you reach 18, you have a right to apply to see your birth record and to use the Adoption Contact Register. The Register helps adopted people get contact details of birth relatives who have also registered.

To apply to the Adoption Contact Register, write to: Adoption Section, Room C201, The General Register Office, Trafalgar Road, Southport PR8 2HH.

Alcohol

It is an offence to give alcohol to a child under five (unless it is given by a doctor on health grounds). If you are five or over and under 16, there is no legal restriction on your drinking alcohol at home or on other private premises.

If you are under 14, you cannot normally go into a pub or other licensed premises where alcohol is sold and consumed during opening hours unless you are the landlord's child or live on the premises. However, a publican can apply for a children's certificate that will allow children under 14 to be taken into a pub by an adult. Children would normally have to leave by 9 p.m.

If you are aged 14 or 15 you can go into a pub but cannot buy or drink alcohol there. If you are aged 16 or 17, you can buy or drink wine, beer, cider or perry (but not spirits) with a meal in a hotel or restaurant or part of a pub set apart for eating meals.

It is normally an offence for a person under 18 to buy alcohol and drink alcohol in a pub – but see paragraph above. It is also an offence for a person to buy alcohol on behalf of a person under 18 that is to be drunk in the street. Anyone working in a pub will be committing an offence if they sell or allow a person under 18 to drink alcohol in a pub. However, they will have a defence if they can prove that they had no reason to suspect that the person was under 18.

If police suspect a young person of possessing alcohol (or something they believe to be alcohol) in a 'relevant place', they can confiscate it. A 'relevant place' is any public place (except licensed premises) or a place to which someone has gained access unlawfully. The police can also confiscate alcohol or what they think may be alcohol from a person of any age if they suspect some of it has been, or is intended to be, drunk by someone under 18 in a 'relevant place'. The police can arrest anyone who tries to prevent them confiscating what they believe to be alcohol.

Anti-social behaviour

Anti-social behaviour is behaviour likely to cause alarm, distress, or harassment. Examples of anti-social behaviour include vandalism, graffiti, throwing fireworks in the street, throwing stones at trains, and causing a nuisance to others.

The following measures can be taken to address anti-social behaviour by children and young people:

- parents can be asked to enter into a parenting contract to help improve their child's behaviour. A parenting contract may involve the parent attending counselling or guidance sessions
- the police and community support officers can take action. For example, an officer can order someone to stop cycling on the pavement and disperse groups of young people. It is a criminal offence to refuse to follow these instructions
- the police and community support officers can issue an on-the-spot fine (penalty notice) to anyone aged 16 or over (ten or over in some areas)
- bodies such as a local authority, the police and registered social landlords can apply to court for an anti-social behaviour order. It is a criminal offence to disobey an anti-social behaviour order
- a parenting order can be made if a child is convicted of an offence or if a

young person has been involved in anti-social behaviour. It is a criminal offence for a parent to disobey a parenting order.

Banking, credit and borrowing money

There is no legal age limit at which you can open a bank account but a bank manager can decide whether to allow a child or young person to open an account. There are restrictions on opening certain kinds of account – for example, as a young person you are not normally legally responsible for your debts so you are unlikely to be granted an overdraft.

If you are under 18, it is a criminal offence for anyone to send you material inviting you to borrow money or obtain goods or services on credit or hire purchase. However, if you are over 14 but under 18, you can enter into a credit or hire purchase agreement if an adult acts as your guarantor.

You can borrow money at any age, but access to loans may be limited because a contract between a lender and a young person will not usually be enforceable.

If you apply for a credit card when you are under 18, you will have your application turned down.

Benefits

Usually, you cannot get benefits until you are 18 or over. However there are some exceptions. For example, some 16- and 17-year-olds who are unemployed and not in full-time education may be able to claim Jobseeker's Allowance. If you are 16 or 17 years old, you may get Income Support if you have a child or are pregnant or if you are sick.

Depending on your income, you may be able to claim Housing Benefit to help you pay the rent, but the amount you can get if you are a single person aged under 25 with no children is restricted.

If you are a young person with a disability, there are a number of different benefits and tax credits you may be able to claim. Usually, your parents would claim the benefit on your behalf.

As a young person, you may be able to claim a crisis loan from the Social Fund if there is an emergency and you are unable to pay for your immediate needs. You do not have to be receiving any other benefits to be able to claim.

If you are 16 or over, you may be able to claim tax credits. To get Working Tax Credit, you must work 16 hours or more a week, be on a low income and either have a disability which puts you at a disadvantage in getting a job or be responsible for a child.

If you are 16 or over you can get Child Tax Credit if you are responsible for a child under the age of 16. If you are under 16 yourself and responsible for a child, you cannot claim Child Tax Credit in your own right. However, your parents or someone who is responsible for you can include you in their own claim.

Betting and gambling

It is an offence for anybody to have a betting transaction with a person they know, or ought to know, is under 18. This includes gambling on the internet.

Betting shops, gaming clubs and bingo

If you are under 18, you may not enter a public betting shop or gaming club. You can go into a licensed bingo club where bingo is played as long as you do not take part in the game.

Fruit machines

If you are under 16, you can go into arcades but must not play on fruit machines giving a £10 or more cash payout.

If you are between 14 and 18 you can go into a pub, but you are not allowed to play on fruit machines with a cash payout of £10 or more. A sign stating that the machines are restricted to over-18s must be displayed.

There is no lower age limit for playing on fruit machines with a maximum cash or token prize of up to £8.

Lottery tickets and scratch cards

If you are under 16, you may not buy tickets (or scratch cards) in a registered public lottery. You may buy tickets in a private lottery.

Blood and organ donation

You are not allowed to donate blood unless you are considered to have sufficient understanding of what is involved.

If you are under 18, you can donate your body and organs on death, but if you are under 16 you need to get your parents' consent to carry a donor card. Parental consent is also required before the organs can be used.

Body piercing

There are no legal restrictions on the age at which you can have your ears or other body parts pierced. However, some establishments may operate their own informal guidelines on obtaining parental consent.

Butane lighter fuels

It is illegal to sell a lighter fuel refill canister containing butane to children and young people.

Changing your name

You cannot change your name until you are 16 years old. Between 16 and 18 you can complete a change of name deed with parental consent.

Cigarettes

You can smoke cigarettes in private at any age. However, it is an offence punishable by a fine to sell tobacco, cigarettes or cigarette papers to anyone under 18. If you are aged 18 or above, you are subject to the usual rules about smoking. For example, there is a smoking ban in nearly all enclosed public places and workplaces, whatever your age.

Civil partnerships

A civil partnership is a legal relationship which can be registered by two people of the same sex. If you are in a gay or lesbian relationship, registering a civil partnership will give your relationship legal recognition.

You are not allowed to register a civil partnership if one of you is under 16. If you are a young person of 16 or 17 who wants to register a civil partnership, you can usually do this only if you have the consent of your parents, although in some cases the court could give you permission.

Contraception

There are no age restrictions on giving contraceptive advice and supplies. As long as you understand the possible risks, a doctor is allowed to prescribe contraception if you are under 16 without the consent or knowledge of a parent. Your doctor has to encourage you to discuss with your parents the fact you have sought advice about contraception. But it is only in exceptional circumstances that the doctor will tell your parents or another adult about your visit. An example would be if the doctor believes you are at risk of serious harm. The doctor would always discuss this with you first before telling anyone else.

Courts and young people

Criminal proceedings

A child under ten is not considered to be capable of deciding whether an action is right or wrong. They cannot be taken to court and charged with a criminal offence. If you are aged ten but under 14 years old, you are considered to be responsible for a criminal offence and are treated in the same way as any young person under 18. This means that you can face criminal proceedings, although your case will normally be dealt with in a youth court.

Civil proceedings

If you are under 18, you cannot normally start court proceedings in your own name, and a litigation friend – usually a parent – must act on your behalf.

As a child or young person you cannot normally be sued for breach of contract because, in most circumstances, you cannot enter into a contract that is enforceable in a court.

Negligence

As a child or young person you can be sued for negligence through your parent. Negligence is defined as failure to act with reasonable care so as not to cause damage to other people or property. An injured party has the right to sue for compensation. An example of negligence is riding a bicycle in a manner that results in personal injury or damage to property.

Legal aid

A child or young person can apply for legal aid. In some cases only the applicant's financial circumstances will be taken into account. In other cases the financial circumstances of the applicant's parents will also be taken into account.

A child or young person who has been arrested for a criminal offence has the same rights to legal advice (including criminal legal aid) as an adult. If you are under 18, you do not have to meet certain financial eligibility conditions that adults might have to meet.

Being a witness

If you are 14 or over, you will normally be expected to give evidence at court as a witness under oath. If you are under 14, you will normally give evidence without swearing an oath.

If you are under 17 and the court agrees, you will be allowed to present your evidence to the court by video recording or live TV link. You have to be available for cross-examination. This would apply in a sexual abuse case, in a case of violence or neglect and in certain other cases.

Who can help?

The **Law Centres Federation** (020 7428 4400; www.lawcentres.org.uk) can provide addresses of local law centres.

Debt

As a child or young person you cannot normally be taken to court for debt. This is because you cannot usually make a legally enforceable contract. The exception is when debts are incurred for necessities – for example, food, clothing and shelter.

As a parent you are not usually under any obligation to pay the debts of your child. However, if you acted as a guarantor for a contract they entered into, you will be responsible for any debts under the agreement, even where the contract is not legally enforceable against the young person.

Discrimination

It is against the law to discriminate against anyone, including a child or young person, because of their:

- race, colour, nationality, or ethnic or national origins
- sex
- disability
- sexuality
- religion or belief
- age (only at work).

Some of the places where you are protected against discrimination include work, schools and colleges, shops, clubs, pubs, hospitals and clinics, and council services. You are protected against discrimination regardless of whether you are buying something or getting it for free.

In certain circumstances, there are some exceptions to these rules which mean that discrimination is allowed. For example, the rules banning age discrimination apply only at work.

If you have experienced discrimination, including sexual or racial harassment, you may be able to take action against the organization or person responsible.

Driving

There are rules about the age at which you can drive a particular type of vehicle. For example, you can ride an electrically assisted pedal cycle from the age of 14, or a moped or invalid carriage from the age of 16, and drive a motorbike, car or certain classes of van and lorry from the age of 17.

You are not allowed to supervise a learner driver until you are 21 and have had a licence yourself for three years.

If you drive a vehicle when you are 17, you must have third-party liability insurance, even though you cannot usually enter into a contract until you are 18.

Drugs

If you are in possession of illegal drugs you may face prosecution, depending on your age.

Films, DVDs and videos

Film classification

There are restrictions on the films you can see in a cinema. The British Board of Film Classification (BBFC) issues certificates for all films as follows:

- U (universal) – suitable for all those aged four years or over
- PG – unaccompanied children are admitted but parental guidance needed as some scenes are unsuitable for young children

- 12A – no one under the age of twelve will be admitted, unless accompanied by an adult
- 15 – no one under the age of 15 will be admitted
- 18 – no one under the age of 18 will be admitted.

As well as these restrictions, a cinema manager has discretion over admission of any member of the public. In general, children under five outside London and under seven in London are not allowed in a cinema unless accompanied by an adult.

DVD and video classification

Most pre-recorded English language DVDs and videos have to be classified and labelled according to their suitability for viewing by different age groups. The classification categories are:

- Uc (universal) – particularly suitable for pre-school children
- U (universal) – suitable for all those aged four years or over
- PG (parental guidance) – for general viewing but some scenes may be unsuitable for young children
- 12 – only suitable for people aged twelve years or over; not to be supplied to anyone below that age
- 15 – only suitable for people aged 15 years or over; not to be supplied to anyone below that age
- 18 – only suitable for people aged 18 years or over; not to be supplied to anyone below that age
- Restricted 18 – only to be supplied in licensed sex shops to people aged 18 or over.

It is an offence to supply a classified DVD or video to someone who is below the age specified in the classification.

It is an offence to supply an unclassified DVD or video unless it is exempt from classification.

PC and video games

Some video games may need classification by the British Board of Film Classification (BBFC), for example, if they depict gross acts of violence towards humans or animals or if they show criminal behaviour. The BBFC could refuse to classify the game, in which case it is an offence to supply the game in the UK.

There is a European-wide voluntary rating system in operation for video games that do not need to be classified. This is called the PEGI system and it is administered in the UK by the Video Standards Council (www.video standards.org.uk).

Flying

You are allowed to fly a glider from the age of 16. You can hold a private air pilot's licence from the age of 17 and a commercial air pilot's licence from the age of 18.

Glue sniffing

It is illegal to sell solvents to anyone under 18, but glue sniffing is not against the law. However, as a child or young person you can be arrested for glue sniffing in a public place and charged with breach of the peace.

Income tax

You are taxed independently on your income, in the same way as an adult. However, in general, if you are under 16, your parent enters details of your income on their own tax return.

If you are unmarried and under 18 and your parent gives you money that produces investment income – for example, money in a National Savings account – any resulting income over £100 will normally count as your parent's income and should be entered on their tax return.

If you are under 16 and want to make a claim to HM Revenue and Customs for repayment of overpaid tax, your parent, guardian or trustee must make the claim.

If you are under 16 and have a bank or building society account that pays interest, your parent can register to stop tax being automatically deducted from the interest, if you are a non-taxpayer.

Internet use

There is no central body that monitors content on the internet. However there are various laws about children and the internet. For example, it is against the law to show or download indecent images of children and young people on the internet. Grooming is where an adult uses the internet to gain the trust of children or young people – this is against the law. It is against the law for online gambling websites to allow anyone under 18 to gamble. It is also a criminal offence to sell pornography over the internet with no means of checking whether the customer is under 18.

There is parental control software that can be installed if you are concerned about your child's access to the internet. You may want your child to use only moderated chatrooms where a specially trained adult is present to stop any improper communications.

The children's charity NCH (www.nch.org.uk) has useful information for parents about their child's use of the internet. You can report illegal content on the internet to the Internet Watch Foundation (www.inf.org. uk).

Leaving home voluntarily

In most circumstances you can leave home without the consent of your parents or anyone with parental responsibility when you are 16. A parent or person with parental responsibility could take wardship proceedings in court, but it is unlikely that any court would order you to return home if you did not want to.

Local authority care

You can only be taken into care if you are under 18 and the local authority has obtained a court order. You have a right to know why you are in care, under what law, and how long you are likely to remain there.

You can be accommodated by a local authority without a court order if a parent requests it or gives permission. However, the local authority must take your wishes into account.

Marriage

If you are under 16 and marry, it will not be recognized by law unless your marriage took place in a country with a lower marriage age limit than 16.

If you are 16 or 17 and want to get married in a register office, you need the written permission of a parent. If they refuse permission, you can apply to a magistrates' court, county court or the High Court for permission to marry. If you are 16 or 17 and want to get married in a church, you need parental permission. This too may need to be in writing. Anyone aged 18 or over can be married without parental permission.

Although two people of the same sex cannot get married, they can register a civil partnership (see *Civil partnerships*, p. 20).

Medical treatment

Registering with a GP

If you are under 16, you have no right to choose your own GP and must be registered by a parent. If you are aged 16 and over you can choose your own GP.

Confidentiality

If you are under 16, you are entitled to a confidential consultation with a doctor. The doctor will only tell your parents or another adult that you have been to see them in very exceptional circumstances. An example of exceptional circumstances is when a doctor believes you are at risk of serious harm. They would always discuss this with you first, before telling anyone else.

Consent to medical treatment

If you are under 16, you can give your own consent to medical treatment provided you fully understand what is involved. If a doctor decides that you do not fully understand what is involved in giving consent, a person with parental responsibility for you can give consent on your behalf.

If you are under 18 and refuse treatment, a person with parental responsibility or medical staff may seek a court order to override you.

NHS charges

If you are under 16 (or are 16, 17 or 18 and in full-time education), you are entitled to free dental treatment (including check-ups), eye tests, vouchers for glasses and free wigs and fabric supports. In England, this also applies to prescriptions. In Wales, no one has to pay for prescriptions.

If you are aged 16 or 17 and are not in full-time education, you are entitled to free dental treatment (including check-ups). You may also qualify for help with other NHS treatment if you are on a low income.

If you are aged 16 or 17 and maintained financially by the local authority (either wholly or partly), you are entitled to eye tests, vouchers for glasses, wigs and fabric supports. In England, this also applies to prescriptions. In Wales, no one has to pay for prescriptions.

Sexually transmitted diseases

If you think you have a sexually transmitted disease (STD) and want advice or treatment, go to a family doctor, family planning clinic, pregnancy advisory service or STD clinic. If you are under 16, you are entitled to see a doctor and get treatment in confidence without your parents or another adult being informed. However, in exceptional circumstances, a doctor may tell your parents or another adult if the doctor believes that you are at risk of serious harm. They would always discus this with you before telling anyone else.

HIV/AIDS

If you want advice about HIV/AIDS, you will need to seek specialist advice – for example, from the Terrence Higgins Trust (0845 1221 200; www.tht.org.uk).

Mobile phones

If you are under 18, you cannot enter into a monthly contract for a mobile phone. However, you can buy a pay-as-you-go mobile phone as this does not require a contract.

Parents aged under 16

Mothers aged under 16

If you are under 16 and have a baby you have the same legal rights and responsibilities towards the child as any mother.

Benefits and Tax Credits

If you live with your parents and they are claiming Child Tax Credit, both you and your child can be included in the claim. Your parents may also be able to claim a Social Fund Maternity Grant for you and your child. If they are claiming Housing Benefit, they can include you and your child in their claim.

As a young mother, you can claim Child Benefit once the baby is born.

If you are at least ten weeks pregnant, your parents can get vouchers for free milk, fruit and vegetables for you. It doesn't matter what their income is.

Once you have had the baby, your parents can continue to get vouchers for you but only if they get Income Support, income-based Jobseeker's Allowance or Child Tax Credit and have an annual income below a certain amount.

Education

Local education authorities have a duty to ensure that all children under 16 receive an education. They still have this duty to you, even if you become a mother.

Housing

As a young mother you will not normally be able to obtain privately rented or council accommodation because you are too young to be granted a tenancy. However, you can contact the local authority social services department and ask it to accommodate you, provided your parents agree.

Maintenance

As a young mother you can apply to the Child Support Agency for a maintenance assessment to be carried out in respect of your child. This applies only if you are not living with the father of your child.

Fathers aged under 16

As a father aged under 16, you may want to have a formal relationship with your child by applying for a parental responsibility agreement, residence order or contact order.

Maintenance

If you are aged under 16 and father a child, the Child Support Agency (CSA) can expect you to pay maintenance for the child if you do not live with the child's mother. Once the CSA is satisfied that you are the father, you will be expected to make maintenance payments when you begin earning or receiving a benefit.

Passports

Everyone who is travelling outside the UK must have their own passport. This includes babies and children.

You must have the consent of a parent to have a passport if you are under 18, unless you are married or a member of the armed forces.

Personal records

At any age, you have the right to see information kept about you, unless the person looking after the information considers you incapable of understanding the nature of the request you are making. If you are refused access to your records, you can complain to the Information Commissioner (08456 306060; www.ico.gov.uk).

As a parent you do not usually have the right to see information about your child kept on a computer record. This will only be allowed if the person looking after the information knows that the child has authorized the request, or – if the request is being made on behalf of a child or young person – is considered incapable of understanding the nature of the request.

Pets

There is no lower age limit for owning a pet. However, if you are under 16, you cannot buy one without a parent being present.

Police

If you are over the age of ten you can be fingerprinted, photographed and searched while you are in police custody. If you are 16 or over and have been involved in anti-social behaviour, you may be issued with a penalty notice. This is a notice for an on-the-spot fine. Community support officers can also take action against young people if they are behaving in an anti-social way.

The procedures governing the treatment of children and young people by the police are set out in the codes of practice made as a result of the Police and Criminal Evidence Act (the PACE codes). If these procedures are not followed, the case may be dismissed. Disciplinary proceedings can be brought against police officers who break these codes of practice.

You should seek advice in these circumstances from a local law centre – see p. 529.

Proof of age

There are many schemes that provide cards to help prove your age. Many local authorities and local colleges run card schemes.

It is against the law for someone under 18 to buy or be sold alcohol and the Proof of Age card provided by the Portman Group can help you prove you are old enough to buy or be sold alcohol if you are 18 or over but do not look your age. You must pay a fee to apply, complete a form and provide a photograph. A professionally qualified person must countersign both the form and the photograph. The form is available from some retailers or directly from the Portman Group (020 7907 3700; www.portmangroup.org. uk).

Punishment

Parents

Parents have a legal right to smack their child. However, if the violence they use is severe enough to leave a mark, for example a scratch or a bruise, they can be prosecuted for assault, or their child can be taken into local authority care.

School

No teacher in a school is allowed to inflict corporal punishment on a student of any age.

The head teacher and teachers can use reasonable non-physical means to punish a pupil for unacceptable conduct or behaviour. Any punishment must be fair, reasonable and within the school's policy. Examples of reasonable punishment are extra work during school hours or being told off.

A member of staff can use reasonable physical force to break up a fight between pupils or to stop pupils endangering themselves, other pupils or school property, or to prevent a pupil from committing a criminal offence.

In care and other institutions

Corporal punishment must not be inflicted on any child or young person living in a children's home, secure unit, foster home provided by the local authority or voluntary organization, residential care home or young offender institution. If a child or young person lives in a private foster home, nursing or mental nursing home, or a youth treatment centre, mild smacking is allowed as long as it does not leave a mark.

Registered childminders

A registered childminder is not allowed to smack a child in their care.

Religion

A parent has the right to choose which religion their child will follow at home and at school or to choose that they shall follow no religion at all. However, a child or young person may choose their own religion if they have sufficient understanding. If a parent considers the child's chosen religion to be harmful, a court can be asked to intervene.

There is a general requirement that schools should provide religious education but it is possible for an individual child to be withdrawn from religious education. There are laws prohibiting religious discrimination but in some cases faith schools can still discriminate against pupils of another religion when they decide who can be admitted to the school.

Seat belts

Children under twelve travelling in the rear or front seats of a vehicle must normally wear a child restraint. Passengers aged twelve or over must normally wear a seat belt. Even if you are under twelve, you have to use a seat belt if you are over a certain height.

If you are under 14, the driver of the vehicle is responsible for making sure that you wear a seat belt or restraint where this is required by law. Everyone over the age of 14 is responsible for wearing a seat belt when this is required by law. The driver or owner of the vehicle is not responsible for passengers over this age.

Sex and sexuality

It is legal for two people of the opposite sex or the same sex to have a sexual relationship if both of them are 16 or over and both of them consent to the sexual activity.

It is a criminal offence for someone of either sex to take part in sexual activity with someone under the age of 16, unless it is reasonable to believe that that person is 16 or older. Sexual activity includes sexual intercourse and intentional sexual touching. The penalties for an offence of this type are more severe if it is committed by someone who is 18 or over rather than someone who is under 18.

Where both people are under 16, each will be committing an offence if they have a sexual relationship. However, it is unlikely that there will be any prosecution if the sexual activity was mutual and non-exploitative. If someone under the age of 16 is sexually involved with someone else aged 16 or over, the younger person will not be committing an offence. However, the person over 16 could be charged.

Incest means sexual intercourse between close relatives and it is a criminal offence.

Child abuse can include physical or emotional neglect, physical injury or sexual abuse.

If you are worried about child abuse or incest, you should consult an experienced adviser.

Tattooing

It is an offence to tattoo anyone under 18 unless a qualified medical practitioner does it for medical reasons. Someone who tattoos anyone under 18 can be prosecuted unless they show they had good cause to believe the person was over 18.

Wills

If you are under 18, you cannot make a valid will unless you are in the armed forces or a seafarer. No one under the age of 18 can act as a trustee, executor or administrator of a will, but you can appoint a guardian to act on your behalf.

Who can help?

The Office of the Children's Commissioner (0844 8009113; www.11million.org.uk) is an independent organization that was set up by the government. They look after the interests and act as the voice of children and young people in England.

The **Children's Commissioner for Wales** (01792 765600; www.childcom. org.uk) can give children and young people living in Wales advice about their rights and welfare. The Commissioner can also help you make a complaint about your treatment if you are using the usual complaints procedure of an institution such as a school, care home or social services department. If your complaint is unsuccessful, the Commissioner may be able to carry out a separate investigation.

2
Health

CONTENTS

INTRODUCTION

It is hard to imagine what life must have been like, especially for poor families, prior to the National Health Service (NHS). Before then, some workers on low pay were entitled to see a doctor for free, but this benefit often did not stretch to their wives or children. Hospitals charged patients and, although sometimes poorer families would be reimbursed, it still meant paying in the first place, which many people simply could not do. People with mental health problems were locked away, out of sight and out of mind. Many older people who could no longer care for themselves ended up in the workhouse, doing unpaid work in return for food and a roof over their heads.

The new NHS – free to all at the point of delivery – was born on 5 July 1948, bringing access to healthcare services to the whole population, regardless of their ability to pay. It would be difficult to exaggerate the impact that the NHS has had on the health of the nation, cradle to grave – from establishing a vaccination programme for babies and children that protects the whole community to delivering appropriate care for older people approaching the last part of their lives. Huge medical and technological advances in recent years, such as IVF treatments, gene science, and successes in heart and liver transplant surgeries, have brought new challenges and an expansion in the demand for and provision of health services. The NHS is now the largest organization in Europe and is recognized as one of the best health services in the world by the World Health Organization.

This chapter covers the services provided by the NHS, how the system works and who to turn to if things go wrong.

JARGON BUSTER

GP	general practitioner or doctor
NHS	National Health Service
PCT	Primary Care Trust. There are no PCTs in Wales – Local Health Boards in Wales have similar functions
A&E	Accident and Emergency
PALS	Patient Advisory Liaison Service
ICAS	Independent Complaints Advocacy Service

NHS NUMBERS AND MEDICAL CARDS

NHS numbers help staff across the NHS get up-to-date information on patients' health. However, if you do not have an NHS number, you can still get NHS treatment.

A hospital should give your baby an NHS number shortly after birth. If the baby was not born in hospital, a number will be given once the hospital has been told about the birth. If your baby was born abroad and does not have an NHS number, you can get one by registering with a GP.

To get a medical card for your baby, you may need to give their NHS number to a chosen GP. However, procedures for getting medical cards vary from area to area. If in doubt, you should ask your GP. If you do not have a medical card, or have lost it, you should contact your local Primary Care

Trust (PCT), giving your name, address and date of birth, and the name and address of your previous GP. If possible, you should also give your NHS number.

You can register with a GP without a medical card by completing a form supplied by the GP. The PCT will then send you a new medical card.

GENERAL PRACTITIONERS (GPs)

Registering with a GP

If you are ordinarily resident in the UK, even if you are from abroad, you have the right to be registered with a GP. You can choose which GP you want to register with. The GP does not have to accept you. However, if they do refuse to accept you, they must have reasonable grounds for refusing and they must give you their reasons in writing.

You can obtain a list of local GPs from the PCT or the local community health council in Wales. You can also find details of GPs from NHS Direct and NHS Direct online (0845 4647; www.nhsdirect.nhs.uk in England or www.nhsdirect.wales.nhs.uk in Wales). The list will describe the services offered by the GP and may also contain information on whether any alternative therapies are available within the practice. It may also give details of surgery hours, whether there is an appointment system and whether there are any special clinics run at the surgery.

You should take your medical card to the GP's surgery in order to register with the GP of your choice. You will need to fill in part A of the card and hand it to the GP or practice staff. A GP may wish to see you before agreeing to register you. The GP will forward the medical card to the PCT (or local health authority in Wales), which will send you a new medical card.

Children under 16 should be registered by their parent(s), but they do not have to register with the same GP as the rest of their family.

If you are staying somewhere in the UK for less than three months, you can ask to be registered with a GP on a temporary basis. You can also register temporarily if you move around the country and have no permanent address.

Unless the GP's register is full, or you live too far away for home visits, it is unlikely that the GP will refuse to register you. However, if the GP does refuse to accept you, they must have reasonable grounds for doing so. These grounds must not have anything to do with race, gender, social class, age, religion, sexuality, appearance, disability or medical condition. The GP must give you the reasons for their decision in writing.

If you have been unable to register with a GP, you should contact the local PCT. You should send your medical card, with a letter giving the names of any GPs who have refused to register you, and of any GPs with whom you would prefer not to be registered.

The PCT will try to find a GP who is prepared to accept you. This will not necessarily be a GP of your choice. Once you have been allocated a GP, the GP must accept you and treat you, and can only remove you from their list under certain circumstances (see *If your GP removes you from their register*, p. 87). The PCT will then have to find you another doctor. The PCT cannot help you find another GP if you are already registered with one.

Treatment from a GP

You are entitled to treatment from a GP at the surgery where you are registered. You have no automatic right, however, to see your own GP.

A GP must provide any treatment which is immediately necessary in an emergency, even if you are not registered with them.

Outside surgery hours

All GPs must make sure that a service is provided for their patients when they are off duty. This service could be provided by, for example, other partners in a group practice, a rota between GPs, a commercial deputizing service (a locum), or a telephone number that patients can use out of hours.

Primary Care Trusts are responsible for ensuring that the standard of care provided by commercial deputizing services is satisfactory. If you are unhappy about the standards of treatment you have received, you should contact the PCT responsible for commissioning the deputizing service.

Home visits

You cannot insist that a GP visits you at home. A GP will only visit you at home if they think that your medical condition requires it. A GP can also decide how urgently a visit is needed.

If you were to become seriously ill after a GP had refused a home visit, the GP could be found to be in breach of their contract with the NHS, or could be found to have been negligent. You might therefore wish to make a complaint.

You can be visited at home by a community nurse if you are referred by your GP or by a hospital consultant. If you are not an urgent patient, you can make an appointment and should be visited on the day arranged.

You should also be visited at home by a health visitor if you have recently had a baby or if you are newly registered with a GP and have a child under five years.

Medication

If a GP decides you need medication, they will usually give you a prescription. In some cases – for example, if the surgery is in an isolated area – the GP may provide the medication themselves.

A GP must supply any drugs needed for immediate treatment in an emergency. There is no prescription charge for these.

Alternative therapies

Some GPs are qualified in alternative therapies and may offer these as part of their NHS treatment. In some areas GPs may be able to refer a client to alternative practitioners, but this option will not always be available.

Second opinions

You can ask your GP to arrange a second opinion from either a specialist or another GP. However, the GP does not have to do this if they do not think it necessary. You have no right to a second opinion.

You do have the right to see a GP competent to deal with your particular case. If a GP refers you for a second opinion, you cannot insist on seeing a particular practitioner. However, you should not be referred to someone you do not wish to see.

If the GP refuses to arrange a second opinion, you may wish to change your GP.

If a GP is unsure about a diagnosis, they could be found negligent if they failed to refer you to a specialist and you suffered as a result. If you have not been referred for a second opinion and have suffered as a consequence, you may wish to complain.

GP charges

Anyone living in the UK normally qualifies for free treatment from a GP. However, visitors do not usually qualify for free treatment. For example, if you used to live in the UK and then went to live abroad, you would not normally get free treatment if you came back for a visit. There are some exceptions to these rules – for example, if you need emergency treatment.

A GP may, in practice, be flexible in deciding whether you are resident in the UK in order to qualify for free treatment. You will usually have to show that your stay in the UK has some degree of permanence and stability.

If you are a visitor in the UK for a period that is less than three months, a GP may accept you as a temporary resident. Otherwise, a GP may offer to accept you as a private patient and you will have to pay for treatment.

Even if you do live in the UK, you may be charged for certain GP services – for example, check-ups for employees and vaccinations for travelling abroad.

Changing your GP

You can change your GP at any time you wish without having to give a reason. If you tell the PCT that you want to change your GP, the PCT must give you details of how to do so and provide you with a list of alternative GPs.

You do not need the consent of your GP to change GPs. When you have found another GP willing to accept you, you should take your medical card to the new GP to be registered. You can then make an appointment to see the new GP immediately.

If you wish to change your GP, but cannot find a new one who will accept you, you should contact the Primary Care Trust, who should find you an alternative.

If your GP removes you from their register

A GP may be able to remove you from the patient register in some situations – for example, because you move out of the practice area or are physically or verbally abusive to people at the practice. In most cases, the GP must have given you a warning, and given you reasons for your removal from the register. The removal from the register takes effect from the eighth day after the PCT receives the GP's notice, or from the date that you are included on another register, if this is sooner. You are entitled to emergency treatment, or the continuation of treatment that is occurring more than once a week, until you are accepted by another GP. If you have been violent, or have threatened to be violent, towards your GP or practice staff, and the police have been informed, you can be removed immediately from the GP's list. You will only be accepted for emergency treatment by the GP who has removed you if the GP is satisfied that it is clinically necessary.

If you have been removed from a GP's list, you may wish to complain if you feel it was unreasonable to remove you.

If you move out of GP's area

If you are changing address, but are not moving too far, you may wish to stay with your current GP. You should ask the GP if they are willing to continue treating and visiting you at the new address. A GP can continue to treat you if you have moved out of their practice area, but they will have to assure the PCT that they are willing to continue visiting and treating you.

NHS DIRECT

NHS Direct is a confidential service offering advice and information about health problems and services. It provides 24-hour access to free health advice from experienced nurses. The line is intended to help people care for themselves by advising on the next course of action – for example, whether to stay at home and what self-treatment to take or whether to visit a GP or a hospital. They can also give you information about:

- local charter standards
- local medical services
- waiting times
- common diseases, conditions and ailments
- how to complain about NHS services
- maintaining and improving personal health.

NHS Direct can be contacted by telephone on 0845 4647 (all calls are charged at local rate) or at www.nhsdirect.nhs.uk in England or www.nhsdirect.wales.nhs.uk in Wales.

Other information about NHS services

You can also get information about NHS services from NHS Choices (www.nhs.uk).

MATERNITY SERVICES

If you are pregnant, you will be able to receive services from one or more of the following:

- midwives, based either in a hospital or in a local health centre or clinic.

Midwives are responsible for the care of all normal pregnancies and labours. You do not need to be referred to a midwife by your GP

- a GP. Not all GPs provide antenatal care and arrange for delivery. If your GP does not provide this service, you may wish to register with another GP for your maternity care. The PCT can provide details of GPs who offer maternity care
- an obstetrician based in a hospital. Generally, an obstetrician will only get involved if there are complications. However, you can request to see an obstetrician, even if the midwife or GP is providing all the care.

You may have a range of options to choose from on the type of antenatal care you want and where you give birth. How much choice you have will depend on the area in which you live, but could include:

- full hospital care. This would only happen, in practice, if you require a high degree of medical intervention
- shared care between a GP and hospital staff. Normally, you would return home shortly after the birth
- a home birth, with the birth attended by, and antenatal care provided by, a midwife and possibly a GP. You have the right to have your baby at home and may need to contact the supervisor of midwives to arrange for this. Alternatively, you could register with an alternative GP just for your maternity care.

Information on local maternity services can be obtained from your PCT, a community midwife, a health visitor or a GP. This information will include, for example, the type of care offered, where the birth can take place, what pain relief is offered and what tests are available and what they are for. In some areas, there are maternity charters that set out the rights of pregnant women and new mothers, and the standards of service you can expect.

If you are having difficulty obtaining the type of care you want, or you require more information on how maternity services are organized in your area, you should contact the supervisor of midwives at your local maternity hospital or at the PCT.

HOSPITAL TREATMENT

Emergencies

If you need urgent medical attention, you can go directly to the accident and emergency (A&E) department of a hospital without needing a referral from your GP. Not all hospitals have A&E departments.

If you need an ambulance to get to hospital in an emergency, this should arrive within a few minutes. The NHS plans give target maximum times for ambulance arrival, which differ between urban and rural areas.

It is the responsibility of the hospital providing the emergency treatment to meet the cost of treatment. If emergency admission as an in-patient is needed, the cost will be met by the PCT where you live.

Waiting times in an emergency

If you go into an A&E department, you should be assessed immediately.

You should be given a bed as soon as possible. Staff will try to ensure you do not wait more than four hours between attending the A&E department and admission, treatment or discharge, but this is not guaranteed. If you are using an out-patients' department, you should be given a specific appointment time.

Hospital treatment that may not be available on the NHS

Access to some forms of treatment – for example, in-vitro fertilization – may be subject to the PCT's priorities. Some treatment may not be provided in your area. Access to some treatment may depend on your need. You can obtain details of those services not provided, and any prioritizing criteria, from the PCT.

If you are unhappy because a certain form of treatment is not available, you should complain.

Consultants

You have no right to see a consultant or a particular doctor, although this can be requested. Your GP cannot insist that you see a particular consultant or doctor. You do have the right to see a doctor competent to deal with your case. If you have special reasons for seeing a particular consultant – for example, if your child is the consultant's patient – you could ask for an appointment, explaining your reasons for wanting to see them. If you still have difficulty in seeing the consultant, you could write to the hospital administrator or the consultant's secretary asking for their help.

You may wish to get a second opinion after seeing a consultant, either as an out-patient or as an in-patient. You will need to request this from the consultant, who may arrange for you to see someone else. If the consultant does not agree, you could ask your GP to help.

Choose and Book

In England, you have the right to be offered the choice of at least four hospitals when you need to see a specialist for further treatment.

You can book the appointment yourself. Your GP must give you an appointment request slip first. This must have a reference number and password which you use when you make your booking.

Choose and Book (0845 608 8888; www.chooseandbook.nhs.uk) helps you to choose a hospital appointment at a convenient hospital and at a convenient time for you. It also means you can choose a hospital with a shorter waiting list.

Right to hospital treatment

You cannot receive NHS hospital treatment without being referred by your GP, unless you are attending a special clinic (for example, for the treatment of sexually transmitted diseases) or you need urgent medical attention in an emergency.

If you are violent and/or abusive to NHS staff, you may be refused NHS hospital treatment, or given a verbal or written warning before treatment is withheld or withdrawn. Violent or abusive behaviour could include verbal abuse, threats, violence, drug or alcohol abuse in hospital, and destruction of property. Each PCT can decide which types of behaviour could lead to treatment being withheld or withdrawn and how such policies are implemented. If you are violent or abusive to NHS staff and have severe mental health problems or are suffering life-threatening conditions, you will not be denied treatment.

Waiting lists

You may be unable to receive the hospital treatment you need immediately and may have to go on a waiting list. There are maximum waiting times for in-patient treatment. If necessary, treatment may be arranged in an alternative hospital to meet this guarantee.

There are also waiting time standards for a first appointment as an out-patient.

Waiting lists do not operate on a 'last come, last served' basis. Where you are on a waiting list depends on a range of circumstances and may change. If your condition deteriorates dramatically, your GP may recommend you be seen as a matter of greater urgency. How long you will have to wait for a date to see a specialist or have an operation will therefore depend on the severity of your condition, how busy the specialist is and other demands on the hospital facilities.

You can find out about waiting times at particular hospitals through the NHS Direct website. In Wales, information is available from the Health of Wales Information Service website (www.wales.nhs.uk).

If you are waiting to be admitted to hospital, you should contact the hospital appointments department or the consultant on a regular basis, reminding the hospital staff that you are still waiting. If you are prepared to go into hospital at short notice you should say so, in case a cancellation occurs. You should also keep your GP informed of your condition, particularly if it deteriorates.

Operation cancellations

If your operation is cancelled, you should be offered an alternative date. In most cases, this should be within 28 days of the original date, and sooner for life-threatening conditions. If this does not happen, you may want to complain.

An appointment for an operation should not be cancelled for non-medical reasons on the day that a patient goes into hospital. If it is cancelled on the day – for example, if the surgeon is unavailable or there is insufficient theatre time – an alternative date should be offered.

Visits

Most hospitals have visiting hours during which visits to patients can be made. A person has no automatic right to visit you, and your doctor may decide that visits would be detrimental to your health. There is usually also a limit to the number of people who can visit at any one time. The restrictions on visits from children are the same as those for other visitors.

If someone wishes to visit you outside visiting hours, they should discuss this with the ward sister. If they cannot get permission from the ward sister, they should contact the hospital administrator if they wish to pursue the matter.

Financial help with visits

If you are receiving Income Support or income-based Jobseeker's Allowance, you may be able to get help with travel costs from the Social Fund to visit a sick relative.

Children

There are things to consider if your child is going into hospital – for example, whether you can stay with your child, how much help you can give with feeding and looking after your child, and what will happen to your child's education. Action for Sick Children (0800 0744519; www.actionforsickchildren.org) may be able to advise on all these issues. It also produces a leaflet for parents whose child is going into hospital for the first time.

The Department of Health has strongly recommended to hospitals that they allow unrestricted visiting on children's wards. Hospitals should also allow parents to be with their children as much as possible. This could include allowing you to stay overnight at the hospital. You should make enquiries before your child goes into hospital about what arrangements can be made. If you are finding it difficult to visit a child in hospital – for example, if you have other children at home – you may wish to discuss this with the medical social worker at the hospital.

Single-sex wards

You do not have the right to be cared for in a single-sex ward. However, you do have the right to be informed before you go into hospital (unless it is an emergency or you are admitted to an intensive care unit) whether you will be in a mixed ward. If you wish to be cared for in a single-sex ward, you may have to delay your admission to hospital if this is not available immediately.

If a patient dies in hospital

If a patient dies in hospital, NHS staff should inform relatives and the patient's GP as soon as possible and advise the relatives of the arrangements that need to be made.

An NHS Trust may be responsible for the funeral arrangements if there are no relatives or the relatives are unable to afford the cost and do not qualify for a funeral payment from the Social Fund.

Hospital charges

There is no charge for most hospital treatment for NHS patients who live in the UK. There are charges for visitors from overseas, except in the case of an emergency. However, there are charges for the emergency examination and treatment of people involved in road accidents. There are also charges for certain services – for example, beds with more privacy, alternative menus, patients' telephones and televisions.

Financial help for hospital patients

If you are entitled to benefits or tax credits, your entitlement may be affected by your being in hospital.

If you are concerned about the effect of hospitalization on benefits or tax credits, you should consult an experienced adviser – for example, at a CAB.

If you are on a low income, you may be able to get help with travel costs to hospital and with the cost of wigs and fabric supports. In England, this includes the costs of prescriptions. In Wales, prescriptions are free.

Discharge from hospital

You should not be discharged from hospital until your care needs are assessed and arrangements made to ensure that you will receive any necessary services when you are discharged.

Any assessment should take into account your wishes, the wishes of your family and of any carer. You should be kept fully informed and involved, be given sufficient time to make decisions, and be told how to seek a review of any decisions made. You can ask for a reassessment of your needs if circumstances change in the future.

You may not be satisfied with arrangements for your discharge from hospital because, for example:

- you feel that you need to remain in hospital for further in-patient treatment
- you are not satisfied with the community care services that have been arranged for you when you are to leave hospital
- you do not want to be sent to a care home.

Before discharge takes place, you, or your family, carer or representative, have the right to ask for a review of the decision which has been made about your eligibility for continuing NHS care. In England, you can also ask for a review after discharge.

If you are not satisfied with arrangements that have been made for you after you have been discharged, you can complain. If you are not satisfied with any medical services you are receiving from the NHS, you should use the NHS complaints procedure. If you are not satisfied with community care services that have been arranged or provided by the local authority, you should complain to the local authority using its complaints procedure.

CONSENT TO MEDICAL TREATMENT

You should not be examined or given any treatment or operation without your consent, unless:

- you have a notifiable disease or are a carrier of a notifiable disease
- you have been detained under the Mental Health Act, in certain circumstances
- your life is in danger, you are unconscious and you cannot indicate your wishes
- you are a child who is a ward of court and the court decides that a specific treatment is in your interests
- a court or someone who has parental responsibility authorizes treatment. A person whose treatment is authorized by a court must be given an opportunity to defend their case against treatment in court.

In some cases, it is good practice to ask you, the patient, to sign a consent form, but in other cases consent can be obtained orally. For example, it is good practice to obtain written consent for any procedure or treatment carrying substantial risk or side effects. It is also good practice for the hospital to obtain your written consent for general anaesthesia, surgery and certain forms of drug therapy (if you are capable of giving the consent). Oral or written consent should be recorded in your notes with relevant details of health professionals' explanations.

The doctor must inform you of the nature, consequences, and any substantial risks involved in the treatment or operation, before you give your consent. It is for the doctor to decide exactly how much to tell you, the patient.

Even if you sign a consent form, the signature may not be a valid form of consent if you have not been given appropriate information to be able to give informed consent. Similarly, consent for one procedure does not imply consent for a further procedure or form of treatment.

Children

Young people aged 16 or 17 can give independent consent to their own treatment. It is not necessary to obtain the consent of a parent or guardian. A young person can be overruled by a court order.

However, if the young person is incapable of giving their own consent – for example, if they are severely disabled – the consent of their parent(s) or guardian(s) must be obtained.

Children under 16 can give their own consent to treatment provided they are judged capable by a doctor or PCT of understanding what is involved. There is no general test for assessing this capacity, and each case will be decided on its own merits.

If a child under 16 does not have sufficient understanding, parental consent (or a court order) will be required for any treatment, except in an emergency. If a child under 16 who does have sufficient understanding refuses treatment, treatment can still be given with the consent of their parent(s) or guardian(s) or by a court order.

Children or young people under 18 cannot give their own consent to experimental operations and blood donations, unless they have sufficient understanding of what is involved.

Experiments, medical research and teaching

In general, if a doctor wishes to carry out research on you, your consent has to be given. You should be given a full explanation of the procedures and risks involved. It should also be made clear to you that you can withdraw from the research at any time. Appropriate safeguards should always be in place to protect patient confidentiality.

No one can consent to research being carried out on another person. If your consent cannot be obtained, the research should not be done. However, if a child under 16 is not competent to decide, a parent or court can consent to the research on their behalf.

You have the right to refuse to participate in teaching without your treatment being affected. If you do not want to be involved in teaching, it is advisable to inform the hospital in advance.

Removal of organs after death

Unless you have said you do not want parts of your body used for research or donated to others after your death, whoever is legally responsible for the body can allow organs to be donated. This will usually be your personal representative. Before organs can be removed from the body, medical staff must be certain that brain death has taken place, and a death certificate must be issued.

Right to refuse treatment

You can refuse any treatment if you wish (but see *Consent to medical treatment*, p. 95, for exceptional circumstances). The doctor cannot act against specific instructions, so you should tell the doctor about any treatment you do not want.

If there are a number of alternative treatments that can be used to treat your condition, you should be given information on these. However, you cannot insist on a particular treatment if the doctor or consultant thinks this is not appropriate.

Sometimes a doctor needs to treat someone who does not have the mental capacity to say whether they want a particular treatment or not. If you have mental capacity, and you are 18 or over, you can make an 'advance decision' about the treatment you want in the future. The decision will apply even if you lose your mental capacity. If you want to refuse treatment which may help keep you alive, the advance decision has to:

- be in writing (although it can be written by someone other than yourself or recorded in your medical notes); *and*
- be signed by you and witnessed by another person; *and*
- state clearly that the decision applies even if your life is at risk.

If you receive compulsory treatment because of mental illness, this treatment can override an advance decision.

Forcing treatment on you against your will is assault. If you are assaulted, you should make a complaint. You may also wish to involve the police.

I have a terminal illness the symptoms of which mean that a time will come when I can no longer communicate. If I want to refuse further treatment at that stage, how can I make my wishes known?

You have a right to refuse or stop treatment at any time, even if this means you may die. It is illegal for a doctor actively to cause death – for example by massively increasing dosages of drugs which may bring about an earlier death. There are, however, some exceptions to this general rule – for example, a House of Lords case decided that it was lawful for a doctor to end life support treatment because the treatment was futile, as the patient was unconscious and there was no prospect of any improvement in his condition. It may also be lawful to end life-prolonging treatment if a patient lacks mental capacity and treatment would cause extreme pain, discomfort or indignity.

If you are concerned that you will be unable to make your wishes known at a later stage in an illness, it may be wise to inform the doctor in advance at what stage you want to stop treatment. This is called making an advance decision. There are certain formalities that have to be followed if the advance decision would lead to your refusing life-sustaining treatment – see p. 97.

You have the right to refuse medical treatment in most situations. However, consent to treatment is not needed if you have a notifiable disease, have been detained in certain circumstances for psychiatric reasons (usually called being sectioned) or are unconscious and in need of lifesaving treatment and are unable to indicate consent. In fact, your consent is needed for most medical matters, but simply going to see a doctor can be regarded as implied consent for an examination or treatment. If you are concerned about a specific type of treatment, the doctor is obliged to describe other forms of treatment that are available. Forcing treatment on a patient who has refused can be considered assault.

Refusing treatment for a child

If a parent, guardian or child refuses to give consent for treatment which a doctor thinks is necessary, the doctor is still obliged to treat the child. The action the doctor takes will depend on how urgently the treatment is needed.

When a child's life is in danger, the doctor has the right to do whatever is needed to save the child's life, although the doctor may need to obtain a court order. If a parent or a guardian either fails to provide medical help for a child, or unreasonably refuses to allow treatment, they can be prosecuted for neglect.

RIGHT TO DIE

The law concerning whether a person has the right to die is unclear.

You have a right to refuse or stop treatment at any time, even if this means that you may die. However, it is illegal for a doctor to omit or carry out treatment with the specific intention of inducing or hastening death. There are some exceptions to this general rule – for example, a House of Lords case decided that it was lawful for a doctor to end life support treatment because the treatment was futile, as the patient was unconscious and there was no prospect of any improvement in his condition. It may also be lawful to end life-prolonging treatment if a patient lacks mental capacity and treatment would cause extreme pain, discomfort or indignity.

If you believe you may become so ill that you could no longer make the decision about treatment, you can draw up a written document setting out for the doctor at what stage you would want treatment to stop (an advance decision). An advance decision refusing treatment is legally binding on healthcare professionals. See p. 97 for more details.

ACCESS TO MEDICAL REPORTS AND HEALTH RECORDS

You have the right to see most health records held about you, subject to certain safeguards. You are entitled to be informed of the uses of the information, who has access to them and how you can arrange to see your records. You have a right, subject to certain safeguards, to see any medical report written for an employer, prospective employer or insurer by a medical practitioner who has responsibility for your ongoing care – for example, your GP or consultant and any medical practitioner who has treated you in the past. Information about your medical history should be kept confidential and should not be released without your consent to people who are not involved in your medical care. This includes your relatives, unless you are unable to give consent yourself.

HELP WITH HEALTH COSTS

Most NHS treatment is free, but there are a number of things for which there are usually charges. In some situations – for example if you are in receipt of certain state benefits or are a certain age – you may be able to get help with:

- prescription charges in England (these are free in Wales)
- NHS dental charges, including check-ups
- sight tests
- vouchers towards the cost of glasses and contact lenses
- travel costs to and from hospital for NHS treatment
- travel costs if travelling abroad for treatment
- wigs and fabric supports – for example, abdominal and spinal supports, and support tights. In Wales, you can get a free NHS wig or fabric support, if you have been prescribed one, whatever your age, income or personal circumstances.

Help with prescription charges

Free prescriptions

In Wales, everyone is entitled to free prescriptions. In England, you are entitled to get prescriptions free of charge if, for example, you:

- get certain benefits, such as Income Support. If you are getting Working Tax Credit and/or Child Tax Credit, you may be entitled to free prescriptions, depending on your income
- are 60 or over
- are under 16
- are in full-time education and are aged 16, 17 or 18.

If none of these categories applies to you, you may still be able to get free prescription on the grounds of low income – see *Help with health costs if you are on a low income* (p. 101).

Prepayment certificates

If you need frequent prescriptions but do not qualify to get them free of charge, you can buy a prepayment certificate which will save you money. You can get a certificate that lasts for either four or twelve months. You will usually benefit from buying a prepayment certificate if you have to pay for more than five prescription items in a four-month period, or more than 14 items in a twelve-month period.

Before buying a prepayment certificate, check that you are not entitled to free prescriptions as it is very difficult to get a refund once you have paid for your certificate.

In England, there are a number of ways to buy a prepayment certificate:

- over the phone from the NHS Business Services Authority (0845 850 0030)
- from the NHS Business Services Authority website (www.ppa.org.uk)
- from the pharmacist
- from your PCT.

In Wales, prescriptions are free, so you do not need a prepayment certificate.

Help with health costs if you are on a low income

If you have difficulty in meeting your health costs and do not qualify for any other kind of help, you may be able to get help under the NHS low income scheme.

The amount of help you get will depend on the amount of income you have. You might not be entitled to any help at all if you have too much capital. There are two types of certificate: a full help certificate (HC2), and a limited help certificate (HC3), which tells you how much you have to pay.

To apply for either a full help certificate (HC2) or a limited help certificate (HC3), complete form HC1, which is available from local Jobcentre Plus offices, NHS hospitals, dentists, opticians and pharmacists. You do not have to wait until you need treatment before you apply for a certificate. Send the completed form HC1 to the NHS Business Services Authority (0845 850 1166).

NHS HOSPITAL CHARGES AND PEOPLE FROM ABROAD

Your entitlement to free NHS hospital treatment depends on the length and purpose of your residence in the UK, not your nationality. Any free NHS hospital treatment you receive, or any help with NHS costs, does not affect your immigration status.

If you are entitled to it, you can obtain free treatment immediately. There is no qualifying period.

Hospital treatment that is always free of charge

Some hospital treatment is free of charge for everyone who needs it, regardless of how long they have been or intend to stay in the UK. This is:

- treatment for accidents and emergencies as an out-patient in a hospital's casualty department, or in a walk-in centre
- compulsory psychiatric treatment
- treatment for certain communicable diseases, such as tuberculosis, cholera, food poisoning, malaria and meningitis. Testing for the HIV virus and counselling following a test are both free of charge, but any necessary subsequent treatment and medicines may have to be paid for
- family planning services.

Who can receive all NHS hospital treatment free of charge?

Some people from abroad can receive all NHS hospital treatment free of charge. If you are entitled to free NHS hospital treatment, your husband, wife or civil partner will also be able to receive free treatment, but only if they live with you permanently in the UK.

You can receive free NHS hospital treatment if you:

- have been living legally in the UK for at least twelve months when you seek treatment, and did not come to the UK for private medical treatment. Temporary absences from the UK of up to three months are ignored
- have come to the UK to take up permanent residence – for example, if you are a former UK resident who has returned from abroad – or if you have been granted leave to enter or remain as a spouse
- have come to the UK to work, either as an employee or as a self-employed person. This does not include people on short business trips
- normally work in the UK, but are temporarily working abroad, have at least ten years' continuous residence in the UK, and have been abroad for less than

five years. However, if you are studying abroad, you are not entitled to free NHS treatment

- are receiving a UK war pension
- are an asylum seeker or have been granted discretionary leave to remain or refugee status
- are imprisoned in the UK or detained by UK immigration authorities
- are a UK state pensioner who spends at least six months a year living in the UK and up to six months a year living in another EEA state (but are not a resident of that state)
- are working in another EEA country, or in Switzerland, but are paying compulsory UK national insurance contributions. For a list of EEA countries, see p. 502
- are a student following a course of study that lasts at least six months or is substantially funded by the UK government.

Visitors who can receive NHS hospital treatment free of charge

If you are a visitor, you and your dependants are entitled to free NHS hospital treatment if your need for it arose during your visit to the UK. A medical opinion may be needed in order to decide if treatment should be provided free of charge. This applies if:

- you are a national of an EEA country, living in an EEA state or Switzerland, or a refugee or stateless person living in an EEA state, or you are a non-EEA national who lives in an EU state and pays national insurance contributions there
- you normally live abroad in a non-EEA state, and are receiving a UK state pension or other benefit, and have lived in the UK in the past for at least ten years
- you have lived in the UK for at least ten years in the past, but now live in an EEA state or Switzerland, or in a non-EEA state with which the UK has a reciprocal agreement
- you are a national or a resident of certain non-EEA countries with which the UK has a reciprocal agreement.

For a list of EEA countries, see p. 502.

In addition, people from some countries can get free hospital treatment if they have been referred to the UK for that treatment under the terms of the reciprocal agreement. There are also special arrangements with certain countries that enable people from outside the UK to get free treatment.

The Department of Health can give details of countries with which the UK has a reciprocal agreement and for which there are special arrangements.

Paying for NHS hospital services if you are a visitor

Once the hospital has established that you must pay for treatment, you will usually be asked to pay the full cost in advance, unless emergency treatment is required immediately.

If you cannot pay in advance, the hospital will ask for a written undertaking to pay.

If you cannot provide proof that you can afford to pay, treatment will be refused and you may be offered the chance to be treated privately.

Refusal of hospital treatment

If you are not entitled to receive free NHS hospital treatment, you will not be refused medical treatment that stabilizes a life-threatening condition – for example, for renal failure. Treatment will be given to deal with the emergency but you will be expected to return home for it to be completed once the emergency is over.

Refunds

If you have paid for hospital treatment but are entitled to free treatment, you should contact the Primary Care Trust for a refund.

I am coming to the UK from abroad. Can I get free NHS treatment?

Free treatment is available, but not automatically for every person who enters the UK from abroad. Emergency, compulsory psychiatric and contagious or infectious disease treatments are free. HIV diagnosis is free but treatment may not be.

As with UK residents, some NHS treatments have to be paid for (such as dentists and opticians), although help is available if you cannot afford to pay. People living or working in the UK are entitled to free treatment, but so are people who are taken ill while in the UK for a short stay. Some countries have an arrangement whereby UK residents can get free medical treatment there, and residents of that country can get the same in the UK – this is called a reciprocal agreement.

If you cannot pay for NHS treatment, urgent treatment will still be carried out on the NHS, but you will have to return home for continued treatment. If the need is not urgent, NHS treatment may be offered, but not for free.

Unless you have come to the UK specifically for medical reasons, this entitlement to free treatment extends to GP services, community nurses, midwifery and ambulances, although a GP may require proof of how long you intend to stay in the UK.

MAKING A COMPLAINT ABOUT THE NHS

You have the right to make a complaint about any aspect of NHS treatment using the NHS complaints procedure. To use the procedure you must usually be a patient or a former patient of the practitioner or institution concerned, although it is possible to complain on behalf of someone else. If you want to complain on behalf of another person, the hospital or practice must agree that you are a suitable representative.

There is a set procedure to follow to make an NHS complaint. Get hold of the procedure from your GP, hospital or PCT.

You should make your complaint as soon as possible after the problem incident. There are time limits for complaints.

It is not possible to get any financial compensation through the NHS complaints procedure. If you are seeking financial compensation, you will need to take separate legal action.

Help with your complaint in England

The Independent Complaints Advocacy Service (ICAS) is a free, confidential and independent service that can help you make a formal complaint about your NHS experience. You can contact your local ICAS office direct, or through NHS managers at hospitals and GP practices, NHS Direct, and the Patient Advice and Liaison Service (PALS).

Contact numbers for local ICAS offices are:

London   0845 120 3784
South-East   0845 600 8616

Eastern (Bedfordshire and Hertfordshire)	0845 456 1082
Eastern (Cambridgeshire, Norfolk, Suffolk)	0845 456 1084
Eastern (Essex)	0845 456 1083
South-West	0845 120 3782
West Midlands	0845 120 3748
East Midlands	0845 650 0088
North-East	0845 120 3732
North-West	0845 120 3735
Yorkshire/Humberside	0845 120 3734

The Patient Advice and Liaison Service (PALS) gives general advice on how to complain and may be able to help you resolve a complaint. However, PALS is not able to take up formal complaints on your behalf.

You can contact your local PALS from:

• your local hospital, clinic, GP surgery or health centre;
• NHS Direct (0845 4647; www.nhsdirect.nhs.uk).

You can also get help from your local CAB to make a complaint about your NHS practitioner.

Help with your complaint in Wales

In Wales, Community Health Councils (CHCs) provide a free advice and advocacy service for people who want to complain about NHS services. Contact details of your local CHC can be obtained from the Board of Community Health Councils in Wales (0845 644 7814; www.patienthelp. wales.nhs.uk).

Going to the Ombudsman

In England, you may be able to take your complaint to the Health Service Ombudsman (see p. 487).

In Wales you may be able to take your complaint to the Public Services Ombudsman for Wales (see p. 484).

Taking legal action about your NHS complaint

If you are considering taking legal action about your NHS complaint, you will need to consult a solicitor.

You should be aware that these actions are costly and complex. All family practitioners are insured and legal action will usually be contested by an insurance company. When the legal action is about the actions of an NHS employee of a trust or PCT, the NHS institution will be responsible for deciding whether to contest the action.

Complaints about professional misconduct

If you think that an NHS practitioner has been guilty of professional misconduct, it may be possible to complain to the practitioner's professional or regulatory body. Each body has a disciplinary committee that can investigate complaints. If a practitioner is found guilty of professional misconduct they can be prevented from practising in the future.

To find out more about the appropriate professional body, you can look at a leaflet produced jointly by all of the regulatory bodies including the General Medical Council. The leaflet outlines which regulatory body is responsible for monitoring each profession and what regulation means. It also provides contact details for all of the organizations. To download a copy of the leaflet, go to the website of the General Medical Council (www.gmc-uk.org).

A–Z OF NHS AND LOCAL AUTHORITY SERVICES

Abortion

Certain women may be able to obtain an abortion through the NHS. General advice and help is available from GPs and family planning clinics. Help is also available from voluntary organizations, such as the British Pregnancy Advisory Service (08457 304030; www.bpas.org.uk.), which runs its own clinics.

Aids and adaptations

Aids for disabled people are available from hospitals and local authorities' social services departments, as well as a number of voluntary organizations, including the British Red Cross. Council tenants should contact their local authority housing department for more information.

Alternative medicine

Some forms of alternative medicine (also known as complementary medicine) are available through the NHS from certain GPs and hospitals. The therapies most frequently available through the NHS are acupuncture, osteopathy, homoeopathy, chiropractic and aromatherapy.

Ambulances

Most ambulances are provided for patients by the NHS for both emergency and routine patient transport. Emergency ambulances can be contacted through the emergency telephone (999) service. Ambulances for routine journeys can be arranged through GPs or hospitals.

Breast cancer screening

Breast cancer screening is available through the NHS at three-yearly intervals for women aged between 50 and 64. Women aged over 64 can be screened on request.

Cervical screening

Cervical screening is available through the NHS every three to five years for women aged between 20 and 64. Women over 64 can be screened on request.

Chiropodists

Chiropody may be available on the NHS free of charge, although this depends on your PCT. Each case is assessed on an individual basis. If your health or your mobility is not affected, you are considered to be 'low risk' and you may not get NHS chiropody. If you have diabetes, you are treated as a high priority case. You must normally be referred to a chiropodist by a GP or clinic.

Community nurses

Community nurses are employed by the NHS to provide home nursing care for patients. They are based at GP surgeries and health centres and can also be contacted through local community nursing offices.

Contraception

Contraceptive advice and supplies are available free on the NHS through GPs and family planning clinics. Free advice and supplies are also available from some voluntary organizations, such as the British Pregnancy Advisory Service (08457 30 40 30; www.bpas.org.uk).

Counselling services

Some GP practices provide free counselling services through the NHS.

Day centres

Local authority social services organize day care services for people with mental, physical and learning disabilities and for older people. There is usually a charge for these services.

Dentists

Lists of dentists who provide NHS treatment can be obtained from PCTs and, in Wales, community health councils. They can also be obtained from NHS Direct. Some groups of people are entitled to free treatment.

Disease and pest control

Local authority environmental health departments are responsible for investigating outbreaks of food poisoning and certain infectious diseases. They are also responsible for vermin control and the control of other health hazards – for example, excessive noise, dust or smoke.

General Practitioners (GPs)

Everyone is entitled to be registered with a GP. For help in finding a GP, contact your local health authority or NHS Direct. As well as providing health advice and treatment, GPs provide check-ups, take cervical smears, do immunizations and sign certificates for people unable to work because of illness. Many GPs also provide health promotion clinics, contraceptive services, minor surgery, counselling, maternity services and medical examinations for insurance and other purposes (for which they may make a charge).

Health services in prison

Prisoners should have access to the same range and quality of health services as the general public receives from the NHS. This includes mental health services.

Health visitors

Health visitors provide support through the NHS for families with children under five and for older patients. They are normally based at GP surgeries.

Home care

Local authority social services departments are responsible for providing home care (formerly called home help) services for older people and other people who need help at home with personal care – for example, washing and dressing. There is normally a charge for these services.

Hospitals

Most NHS hospital admissions and appointments take place through referrals by GPs but patients can attend an NHS hospital without a GP referral by visiting an Accident and Emergency department or by attending a special clinic for the treatment of sexually transmitted diseases.

Immunizations

The NHS provides immunizations for children and some adults. A charge may be made for immunizations needed for overseas travel.

Infertility treatment

If you need infertility treatment, and your GP refers you to a specialist for further tests, the NHS will pay for this. You have the right to be referred to an NHS clinic for a first investigation. However, infertility treatment is not widely available on the NHS and there can be long waiting lists. The treatment available also depends on where you live and what the problem is. Your GP will tell you if you are eligible for NHS treatment.

Maternity services

Antenatal and postnatal care is available through the NHS from GPs, midwives and hospitals. Expectant mothers are also entitled to free prescriptions and dental treatment from the time when the pregnancy is confirmed until one year after the birth. If you are on a low income, you might also get other help if you are pregnant, such as vouchers to help with the cost of milk, fruit or vegetables. If you are under 18 and pregnant, you can get this help whatever your income.

Older people's services

A number of NHS services are available for older people. GPs should offer annual health checks to patients aged 75 and over. Help is also available from health visitors and district nurses. Local authority social services departments and some voluntary organizations – for example, Age Concern – provide various services, including meals on wheels and lunch clubs.

Optical services

You have to pay for eye tests, glasses and contact lenses. But some people can get free eye tests and vouchers towards the cost of glasses or contact lenses. This includes all children under 16, some young people under 19, people aged 60 or over, people with certain eye conditions, people entitled to certain benefits and anyone else on a low income.

Pharmacists

Pharmacists (also known as chemists) are responsible for dispensing medicines. They can also provide information and advice about many common medical problems.

Physiotherapy

Physiotherapy is available through the NHS to patients referred for treatment by GPs or hospitals.

Prescriptions

Doctors, dentists and some nurses can prescribe a range of drugs and appliances on the NHS but can normally only prescribe a limited quantity of a drug at any time (usually one month's supply).

School health

Health checks on school children are carried out by the school nurse. These tests include tests on hearing, sight and growth. Parents have the right to be present at these checks. School nurses also provide health education and general advice on managing health problems in school.

Sexual health clinics

The NHS provides special clinics to treat sexually transmitted diseases and genito-urinary infections. Most clinics are based in hospitals and patients need not be referred by their GP. For details of your nearest clinic, contact NHS Direct.

Terminal care

Terminal care (sometimes called palliative care) is the treatment of symptoms where cure is no longer considered an option – in other words, when someone is dying. Terminal care concentrates on:

● controlling pain and other symptoms
● improving the quality of life for the patient and their family
● meeting the patient's social, emotional and spiritual needs.

NHS terminal care may be given in hospital or at home. There are also a number of NHS hospices providing care for patients as well as hospices run by voluntary organizations.

Hospice Information (0870 903 3 903; www.hospiceinformation.info) can help you find a hospice.

Travel to hospital for treatment

You may be able to get essential travel costs paid to and from hospital for NHS treatment – for example, if you are on a low income or getting benefits like Income Support or income-based Jobseeker's Allowance.

Walk-in centres

Walk-in centres are NHS centres staffed by nurses where patients can attend without an appointment for free advice and treatment for minor injuries. For the address of your nearest centre, contact NHS Direct.

Who can help?

Further information about NHS services can be obtained from:

● the **NHS Choices** website (www.nhs.uk)
● **NHS Direct** (0845 4647) or at www.nhsdirect.nhs.uk (in England) or www.nhsdirect.wales.nhs.uk (in Wales).

3
Housing

CONTENTS

INTRODUCTION

Shelter – a roof over your head – is one of our most basic human needs and the conditions in which we live profoundly affect the quality of our lives. Yet the current council house waiting list stands at 1.6 million and the specialist housing and homelessness charity Shelter warns that this could rise to 2 million within three years. According to official figures, nearly 1 million private rented homes fail the government's decent homes standard and are in need of repair. A lack of secure, long-term, adequate housing has a huge impact on health.

Knowing how to tackle the housing problems you face is a good place to start in trying to tackle the above problems. With many of us spending a large percentage of our monthly incomes on paying for our housing, through rent or mortgage repayments, making sure that we can live as comfortably as possible for what we can afford is important to everyone.

Whether you rent your place, either privately or from a social landlord or the council, own it or want to get your foot on the property ladder, this chapter will help you to find – and keep – a home that you can call home.

And, as the song says, everybody needs good neighbours, but unfortunately we don't all get them, so we take a look at common neighbour disputes and how to go about resolving them.

BUYING A HOME

The first thing to do is decide how much you can afford. You will need to look at how much money you have available yourself and how much you can borrow. There are a number of different financial institutions that offer loans to people buying a property, like building societies and banks, that will tell you whether they'll lend you money and if so, how much.

Some building societies now provide buyers with a certificate that states that a loan will be available provided the property is satisfactory. You may be able to get this certificate before you start looking for a property. Building societies state that this certificate may help you to have your offer accepted by the seller.

Before finally deciding how much to spend on a property, you need to be sure you will have enough money to pay for all the additional costs. These include:

- survey fees
- valuation fees
- stamp duty. This is payable on properties costing more than £125,000 and is at least 1 percent of the purchase price. In some areas, designated as 'disadvantaged' areas, it is payable only on properties which cost £150,000 or more
- land registry fee
- local authority search
- fees, if any, charged by the mortgage lender or someone who arranges the mortgage, for example a mortgage broker
- your solicitor's costs
- VAT
- removal expenses
- any final bills, such as gas and electricity, from your present home that will have to be paid when you move.

On some properties, the seller has to provide the buyer with a Home Information Pack (HIP). The buyer does not have to pay for this. HIPs contain essential information about the property you want to buy. They include an energy performance certificate which assesses how energy-efficient the property is, as well as other compulsory documents such as an index of contents, a sale statement, searches and evidence that the seller owns the property. If the house comes with a HIP, this would reduce the buyer's costs.

You should be aware that if you start the process of buying a property and the sale then falls through, you may have already paid for a valuation or a survey. You will not get this back. If the solicitor has started any legal work, you may also have to pay for the work done.

You will also have to pay a deposit on exchange of contracts, up to 10 per cent of the purchase price, a few weeks before the purchase is completed and the money is received from the mortgage lender.

Freehold, leasehold and commonhold

Freehold property

If the property is freehold, this means that the land on which the property is built is part of the sale and no ground rent or service charge is payable.

Leasehold property

A property may be leasehold, which means that the land on which the property is built is not part of the sale. You have to pay ground rent to the owner of the land, who is called the freeholder.

The length of a lease can vary and you should check that the length of the lease on the property you are interested in buying is acceptable to the mortgage lender.

In addition to ground rent on a leasehold property, you may have to pay an annual service charge. This usually happens with a flat. The service charge covers such items as maintenance and repairs to the building, cleaning of common parts and looking after the grounds.

A group of leaseholders living in the same building may have a right to buy the freehold of the building jointly or take over its management.

I am a leaseholder and I pay an annual service charge. The freeholder wants to increase his charge to cover repairs to the building. Do I have to pay?

A lease is a legal contract and you can only be charged for services if they are specified in the lease. You should check your lease carefully to see what has to be paid for and how much you can be charged.

The law gives you certain rights where your lease says that you have to pay for services, repairs, maintenance, insurance or management costs in addition to ground rent. These rights include the right to be given a summary of the costs on which any charge is based, the right to look at the accounts and receipts for the charge, the right to be consulted about major, non-urgent works and the right to challenge unreasonable charges.

If you are asked to pay for something that is not covered by your lease, or you think that a charge is too much, you should start by writing to the freeholder explaining why you think the charge is wrong. If you are not satisfied with the response you can challenge the amount by applying to a leasehold valuation tribunal. You can

> make a challenge either when the work is proposed or when you receive a bill, but not if you have already agreed to make the payment.
>
> You and the other leaseholders in your block may wish to form a tenants' or residents' association and negotiate jointly with the freeholder through that association.

You can get further advice about leasehold from the Leasehold Advisory Service (020 7374 5380; www.lease-advice.org.uk).

Commonhold property

If the property is commonhold, this means that you can buy the freehold of a flat and own the common parts of the building jointly with the owners of other flats in the building (known as a commonhold association).

In commonhold, a ground rent or service charge is not payable. However, a share of the commonhold association's expenditure on maintenance, insurance and administration will be payable for the common parts of the building.

Making an offer

When you decide you would like to buy a particular property you do not necessarily have to pay the price being asked for it by the owners. You can offer less if, for example, you think there are repairs to be done that will cost money.

If the property is being sold through an estate agent, you should tell the estate agent what you are prepared to pay for the property. The estate agent will then put this offer to the owners.

If the owners do not accept the first offer put to them, you can decide to make an increased offer. There is no limit on the number of times you can make offers on a property. If you make a written offer it will always be made subject to contract. This means that you will not be committed to the purchase before finding out more about the state of the property. If you make an oral offer, this is never legally binding.

When your offer for the property has been accepted you will have to consider the following:

- whether a holding deposit is payable
- arranging a mortgage

- whether a survey is necessary
- who will do the necessary legal work
- whether you want to buy with someone else.

Once the owners have accepted your offer, you may be asked to pay a small deposit to the estate agent. This is usually between £500 and £1,000. It is meant to show that you are serious about going ahead with the purchase. It is repayable if the sale does not go ahead.

Arranging a mortgage

If you have not already begun to arrange a mortgage, you should start to do this now. It should take about three weeks from the application for the mortgage to the formal offer being made by the lender. However, this timescale may vary.

Whoever agrees to lend the money will want to have the property valued. This is to make sure that the lender could get the loan back if for any reason you stopped paying your mortgage and the property had to be sold again. The valuation will be done by a surveyor on behalf of the lender but you will have to pay for this valuation. The fee will be payable in advance, usually when you send a completed mortgage application form to the lender.

If the amount of money to be borrowed is more than a certain percentage of the valuation of the property (usually 75–80 per cent), your lender may make it a condition of the loan that you take out extra insurance to cover the extra amount. You pay a single premium to your lender, which is usually added to the loan. This is known as a higher lending charge.

Arranging a survey

The valuation that is done for whoever is lending the money is not a survey. You should consider whether or not to have an independent survey carried out in addition to the valuation. The survey would not only consider the value of the property but would also examine the structure of the property and should identify any existing or potential problems.

If the surveyor reports that there are some problems with the property, you will have to consider whether you still want to go ahead with the purchase or want to negotiate further with the seller about the price. The surveyor will usually advise you as to how any problems they have identified should be dealt with and the likely costs of this. You can find more useful information about property surveys from the Royal Institution of Chartered Surveyors (0870 333 1600; www.rics.org).

Getting the legal work done (conveyancing)

The legal process of transferring the ownership of the property from the present owner to the buyer is known as conveyancing. You should decide who you want to do the conveyancing work. You can choose to do it yourself, although this can be complicated, or:

• use a solicitor
• use a licensed conveyancer.

Before making a choice as to who will do the conveyancing, you should find out the probable costs. It is advisable to contact more than one solicitor or licensed conveyancer as there is no set scale of fees for conveyancing.

Using a solicitor

Most firms of solicitors offer a conveyancing service. Although all solicitors can legally do conveyancing, it is advisable to choose a solicitor who has experience of this work.

Using a licensed conveyancer

You can use a licensed conveyancer to do your conveyancing. Licensed conveyancers are not solicitors but are licensed by the Council for Licensed Conveyancers (01245 349599; www.conveyancer.org.uk), which you can contact to find out if a local conveyancer is licensed.

Buying with someone else

Legal ownership

If two or more people are buying the property jointly they will be joint *legal owners*. The agreement of all legal owners is needed if the property is to be sold, although if there is a dispute an owner can apply for a court order to decide how the property sale should be handled.

Beneficial ownership

As well as the legal ownership of property, there is the 'beneficial ownership' to be considered. This means the shares in the property to which the owners are entitled.

There are two types of beneficial ownership: joint tenancy and tenancy in common. The most important difference is what happens when someone dies. Joint tenants all own all of the property, so if a joint tenant dies their share passes automatically to the remaining joint tenant(s). Tenants in common each have a share in the property that they can dispose of as they wish, either while they are living or through their will.

Steps in the legal work of buying a property

From having an offer accepted to exchange of contracts can take up to seven weeks and from exchange of contracts to completion can take up to four weeks. However, if there are any problems the time taken may be longer. Some properties might come with a Home Information Pack (HIP) – see p. 127. If so, the time taken might be less.

Once you have instructed the solicitor or a licensed conveyancer, the seller's solicitor or conveyancer draws up a contract that will eventually be signed by you and the seller. However, before the contract can be signed, your solicitor or licensed conveyancer must make sure that there are no problems with the ownership of the property, rights of way, access or future developments in the area that might affect the property.

While the solicitor or licensed conveyancer is making the enquiries, you should sort out how you will pay the deposit that has to be made when the contracts are exchanged. This deposit is usually 10 per cent of the price of the home.

Exchange of contracts
The final contract between you and the seller is prepared when:

- the solicitor (or licensed conveyancer) and you are satisfied with the final outcome of all the enquiries
- any surveyor's report has been received and any necessary action taken
- the formal mortgage offer has been received
- arrangements about the payment of the 10 per cent deposit have been made
- the date of completion has been agreed.

You and the seller each have a copy of the final contract which you must sign. These signed contracts are then exchanged. At exchange of contracts both you and the seller are legally bound by the contract and the sale of the house has to go ahead.

Completion

Completion of the purchase usually takes place about four weeks after exchange of contracts. On the day agreed for completion:

- the mortgage lender releases the money
- the deeds to the property are handed over to your solicitor or licensed conveyancer
- the seller must hand over the keys and leave the property by an agreed time.

The solicitor or licensed conveyancer will usually send their account to you on, or soon after, the completion date. You are in and the house is yours!

The right to buy your council-owned property

As a public sector tenant you will probably have the right to buy if you are a secure tenant of:

- a local authority
- a non-charitable housing association
- a housing action trust.

You have the right to buy if you have been a public sector tenant for at least two years. However, if your tenancy began on or after 18 January 2005, you must have been a public sector tenant for at least five years. This need not necessarily have been in your present accommodation. A tenancy with another public sector landlord can be included in this time.

As a tenant you will *not* have the right to buy if:

- you are a housing association tenant whose tenancy began on or after 15 January 1989
- you are a tenant of sheltered housing or housing specifically designated for the elderly
- you are bankrupt or about to go bankrupt. If you have rent arrears, you can apply to buy, but you have to clear the arrears before the sale can go ahead
- your landlord has applied to court for a suspension order (suspending your right to buy) if you have been involved in, or have threatened, anti-social behaviour.

If you are not sure whether you have the right to buy, you should check with your landlord.

Discounts

As a tenant with a right to buy, you will get a discount on the price of the property. If you live in a house the discount will be between 32 and 60 per cent, depending on how long you have lived there. If you live in a flat the discount will be between 44 and 70 per cent, depending on how long you have lived there. The discount will not exceed the regional upper limits, which range from £16,000 to £38,000.

If you exercise the right to buy and then sell the property within five years, you may have to repay all or some of the discount – check the rules with your local authority.

How to pay

As a tenant who wants to exercise your right to buy, you should try to get a mortgage from a building society or high street bank. You could also contact a mortgage broker to see if they can arrange a mortgage.

However, if you cannot afford to buy the property outright, you can still buy under the *rent to mortgage* scheme. Under this scheme you can buy a share of the property and make mortgage repayments on the amount you have borrowed for this. The landlord will retain ownership of the remaining share of the property.

How to apply

If you want to apply for the right to buy, you should ask your landlord for the Right to Buy Claim Form (Form RTB1), which the landlord must provide.

The right to acquire

As a secure or assured tenant of a registered social landlord – for example, a housing association or a local housing company – you may have the right to buy your home under a different scheme called the *right to acquire*. The right to acquire only applies to a limited number of properties – for example, homes built with public funds on or after 1 April 1997.

For more information about the right to acquire in England, speak to your landlord or contact the Housing Corporation (0845 230 7000; www.housingcorp.gov.uk). In Wales, you should contact the Welsh Assembly Government (0845 010 3300; www.new.wales.gov.uk).

Schemes to help people who cannot afford to buy a home

There are various schemes aimed at helping people who otherwise would not be able to afford to buy a home. The terms of the schemes differ but you may qualify if you are a:

- local authority tenant
- housing association tenant
- key worker
- first-time buyer.

In one scheme, you can buy a share of the property and pay rent to your landlord for the rest. In other schemes, you have to raise your own finance to buy a certain share in a flat or house and you get help with a loan for the rest.

To find out more about these schemes, contact the Housing Corporation (0845 230 7000; www.housingcorp.gov.uk), or ask your local authority or housing association.

MORTGAGES

If you want to buy a home, you may be able to borrow money to do this. The borrower offers the home as security against the loan. The lender has a legal charge against the property – that is, if you do not keep up the agreed repayments, the lender can take possession of the property. This is known as a mortgage. The loan will be for a fixed period and the borrower will be charged interest on the loan.

There are several types of mortgage available. The most common are:

- repayment mortgage. This is a mortgage in which the capital borrowed is repaid gradually over the period of the loan. The capital is paid in monthly instalments together with an amount of interest. The amount of capital that is repaid gradually increases over the years while the amount of interest goes down
- endowment mortgage. This mortgage consists of two parts: the loan from the building society and an endowment policy taken out with an insurance company. You pay interest on the loan in monthly instalments to the building society but do not actually pay off any of the loan. The endowment policy is also paid monthly to the insurance company. At the end of the period of the mortgage the policy matures and produces a lump sum which pays off the loan to the building society. There is a risk that the endowment policy will not

be worth enough to pay off the loan at the end of the mortgage period. If you have been told by your endowment provider that your policy will not be enough to pay off your loan, you should seek independent financial advice. You can get information about dealing with endowment policies from the Financial Services Authority (FSA; www.moneymadeclear.fsa.gov.uk)

- pension mortgage. This mortgage is primarily for self-employed people. The monthly payments consist of interest payments on the loan and contributions to a pension scheme. When the borrower retires there is a lump sum to pay off the loan and a pension
- the government-backed Open Market HomeBuy scheme, which helps certain people such as key workers to borrow extra money to buy a home. For more information, contact the Housing Corporation (0845 230 7000; www.housingcorp.gov.uk).

A mortgage could be available from a number of different sources, such as banks, building societies, insurance companies (although they only provide endowment mortgages), finance houses and specialized mortgage companies. Some large building companies might arrange mortgages on their own new-build homes.

I have an endowment mortgage and have been told that there won't be enough money at the end of the mortgage term to pay for the house. What can I do?

There are over 10 million endowment policies linked to mortgages in the UK. An endowment mortgage combines an interest-only mortgage and an investment (the endowment policy). Throughout the term of the mortgage (usually 20 or 25 years), interest is paid on the amount borrowed to your mortgage lender and a monthly premium is paid on your endowment policy. The endowment premiums are invested with the intention that the endowment produces enough capital at the end of the term to pay off the mortgage. If your endowment policy doesn't reach this target you will have a shortfall and will need to pay part of the capital owed on your mortgage another way.

Many people were mis-sold endowment policies because the policy was not suitable for them. There are many reasons why an endowment policy may not have been right for you but, broadly, if you were not informed of the risks associated with using an investment product to repay your mortgage you have grounds for complaint. Find out more about problems with endowment mortgages from the Financial Services Authority (0845 606 1234; www.moneymadeclear.fsa.gov.uk).

Using a broker to get a mortgage

Instead of going directly to a lender such as a building society for a mortgage, a broker could be used. A broker may be an estate agent, or a mortgage or insurance broker. They will act as an agent to introduce people to a source of mortgage loan to help them buy a home.

A broker may be used when it could be difficult obtaining a mortgage directly from a lender, for example when:

- the mortgage required is particularly large
- the property is unusual in some way
- more than two people wish to purchase the home jointly
- you are self-employed and your income fluctuates.

Brokers can charge for their services and must tell you how much the fee will be.

SELLING A HOME

Finding a buyer yourself

If you wish to find a buyer for your home yourself, you must first decide what price you want to ask for the property. Many estate agents do free valuations, so it is always possible to arrange for two or more local estate agents to provide this information. If you want a formal valuation, you could arrange for an estate agent to provide this but you would have to pay a fee.

In addition, you can find out about the cost of houses locally by looking at local papers, estate agents' windows and similar houses in the area.

You should also decide in advance if you are prepared to include any extras in the sale, such as curtains and carpets. These are known as fittings. A price for these can be included in the asking price or a separate price can be asked in addition.

There are some items that you must sell as part of the house unless you make it clear to the buyer that such items are not included in the sale. These are known as fixtures and include such items as fireplaces and a central heating system. However, in some cases it is not always clear whether something is a fixture or fitting so it would be useful for you to draw up a list of any items you intend to remove or are prepared to sell to avoid problems later.

Home Information Packs

Before you put your house on the market, you may need to have a Home Information Pack (HIP).You can get your estate agent or solicitor to compile a HIP or compile one yourself. You must make the HIP available to people who might buy the property. HIPs contain essential information about the property. They include an energy performance certificate which assesses how energy efficient the property is, as well as other compulsory documents such as an index of contents, a sale statement, searches and evidence that you own the property. For more information about HIPs and the sorts of properties which must have one, go to www.homeinformation packs.gov.uk.

Using an estate agent

If you wish to use an estate agent, you should enquire about local estate agents and find out the following information:

- what type of property the estate agent specializes in
- whether the estate agent belongs to a professional association
- how much the estate agent will charge
- the reputation of the local estate agencies, if possible.

Estate agents' charges

Nearly all estate agents calculate their fees as a percentage of the final selling price of the property, usually between 1½ and 2½ per cent. This is known as the rate of commission and the estate agent must confirm the charges that will be made and the rate of commission when they agree to act for you.

Types of agreement you have with an estate agent

When you use one estate agent to handle the sale it is known as 'sole agency'. It is usual for the agreement to state that commission is only paid to the estate agent if they sell the property. If you find a buyer yourself, you don't have to pay the commission. If the agreement gives the estate agent 'sole selling rights' the agent is the only person who can sell. You would have to pay the agent under this type of agreement even if you find the buyer yourself.

If you appoint two or more estate agents to act together for you in selling the property, this is known as 'joint agency' or 'joint sole agency'. The estate agents involved share the commission when the property is sold regardless of which estate agent actually finds the buyer. The commission for the joint agency agreement is usually higher than for a sole agency.

If you appoint two or more estate agents independently, but the commission is only paid to the estate agent who finds the buyer, this is known as 'multiple agency'.

What does the estate agent do?

The estate agent first of all visits the house in order to value it and decide on an asking price with you. You may wish to ask more than one estate agent to call and value the house. It is also advisable for you to check the price that the estate agent suggests by comparing it to similar houses in the local paper.

The estate agent will prepare details of the house to send out to people who are interested in buying it. These details will include the number and size of the rooms and all the fixtures and fittings that will be left in the house. The estate agent also arranges for the property to be advertised and can arrange for a Home Information Pack (HIP) to be compiled if you need one.

Deciding who to sell to

Whether you have arranged to sell the house yourself or used an estate agent you may find that you receive more than one offer for the house. You can sell the house to whoever you want and do not have to sell to the buyer who offers the most money. You may wish to take into account whether the buyer:

- is a first-time buyer – this means they are unlikely to be in a chain of buying and selling and the sale may be more simple
- has found a buyer for their own property. If so, is it part of a chain of buying and selling and how long is the chain?

- is paying cash or is likely to get a mortgage
- wants to move at the same time as you.

If you are using an estate agent, it is often easier for the estate agent to find out this information from the buyer.

It is against the law for a seller who uses an estate agent to discriminate against a prospective buyer on grounds of race, sex, disability, sexuality or religion or belief, either by refusing to sell the property, or by offering it on less favourable terms.

If you are using an estate agent, the agent negotiates with the potential buyer(s) about the price. The estate agent should try and obtain the best possible price for you. If you are acting alone, you must negotiate yourself. You do not have to accept the first offer put to you and should not be rushed into making a decision quickly.

Accepting an offer

Even if you have accepted an offer, there is nothing in law to prevent you from changing your mind and accepting a higher offer from someone else. You should also bear in mind that when an offer is made and accepted, the potential buyer can also withdraw – for example, they may not get a mortgage, or the survey may show up some structural problem.

If you are handling the sale yourself, it may be a good idea to keep the names and addresses of all potential buyers who make offers, in case the one you accept falls through.

COMMON PROBLEMS BUYING AND SELLING A HOME

Chains

A buyer or seller may find that they have problems because they are involved in a chain of buying and selling. This happens when a buyer or seller is selling and buying at the same time and the other people involved are also buying and selling. This creates a chain of buyers and sellers that may be very long and so delays may occur. It depends on the reasons for the delays as to what, if anything, you can do about them. If the problem is with a buyer further down the chain, the seller could look for another buyer or consider arranging a bridging loan until the property is sold.

Estate agents

If an estate agent is selling a property for you, there is a contractual agreement between yourself and the estate agent. If you have a problem with an estate agent, it is usually necessary to check a copy of any written agreement between you both and establish what verbal agreements, if any, were made.

As the seller, you pay the estate agent for their services and the estate agent is therefore acting on your behalf. It is the seller's interest they will represent and the buyer should bear this in mind if they are interested in a house being sold through an estate agent.

The estate agent's bill is too high

You may think that the bill from the estate agent, after the sale is completed, is too high. It is important to check that the bill gives a clear breakdown of the costs – for example, the commission fee, advertising and VAT. Check the bill against the original agreement you made with the estate agent.

You decide not to sell

If you decide not to continue with the sale of your home, you may have to pay some estate agents' charges – for example, to cover any costs the estate agent has already incurred. This will depend on the original contract between you and the estate agent.

You want to use an additional estate agent

If you have been using one estate agent this is known as 'sole agency'. When you agree a sole agency with an estate agent the contract will usually state how long this period of sole agency will last. At the end of this period you are free to use one or more additional estate agents.

If you use one or more additional estate agents before the period of sole agency has come to an end, you are breaking the contract with the original estate agent. This means that if the new estate agent finds a buyer for the house you would have to pay commission not only to the new estate agent but also to the agent with whom you had the sole agency agreement. If the original agent found a buyer, the amount of commission that you would have to pay to the new estate agent would depend on the type of agreement you had with them.

However, you may be able to negotiate changing the sole agency agreement to a joint sole agency agreement with the original estate agency.

You want to change estate agents

You may want to change your estate agent. You should check the terms of the agreement you have with the estate agent to see if this is possible. If it is possible, you may still have to pay some charges to the estate agent to cover costs, such as advertising, that the estate agent has incurred.

You have found your own buyer

You may have found your own buyer for the property who has not come through the estate agent – for example, a friend may want to buy the property. You are entitled to sell to a buyer who has not been found by the estate agent but you may find that you will still have to pay the estate agent. What you have to pay will depend on your contract with the estate agent.

You are not satisfied with the service provided

You may not be satisfied with the service the estate agent is providing, for example:

- the estate agent may not be sending out details of your property to potential buyers
- the advertising is not what you wanted
- the details about the house are inaccurate or inadequate.

You may wish to consider complaining to the estate agent in writing or changing to a different estate agent.

If you are not satisfied with the estate agent's response to your complaint, you might be able to complain to the Ombudsman for Estate Agents – see p. 489.

Gazumping

The seller may accept an offer for their house and then inform you as the buyer that they have been offered a higher price by someone else. This is known as 'gazumping'. You may decide to offer a higher price in order to try and secure the house but there is no guarantee that you will not be gazumped again. There is nothing illegal about gazumping and the purchase price of a house is only legally settled when contracts are exchanged. You may, however, have entered into an agreement with the seller that the seller will not consider other offers during a set period before the exchange of contracts. If such an agreement exists, and you are gazumped during this period, you will be able to sue the seller for breach of contract.

Lenders

You are having difficulty in getting a mortgage

As the buyer, you may be having difficulty in getting a mortgage – for example, your salary is not enough or the property is unusual. Different lenders have different rules about giving mortgages and it may be worth your trying some other lenders.

The lender's valuation is less than the purchase price of the house

The lender may decide that the security value of the house is less than the amount that you have agreed to pay for it. This means that the lender will not lend as much money as you had requested. You may therefore try to negotiate a lower price with the seller. If the seller will not drop the price and you still want to go ahead with the purchase, you may have to borrow the difference from elsewhere if you do not have the extra money available.

If the seller will not lower the price, or you cannot pay the difference, you may consider if another lender would give the house a higher valuation.

There are delays in getting a mortgage offer

There may be a delay in the lender making a formal mortgage offer to you. Until the mortgage offer is made, contracts cannot be exchanged. You should contact the lender to find out if there is any reason for the delay – for example, if the lender is waiting for salary details from your employer. It may be possible for you to do something about the problem, such as contacting your employer yourself.

Offers

The offer to buy is withdrawn

The buyer may withdraw the offer they have made before contracts are exchanged. Until contracts are exchanged, the buyer is under no legal obligation to buy the home and does not have to pay for any of the costs that you, as the seller, may have incurred. However, you may wish to ask the buyer to contribute towards these costs.

The price offered is reduced

The buyer may decide to reduce the offer they have made for the house. If they do this before contracts are exchanged, it is up to you as the seller to decide whether or not you want to accept this lower offer. However, once contracts have been exchanged the buyer is legally committed to paying the price stated in the contract. If they try to drop the price at this stage, you do not have to accept this lower price. If the sale is not then completed, the buyer will forfeit the 10 per cent deposit they paid when contracts were exchanged and you could also sue the buyer for any additional loss.

The seller withdraws their acceptance of the offer

The seller may withdraw their acceptance of the offer any time before contracts are exchanged – for example, if they have found another buyer or have decided not to sell. There is nothing you as the buyer can do about this but you could ask the seller for a contribution towards any costs you have incurred, such as survey fees.

The seller accepts more than one offer (contract race)

The seller may accept more than one offer and instruct their solicitor to send draft contracts to more than one potential buyer. The solicitor must inform all potential buyers that more than one contract has been sent out and that the first contract that is returned, signed and ready for exchange will get the house. This is known as a contract race and is quite legal. There is nothing you as the buyer can do except withdraw if you do not want to incur the necessary costs in getting the contract completed quickly.

Property

The buyer is dissatisfied with the state the property was left in

As the buyer, you may be dissatisfied with the state of the property when you move in – for example, it is dirty. There is nothing you can do about this because the seller is under no legal obligation to leave the house in a clean state. However, the seller is under an obligation to empty the house of all their furniture and belongings. If some belongings have been left in the house, you should ask the seller to remove them. If the seller cannot or will not remove the items you will have to arrange to have them moved. Moving the items may cost you money and you could try to recover this from the seller. However, if the seller refuses to cover the costs you may have to take them to court to recover the money and this is unlikely to be worthwhile.

The seller's property is worth less than they paid for it (negative equity)

As the seller, you may find that the value of your house has dropped since you bought it. This may mean that if you sell it at its current value you will still owe money to your lender. This is called 'negative equity'.

There are a number of different schemes that have been designed to help someone with negative equity. For example, it may be possible to transfer the existing mortgage to a new property rather than pay it off and take out a new one. Different lenders will offer different schemes and you should discuss the situation with your lender.

Furniture and fittings have been removed

The seller must leave all the fixtures – for example, a fireplace – and any fittings that they agreed would either be included in the sale or paid for separately – for example, fitted carpets. If, as the buyer, you find that something has been removed you should check with your solicitor or licensed conveyancer whether or not the item should have been left. The solicitor or licensed conveyancer may be able to resolve the problem.

The property has been damaged between exchange and completion

A house may be damaged after contracts have been exchanged but before the sale is completed – for example, there might be a burst pipe or a broken window. It is the seller's responsibility to inform the buyer of any damage. It is, however, the buyer's responsibility to insure the property from the date of exchange of contracts and to have the repairs carried out. The buyer will then have to make a claim on their insurance policy.

Solicitors and conveyancing

There are delays in conveyancing

As the buyer or seller, you may think that there is an unreasonable delay in the conveyancing. You should find out from your solicitor or licensed conveyancer the reason for any delay. If the delay is unreasonable, you should take this up with the Legal Complaints Service (0845 608 6565; www.legalcomplaints.org.uk) or the Council for Licensed Conveyancers (01245 349599; www.conveyancer.org.uk).

The solicitor is not passing on the interest on the deposit

When a buyer pays a deposit on a property, this is held by the seller's solicitor or licensed conveyancer. Any interest earned on the deposit during the period is kept by the solicitor or licensed conveyancer and should be passed on to the seller at completion. The seller may need to ask for the interest as it is not always passed on. If the solicitor or licensed conveyancer refuses to pass on the interest, the seller should take this up with the Legal Complaints Service (0845 608 6565; www.legalcomplaints.org.uk) or the Council for Licensed Conveyancers (01245 349599; www.conveyancer.org.uk).

The bill for the conveyancing is too high

If you, as the buyer or seller, think that the solicitor's or licensed conveyancer's bill is too high, you should not pay the bill but should first check that all the various costs are clearly itemized. You should ask the solicitor or licensed conveyancer to explain anything you do not understand. If you are still not satisfied with the amount of the bill, you may wish to consider taking further action against the solicitor or complaining to the Legal Complaints Service (0845 608 6565; www.legalcomplaints.org.uk) or the Council for Licensed Conveyancers (01245 349599; www.conveyancer.org.uk).

You think your solicitor or licensed conveyancer has been negligent

As the buyer, you may think that the solicitor or licensed conveyancer has been negligent. For example, after the sale has been completed, you may discover there is a problem with the boundary wall or there is a road-widening scheme that will reduce the size of the garden, and this might mean that the value of your house is reduced. If this happens and you want compensation, you should seek legal advice about suing the conveyancer.

If you have a complaint regarding poor service or behaviour, you should follow any internal complaints procedures of the firm concerned. If you are not happy with the outcome you should complain about a solicitor to the Legal Complaints Service (0845 608 6565; www.legalcomplaints.org.uk).

You will need to contact the Legal Complaints Service within six months of the end of the work your solicitor did for you, or within six months of your solicitor's final response to your complaint.

If you want to complain about a licensed conveyancer, you should contact the Council for Licensed Conveyancers (01245 349599; www.conveyancer.org.uk).

Surveys and valuations

Carrying out the survey and/or valuation

If you are selling your property, a potential buyer will usually want a valuer and/or surveyor to inspect the property. You will have to allow the valuer/surveyor to look round the property if you want the sale to go ahead.

The circumstances in which a surveyor or valuer can be held legally responsible for any financial loss suffered by the buyer as a result of the survey or valuation are limited.

RENTING A HOME

Local authority help for homeless people

Local authorities have a legal duty to provide help to certain people who are homeless or threatened with homelessness. Certain people do not qualify for help because they are not 'eligible for assistance'. If you are 'eligible for assistance', you also have to be legally homeless or threatened with homelessness, in priority need and not intentionally homeless. The local authority may also investigate whether you have a local connection with the area.

Local social services authorities also have responsibility for some homeless people. They have a duty to provide accommodation for children and young people over 16 who are leaving care, or who are in need for other reasons.

Applying to rent local authority accommodation

If you are looking for local authority accommodation, you should first check whether you qualify. Many people from abroad – for example, most asylum seekers and people who have spent significant time living away from the UK, even if they are UK citizens – do not qualify for housing. The rules on who can qualify for local authority housing are complicated, especially if you have just arrived in, or returned to, the UK from abroad.

Most local authorities have a housing register or waiting list of people who have applied to rent local authority accommodation. This is usually the only way you can apply for local authority accommodation.

Local authorities use different systems to give priority to applicants on their waiting lists. How priorities are allocated varies from one local authority to another, but factors normally taken into account will be:

- poor health made worse by housing conditions
- lack of or shared use of some facility – for example, a bathroom or toilet
- an inadequate number of bedrooms for the size of your family
- length of time you have lived in the area
- age (where access to sheltered or warden-supported accommodation is under consideration)
- length of time on the waiting list
- separation from your family (including a family that is overseas) because of inadequate accommodation
- homelessness – see *Local authority help for homeless people*, p. 136.

Once accepted on a local authority waiting list, you may have to wait a long time before you are offered accommodation. Your local authority should be able to give you a rough idea of how long you will have to wait. You should make sure that you keep them informed of any changes likely to affect your application – for example, changes in the number or ages of your children. You may also have to renew your application regularly.

When you are made an offer, it may be accommodation owned by the local authority or by a housing association. In an area where the local authority's housing has all been transferred to a housing association, this may be the only option offered.

You will usually only be able to turn the offer down if it is unsuitable for your needs – for example, if you are disabled and there is no lift. However, there is usually a limit to the number of offers a local authority will make.

Housing associations

Housing associations are 'not-for-profit' organizations that provide housing for rent. There are many housing associations providing a range of accommodation. Some provide housing for certain types of people – for example, single parents or disabled people. Others provide general housing in the same way as a local authority.

Only some housing associations accept direct applications. Most require you to be nominated by the local authority, which means that you will need to apply to go on the local authority waiting list and ask to be nominated. Where a housing association does not insist on this, it may require that you are nominated by a local agency, such as an advice agency or the social services department. If a housing association does accept direct applications, the criteria each has for selecting tenants will vary.

In some areas the housing associations and local authority have joint waiting lists. This means you can register with the local authority and housing associations on the same form.

Who can help find rented accommodation?

Help the Aged (020 7253 0253; www.helptheaged.org.uk) and **Age Concern** (020 8756 7200; www.ageconcern.org.uk) both produce free publications giving advice about housing matters for older people, including information about care homes.

The **Shelternet** website (www.shelternet.org.uk) provides information about a range of housing options, including help for homeless people, private renting and home ownership.

Housing advice centres can offer advice and information about all aspects of housing. Some are run by local authorities while others are run by voluntary organizations. Details of independent housing advice centres are available in England from **Shelter** (0808 800 4444; www.england.shelter.org.uk) or in Wales from **Shelter Cymru** (0808 800 4444; www.sheltercymru.org.uk).

Accommodation agencies

An accommodation agency may be able to help you find accommodation owned by a private landlord. If you register with an agency, you will be asked about the type of property you are looking for and how much rent you are willing to pay. You will normally be asked to give details of your job and income, and may also be asked to provide references from your employer, bank, and present or previous landlord.

When you register with an accommodation agency, it is only legally allowed to charge a fee when it finds you somewhere to live. Once you have signed a contract to accept the tenancy of a property, the fee the agency can charge is unlimited. As part of their fees, some agencies are allowed to include an administrative charge for preparing a tenancy agreement, making an inventory, and other costs of setting up a tenancy agreement.

It is against the law for an agency to ask for payment for:

- putting your name on its list or taking your details
- providing a list of properties available for renting
- a deposit that will be returned if no suitable accommodation is found.

If you are offered accommodation by an agency, you should inspect the property before accepting it and ensure you have full details about:

- the terms of the tenancy agreement
- the amount of rent you will have to pay, and whether it includes any services, fuel and water charges
- how much rent you will have to pay in advance
- whether you will have to pay a premium and/or a security deposit and, if so, how much and what tenancy deposit protection scheme is being used
- whether the property has a mortgage. You can lose your accommodation if the property is repossessed due to the landlord's failure to keep up mortgage payments
- the name and address of the landlord.

Where possible, you should use an agency that has signed up to the National Approved Letting Scheme (01242 581712; www.nalscheme.co.uk). Agencies belonging to this scheme have agreed to follow a set of standards that include a complaints procedure.

Organizations that belong to this scheme include the National Association of Estate Agents (01926 496800; www.naea.co.uk), the Royal Institution of Chartered Surveyors (0870 333 1600; www.rics.org), and the Association of Residential Letting Agents (0845 345 5752; www.arla.co.uk).

An accommodation agency can refuse to register you. It may do this, for example, because:

- you are unemployed
- you are on benefits
- you are looking for accommodation for a family.

If you experience discrimination for these reasons, you may be able to take action under human rights law. You should get specialist advice.

It is against the law for an accommodation agency to discriminate on grounds of disability, sexuality, religion, race or sex, even where a landlord has said, for example, that they do not want a tenant of a particular race or sex, or with a disability.

Tenancy agreements

A tenancy agreement is a contract between you and your landlord. It may be written or oral. The tenancy agreement gives certain rights to both you and your landlord – for example, your right to occupy the accommodation and your landlord's right to receive rent for letting the accommodation.

You and your landlord may have made arrangements about the tenancy, and these will be part of the tenancy agreement as long as they do not conflict with law. Both you and your landlord have rights and responsibilities given by law. The tenancy agreement can give both you and your landlord more than your statutory rights, but cannot give you less than your statutory rights. If a term in the tenancy agreement gives either you or your landlord less than your statutory rights, that term cannot be enforced.

The tenancy agreement is a form of consumer contract and as such it must be in plain language that is clear and easy to understand. It must not contain any terms that could be 'unfair'. This means, for example, that the tenancy agreement must not put either you or your landlord in a disadvantageous position, enable one party to change terms unilaterally without a valid reason or irrevocably bind you to terms with which you have had no time to become familiar. An unfair term is not valid in law and cannot be enforced.

A tenancy agreement can be made up of:

- *express* terms. These include what is in the written tenancy agreement, if there is one, what is in the rent book, and/or what was agreed orally
- *implied* terms. These are rights given by law or arrangements established by custom and practice.

'Express' terms of tenancy agreements

Most tenants do not have a right in law to a written tenancy agreement. However, social landlords such as local authorities and housing associations give written tenancy agreements as a matter of good practice.

If you have a written agreement, it should indicate the type of tenancy you have. The tenancy agreement should be signed by both you and your landlord. Each tenant, if there are joint tenants, should receive a copy of the agreement.

Your landlord is obliged by law to give their address.

It is good practice for a written tenancy agreement to include the following details:

- your name and your landlord's name and the address of the property that is being let
- the date the tenancy began

- whether other people are allowed the use of the property, and if so, which rooms
- the duration of the tenancy – that is, whether it runs out on a certain date
- the amount of rent payable, how often and when it should be paid, and how often and when it can be increased. The agreement could also state what the payment includes – for example, council tax or fuel
- whether your landlord will provide any services – for example, laundry, maintenance of common parts or meals – and whether there are service charges for these
- the length of notice you and your landlord need to give if the tenancy is to be ended. Note that there are statutory rules about how much notice should be given and these will depend on the type of tenancy and why it is due to end.

The agreement may also contain details of your landlord's obligations to repair the property, although it is rare for agreements to go into details. Your landlord's obligations to repair depend on the type of tenancy.

A tenancy agreement exists even if there is only an oral agreement between you and your landlord. For example, you and your landlord may have agreed at the start of the tenancy how much the rent would be and when it is payable, whether it includes fuel and bills such as water rates or whether your landlord can decide who else can live in the accommodation. Oral agreements can be difficult to enforce because there is often no proof of what has been agreed, or a particular problem may have arisen that the agreement did not cover.

'Implied' terms of tenancy agreements

There are obligations you and your landlord have that may not be set down in the agreement but which are given by law and are implied in all tenancy agreements. These terms form part of the contract, even though they have not been specifically agreed between your landlord and you.

Some of the most common implied terms are:

- your landlord must carry out basic repairs
- your landlord must keep the installations for the supply of water, gas, electricity, sanitation, space heating and heating water in good working order
- you have the right to live peacefully in the accommodation without nuisance from your landlord
- you must take proper care of the accommodation.
- you must not be discriminated against because of your sex, race, disability, religion or sexuality.

Rights given by law will vary according to the type of tenancy.

What documents and information the tenant must receive

By law, as a tenant, you must be given the following information:

- if you have a weekly tenancy (not a fixed-term or monthly tenancy), your landlord must provide a rent book or similar document. Your landlord commits a criminal offence if they fail to do so
- your landlord's address
- if you do not know the name of your landlord, you can make a written request to the person who receives the rent for the full name and address of your landlord. The agent must supply you with this information in writing within 21 days, after which they commit an offence
- if the tenancy is an assured shorthold that started on or after 28 February 1997, your landlord must provide basic written terms of the agreement within 28 days of your requesting this in writing.

Sham tenancy agreements

The rights laid down by law always override those which are stated in a written or oral agreement. An agreement which suggests that you or your landlord have fewer rights than those given by common law or statute is a sham tenancy agreement.

What an agreement states and what the tenancy actually is may be different. For example, your landlord may claim that the sort of tenancy you have is another sort which gives you fewer rights. This is an example of a sham tenancy agreement. If you think your tenancy agreement might be a sham agreement, get expert advice about what to do.

PRIVATE SECTOR TENANCIES

Different types of tenancy agreements

Because of changes to housing law, the kind of tenancy agreement you have, and the rights that you and your landlord have under that agreement, depend on when the agreement was made. Understanding what those rights are can be complicated.

The tenancy began on or after 15 January 1989 but before 28 February 1997

If your tenancy is a private or housing association tenancy that began on or after 15 January 1989 but before 28 February 1997, you may be:

- an assured tenant
- an assured shorthold tenant
- an occupier with basic protection (see *Occupiers with basic protection*, p. 146.

Assured tenants

An assured tenant will not normally have a resident landlord and the landlord will not provide food or services. As an assured tenant, you will be paying rent for accommodation that you occupy as your only or principal home.

You are not an assured tenant if your accommodation is:

- a student let
- a holiday let
- a company let
- business premises
- a Crown tenancy
- private accommodation arranged by the local authority because you are homeless.

As an assured tenant you have the right to stay in your accommodation unless your landlord can convince the court there are good reasons for eviction – for example, rent arrears or damage to the property – or that another of the terms of the agreement has been broken.

As an assured tenant you can enforce your rights – for instance, to get repairs done – without worrying about getting evicted.

As well as the right to stay in your home as long as you keep to the terms of the tenancy you will also have other rights by law, including:

- the right to have the accommodation kept in a reasonable state of repair
- the right to carry out minor repairs yourself and to receive payment for these from your landlord
- the right for your partner to take over the tenancy on your death (the right of 'succession'). This applies whether you were married partners or civil partners or even if you were just living together as partners.

Assured shorthold tenants (before 28 February 1997)

You will be an assured shorthold tenant if your tenancy is for a fixed period of not less than six months.

This is a less secure type of tenancy than an assured tenancy. After the fixed period ends, your landlord can apply to the court for possession as long as they have given two months' notice. If your landlord does not renew the agreement, you can stay on until your landlord serves notice that they want to repossess the property.

If you were not given a Notice of an Assured Shorthold Tenancy, or were given it after the tenancy started, you are an assured tenant.

You are not an assured shorthold tenant if the accommodation:

- is a holiday let
- is a company let
- is rented by you and you are a student from a university or college
- is private temporary accommodation in which you are housed because you are homeless
- has a resident landlord
- is accommodation for which you pay no rent.

As an assured shorthold tenant you have the right to stay in the accommodation until the fixed term ends unless your landlord can convince the court there are reasons for eviction – for example, rent arrears or damage to property, or that one of the other terms of the agreement has been broken. You can stay on after the end of the fixed term, even if the agreement is not renewed, until your landlord gives you notice.

As an assured shorthold tenant you can enforce your rights – for instance, to get repairs done – but if you do, your landlord may decide not to renew the tenancy agreement at the end of the fixed term.

As well as the right to stay in your home for the fixed period as long as you keep to the terms of the tenancy, you will also have other legal rights, including:

- the right to have the accommodation kept in a reasonable state of repair
- the right to carry out minor repairs yourself and the right to deduct the cost from the rent
- the right for your partner to take over the tenancy on your death (the right of 'succession'). This applies whether you were married partners or civil partners or even if you were just living together as partners.

You may have a written tenancy agreement that may give you more rights than the minimum provided by law.

The tenancy began on or after 28 February 1997

Any new tenancy created on or after this date will automatically be an assured shorthold tenancy, unless:

- you are an occupier with basic protection (see below for more information)
- it was created following a contract made before 28 February 1997; *or*
- your landlord serves a notice on you stating that the tenancy is to be an assured tenancy; *or*
- there is a clause in the tenancy agreement stating that it is to be an assured tenancy; *or*
- the tenancy is one created by the death of a former protected tenant (see below for more information about protected tenancies); *or*
- the tenancy was previously a secure tenancy and became an assured tenancy.

This list of exceptions is not exhaustive. Only the most important exceptions are given.

If the tenancy is not an assured shorthold tenancy for one of the reasons given above, it will be an assured tenancy. Assured shorthold tenancies created on or after 28 February 1997 do not have to have a fixed-term period at the beginning of the tenancy, although your landlord may give a fixed term if they want. No written agreement or notice is needed to create an assured shorthold tenancy on or after 28 February 1997. An oral agreement is sufficient.

You will have the same rights as other assured tenants whose tenancy began before 28 February 1997 but after 15 January 1989.

However, there is one additional right to a statement from your landlord of the terms of the agreement. Your landlord must provide a written statement of the basic terms of the tenancy that are not already provided in writing. Failure to provide the statement is a criminal offence.

The tenancy began before 15 January 1989

If your tenancy began before 15 January 1989 you could be either:

- a protected tenant; *or*
- an occupier with basic protection.

Protected tenants
If you are a protected tenant you will:

- be paying rent for the accommodation; *and*
- not normally have a resident landlord; *and*
- not be provided with food or services by your landlord.

You will not be a protected tenant if your accommodation is:

- a bed and breakfast letting
- a 'company' let.

Protected tenants have the strongest rights of any private tenants. As a protected tenant you have the following rights:

- security of tenure. Your landlord can only repossess the accommodation in certain specified circumstances
- the right to have the rent fixed by the rent officer
- the right to have rent increased only in certain circumstances
- the right to have the accommodation kept in a reasonable state of repair
- the right of a partner or another family member to take over the tenancy on your death.

Occupiers with basic protection

If you are not an assured tenant, assured shorthold tenant, or protected tenant, you may be what is called an occupier with basic protection. You may have basic protection if you have:

- a 'company' let (where a company holds the tenancy and provides accommodation for you as a member of staff)
- a student let granted by an educational institution
- a resident landlord who does not share living accommodation with you, the accommodation is your landlord's only or main home and your landlord has been living there since the tenancy began and lives there when the tenancy ends. If your landlord shares living accommodation with you, you will not have basic protection – see *The right to stay in accommodation*, p. 152
- accommodation provided by the Crown or a government department
- accommodation provided by some housing co-ops and almshouses
- accommodation provided by your employer in order for you to carry out your job. If you occupy accommodation because of your job (for example, a launderette assistant or a caretaker), you may not necessarily have to give up the accommodation if you leave the job.

The above list is not exhaustive.

Deposits and premiums

There are two types of deposit that you may be asked to pay by a landlord or an accommodation agency acting on their behalf. They are a holding deposit and a security deposit.

Holding deposits

A holding deposit is money a landlord or accommodation agency asks you to pay when you agree to rent a property but have not yet taken up the tenancy. This deposit will probably be deducted from the security deposit you pay when you move into the property.

Before making any payment, you should be sure you want to take up the tenancy as a holding deposit cannot be returned unless you are unable to move in for reasons beyond your control. Examples of this are if the landlord asks for more rent than was originally agreed, or the accommodation is not ready on the date the tenancy is due to begin.

Security deposits

A security deposit is money paid to a landlord (or an accommodation agency acting on their behalf) as security against, for example, rent arrears, damage to property or removal of furniture.

If you are asked to pay a security deposit, you should check the condition of the property and its contents carefully. This is because, when the tenancy ends, you may be held responsible for anything that is missing or damaged, and may lose all or some of your deposit.

When a tenancy ends, the security deposit should be returned to you. It is reasonable for deductions to be made to cover, for example, damage to the property or furniture, missing items listed on the inventory, or outstanding rent you owe.

> *I paid a deposit when I moved into my rented house. I have now moved out but the landlord will not return the deposit. What can I do?*
>
> A deposit is usually paid to a landlord or letting agency at the start of the tenancy. When the tenancy ends the landlord or agent should inspect the property and can make deductions from the deposit for any reasonable losses, such as rent arrears, damage to the property or furniture, or missing items.

Deductions should not be made for fair wear and tear.

If the landlord does not return the deposit or you disagree with the amount that has been deducted, what you can do about it depends on when you paid the deposit. If it was before April 2007, you can just try to negotiate. If that does not succeed, then consider taking court action against the landlord. If you paid the deposit on or after 6 April 2007, the landlord has to take part in a tenancy deposit protection scheme which will have a procedure for dealing with disputes. Your landlord has to tell you which scheme covers you.

If you pay a deposit to a private landlord or accommodation agency on or after 6 April 2007, your landlord must place it in a tenancy deposit protection scheme. This means you can be sure that you will get your deposit back at the end of the tenancy, as long as you are entitled to it. The scheme also provides a service to sort out any disagreements about the deposit between you and your landlord, without going to court.

Premiums

A landlord can charge you a premium, or 'key money', for granting a tenancy. There is no limit on what can be asked by a landlord. If the amount appears unreasonable, you have no choice other than not to take the accommodation.

Rent deposit guarantee schemes

Some local authorities, housing associations and charities offer loans to pay a deposit of a month's rent on a private flat. Most schemes operate by lending the rent in advance, which you repay to the scheme. This may be through Housing Benefit. Other schemes guarantee that any outstanding rent will be paid to the landlord if required, but no money is exchanged. Most schemes guarantee to pay for any damage to the accommodation at the end of the tenancy.

You can get details of rent deposit schemes from the Crisis Smartmove website at www.crisis.org.uk. Or contact your local authority housing department.

Discrimination and rented property

If you are renting property, you may find that you face discrimination. People who are letting property must not discriminate against you because of your race, sex, sexuality, religion or disability. They are probably breaking the law if, because of your race, sex, sexuality, religion or disability, they:

- refuse to let a property to you or offer you a property for rent on worse terms than other people
- treat you differently on a housing waiting list
- treat you differently from other tenants in the way you are allowed to use benefits or facilities such as a laundry or a garden
- evict or harass you.

There are some circumstances where the general rules about discrimination may not apply – for example, if your handlord lives in the same property as you.

A landlord's duty to make reasonable adjustments for disabled people

If you are disabled, you can ask your landlord (or future landlord) to make certain changes when this is necessary for you to be able to live in the property. These changes are known as reasonable adjustments. Landlords who refuse to make reasonable adjustments are discriminating against you and are breaking the law, unless they can justify this – for example, on health and safety grounds. Reasonable adjustments can include providing aids and services, such as a temporary ramp for a wheelchair user with a small step up to their flat. It could also include changing policies. For example, a parking policy could be changed. What is reasonable will depend on the individual circumstances.

Your landlord does not have to undertake any major works such as putting in a permanent, concrete ramp or a lift.

It also counts as discrimination if your landlord tries to evict you or increase the rent because of the cost of an adjustment you have asked to be made.

Your landlord does not usually have to make reasonable adjustments for you if they live in the same property as you.

Fixing and increasing the rent

Assured tenants

As an assured tenant you must pay whatever rent you agreed with your landlord when the tenancy began. Your landlord cannot normally increase the rent unless you agree or the tenancy agreement allows it. If the tenancy agreement allows your landlord to increase the rent, it should contain information about when and how the rent can be increased.

If a rent increase has not been agreed with your landlord, or if the tenancy agreement does not allow an increase, you may have the right to appeal to a local Rent Assessment Committee if you think the rent increase proposed by your landlord is too high. You can only do so if your tenancy is not fixed term (that is, it does not run for a specific period only, such as six months or a year) and if your landlord uses a special procedure to increase the rent. If the tenancy agreement allows the rent increases, you cannot apply to a Rent Assessment Committee. Also, a Rent Assessment Committee can set a rent that is higher than that proposed by your landlord.

If you cannot afford to pay your rent, you may be able to apply for Housing Benefit. You may also be entitled to other benefits if you are unemployed or on a low income.

Assured shorthold tenants

As an assured shorthold tenant you must pay whatever rent you agreed with your landlord when the tenancy began.

Your rent cannot normally be increased unless you agree or the tenancy agreement allows it.

In certain cases, your landlord can instead use a special procedure to increase the rent, which involves giving you a formal notice whose details are set down by legislation. It is in theory possible for certain types of assured shorthold tenant to appeal to a Rent Assessment Committee as assured tenants, but assured shorthold tenants have very little protection from eviction, and antagonizing your landlord can put you at risk of losing your home.

If you cannot afford to pay your rent, you may be able to apply for Housing Benefit. You may also be entitled to other benefits if you are unemployed or on a low income.

Protected tenants

As a protected tenant you must pay the rent you agreed with your landlord when the tenancy began. However, either you or your landlord can subsequently ask the Rent Officer to fix a 'fair rent'.

Your landlord cannot increase your rent if it has been registered as a fair rent by the Rent Officer. If no fair rent has been registered, your landlord cannot increase the rent unless you agree formally in writing, or either you or your landlord apply to the Rent Officer and the Rent Officer fixes a fair rent.

If you cannot afford to pay your rent, you may be able to apply for Housing Benefit. You may also be entitled to other benefits if you are unemployed or on a low income.

Occupiers with basic protection

As a tenant with basic protection you must pay the rent you agreed with your landlord when you moved into the accommodation. You cannot apply to the Rent Officer or to the Rent Assessment Committee to have the rent reduced. If your landlord wants to increase the rent, you could try and negotiate. If you refuse to pay the increase this could lead to your landlord evicting you.

> ### I rent my flat privately and the landlord wants to increase the rent. Can he do this?
>
> It all depends on the type of tenancy agreement that you have. If your tenancy is for a fixed term (for example, six months), the rent cannot be increased during the fixed term unless the agreement states that it can, or you agree to the increase. When the fixed term ends, the landlord may ask you to sign a new tenancy agreement which charges a higher rent.
>
> If your tenancy is not for a fixed term, the landlord can charge a higher rent if you agree, or if the agreement allows for this, or by giving you the correct written notice. If the agreement allows for an increase, it should say when and how this should happen, such as annually.
>
> In some cases you can appeal against an increase if you think the amount of the increase is too much or if you think the notice of the increase was not issued correctly. If you start to pay the increased

amount, this means you have agreed to it and you cannot appeal against it.

Some tenants have very little protection against eviction and could risk losing their homes if they disagree with the landlord about the amount of rent to be paid. If you cannot afford to pay your rent, remember you may be able to claim Housing Benefit.

The right to stay in accommodation

Your right to stay in the accommodation will depend on the type of tenancy you have.

Protected and assured tenants

Your landlord can only repossess the property if they can convince the court that there are reasons why you should be evicted – for example, you have rent arrears, you have damaged the property or you have broken one of the terms of the agreement.

Assured shorthold tenants

Tenancy began before 28 February 1997

As an assured shorthold tenant you have the right to stay in the accommodation for the duration of the initial fixed term unless you breach a term in the tenancy agreement or, for example, you are in rent arrears, or you have damaged the property.

If you stay in the home after the initial fixed term ends and your landlord does not intend to renew the agreement and wants possession, they will have to give you at least two months' notice to leave the property and will have to go to court for possession of the property if you do not leave. If your landlord takes no action, you will become a statutory periodic assured shorthold tenant and your landlord will not be able to regain possession of the property without going through this procedure.

Tenancies created on or after 28 February 1997

Your landlord cannot evict you during the first six months of the tenancy, or during the initial fixed term, whichever is the longer, unless they have grounds for doing so, as for tenancies created before 28 February 1997.

At the end of this period your landlord can automatically get a court order to evict you, as for tenancies created before 28 February 1997.

Occupiers with basic protection

If you are a tenant with basic protection and you do not move out when your landlord has given you notice to quit and the notice period has expired, your landlord has to go to court for a possession order. This will normally be granted. If the tenancy is for a specified fixed term (for example, it is agreed that it lasts for six months or a year), your landlord does not have to give you notice to quit at the end of that term. However, your landlord still has to apply for a possession order to evict you. They can only apply once the fixed term has ended.

PUBLIC SECTOR TENANCIES

You are a public sector tenant if you are a tenant of:

- a local authority (these are district councils and London borough councils)
- a Housing Action Trust (HAT)
- a housing association (if the tenancy began before 15 January 1989)
- a housing co-operative (if the tenancy began before 15 January 1989).

If you are a tenant of one of the above bodies, you will be a secure tenant. However, HAT and local authority tenants may be introductory tenants for the first twelve months that they occupy their property.

If you are a housing association or housing co-operative tenant and your tenancy began on or after 15 January 1989, you will be an *assured* tenant.

Rights of secure tenants

As a secure tenant you have the right to stay in the accommodation unless your landlord can convince the court that there are special reasons to evict you – for example, if you have rent arrears, have damaged property or broken some other term of the agreement.

As a secure tenant you can enforce your rights – for example, to get repairs done – without worrying about being evicted. As well as the right to stay in your home as long as you keep to the terms of the tenancy, you will also have other rights by law, such as to sub-let with your landlord's permission and for your partner or a resident member of your family to take over the tenancy on your death (the right of 'succession').

You will usually have a written tenancy agreement that may give you more rights than those set out above.

As a secure tenant you also have the right to complain to an ombudsman about certain problems. If you are a local authority tenant, this will be the Local Government Ombudsman. If you are a housing association tenant, it will be the Housing Ombudsman.

Rights of assured tenants

As an assured tenant you have the right to stay in your accommodation unless your landlord can convince the court there are good reasons for eviction – for example, rent arrears or damage to the property, or that another of the terms of the agreement has been broken.

As an assured tenant you can enforce your rights – for instance, to get repairs done – without worrying about getting evicted.

As well as the right to stay in your home as long as you keep to the terms of the tenancy you will also have other rights by law, including:

- the right to have the accommodation kept in a reasonable state of repair
- the right to carry out minor repairs yourself and to receive payment for these from your landlord
- the right for your partner to take over the tenancy on your death (the right of 'succession'). This applies to married partners and civil partners, and even if you were just living together as partners.

Fixing and increasing the rent

Secure tenants
Local authority tenancies
Rents for local authority tenants are fixed according to the local authority's housing policy and the amount of money it gets from central government. You cannot control the amount of rent payable, but may be able to claim Housing Benefit to help pay it.

Housing association and housing co-operative tenancies that began before 15 January 1989
The housing association or co-operative will usually have had the rent registered as a fair rent by the Rent Officer.

Once a rent has been registered, a new rent cannot usually be considered for the accommodation for two years. The rent can only be increased if:

- you ask for a new fair rent assessment after two years
- your landlord asks for a new fair rent assessment after one year and nine months, although any new rent would not become effective until the end of two years.

An application for a rent increase can be made earlier, but only if the tenancy has changed drastically or if you and your landlord apply together.

If you need help paying the rent you may be able to claim Housing Benefit.

Assured tenants

Housing association or housing co-operative tenancies that began on or after 15 January 1989

As a housing association tenant whose tenancy started on or after 15 January 1989, your rent is the rent you agreed to pay your landlord at the beginning of the tenancy. It should be covered in your tenancy agreement. The tenancy agreement should also state when and how the rent can be increased. Most housing associations and housing co-operatives are registered with the Housing Corporation and are known as 'registered social landlords'. They must follow standards and procedures set down by this regulatory body. They should try to set rents that are affordable to people in low-paid employment. They should also provide each tenant with information on their policies, including those for setting rents. This information is often in the form of a handbook.

There is also a model tenancy agreement for registered social landlords' assured tenants, produced by the National Housing Federation, which says that assured tenants' rents should not be increased more than once a year.

If your tenancy agreement does not cover rent increases, you have the right to apply to a Rent Assessment Committee if you do not agree to the increase. However, the Rent Assessment Committee may agree to the rent increase, or may set an increase that is higher than that proposed by your landlord.

The right to stay in accommodation

Secure tenants

As a secure tenant you have the right to stay in the accommodation as long as you keep to the terms of the tenancy agreement with your landlord. However, if the tenancy agreement is broken – for example, because of rent arrears or nuisance to neighbours – your landlord can serve a notice on you and apply to the county court for eviction.

A public sector landlord can only evict you if they give you the proper notice and if one of the 'grounds for possession' applies.

What constitutes 'grounds for possession' is complicated. The landlord must apply to the county court to seek possession of the property and a secure tenant can only be evicted if the court grants a possession order to the landlord.

Assured tenants

If a housing association or housing co-operative tenancy began after 15 January 1989, it will be an assured tenancy. There will usually be a model housing association tenancy agreement, giving similar rights to those of secure tenants. In order to evict you, the housing association will have to give proper notice that it is going to seek possession. The housing association will then have to obtain a possession order from the county court by proving that one of the 'grounds for possession' applies.

Introductory tenants

Some local authorities and Housing Action Trusts (HATs) make all new tenants introductory tenants for the first twelve months of the tenancy. Introductory tenants have some but not all of the rights of secure tenants.

At the end of the twelve months, provided there have been no possession proceedings against you, the introductory tenancy will be converted by your landlord to a secure tenancy. However, if the tenancy started on or after 6 June 2005, your landlord may be able to extend the introductory tenancy for a further six months.

It is very easy for a landlord to evict an introductory tenant.

COMMON PROBLEMS WITH TENANCIES

Sounds silly, but I don't know who my landlord is!

If you do not know the identity of the landlord, you can write to the person who last collected your rent asking for your landlord's full name and address. You should send this letter by recorded delivery and keep a copy. If the person to whom you have written does not reply within 21 days, this is a criminal offence. You can inform the Tenancy Relations Officer of the local authority, who can prosecute the person who has failed to provide the information.

Before contacting the Tenancy Relations Officer, you should consider whether this might provoke your landlord into retaliating with threats or attempted eviction.

If you need to find out your landlord's identity because of an emergency, such as a burst pipe, it may be quicker to inform the local authority of the emergency. The local authority has special powers to enter and carry out any necessary work, and can take steps to find out who your landlord is in order to recover its costs.

My landlord thinks he can come and go as he chooses. Can he do that?

Your landlord has a right to reasonable access to carry out repairs. What 'reasonable access' means depends on why your landlord needs to get access. For example, in an emergency, your landlord is entitled to immediate access to carry out any necessary work.

Your landlord also has a right to enter the property to inspect the state of repair, but they should always ask for your permission and should give you at least 24 hours' notice.

If you are staying in lodgings where it is agreed that your landlord provides a room-cleaning service or where you share a room with other lodgers, your landlord can enter without permission.

Your landlord does not have a right to enter in any other circumstances unless they have a court order.

We feel harassed by our landlord

It is an offence for your landlord to do anything that they know is likely to make you leave the home or prevent you from exercising your legal rights.

This would include, for example, repeatedly disturbing you late at night or obstructing access to the home, creating noise, disconnecting supplies of water, gas or electricity where your landlord knows that this is likely to drive you out or discourage you from insisting on your legal rights.

If you are subjected to harassment, the matter should be reported to the Tenancy Relations Officer of the local authority or to the police.

We rent a house and want to take in a lodger or sub-tenant. Can we do that?

A lodger is someone who lives with the person who occupies the accommodation, is provided with meals and services (such as cleaning and provision of linen), and who may not have any separate accommodation of their own. A sub-tenant has their own separate accommodation (at least one room) and will not normally be provided with meals and services.

Secure tenants can take in lodgers without the landlord's permission. Private tenants should look at their tenancy agreement to see if they are prohibited from taking in lodgers.

As a secure tenant, you have to get your landlord's permission to sub-let part of your accommodation to sub-tenants, but your landlord cannot refuse unreasonably. Sub-letting all of the accommodation can be a ground for possession. This means your landlord can evict you.

In other cases, the right to sub-let depends on the tenancy agreement. If you are a private tenant, you should seek your landlord's permission before sub-letting unless the tenancy agreement specifically allows this. There is no appeal against a private landlord's refusal to allow sub-letting.

Our landlord wants to bring in another tenant – the house is already overcrowded. What can we do?

A home is considered overcrowded if:

- there are more than the 'permitted number' of people living there (the 'permitted number' will depend on the size of the accommodation); or
- two or more people of the opposite sex aged ten or over, who are not living together as husband and wife, have to sleep in the same room.

The local authority can, in certain circumstances, prosecute both the landlord and the occupier of an overcrowded dwelling.

If you are in privately rented accommodation and you are on the local authority housing register/waiting list, you should inform the housing department that you are living in overcrowded accommodation. If you are not on the housing register/waiting list, you should apply to go on it. If you are living in local authority accommodation, you should inform the housing department of your situation and ask for a transfer.

We have just rented a flat as 'furnished' but it has very little furniture in it. How furnished does a furnished flat have to be?

If a property is let furnished, as a tenant you could expect a level of furnishing that would be reasonable to allow you to live in the accommodation. This would include:

- table and chairs in the kitchen/living room
- sofa and/or armchairs in the living room
- a bed and storage for clothes in each bedroom
- heating appliances
- curtains and floor coverings
- a cooker, fridge, kitchen utensils and crockery.

If you think that the provision is not adequate, you can provide your own furniture, unless the tenancy agreement does not allow this.

If you are not happy with the condition of the furniture when you move in, you could consider discussing this with your landlord. Your landlord might agree to replace it. You could check what was listed in the inventory, if one exists, or tenancy agreement about the condition of the furniture.

Any furniture provided by your landlord must be fire-resistant, unless the landlord is letting a room in their own home, or letting the whole home on a temporary basis.

All new and second-hand upholstered furniture sold should meet the fire safety regulations, and carry a label to say so. The labels should be permanently attached to a hidden part of the item. If a piece of furniture does not carry a label saying that it meets the regulations, it is likely that the item does not meet the regulations and must be replaced. The landlord is committing a criminal offence if the furniture does not meet the fire safety regulations.

The landlord is not providing the services we think they should. Can we make them?

If the tenancy agreement specifies that your landlord should provide certain services – for example, gardening or lighting common parts – you must make them do so.

If your landlord is not providing the agreed services, or is providing an inadequate level of service, you may wish to negotiate with the landlord to enforce the agreement.

Who is responsible for repairing any damage to the property?

Your landlord is usually responsible for external and major structural repairs. You are usually responsible for internal decoration and for making sure that furniture and other contents, and fixtures and fittings, are not damaged because of your negligence.

You will not usually be responsible for making good any deterioration caused by 'fair wear and tear'. Your exact responsibilities will normally be described in the tenancy agreement.

You must take care of the property by doing the little jobs that can reasonably be expected of you – for example, unblocking drains and mending fuses.

You should also inform the landlord about any situation that could cause damage to the property, such as a leak in the roof.

If your landlord claims that you have damaged the property, they will normally keep all or part of any deposit you may have paid to cover the cost of damage.

Who is responsible for 'wear and tear'?

Over a period of time, most household furniture and contents deteriorate as a result of normal use – for example, floor coverings will become worn. This is known as 'wear and tear', and you would not be responsible for replacing these items.

If the extent of the wear and tear means that it causes a hazard – for example, springs in an armchair begin to stick through the upholstery – your landlord should repair or replace such items.

If your landlord has supplied an appliance such as a cooker or a washing machine that was working at the beginning of the tenancy, they have a responsibility to repair or replace it if it breaks down, unless this is the result of your negligence.

What about insurance for contents?

If there is damage or loss of furniture or contents, the cost may be covered by your landlord's or your own insurance.

The tenancy agreement may state who is liable for any damage or loss to contents. The liable person should consider arranging an insurance policy to cover this liability.

You are responsible for arranging insurance cover for any contents or possessions that you own.

Our landlord wants us to move out while he does repairs. Do we have to?

If your landlord wants to carry out improvements, they must either get your permission to enter the home and do the work, or get a court order authorizing them to take possession of the home. This also applies if the repairs are so extensive that they cannot be done unless you move out. Your landlord may have to provide alternative accommodation for you. If you do not want to move, your landlord has the power, in some circumstances, to apply to the county court to repossess the property.

If your landlord wants you to leave so that improvements or repairs can be done, you should not agree to this until you have obtained independent advice on your rights.

We think we are going to have trouble getting our deposit back at the end of the tenancy. What are the rules?

If you paid a deposit to your landlord at the start of a tenancy as security for any rent arrears or damage to property, this should be returned at the end of the tenancy if the accommodation has been left in good condition and there are no arrears.

If your landlord refuses to return the deposit or makes deductions, you should check the terms of the tenancy agreement or the agreed inventory (if there was one) to see what the deposit was supposed to cover. In cases of damage to property, it will often be cheaper for you to make good the damage before your landlord comes to inspect the property than for your landlord to charge for the cost of getting repairs done.

If your landlord persists in refusing to return a deposit, the way to solve the problem depends on when you paid the deposit. If it was before 6 April 2007, you could use the small claims procedure in the county court to try and get it back. If you paid the deposit on or after 6 April 2007, your landlord had to join a tenancy deposit guarantee scheme. This will include a procedure for dealing with disputes about the deposit. Your landlord has to tell you which scheme covers your deposit.

Can I keep a pet in my rented flat?

You can keep pets as long as it is not specifically forbidden in the tenancy agreement and it does not cause a nuisance to neighbours. However, you should normally seek your landlord's permission because, even if you have a legal right to keep pets, if your landlord does not approve, they may seek to evict you for some other reason.

If you are disabled and need an assistant dog, and your tenancy agreement says you cannot have pets, your landlord should change this term. Otherwise this could be disability discrimination, which is against the law.

Can I pass my tenancy on to someone else?

Passing on a tenancy to someone else is called assignment. The rules about who can and who cannot assign tenancies are very complex.

When a tenant dies, there are rules that may allow the tenancy to be passed on to the tenant's partner or, sometimes, another member of the family who has been living with the tenant. These rules apply regardless of anything stated in a tenancy agreement. A tenancy agreement can increase the basic rights of a tenant, but it cannot take these rights away. The rules are different for different kinds of tenancy.

I left some property in my rented flat after I left and the landlord is being difficult about me getting it back

Property you left behind still belongs to you and normally should be returned to you when you ask for it.

If you leave things behind when you give up a tenancy, your landlord may charge for the cost of clearing them out of the home.

ENDING A TENANCY

Tenancy ended by landlord

There are many rules that govern the notice needed to end a tenancy agreement. The rules cover the length of notice needed, the form in which it must be given and the dates on which it must take effect.

In most cases, your landlord has to serve a special notice on you before they can apply to the court for an order to evict you from your home (this is called a possession order). The rules vary depending on what kind of tenancy it is and, in some cases, more than one notice is needed.

If a private landlord wants to end a tenancy on the date the agreement expires, they must usually serve a notice conforming to special rules.

Tenancy ended by tenant

You generally have to give the same amount of notice as your landlord to end the tenancy agreement.

If you want to end a fixed-term agreement before it is due to expire, you can only do so with the permission of your landlord or if there is a term in the agreement that allows for this. Otherwise you may end up liable for the rent for the remainder of the time covered by the fixed-term agreement.

If you have given notice to your landlord and then change your mind and want to stay on, there are different rules on this for different kinds of tenancy.

If you leave without giving proper notice, your landlord may be entitled to charge rent up to the date when notice should have expired, or up to the end of the tenancy agreement if it is a fixed-term agreement and you did not give any notice at all. The landlord does not have to minimize their loss – they don't have to try to re-let the accommodation and can claim the whole amount of money you owe.

Facing eviction

How your landlord can evict you and get possession of the accommodation will depend on the type of tenancy you have.

Once your landlord or you have given notice, this does not necessarily mean you can be evicted. In nearly all cases a court order is needed, and further notice of court proceedings is often required. Whether the court will allow the eviction will depend on the kind of tenancy and the reasons for seeking eviction. However, in some cases a court order may not be necessary. For example, a court order for eviction is not needed to evict you from your home if you have a resident landlord and the tenancy started after 15 January 1989.

If your landlord has an order from the court giving them possession of the property, you do not have to leave until the date on the order.

If you are threatened with eviction you should always get advice.

REPAIRS

If you are living in rented property that is in an unsatisfactory condition, there are several ways of getting repairs or improvements done.

This is a very complex area of the law and trying to get a repair done may put a tenant at risk, so what action you take will depend on your housing security. It will also depend on which repair responsibilities are yours and which are your landlord's.

You should not stop paying your rent because of bad housing conditions. If you are in rent arrears, your landlord may take action to get you evicted.

The landlord's general responsibilities

By law, your landlord has a number of repairing responsibilities, including repairing and keeping in working order:

- the structure and exterior of the premises, including drains, gutters and external pipes
- the water and gas pipes and electric wiring (including, for example, taps and sockets)
- the basins, sinks, baths and toilets
- fixed heaters (for example, gas fires) and water heaters (but not gas or electric cookers).

Your landlord has these duties by law, no matter what is written in the tenancy agreement. However, if you ask your landlord to do these repairs they may attempt to regain possession of the property or not renew the agreement when it expires. Before attempting to use this general right to repairs, you should consult an experienced adviser.

The tenancy agreement may specify additional repairing obligations.

Common parts

Your landlord is normally also responsible for repairs to common parts of the building – for example, stairways, lifts, hallways or garden paths shared with other tenants or your landlord.

Electrical and gas appliances

Your landlord is responsible for ensuring that any electrical appliances supplied with the accommodation are safe. This includes heaters, cookers, kettles, and any other electrical goods.

If you are concerned that an electrical appliance is not safe, you could contact Consumer Direct (0845 404 0506).

Your landlord must also arrange and pay for safety checks on gas appliances and any necessary work to be carried out on appliances at least once every twelve months. The checks must be carried out by a person who is registered with the Confederation of Registered Gas Installers (0800 915 0485; www.trustcorgi.com).

Your landlord must keep a record of inspection dates, any defects identified and any remedial action taken. You must be given a copy of this record.

If your landlord does not carry out regular inspections of gas appliances, or if they refuse to give you a copy of the inspection record, you could contact the local office of the Health and Safety Executive (HSE: 0845 345 0055; www.hse.gov.uk), which has a duty to enforce the safety requirements. The HSE also operates a special Gas Safety Advice Line (0800 300363 – 24-hour freephone).

Discrimination and repairs

If you are renting your property, your landlord must not discriminate against you because of your sex, race, sexuality, religion or disability. If your landlord refuses to carry out repairs because of any of these reasons, this is against the law. If you think your landlord is discriminating against you, get expert advice about what action to take.

Disabled tenants

If you are a disabled tenant, you may be able to get a grant to make your home more suitable. Alterations could include the installation of a stair lift or hoist or adaptation of a bathroom or toilet.

You will first have to get the need for any alterations assessed by the social services department of your local authority.

If you want to make alterations yourself to make your home more suitable, you will need to get permission from your landlord first. Your landlord must not refuse permission without good reason.

If the alterations you need do not involve major work to your home, your landlord may have a duty to make these changes. If the landlord does not agree, this could be disability discrimination.

Local authorities' duties and unfit property

Local authorities have a duty to take action against private landlords, housing association landlords, or registered social landlords if:

- the condition of the property affects the health of the occupier – for example, if it is damp, infested with insects or has dangerous wiring; or
- the property causes a 'nuisance' to people living nearby – for example, if damp is coming into a person's property from next door, or if rotten windows may fall into the street and injure others.

This duty covers disrepair in common parts of blocks of flats, such as unhygienic rubbish chutes and noisy central heating.

If you think that the condition of the property is either affecting health or causing a nuisance, you should complain to the Environmental Health Department of the local authority. They must investigate and, if appropriate, give your landlord a notice instructing them to carry out the necessary repairs. If your landlord does not comply with the notice they could be prosecuted and the local authority can carry out the repair work itself.

> *The house I rent is very damp. I told the landlord but they have not done anything about it. What else can I do?*
>
> As a tenant, you have the right to have the structure of your home kept in good repair by the landlord. This includes some of the installations in the home such as heating and hot water systems. You will often be responsible yourself for repairs to internal decoration and for minor repairs such as a blocked sink. Details about repairs are usually set out in a written tenancy agreement that describes the landlord's and tenant's responsibilities. If you do not have a tenancy

agreement, the law may still give you some basic rights. However, you should always check what sort of tenancy agreement you have before you complain about housing conditions, as some landlords try to evict tenants who wish to enforce their legal rights to repair.

When you have decided that your repair should be done by the landlord, you must tell them about the repair that is needed. You should write out a description of the problem and collect evidence such as photographs, a report from environmental health officers, and medical reports if the disrepair is affecting your health or the health of someone in your household.

If the landlord still fails to carry out the work, you could consider contacting the Environmental Health Department at your local authority, or you could take the landlord to court. If your landlord is a registered social landlord such as a housing association or is a private landlord, the local authority may be able to force them to take action. If you are a tenant of the local authority itself, then you should make a complaint using the authority's complaints procedure.

You should carry on paying your rent while you try to get the repair work done, as your landlord may try to evict you if you have rent arrears.

The local authority also has a duty to take action against a private landlord, housing association landlord or registered social landlord if the property does not meet certain housing standards and is 'unfit for human habitation'. A property must:

- be structurally stable; *and*
- be free from serious disrepair; *and*
- be free from dampness prejudicial to the health of the occupier; *and*
- have adequate heating, lighting and ventilation; *and*
- have an adequate supply of piped, wholesome water; *and*
- have satisfactory facilities for preparing and cooking food, including a sink with a satisfactory supply of hot and cold water; *and*
- have a suitably located toilet, for the exclusive use of the occupier; *and*
- have a suitable sewer and drainage system; *and*
- have a suitably located fixed bath or shower and hand basin, each of which has a satisfactory supply of hot and cold water for the exclusive use of the occupier.

If your property does not meet these standards, it will be declared unfit and your landlord will be ordered to do the necessary repairs. If your property cannot be repaired, the local authority may order that it is not to be occupied or that it is demolished. In this case, it will rehouse you.

Right to Repair schemes

Tenants of local authorities and registered social landlords (including housing associations) can use 'right to repair' schemes to claim compensation for repairs that the landlord does not carry out within a set timescale.

If you are a tenant of a registered social landlord, you are entitled to compensation if you report a repair or maintenance problem that affects your health, safety or security and your landlord fails twice to make the repair within the set timescale. There is a flat rate award, plus a daily rate up to a maximum amount, for each day the repair remains outstanding. A maximum cost for an eligible repair may be set by the individual landlord. You should contact your landlord for more details about the scheme.

Local authority tenants have a Right to Repair scheme similar to that of registered social landlord tenants. Under this Right to Repair scheme, if repairs are not carried out within a fixed timescale, you can notify the landlord that you want a different contractor to do the job. The local authority must appoint a new contractor and set another time limit. You can then claim compensation if the repair is not carried out within the new time limit.

As a local authority tenant you can currently use this Right to Repair scheme for repairs that your landlord estimates would cost up to £250. You can also claim up to £50 compensation. There are twenty types of repairs that qualify for the scheme, including insecure doors, broken entry-phone systems, blocked sinks and leaking roofs.

A repair will not qualify for the scheme if the local authority has fewer than a hundred properties, is not responsible for the repair or decides it would cost more than £250.

Taking action about repairs

If you are a tenant thinking of taking action about disrepair in your home you should seek the advice of an experienced adviser. If you think you have been discriminated against, make sure you mention this to the adviser. The adviser will be able to advise you on the possible courses of action, including one or more of the following:

- negotiating with your landlord
- using the law
- using the Ombudsmen
- campaigning with others.

Negotiating with the landlord

If you think your landlord has an obligation to carry out a repair, you should first consult an experienced housing adviser to check whether you can try to have the repair done without risking losing your accommodation. An adviser will also be able to check whether your landlord is obliged by law to carry out the repair.

It may be worth trying to negotiate amicably with your landlord, even if they do not have a legal duty to carry out a repair.

It is also advisable to put a repair request down in writing. You should keep copies of letters written to your landlord.

If you are a tenant of a local authority, housing association or registered social landlord, you should find out how long your landlord usually takes to carry out repairs. This may depend on the urgency of the repair. If your landlord refuses to do repairs or delays carrying out agreed repairs, you should try to negotiate. You may need specialized help to do this. If negotiations fail, you may need to take legal action to enforce your rights to repair.

Using the law

There are a number of laws that cover your right to have your property repaired. These laws are very complex. Before starting legal action you will, in most cases, need an expert's report on the disrepair.

Private prosecutions

If you are affected by the poor condition of a property, you can take out a private prosecution against your landlord. If the prosecution is successful, your landlord will be ordered to do the repairs and will be guilty of a criminal offence if they do not carry them out. This is useful for local authority tenants, who may not be able to use other types of action against the local authority. However, criminal legal aid is not available to pay for your legal costs.

Civil court action

If a property is in poor condition, your landlord may have broken the tenancy agreement by failing to carry out repairs. Your tenancy agreement may include specific details of what repairs your landlord has agreed, either in writing or orally. In addition, even if there are no specific terms in the tenancy agreement, certain repairing responsibilities will be implied by legislation. If your landlord has broken the tenancy agreement, you can sue your landlord and, if successful, get a court order requiring your landlord to carry out the repairs. You may also be able to get compensation. If the reasons for not carrying out repairs is discrimination because of race, sex, sexuality, disability or religion, you might also be able to take civil court action. Legal aid may be available to help with your legal costs.

If you intend to take action, you must give your landlord written notice of the repairs that need doing. You will not be able to start court action until a reasonable time for your landlord to carry out the repairs has elapsed.

Using the Ombudsmen

Local Government Ombudsman

The Local Government Ombudsman investigates cases of management inefficiency and unreasonable delay by local authorities. As a local authority tenant you can complain to the Local Government Ombudsman if you are dissatisfied with any aspect of how a problem over a repair has been dealt with. Tenants of other landlords can only complain about dissatisfaction they have with the authority's exercise of, or failure to exercise, its duties. If you think discrimination was involved, you can complain about this too.

You cannot complain to the Local Government Ombudsman until you have gone through the local authority's own complaints procedure. A complaint to the Ombudsman may take quite a long time to be investigated, but usually no more than three months. The Ombudsman can also make a recommendation for a local authority to pay compensation. The Ombudsman's recommendations cannot be enforced but local authorities do usually comply.

Contact details of the Local Government Ombudsmen for your area are listed in the chapter on Civil Rights (p. 485).

Independent Housing Ombudsman

In England, all registered social landlords are members of the Independent Housing Ombudsman scheme, including housing associations and local housing companies. Some private landlords may also be members. You can complain to the Independent Housing Ombudsman about any aspect of the way in which a landlord has handled a request for a repair. If you think discrimination was involved, you can complain about this too. You cannot complain to the Independent Housing Ombudsman until you have gone through your landlord's own complaints procedure. Contact details of the Independent Housing Ombudsmen are listed in the chapter on Civil Rights. Complaints about maladministration by registered social landlords in Wales should be made to the Public Services Ombudsman for Wales – see p. 484. If you are also dissatisfied with the way in which the local authority carried out, or did not carry out, its legal obligations or powers, you can also complain to the Local Government Ombudsman – see p. 485.

Campaigning with others

If you know that there are a number of tenants affected by the disrepair, it may be effective to start a campaign against your landlord. This is likely to be more effective if your landlord is a local authority or a registered social landlord (including a housing association), which could be sensitive to bad publicity. A successful campaign should involve as many people as possible and publicity in the local or national media can be effective. It may also be useful to lobby local councillors, MPs and the chair of the housing committee (if your landlord is a local authority).

HOME IMPROVEMENTS

A local authority can offer different types of help with home improvements. It will have its own rules about the types of help it will offer, and about the conditions you must meet in order to qualify for help. To find out if you can get help with home improvements, and the help available in your area, contact your local authority. Your local authority can give you help to:

- adapt, improve, or repair your home. This could be in the form of a grant or loan. It could be by providing labour, tools, or cheap materials to help you carry out the work. It could be by providing details of builders who can carry out the work, or by providing free or low-cost surveys, or advice on carrying out repairs
- buy a new home if it decides that this would be a better way of improving your living conditions than carrying out work on your current home. The help could be in the form of a grant or loan

- buy a new home if it has decided to buy your current home. The help could be in the form of a grant or loan
- demolish your home, or build a new home if your previous home has been demolished. The help could be in the form of a grant or loan.

If you or someone you live with are disabled, you may be able to get a disabled facilities grant to help you adapt, improve or repair your home – see below.

Your local authority can help improve a building, part of a building, a caravan, or a boat, as long as the property is your home, or it is available for you to live in as your home.

Your local authority will have its own rules about the conditions you must meet in order to get help. For example, it might say you cannot get a grant if your savings are over a certain limit. Although the local authority can have its own rules, it cannot have rules which are completely rigid or unreasonable. For example, it cannot say it will never give any grants, and it must take your individual circumstances into account if you apply for help.

If you rent your home and apply to your local authority for help with home improvements, you will need to get your landlord's permission before the local authority will agree to help you. If you are disabled and the home improvements are to do with your disability, your landlord must not refuse permission without a good reason. If your home is in need of repair, your landlord may have to do the repairs you need. If your home is in need of serious repair and you apply for help, your local authority may decide it is unfit for human habitation.

Disabled facilities grants

There are special rules for getting a disabled facilities grant and these are different from the rules above that apply for getting help with home improvements.

A disabled facilities grant is a grant that you can get from your local authority for work that is essential to help a disabled person live an independent life. You can, for example, get a disabled facilities grant for the following things:

- making it easier to get in and out of your home – for example, by widening doors or providing ramps
- making it easier to get to a living room, bedroom, toilet, bathroom or kitchen – for example, by putting in a stair lift, or providing a downstairs bathroom

- providing suitable bathroom or kitchen facilities
- providing or improving a heating system
- ensuring your safety – for example, by providing a specially adapted room in which it would be safe to leave you unattended, or by providing improved lighting for better visibility
- helping you get around at home so you can care for someone who lives with you and needs care.

A local authority must give you a disabled facilities grant if you meet the conditions for getting one.

Owner-occupiers, landlords, tenants, licensees, and occupiers of some houseboats and park homes can apply for a disabled facilities grant, provided the work is for the benefit of a disabled person who lives or will live in the property.

To apply for a disabled facilities grant, you need to fill in a form that you can get from your local authority. They may ask for information or for tests to be carried out before you make a formal application. You may also need to get approval for building regulations, planning, listed building or conservation area purposes.

Your local authority may have a list of local architects, surveyors and builders who specialize in renovation work that you could ask to see when choosing a contractor for the work to your home. If you intend to carry out the work yourself, you will not be able to claim for the cost of your labour.

Once you have applied for a grant, your local authority must tell you about its decision in writing as soon as it can, and no later than six months after you applied.

You can only get a disabled facilities grant if the work you need done on your home is:

- necessary and appropriate to meet your needs. Your local authority will normally ask an occupational therapist for their opinion on whether or not you need the work done. *And*
- reasonable and practicable, given the age of your home and the condition it is in. For example, if your home is in a serious state of disrepair, it might not be practical to do the work you need.

A disabled facilities grant will be no more than £25,000 in England and £30,000 in Wales, although your local authority can top this up as it can give you other help with home improvements. The amount of grant you get depends on your income and savings unless the work is to meet the needs of a disabled person under 16, or, in some cases, over 16 but under 19.

If you live in rented accommodation and are applying for a disabled facilities grant for work to a communal area of the property in which you live, you should make sure that you are responsible for doing the work. If your landlord is responsible for doing the work, you will not be able to get a grant and your landlord may be able to apply for a grant instead.

If you rent your home and apply to your local authority for a disabled facilities grant, you will need to get your landlord's permission before your local authority will agree to help you. Your landlord must not refuse permission without a good reason, otherwise this could be disability discrimination, which is against the law. If your home is in need of repair, your landlord may have to do the repairs you need. If your home is in need of serious repair and you apply for a disabled facilities grant, your local authority may decide it is unfit for human habitation.

If you wish to challenge a decision by your local authority on a disabled facilities grant, the Royal Association for Disability and Rehabilitation (020 7250 3222; www.radar.org.uk) may be able to help you do this. Or you could contact the Equality and Human Rights Commission (EHRC: 08457 622633 in England, 0845 604 8810 in Wales; www.equalityhumanrights.com).

The rapid response adaptations programme in Wales

If you live in Wales, and are physically disabled or aged 60 or over, you may be able to get help under the rapid response adaptations programme. You can get help with small-scale alterations to your home so that you can be discharged from hospital and return to live safely at home. You may also be able to get help if you are not in hospital. You can get various adaptations to your home under the programme.

You must be referred to the programme by a health professional. You cannot apply directly yourself. To get help, you have to be a homeowner or a tenant. You must usually be aged 60 or over, and/or have a physical disability, and:

- be in hospital; *or*
- have recently been discharged from hospital; *or*
- want to carry on living independently at home.

The work to your home should be finished within 15 days of the day you were referred to the programme.

The rapid response adaptation programme is run by Care and Repair Cymru (029 2057 6286; www.careandrepair.org.uk).

Home improvement agencies

Home improvement agencies (HIAs) are not-for-profit organizations run by housing associations, local authorities and charities. They can help people who own their own homes, or who live in privately rented accommodation, and who are elderly, disabled or on a low income, to repair, maintain or adapt their home.

For example, an HIA can:

- arrange for repairs to be carried out to your home
- help you to get funding for repairs to be carried out to your home
- give you advice about a range of issues that affect your living conditions
- organize the fitting of small aids and adaptations to help you live independently in your home
- install security measures to your home such as door and window locks, door chains and viewers.

Foundations (in England: 01457 891909; www.foundations.uk.com) and Care and Repair Cymru (in Wales: 029 2057 6286; www.careandrepair. org.uk) can put you in touch with your local organization, if one exists.

Home energy efficiency scheme

The home energy efficiency scheme (HEES) provides grants that help to cover the costs of home insulation and of improving energy efficiency. It is available to owner-occupiers and people renting accommodation. You may also be able to get other help with insulating your home.

PLANNING AND PLANNING PERMISSION

Planning laws are there to protect the environment in towns and the countryside. It is a very complex area and the rules differ from area to area, so it is important to check with the planning department of your local authority whether planning permission is required before you start making any changes to your house or land.

If you carry out work without the proper permission, there can be serious consequences and the local authority has powers to enforce planning laws. For example, it could order you to knock down a building erected without permission.

The local authority has the responsibility to ensure that 'development' of land is carried out in the public interest and that the character of an area is not adversely affected by new buildings or changes in the use of existing buildings or land. 'Development' is building or engineering work, or changes in the use of land. For the purpose of planning permission 'buildings' include any structure or erection, which would cover, for example, fences, flagpoles, and a steel structure covering a swimming pool. Local authorities have a development plan for their area that sets out the local planning authority's policies and proposals for development in the use of land in their area.

If planning permission is required, and the local authority refuses to grant it, you can appeal. In most circumstances, other people can object to the granting of planning permission and the local authority has to take these objections into account.

When is planning permission always required?

A planning application is always needed:

- for additions or extensions to a flat or maisonette
- if you want to change the use of the property – for example, if you want to divide off part of the house to rent out as a separate home for someone else to live in
- if you want to use a caravan in your garden as a home for someone else
- if you want to start up a business at home, so that the main use of the property is no longer residential.

In some situations, you may need planning permission even if otherwise you would not need to apply. Common examples are:

- if you live in a conservation area. A conservation area is an area of 'special architectural or historic interest whose appearance or character it is desirable to preserve or enhance'. The rules about planning permission for houses in conservation areas may be different to other areas
- if you live in a national park
- if you live on the Norfolk or Suffolk Broads
- if you live in an area of outstanding natural beauty
- if you live in a listed building. A listed building is a building designated by the

Government as a building of special architectural or historic interest. If you live in a listed building, there are two separate systems of controlling work to or near the building. The two systems are *planning permission* and *listed building consent.*

If you are extending a house – for example by adding a conservatory or doing a loft conversion – you will need planning permission if:

- more than half of the area of the land around the original house will be covered by additions or other buildings
- the extension or addition is bigger than certain prescribed limits. In all cases, 115 cubic metres is the maximum that can be added to the volume of the original house without making a planning application
- if the extension or addition is higher than certain prescribed limits.

These are only some common examples. There are other situations where you need planning permission if you want to extend a house.

When is a planning application not usually required?

The right to carry out work in some circumstances without making a planning application is called a *permitted development right.* However, the local authority can decide to withdraw some or all of these permitted development rights in its area.

A planning application is not usually required for:

- a normal domestic television or radio aerial. However, a planning application is necessary to install a satellite dish or antenna if it is going on a chimney and it would be more than 45 centimetres in any dimension (diameter, depth, width), excluding mounting brackets
- repairs or maintenance
- minor improvements, such as painting the house
- internal alterations
- putting in windows, skylights or rooflights, provided that they do not alter the shape of the house or alter the shape of any roof facing a highway. However, if you want to put in a new bay window, this will be treated as an extension of the house
- the installation of solar panels that do not project significantly beyond the roof slope
- re-roofing the house. However, any additions to the roof are treated as extensions to the house.

Applying for planning permission

There are several things that you can do to try to ensure that your application is successful. Your local planning department may be able to give you an informal opinion and some local authorities will make an informal site visit if you request. It might be helpful to discuss your proposals with neighbours before applying, so you can take their comments into account. Your neighbours may even agree to write in support of your application.

If the proposal is controversial, you could consider applying for planning permission that would be limited to you. This would mean that only you could carry out the works or use the building in a different way. (Usually, a planning decision applies to the land and not to the individual applicant so that if a new owner buys the land, they are subject to the decision and may make use of it.)

To make a planning application, you will need to fill in an application form for the planning department of the local authority. You have to pay a fee to apply. You may be able to fill in and submit an application form online. You may also be able to follow the progress of a planning application online. Go to www.planningportal.gov.uk to find out how to do this.

The planning department should usually determine a planning application (make a decision) within eight weeks. However, it may ask to extend this period – for example, if the issues involved are complex or a lot of people will be affected by the decision.

You can appeal if the local authority refuses an application for planning permission.

Other types of approval

Whether or not you need planning permission to carry out work, you may need another sort of approval. For example:

- listed building consent. It is a criminal offence to carry out work that needs listed building consent without first obtaining it
- conservation area consent
- consent to prune or chop down a tree
- building regulations approval if you are putting up a new building, extending a building or changing the use of a building, even if no construction work is involved. Building regulations approval is completely separate from planning permission and a different department of the local authority will deal with it. This will normally be the building control department and you should

contact this department before carrying out work if there is any doubt about whether building regulations approval is required
• if work would obstruct a right of way.

Planning and wildlife

If bats or other protected species of animals live in the roof of your property, you must notify English Nature or the Countryside Council of Wales if you wish to carry out any work that might disturb the animals, and obtain a licence before carrying out the work.

Planning and phone masts

Each mobile phone company operates a network of phone masts, which carry mobile phone messages across and beyond England and Wales.

A mobile phone company can erect a mast of up to 15 metres. However, it must make a planning application, and the local authority will then give members of the public 56 days in which to make representations about the application.

When deciding whether to allow the application, the local authority must take into account health and environmental concerns. It must also consult with any nearby school or college. Local authorities must also encourage the sharing of masts by multiple companies.

If you are concerned about a planning application for a mast, you can object to the local authority. You may also want to contact the mobile phone company direct.

Who can help?

If you are concerned about the possibility of health risks resulting from a mobile phone mast, you can seek advice from the **Health Protection Agency** (01235 831600; www.hpa.org.uk/radiation).

In England, the **Department for Communities and Local Government** (020 7944 4400; www.communities.gov.uk) publishes guidance on the erection of masts, entitled 'Planning Policy Guidance Note 8: Telecommunications', and a 'Code of Best Practice on Mobile Phone Network Development'.

In Wales, the **Welsh Assembly Government** (0845 010 3300; www.new.wales.gov.uk) has published guidance entitled 'Technical Advice Note (TAN) 19 – Telecommunications'.

In England, the **Campaign to Protect Rural England** (020 7981 2800; www.cpre.org.uk) can also provide information and advice about challenging planning applications for telecommunications masts.

Objecting to proposals

Your local planning authority must have a development plan for its area, and all large-scale development that takes place – for example, the construction of a housing development or a hypermarket – must comply with the local development plan. If the development plan shows, for example, that a particular area of land is designated for residential use, it should not be used for a large commercial enterprise. In most circumstances, any large- or small-scale development or building activity must be compatible with both planning law and building regulations.

If you are concerned about the environmental impact of any form of development or building work, you should contact the planning department at the local authority.

If you wish to object to the proposals of a neighbour or commercial developer, you should first of all try to discuss the matter and suggest alterations to the scheme that would be mutually acceptable.

If this is not successful, there are several possible options to consider. Before deciding which option to pursue, you should find out as much detail as possible about the proposal by inspecting the application. You could also ask the planning department to send you a copy of the application and drawings. The local authority has to send copies to people who are unable to visit the office – for example, because of mobility difficulties – and is likely to charge a fee. Ask in advance how much the fee is. It is, however, best to visit the office if possible, since you could then find out about other proposals affecting the same site and look at any previous decisions that might be relevant.

Any objections to the proposal should be sent in writing to the planning officer dealing with the application. You could also make contact with the local residents' or tenants' association or other local organizations that might support the objection.

We have just bought a house on a private estate and have been told by our new neighbour that we are not allowed to put up a fence around our front garden without planning permission. Can this be right?

When the local authority originally gave planning permission for the building of your estate, they may have done so on the condition that no fences were put up. These conditions may restrict your right to carry out work which you would normally be allowed to do without planning permission. The planning department of the local authority will have a record of all existing planning permissions and you should contact them to see whether you need to make a new application for planning permission to carry out the work.

Who can help?

Planning Aid (0121 693 1201; www.planningaid.rpti.org.uk) is a free service providing independent professional advice on town planning for community groups, residents' associations and individuals who cannot afford professional fees.

The government planning website at www.planningportal.gov.uk puts you in touch with your local planning authority and also includes useful visual aids and calculators to help you make a planning application.

COMMON DISPUTES WITH NEIGHBOURS

It is not possible to provide a standard set of guidelines for how to deal with every neighbour problem, because the problems are so varied and the solution to any particular dispute will depend on the individual circumstances.

So this section is in two parts:

- common neighbour disputes, which describes some common disputes and indicates which of the alternative courses of action would be most suitable in each case
- how to deal with a neighbour dispute. This outlines the range of actions that may need to be taken to resolve a neighbour dispute.

Access to a neighbour's land for repairs

If you want to carry out repairs to property or land, you may need to have access to neighbouring property or land in order to carry out these repairs.

There may be a right of entry specifically for the purposes of inspection or repair in the property's legal documents. If there is no such right, or no agreement can be reached, the law allows you as the person wishing to carry out repairs to apply to the county court for an access order allowing you to enter your neighbour's land to carry out the repairs. There is a fee for the application.

Amenities that are shared

There may be amenities shared between two or more properties – for example, drains and pipes, shared drives or the roof of a block of flats. Responsibility for maintaining them and rights to use them – for example, putting up an aerial on a shared chimney – are usually outlined in the property's legal documents.

The legal documents may give you as a property owner rights over your neighbour's property. Sometimes these rights are not included in the legal documents but have arisen out of long, continuous and unchallenged use (usually 20 years). A right to use, for example, a pipe through a neighbour's property implies a right to go on that neighbour's property to undertake repairs, although any damage incurred to that property must be made good. If access is refused, an application can be made to a county court for an access order – see above.

Where there is a shared amenity that is in need of repair, the first step is to find out who is responsible for repairs. However, the legal documents may not always provide clear evidence and, in this case, it is probably best to settle in advance that the costs will be shared between owners.

The next stage will probably be to get a surveyor or architect to inspect and report on the part of the property requiring repairs. Estimates will have to be sought and finally a contract made with builders. It is essential that at each stage when a cost is incurred the household initiating the repairs has the consent of the other parties responsible.

If some or all of the property involved is rented, the landlord may be liable for repairs.

Boundaries, fences and walls

If a dispute arises between neighbours about the boundary between their properties, it will be necessary to establish who owns the disputed land. The primary evidence will be contained in the legal documents. Clear evidence of this kind is normally conclusive.

However, the boundaries between properties can differ from those described in the title documents or lease in certain circumstances. The most common are where they have been changed by agreement or by encroachment (occupation without permission). For more useful information about boundary disputes, see the Royal Institution of Chartered Surveyors' website (www.rics.org).

Duty to erect a barrier

Generally, as a property owner you do not have to erect and maintain any type of barrier, such as a fence, wall, trellis or railing, around your property. Some of the exceptions include when:

- there is a clause in the title documents or lease which says a barrier has to be erected and maintained
- the property is next to a street and may cause danger
- the land is used for dangerous purposes – for example, storing chemicals
- a barrier is necessary to prevent animals, other than domestic pets, from straying.

Who can use or repair a barrier

In order to decide who can use and repair a barrier, it is first necessary to establish who owns it. The rules for working out ownership are the same as for other boundaries. In other words, the legal documents may specify who owns the fence, or you may have evidence that it belongs to you.

If the barrier belongs to you alone, you can use it as you wish, without your neighbour's consent, providing it is safe. The neighbour has no rights over the barrier. For example, they could not use it to support trailing plants without your permission. If a fence is jointly owned, each neighbour can use it for support, provided neither makes it unsafe. Any repairs should be financed jointly.

As a property owner you do not have to repair your barrier unless the title documents or lease contain such obligations. However, if the barrier causes damage or injury, your neighbour could take you to court for compensation.

If, as a property owner, you have a barrier next to the street, this should be kept in good repair to prevent it becoming a nuisance or danger to people using the street. If a passer-by is injured by the barrier – for example, if it has barbed wire, or falls down on someone in the street – that person can take you to court for compensation.

Party walls

There are special rules covering structural work to walls that stand across the boundary of land belonging to different owners, or which are used by two or more owners to separate buildings. The owner must notify neighbours about any work they intend to carry out. These rules allow for the agreement or objection to any work within certain time limits, and compensation and temporary protection for buildings and property. If there is no agreement, an independent surveyor can be appointed to decide what work can be done, and how and when. For more useful information about party walls, see the website of the Royal Institution of Chartered Surveyors (www.rics.org).

Planning restrictions on barriers

Planning permission is not generally needed before erecting a fence or wall, provided it is no more than one metre in height if next to a highway, or two metres elsewhere. If you wish to exceed these limits, you will need to get planning permission from the local authority.

Children

Noisy children

Noisy children in themselves are not a 'nuisance'. If someone is disturbed by a neighbour's children – for example, a shift worker who wants to sleep during the day – the only real solution is a conciliatory approach to the neighbour.

Damage done by children

If a neighbour's child causes damage to a property, a conciliatory approach to settle the matter is probably the best solution. Legally, the child can be sued for damages if they are old enough to know what they were doing. In practice, this is unrealistic since few courts would look favourably on such an action, and a child is unlikely to have much money to pay any damages. However, the parents of the child may be liable for negligence and damages if they have trusted the child with something dangerous that was beyond their capability to use responsibly, such as an airgun. The parents may also be liable if they have failed to exercise the control that would be expected of a parent given the child's age.

Balls and ball games

If a child throws a ball into a neighbour's property, the neighbour should either hand it back or allow it to be collected. However, as it is a trespass for the ball to cross the neighbour's boundary, even if it was unintentional, the neighbour would be entitled to financial compensation if any damage had been caused.

Noise

Dealing with noisy neighbours

As a first step, you should talk to your neighbour making the noise and ask them to reduce the noise. If the noise is not reduced and your neighbour is a tenant, it may be worth contacting your neighbour's landlord. If the problem persists, it is useful to keep a record/diary of the disturbances that can be used as evidence in any future action.

Local authorities have extensive powers to deal with noise nuisances. You can ask the Environmental Health Officer (EHO) to investigate the noise. They are able to measure the level of noise and to give an expert opinion on how it rates as a noise nuisance. Local authorities have powers to seize noise-making equipment.

If the EHO considers there is a noise nuisance and has been unable to resolve the matter by discussion, the authority can then serve a notice on the person causing the noise, or on the owner or occupier of the property. If the person causing the noise does not comply with the notice, the local authority can prosecute them. The local authority can also apply for an injunction. (An injunction is a court order that forbids a particular person taking a particular action.)

Local authority tenants who suffer noise nuisance can contact the Local Government Ombudsman, who may be able to recommend compensation if the local authority has failed in one of its duties. Tenants of housing associations and other registered social landlords (and of some private landlords) can contact the Independent Housing Ombudsman. See *Civil Rights*, p. 481, for details of how to complain to the Ombudsman.

Noise in the neighbourhood

Loudspeakers (except for the police, ambulance and fire brigade) must not be used in the streets between 9 p.m. and 8 a.m. It is illegal to use loudspeakers in the street at any hour for advertising, entertainment, trade or business. There is an exemption from this rule for vehicles that sell food (such as ice cream), but loudspeakers or chimes on these vehicles may only be used between the hours of noon and 7 p.m. in such a way as not to annoy people nearby. Any complaints about noise from loudspeakers or chimes should be made to the police or to the environmental health department of the local authority.

All local authorities have the power to deal with noise nuisance from vehicle alarms and other street noise, such as music. This includes the power to break into the vehicle and silence the alarm if it is creating a nuisance.

The local authority also has the power to deal immediately with noise coming from licensed premises at night (between 11 p.m. and 7 a.m.). First of all, it will formally warn whoever is responsible for the noise and then, if they do not stop within the time set out in the warning (usually ten minutes), the local authority can impose a fixed penalty fine on them or prosecute them. The local authority can also seize the equipment making the noise.

Burglar alarms

A local authority has the power to enter a building and silence an alarm, where the alarm has been operating non-stop for 20 minutes or on and off for an hour and is causing a noise nuisance. A local authority officer can only enter a building by force with a warrant. The authority can recover the cost of silencing the alarm from the occupier of the premises.

A local authority can also make an area an 'alarm notification area'. This means that the owner or occupier of every building in the area which has an alarm must have a keyholder and must give their contact details to the local authority. The local authority can ask the keyholder to switch off the alarm. If you live in an alarm notification area, it is a criminal offence not to stick to these rules. Your local authority should put a notice in the paper and put a copy through your door if they plan to introduce these rules in your area.

The National Society for Clean Air and Environmental Protection (01273 878770; www.nsca.org.uk) can provide general advice on noise. It also produces a series of leaflets on noise pollution.

Parking space

Unless there are local parking restrictions giving a right to a particular space, residents do not have automatic rights to a parking space on a public road. However, they do have a right of access to their drive. If there is a shared drive, then each person has a right of access and neither should block the drive. The local authority and the police have wide powers to remove vehicles that are illegally parked, are causing an obstruction on the highway or have been abandoned.

Trees

Overhanging branches

If your neighbour's tree hangs over your property, the neighbour should be asked to trim back the tree. If this is not done, you have the right to trim the tree back to the boundary line (but see *Tree preservation orders*, p. 188). Any branches and/or fruit removed belong to the tree's owner and should be returned.

An overhanging tree may also be a danger. For example, most parts of a yew tree are poisonous. If you suffer any damage or injury, the tree owner will be liable to pay compensation if you take court action.

Dangerous trees

Local authorities have powers to deal with trees on private property that are in a dangerous condition. A local authority can:

- make any tree safe, if asked to do so by the owner of the land on which the tree stands – the local authority will recover the costs of doing this from the owner; *and/or*
- make a tree safe on someone else's land, if asked to do so by a neighbour whose property is threatened by the tree and the owner of the land on which the tree stands is not known; *and/or*
- serve a notice on someone who has a tree in a dangerous condition that is threatening to damage the property of a neighbour if that neighbour asks the local authority to take action. The owner of the tree must comply with the notice. If they do not, the local authority will do the necessary work and recover the costs from the owner. The owner can appeal to the county court against the notice.

If you want the local authority to take action, you should contact the planning or technical services department, who will check the condition of the tree. It is up to the local authority to decide if the tree is in a dangerous condition. If it considers it to be safe, it does not have to take any action.

Roots

If the roots of your neighbour's tree spread into your property, they can be removed using the least damaging method available, unless there is a tree preservation order on the tree – see below. If you have to enter the tree owner's property to do this, you must give reasonable notice.

You may also wish to consult your insurers, if there is a possibility that your property may be damaged by the roots. If the roots have already caused damage, the tree owner is liable to pay compensation but it must be shown that the tree owner knew, or ought to have known, of the danger.

Tree preservation orders

If you wish to prevent a tree being lopped by your neighbour, you could contact the local authority to see if they will place a tree preservation order on it. All trees in an area designated as a Conservation Area are automatically protected.

Hedges

If a neighbour's hedge is tall and blocks out light, the person affected by the nuisance can prune the roots or branches. However, no one should attempt to reduce the height of a hedge without obtaining advice from a solicitor. In addition, some hedgerows are protected by law.

If you have a problem with a neighbour's high hedge and you have not been able to solve the problem with the neighbour themselves, you can get the local authority involved. For a fee, the authority will look into the problem and may order the neighbour to cut the hedge back down to two metres.

Hedgeline (01924 36 74 67; www.hedgeline.org) is an organization that can give advice to victims of hedge nuisance who are members of the organization.

How to deal with a neighbour dispute

Approach the neighbour

You should first make a complaint to the neighbour. If it seems that either of you will be unable to keep their temper during such a meeting, it may be advisable to write.

Sometimes a neighbour may be made to see that their behaviour is anti-social if representations come from a group of neighbours.

If an initial approach to the neighbour has failed, there may be local mediators who are able to help. For information about local mediators, go to the website of ADR Now (www.adrnow.org.uk).

Contact the landlord

If the offending neighbour is a tenant and refuses to co-operate when approached directly, it may be appropriate to contact the landlord.

If the property is owned by the local authority, the authority's housing department should be approached. It may be prepared to contact the offending neighbour to help resolve the problem.

If the property is owned or run by a housing association, it may have a housing welfare officer who deals with disagreements between tenants.

A private landlord can also apply for possession on the grounds that a tenant has been a nuisance to neighbours. If it is possible to find out who the landlord is, they might be prepared to talk to the tenant about the problem.

Call the police

You can call the police if it is possible that a criminal offence is being committed. The most likely offences in the case of neighbour disputes are breach of the peace or assault.

Contact the environmental health department

In cases where neighbours may be breaching public health or pollution laws, you can approach the local authority environmental health department.

An environmental health officer will usually contact the neighbour and attempt to resolve the matter informally. If this fails, a notice may be served on the neighbour, requiring the abatement of the nuisance. This means they are required to stop, or deal with, the nuisance.

Contact the planning department

The local planning department has the power to investigate if there has been a breach of planning control. The authority can issue an enforcement notice if the neighbour has carried out building work without permission or is using the land for an unauthorized purpose.

Consult a solicitor/take court action

Solicitor's letter

A letter from a solicitor may be helpful in making a neighbour realize that you are serious about your complaint. It may be particularly effective in making tenants realize that the next stage might be eviction by their landlord. It may also be necessary when, for example, there is genuine disagreement as to who is responsible.

Taking court action

Although a particular dispute may be resolved successfully through the courts, the relationship between neighbours may be damaged irretrievably. It can also be very expensive unless you are eligible for legal aid.

ANTI-SOCIAL BEHAVIOUR

Anti-social behaviour is acting in a way that causes or is likely to cause harassment, alarm or distress. To be anti-social behaviour, the behaviour must be persistent. There can be a fine line between anti-social behaviour and disputes between neighbours over relatively minor inconveniences. Anti-social behaviour can include:

- intimidation of neighbours and others through threats or actual violence
- harassment, including racial harassment
- verbal abuse
- homophobic behaviour
- noise
- dumping rubbish
- animal nuisance
- vandalism, property damage and graffiti.

If you want to take action about anti-social behaviour, you should first try and establish who is responsible for the behaviour. It is also important to establish whether the behaviour is deliberate or unintentional.

To deal with anti-social behaviour you can do one or more of the following:

- take action yourself, including going to court if you want compensation or an order to stop the behaviour from recurring
- get the landlord to take action
- get the local authority to take action
- get the police or a community support officer to take action.

Taking action yourself

If you want to take action about anti-social behaviour you can:

- contact the tenants' association where you live (if there is one), particularly over behaviour that may also be affecting other people
- seek mediation
- start a criminal prosecution in court, which could lead to the perpetrator being fined or imprisoned
- take civil proceedings in court to claim compensation or apply for an order to stop the perpetrator continuing with their behaviour.

If you are thinking of taking any legal action you should get advice first.

If you just want the behaviour to stop and do not wish to take legal action, you could consider a mediation scheme. Mediation is a process in which a neutral third party helps two or more people in dispute to seek a mutually acceptable solution informally. Community mediation services deal with disputes between neighbours and in the community, including noise, children, pets, parking and burglaries. Mediation is usually free.

Mediation is an appropriate course of action if both parties are willing to go through with it. Mediation can take the form of direct, 'round the table' discussion, where the parties in dispute meet on neutral ground. If they are unwilling to meet, the mediators will act as intermediaries, conveying messages between each of the parties.

For information about local mediation schemes, go to the website of ADR Now (www.adrnow.org.uk).

Asking the landlord to take action

You can ask your landlord to take action. You should find out whether the landlord has a policy and procedures for dealing with anti-social behaviour. Any landlord can take action against anti-social behaviour, although it is more likely that local authorities and registered social landlords (including housing associations) will be willing to take action. Remember that landlords have discretion to take action, not a duty to do so.

A landlord could:

- ask the police or the local authority to take action
- go to court to get the person behaving in an anti-social way evicted, if they are a tenant or leaseholder
- apply to court for an anti-social behaviour order, if the landlord is a local authority or housing association
- rehouse the victim, or the person behaving in an anti-social way. This is very unlikely unless the landlord is a local authority or a registered social landlord.

A local authority landlord can also extend the period of an introductory tenancy, suspend a tenant's right to buy, or refuse to allow them to exchange with another tenant. Local authority and registered social landlords can also apply for a court order to 'demote' someone's tenancy. This will make it easier for the landlord to evict a tenant whose behaviour does not improve.

The person you are complaining about may have a tenancy agreement which forbids certain types of behaviour – for example, harassment, drug dealing or noise. Breaking any of these conditions could lead to their being evicted.

If you are a local authority or registered social landlord tenant, you will normally have a housing officer to whom you can refer a complaint about anti-social behaviour of a neighbour. If you have a private landlord, you will have to contact the landlord or their agent.

What the local authority can do

If you are suffering anti-social behaviour, you can ask the local authority to deal with it, regardless of whether you are a local authority tenant or not. The local authority can:

- apply to the county court for an order to stop or prevent certain anti-social behaviour
- apply to a court for an order to stop public nuisance, which includes drug-dealing
- take action to stop noise, nuisance and threats to health
- take action to evict the person responsible for the behaviour, if they are a local authority tenant
- prosecute where the behaviour is a criminal offence

- apply for an anti-social behaviour order
- take over management of a property where there are particularly serious anti-social behaviour problems.

What the police can do

The police can take action about any anti-social behaviour that is a criminal offence and can charge someone who has:

- attacked another person, causing physical or psychological damage
- wilfully damaged someone else's property
- behaved in a threatening or intentionally abusive way
- incited racial or religious hatred by, for example, distributing racist leaflets.

The police can also get a court order to close down properties that have been taken over by drug dealers. Entering the property will then become an offence and the property will be sealed.

You should bear in mind that although the police may charge someone, there is discretion whether or not a prosecution will follow the charge.

The police can issue on-the-spot fines (penalty notices) for some types of anti-social behaviour and can also apply to court for an anti-social behaviour order.

What community support officers can do

Community support officers can take action about anti-social behaviour in certain circumstances. For example, they can order people to stop cycling on the pavement, disperse groups of young people who are gathering in a public place and escort young children home if they are out unattended late at night.

4
Education

CONTENTS

INTRODUCTION

Some parents are voicing concern over increased testing and others are jailed for allowing their children to skip school. MPs are arguing over student fees, and in Wales a new baccalaureate-style system is being rolled out. The educational landscape is very different from 1870, when free primary schooling was first introduced. The 1944 Education Act delivered free secondary education and comprehensive education became government policy in the 1960s.

Today, the numbers of young people going on to further education are at an all-time high and the range of part- and full-time courses available to adult learners is vast. But with increased opportunity and the extension of choice comes an ever more complicated education system. In this chapter, we look at what kinds of education are available, who has a right to free education and the funding available for those who don't, the responsibilities of parents and what happens if they fail in their duties, and how to deal with problems at school. We look at further and higher education choices and how to secure financial help to carry on studying, as well as bullying, home education and what happens if you take a gap year.

Note: the term 'parent' is used throughout this chapter to describe either or both parents, or the child's guardian, or another person who has custody of the child.

JARGON BUSTER

National Curriculum:

Foundation stage	The first stage of the National Curriculum for children aged three to the end of the reception year at school
Key Stage 1	The second stage of the National Curriculum for children between the ages of five and seven
Key Stage 2	The third stage of the National Curriculum for children between the ages of seven and eleven
Key Stage 3	The fourth stage of the National Curriculum for children between the ages of eleven and 14
Key Stage 4	The fifth stage of the National Curriculum for students between the ages of 14 and 16
DCSF	Department for Children, Schools and Families (formerly Department for Education and Skills)
DIUS	Department for Innovation, Universities and Skills (formerly Department for Education and Skills)
LEA	Local Education Authority
ELB	Education and Library Board – Northern Ireland

OFSTED	Office for Standards in Education
SEN	special educational needs
EWO	education welfare officer
EMA	external marking agency
CTC	City Technology College
LSC	Learning and Skills Council
CETW	National Council for Education and Training in Wales
UCAS	Universities and Colleges Admissions Service

THE BASICS

Types of school

There are two main types of school to choose from – local education authority (LEA) maintained schools and independent schools.

The bulk of LEA-maintained schools are *community schools*, owned and funded by the LEA but run by the school's own governing body. Admissions policies are set and administered by the LEA.

Other types of LEA-maintained schools are:

- voluntary controlled schools, owned by a voluntary organization, usually a church or other religious body, run and funded by the LEA. The admissions policy is usually set and administered by the LEA. These schools are often called faith schools
- voluntary aided schools, owned by a voluntary organization, usually a church or other religious body, and run by the governing body. The school is funded partly by the LEA, partly by the governing body and partly by the voluntary organization. The admissions policy is set and administered by the governors in consultation with the LEA and other schools in the area. These schools are often called faith schools
- foundation schools, owned and run by a governing body, but funded by the LEA. The admissions policy is set and administered by the governors, in consultation with the LEA and other schools in the area.

An independent school is funded by fees, sometimes quite substantial, paid by parents and, sometimes, by charitable trust funds. The governing body runs the school and, along with the head teacher, sets the admissions policy.

There are other types of schools not maintained by the LEA, such as:

- city technology colleges (CTCs), which are independent non-fee-paying schools in urban areas, funded by commercial sponsors and the Department for Children, Schools and Families (DCSF)
- specialist schools, which have a special focus on their chosen subject area, but

must meet the full National Curriculum requirements and deliver a broad and balanced education to all pupils

- city academies, which are independent schools providing a free education for local pupils. In a city academy, the DIUS funds the school's running costs, the governing body employs the staff and the pupils do not have to follow the National Curriculum
- special schools for pupils with special educational needs (SEN). Some schools for pupils with SEN are not maintained by the local education authority and our information about independent schools applies. In some circumstances, the LEA may pay the fees so that a pupil with special educational needs may attend one of these schools if this school best meets their needs
- early learning organizations. They could be independent playgroups, private day nurseries or independent schools for three- and four-year-olds. A part-time place might be free if your child is three or four, but you'll usually have to pay fees if you want your child to go on a full-time basis.

Compulsory school age

Everyone between the ages of five and 16 must receive full-time education, either at school or out of school, and your LEA has to find a school place for your child. Plus, the LEA must provide full-time education to anyone who wants it between the ages of 16 and 19, at a school or sixth-form college. That includes children who are living in the area temporarily, like a child whose parent is in the armed forces, or who has come from abroad.

By the same token, it is up to you to make sure that your child receives education during the compulsory school age years. If you fail in that duty, legal action could be taken against you.

When does my child have to start school?

A child does not have to attend school until the beginning of the term following their fifth birthday, although most LEAs accept children into school at the beginning of the term during which the child becomes five. All young people can leave school on the last Friday in June of the school year that they reach 16. In addition, some schools allow some 14- to 16-year-olds to drop compulsory subjects and, instead, attend up to a day a week in a workplace, or at college.

Pre-school education

You may want (or need) to find your child a place in a nursery, or other early education setting, prior to their reaching compulsory school age. You can find out what is on offer in your area via the LEA. A range of places provide early education, such as nursery schools, nursery classes in primary schools or reception classes in primary schools, playgroups, private day nurseries and independent schools.

Every three-year-old and four-year-old is entitled to a free early education place. It should be for at least two and a half hours each day, for five days a week, during normal term times. Even if the place would normally charge fees, you will not have to pay for at least two and a half hours each day, but if your child attends for longer than that, you may have to pay for extra hours. Schools and groups in the scheme will provide information about how to apply for a place and about the education they offer.

STARTING SCHOOL

Choosing a school

You have the right to express a preference for your child's school (but don't have to). Expressing a preference does not mean that your child will be offered a place at that school but the LEA usually has a duty to try to comply with your choice, subject to the school's admission policy.

When you have decided which school you'd like your child to go to, you will need to tell either the school or the LEA, depending on what type of school you have chosen. The school or LEA will be able to supply you with the relevant application form.

Admissions policies

The policy will vary from one school to another but criteria often include:

- if your child has a brother/sister already attending the school
- how far your child lives from the school
- whether your child lives within the 'catchment area' of the school
- whether the school is a faith school, and whether your child follows that particular religion. It is not against the law for faith schools to discriminate against pupils of a different religion when drawing up their admission policy,

although it is against the law for other schools to discriminate on the grounds of religion

- whether the school gives priority to parents who express a preference for a single-sex or co-educational school
- whether your child has been excluded from two or more schools. The LEA or governing body can refuse to admit pupils who have been excluded from two or more schools
- whether the school selects its pupils on the basis of academic ability. Grammar schools select pupils wholly on academic ability. Some other schools select some pupils on their academic ability.

What you can do if your choice of school is refused

If your child does not get offered a place at the school of your choice, the school or LEA must tell you why. It may be because a particular school is popular and therefore over-subscribed.

You can talk informally to the LEA or governing body about changing the decision, which may avoid using the formal appeals procedure and might resolve the matter more quickly. There is usually a time limit on appeals, so be careful if you have informal discussions that there is still time to appeal after that.

If, after discussion and negotiation, the LEA or school still refuses to accept your choice of school, and they are offering your child a place at a school that you find unacceptable, you can appeal to a local appeal committee. The school or LEA should give you information about how to appeal against a decision, and what the time limits are.

Children with special educational needs (SEN)

Pupils are defined as having SEN if they have a learning difficulty that requires special educational provision to be made or if they have a disability which means that they cannot make full use of the general educational facilities provided for pupils of their age.

Pupils with SEN, between the ages of two and 19, are entitled to receive full-time education appropriate to their needs and that may be in a special school or a mainstream school, or somewhere else. You can educate your child at home if you choose, as long as the education is satisfactory and has been approved by the LEA. If your child has SEN, or you feel they may have, contact your LEA to discuss those needs as soon as possible prior to their starting school. There are also a number of organizations who can offer advice and support, such as the Centre for Studies on Inclusive Education (0117 328 4007; http://inclusion.uwe.ac.uk), which gives SEN information and advice for pre-school children and school pupils up to the age of 19. Parents for Inclusion (0800 652 3145; www.parentsforinclusion.org) is a self-help organization giving information, advice and support on education matters to parents of children with learning difficulties. Contact a Family (0808 808 3555; www.cafamily.org.uk) links up parents of children with learning difficulties to other individual families and to local support groups.

My daughter has just been diagnosed as autistic. Can she continue to go to our local primary school?

Your daughter should be assessed by the LEA and may be given a statement of special educational needs (SEN). All children with SEN should be provided with education that suits their needs. This education may be in your local primary school, a special school or somewhere else, depending on her needs. If you do not feel that the education being offered to your child is best suited to her, you have a right of appeal over any decision made. You can get more advice and support from the Centre for Studies on Inclusive Education on 0117 328 4007; http://inclusion.uwe.ac.uk).

Children with a disability

Schools must not treat children with a disability less favourably than other children, and this applies to both pupils and prospective pupils. You can find out more about discrimination and education in the chapter on Civil Rights. More information is also available from the Equality and Human Rights Commission (www.equalityhumanrights.com). Other organizations who offer advice and support are the Council for Disabled Children (020 7843 1900; www.ncb.org.uk), an information service to parents and professionals on the needs of disabled pre-school children, pupils and students; Disability Wales (029 2088 7325; www.disabilitywales.org); and the Royal National Institute for Deaf People (RNID) (0808 808 0123; textphone: 0808 808 9000; www.rnid.org.uk). The RNID Information and Casework Service provides information to deaf and hard-of-hearing people who may have been discriminated against in education.

EDUCATION OUTSIDE SCHOOL

Home education

Some people decide, for a variety of reasons, that the education on offer within a school environment is not what they want for their child and decide to educate at home. This is perfectly legal. Although you do not have to tell the LEA that you are educating your child at home, if you do not do this, the LEA may make enquiries to find out what education you are providing. They have a duty to take action if it comes to their attention that a child in their area is not getting suitable education.

If you are educating your child at home, you do not have to keep to school hours or follow the National Curriculum. However, you must be able to show that your child's education is 'efficient'. This must take into account your child's age and ability, and any special educational needs your child has.

Organizations who can support you, if you are considering home education, are the Home Education Advisory Service (01707 371 854; www.heas.org.uk) and Education Otherwise (0870 730 0074; www.education-otherwise.org.uk).

Can I educate my child at home?

Yes, you can. An LEA must provide a full-time education for a child of 'compulsory school age' by law and a parent must make sure that their child of 'compulsory school age' receives an education. But the law does not say a child must go to school and you can arrange for your child to be taught at home. You must be able to show that your child's education is 'efficient'. This must take into account your child's age and ability, and any special educational needs your child has.

Pupils who have been permanently excluded (expelled) from school

If your child is permanently excluded (expelled) from any school, the LEA has a duty to provide other suitable education from the sixth day of their exclusion. This may be a place in another school or at a special educational unit (sometimes called pupil referral units, PRUs), or provision of home or individual tuition. If you want your child to go back to the same school, you have a right to appeal against your child's exclusion. If you find yourself in this position, seek advice from the Advisory Centre for Education (ACE) exclusion line (020 7704 9822) or your local CAB.

Illness

If your child cannot attend school because of sickness or injury, the LEA must arrange suitable education for them. It might be in a hospital school or hospital teaching unit, or at home. A child who is admitted to hospital should have their educational needs assessed as soon as is reasonable after admission. They should be given tuition as soon as their condition allows.

Children should not be home unwell for more than three weeks (four weeks in Wales) without home tuition. If your child is absent from school for less time, the school is expected to provide work for your child to do at home.

Education during and after pregnancy

If your daughter cannot attend school because she is pregnant, your LEA still has a duty to provide suitable alternative education, for example home tuition. It would be reasonable to expect a minimum of ten hours a week. In practice, you may find that the provision is more limited. Many LEAs provide only one session each week and others none at all. However, lack of resources is not a sufficient reason for failure to provide suitable alternative education. If you feel she is not receiving suitable education in these circumstances, you can get advice and support from the Advisory Centre for Education (ACE: 0808 800 5793; www.ace-ed.org.uk).

LEARNING

From learning by rote to letting pupils decide whether to attend lessons at all, what our children learn and how they learn it has been the subject of hot debate since education became compulsory.

National Curriculum

What we do know is that all pupils in LEA-maintained schools must follow the National Curriculum, whereas those in independent schools need not. Most LEA-maintained schools will teach other subjects alongside the National Curriculum, and a pupil will usually be able to choose which of these they study. If the school does not offer a subject or combination of subjects your child wants to study, you can try and persuade the school to offer them. The school may be able to re-timetable subjects if a particular combination of subjects is asked for, or you could suggest that your child studies a subject at another school. If a restriction on the choice of subjects offered is affecting other pupils, you may wish to consider involving the parents' association.

Key stages

The Foundation stage is the first stage of the National Curriculum and is for children aged three until the end of the reception year of primary school.

Key Stage 1 lasts two years and covers the education for children between the ages of five and seven.

Key Stage 2 covers National Curriculum learning over four years, when your child is aged between seven and eleven.

Moving to secondary school is a big step and marks the beginning of Key Stage 3, which covers the ages 11–14.

Key Stage 4 covers the last two years of compulsory education (14–16 years).

Students whose first language is not English

If English is not your child's first language, you might feel he or she needs extra tuition to improve the standard of their written and spoken English, or you may wish them to have teaching in their first language at school. However, there is no requirement for LEAs or governing bodies to teach

English as a second language, or, in England, to provide teaching in a first language other than English. Welsh is a subject in the National Curriculum and is compulsory at all schools in Wales for pupils up to the age of 16. It is taught either as a first language (in Welsh medium schools) or as a second language (in English medium schools).

Sex education

My child's class is to be shown a sex education video, but I feel my child is too young for 'the birds and the bees'. Is there anything I can do?

In most primary schools, governing bodies must consider whether to offer sex education and at what age to do this. They should have a written sex education policy for parents to see. In LEA-maintained secondary schools, sex education (including education about HIV and AIDS and other sexually transmitted diseases) must be provided for all registered pupils. You can withdraw your child from all or part of the sex education provided, if you wish, but not from those aspects of the National Curriculum which cover the reproductive process, usually in science lessons.

There is no requirement to provide sex education at an independent school.

Religious education and collective worship (assembly)

Religious education must be taught in all schools, except independent schools, and information should be given to you about the religious education your child will receive at a particular school.

Most schools must teach an agreed syllabus for religious education, which reflects the fact that religious traditions in England and Wales are mainly Christian, although it must take account of the other principal religions in Britain. Teaching should be non-denominational, although individual lessons about particular denominations are allowed.

An act of collective worship, what used to be called assembly, must take place each school day in community schools, voluntary schools and foundation schools. The form the 'collective worship' takes will depend on the type of school, but it must be mainly of a broadly Christian character and non-denominational. City technology colleges (CTCs) are expected to make broadly similar provision for collective worship as other state schools. Independent schools are not obliged to hold a daily act of collective worship.

There are rules which prohibit discrimination against pupils on the grounds of their religion. However these rules do not cover religious education or collective worship.

Homework

Your child may be pleased to hear that pupils do not legally have to do homework. However, schools are encouraged to draw up reasonable homework policies that detail sanctions for not doing homework. If the pupil does not do homework, as set out in these policies, the school could argue that the pupil is in breach of school policy and rules and could take steps to discipline them.

Home–school agreements (HSAs)

A home–school agreement is a document drawn up by a school's governing body in consultation with the parents of all registered pupils. Parents and perhaps pupils will be invited to sign the HSA, but if parents refuse or fail to sign they or their children should not be penalized in any way and the terms of the HSA are not legally binding.

SCHOOL LIFE

Charges

All schools, except of course independent schools, must provide free education. Also they must not charge for any activity (or materials, books, exam entry fees or equipment connected with an activity) that is an essential part of the National Curriculum or the religious education syllabus or is part of the syllabus for a prescribed examination. They cannot charge for something that takes place wholly, or mainly, during school hours.

What activities can the school charge for?

It is common practice for schools to request a voluntary contribution from parents towards the cost of school equipment, for example. They should make the voluntary nature of the contribution quite clear and state that the children of parents who do not contribute will not be discriminated against in any way. Sometimes a school may ask for voluntary contributions for an activity or trip and will specify that the trip will not go ahead unless the majority of parents agree to contribute. You may feel that this is unfair pressure, but it does not amount to discrimination.

The LEA and governing body must make it clear which activities they will charge for and where circumstances mean they will not – for example, if a parent is on a low income. If you have a problem about being asked to pay for activities, you might want to seek advice from the Advisory Centre for Education (ACE: 0808 8005793; www.ace-ed.org.uk) or your local CAB.

School records

LEAs and schools are required to keep information on each pupil's educational progress. They may also keep a record of other information about the pupil's medical history, family background, personality and predictions of future potential. Some will store all the information on computer, while others will keep manual records. You and your child are entitled to see school records. The record must be disclosed within 15 days of the written request for it being received and you should not be charged more for it than the cost of photocopying or postage. In Wales, the head teacher can arrange for the record to be translated into Welsh, English or any other language that they feel to be appropriate. If a fee is charged for the translated record it should be no greater than for the original record.

If you think that any part of the school record is inaccurate, write to the LEA or school holding the record. If it is inaccurate it must be amended.

School records will not be disclosed if the record would give information about another pupil, if disclosure would cause serious harm to the pupil in question or to someone else or if the record holder believes the record is relevant to whether the pupil is at risk of child abuse, or has been a victim of child abuse.

Holidays during term-time

You are allowed to take your child out of school for two weeks' annual holiday (in any one year) during term time, but only with the agreement of the school.

If you want to take more time off for a holiday during term, you'll have to get the permission of the head teacher. If your request is refused, you can ask the governing body to consider your request. However, most governing bodies will only agree to allow more than two weeks' holiday in what they consider to be exceptional circumstances. Even if they do agree, you should bear in mind that your child may not be allowed to return to the school after the holiday. If you do take your child out of school without the head teacher's permission, you could be fined and the fine will be doubled if you do not pay within 28 days. Failure to pay the fine within 28 days could also result in prosecution.

> ### Can I take my children out of school to celebrate Islamic festivals like Eid at the end of Ramadan?
>
> Yes, you can. Pupils are allowed time off school to celebrate major religious occasions, even if they also attend the school's own acts of collective worship. It is good practice to let the school know in advance if your child will be absent for these reasons.

School uniform

Whether or not your child has to wear a school uniform depends on the school they attend. Many schools do have a school uniform policy stating that certain items must be worn, while others cannot. Governmental guidance says that the uniform chosen should be affordable. It should not be so expensive that it prevents a pupil applying to the school. The school should consider the cost of including branded items before insisting they must be worn.

A school's uniform policy must be reasonable and must not discriminate on grounds of sex, race, disability, sexuality or religion. Religious and cultural requirements must also be considered when drawing up a school uniform policy.

Some LEAs give help with the cost of school clothing in the form of one-off grants when the pupil starts school, while others pay regular grants as the pupil grows and needs new clothing. Some are cash grants while others give vouchers to be used at local shops. In Wales, a one-off grant for clothing is available to all pupils entering secondary school as long as they are eligible for free school meals. The grant is also available to pupils in Wales who are aged 11 and are in special schools, special needs resource bases and pupil referral units. You can get this grant on top of any other help you get.

Some schools keep a stock of second-hand clothing that it gives to pupils who fall within its criteria for help, or run a second-hand uniform shop where the clothing can be bought cheaply by any parent.

If your child is disabled and you are on Income Support or income-based Jobseeker's Allowance, you may be eligible for a community care grant from the Social Fund to help with the cost of school clothing. Contact your local CAB for advice.

Meals at school

All schools must make provision for meals in the middle of the day. They must provide free supervised facilities for pupils to eat a packed lunch and may provide school meals for all pupils. A school that decides to provide school meals for all pupils can decide how much to charge.

Meals provided by all local authority schools must meet certain government standards which are aimed at making the meals healthier. This means that some types of food like sweets, chips and chicken nuggets cannot be served or are restricted.

The government standards also say that menus for school lunches at local authority schools should include healthier types of food, such as fruit and vegetables, oily fish and bread.

Your child may be eligible for free school meals if you get income-based Jobseeker's Allowance or Income Support, or if you are receiving support as an asylum seeker, or if you receive Child Tax Credit and your income is below a certain level.

At City Technology Colleges (CTCs), the governing body decides whether or not to provide free school meals and, if so, to whom. So if your child is a student at a CTC, you should check what provision that particular school makes.

Safety at school and on school trips

You might be surprised to know that schools do not have to provide insurance cover for accidents to pupils. You may wish to arrange individual accident insurance for your child. Speak to your LEA as some negotiate special terms with insurance companies.

However, teachers have a duty of care towards pupils while they are on the school premises or taking part in a school activity, such as a school trip. This duty of care will apply even if you have given permission for your child to take part in the activity. You should inform the school if your child has a medical condition or disability which means that they are more likely to be injured or that extra care should be taken – for example, if your child is a haemophiliac. All accidents should be recorded by the school.

Examinations

If your child is unhappy with the results of their external examinations, such as GCSEs or A levels, you can ask the head teacher to submit an 'enquiry on results' or appeal to the examinations board on their behalf, no later than 20 September following the summer GCSE/A level examinations.

Your child is entitled to re-sit an exam if they missed it the first time, or if they want to try to improve their grade, but you may be required to pay the examination fee.

PROBLEMS AT SCHOOL

Most problems at school can be resolved by talking to your child's teacher or their year tutor, who will usually be able to clarify the problem and provide more information and may be willing to support and work with you, if this is in the best interest of your child. The vast majority of problems or areas of concern can be resolved in this way.

If you feel you need to take it further, you can go to the head teacher or the governing body, via the clerk of the governing body or a parent governor. All LEA-maintained schools in England must have a formal complaints procedure and you can ask the school for a copy of their procedure.

If the matter remains unresolved, or you are still not happy, you may be able to appeal to the LEA or to the organization that set up the school. For example, if your child is at a church school, you may be able to appeal to a local diocesan board. If the right of appeal is to the LEA, you could talk to your local councillors before the appeal as they may be on the appeal committee or may be willing to give advice and support. If you are considering appealing, you may want to speak to a CAB adviser.

Harassment and discrimination at school

Incidents of harassment by pupils or teachers should be reported to the head teacher. For example, sexual harassment could amount to unlawful discrimination. Harassment by teachers is gross misconduct and could lead to them losing their jobs.

Some schools have clear anti-discrimination policies and will, for example, take positive steps to discourage racism and stop racist attacks, either at school or on the way to and from school. It is important that parents bring all incidents to the head teacher's attention.

It is against the law for a school, or any other provider of education, to discriminate against both current and prospective pupils because of their race, sex, disability, sexuality or religion. For example, LEAs must develop plans to make schools accessible to disabled pupils. Another example is that schools must not discriminate against lesbian or gay students or against the children of lesbian or gay parents. There are some exceptions to these rules. For example, faith schools can select pupils on the grounds of their religion.

You can find more information about discrimination at school in the chapter on civil rights – see p. 459.

Punishment

Corporal punishment is unlawful in all schools (including independent schools) and for children receiving nursery education, although staff can use reasonable physical force to break up a fight between pupils, or to stop pupils endangering themselves, other pupils or school property, or to prevent a pupil from committing a criminal offence.

Teachers can, however, use 'reasonable non-physical' means to punish a pupil for unacceptable conduct or behaviour. That might mean extra work during school hours or being told off. Detention after school hours is allowed, whether or not a parent consents to the detention, as long as it is known by both pupils and parents that detention is a disciplinary measure, that the detention is carried out by an authorized teacher, the detention is reasonable, the school takes the pupil's safety into account and the pupil's parent has been given 24 hours' written notice of the detention (although this does not apply to lunch-time detentions). The pupil must be aged under 18 and the detention must be on a school day. It can also be on a Saturday or Sunday during term-time as long as it is not just before or after half term or a day set aside for staff training.

Confiscation of belongings

Disciplinary penalties may include confiscation and/or disposal of items such as MP3 players or mobile phones. The confiscation has to be reasonable in the circumstances. For example, if a pupil is playing loud music on an MP3 player, it would be reasonable to take it away and return it at the end of the day. But it would not be reasonable to destroy it.

Misbehaviour out of school

Head teachers have the power to regulate pupils' behaviour off school premises if this is reasonable. This includes disruptive behaviour from pupils on their way to and from school. Although schools can regulate misbehaviour off school premises, they can only give punishments such as detention when the pupil is on the school site or under the control of a member of staff – for example, on a school trip. Otherwise pupils cannot be punished until they are back at school.

Special units

Some schools have special units attached to the school that specialize in helping pupils with disruptive behaviour.

Bullying

My child is being bullied at school; what can I do?

First of all, talk to your child to hear what they have to say. Then arrange to speak to the child's teacher. You should find out how they usually deal with a problem about suspected bullying and how they are going to take the matter forward. The school should have a written policy about what they do to eliminate bullying. If your child is being bullied, ask to see the policy.

If you are not satisfied with the teacher's response, ask to see the head teacher. If you are still not happy, you could contact the governing body of the school and/or the LEA. If the bullying is really severe, it is possible that it could be considered a criminal activity.

There are several organizations that may be able to help you and provide support if you think your child is being bullied. Advice is available from www.dfes.gov.uk, http://new.wales.gov.uk and www.parentscentre.gov.uk. You can also contact Bullying Online (www.bullying.co.uk).

Exclusion from school (being expelled)

> ### *What can I do if my child is expelled from school?*
>
> Children can be excluded from school for a short time if they have broken a rule that the school considers important. They can be permanently excluded (expelled) if the school decides that their behaviour has been very unacceptable. The ways in which this happens will depend on what sort of school your child goes to and the ways to appeal will also vary according to the type of school. If they are permanently excluded from any school, your LEA still has a duty to provide them with other suitable education from the sixth day of their exclusion. The Advisory Centre for Education runs a dedicated exclusion helpline on 020 7704 9822.

Truancy

If you find out that your child is truanting, try to resolve the problem by talking to the school. The LEA education welfare officer (EWO) may be asked by the school to visit your child at home to find out why they are truanting and offer advice.

If the problem continues, the LEA or the school's governing body can enter into a parenting contract with the parent. This sets out steps that you agree to take to improve your child's attendance at school. It is not compulsory to enter into a parenting contract but if you fail to agree to this or to keep to the terms of the contract, further action might be taken against you.

If the pupil continues to truant, the EWO may send the parents a warning that court action will be taken by the authorities. A school can exclude a pupil from school for persistent truancy, although in practice this is rare.

LEAs, head teachers and the police can also issue a penalty notice against you if your child is truanting. This is a sort of fine and if you do not pay it, the LEA can decide to prosecute you.

If the police believe that a child or young person is of compulsory school age and is absent from school without permission, they can take the child or young person back to school.

HELP WITH THE COSTS OF EDUCATION

You and your family may be entitled to financial help, depending on your financial circumstances, from the LEA, the governing bodies or parents' associations. Some charities give out grants to parents, but often have a limited amount of money to give and usually have very specific criteria that must be met in order to get a grant.

Your child may be entitled to free school meals, school milk, school clothing or school transport. You might get the costs of visiting your child at special school.

You can apply for help whenever you think you may be eligible, but you might find the amount of money available for the year is limited, so the sooner you apply in the school year, the better. Speak to the LEA or the school about what help is available.

School milk

Schools may provide milk to pupils, but you have to pay for it unless you are entitled to free school meals (see p. 209). Some schools take part in schemes that offer free school milk to all children under five; in Wales, all Key Stage 1 pupils are entitled to free school milk.

School transport

Your child's transport costs will be paid, until they are 16, if the LEA considers that transport is needed to get to the nearest suitable school. This is the case even if the nearest suitable school is in a different LEA area, or it is an independent school.

A car allowance may be paid to you if you take your child to school or to a pick-up point agreed by the LEA.

Visiting a pupil at a maintained special school

Your LEA may pay all or some of your travel costs to visit your child, if they board at an LEA-maintained special school that is some way from your home. You may need to get a letter of support from your doctor, social worker or child's teacher.

Grants for other needs

LEAs have a very wide discretion to make grants to enable pupils in maintained schools to take advantage of the educational facilities available to them without causing hardship to their families. However, the money available for these grants is likely to be limited and usually will be given only for activities or items that are not part of the school curriculum – for example, a grant may be given for travelling costs to attend an interview or towards the costs of a musical instrument. Contact your LEA for more details.

Sixteen-year-old students staying on at school or college in England are entitled to a means-tested educational allowance. This is called an Education Maintenance Allowance – see p. 222.

EDUCATION CHOICES AT 16

More and more young people are choosing to continue their studies after the age of 16, to increase their chances of better-paid and more satisfying employment during their working lives.

Where to study

The LEA only has a duty to provide full-time education for students up to the age of 16, so not all schools in your area will have provision for 16- to 19-year-olds. The extent to which you can choose where to study may therefore depend on what is available in the local area. Schools and colleges offer a range of different types of courses. Sixth form colleges and colleges of further education usually provide a wider variety of courses than those normally available in school sixth forms. Further education and specialist colleges are more likely to offer vocational courses than are schools and sixth form colleges.

What to study

Courses that may be available include GCSE courses, A levels, AS levels and vocational courses.

Vocational courses, which often prepare you for a particular job, include:

- Business and Technology Education Council courses (BTEC)

- City and Guilds of London Institute courses
- Royal Society of Arts (RSA) courses
- General National Vocational Qualification (GNVQ) and National Vocational Qualification (NVQ) courses
- specialized foundation courses – for example, in art and design or accountancy.

For more information about your choices at 16, speak to your school or the Connexions service (www.connexions.gov.uk). Or look on www.direct.gov.uk. This gives you links to your local education authority so you can see what is available locally.

Students with learning difficulties or disabilities

I am a wheelchair user and want to go to college after my A levels. What do I need to consider?

You should contact the colleges that interest you and get hold of their prospectuses. Read each prospectus carefully to find out how accessible the college is for wheelchair users and how it caters for the needs of wheelchair users. If the prospectus does not tell you all you want to know, contact the college concerned for further information. You may wish to ask for an interview to discuss accessibility. If your course requires you to go on a work placement, contact the National Bureau for Students with Disabilities (SKILL) (in England, 020 7450 0620; in Wales, 029 2078 6506; www.skill.org.uk) for more advice.

If you have a statement of special educational needs and stay on at school, the LEA must provide the special education specified in your statement. However, if you continue your education at a college outside the control of the LEA, like a sixth form or tertiary college or other further education college, that college does not have to comply with your statement.

It is against the law for any school or provider of further education or higher education to discriminate against disabled pupils. Providers of post-16 education must also supply assistance to disabled students if needed – for example, equipment or a sign language interpreter. If you have particular support needs, you should discuss these at an early stage with the school or college you are interested in attending, so that any necessary arrangements can be made.

You may find it useful to speak to SKILL (in England, 0207 450 0620; in Wales, 029 2078 6506; www.skill.org.uk), which gives advice and information for students with disabilities and special educational needs. Some Connexions offices have a careers officer to advise students with special educational needs.

I've been refused a place at my local college. Can I appeal?

You have no right of appeal but colleges will normally have appeal procedures which you could use. Incidentally, if you had applied to another school (rather than a college) and been refused a place, you could have appealed.

Further information and advice

If you are a student aged between 16 and 19 you can get further information and advice from:

- your school, which can usually offer advice on courses that are available and career options. The school may have a careers teacher and may keep careers information in the school library
- your local Connexions office, which provides careers guidance for 13- to 18-year-olds. Information is available about courses, entry requirements and grants. Go to their website at www.connexions.gov.uk
- libraries. Some branch libraries and all central reference libraries will have up-to-date prospectuses for all local colleges as well as general careers guides
- local colleges, which produce a prospectus with details of courses available and will also give advice on entry requirements and the purpose of courses
- the government website (www.direct.gov.uk), which includes useful links to local education authorities and colleges where you could study.

EDUCATION CHOICES AT 18

This section looks at what your choices are if you are 17 or over and are currently in education and have just taken or will be taking A level or AS exams, a BTEC National Certificate or Diploma or a General National Vocational Qualification (GNVQ) course. The information also applies if you have been out of education for a while but have qualifications or work experience equivalent to the normal higher education entry requirements.

Higher education qualifications

There are three categories of qualification for which you may study at this level:

Diplomas and certificates

Courses that lead to a higher education diploma or certificate are usually vocational courses in business or technology subjects. The diploma or certificate may be awarded by the college or may be a national qualification. The most common are the BTEC Higher National Certificate and Higher National Diploma, which are awarded by the Business, Technology and Education Council, part of Edexcel, and the Diploma of Higher Education, which is awarded by universities and colleges of higher education under their own validating powers.

Degrees

Degree courses usually concentrate on one or two subjects and may be vocational (for example, medicine or engineering) or academic (for example, English or history). It is becoming increasingly possible to study a combination of subjects that may or may not be related.

If you attend a university, the degree will be awarded by the university. If you attend a college of higher education, the degree will be awarded by a body that has degree-awarding powers, such as a local university or the Open University.

Access courses

Some local colleges may run access courses for people who did not get qualifications at school. An access course lasts for one year and will count instead of GCSE and A levels for entry to a degree course.

Foundation degrees

Foundation degrees often combine academic study with workplace learning. They are available on a full-time or part-time basis and also by distance learning or on the internet. There are no national entry requirements and individual institutions can set their own. These courses can provide a route into university or college.

Professional qualifications

Professional qualifications are needed to work in a wide range of professions – for example, teaching, architecture, medicine, accountancy and surveying. Qualifications for some professions are laid down by law – for example, medicine and teaching. Other professions have set up their own standards and qualifications (for example, accountancy and surveying).

Applications to do a professional qualification course leading to a full-time Diploma of Higher Education, a Higher National Diploma or a degree should be made through UCAS – see p. 220.

Help to choose the right course

Further information and advice on choosing an appropriate course can be obtained from a variety of sources, including:

- the school or college where you are currently studying, as it is likely to have a careers adviser and/or reference materials in the library
- your local Connexions service
- libraries. Some branch libraries and all central reference libraries keep up-to-date prospectuses for the local colleges and usually for most other universities and colleges. They often also have independent guides to careers and courses
- the universities or colleges you are interested in. Write or telephone for a free prospectus. You may be able to speak to one of the course tutors. Open days are often held where you can meet the course tutors and other students on the course and find out what the campus is like
- UCAS – see p. 220
- students' unions. Many students' unions produce alternative prospectuses and guides to their university or college. These can be obtained from the students' union and will usually have to be paid for
- the professional body for the career you are interested in following
- educational organizations that give general advice and information
- the government website (www.direct.gov.uk). This website includes links to universities and colleges and gives more information about the sorts of courses available.

Applying for university – Universities and Colleges Admissions Service (UCAS)

You can apply for up to six courses, although for some subjects, such as medicine, you can apply for only four courses. Applications are not made to individual colleges and universities, but to the Universities and Colleges Admissions Service (UCAS (0870 1122211; www.ucas.com)). This is the central administrative system for admissions to universities throughout the United Kingdom and UCAS is not involved in actually selecting students. Applications can be made only online. There is a deadline for applications. Universities and colleges can consider late applications at their discretion. If you apply after June, you will be dealt with by the Clearing process (see below).

UCAS sends your application form to each of the universities or colleges you have chosen. Each university or college will only have details of the course or courses you have applied for at that university or college. They will not know of your other choices until much later in the application process and they are not allowed to ask you for details of your other choices.

You will usually receive offers from your universities by the end of March. Conditional offers are tied to you achieving certain grades in your exams. If you do not get high enough grades, you may not be accepted. An unconditional offer means you have already satisfied entry requirements and can be accepted to study.

You can only accept two offers at the most – one firm acceptance, and one insurance acceptance. There is a deadline for replying to offers – the letter you get with the offer tells you when to reply. If you do not reply by the deadline, you may lose the offer.

If you do not get an offer from your initial application, you can use the UCAS Extra service from March until the end of June – look on their website for further details.

If the UCAS Extra service does not produce a suitable offer, you can go through the Clearing system, where universities and colleges advertise – and fill – their last-minute places. Vacancies are advertised on the UCAS website and in the national press.

There is no right of appeal against the refusal of a place by a university or college unless you think you were discriminated against on grounds of sex, race, disability, sexuality or religion. However, once you have received a conditional offer of a place (for example, on condition you get two B grades and one C at A level), if you meet the precise terms of the offer, the college or university is committed to take you.

Help! My A level results are lower than expected. What can I do?

If your A level or other exam results are lower than you expected, you may not have good enough grades to get the place you have been offered by a university or college. However, the institution may still offer you a place. This may happen if the other applicants have also got lower results than they expected, or other applicants have taken up other offers, which leaves the course undersubscribed. It is important to act quickly. Telephone the university or college that offered you a place to check whether they will still accept you. Or you could try to get a place on another course at a different college. From the day the A level results come out, course vacancies are advertised on the UCAS website and in the national press. You can apply for any course that has free places and you do not need to stick to the subjects you originally applied for.

Once you have made a list of courses you like, contact the university or college directly. Look on the UCAS website (www.ucas.com) for more information about Clearing.

Taking a gap year

You can apply for deferred entry to university or college, which means that you apply in the normal way but do not start the course for a year or more. You may want to defer entry to gain work experience or to travel abroad. Most universities and colleges will accept deferred entry and many positively encourage it, particularly if what you propose to do during this period is linked to the course you are applying for. Before applying on the UCAS application form for deferred entry, check with the individual course admissions tutor that you can do this. If you make an ordinary UCAS application and then decide you want to defer entry to university or college, you need to contact the individual college or university directly.

FEES AND FINANCIAL SUPPORT FOR STUDENTS

Fees

Full-time students aged between 16 and 18 who are studying at an LEA-maintained school or college will not be charged tuition fees. Other students may be charged tuition fees and the amount will vary between individual colleges, although there is a maximum that can be charged for full-time Higher Education students and you may be eligible for a loan to cover tuition fees. In some cases, your college might give you a bursary to help pay the tuition fees.

Financial support for living expenses

Depending on your circumstances and the sort of course, help for living expenses might include:

- an Education Maintenance Allowance – see below
- Income Support, income-based Jobseeker's Allowance, Housing Benefit and Council Tax Benefit
- loans to cover your living costs
- a non-repayable Maintenance Grant for full-time Higher Education students
- if your home is in Wales, an Assembly Learning Grant
- help if you are disabled
- travel expenses
- help if you are an asylum seeker or refugee
- sponsorship.

If you take out a student loan, it need not be repaid until you start earning over a certain amount when you leave college or university.

Full and up-to-date information about financial help for students is available at the government website (www.direct.gov.uk).

> ### Can my child get financial help to go to college after their GCSEs?
>
> An LEA does not have to give financial help to any student over the age of 16. However, it does have the power to help if it chooses to. Each LEA has its own rules for helping students in further education. They may give your child an LEA grant. Also your child may be able to get an Education Maintenance Allowance of up to £30 a week,

with extra bonus payments from time to time. To find out more about EMAs, go to the government website (www direct.gov.uk).

It is also possible that your child may get Income Support, income-based Jobseeker's Allowance, Housing Benefit or Council Tax Benefit. However, the rules for claiming these benefits if you are a student are restricted to certain kinds of student and most will not be able to get help in this way.

Colleges also have their own funds that can be used to help individual students. Each college has its own rules for giving out these funds. Your child can find out more about these from the college itself.

State benefits and tax credits

The rules about students and benefits are complicated. If you are a student and want more information about benefits, contact the National Union of Students (England 0871 221 8221, Wales 029 2068 0070; www.nusonline.co.uk) or a Citizens Advice Bureau.

WHO CAN HELP?

You will find contact details for other relevant organizations in the appropriate sections above. The help given by these organizations, and those listed below, is free unless otherwise stated. However, most will make a charge for publications. The address and telephone number of your LEA will be in the local telephone directory or you can find a link on the government website (www.direct.gov.uk).

Organizations giving general advice

The **Advisory Centre for Education** (ACE: 0808 800 5793; www.ace-ed.org.uk) is an independent information and advice service for parents, governors, teachers and others in England and Wales.

The **British Council** (in England, 0161 957 7755; in Wales, 029 2039 7346; www.britishcouncil.org) gives information and advice on all forms of educational visits, exchanges and working holidays.

Childline (0800 1111; www.childline.org.uk) provides a free confidential phone counselling service for any child with any problem 24 hours a day, every day.

11 Million (the Children's Commissioner for England: 0844 800 9113; www.11million.org.uk)

Children in Wales (029 2034 2434; www.childreninWales.org.uk) has been responsible for guiding policy decisions that affect young people in Wales.

The **Children's Legal Centre** (0845 345 4345; www.childrenslegalcentre. com) provides legal advice and representation to children

The **Gifted Children's Information Centre** (GCIC: 0121 705 4547) offers a free telephone advice and information service and will deal with written enquiries on receipt of an SAE. GCIC have a particular interest in dyslexia and left-handedness, Attention deficit/Hyperactivity disorder (ADHD) and Asperger syndrome.

The **National Association of Gifted Children** (NAGC: 0845 450 0221; www.nagcbritain.org.uk) offers support to parents and others on how to deal with a gifted child from the age of about 18 months to 14 years.

The **National Association of School Governors** (NASG: 0121 643 5787; www.nagm.org.uk) gives information and advice to parents and governors on all aspects of being a governor and the work of governing bodies.

Parentline Plus (0808 800 2222; www.parentlineplus.org.uk) runs courses for parents, produces books and leaflets and has a free, confidential helpline for anyone looking after a child.

The **Welsh Assembly Government** website provides information about education in Wales (www.new.wales.gov.uk).

Young Minds (020 7336 8445; Parents Information Line: 0800 0182138; www.youngminds.org.uk) provides a service for parents or carers of children and young people experiencing difficulties at school owing to mental health problems.

Organizations for students

The **Association of Commonwealth Universities** (ACU: 020 7380 6700; www.acu.ac.uk) provides an information service about universities in Commonwealth countries.

The **British Council** (in England, 0161 957 7755; in Wales, 029 2039 7346; www.britishcouncil.org) offers youth exchange grants to help organized groups of young people, usually between the ages of 14 and 30, to establish continuing links with a group of similar background and interests from another country.

The **British Universities Transatlantic Exchange** (BUTEX: 0191 209 1162; www.butex.ac.uk) programme covers some 80 higher education institutions in the UK, most of which have exchange arrangements with universities and colleges in North America.

Connexions service (www.connexions.gov.uk) gives information and advice for 13- to 19-year-olds about learning and personal life.

The **Fulbright Commission** (020 7404 6880; www.fulbright.co.uk) gives information and advice to British students who want to study at an American university.

The **National Union of Students** (NUS: England: 0871 221 8221; Wales: 029 2068 0070; www.nusonline.co.uk) gives information and advice on most educational and welfare issues affecting students, including help to a student who is having a problem getting a grant.

The **National Academic Recognition Information Centre for the United Kingdom** (0870 990 4088; www.naric.org.uk) provides an advisory service for people who need to relate overseas academic qualifications to qualifications awarded in the UK. There is a fee charged for this service.

UK Council for International Student Affairs (UKCISA: 020 7107 9922; www.ukcosa.org.uk) provides support for people who work with international students and acts as a facilitator for the exchange of ideas on international education.

Universitas 21 (0121 415 8872; www.universitas21.com) is a multinational consortium of higher education institutions. It offers students the opportunity to spend time studying abroad.

Adult education: organizations that give help and advice

Information about local adult education is available from colleges, libraries and the LEA.

The **Basic Skills Agency** (020 7405 4017; www.basic-skills.co.uk) will answer enquiries about basic education (reading, writing, numeracy) where the LEA or library is unable to provide it.

Learndirect (0800 101 901; www.learndirect.co.uk) is a government scheme to encourage people to learn new skills and improve existing skills. It offers courses in basic computer skills as well as numeracy and literacy courses. Courses are available full- or part-time, both to those working and to those studying full-time.

The **Open University** (0845 300 60 90; www.open.ac.uk) is a university for part-time students who wish to take a course leading to a qualification such as a diploma or degree. Students study at home and are provided by the university with study materials.

Distance learning and home study courses

The **Open and Distance Learning Quality Council** (020 7612 7090; www.odlqc.org.uk) sets standards for distance learning and home study courses.

The **Association of British Correspondence Colleges** (020 8544 9559; www.homestudy.org.uk) is a voluntary association of correspondence colleges that comply with a code of ethics guaranteeing certain standards of service in their dealings with students.

Organizations for employees and trade union members

The **Workers' Educational Association** (WEA: 020 7426 3450; www.wea.org.uk) has local branches which run day, evening and residential courses and summer schools.

The **TUC Education Service** (in England, 020 7636 4030; in Wales, 029 2034 7010; www.tuc.org.uk) runs courses for shop stewards, union officers and health and safety representatives.

Supervisory and standards setting bodies

OFSTED (England: 08456 404045; www.ofsted.gov.uk); **ESTYN** (Wales: 029 2044 6446; www.estyn.gov.uk).

Daily Life

Daily life

1

Employment

CONTENTS

INTRODUCTION

Work: it's a four-letter word but most of us do it at some stage, paid or unpaid. The majority of men, women and children have always worked to survive, on land and sea, and then in the sprawling cities that grew up from the Industrial Revolution. Low wages and appalling conditions drove workers, like the Tolpuddle Martyrs, to form trade unions, which have done so much to secure decent wages and safer conditions for working people. Successive governments of all political persuasions have legislated and regulated working terms and conditions. Huge social changes, such as the rise of paid female employment and part-time employment, have been the motivation for new rights designed to deliver a work–life balance, and the deregulation of many industries has spurred the introduction of the National Minimum Wage. In recent years, Europe has been the source of many individual employment rights, such as the Working Time Directive (with its right to paid holidays), health and safety law, and rights to consultation. This chapter includes what your basic rights at work are, finding work, a self-employment checklist and what to do if you think you have been unfairly treated at work. There is also some information that might be useful to you if you are a migrant worker.

JARGON BUSTER

Statutory rights	by law; already on the statute book
Contractual rights	for example, written into your contract of employment given to you by your employer
Occupational	something specific to your trade or profession
NMW	National Minimum Wage: the minimum hourly rate that a UK worker can be paid
SSP	Statutory Sick Pay: a minimum fixed amount payable to workers who are off sick

SMP	Statutory Maternity Pay: a minimum fixed amount payable to women on maternity leave
Whistle-blowing	when an employee makes public a concern about malpractice
Employment tribunals	legal bodies that deal with complaints about employment rights

RIGHTS AT WORK

Your rights at work will depend on:

- your statutory rights – the rights you have by law; *and*
- your contract of employment.

Your contract of employment cannot take away rights you have by law (statutory rights). So if, for example, you have a contract that states you are only entitled to ten days' paid holiday each year, when by law employees are entitled to 24 days' paid holiday each year, that part of your contract is invalid and does not apply and your right under law (to 24 days' holiday in this case) applies instead.

If your contract gives you greater rights than you have under law – for example, more holiday than the minimum allowed by law – then your contract applies.

Statutory rights

Statutory rights are legal rights based on laws passed by Parliament and nearly all workers, regardless of the number of hours they work each week, have certain legal rights.

Statutory rights that most workers have are:

- the right to a *written statement of the main terms of employment*. All employees, regardless of the number of hours they work each week, are entitled to receive a written statement from their employer, within two months of starting work, that describes the main terms of their contract of employment. The statement must give details about job title, wages, hours of work, holiday entitlement, sick pay, pension schemes, notice and the company or organization's grievance and disciplinary procedure
- the right to an *itemized pay slip*. All employees are entitled to an individual written payslip, at or before the time they are paid. The payslip must show gross pay (that is, pay before any tax or National Insurance has been taken off) and take-home pay, after deductions such as tax, National Insurance, pension

and union dues. Deductions that change from week to week – for example, tax and National Insurance – must be listed each time, with the amount of the deduction and what the deduction is for. Deductions that do not change, such as union dues, only have to be shown once a year. This applies from the day you start work

- the right to be *paid at least the National Minimum Wage*. This applies from the day you start work

- the right *not to have illegal deductions made* from pay. This applies from the day you start work

- if you are a full-time employee, the right to at least *24 days' holiday* (going up to 28 days from 1 April 2009) each year. Most workers are entitled to paid holiday, including migrant workers, fixed-term workers or workers in their first year of employment. Part-timers get paid holiday on a pro rata basis

- the right to *time off for trade union duties and activities*. This applies from the day you start work. The time off does not necessarily have to be paid. Employees also have the right to be accompanied by a trade union representative to a disciplinary or grievance hearing

- the right to *paid time off to look for work if being made redundant*. This applies once you have worked for two years for the employer

- the right to *time off for study or training for 16- to 17-year-olds*. This applies from the day you start work

- the right to *paid time off for antenatal care*. This applies from the day you start work

- the right to *paid maternity leave* and the *right to return to work* after this maternity leave. This applies from the day you start work. How long you can take as maternity leave depends on when your baby was due. If your baby was due after April 2007, you have the right to 52 weeks' maternity leave

- the right to paid paternity leave

- the right to paid adoption leave

- the right to ask for flexible working so you can look after your children or an adult dependant

- the right to take *unpaid parental leave* for both men and women (if you have worked for the employer for one year) and the right to reasonable time off to look after dependants in an emergency (applies from the day you start work)

- the right under health and safety law to work a *maximum 48-hour working week*. This applies from the day you start work

- the right under health and safety law to *weekly and daily rest breaks*. This applies from the day you start work. There are special rules for night workers

- the right *not to be discriminated against* on grounds of sex, race, disability, religion, age or sexuality. This applies from the day you start work

- the right to carry on working until you are at least 65

- the right to *notice of dismissal,* provided you have worked for your employer for at least one calendar month
- the right to *written reasons for dismissal* from your employer, provided you have worked for your employer for one year. Women who are pregnant or on maternity leave are entitled to written reasons without having to have worked for any particular length of time
- the right to claim *compensation if unfairly dismissed.* In most cases you will have to have worked for one year to be able to claim unfair dismissal.
- the right to claim *redundancy pay* if made redundant. In most cases you will have to have worked for two years to be able to claim redundancy pay
- the right *not to suffer detriment or dismissal for 'blowing the whistle'* on a matter of public concern (malpractice) at the workplace. This applies from the day you start work
- the right of a *part-time worker* to the *same contractual rights* (pro rata) as a comparable full-time worker
- the right of a *fixed-term employee* to the *same contractual rights* as a comparable permanent employee
- many employees will be entitled to *Statutory Sick Pay* if they are off work due to sickness. In addition, some employees may receive occupational sick pay from their employer but this will depend on their contract of employment. You may also have additional rights that may be set out in your contract of employment.

Workers not entitled to statutory rights

Not everyone is entitled to these statutory rights. These people include:

- anyone who is not an employee – for example, an agent or freelance worker. However, some workers are entitled to certain rights such as the National Minimum Wage, limits on working time and other health and safety rights
- employees who normally work outside the UK
- members of the police service. However, members of the police service are covered by discrimination law
- members of the armed forces. However, members of the armed forces are covered by discrimination law
- merchant seamen or share fishermen
- workers in inland waterways or lake transport are not entitled to paid holidays or limits on their working hours by law and have to rely on their contract
- junior doctors are not entitled to paid holidays. They have to rely on their contract for rights to holidays. They are also limited to working a 56-hour week, rather than 48 hours.

When is a worker not a worker?

If you are a subcontractor, freelancer or a casual or agency worker, you are probably not an employee, but a worker. Sometimes it is not obvious whether someone is an employee – you may be, even if the person you work for calls you something else. If you have any doubt about your status, you should seek advice.

Rights under the contract of employment

The contract of employment is the agreement made between you and your employer. This could be in the form of a written or of a verbal agreement. In addition, the contract of employment will also include 'custom and practice' agreements. These are how things are usually done in the workplace – for example, if the employer always gives the employees a day's holiday in August, even though this is not mentioned in the written contract, this will form part of the contract of employment as it is the usual practice.

If the written contract says one thing, but in practice all the employees have been doing something else with the employer's knowledge, the 'custom and practice' would form the contract rather than the written statement.

A trade union may have negotiated an agreement with an employer about conditions at work. The negotiated agreement will often form part of a contract of employment, particularly if the conditions negotiated are more favourable than the previous ones.

Illegal contracts of employment

Some contracts of employment will be illegal if:

- the employee gets all or part of their wages as 'cash in hand'; *and*
- tax and National Insurance contributions are not paid; *and*
- the employee knows they are getting paid in this way to avoid paying National Insurance and tax.

WAGES

There are a number of statutory rights associated with wages.

Rights to pay

All workers are entitled to be paid for the work they have done. They are also entitled to be paid if they are ready and willing to work but their employer has not provided them with any work to do.

Workers are also entitled to be paid if they cannot work because they are off sick or on holiday, or away from work on maternity leave, paternity leave or adoption leave, or parental leave. In most of these situations, the worker will be entitled to their usual wage while off work. There are some exceptions to this rule, such as:

- a parent on maternity leave, paternity or adoption leave, or parental leave, is entitled to a certain amount of paid leave but the law sets out the rate at which this must be paid and it may not be as much as their usual wage
- an employee on sick pay. By law, most employees are entitled to the legal minimum Statutory Sick Pay. Their contract may give them more pay than this. In either case their sick pay may be less than their usual pay
- workers may be entitled to unpaid time off work in other circumstances – for example, in a family emergency, or on jury service.

There is no legal right to have wages paid in any particular way – for example, for an employee to have their wages paid direct into their bank account.

Salary sacrifice schemes – childcare vouchers

An employer can offer childcare support to employees under a 'salary sacrifice' scheme. This is a scheme which allows you to give up part of your salary in return for vouchers to pay for childcare. There are tax advantages to these schemes but receiving a childcare voucher instead of pay may reduce your pay to a certain limit and this could affect your right to certain benefits.

National Minimum Wage

In the UK, most workers aged 16 or over are entitled to a National Minimum Wage (NMW). The minimum wage covers you whether you are in a permanent job, working for an agency or on a short-term contract.

Some workers are not covered by the NMW, including:

- workers under the age of 16
- some apprentices
- au-pairs and nannies if they are living with a family and not paying for accommodation or meals
- self-employed people
- members of the armed forces
- voluntary workers
- some trainees on government schemes.

How much is the NMW?

There are three different rates of pay under the NMW. The rates go up every year – from October 2007, they are:

- for workers aged 22 and over, the rate of pay is £5.52 an hour
- for workers aged between 18 and 21, the rate of pay is £4.60 an hour
- for workers aged 16 and 17, the rate of pay is £3.40 an hour.

The NMW is an average hourly rate that must be paid for each hour worked over a certain period of time. If you are paid weekly, this period of time is a week, and if you are paid monthly the period is a month. As long as your average pay an hour is not below the NMW during this period, you may earn less than the NMW for some hours.

If you think you are not getting the NMW

If you think you should be getting the NMW but aren't, you can ask your employer to tell you why not.

If you are a member of a trade union, you could ask for advice from your representative. If your employer will not talk about the NMW, or you don't feel able to approach them, you can contact the National Minimum Wage Helpline on 0845 600 0678 (local rates apply); minicom 0845 915 3296.

If you think your employer is aware of the NMW and is not paying it, you can contact the NMW Helpline, who will tell the NMW enforcement agency. This agency is run by HM Revenue and Customs and can investigate employers who do not pay NMW to their workers. If you do not want your employer to know that you have contacted the NMW enforcement agency, you must tell them that you want to remain anonymous. In some cases, reporting an employer can lead to bullying or unfair treatment at work.

You cannot be forced to agree to a wage that is lower than the NMW. If your employer has tried to force or persuade you to sign an agreement that gives you less than the NMW, this agreement will not be legally binding.

There is a website which can help you calculate whether or not you are receiving the NMW. Go to www.worksmart.org.uk.

Wages for agricultural workers

Agricultural workers are entitled to a set minimum hourly pay depending on how old they are and the kind of work they do. They have a set rate for standard pay and a set rate for overtime pay.

If you think you are an agricultural worker and are entitled to a particular level of pay, in England and Wales you should contact the Agricultural Wages Helpline for more information on 0845 000 0134 (calls charged at local rate).

Deductions from wages

By law, your employer is only entitled to make certain deductions from your pay. If an employer does not pay their employee at all, this counts as a 100 per cent deduction. There are rules about what counts as pay for the purposes of when the employer can make deductions.

In most cases, an employer can only lawfully make a deduction from an employee's pay if the deduction is:

- required to be made by law. For example, employers are required to deduct tax and National Insurance from their employee's pay by law. *Or*
- allowed for by the employee's contract. This means that there must be a specific clause in the contract which allows for that particular deduction to be made. The deduction can then only be made lawfully if the employee is given a written copy of that term in the contract before any deduction is made under it. This would cover deductions such as union dues or payments to a pension scheme. *Or*
- the deduction has been agreed to in writing by the employee before it is deducted.

There are particular additional rules for shop workers that make it unlawful for an employer to deduct more than 10 per cent from the gross wages of a shop worker, if the deduction is for stock shortages or cash shortages.

There are particular deductions an employer can make that do not have to fit into the categories listed above. These deductions are:

- a deduction because the employee has been genuinely overpaid
- a deduction made because the employee took part in industrial action
- a deduction made by an employer under a court order or an order from an employment tribunal, such as an attachment of earnings order.

What counts as pay?

When considering whether your employer can make a deduction from your wages, the following all count as wages:

- normal pay, including fees, bonuses and commission
- holiday pay
- payments ordered by an employment tribunal, such as payment of wages between an employee being dismissed and being given their job back
- payments that have to be made by law instead of wages, such as guarantee payments when the employee takes time off to do union work or look for a job if they are to be made redundant
- Statutory Sick Pay
- Statutory Maternity Pay, Statutory Paternity Pay and Statutory Adoption Pay.

Tips and service charges

Tips in cash that are voluntarily given by a customer to a worker, such as a waiter, count as a gift from the customer to the worker and therefore do not form part of the worker's pay.

If a service charge is compulsory – that is, it is added to all bills automatically – it is the property of the employer. The employer can share it out between the workers as the employer wishes, and if a worker is paid part of this compulsory service charge, it will form part of the worker's wages.

If a tip is paid by a customer voluntarily by adding an extra amount to a credit card or cheque payment, the tip is the property of the employer. The employer can share it out between the workers as the employer wishes and if a worker is paid part of this voluntary additional payment, it will form part of the worker's wages.

Bank holidays

Unless your contract of employment gives you bank holidays *in addition* to the 24 days' statutory paid holiday that full-time workers get (28 days from 1 April 2009), bank holidays are included when calculating the 24 days' holiday. So if, for example, you have five days off in a year for bank holidays, and you do not get these bank holidays in addition to statutory holiday, you will be entitled to these five days plus another 19 days' holiday.

I am confused about whether I am entitled to have bank holidays off work.

Most workers are entitled to 24 days' paid holiday. However, there is no automatic right to have any bank or public holidays off or to be paid for them. Any rights that you have to time off for bank or public holidays will depend on what it says in your contract of employment.

If you are given bank or public holidays off, they can count as part of your 24 days' holiday, unless your contract of employment specifically says that you get these holidays in addition to your 24 days' holiday.

There is useful information about paid holiday on the ACAS website (www.acas.org.uk).

Lay-offs and short-time working

If your employer has no work for you to do, they may put you on short-time working or lay you off. Short-time working means you will receive only part of your normal wage. If you are laid off, you will not usually get paid. A person who is laid off or put on short-time working may be entitled to a payment from their employer, called a 'guarantee payment'.

Sickness

Being paid for time off sick

If you earn more than a certain amount each week, you will be entitled to Statutory Sick Pay (SSP). This is money paid by employers to employees who are away from work because they are sick. It is the minimum amount you can be paid when you are off work because you are sick. Your contract of employment may give you extra rights to more sick pay than this, called contractual sick pay. You should check your contract to see what you are entitled to.

To qualify for SSP you must be a worker aged between 16 and 65. This includes agency workers, workers on fixed-term contracts and part-time workers. You will not get SSP for the first three days that you are unable to work, unless you were getting it within the last eight weeks. If you were off sick and getting SSP within the last eight weeks, you will get it again from your first day off work without having to wait for three days.

SSP can last for up to 28 weeks. Contractual sick pay may last for longer. You will need to check your employment contract to see if this applies to you.

If you cannot get SSP, or if you have been off sick for more than 28 weeks, your employer will give you form SSP1 or their own version of it. You can use this form to claim Incapacity Benefit from your local Jobcentre Plus office if you are not entitled to either SSP or contractual sick pay.

How much sick pay will you get?
Either you will be paid SSP or, if your contract of employment gives you more pay when you are off sick, you will be paid what it says in your contract. This might not be your normal rate of pay, but it should not be less than SSP. SSP is paid at a fixed weekly rate. If SSP is your only income while you are off sick, you may be able to claim other benefits, such as Housing Benefit.

Your employer can decide how you provide evidence that you are not able to work when you are off sick. You may have to fill in a form provided by your work for the first week you are unable to work. After that you will usually have to provide a doctor's certificate.

If you are off sick because of a disability
If you are disabled and your employer refuses to give you sick pay when you are off sick for a reason connected with your disability, your employer could be breaking the law and you may be able to make a complaint to an employment tribunal for unfair treatment because of your disability. You may have to raise a written grievance with your employer first. For help, contact ACAS (08457 474747; www.acas.org.uk) or the Equality and Human

Rights Commission (EHRC: 08457 622 633 in England; 0845 604 8810 in Wales; www.equalityhumanrights.com).

If you are off for several short periods of time

If you are off sick for more than four short periods (four to seven days) in a year, your employer can contact Medical Services to look into the reasons you have given for missing work. Medical Services are contacted by your employer through HM Revenue and Customs. They may contact your doctor to ask for information about your illnesses. Medical Services cannot contact your doctor unless you give them permission to do so. If the Medical Services report says you have been off work without good reason, your employer may refuse to pay you SSP. You can appeal against this decision if you think it is wrong.

If you are off for long periods of time

If you have long periods of time off work, your employer can contact Medical Services to decide if you are fit enough to do your job. If the Medical Services report says you have been off work without good reason, your employer may refuse to pay you SSP. You can appeal against this decision if you think it is wrong.

What you can do if your employer won't pay you SSP

If you think your employer did not pay SSP when they should have done, or paid you too little, you can ask them for a written statement that tells you:

- the days you got SSP, if any
- how much SSP you got for each of those days
- why they did not pay you for days when you were sick.

If you still think you should have been paid SSP and cannot sort it out with the employer, you should get in touch with the nearest HM Revenue and Customs National Insurance Contributions Office and ask for a formal decision. This must be done within six months of the first day when you think that SSP should have been paid. You will need to send a copy of any information provided by your employer. You should think carefully about doing this, as it may have a negative effect on your relationship with your employer, or even put your job at risk. You should get specialist advice first.

I spent the whole of my holiday from work in bed sick!

If you become ill while you are on holiday leave, you may be able to get time off at a later date to make up for losing your holiday, if your contract of employment allows for this. If this applies to you, you should get SSP while you are sick. If you become ill while on holiday and your employment contract does not allow you to take time off at a later date, you should get a mixture of SSP and holiday pay to make up your wages to your normal amount of pay.

If you are dismissed for taking time off sick

If you are dismissed while you are receiving SSP, your employer must go through a proper dismissal process and must give you form SSP1. This explains why SSP is no longer being paid. You should complete the form and take it to your local Jobcentre Plus office to claim either Incapacity Benefit or Income Support. If you believe you have been dismissed because you are ill, or because you have asked for SSP, you may be able to complain to an employment tribunal. You should get advice immediately as there are strict time limits to make a tribunal claim.

If you are dismissed because of your disability

If you are disabled and your employer dismisses you for taking time off sick for a reason connected with your disability, your employer could be breaking the law. You may be able to make a complaint to an employment tribunal for unfair treatment because of your disability. You should get advice immediately as there are strict time limits for making a claim to an employment tribunal.

Unpaid time off work

Almost all employees have rights to take time off work, not necessarily with pay, for the following:

- to participate in trade union activities
- to perform 'public duties', such as being a JP, local authority councillor or school governor
- to care for their children. People who have worked for their employer for one year have the right to 13 weeks' unpaid parental leave. Generally, leave must be

taken before a child is five years old. However, if your child is disabled, you get 18 weeks' leave, which must be taken before the child is 18. You are entitled to paid maternity leave, paternity leave and adoption leave

- to attend to unexpected problems with dependants – for example, when child-minding arrangements break down. A dependant includes anyone who reasonably relies on the employee.

PARENTAL RIGHTS AT WORK

'Work–life balance', 'family-friendly': call it what you will. Working parents have the right to:

- maternity leave
- paternity leave
- adoption leave.

In most cases, some, if not all, of this leave may be paid, although it may not be paid at your usual rate.

You also have the right to request flexible working hours so you can care for your children or adult dependants.

These rights are in addition to your right to:

- unpaid parental leave for parents of children under five (18 if your child has a disability)
- unpaid time off to care for dependants.

MATERNITY RIGHTS

Statutory maternity rights

There are a number of rights for pregnant women given by the law. These are known as statutory rights:

- the right of all pregnant women to take time off work for antenatal care
- the right of all pregnant women to work in a safe environment
- the right of all pregnant women to claim unfair dismissal and/or sex discrimination if dismissed because of pregnancy
- the right of all pregnant women to take up to 52 weeks' maternity leave. How long you can actually take depends on when your baby was due
- the right of some pregnant women to Statutory Maternity Pay
- the right to return to work after you have had the baby.

The statutory rights outlined above are minimum rights and many women will have better rights in their contract of employment.

Workers who do not have statutory maternity rights

Some workers do not have any statutory maternity rights. These include:

- women who are normally employed abroad (unless they have a work connection with the UK)
- self-employed women
- policewomen and women serving in the armed forces are entitled to Statutory Maternity Pay and can claim sex discrimination but are not entitled to the other rights for pregnant women workers.

Time off for antenatal care

Any woman (except those listed above) who is working and pregnant will qualify, regardless of how long they have worked for their present employer, and regardless of how many hours they work each week.

You can have time off for appointments for antenatal care if your doctor, midwife or health visitor advises that it is needed. Your employer should pay your usual wage for the time off, as long as you only have a reasonable amount of time off. However, if you take a lot of time off you may be treated as if you are off sick and will only get paid if your contract of employment allows for you to be paid sick pay. If you are off sick, you may qualify for Statutory Sick Pay or Incapacity Benefit.

After the first antenatal appointment, you will have to show your employer, if requested, a medical certificate stating that you are pregnant and an appointment card for the antenatal care.

If your employer refuses to allow time off for an antenatal care appointment or refuses to pay, you can complain to an employment tribunal within three months of the appointment. You should get advice immediately as there are strict time limits for making a tribunal claim.

There is no legal right for your partner to have time off work to attend your antenatal appointments with you. However, the government recommends that employers allow fathers either to take paid time off, or to make up lost time later.

Right to work in a safe environment

An employer is under a legal duty to make the working environment safe for all employees, and particularly for women of childbearing age, to work in.

This means that the employer must assess what health and safety risks there are in the workplace and, specifically, what risks may be posed to pregnant women, women who are breastfeeding and women who have given birth in the past six months.

Where there is a health and safety risk in the workplace, the employer must take action to eliminate the risk by:

- taking any legal action required – for example, ensuring that pregnant women do not come into contact with hazardous chemicals
- altering your working conditions or hours of work so you are not put at risk – for example, a shop assistant could be given a chair so she does not have to stand for long periods
- if altering your working conditions or hours is not possible, the employer must consider offering you different work, at the same pay
- if offering you different work is not possible, your employer must suspend you on medical grounds and pay you full pay while you are suspended.

Dismissal or unfair treatment because of pregnancy

If you are dismissed because of pregnancy and you are an employee, you can claim unfair dismissal and sex discrimination. It does not matter how long you have worked for your employer or whether you work full- or part-time. This is because the law says that it is automatically unfair to dismiss a woman because she is pregnant.

If you are unfairly treated in connection with your pregnancy or maternity – for example, you are passed over for promotion – you should follow the special three-step grievance procedure which all employers are required to have by law. This means you must:

1 send your employer a written statement, setting out your grievance, and give them at least 28 days to respond

2 meet with your employer to discuss your grievance

3 appeal against your employer's decision if you are not happy with it.

If you have followed this procedure and are still not happy with the outcome, you can take your case to an employment tribunal. You should make a claim for both unfair treatment because of pregnancy/maternity, and sex discrimination. You should bear in mind that if you have not followed the grievance procedure properly first, the employment tribunal may decide to reduce any compensation it awards you.

Dismissal because of pregnancy does not affect your entitlement to any of the other maternity rights. If you qualify for statutory maternity pay and for the right to return to work, you will still qualify if you are dismissed because you are pregnant.

For help, contact the Equality and Human Rights Commission (EHRC: 08457 604 6610 in England; 0845 604 8810 in Wales; www.equalityhuman rights.com). ACAS (08457 47 47 47; www.acas.org.uk) can also help.

Maternity leave

If your baby is due after April 2007, most women employees have the right to take up to one year's (52 weeks') maternity leave. This does not depend on how long you have worked for your employer. The only employees who do not have this right are listed under *Workers who do not have statutory maternity rights* above. Women whose babies were due before April 2007 get less maternity leave.

You can choose how long you take off work for maternity leave, up to a maximum of 52 weeks. However, the law says that you must take at least two weeks immediately after the baby is born. If you work in a factory, you must take at least four weeks.

The first 26 weeks of maternity leave are called Ordinary Maternity Leave (OML). During OML, you will still get all the same rights under your contract of employment as if you were still at work. The only exception is that you will not get your normal pay unless your contract allows for it. But you will, for example, still be entitled to build up holiday and to get any pay increase.

Though you are not entitled to your normal pay, most women employees are entitled to Statutory Maternity Pay or Maternity Allowance.

As well as OML, you can also take an additional 26 weeks' maternity leave. This is called Additional Maternity Leave (AML). This gives a total of up to 52 weeks' maternity leave. If you're taking AML, this must follow on directly after OML and there must be no gap between the two.

Your contract of employment will also continue throughout AML unless either you or your employer ends it or it runs out. However, unlike during OML, you will not keep all of your rights under your employment contract.

Some of the terms and conditions of your employment contract which will still apply during AML include your right to any redundancy pay if you're made redundant, and any terms and conditions in your contract of employment about disciplinary or grievance procedures will continue to apply.

There are other terms and conditions which will not apply unless your employer agrees otherwise. For example, you will not have the right to normal pay or to contractual holiday pay (though you are still entitled to build up statutory holiday) or to a pay increase unless your employment contract gives you these rights.

Returning to work early after maternity leave

If you decide you want to return to work earlier than the date your maternity leave is due to end, you must give your employer eight weeks' notice of your new date of return to work.

Keeping in touch with your employer during your maternity leave

When you are on maternity leave, your employer should keep you informed of issues which may affect you. For example, you should be informed of any relevant promotion opportunities or job vacancies that arise during your maternity leave. The amount and type of contact between you and your employer must be reasonable.

During your maternity leave, you are also allowed to work for up to ten days without it affecting your maternity pay. These are called 'Keeping in Touch Days'. You are under no obligation to work these days and your employer is under no obligation to offer them to you. The rate of pay for Keeping in Touch Days is a matter for agreement with your employer. It may be set out in your employment contract or agreed on a case-by-case basis. However, you must be paid at least the National Minimum Wage.

Your right to return to work after maternity leave

All women have the right to return to their old job after 26 weeks' OML.

After 26 weeks' OML, you do not have to give your employer notice that you are returning to work. You can just turn up for work on the day you are due back.

If your employer refuses to let you return after your Ordinary Maternity Leave

If you are not allowed to return to work after your OML, you can claim your dismissal is automatically unfair for a reason to do with your pregnancy or maternity leave. You could also claim sex discrimination. Both of these claims can be made regardless of how long you have worked for the employer or how many hours a week you work.

Right to return to work after your Additional Maternity Leave

If you wish to return to work after AML, you should be offered your old job back, unless this is not reasonably practical. If it is not reasonably practical to offer you your old job back, you must be offered a job that is suitable for you and appropriate in the circumstances, on the same terms and conditions as your old job. For example, your pay must be at least the same as for your old job.

You do not have to inform your employer of the date you intend to return after your AML, as it will be expected that you will return at the end of your AML. This is the date your employer told you your maternity leave ended. If you want to return to work earlier than this date, you must inform your employer of this, in writing, at least eight weeks before you want to return.

Right to return part-time

You have no automatic right to return to work part-time after maternity leave. However, you may have the right to ask for flexible working and this request must be considered seriously by your employer. If they do not consider it seriously, this could be sex discrimination.

Maternity leave and continuous employment

Some employment rights, such as the right to claim statutory redundancy pay, depend on how long you have worked for your employer. The length of time you have worked for your employer is the length of your 'continuous employment'. It is important, therefore, to note that time spent on maternity leave counts when calculating how long you have been with your employer.

Statutory maternity pay

Who can claim it?

Some women cannot claim Statutory Maternity Pay (SMP) from their employer because they have no entitlement to maternity leave. They are those listed under *Workers who do not have statutory maternity rights* above.

You can claim SMP if:

- you have worked for the same employer for 26 weeks continuously into the 15th week before your baby is due. It does not matter how many hours each week you work. For example, if your baby is due the week beginning 5 May

2008 (expected week of childbirth), 15 weeks before that is the week beginning 21 January 2008 (the qualifying week), and 26 weeks before the qualifying week is the week beginning 23 July 2007. So you would have to have started work on or before 23 July 2007 in order to qualify for SMP if your baby is due in the week of 5 May 2008. *And*

- you are pregnant at, or have had the baby by, the eleventh week before the week the baby is due; *and*
- you have average weekly earnings of at least the National Insurance lower earnings limit. This is worked out on your average earnings in the eight weeks up to the 14th week before your baby is due. There is a helpful calculator on the TIGER website that can help you calculate if you are entitled to SMP. You can access the calculator via the government website (www.direct.gov.uk).

If you are not entitled to Statutory Maternity Pay, you may be entitled to Maternity Allowance paid by the Department for Work and Pensions (DWP).

When is SMP paid?

SMP is paid for up to 39 weeks. The earliest that you can start your maternity leave and therefore start getting SMP is the eleventh week before the baby is due. The latest you can start your maternity leave and therefore start getting SMP is the week after the week when the baby is born. You can choose when you want your SMP to start within this period, unless you are sick.

If you are sick with a pregnancy-related illness in the six weeks before your baby is due, the SMP will start the week following the week you become sick. If you are sick with a non-pregnancy-related illness you can claim Statutory Sick Pay until the week the baby is due.

How much is SMP?

For the first six weeks of maternity leave, SMP is paid at 90 per cent of your average gross weekly earnings (that is, before tax and National Insurance contributions are deducted). For the remaining weeks, it is paid at 90 per cent of your gross weekly earnings or £112.75, whichever is lower.

To claim SMP you must tell your employer at least 28 days before you decide to start maternity leave that you will be off work because of the birth. Your employer will want to see a medical certificate (an MATB1) and you must get one and show it to your employer. SMP is paid by your employer in the same way and at the same time as your wages are normally paid, for example weekly or monthly. Your employer then claims the money back from the government.

If your employer refuses to pay SMP, you can complain to HM Revenue and Customs. They will decide whether or not you should be getting SMP.

Statutory maternity pay and returning to work

The right to Statutory Maternity Pay does not depend on going back to work. You will still receive it, even if you do not go back. You will not have to pay back any SMP if you do not return to work.

Contractual maternity pay

You may have both contractual rights and statutory rights to maternity leave. Contractual rights will usually be better than statutory rights. If they are not, you can ignore them and rely on your statutory rights.

You will need to look at your contract of employment to find out what your contractual rights are to maternity leave and maternity pay.

If you are in one of the groups which do not qualify for statutory maternity rights, you may still be entitled to contractual maternity rights. If you think you have contractual maternity rights but you are not sure how to enforce them, or if you are not sure what your contractual maternity rights are, you should seek advice.

Benefits and tax credits

Working Tax Credit and Child Tax Credit

You can claim Working Tax Credit or Child Tax Credit if you are receiving Statutory Maternity Pay or Maternity Allowance. You can claim Child Tax Credit if you already have a child, or once the new baby is born if it is your first child.

Maternity Allowance

If you do not qualify for Statutory Maternity Pay, you may be entitled to Maternity Allowance paid by the Department of Work and Pensions.

Income Support

If you are on maternity leave, you may be able to claim Income Support if your income is below a certain level. This may apply even if you are getting Statutory Maternity Pay or Maternity Allowance.

If you are entitled to Income Support, you may also be entitled to a lump-sum payment for maternity needs from the Social Fund.

Who can help?

The **Department for Business, Enterprise and Regulatory Reform** (DBERR) has useful leaflets about maternity rights. They are available on their website at www.berr.gov.uk. There is also a version for employers. The **TIGER** website at www.direct.gov.uk can help you calculate maternity and paternity leave.

Further advice on pregnancy and maternity rights is available from the **Equality and Human Rights Commission** (EHRC: 08457 604 6610 in England; 0845 604 8810 in Wales; www.equalityhumanwrights.com)

PATERNITY LEAVE

Statutory paternity rights

If you are a working father you are entitled to one or two weeks' paternity leave when you and your partner have a child. You can also qualify for paternity leave when you adopt a child. This right has now been extended to the partner of a woman who is having a baby if you are in a lesbian relationship, whether or not you are in a civil partnership. Most people who get paternity leave will be entitled to Statutory Paternity Pay. Statutory Paternity Pay is paid at the same rate as Statutory Maternity Pay.

To qualify for paternity leave for a birth you must:

- be employed by your employer for at least 41 weeks by the time your baby is due
- be the biological father of the child. Or you must be married to or be the partner of the baby's mother. This right extends to same-sex partners
- have some responsibility for the child's upbringing
- have given your employer the correct notice to take paternity leave.

To qualify for paternity leave for an adoption you must:

- be employed by your employer for at least 26 weeks by the time you are matched with your child for adoption. (You will not be entitled to paternity leave or pay if you already know the child – for example, if it's your stepchild)
- not be taking adoption leave. When you and a partner are adopting a child, one of you can take adoption leave and the other can take paternity leave

- have some responsibility for the child's upbringing
- have given your employer the correct notice to take paternity leave.

When can you take paternity leave?

If you are taking paternity leave for a birth, the leave can start either on the day the baby is born or on a date that has been agreed in advance with your employer. Your paternity leave cannot start before the baby is born and, if you are agreeing a date later than the birth of your baby, it must be completed within 56 days of the birth.

If you are taking paternity leave for an adoption, the leave can start either on the day that the child is placed with you, or on a date that has been agreed in advance with your employer. If you are agreeing a leave date later than the date the child was placed with you, the leave must be completed within 56 days of the adoption date.

Telling your employer about your paternity leave

You need to be able to show your employer that you are entitled to paternity leave. To do this you must give the employer the following information:

- your name
- the date the baby is due or the date of the birth. If you are adopting a child, you should give the date that you were matched with your child or the date on which the child is placed with you
- the date when you would like your paternity leave (and pay) to start
- whether you are taking one or two weeks' paternity leave
- a declaration that you are entitled to paternity leave
- a declaration that you are taking leave to support the mother or care for the child.

(There are self-certificates available on the website of the Department for Business, Enterprise and Regulatory Reform (DBERR: www.berr.gov.uk) that you can use to provide this information to your employer.)

You must also give your employer notice that you want to take paternity leave. The notice must be in writing if your employer asks for written notice. You must give notice 15 weeks before the baby is due or, if this is not practical, as soon as possible once you know you want to take leave. If you are adopting a child, you must give notice no later than seven days after the date you are matched with your child for adoption. If this is not practical, you must give notice as soon as possible once you know you want to take paternity leave.

If you change your mind about when you want to take paternity leave you can, but you should give your employer 28 days' notice of the changed date.

The website of the Department for Business, Enterprise and Regulatory Reform (DBERR: www.berr.gov.uk) has more information about paternity leave. The TIGER website can help you calculate paternity leave and pay – you can access it via the government website (www.direct.gov.uk). An organization called Working Families has a text and e-mail service for fathers which gives more information about their rights at work. The text number is 0780 000 4722 and the e-mail address is edads@workingfamilies.org.uk.

ADOPTION LEAVE

If you are a working parent matched with a child for adoption, or who has a child placed with you for adoption, you may be entitled to adoption leave. You must have worked for your employer for at least 26 weeks ending with the week in which you were notified that you had been matched with your child.

If you adopt a child from overseas, you must also have worked for your employer for at least 26 weeks: either 26 weeks ending with the notification of a match or 26 weeks from the start of your employment if you've changed jobs since you were notified of the match.

Adoptive parents who adopt after April 2007 are entitled to up to 52 weeks' adoption leave. Most parents will be entitled to Statutory Adoption Pay for 39 weeks and it is paid at the same rate as Statutory Maternity Pay (see p. 249). Additional adoption leave is usually unpaid, although you may be entitled to some contractual adoption pay during this leave. If you adopted before April 2007, you are entitled to less leave.

You must notify your employer that you want to take adoption leave no more than seven days after you have been notified that you have been matched with a child for adoption, or as soon as is practical after this. You must tell your employer the date on which you expect the child to be placed with you and the date on which you want your statutory adoption leave to start.

Where a couple adopts a child, only one parent is entitled to take adoption leave. The other parent may be able to take paternity leave and pay. This applies to same-sex couples as well as opposite-sex couples.

Again, the website of the Department for Business, Enterprise and

Regulatory Reform (DBERR: www.berr.gov.uk) has more information about adoption leave. The TIGER website can help you calculate adoption leave and pay – you can access this website via the government website (www.direct.gov.uk).

FLEXIBLE WORKING

If you are the parent of a child under six (or under 18 if your child is disabled), you have the right to ask to work flexibly and your employer should consider your request seriously. You also have the right to ask for flexible working so you can care for an adult dependant, such as your husband, wife, civil partner or a near relative. This right could extend to someone with whom you share the same address.

It is important to understand that, although you have the right to ask for flexible working hours, you do not have the right to flexible working. This will depend on your employer, who must consider your request seriously but is not compelled to grant it. You must also have worked for your employer for at least 26 weeks and must be responsible for your child on a day-to-day basis. You can make one request to work flexibly each year. Flexible working can include working part-time, working school hours, working flexitime, home working, job sharing, shift working, staggering hours and compressing hours (where you work your total number of agreed hours over a shorter period).

There is a standard procedure that employees and employers must follow when making a request to work flexibly and considering the request. ACAS (08457 47 47 47; www.acas.gov.uk) can give you more information about flexible working rights.

HEALTH AND SAFETY

All employers have a statutory duty to take care of the health and safety of all their employees: for example, they should provide first-aid equipment, protective clothing and adequate means of escape in case of fire, and ensure all machinery is safe.

In addition, there are specific rules covering the following:

- fire safety
- cleanliness
- noise

- machinery
- lifting and carrying heavy weights
- hazardous substances
- toilets
- washing facilities
- drinking water
- seating
- first-aid facilities
- temperatures
- computers
- smoking in an enclosed space at work (this is banned).

Hours and rests

Nearly all workers have the right not to have to work for more than 48 hours on average a week. Night workers cannot work an average of more than eight hours in each 24-hour period. Workers aged 18 and over (adult workers) are entitled to one day off each week. Workers aged 16–18 (adolescent workers) are entitled to two days off each week. Adult workers are entitled to eleven hours' consecutive rest each day, and a minimum 20-minute rest break if their working day is longer than six hours. Adolescent workers are entitled to twelve hours' consecutive rest each day, and a minimum 30-minute rest break if they work for longer than four and a half hours.

The Health and Safety Executive (0845 345 0055; www.hse.gov.uk) provides information on workers' rights and responsibilities. If you believe your workplace is unsafe or unhealthy, you should contact the local Health and Safety Executive or the local authority's environmental health department.

HARASSMENT AND DISCRIMINATION

It is unlawful to discriminate against someone at work because of their:

- sex (this includes transsexuals)
- race
- disability
- colour
- nationality
- ethnic or national origin

- religion
- sexuality
- age.

Discrimination can be either direct or indirect. Direct discrimination occurs when a person is treated less favourably at work because of their sex, race, religion, sexuality, age or disability. For example, if an Asian employee is not selected for promotion because of their race, this is direct discrimination.

Indirect discrimination occurs where a particular employee cannot meet a requirement that is not justifiable in terms of the work and they are at a disadvantage as a result. For example, if the employer only gives training to full-time workers, this would indirectly discriminate against women, as most part-time workers are women.

Harassment is also a form of discrimination. Harassment can include verbal abuse, suggestive remarks and unwanted physical contact. You may also be discriminated against if you are victimized because you have tried to take action about discrimination, either on your own behalf or on behalf of someone else.

If you have been discriminated against or harassed at work, you can take legal action – see below.

Discrimination on grounds of sex

Employment and training

It is unlawful for an employer to discriminate on the grounds of sex. Employment is defined as employment under a contract, which includes employees and self-employed people contracted to do a job personally. Discrimination in employment also includes discrimination in recruitment and in vocational training.

If you think you have been discriminated against because of your sex, you may want to seek advice as soon as possible because there is a strict time limit for taking legal action on these grounds.

Equal pay

A form of unlawful discrimination occurs where a female or male employee is paid less than an employee of the opposite sex for doing the same or similar work.

The Equal Pay Act 1970 gives a person the right to be treated equally in terms of pay in comparison to a member of the opposite sex. The people who are being compared must be working in the same place or working at different establishments for the same employer. A woman who believes she is being discriminated against would have to show that she is employed:

- in *like work* – that is, work that is the same or broadly similar to a man's; *or*
- in work that has been rated as equivalent to a man's job under a job evaluation study; *or*
- in work which is of equal value to that of a man in terms of, for example, effort, skill and decision making.

Pregnancy and maternity leave

It is direct sex discrimination to dismiss a woman because she is pregnant or for a reason connected to maternity leave. As only a woman can become pregnant or go on maternity leave, dismissal on the grounds of pregnancy is automatically discrimination on grounds of sex.

A woman who is dismissed because she is pregnant can also claim that she has been unfairly dismissed, regardless of how long she has worked for her employer. There is a maximum limit on the compensation that can be awarded for unfair dismissal but no limit on compensation for sex discrimination. Therefore a woman dismissed for being pregnant or a reason connected with maternity leave should claim sex discrimination as well as unfair dismissal.

Transsexual people

It is unlawful to discriminate in employment and vocational training against someone who intends to undergo, is undergoing, or has already undergone gender reassignment.

Marriage and civil partnerships

In the case of employment, it is sex discrimination to discriminate against a person of either sex for being married or being in a civil partnership. There is no provision covering discrimination against a person for being single.

Positive action

The law against sex discrimination does allow positive action in favour of one sex, particularly in training and advertising. Positive action is intended to redress the effects of previous unequal opportunities by providing special encouragement to the minority sex without actively discriminating against the majority sex. Examples of positive action are:

- a training agency may use positive action if it appears that very few or no people of one sex have been engaged in a particular kind of work over the past twelve months
- an employer who has very few or no employees of one sex engaged in a particular job, or in management positions, may use positive action to provide training for that work to employees of the minority sex only
- a trade union or political party is allowed to use positive action to ensure that members of both sexes are represented at all levels of the organization. A trade union can, for example, reserve seats on a committee for one sex where it is under-represented.

Discrimination on grounds of race

It is unlawful for an employer to discriminate against someone on the grounds of race. This includes all employers, no matter how small. Most workers, including employees, trainees and those who are self-employed, have legal protection from race discrimination in all aspects of employment, including recruitment, selection, promotion, training, pay and benefits, redundancy, dismissal, and terms and conditions of work.

Trade unions have a duty not to discriminate against their members or those wishing to become members.

If you think you have been discriminated against because of your race, you may want to seek advice as soon as possible because there is a strict time limit for taking legal action on these grounds.

When race discrimination is not illegal

There are some situations where race discrimination is permitted.

If certain conditions or requirements in employment can be shown to be a 'genuine occupational qualification' they may not be discriminatory. For example, it may be justified for the owner of a Chinese or a Greek restaurant to ask for a Chinese or a Greek waiter because the restaurant setting requires this. It is justifiable for a hostel for Asian women who have suffered violence to specify that it wants only Asian women workers on the grounds that the women would find it easier to relate to and communicate with people of the same racial group.

Race discrimination is not unlawful if the job involves working for a private household, working abroad for most of the time or when, with regard to certain jobs, the Crown is the employer.

Discrimination on grounds of disability

It is against the law for an employer to:

- discriminate directly against a disabled person
- treat a disabled person less favourably because of their disability, unless the treatment can be 'justified' (see below)
- fail to make 'reasonable adjustments' to the workplace to enable a disabled person to work or to continue in work (see below)
- harass a disabled person – for example, by making jokes about their disability
- victimize a disabled person for taking action under the Disability Discrimination Act, or for helping someone else take action.

An employer can only treat a disabled person less favourably if they have a justifiable reason for doing so that cannot be overcome by making 'reasonable adjustments'. For example, an employer would be justified in rejecting someone with severe back pain for a job as a carpet fitter, as they cannot carry out the essential requirements of the job.

The Disability Discrimination Act gives examples of the types of adjustments that an employer might have to make. These include:

- making physical adjustments to the premises
- supplying special equipment to help a disabled person do their job
- transferring a disabled person to a different post or workplace
- altering a disabled person's hours of work or giving them extra time off.

When an employer is deciding whether an adjustment is reasonable they can take into account several considerations, including the cost of making an adjustment and the size of their business. In the case of an existing employee, an employer can also take into account the disabled person's skills and experience and the length of time they have worked for the employer.

If you think you have been discriminated against because of your disability, you may want to seek advice as soon as possible because there is a strict time limit for taking legal action on these grounds.

Discrimination on grounds of sexuality

It is against the law for an employer to discriminate against you on the grounds of your sexuality. This means that you cannot be discriminated against or harassed in the workplace because you are gay, lesbian, bisexual or heterosexual. You are protected whatever your sexual orientation.

If you think you have been discriminated against because of your sexuality, you may want to seek advice as soon as possible because there is a strict time limit for taking legal action on these grounds.

You can find more information on the website of the Advisory, Conciliation and Arbitration Service (ACAS: 08457 47 47 47; www.acas.org.uk). Or contact the Equality and Human Rights Commission (EHRC: 08457 604 6610 in England; 0845 604 8810 in Wales; www.equalityhumanwrights.com).

Discrimination on grounds of religion and belief

It is unlawful for an employer to discriminate against you on the grounds of your religion or belief or your lack of religion. Religion or belief generally means any religion, religious belief or similar philosophical belief. It does not include purely political beliefs. You are also protected from discrimination whatever your employer's religion or belief, and whether you are already working for them or are applying for a job.

If you think you have been discriminated against because of your religion or belief, you may want to seek advice as soon as possible because there is a strict time limit for taking legal action on these grounds. You can find more information on the website of the Advisory, Conciliation and Arbitration Service (08457 47 47 47; www.acas.org.uk). Or contact the Equality and Human Rights Commission (EHRC: 08457 604 6610 in England; 0845 604 8810 in Wales; www.equalityhumanwrights.com).

I think I'm being treated unfairly because of my religion. Is this legal?

I'm Jewish and need to take Friday afternoons off work in winter to get home before dark and prepare for the Sabbath. At the moment, my boss is happy to let me do this and make up the time during the rest of the week. However, he is thinking of introducing a new shift pattern which means I will not be able to do this any more. Can he do this?

It is unlawful to discriminate against any worker because of their religion or belief. For example, if your employer is introducing a new shift pattern which will be difficult for you because of your religion, it may be that you are the victim of indirect discrimination on religious grounds. Your employer would have to show exactly why it is essential for you to work on Friday afternoons. If he is unable to show that there is no other reasonable way to reorganize your work, his behaviour towards you may count as discrimination on religious grounds.

Discrimination on grounds of age

It is against the law to discriminate against you at work because of your age, either for being too young or for being too old.

The law applies to you if you are in work or if you are applying for a new job. It applies to you if you are an agency worker. It also applies to you if you need to get a reference from a company you used to work for.

The law applies regardless of how many people work for your employer or how long you have been working for them. However, the law does not apply to you if you are in the armed forces or if you are an unpaid volunteer.

The law means that:

- an employer is not allowed to refuse to employ you because of your age
- your employer is not allowed to treat you unfairly at work because of your age
- your employer is not allowed to force you to retire before the age of 65
- there is no upper or lower age limit for getting redundancy pay
- your employer is not allowed to dismiss you because of your age.

There are some exceptions to the general rules. An employer may be allowed to discriminate against someone because of their age if they can show this is justified. For example, an employer could argue that it does not make business sense to recruit people over 60 when there is a long and expensive training period involved in the job. Not many employers will be able to justify discrimination.

Retirement

Your employer can force you to retire at the normal retirement age. This is 65 or higher, depending on what your contract says. There are rules about how your employer can force you to retire. These include giving you written notice of the date you are due to retire. You have a right to request to stay on beyond that date and your employer has to consider your request seriously but they do not have to agree.

If you want to retire before you are 65, you are allowed to do this as long as your employer agrees.

The law does not affect the age at which you can get state retirement pension. This is currently 60 for women and 65 for men.

Job applications

There is nothing to stop a company asking your date of birth on an application form. But if you do not get the job and you think it is because of your age, you can use the fact that they asked you for your date of birth as possible evidence of age discrimination, which is against the law.

Pension schemes

Employers are allowed to include rules about age in their work pension schemes. This does not count as age discrimination. For example, if your work pension scheme says that you cannot get your pension before you are 60, this is not against the law. Your company can set the age at which you can get your work pension, as long as it is over 50.

Bullying at work

Your employer should protect you from being bullied at work. The Advisory, Conciliation and Arbitration Service (08457 47 47 47; www.acas.org.uk) has useful guidance about workplace bullying and harassment and, if you are a member of a union, they will also be able to provide information and help. If you are being harassed or victimized at work because of your sex, race, disability, sexual orientation or religion, seek advice as soon as possible. Bully Online (www.successunlimited.co.uk) can also provide information on bullying.

TRADE UNIONS

You have the right to join a trade union, and should not be refused a job, dismissed, harassed or selected for redundancy because you are a member of, or wish to join, a trade union.

You also have the right not to join a trade union if you wish, and should not be refused a job, dismissed, harassed or selected for redundancy because you refused to join.

A member of a trade union has the right to take part in trade union activities, such as recruiting members, collecting subscriptions and attending meetings. Any form of industrial action – for example, going on strike – is not considered a form of trade union activity.

Trade union activities must take place either outside the employee's normal working hours or at a time agreed with the employer. An employee has no right to be paid for this time off work unless their contract allows for this.

You can get further information and advice about trade unions from the Trades Union Congress (020 7636 4030; www.tuc.org.uk).

WHISTLE-BLOWING AT WORK

There is some protection for workers who are concerned about malpractice at work and who publicly disclose information about their employer's activities. This is called 'whistle-blowing'. The information disclosed must relate to one or more of the following:

- a criminal offence
- a failure to comply with a legal obligation
- a miscarriage of justice
- a health and safety issue
- damage to the environment
- an attempt to cover up any of the above.

For further information and help, contact Public Concern at Work (020 7404 6609; www.pcaw.co.uk).

SURVEILLANCE AT WORK

Employers have the right to monitor the following activities of their employees:

- postal communications
- telephone calls
- faxes
- e-mails
- internet use
- workplace behaviour (by CCTV).

Surveillance is only permitted by law if:

- the monitoring is relevant to the employer's business
- the telecommunications system is provided for use partly or wholly in connection with the employer's operation
- the employer has made all reasonable efforts to inform users that their communications will be intercepted.

Ideally, an employer should have a code of conduct or policy about surveillance. If it has been agreed with the employees, it will form part of the contract of employment and can be the basis for disciplinary action.

Some employers monitor their workers without informing them that this is happening – for example, by use of hidden cameras or audio devices. This is very rarely legal and guidance under data protection law says that secret monitoring should not be allowed in private areas at work, such as staff toilets, unless there is serious crime involved, such as drug dealing. If you think that your employer has been monitoring you in a way that is not allowed, you can contact the Information Commissioner (01625 545 745 or visit www.ico.gov.uk) to assess whether your employer is meeting their obligations under data protection law. There is no charge for this. If the Commissioner decides that your employer is not complying with the law, recommendations can be made to them or an enforcement notice can be issued. The Information Commissioner cannot award you compensation.

SUNDAY WORKING

Shop workers (including betting-shop workers) have certain rights if they are asked to work on Sundays but only if they work in large shops (over 280 square feet) or were employed before 1994.

Employees of a catering business do not count as shop workers and are not protected from having to work on Sundays. This includes employees of pubs, restaurants and cafés.

MIGRANT WORKERS

A migrant worker is someone who has come from abroad to work in the UK. Migrant workers often work in hotels or restaurants, food packaging or processing, crop or fruit picking, or shellfish gathering.

If you are a migrant worker, you may be working here legally – that is, you have permission from the UK immigration authorities to work in the UK –

or you may be working here illegally – that is, you do not have permission to work here. If you are from one of the European Union countries, you will almost certainly have permission to work in the UK, although you may have had to register on the Workers Registration scheme first. The rules are different if you come from Bulgaria or Romania.

It is very important to know whether you have permission to work in the UK because this seriously affects your rights while you are here. If you are working in the UK illegally, or are not sure whether you have permission to work here, you **must** get advice as soon as possible from an expert adviser. The following information is written for people who have a right to work in the UK.

There are rules about how your employer is allowed to treat you and there are things you can do about it if your employer breaks these rules. Everyone who works in the UK has these rights from their first day of work. This includes people who work for an agency. If you are having problems at work, it is best to get advice first before you tackle your employer. Go to your local Citizens Advice Bureau. You have other rights too (see p. 232) but some of the issues that may affect you the most are described below:

- wages. You have the right to a minimum wage – see p. 237. If you are doing agricultural work – for example, crop or fruit picking – the rules about how much you should get are slightly different from other types of job. Your employer must give you a pay-slip, telling you how much you have been paid. They must pay you all the money you are owed. If you think you are being paid less than the minimum wage, you can report this to the National Minimum Wage Helpline on 0845 600 0678. You do not have to give your name if you do not want to
- deductions from wages. There are rules about how much money your employer can take from your wages to pay for things like your accommodation, travel to the UK and travel to work. There is a set amount of money below which your wages must not go. There is a maximum amount for accommodation which can be taken into account when calculating whether you are getting the minimum wage. If your employer is taking money from your wages, they can only do this if you have agreed to it in writing. But even if you have agreed to this, your employer is not allowed to pay you less than the minimum wage. If you think you are not being paid all the money you are owed, you should get advice
- maximum hours of work – see p. 233. There are special rules for people doing agricultural work
- the right to paid holiday – see p. 233
- the right to health and safety protection – see p. 255

- the right to be protected from discrimination – for example, you must not be treated unfairly because of your nationality – see p. 256
- the right to leave your job. You must be allowed to leave your job if you no longer want to work there. No one, including your employer, can stop you from doing this. Some migrant workers are not allowed to find other work if they leave their job or if they are sacked. If you want to leave the UK before the date that you have agreed with the person you work for, you may find that you cannot change the date of travel on your plane ticket. This may happen if your travel to the UK has been paid by someone else, such as an agency. If you are in this situation, you should get advice
- the right to have your own passport. Your employer or employment agency is not allowed to hold on to your passport or any of your other official documents for any longer than a day. If your employer is holding on to your passport without your agreement, they could be breaking the law.

Problems with employment agencies and gangmasters

You may have come to work in the UK because an employment agency found work for you. Sometimes employment agencies do not tell you the truth about the work they have found for you. You may find that you are not being paid as much as you expected, or the working conditions are not as good as you were led to believe. If you think an employment agency has not told you the truth about your job, you may be able to complain to the Employment Agency Standards Inspectorate (EASI) by phoning 0845 955 5105. However, you can only do this if the agency has offices in the UK. If the agency does not have a UK office, there is usually nothing you can do.

You may work in the UK for a gangmaster. A gangmaster is someone who organizes work for people such as on farms, in hotels, restaurants, building work and hospitals. If you are having problems with your gangmaster, you can report them to the Gangmasters Licensing Authority (GLA) on 0845 602 5020. But you should get advice first.

You can get free, independent advice about employment problems from a local CAB. They may be able to arrange for an interpreter if you have problems with English.

MAKING A COMPLAINT TO YOUR EMPLOYER

Grievance procedures enable you to raise concerns with your employer about your job, your terms and conditions, or the way your employer or people at work treat you.

Your employer must by law have a grievance procedure to allow you to raise concerns, and must tell you what it is. Within two months of starting work, a new employer must give you written details about the job, including information about terms such as pay and hours. This statement must also set out the employer's disciplinary and grievance procedures and tell you who to go to if you have a grievance. If you do not follow these procedures, it could seriously affect your rights if you later make a claim to an employment tribunal . You may not be able to begin an employment tribunal claim, or if you take a case to an employment tribunal and if they decide it was your fault that procedures were not followed properly, compensation awarded to you will be reduced by at least 10 per cent and possibly up to half.

If you have a problem with your employer, you should usually try to sort it out informally first. Raise the matter with the person named in the grievance procedure or, if this isn't possible, go to the next most senior person after the named person. If you cannot sort the problem out informally and want to pursue the grievance, you must follow the statutory minimum grievance procedure. Usually, you will also have to use this procedure to raise a grievance if you have already resigned but want to follow up a complaint with your ex-employer.

The standard three-step grievance procedure is:

1. The written statement
2. The meeting
3. The appeal meeting

1. The written statement

You must send your employer a written statement, setting out your grievance. It should include as much detail as possible, including dates and times. You must keep a copy of this written statement. As a general rule, you will not be able to take your grievance to an employment tribunal later on unless you have provided the information about the grievance to your employer and waited for at least 28 days.

You may find it helpful to state in the written grievance how you would like the matter to be resolved. Be positive – suggest options if you think there are different ways of solving the problem that you would be happy with.

You can find a sample grievance letter for you to adapt and use on the website of the Department for Business, Enterprise and Regulatory Reform (DBERR; www.berr.gov.uk).

2. The meeting

Once you've sent your employer the written statement of your grievance, they must arrange a meeting with you to discuss the issue. Your employer should be allowed enough time to think about what you have said but should not delay the meeting for an unreasonable time.

You have a right to be accompanied at the meeting by someone who works with you or by a trade union official. You have a duty to attend the meeting, which must be held at a time and place that is reasonable for you and anyone accompanying you. If either of you is disabled, your employer must ensure that you have no problems getting to or joining in the meeting.

If you do not attend, a tribunal may later find you at fault for not completing the procedures and reduce your compensation.

If, for an unforeseeable reason, you or the person accompanying you cannot attend, the employer must arrange another meeting and you must attend. If this meeting also has to be cancelled for an unforeseeable reason, then no further meetings need to be held and the necessary procedures would have been complied with.

Prepare carefully for the meeting and discuss the matter fully with anyone accompanying you. If there is anyone there you don't know, ask your employer to introduce them.

Set your case out calmly and clearly and explain what you have done to try to resolve the problem informally. You could also make some further suggestions as to how the problem might be resolved. Try to keep the discussion to the point of the grievance.

After the meeting, your employer must tell you their decision and what action they are going to take.

You have the right to appeal against the decision. You must use your right of appeal before you take a claim to an employment tribunal. If you do not, any compensation award will be reduced.

3. The appeal meeting

If you decide to appeal, you must tell your employer. It is advisable to do this in writing. Keep a copy of the letter, as you may need it if your case goes to an employment tribunal. Your employer must arrange a further meeting to discuss your appeal. Again, it must be at a reasonable time and place and you have a right to be accompanied.

Where possible, a more senior manager should deal with your appeal.

You have a duty to attend the meeting. If you do not attend, a tribunal may later find you at fault for not completing the procedures and reduce your compensation.

After the meeting, your employer must decide what they are going to do and tell you what it is. This is their final decision, and if you are not happy with it and you think your rights have been infringed, you may be able to take your case to an employment tribunal.

If an employer does not follow proper procedures, a tribunal may decide they have acted unreasonably. This would mean you would have been unfairly dismissed.

There are some situations where you will not need to follow the formal grievance procedure. You will not need to follow it if:

- you have been dismissed (unless you are claiming constructive dismissal – see p. 277)
- more than one employee is affected by the same grievance and the matter is being dealt with by the recognized trade union
- you have suffered harassment and it's reasonable to believe that you will suffer further harassment if you use the formal grievance procedure
- it is reasonable to assume that there is a serious threat of violence or damage to property by one of the parties to the grievance
- it is impracticable to begin or to complete the procedure within a reasonable time, or – where you have resigned – to deliver a written grievance to your ex-employer.

DISCIPLINARY ACTION AND DISMISSAL

The statutory minimum disciplinary and dismissal procedure

Your employer must by law have a disciplinary and dismissal procedure and must tell you what it is. Within two months of starting work, a new employer must give you written details about the job, including information about terms such as pay and hours. This statement must also set out the employer's disciplinary and dismissal procedure or refer you to a document which sets out the procedure.

By law, if your employer is considering taking disciplinary action or dismissing you, they must comply with the statutory minimum three-step disciplinary procedure detailed below. Your employer's disciplinary and dismissal procedure may have more steps than the statutory minimum procedure. If so, your employer should follow this fuller procedure.

The standard three-step dismissal and disciplinary procedure is:

1. The written statement
2. The meeting
3. The appeal meeting

1. The written statement

If your employer is considering disciplinary action or dismissal, their first step should be to send you a written statement, setting out exactly the complaint made against you. If you think information is missing – for example, the date of the misconduct – then ask your employer to provide it in good time for the hearing.

It would usually be reasonable for your employer to provide you with evidence from any investigation that has been held so you have an opportunity to consider the information.

Read the statement and any other documents carefully.

2. The meeting

Once your employer has sent you the statement, they must arrange a meeting with you to discuss the issue. You should be allowed enough time to think about what your employer has said but should not delay the meeting for an unreasonable time. The employer must not take any disciplinary action before the meeting.

You have a right to be accompanied at the meeting by someone who works with you or by a trade union official. You have a duty to attend the meeting, which must be held at a time and place that is reasonable for you and anyone accompanying you. If either of you is disabled, your employer must ensure that you have no problems getting to or joining in the meeting.

If you do not attend, a tribunal may later find you at fault for not completing the procedures and reduce your compensation.

If, for an unforeseeable reason, you or the person accompanying you cannot attend, the employer must arrange another meeting and you must attend. If this meeting also has to be cancelled for an unforeseeable reason, then no further meetings need to be held and the necessary procedures would have been complied with.

Prepare carefully for the meeting and discuss the matter fully with anyone accompanying you. If there is anyone there you don't know, ask your employer to introduce them. Your employer should explain how the meeting will be held, who will speak and when. They should then set out the allegations made against you and the evidence that supports them. Listen to what your employer has to say and give your side of the case calmly and clearly when asked to do so. The employer must give you the opportunity to set out your case at the meeting.

Preparing a written note before the hearing may help – your companion or a CAB can help you with this.

Take notes of what is being said and done – your employer will not always take notes and they may be needed later.

After the meeting, your employer will tell you their decision and what action they are going to take.

You have the right to appeal against the decision. You must use your right of appeal before you take a claim to an employment tribunal. If you do not, any compensation award will be reduced.

3. The appeal meeting

If you decide to appeal, you must tell your employer. It is advisable to do this in writing. Keep a copy of the letter, as you may need it if your case goes to an employment tribunal. Your employer must arrange a further meeting to discuss your appeal. Again, it must be at a reasonable time and place and you have a right to be accompanied.

Again, if you do not attend, a tribunal may later find you at fault for not completing the procedures and reduce your compensation.

You have a duty to attend the meeting. If, for an unforeseeable reason, you or the person you have chosen to come with you cannot attend, the employer must arrange another meeting and you must attend it. If this meeting also has to be cancelled for an unforeseeable reason, then no further meetings need be held and the necessary procedures will have been complied with. Prepare carefully for the meeting and discuss the matter fully with the person accompanying you. Take notes at the meeting.

After the meeting, your employer must decide what they are going to do and tell you what it is. This is their final decision, and if you are not happy with it and you think your rights have been infringed, you may be able to take your case to an employment tribunal.

If your employer sacks you without following the proper procedures, and you have been employed for more than one year, an employment tribunal could decide that your dismissal was automatically unfair.

Warnings

Employers often use a system of verbal and written warnings in disciplinary action, which will increase in seriousness, leading to final written warnings or dismissal. Your employer is not required to follow the three-step procedure above if they simply want to issue a warning to you – even a final written warning. However, if they are thinking of taking any other action, such as deducting wages or demotion, they do have to follow the procedures.

Suspensions

Your employer can suspend you on full pay without having to go through the procedures. However, if your pay is reduced the procedures will have to be followed.

If you are unsure about how to proceed, seek advice from your local CAB, ACAS or your union rep.

Unfair dismissal

A dismissal may be fair or unfair depending on the circumstances of the dismissal.

Have you been unfairly dismissed?

You need to work through the following steps to identify whether you can make a claim for unfair dismissal:

- Step 1 – do you have the right to make a claim for unfair dismissal?
- Step 2 – have you actually been dismissed?
- Step 3 – have you been discriminated against?
- Step 4 – was the reason for the dismissal one which means the dismissal was automatically unfair?
- Step 5 – if the dismissal was not for one of the reasons in step four, was the

dismissal fair or unfair, and did your employer act reasonably in dismissing you? You may be able to claim that you have been unfairly dismissed to an employment tribunal, provided you have worked for your employer for one year. Only an employment tribunal can decide if a dismissal was fair or unfair, taking into account all the circumstances of the case. You can also make a claim for unfair dismissal if your employer did not follow proper procedures, which include consulting you before dismissing you.

In all cases, if you make a claim of unfair dismissal to an employment tribunal and you win your claim, the employment tribunal can award you compensation for the unfair dismissal from your employer and/or tell your employer to give you your job back. It is very rare, however, for tribunals to tell employers to give an employee their job back. It is much more usual for the tribunal to award compensation to the employee.

In all cases, when making a claim to an employment tribunal the claim for unfair dismissal must be made within a very strict time limit.

Step 1: Who cannot claim unfair dismissal?

There are some employees who can never claim unfair dismissal. They are:

- people who are not employees, such as independent contractors or freelance agents. Employers often claim that people who are actually employees are self-employed. It is important to check the relationship between the employee and their 'employer', because this will determine the employee's actual employment status
- police officers
- members of the armed forces
- share fishermen
- people who work outside Great Britain
- registered dock workers.

There is no upper age limit on who can make an unfair dismissal claim. However, if you are over the normal retirement age (65 for both men and women) and you are dismissed on the grounds of retirement, this will not be regarded as unfair dismissal if the employer followed the proper procedure before dismissing you.

Step 2: Have you actually been dismissed?

All the following count as dismissal:

- your employer ends your employment with or without notice
- your employer does not renew a fixed-term contract that has run out

- you are made redundant, including if you take voluntary redundancy
- your employer refuses to take you back after a strike or lockout
- constructive dismissal. This is when your employer makes it impossible for you to carry out your work so you resign
- you resign under pressure from the employer
- you are a woman on maternity leave, and your employer refuses to allow you to return to work after maternity leave
- self-dismissal. An employer may argue that you have dismissed yourself by behaving in a way that brings the contract to an end. However, unless it is obvious that you have actually resigned, you will have been dismissed by your employer
- you have been laid off or put on short-time working when your contract does not allow for this.

The following will not count as dismissal:

- you resign without any pressure from your employer or leave by mutual agreement
- you are suspended on full pay
- your employer withdraws a job offer before you start work
- circumstances change and you can no longer continue to work for your employer (known as frustration of contract)
- you are laid off or put on short-time working and your contract allows for this, and then you claim redundancy. You are then actually resigning
- you receive an ambiguous dismissal from your employer and it is not clear if the employer is dismissing you or not.

Step 3: Have you been discriminated against?

You may believe that you have been dismissed because of your sex, race, disability, age, religion or sexuality. You can make a claim for discrimination to an employment tribunal instead of, or in addition to, a claim for unfair dismissal. You do not have to have worked for any particular length of time to be able to claim discrimination.

If you have been dismissed for a discriminatory reason, you will almost always have been unfairly dismissed. However, in order to claim unfair dismissal, you will need to have worked for your employer for one year.

Step 4: What is the reason for the dismissal and is it one that means the dismissal is automatically unfair?

The reason for the dismissal dictates what action you can take. The reason your employer has given you may not be the real reason for the dismissal.

In most circumstances, if your employer wants to dismiss you, they must follow proper dismissal and disciplinary procedures laid down by law – see p. 270. If they do not, and you have worked for your employer for at least a year, your dismissal will be automatically unfair.

Automatically unfair dismissal (where it does not matter how long you have worked for the employer). If the reason for the dismissal was any of those listed below, an employment tribunal will automatically decide that the dismissal was unfair. If you were dismissed for one of the following reasons you can still claim unfair dismissal regardless of how long you have worked for the employer:

- because you are pregnant or on maternity leave or a related reason
- for trying to enforce a right you have under law
- for taking action over a health and safety issue
- for refusing to work on a Sunday (this applies only to some shop workers)
- for carrying out your duties as a trustee of an occupational pension fund
- because you are a trade union member or have taken part in trade union activities including official industrial action, or have acted as an employees' representative
- because you have 'blown the whistle' on a matter of public concern at work.

Automatically unfair dismissal (where you must have worked for your employer for one year). If you have not been dismissed for one of the reasons listed above, but have been dismissed in any of the following circumstances, an employment tribunal will automatically find that you have been unfairly dismissed. However, in order to bring a claim, you must have been employed by your employer for at least one year:

- if your employer has not followed proper dismissal or disciplinary procedures before dismissing you (see section above)
- if the dismissal is as a result of the business you work for having been taken over by a new owner, the dismissal will be automatically unfair and you can make a claim provided you have worked there for one year
- if the dismissal is as a result of your not declaring a spent conviction.

Remember: a claim to an employment tribunal must be made within three months of the date of the dismissal.

Step 5: Is the reason for the dismissal one that is not automatically unfair? If you have not been dismissed for one of the reasons in Step 4, then the dismissal may have been fair or unfair depending on the reason for it and the procedures followed by your employer in dismissing you. If the reason for the dismissal was not one of those in step 4, you will have to have worked for one year for your employer in order to make a claim to an employment tribunal.

Reasons for claiming unfair dismissal where you will have to have worked for one year are:

- your employer says you are not capable of doing the job
- your employer says you do not have the necessary qualifications to do the job
- your employer says your conduct has been poor
- your employer says you have done something illegal
- your employer says you are redundant
- your employer has given some other reason for dismissing you.

It is important to remember that there is a three-month time limit, starting from the date the employee is dismissed, during which any claim must be made to an employment tribunal.

Constructive dismissal

Constructive dismissal occurs if you resign because your employer breaches the employment contract, by taking action such as cutting your pay, changing your working conditions, and so on, and so makes it impossible for you to continue working. Constructive dismissal is a type of unfair dismissal and you will therefore have to have worked for your employer for one year to be able to make a claim to an employment tribunal.

Notice periods

Most employees have a legal right to a period of notice if dismissed. Many employees will have extra rights to notice under their contract of employment. There will always be a contract of employment, even if there is nothing written down. Even if the law or your contract of employment does not give you the right to a minimum amount of notice, you are still entitled to 'reasonable' notice. In most circumstances, if your employer wants to dismiss you, they must follow the proper dismissal and disciplinary procedures set out above which are laid down by law.

Who has no legal right to minimum notice?

Some employees have no legal right to a minimum period of notice (but see also under 'Reasonable notice' section, below). These include:

- those employed for less than one calendar month by their employer. Employees on fixed-term contracts who have worked for their employer for one month have the right to notice
- Crown servants
- seamen employed on a ship registered in the United Kingdom under a crew agreement
- employees who have been dismissed for gross misconduct. If you have been accused of gross misconduct, you may wish to make a claim to an employment tribunal. There is a strict time limit for doing so.

If you have no legal right to notice, you will still be entitled to 'reasonable' notice or the notice your contract gives you, except when you have been dismissed for gross misconduct, when you will not be entitled to any notice under your contract or any 'reasonable' notice. For this reason, it is important to check the real reason for the dismissal.

How much notice should you get?

The law gives all employees the right to a minimum amount of notice, except those listed above. This period of notice is:

- one week for employees who have worked for their employer for one month but less than two years
- two weeks if the employee has worked for their employer for two whole years; *and*
- one extra week for each further whole year's employment at the date the notice period expires, up to a maximum of twelve weeks' notice in total
- between six and twelve months if you are due to retire.

Contractual notice

Your contract of employment may give you more notice than the minimum the law gives you. However, you can never get less than the minimum, no matter what your contract says.

If your contract does not specify a period of notice, you may still have the right to a minimum period of notice because of custom and practice. For example, if everyone who works for your firm has always been given at least three weeks' notice, you would have the right to this much notice.

'Reasonable' notice

If the law does not give you the right to notice, and there is no notice period in your contract (whether written, spoken or through custom and practice), you will still be entitled to 'reasonable' notice. What is reasonable will often depend on your pay period. For example, if you are paid weekly, you could argue that a week is reasonable, and if you are paid monthly, you could argue that a month is reasonable. You won't be entitled to reasonable notice if you have been dismissed for gross misconduct.

How much notice is an employer entitled to?

The notice you should give your employer before resigning should be in your contract. If your contract does not say how much notice you must give your employer then, if you have worked for one month or more, the minimum notice you should give is one week. If you have worked for less than one month, the notice period should be reasonable. If your contract says you must give your employer more notice than this, you must give the amount of notice in your contract. Your contract may set out how much notice you must give, whether it must be written, and when you should give it.

If you leave your job without giving proper notice, your employer may try to withhold part or all of the money owed to you. In general, employers are not legally entitled to withhold money owed but it will depend on what it says in your contract.

Pay

Pay during your notice period

If you work your normal working hours in your notice period, you are entitled to be paid your normal pay.

You may not be able to work during the notice period because you are:

- willing to work but are given no work to do
- on holiday
- off work through sickness or injury.

If you do not work during the notice period for one of the reasons above, the law says you should usually still get your normal wage. However, there is an exception to this rule. If your contract gives you at least one week's notice more than the law gives you, you lose your legal right to be paid during the whole of the notice period. In this case you would just be entitled to the pay specified in your contract.

Pay in lieu of notice

If your employer has dismissed you without giving you notice that the law or your contract says they should have, your employer should pay you in lieu of notice. 'In lieu' means 'instead of'. This is also called severance pay. The only exception to this is when you have been dismissed because of gross misconduct.

The amount of pay in lieu of notice you should get will depend on how much notice you are entitled to. You should get pay in lieu at the rate of your normal wages. For example, if you are entitled to four weeks' notice, but are only given one, you will be entitled to three weeks' pay in lieu of notice. You may be entitled to more than this, depending on what your contract says.

ENFORCING RIGHTS AT WORK

Employment tribunals

Employment tribunals are legal bodies that deal with complaints about employment rights. A tribunal is made up of a legally qualified employment judge and two other people representing the employer's and the employee's sides of industry.

If you wish to enforce your rights at work, you can complain to a tribunal. A tribunal can deal with problems on the following:

- written statement of terms and conditions
- maternity rights
- holiday rights
- itemized pay statements
- unpaid wages
- sex discrimination/equal pay
- race discrimination
- disability discrimination
- discrimination on grounds of sexuality
- age discrimination
- discrimination on grounds of religion or belief
- some health and safety issues

- unfair dismissal and redundancy.

If you complain to an employment tribunal, you may risk losing your job. There are time limits within which you must take a case to a tribunal. These vary but generally a claim for unfair dismissal/illegal deduction from wages/ discrimination must be made within three months of the last day worked, or of the date of the last deduction or of the date of the discriminatory act. This time limit may be extended if you have raised a written grievance with your employer. If you are applying for a redundancy payment, special time limits apply. These are complicated and you can get further advice from the Redundancy Payment Helpline (0845 600 0678). It is very important that, if you are considering making a claim to an employment tribunal, you get help from an experienced adviser as soon as possible – for example, at a Citizens Advice Bureau.

What is wrongful dismissal?

If your employer does not give you the rights you are entitled to under your contract of employment – for example, your employer does not give you the correct notice of dismissal that you are entitled to under your contract – this is known as a breach of contract.

Your employer may pay you an amount of money as compensation instead of giving you notice of dismissal or allowing you to work out your notice. This is called pay in lieu of notice. If there is a term in your contract that allows your employer to pay you 'pay in lieu of notice' instead of giving you notice, then provided you are paid the correct amount of pay in lieu, there will be no breach of contract.

If your employer does not give you the correct notice and does not pay in lieu instead, or does not pay the right amount of pay in lieu of notice, you may be able to claim compensation for the breach of contract by making a claim for wrongful dismissal. You can make a claim for breach of contract to the employment tribunal at the same time as making a claim for unfair dismissal. Your employer should follow the three-step dismissal procedure before dismissing you (see p. 270). Otherwise, the dismissal will be automatically unfair and you will be entitled to extra compensation, as long as you have worked there for one year.

You can claim compensation for breach of contract for other things, such as if your employer takes back your company car when it is a term of the contract that you have a company car for all the time that you are an employee (including your notice period).

REDUNDANCY

Redundancy is a form of dismissal. Therefore, in order to claim redundancy, you must normally have been dismissed from your job. You must have been dismissed because you are genuinely redundant, otherwise you will have been unfairly dismissed.

If you resigned, you will not be redundant. You may, however, be able to argue that, although you have resigned, you have actually been dismissed. This is called constructive dismissal and occurs when you have been put in a position where you have no choice but to resign – for example, you have been made to resign under pressure or you have been made to take another job that is not suitable.

If you volunteered for redundancy, this will usually count as a dismissal. There are special rules that apply if you have been dismissed because the business has been transferred to a new owner. There are also special rules that apply if you think you may have been dismissed or chosen for redundancy for a discriminatory reason – for example, if all the people chosen for redundancy are part-time, this would usually be sex discrimination.

If you are facing redundancy and are a member of a trade union, the trade union is the first place you should go for help. You should get advice as soon as possible.

Redundancy procedure

Where a job disappears, or is moved, causing a redundancy, the employer must follow a recognized procedure when selecting who is to be made redundant. The employer must also follow a proper procedure when dismissing an employee.

There are special rules if an employer is making 20 or more employees at one workplace redundant. This is called a 'collective redundancy'. An employer making a collective redundancy must consult with a recognized trade union where there is one. Where there is no recognized trade union, an employer must consult with employee representatives before issuing redundancy notices.

Before making you redundant, your employer must:

- send you a written statement, telling you why they are making you redundant
- hold a meeting with you to discuss the matter
- hold an appeal meeting with you, if you want to appeal against your employer's decision.

If your employer does not follow the proper procedures, any dismissal will be automatically unfair and you will be able to make a claim for unfair dismissal to an employment tribunal (as long as you have worked for your employer for at least a year). If you win your case, the tribunal will increase the compensation awarded to you because your employer did not follow the procedure.

The employer must use a procedure that is fair, objective and non-discriminatory, using objective criteria. There is no legal definition of what is a fair and objective procedure, but cases that have gone to employment tribunals have established principles of good employment practice that employers should follow. These are:

- the employer will try to give as much warning of the redundancies as possible
- the employer will use objective criteria when deciding who will be made redundant
- the employer will try to ensure that the selection for redundancy is fair and in accordance with the criteria set
- the employer will try to find alternative employment for the employee.

Unfair selection for redundancy is a type of unfair dismissal. Someone who has been unfairly selected for redundancy may therefore be able to claim compensation for unfair dismissal as well as redundancy pay.

Notice of redundancy

The required statutory notice is one week if you have been employed for at least one month but less than two years, two weeks if you have been employed for two years, three weeks for three years, and so on, up to twelve weeks. After twelve years' service, the statutory notice period is twelve weeks.

Discrimination

It is unlawful to have redundancy selection criteria or a redundancy procedure that involves discriminating on the basis of disability, sex, race, religion, age or sexuality. However, it is not against the law to select someone for redundancy on the basis of how long they have worked for the company. It is against the law to have criteria based on whether employees chosen to be made redundant are part-time or pregnant, as this would be sex discrimination. This is the case even if the criteria or procedure have been agreed with the work force.

You do not have to have worked for your employer for any qualifying period to be able to claim compensation for discrimination from an employment tribunal.

Suitable alternative job offers

If your employer intends to make you redundant, they must consider whether there are other jobs available that you would be capable of doing. If such suitable employment is available, it should be offered to you. If it isn't, normally this would mean that you were unfairly dismissed. Whether an alternative job offered is suitable will depend on the terms of the job offered and your skills, abilities and circumstances. Factors such as pay, status, hours and location are relevant when deciding if a job is a suitable alternative. Your employer does not have to offer a similar position or a position in the same workplace.

The offer of alternative employment must be made before your current job ends. It can be made in writing or can be verbal. It must give you enough details about the new job so you know what the difference is between your existing job and the new job. You must also be offered a trial period in the new job.

Your employer may offer you a number of alternative jobs. Each offer must give sufficient detail and you are entitled to a trial period in each, if you wish.

If you are considering the offer of another job with your employer you have a right to try out the job before you decide whether or not to take it, without losing the right to statutory redundancy pay. You can work in the new job for a trial period of four weeks. The trial period will start immediately the previous job ends. At any time during the period you can decide that the job is unsuitable. If you unreasonably refuse the alternative job after the trial period, you will not have a right to a statutory redundancy payment.

Leaving or getting another job during the redundancy notice period

If you are under notice of redundancy and have found another job, you may leave to take the new job during the notice period. However, you could lose your right to redundancy pay if you leave during the notice period. You need to get expert advice if you are offered a new job and you want to start it during your notice period.

Redundancy pay

A redundancy payment is compensation because an employee's job has disappeared. If you are entitled to redundancy pay, you will get a statutory redundancy payment from your employer. You may be entitled to a larger amount of compensation because your employer has a contractual redundancy scheme.

If your contract gives you less redundancy pay than you are entitled to under law, the statutory amount will apply.

If you have contractual rights to redundancy pay, the way it is calculated and when it should be given will be in the contract.

Who is entitled to a statutory redundancy payment?

Only some employees are entitled to a statutory redundancy payment. To be entitled, you must:

- be an employee. Self-employed people or members of a partnership do not qualify
- have worked for the firm for at least two calendar years continuously since the age of 16
- not be in an excluded occupation (see below).

If you do not meet these conditions, you won't get a statutory redundancy payment, even if you are genuinely redundant. If you are excluded from statutory redundancy pay, you may be entitled to contractual redundancy pay. Check your contract of employment.

Excluded occupations

Most public employees – for example, civil servants and police officers – cannot claim a statutory redundancy payment as they have contractual arrangements that give them similar or better payments. Share fishermen can never claim a statutory redundancy payment.

Losing the right to a statutory redundancy payment

Even if you are entitled to redundancy pay, there are reasons you might not get it – for example, if your employer claims to have offered you a suitable alternative job, you may lose the redundancy pay (see p. 284). If you want to leave before the date your employment is due to end – because, for example, you have found another job, you could lose your redundancy payment. You need to get expert advice if you are offered a new job and want to start it during your notice period.

How much is a statutory redundancy payment?

The amount of a statutory redundancy payment depends on:

- how long you have worked for your employer; *and*
- your age; *and*
- your weekly pay.

Statutory redundancy pay is worked out as follows:

- one and a half weeks' pay for each complete year of employment when you were aged 41 or over
- one week's pay for each complete year of employment when you were aged between 22 and 40 inclusive
- half a week's pay for each complete year of employment when you were aged under 22.

The maximum number of years of employment that can count is 20. Employment is counted up to the relevant date, which is the date your notice expires. If you have not been given any notice, it is the date on which the notice would have expired had you been given it.

Weekly pay

The weekly pay that will be used to work out the redundancy payment will usually be your normal weekly gross pay at the time you were made redundant up to the maximum limit. This means that if you changed from full-time work to part-time work and are then made redundant, your weekly pay will be calculated at the part-time rate. Gross pay is pay before deductions such as tax and National Insurance are made.

A week's pay does not include overtime pay unless the overtime was regular and compulsory. Where earnings vary each week, an average of the twelve-week period leading up to the redundancy will be used. If commission is paid regularly, this should be included in a week's pay. An average should be calculated – for example, an amount that could be expected in a year, divided by the number of weeks worked in a year.

There is a maximum limit on the amount that can count as a week's pay. This applies even if you earned more than the maximum amount. The Department for Business, Enterprise and Regulatory Reform (DBERR) has produced a useful ready reckoner to calculate how much statutory redundancy pay you will get – go to www.berr.gov.uk. The rules about redundancy pay were different if you were made redundant before 1 October 2006 and the DBERR ready reckoner gives you these figures too.

When making a payment, your employer must give you a written statement saying how it is calculated.

Claiming a statutory redundancy payment

Your employer is responsible for paying a statutory redundancy payment to you on, or soon after, the date of your dismissal. You do not need to make a claim unless your employer fails to pay or claims that you are not entitled to the payment.

What to do if your employer refuses to make a statutory redundancy payment

If you have a right to a statutory redundancy payment, but your employer refuses to make it, you will have to make a claim to an employment tribunal within six months of the date of dismissal to get the money. However, remember that if you want to claim unfair dismissal or discrimination, the time limit to apply to an employment tribunal is three months. In most circumstances you will need to raise a written grievance with your employer first before you can make a claim to an employment tribunal.

Benefits, tax and redundancy

A statutory redundancy payment may affect your entitlement to benefits and your tax position.

Claiming redundancy pay if the employer has ceased trading

If your employer is insolvent and a receiver or liquidator has been appointed to deal with the company's affairs, you should claim your redundancy payment from the National Insurance Fund. You can contact the fund on 0845 145 0004.

If your employer has ceased trading but is not insolvent, write to your employer claiming the redundancy payment. If the employer does not pay the statutory redundancy pay, you must apply to an employment tribunal within six months of your dismissal. You will need to raise a written grievance with your employer first – see p. 268. If an employment tribunal decides that you are entitled to statutory redundancy pay but your employer still does not pay it, you can make an application to the National Insurance Fund for your redundancy payment.

Other redundancy rights

Right to notice of redundancy

Because redundancy is a form of dismissal, you will still be entitled to your statutory or contractual period of notice of dismissal, if your employer plans to make you redundant.

Time off to look for work

If you have been given notice of redundancy, you are entitled to paid time off to look for a new job providing that by the time your notice period ends you have worked for your employer for two years. The following employees are not entitled to paid time off to look for work:

- employees who have worked for their employer for less than two years
- overseas employees
- merchant seamen
- share fishermen
- members of the armed forces
- police service employees.

There is no definition of how much time the employer has to give, but it must be reasonable. What is reasonable will vary according to the circumstances – for example, the difficulty of finding work in certain areas, the time and travel involved, and the range of jobs you are looking at. In addition to these legal rights, you may have rights that have been negotiated by the trade union, if any, or from your contract.

SELF-EMPLOYMENT

If you are considering self-employment, you will need to give some thought to the different ways of trading and which would be most appropriate for your business. The business could take one of three legal forms:

- a sole trader. This is the simplest way of starting a business
- a partnership. This is similar to a sole trader except that two or more people run the business
- a limited company. This gives the business a completely separate identity from the people who run the business. It is more complicated to set up.

In addition to one of the above legal forms, self-employment can also involve one of the following trading practices:

- a co-operative. This is a business that is collectively owned and controlled by the people who work in it. At least two people must be involved
- a franchise. A franchise is an agreement that allows the person buying the franchise the right to run a branch of a business that someone else has set up.

It is extremely important that accurate and detailed records of the business are kept. You may be able to keep your own books or employ a bookkeeper or accountant, but if you are trading as a limited company you will need the help of an accountant.

Tax

As a self-employed person, you will be taxed differently to an employee. You will be responsible for paying income tax on your earnings and will usually need the help of an accountant. There are special tax reliefs and allowances that self-employed people can claim. If you are newly self-employed, you should register with HM Revenue and Customs by calling the helpline for the Newly Self-Employed. The helpline number is 08459 154515.

VAT

Value Added Tax (VAT) is a tax on goods and services that is paid to HM Revenue and Customs. Whether or not a self-employed person has to pay, and in some cases has the right to choose to pay, VAT depends on the type of business and how much the business sells. Your accountant should be able to tell you whether you should be paying VAT or not.

Premises

Working from home has the advantage of low costs but you will need to make sure that the tenancy agreement, mortgage agreement or title deeds of the property do not place any restrictions on business use. You may also need to get local authority planning permission. If you are buying or renting property from which to trade, you need to make sure the property has been approved for business use. Planning permission may also be necessary.

As a self-employed person, you have a duty to make sure that your business premises and working environment meet health and safety requirements. Further information is available from the local health and safety executive or environmental health department of the local authority.

Business rates

You have to pay business rates to the local authority on most business premises. These include shops, offices, warehouses and factories. In some cases – for example, in a property which contains a shop and a flat or if you work from home – you may have to pay both business rates and council tax. Some types of business premises are exempt from rates, for example, agricultural land. For more information about business rates in England, see the government's Business Link website (www.businesslink.gov.uk), and for more information about business rates in Wales, contact your local council.

Insurance

Depending on the business and how you trade, you will be required by law to take out certain types of insurance. Other types of insurance are not compulsory but it is important to consider which ones are appropriate. The types of insurance you may need are:

- employer's liability insurance. If you employ other people you must have this insurance. It provides cover for claims made by employees who are injured or become ill as a result of their employment
- vehicles insurance. Vehicles used for business must be insured for business purposes even if already insured for private use
- public liability insurance. This provides cover against claims by members of the public who have been injured or had property damaged as a result of carelessness at work by you or your employees
- premises insurance. Insurance will be necessary for the premises you work from, even if you work from home and there is already a policy. This is because the insurance will usually only cover residential use
- contents, stock and materials insurance. This insurance will be necessary to cover the replacement costs of stock, materials and the contents of the premises even if work is being done from home and there is already a home contents insurance policy
- health and accident insurance. These will pay a regular income or lump sum if you are unable to work because of an accident or sickness.

Immigration status

Setting up in business may affect your immigration status and you should therefore get good advice before doing so.

Employing other people

If you employ other people, you will be responsible for paying wages, tax, National Insurance contributions and Working Tax Credit where relevant. You will have to meet the requirements of employment law and health and safety regulations.

National Insurance contributions

As a self-employed person you may have to pay National Insurance contributions for yourself and any employees. Whether you have to pay contributions for yourself, and if so what type, depends on how much you earn. Whether contributions have to be paid for any employees depends on what they earn. The payment of contributions will affect the benefits you can claim in the future. You can contact a telephone helpline for information about National Insurance contributions, Statutory Sick Pay and Statutory Maternity Pay on 0845 714 3143.

Benefits, tax credits and pensions

As a self-employed person you may be able to claim benefits or tax credits, depending on your income and other circumstances. As a self-employed person, you will get state retirement pension if you have met the contribution conditions.

You could also consider getting a private personal pension.

Trading names and licences

You need to consider whether you wish to use a trading name for the business. If so, there are restrictions on the names businesses can use. You may also need to get a licence, depending on the type of business.

Further help in setting up a business or co-operative

Banks can be useful sources of information and advice if you are thinking of setting up in business.
Chambers of Commerce are local organizations that give information, advice and training to businesses in their town or area. Most give free

advice to members, but charge for services to non-members. Some Chambers of Commerce serve particular ethnic minorities.

The **Enterprise Directorate** (0845 600 9006 helpline) is a government agency providing general information on starting up a small business. It operates the Business Link National Contact Centre (www.businesslink. gov.uk), designed to deliver information and advice to small businesses in the UK. It also operates a network of local providers throughout the UK, which can provide independent and impartial advice.

Inbiz (0800 0321 001; www.inbizonline.co.uk) provides help and support to long-term unemployed people in England who want to become self-employed.

Natural England, previously called the **Countryside Agency** (in England only: 0845 600 3078; www.naturalengland.org.uk) can help small businesses in rural areas. Normally the agency only helps manufacturing or service industries and businesses employing fewer than 20 skilled employees, and will not help agricultural and horticultural businesses.

Local enterprise agencies give free general advice and support to small businesses. Training courses are also available, and are often free. Details of local enterprise agencies are available from the National Federation of Enterprise Agencies (01234 831 623; www.nfea.com or for business advice www.smallbusinessadvice.org.uk).

The **National Federation of Small Businesses** (01253 336 000; www.fsb. org.uk) is a pressure group that promotes the interests of all self-employed people.

The **British Franchise Association** (01491 578050; www.thebfa.org) is the trade association for franchising companies. It was set up to promote franchising and establish standards.

The **Prince's Trust** (0800 842 842; www.princes-trust.org.uk) helps young unemployed people aged 18–30 to set up their own businesses. In Scotland the age limit is 18–25. The Trust can give loans, ongoing business advice and help with marketing. The Trust is particularly interested in helping people from ethnic minorities, disabled people and ex-offenders.

Livewire (0191 261 5584; www.shell-livewire.org.uk) is a national scheme sponsored by Shell, to help young people aged 16–30 to set up in business. Young people with projects can discuss their ideas with local advisers and financial awards may be given. There is usually a closing date for the scheme each year. Each entrant to the scheme will be paired with an adviser who will help them on an individual basis to plan and develop their business idea.

Instant Muscle (0845 1300 930; www.instantmuscle.org.uk) is a charity that helps unemployed people to set up their own businesses or find a job. It provides training, practical advice, help with preparing a business plan, and individual business counselling. Instant Muscle also offers help and support during the first two years of trading.

Co-operatives UK (0161 246 2900; www.cooperatives-uk.coop) is the national federation for worker co-operatives. It produces model rules and model employment contracts that are used by most co-ops in the UK. It gives advice on setting up and running a co-operative, community business or community enterprise, particularly on the legal requirements necessary.

Business Eye (01874 610 054; www.businesseye.org.uk) is responsible for the economic and social development of mid-Wales. It provides advice and support to small businesses, including advice about setting up in business, preparing a business plan and whether the business idea is viable, and can help investigate sources of money, find suitable premises and set up financial control systems, such as bookkeeping.

Equality Direct (0845 600 3444; www.equalitydirect.org.uk) runs a free, confidential advice line for employers. It provides advice and information on equality issues and general people management.

Jobcentre Plus offices sometimes advertise details of self-employment possibilities for unemployed people, including contract work and commission-only vacancies. They may also be able to provide information on starting a small business or arranging a franchise. If you want information you should speak to your Employment Services Adviser.

HELP FINDING WORK

The main government employment schemes are provided through Jobcentre Plus offices, where you can get more details. Some employment schemes are compulsory for people claiming Jobseeker's Allowance (JSA) while others are voluntary. You can also find information at your local Jobcentre Plus office about employment schemes for the self-employed, training schemes, the New Deal and other types of help on offer.

Help for disabled people

Every Jobcentre Plus office has a Disability Employment Adviser (DEA) attached as part of a Disability Service Team (DST), providing specialist advice to disabled people and actual or potential employers. The DEA can advise on practical help through the Access to Work scheme, the Job Introduction Scheme and supported employment.

> *When I was younger I got into trouble with the police. I'm applying for jobs now and I'm worried my conviction will stop me getting work. Do I have to tell employers about my criminal record?*
>
> The information that you have to give will depend on the length and type of sentence that you received and the job that you are applying for. You will always have to declare a prison sentence of more than two and a half years (or an equivalent period of youth detention or custody), if you are asked about any criminal record by an employer. This applies to a suspended or partially suspended sentence too. When you are calculating the time it is the length of the original sentence that counts, not how long you actually spent in custody. So, if the sentence was for five years but you were given parole after two years, you will still have to declare the offence.
>
> You will also always have to declare any conviction if you are applying for a job in which you will be working with children or vulnerable adults. For example, you will have to declare all convictions if you are applying to teach, work in the healthcare sector, or work as a childminder or as a social worker.
>
> However, if you are not working with children or vulnerable people, there are some offences that do not have to be declared after a certain period of time has passed. If your conviction falls into this category the conviction is considered to be 'spent' and does not have to be declared, even if an employer asks you directly about your criminal record. This fixed period is known as a 'rehabilitation period' and runs from the date of conviction. The length of the rehabilitation period depends on the sentence that you received rather than the type of offence that you committed. Some will be spent more quickly than others. You can find more information at www.crb.gov.uk.

2
Communications

CONTENTS

INTRODUCTION

From 1875 when Alexander Graham Bell was granted a patent for his 'multiple telegraph' device, through to the world's first television broadcasts in 1935 and on to the development of the internet by Tim Berners-Lee in the late 1980s, advances in communication are at the heart of modern economic, financial and social life. Few in the developed world are without access to telephones and TV and the internet is central to many people's working lives. But hard on the heels of the benefits come the legislation and the pitfalls, along with concerns about privacy and data protection. In this chapter, we cover what to look out for when you are choosing phone service providers and the standards you can expect from them, television licences, and where to get help to protect your private information from misuse.

JARGON BUSTER

ISP	Internet Service Provider
CPS	carrier pre-selection – a phone service that allows a BT customer to make calls using another phone company
Network operator	the company that allows airtime so that you can make and receive calls
Service provider	the company that buys airtime from the network operator and sells it to shops, outlets or the public
Pay-as-you-go	where calls are paid for in advance

PHONE SERVICES – LAND LINES

You can choose between a range of phone service providers for phone lines and equipment providers for telephone handsets, faxes and switchboards. As well as BT, other phone service providers include Virgin Media and Onetel. Before choosing a phone service provider, find out what phone services are available and how much they will cost. Take into account the cost of equipment rental, line and call charges, and call facilities such as call waiting. Also, check whether cheaper rates are offered for particular payment methods, such as direct debit, the standards the phone service providers offer, any extra help for older or disabled customers and what the company's policies are on debt and disconnection.

Each phone service provider issues a code of practice that covers issues like repairs, maintenance, disconnection and their complaints procedure. Check the code of practice before choosing a service provider. For where to obtain copies of the Codes of Practice of the individual phone service providers, see *Complaints about a land line phone service*, p. 302.

Phone directories and directory enquiries

BT produces a phone directory. You can choose not to be included in this if you do not want to give general access to your phone number.

No charge is made for a listing in the telephone directory.

If you are listed in the directory, your telephone number will also be available from companies that deal with enquiries about telephone numbers. You must pay for calls to directory enquiries unless you are disabled. Disabled phone users must register with the phone service provider before they are eligible for this service.

I'm always getting phone calls from people I don't know. How can I stop them?

If the phone calls are from people trying to sell you something then you can sign up to the Telephone Preference Service. This service is free. Companies should not make phone calls to people who have signed up to this service. For details of how to register, contact the Telephone Preference Service (0845 070 0707; www.tpsonline.org.uk). If the phone calls are from strangers who do not give their name and are being offensive then contact the police. This sort of nuisance call is against the law and people can be prosecuted if they are discovered doing this.

Repairs, rebates and compensation

Each phone service provider has a different policy on repairs, and you will need to check their code of practice to find out more.

Codes of practice on repairs will usually cover issues such as whether there is a time limit during which repairs should be started once a problem has been reported and whether faults are repaired free of charge. This is often the case unless the phone service provider decides the fault was due to damage caused by the customer.

If your phone is not working properly for more than a certain time after being reported, you may have a right to a rental rebate on the standing charge. The phone service provider may also have to pay compensation for the period when the phone service was not available. Details will be in the code of practice.

Claiming the cost of repairs on insurance policies

You may be able to claim on your house contents insurance policy for the cost of repairing or replacing damaged phone equipment if this is not provided free of charge by the phone service provider. Check your policy to find out whether there is an excess or loss of no-claims bonus since the cost of replacing damaged telephone equipment is usually quite low.

Entering land for installation and repairs

If a phone service provider wishes to install cable, telephone poles or pylons or other equipment, it must first get permission in writing from the occupiers of any land concerned, including land needed for access. Various problems can arise:

- you may not want poles on your land or wires going over your property
- you may not want your land dug up for cable laying or may not agree to the phone service provider's plan
- there may be disputes about how near to a building the phone service provider wants to install overhead wires
- you may be willing to allow entry to the phone service provider but want to know if you are entitled to compensation and, if so, how much.

It is worth getting legal advice on this if you want to withhold permission. A previous owner of the land may have agreed to installation of cables or poles and you may be bound by the agreement. If permission is refused, the phone service provider could apply to court for an order allowing installation.

The right to a phone service

BT has an obligation to provide a phone service to anyone who asks for it, unless a prospective customer has been in debt with BT before. In this case, BT can refuse to provide a new service.

If a prospective customer lives somewhere remote, the price of providing a phone service may be extremely high, and the person may not be able to pay the full connection cost.

None of the phone service providers other than BT have an obligation to provide a phone service.

If you want information or advice about changing to a new phone service provider, you could consider contacting OFCOM (020 7981 3040; www. ofcom.org.uk), which can give general information about what to check when considering whether to change to a new phone service provider and provide a list of the licensed phone service providers in your area. OFCOM cannot recommend individual phone service providers.

Number portability

All phone service providers must allow customers to keep their phone number when changing phone service provider. This is known as number portability. This only applies if you are changing the phone service provider you use without changing your address. Some phone service providers offer an additional service where a customer may change address and phone service provider and still keep the same phone number. However, phone service providers are not obliged to offer this service. Phone service providers may make a reasonable charge for providing number portability.

Carrier pre-selection

Carrier pre-selection (CPS) is a phone service that allows a BT customer to make calls using another phone company. You can do this either by dialling a short code or freephone number on your BT phone (which connects you to the other phone company) and then dialling the number wanted. Alternatively, you can have an adaptor plugged between the socket and the phone that allows calls to be diverted to another phone number without your having to dial a code first. Carrier pre-selection must be made available to BT customers. Other phone companies – for example, mobile phone companies – can choose whether to make it available to their customers.

Certain types of call are not included in CPS – for example, emergency numbers, operator assistance, directory enquiries and flat-rate internet access. You will still have the same access to these.

You do not have to make every call using CPS. For example, you may want to use a CPS provider for international calls but another provider for local calls. In such a case, once you have arranged to have international calls put through via a certain provider, you dial the code for that provider before dialling the international number. You can choose four options for CPS: national calls only, international calls only, national and international calls and 'all calls', which includes local, national, international and mobile phone calls.

BT will still own, run and send you the bills for your phone line. Your phone number will not change. However, you will get a separate bill for call charges from each different phone company that you use. More information about CPS is available from OFCOM (020 7981 3040; www.ofcom.org. uk).

Phone bills

Disputing the size of the bill

Your phone service provider may offer an itemized billing service, showing the date, time, duration and cost of calls costing more than a certain amount, or it may show all calls made. You will need to check with your phone service provider to see if it offers such a service, and if there is any charge. This will help you to minimize disputes about the size of the bill.

You may consider that a telephone bill is too high. In general, it is rare for phone equipment to give wrong information but it is possible for there to be a fault. Occasionally a handset may be faulty and fail to disconnect at the end of a call.

If you have a high bill as a result of calls made by someone who is not a joint-account holder – for example, a friend or a lodger – you will have to pursue that person for the money. If the calls were made to premium rate services, you could also contact Phonepay Plus (0800 500 212); www. phonepayplus.org.uk). This is the regulatory body for all premium rate services, and they might be able to help you claim compensation.

Payphones installed by landlords

If a landlord has a payphone put into a property, they are responsible for the rental and for paying the phone service provider for calls made. Some payphones can be programmed (by the landlord) with a special scale of charges. This may be considerably higher than public payphone charges. The landlord must display the charges on or near the payphone. If charges aren't displayed, you can make a complaint to OFCOM (020 7981 3040; www.ofcom.org.uk).

Disconnection

Each phone service provider has its own policy on disconnections and it is vital that you refer to their code of practice.

Rebate, discount and low-cost schemes

Many phone service providers offer a range of special discount and rebate schemes, including schemes for light and heavy users of their phone services. Information on these schemes is available from individual phone service providers.

Phones for disabled people

Someone who is assessed by social services as having a particular need may get help with telephone charges. Some local authorities will pay for installation, others will pay for the rental costs. Phone companies can provide a range of special equipment and services for elderly or disabled people.

Problems in rural areas

There is usually a standard charge for running a phone line into a property and installing a phone. However, if you live some distance from the nearest cable, the phone service provider may charge for part or all of the cost of laying new cable, poles and so on. Contact the phone service provider for details of, for example, how near you are to other customers or phone cables, and the likely costs of connection.

Nuisance calls

Stopping unsolicited phone calls and faxes

All direct marketing companies are banned from making unsolicited phone calls to people who have registered with the Telephone Preference Service (0845 070 0707; www.tpsonline.org.uk). Direct marketing companies in the European Union are not allowed to send unsolicited faxes to anyone who has not given their consent to receive faxes from the company, and this is the case whether or not they have registered with the Fax Preference Service (0845 070 0702; www.fpsonline.org.uk).

Harassing, obscene or malicious phone calls

Making an obscene, harassing or malicious phone call may be a criminal offence. If you receive such a call, report it to the police. The police can, for example, authorize the phone service to trace malicious calls. If the person who is making the calls is prosecuted, you may have to give evidence in court. The phone service provider may have procedures that deal with malicious, obscene or harassing phone calls. Check the phone service provider's code of practice. For example, BT has a special phone number to call – 0800 666700 – for a 24-hour recorded message.

Caller display/caller return

Almost all phone service providers supply a service called 'caller display' or 'caller return'. Caller display shows the number of the caller, provided the phone receiving the call has a visual display unit. Caller return enables the person receiving calls to find out the number of the last caller by phoning 1471. To delete the last incoming number, dial 1475.

Caller return may be of limited use in the case of malicious calls, as the person making the call can withhold their number by dialling 141 before making the call. This does not mean that the number cannot be traced once the police have authorized this. In the case of nuisance calls, the phone service provider can trace the caller's number even if the number from which the call was made has been withheld. You can also decide not to answer a call if the caller's number is not displayed.

Complaints about a land line phone service

The contract covering the service provided by the phone company is covered by the usual law of contract and you will have your usual consumer rights. If you have a problem with the services provided, check the code of practice for details of the complaints procedure you should follow. All phone companies must have a formal customer complaints process. If the company has not got one, you should tell the communications watchdog, OFCOM – see p. 303. If you have made a formal complaint to the phone company and this has not solved the problem, you can try using the company's Alternative Dispute Resolution (ADR) scheme. All phone companies must have an ADR scheme. They are breaking important consumer protection rules if they do not. Your phone company might belong to one of two ADR schemes which have been approved by OFCOM:

- OTELO (the Office of the Telecommunications Ombudsman (08450 501614; www.otelo.org.uk))
- CISAS (Communications and Internet Services Adjudication Scheme (020 7520 3827; www.cisas.org.uk)).

If your phone company will not tell you about its ADR scheme, you can contact OFCOM for details.

If you are still dissatisfied, OFCOM (020 7981 3040; www.ofcom.org.uk) or OTELO (the Office of the Telecommunications Ombudsman: 08450 501614; www.otelo.org.uk) may be able to investigate a complaint.

OFCOM is a government organization set up to regulate telecommunications in the UK. It has various roles, including monitoring the activity of licensed phone service providers and promoting competition between them. OFCOM can also look into or take up complaints by individuals about any aspect of phone service providers. It cannot help negotiate reduced or deferred payment of a bill.

OTELO may be able to help with a complaint about a telecommunications company if the company is a member of OTELO. You must have first used the company's own complaints procedure.

PHONE SERVICES – MOBILE PHONES

There are a number of points to consider before deciding which mobile phone service to choose, such as:

- the cost of calls. This varies depending on the time of day and it usually costs more to phone a mobile from a land line phone than it does to call another land line phone
- the type of contract, and length of the contract
- reception in the area where you live
- what facilities are available, such as voicemail.

Reception signals for mobile phones may be stronger in some areas – for example cities or towns – and weaker in others, such as rural districts. If you are thinking about buying a mobile phone and live in a rural area, you need to find out how good the reception signal will be.

Pay-as-you-go services

Instead of a contract where you pay monthly rental charges and the cost of the calls, you can choose a pay-as-you-go service, where calls are paid for in advance. With these you enter into a contract to pay a set figure for a phone package that includes a handset, battery and free calls for a certain period of time, such as one month, or you may be given a voucher to pay towards the first calls that you make on the phone. When the voucher has been used up, you can top up your credit from the mobile phone company. In this sort of arrangement, you enter into a contract for goods and services when you first buy the package and then into a contract for service each time you top up your credit, even though this contract may be unwritten.

Contracts

It is important to establish who the contract is with in case you:

- want to end your contract for a mobile phone
- have a fault on your mobile phone
- want to make a complaint.

Your contract may be with:

- the network operator, which is the company that allows airtime so that you can make and receive calls. Examples of network operators are O2, T-Mobile, Vodafone and Orange
- the service provider, who buys airtime from the network operator and sells it to shops, outlets or the public
- the outlet that sells mobile phones. Some outlets may also be service providers or they may act as agents for service providers.

Here we use the term 'mobile phone company' to cover whichever type of company your contract is with.

You may find it difficult to arrange a contract if you are not on the electoral register. This is because all mobile phone companies make a credit check and someone not on the electoral register may automatically fail this.

Ending a contract

If you want to cancel your contract, you can only do so if there is a clause in your contract allowing you to cancel. If there is a right to cancel, the mobile phone company may impose a charge. However, there may be other circumstances in which you can cancel your contract free of charge – for example, if you have paid by credit, signed the contract in your own home, or ordered the service by post, phone or over the internet – see *Cooling off periods and your right to cancel*, p. 334 for more details.

Selling a mobile phone to someone else

If you want to sell your handset to someone else, check whether your contract allows this. Someone who wants to buy a second-hand mobile phone handset should check whether it is possible to use airtime that was originally bought by another person. Sometimes the mobile phone company may agree to a transfer, but make a charge. The mobile phone company will also check whether the phone has been stolen before agreeing to transfer the contract.

Stolen mobile phones

If your mobile phone is stolen, immediately inform the mobile phone company and the police. The mobile phone company will usually disconnect the service so that you do not have to pay for unauthorized phone calls. You may still have to pay for line rental for the minimum term of the contract, but check the terms of your contract. If your mobile phone is stolen, it may be covered by your household insurance: check whether a claim can be made.

Broken mobile phones

If your mobile phone breaks, immediately inform the mobile phone company. You should check your contract to find out if you must continue to pay rental charges for this period.

Driving and mobile phones

It is a criminal offence to use a hand-held mobile phone when driving. The ban also applies when you are waiting at traffic lights or in a traffic jam. You can get a fixed penalty (a sort of fine) and three penalty points on your licence if you break the law. You are allowed to use a hands-free mobile phone when you are driving but if you lose control of your vehicle while using it, you could also get a fixed penalty and three penalty points. If a case goes to court, in addition to the points on your licence, you could face disqualification and a fine. These rules apply to motorcyclists as well as vehicle drivers. Drivers of buses, coaches or goods vehicles face a higher maximum fine.

You can find out more about mobile phones and driving on the Department of Transport website (www.dft.gov.uk).

Mobile phone bills

Disputing the size of a bill

It is possible that a fault may have occurred that is the responsibility of the mobile phone company. However, mobile phone companies usually offer an itemized billing service, showing date, time, duration and cost of calls, so you can check whether or not a high bill is due to the calls made or a fault.

How to complain about a mobile phone service

If the mobile phone or phone service is unsatisfactory

If you have a problem with the phone (handset), it is the *seller* and not the manufacturer or the service provider who is responsible for dealing with your complaint. Remember, the law says the handset must be of satisfactory quality, fit for purpose and match its description.

If you have a complaint about your mobile phone company, you should speak to them about it first. If this does not solve the problem, you can make a formal complaint to the company. You can find details of how to do this on the back of your phone bill. If you can't find these details, the company's customer service staff will tell you how to make a formal complaint.

All phone companies must have a formal customer complaints process. If the company has not got one, you should tell OFCOM – see p. 303.

If you have made a formal complaint to the phone company and this has not solved the problem, you can try using the company's Alternative Dispute Resolution (ADR) scheme. All phone companies must have an ADR scheme. They are breaking important consumer protection rules if they do not. Your phone company might belong to one of two ADR schemes which have been approved by OFCOM:

- OTELO (the Office of the Telecommunications Ombudsman (08450 501614; www.otelo.org.uk))
- CISAS (Communications and Internet Services Adjudication Scheme (020 7520 3827; www.cisas.org.uk)).

If your phone company will not tell you about its ADR scheme, you can call OFCOM for details.

If you have a complaint about a premium rate number service, see *Helplines and premium rate phone lines*, below.

If you are still dissatisfied, OFCOM (020 7981 3040; www.ofcom.org.uk) or OTELO (the Office of the Telecommunications Ombudsman: 08450 501614; www.otelo.org.uk) may be able to investigate a complaint. OFCOM can investigate a complaint about any aspect of mobile phone services. OTELO will only be able to investigate if the telephone company is a member of OTELO and you have first used the company's own complaints procedure.

HELPLINES AND PREMIUM RATE PHONE LINES

If you get itemized phone bills, any calls to telephone helplines will be listed. This means that other people in the household with access to your bill will be able to see that you have phoned a helpline. Almost all phone service providers supply a last number redial service which means that other members of the household can check the last telephone number that was called.

Some phone service providers itemize only those calls above a certain limit and so, to protect confidentiality, you could make a very brief call to a helpline and ask them to call you back. Most helplines that do this do not use caller display equipment and they withhold their number when making or returning calls to customers. Calls to freephone numbers beginning 0800 or 0500 are not itemized on the phone bill unless made through a switchboard. If you do not want the helpline to know your telephone number, you should dial 141 before entering the helpline number. This works only if you get through to the helpline immediately; it does not work if you press a 'redial' key. Premium rate services give information and provide entertainment over the phone – for example, weather information, competitions and message exchange services.

Premium rate calls cost more than ordinary phone calls, and rates for calls from mobile phones, telephone boxes and hotels can be higher still. Charges from an ordinary domestic phone must be shown in the advert for the service. Most premium rate service numbers begin with 090 and services of an adult nature begin 0909. Directory Enquiry services which begin with '118' are also premium rate numbers.

You can bar any dialling from your phone line to all UK based 090 premium rate numbers. This will include calls from your home computer, if you have one. If you want to do this, you should contact your phone service provider.

If you have problems with premium rate phone services, contact Phonepay Plus on 0800 500212 (www.phonepayplus.org.uk).

POSTAL SERVICES

The Royal Mail operates to a code of practice and service standards that are described in the customer services section of their website (www.royalmail. com). You can also find out about Royal Mail service standards at your local post office. You can contact Post Office Customer Services (08457 740740) for help and advice about lost, delayed or damaged mail or to make a complaint. You can also e-mail a complaint via the website.

If you have made a complaint and you are not satisfied with the response you have received from Royal Mail, you can contact Postwatch (08456 013 265; www.postwatch.co.uk), the independent watchdog for postal services.

TELEVISION LICENCES

Everyone who uses a television set or DVD/video recorder needs a television licence. You will also need a licence if you use a computer that is capable of receiving authorized broadcast programmes (that is, the BBC, ITV, Channel 4, Channel 5, cable or satellite television). A television licence is not needed if the TV set cannot receive TV programmes and is used only for close circuit monitoring, for watching pre-recorded DVDs or videos, or as a computer monitor. You do need a licence to watch TV on a mobile phone or other battery-operated device.

A television licence allows the person named on it and any member of their household to use one or more television sets or DVD/video recorders. If you only have a black-and-white television, you only require a black-and-white television licence. If you have a colour television or a DVD/video recorder, you will require a colour television licence. This will apply even if the DVD/video recorder is used with a black-and-white television set.

There are set fees for colour and black-and-white television licences. These are increased annually. The increase is effective from midnight on the day of announcement. For details of current fees, contact your local post office or TV Licensing (0870 576 3763; www.tvlicensing.co.uk).

Rules for particular groups

People who are aged 75 or over

Free television licences are available for anyone who is 75 years old or over.

The TV licence reminder includes details of how to apply along with an application form for the free over-75 licence. There is a special helpline to answer queries on 0845 603 6999.

If you are 74, you can apply for a special short-term licence that lasts until you are 75.

People who are registered blind

If you are registered blind by the local authority, you will get a reduction in the cost of your television licence if you produce the local authority certificate or doctor's certification form when you buy the licence. The reduction is 50 per cent of the cost of a colour or black-and-white television licence. If you are registered as partially sighted, you cannot get a reduction.

A TV licence is not necessary in order to install or use a television sound-only receiver. These are made for blind people and are manufactured on behalf of the Royal National Institute for the Blind. Television sound-only receivers are available on loan from the British Wireless for the Blind (01634 832 501).

People living in care homes

If you live in one of the following, you may be entitled to a reduction in the cost of a television licence:

- a registered care home
- sheltered accommodation provided by the local authority or a housing association.

If you live in one of the above types of accommodation, you must also meet the following conditions to be eligible for a reduction in the cost of a television licence. You must:

- be fully retired and aged 60 or over. For people aged 75 years or over, see above; *or*
- have a physical or learning disability, or a mental illness.

This type of licence is called a licence for Accommodation for Residential Care (ARC). It is a group licence and must be applied for by the providers of the accommodation. It can only be obtained from TV Licensing (0870 576 3763; www.tvlicensing.co.uk). The provider of the accommodation is responsible for collecting the licence fee from each person covered by the ARC.

Students

If you are a full-time student living away from home, you will usually need a television licence. If you are living in a hall of residence and use a TV in your room you will need a separate TV licence. You will also need your own licence if you share a house with others but have a TV in your own room for which you have a separate tenancy agreement. If you have a separate tenancy agreement but there is only one TV being used in a communal area, only one licence is needed. If you share a house with others and have a joint tenancy agreement, you will only need one TV licence regardless of where the TV is located in the house.

Students can apply for a refund of an unused portion of their TV licence. If you have bought a licence at the beginning of the autumn term and do not remain in university accommodation or lodgings over the summer, you are entitled to a refund of any unused quarter (three full calendar months).

Buying a television licence

As soon as you get a television set or DVD/video recorder for which you need a licence, you are responsible for buying the licence. You can do this by phoning or writing to TV Licensing and asking for a form to complete. You will not be covered until the licence is issued, even if you have sent a completed application form and payment to TV Licensing. A licence issued for the first time will last for one year from the first day of the month of issue.

You can apply to renew a licence up to a month in advance. The new licence will last for one year from the original date of expiry, not from the date the licence is renewed.

It is the policy of TV Licensing to send reminders to renew licences, but they are under no legal obligation to do so and it is the responsibility of the licence holder to renew the licence. The absence of a reminder is not regarded as a valid excuse for not having a current licence. It is also the licence-holder's responsibility to tell TV Licensing if they move.

If you rent or buy a television set or DVD/video recorder, the trader is under a legal obligation to notify TV Licensing. This also applies if you change a rented black-and-white television for a colour television.

Paying for your TV licence annually

If you make an annual payment for your TV licence, you can pay by:

- cash, at a PayPoint outlet
- cheque, by post to TV Licensing
- debit card. This can be arranged by contacting TV Licensing
- direct debit from your bank account or credit card account. Contact TV Licensing to arrange this or sign up online using the TV Licensing website (www.tvlicensing.co.uk/dd). Direct debits will be made from your account annually, at the current licence fee rate.

Paying for your TV licence in instalments

There are several ways you can pay for your TV licence in instalments. You can pay by direct debit monthly. If you are buying a new licence, you will pay the whole cost over the first six months. After the first six months, you can start paying towards the next year's licence in 12 monthly instalments. Or you can pay by direct debit quarterly. You have to pay extra for this.

If you get benefits such as Income Support or if you are on a low income or if you do not have a bank account, you may be able to pay in weekly or fortnightly instalments. This is called the Cash Easy scheme. Or you could pay for your TV licence in instalments with a TV licensing savings card. You can top up the card by cash or debit card. To apply for a savings card, phone 0845 155 0325.

If you do not have a licence

You can be prosecuted if you do not have a TV licence. You can be prosecuted even if you are not the owner or hirer of the set. If TV Licensing decide to prosecute, the case will be heard in the magistrates' court. If you are found guilty, the maximum fine that can be imposed is £1,000. The court cannot confiscate the television set or order you to pay the television licence fee arrears.

Using a television set or DVD/video recorder away from home

If you have a television set or DVD/video recorder that you use at another address on a temporary basis – for example, at weekends or during holidays – you will need to have a separate licence for it. This is the case even if you already have a licence for a television in your main home.

Television sets or DVD/video recorders in rented accommodation (including guest houses and bed and breakfast)

In rented accommodation, the tenant is responsible for obtaining the licence unless the landlord installed the set, in which case the landlord is expected to obtain the licence. However, the user of the television set or video recorder will always be ultimately responsible for ensuring there is a television licence and could therefore be liable for prosecution. If you are the tenant, make sure there is a licence, either by ensuring the landlord buys the licence or by buying it yourself.

A landlord who lets more than one unit of accommodation with a television set or DVD/video recorder in the building for overnight, as opposed to long-term, accommodation, may be eligible for a hotel licence – see below. If a building is divided into bedsitters or flats, each separate unit of accommodation is regarded as one household unit. This means that each household unit with a set needs a separate television licence. Lodgers, paying guests and other residents, including relatives, who occupy separate accommodation at the same address count as separate households and need a separate licence for their own use of a television.

Where people jointly rent a flat or house, only one licence is required as long as they all live together as part of the same household, sharing all the facilities and the bills. People who live under this type of arrangement may have to produce evidence of this, such as the joint tenancy agreement. The licence will need to be in the name of one individual, and if that person leaves the flat they are entitled to take the licence and transfer it to their new address. A television licence is not transferable from one person to another except in the case of a free over-75 licence.

If a tenant installs a television set, their landlord is under no obligation to ensure that the tenant has a licence.

Television sets or DVD/video recorders in holiday accommodation (including caravans)

Television sets or DVD/video recorders installed by the landlord for the use of temporary guests on holiday must be licensed. A separate full licence must be obtained for each unit of accommodation with a television set or DVD/video recorder. For example, in a house divided into self-contained flats, each flat will need a licence. However, on a caravan site, the proprietor who owns the caravans may be eligible for a hotel licence. If you are a holidaymaker and have a set in a touring caravan, this will be covered by a licence for your home address. If the caravan is static, a licence for your home address provides sufficient coverage if television sets are not used at the same time at home and in the static caravan.

Television sets or DVD/video recorders in hotels

Hoteliers can obtain special comprehensive licences (hotel licences). Only one licence fee is required for television sets or DVD/video recorders provided by the hotelier in up to 15 rooms. Each additional licence fee will cover up to five more rooms. A room may have more than one television set or DVD/video recorder in it without affecting this rule. Guests and staff who are permanently resident in the premises will require separate licences to use their own sets in their rooms. More information about hotel licences can be obtained from TV Licensing.

If you do not use your television set or DVD/video recorder to watch or record authorized broadcast programmes

If you do not use your television set or DVD/video recorder to watch or record authorized broadcast programmes (that is, BBC, ITV, Channel 4, Channel 5, cable television or satellite television), you will not need a licence. This means that you would not need a licence if, for example, you only:

- use the television set as a computer monitor
- use the television set to play electronic games
- watch pre-recorded DVDs and videos, whether these have been bought or recorded by someone else on a licensed DVD/video recorder.

However, the television set or DVD/video recorder must be incapable of receiving all authorized broadcast programmes. This could be done, for example, by making sure that neither the television set nor the DVD/video recorder is tuned into any channels and ensuring that they are not connected to an aerial.

> ### I am going to university soon and I want to take my television with me. Do I need a separate licence?
>
> Most students will need a television licence. There are a few exceptions – for example, if the TV set cannot receive television programmes and you are only using it as a computer monitor. If you are living in a hall of residence and use a TV in your room, you will need your own licence. If you are living in a house with other people you will only need one licence if you all live as one household – that is, you share bills and kitchen and other facilities.
>
> If your house is divided into bedsits or flats with their own facilities, then each unit will need its own TV licence.

3
Consumer Affairs

CONTENTS

INTRODUCTION

There's no doubt about it: we live in a consumer society. Most of us make thousands of buying decisions every year, from choosing a plumber or where to go on holiday to deciding which insurance policy to go for, so understanding our rights as consumers is more important now than it has ever been.

The rights of the consumer really took off in the post-war 'never had it so good' boom of the 1950s, when almost full employment saw more people with more cash to spend. Coupled with that increased spending power was a massive increase in the production of consumer goods, alongside an explosion in the advertising and marketing industries. Add into the mix more recent moves away from state provision of pensions, and the privatization of many previously state-owned suppliers, such as water and energy, and, like it or not, we now make more personal choices over every area of our lives than ever before.

Cheaper foreign travel and the growth of the holiday industry have meant that we are also consumers abroad, bringing the added challenge of understanding foreign consumer law. And buying over the internet is now a fact of life for many of us. But do we understand our rights for this and other forms of distance selling?

This chapter looks at what our basic consumer rights are, how we can enforce them and how to decide what choices to make in the first place.

PROBLEMS WITH SOMETHING YOU HAVE BOUGHT

When you buy goods from a trader, the law says that they must be:

- of satisfactory quality. This means that the goods must be free from faults, including minor ones
- accurately described. It is a criminal offence for a trader to put a false description on goods
- fit for their purpose.

Technically speaking, if one or more of the above conditions is not met, it means that your consumer rights may have been breached.

If there is a problem with something you have bought, deciding what outcome you want is the best place to start. You may want to reject the goods and get a refund, compensation or both, or you may want the goods replaced or repaired. If the trader is not able to replace or repair the goods, you may be able to get some money back, or end the contract you made when you bought the goods.

Even if your statutory rights under consumer law have not been breached – for example, even if the champagne flutes you ordered for your daughter's wedding are of satisfactory quality, have been accurately described and are fit for the purpose, but arrived during the honeymoon – there are still things you can do to resolve your problem. You may be able to take action against the trader for breaking a specific condition of the contract – that is, the agreed delivery date. Or you may be able to use a trade association code of practice or guarantee to help you resolve the problem with your goods. If things have gone seriously wrong, you may need to claim compensation from a trader for injury or damage, and you may want to consider reporting the trader to Consumer Direct (0845 404 0506).

You won't have a case against the trader if:

- you examined the goods, or a sample of the goods, when you were buying them, and the fault you want to complain about was so obvious that you should have noticed it
- the trader pointed out the defect that you now want to complain about
- you have damaged the goods yourself.

There are other situations where you do not have your usual legal rights. These include private sales, business-to-business sales, and where goods have been given to you. Also these rights may not apply if you buy goods at auction (but make sure it is a genuine auction – see p. 338 for information about internet auctions).

Codes of practice

Some traders follow codes of practice. Although not legally binding, they can give you extra protection. If the trader is a member of a trade association and is not following the code of practice, the association may be able to put pressure on them to resolve the problem.

Some codes of practice include an alternative dispute resolution scheme, such as mediation, an ombudsman or an arbitration scheme. If you go to arbitration the outcome is legally binding.

Getting a refund for goods

Goods bought from a shop must be of satisfactory quality, accurately described and fit for their purpose. If any of these conditions is not met, then you may have a legal right to reject the goods and get your money back.

You are allowed a short time to examine goods and try them out, but you must tell the trader about the fault as soon as you discover it. If you know you won't be able to get back to the shop for a few days, you should telephone to let the seller know there's a problem and that you want a refund. If you have kept an item for several weeks without properly checking it and then discover a problem or fault, you might have difficulty in getting a refund because you would have had what is called 'reasonable' time to use the goods. To make matters more complicated, there is no legal definition of what a 'reasonable' time is.

There are some types of sale to which these legal rights do not apply. For example, if you bought the goods from a private individual, you only have a legal right to get your money back if the seller described them wrongly. Also you will not be able to get a full refund if you have continued to use the goods or tried to repair them in some way, so think twice before you do this.

There are some 'grey area' situations in which you may not get a full refund, even if it looks as though one of your consumer rights has been breached – for example, if the goods are faulty, but you have been using them for some time before they show signs of being faulty. In that case, the trader may offer you some money as compensation, instead of a full refund. They may offer you alternatives, such as a repair or an exchange.

Some traders refer you to the manufacturer or say that you should claim on the guarantee. However, you do not have to accept this and you would still be entitled to ask for financial compensation. Remember: it is the person who sold you the goods who is responsible for sorting your problem out, and not the manufacturer, so don't be pushed into claiming on a maker's guarantee, unless you want to.

If you want a refund but the trader does not offer one, you can go to court or use an alternative dispute resolution scheme to enforce your rights. Both these procedures can be straightforward and do not usually need a solicitor; a Citizens Advice Bureau (CAB) will give you the information and advice you need to enforce your legal rights.

When you buy something, the trader may give you additional rights over and above those that the law allows you. For example, some shops allow you to return items to them during a short period after the sale, even if there is nothing wrong with them. Because the shop offers this in addition to your legal rights, you will often be given a credit note or an exchange rather than cash back.

I bought a DVD player in a sale and it's faulty. Can I ask for my money back?

You have just as much right to expect the item that you are buying to be of good quality as if you had bought the item before the sale. The only difference with sale items is that if they were clearly marked as 'shop soiled' or imperfect you would not be able to ask for a refund because you would have been aware when you bought the item that it was not going to be perfect.

All legal rights still apply to goods bought in a sale. They must be of satisfactory quality, fit for the purpose you are buying them for and as described on packaging or labels. That means that if a saucepan is described as non-stick, the egg you are frying should not stick to it, and the 100 per cent cotton blouse you buy should be exactly that.

Repair or replacement of goods – the six-year rule

If one of your rights under consumer law has been breached, you can ask the trader for a free repair or replacement. You can ask for a repair or replacement at any time within six years of buying the goods, as long as it is reasonable for them to have lasted that long. Taking back a T-shirt to a market stall after five and a half years and expecting a replacement is probably not reasonable! If you don't discover the problem within six years of buying the goods, you will not be able to claim a repair or a replacement.

If the trader does not agree that there was a problem with the goods at the time of sale, it is the trader's responsibility to prove this if you have complained within six months of receiving the goods. If you make your complaint after six months, it is your responsibility to show that the problem existed at the time of sale.

A trader who agrees to carry out a repair or provide a replacement must do so within a reasonable period of time, and without causing you any significant inconvenience. If you ask the trader for a repair but this turns out to be impractical or too expensive, the trader will not be obliged to repair your goods, but you can choose to have a replacement instead. In the same way, if you have asked the trader to replace your goods and this turns out to be impractical or too expensive, the trader will not be obliged to replace your goods, but you can choose to have a repair instead.

If neither repair nor replacement is practical, you may be able to get the price reduced, or even to get a full refund if:

- it is impossible to replace or repair the goods
- replacing or repairing the goods would cost more than reducing the price or giving you a full refund
- the trader did not replace the goods or repair them within a reasonable period of time, or was not able to do so without causing you significant inconvenience.

You are likely to get the price reduced if the goods had performed well up until the point when you stopped being able to use them. If you have been unable to use the goods at all, you may be able to give them back and get a full refund.

Compensation for dangerous goods

If you have bought dangerous or faulty goods that have caused damage to property or personal injury to you or someone else, you can claim additional compensation to cover the costs of the damage, as well as getting some money back because the goods were unsatisfactory. Dangerous goods should be reported to Consumer Direct (0845 404 0506).

Compensation for delivery delays

If you have been given a date for delivery, your goods must be delivered by that date. If they are not delivered by then, the trader will have broken their agreement with you and you are entitled to ask for compensation.

If you have not been given a proper date for the delivery, you will not be able to claim compensation. However, if you think you have waited a reasonable time and the goods still have not arrived, you should write to the trader, giving a firm date for delivery. This is called 'making time of the essence'. If the trader does not keep to this date, you can claim compensation.

If you bought your goods by distance sale – for example by mail order or over the internet – your rights will be different.

When you claim compensation for late delivery, the trader may offer you a fixed sum of money. However, you can make additional claims for other losses on top of this, such as the costs of taking a day off work while you were waiting for goods which didn't arrive.

As well as claiming compensation, you would also be entitled to cancel your order and get your money back.

I ordered a scooter for my little boy's birthday, which was last week, and it hasn't turned up. Is there anything I can do to make up for his disappointment?

Under consumer law, delivery dates don't form part of your contract with the trader. However, if you agreed a specific delivery date with the trader and the scooter still failed to arrive, you might consider taking legal action to get some sort of compensation.

Goods that are damaged during delivery

The trader is responsible for goods bought until they are delivered to you. If your goods have been damaged during delivery, you should complain to the trader.

Credit notes and goods

You cannot insist on a credit note, and you do not have to accept a credit note if one is offered. However, if you accept a credit note, you cannot change your mind later and get a full refund, or compensation, even if you were entitled to it.

A credit note does not have to take any particular form. It may be offered as a gift voucher and it can also have conditions attached to it. You may have to use it within a given time limit.

Check the conditions on the credit note and make sure that the trader has goods that you want to buy.

> *I have found a hole in the sleeve of a jumper I bought last weekend and am planning to take it back to the shop. Do I have to accept a credit note?*
>
> If you take goods back to the seller because they are of unsatisfactory quality, not fit for their purpose or do not match their description, you do not have to accept a credit note and you are within your legal rights to ask for your money back.
>
> However, if you accept a credit note when you were entitled to your money back, you cannot later change your mind unless you can prove that you were forced to accept the credit note by the seller.
>
> If you have taken goods back to a seller because you simply changed your mind about them – for example you don't like the colour – then you would have no legal right to ask for your money back. If the seller is offering you a credit note in these circumstances they are doing more than is required by the law.

Guarantees, warranties, servicing and spares

You have no automatic right to a guarantee, a warranty or servicing. In general, a guarantee is given to you free when you buy goods. You often pay for a warranty or a service contract. There is no law that says that spare parts for goods must be available for any length of time, or even at all.

If there is a guarantee or warranty, it may give you rights in addition to your normal legal rights. Guarantees and warranties often have terms and conditions attached to them which limit what they offer you.

However, it might be easier for you to claim under a guarantee or warranty where the trader is refusing to give you what you want, or if you have no legal rights against them. If you have bought goods in a distance sale (over the internet or by telephone, for example), it can be more convenient for you to claim on the guarantee or warranty. Guarantees and warranties can be very useful if you have problems with goods and the trader has gone out of business. Guarantees given free with goods must be written in clear English and be available for you to see. The conditions of the guarantee are legally binding. Both free guarantees and guarantees you pay for may offer you protection in addition to your legal rights.

If a trader sells extended warranties (sometimes called service agreements) to cover domestic electrical goods such as computers, fridges or washing machines, they must display the price of the warranty alongside the goods. You can ask the trader to give you a written quotation for the price of a warranty. They have to honour this quotation if you go back to buy the warranty after you have bought the goods as long as you do this within 30 days of buying the goods. The trader must also inform you of your rights to buy a warranty elsewhere and that the electrical item you bought may already be covered by your own household contents insurance.

If you do choose to buy the warranty from the trader, you have the right to cancel within 45 days and get a full refund, as long as you have not made a claim. If you make a claim on the warranty, you can still cancel and get a pro-rata refund at any time up until the end of the service agreement.

> ## My new washing machine has come with a guarantee. What exactly does this cover?
>
> A guarantee is extra protection over and above your legal rights when you buy an item. The seller does not have to give you a guarantee.
>
> Guarantees given free with goods must be written in clear English and be available for you to see. The conditions of the guarantee are legally binding.
>
> In some cases a guarantee allows you to have faulty goods repaired or replaced. Giving a guarantee does not mean that the seller can ignore your legal rights as a customer – for example, your right to get your money back in certain circumstances if there is a problem with the goods.

If a trader tries to ignore a customer's legal rights they may be committing a criminal offence, in which case you could contact Consumer Direct (0845 404 0506).

What you can do if you have no rights under consumer law

Even if you have no rights you can enforce under consumer law, perhaps because your goods weren't faulty when you bought them, or because more than six years have gone by since you bought them, there are still a few things you could try to get what you want. For example:

- you can try and negotiate with the trader for what you want – you may be able to get a good result
- you can choose to accept a credit note from the trader
- you can use your additional rights under a guarantee, if you have one
- if the trader is a member of a trade association, you may be able to ask that trade association to put pressure on the trader. Some trade association codes of practice include an alternative dispute resolution scheme. These schemes use a third party, such as a mediator or ombudsman, to help the parties reach a solution.

How to go about getting what you want

Once you have decided what outcome you want – for example, refund, repair, replacement or compensation – you will need to contact the trader to put your case. If you approach the trader in the early stages and prepare your case well, your negotiations are more likely to have a successful outcome. You should put together all the information that you will need to pursue your case. This includes information on whether you have any rights in the situation and, if so, what they are.

You will need:

- a description of the goods. This includes anything that was said to you, anything in an advert or anything given to you in writing
- some details about the trader. If the person who sells you the goods is a private individual, you have fewer legal rights
- details of the problem with the goods
- details of how long you have had the goods, or, if you have not had the goods at all, when you were supposed to have received them

- details of when you first noticed the problem
- details of whether the goods have caused any damage to people or property
- details of what you have done about the problem, if anything
- if you have already approached the trader, details of what was said
- copies of any documents – for example, an order form, credit agreement or price quotation
- copies of instructions, an advertisement or a guarantee
- if you have paid anything, a note of how much, together with any bills or receipts
- a note of how you were to pay for the goods, for example by cheque, cash or credit
- copies of any letters between you and the trader, dealing with the problem
- details of where you were when you made the agreement – for example, in a shop, at home, or at work.

Write to the person who sold you the goods first of all, at the address of the shop or the catalogue where you bought them, or e-mail the website if you bought them over the internet. Keep a copy of your letter or e-mail. If the trader has a head office address, send a copy of your letter there. If you bought the goods on credit, send a copy of your letter to the credit company.

Your letter or e-mail to the trader should say:

- what you bought and when, with a full description of the goods and reference numbers if possible
- how much you paid
- what the problems are, and when you first discovered them
- what solution you would like – for example, a full refund, a replacement, a repair, or compensation.

You should also give the trader a firm date by which to reply to you. The date that you give should usually be 7–14 days after you send the letter.

You may prefer to phone the trader, or go and talk to them. Even if you get nowhere with this approach, it is always a good idea to follow up a visit or a phone call with a letter or an e-mail. The letter or e-mail should follow the format suggested above.

Credit where credit's due

If you bought goods costing more than £100 and less than £30,000 on credit, you may be able to enforce your rights against the com-

> pany that gave you the credit, instead of the trader. This can be use-
> ful in situations where you have a claim against the trader who sold
> you the goods, but they have gone out of business or have no
> money to compensate you.

If you've tried negotiating with a trader but are not successful, you may want to consider going to court. Before taking legal action, you should make sure that you have tried all other options for resolving your dispute, like alternative dispute resolution (ADR).

CRIMINAL OFFENCES AND THE SALE OF GOODS

It is a criminal offence for a trader to:

- discriminate on the grounds of sex, race, sexuality, disability or religion when supplying goods
- make a written statement that you have no legal rights
- put a false description on goods
- ignore the safety laws
- try to charge for goods sent that you did not order
- sell short measure or short weight
- give a misleading price, either in writing or verbally.

These are only some of the criminal offences relating to the sale of goods. If you think that a trader has committed a criminal offence, you should report the matter as soon as possible to Consumer Direct (0845 404 0506).

WHAT YOU CAN DO IF THE SUPPLIER GOES OUT OF BUSINESS

Sole traders, partnerships and limited companies

If the supplier of the goods or services has gone out of business, the action you can take will depend on whether the supplier was a limited company, an individual (sole trader) or a partnership. If you have a guarantee, you may find it easier to claim under the guarantee.

Sole trader/partnership

If you were dealing with a sole trader or a partnership, they remain liable even if they have ceased trading. You should continue to negotiate with the owner or partner and could consider suing for compensation if your negotiations fail. Before you take court action, you will need to find out whether the trader is able to pay. If the trader has gone personally bankrupt, there is not much point pursuing them through the courts. If you have already lost money on faulty goods or services, it is not worth losing more money on suing someone who cannot pay you.

Limited company

If the supplier is a limited company, it may have gone into administration or liquidation. Administration is where an administrator is appointed to take control of all the company's assets and sell them for the best possible price. This may mean selling the business as a going concern. However, the company may subsequently have to go into liquidation. A limited company may go into 'voluntary' liquidation following a shareholders' decision that the company is no longer solvent, or go into liquidation because of a court order. Once the company is in liquidation, a liquidator will be appointed to collect and redistribute all the company's assets using the rules set out in the insolvency laws. This is known as winding up. Once the winding up is complete, the liquidator sends the final accounts to the Registrar of Companies and the company is considered to be dissolved (gone out of business) three months later.

Disappeared off the face of the earth?

If you no longer have contact details for the business you have a problem with, contact Consumer Direct (0845 404 0506). If it has them, it may be able to pass contact details on to you for the purposes of court action.

Is the supplier in administration or liquidation?

You can find out whether a supplier is in administration or liquidation and details of the administrator or liquidator from one of the following sources:

- Consumer Direct (see above)
- a local traders' association or chamber of commerce
- a trade association (if the trader was a member)

- Companies House (0870 3333 636; www.companieshouse.co.uk) will tell you whether a company is in liquidation, free of charge
- local firms of accountants or solicitors who deal with administrations
- the local Official Receiver's office.

When a company is in administration or liquidation, you cannot insist that the administrator or liquidator sort out your problem but you should make a claim for compensation, which will only be met if there are assets left after the priority creditors have been paid in full. If the company is a member of a trade association, it may have a bonding scheme that covers you for this situation. For example, the Association of British Travel Agents (ABTA) will repatriate stranded travellers if their travel agency goes into liquidation.

You will have to negotiate with the administrator or liquidator to solve problems, such as:

- return of deposit. You are entitled to ask for your deposit returned, but this is unlikely to happen unless there is any money left after all the secured or priority creditors such as the company's landlord and HM Revenue and Customs have been paid. You should write to the administrator or liquidator enclosing proof such as a receipt, cheque stub or credit card voucher and keep a copy of your letter
- delivery of goods ordered. If the goods you ordered have been earmarked for you by the supplier (for example, they have placed your name on them), you are entitled to have them and should contact the administrator or liquidator to prevent them from being sold. If not, you may be able to negotiate with the administrator to sell you the goods, but cannot insist that this happens. If the company goes into liquidation, the liquidator may sell the goods to raise sufficient money to pay the priority creditors, but will sell you the goods if they are still available once the priority creditors have been paid. You are unlikely to be given a guarantee, but may wish to accept the goods and pay the balance, if they are covered by a manufacturer's guarantee
- work not carried out. If a company has gone into administration, you may be able to have any work it was doing for you completed. You should contact the administrator to see if this is possible, but cannot insist that it happens. Should the company go into liquidation, the liquidator will not be able to guarantee the work and you will have to decide whether to have the work done without a guarantee or lose your deposit. You may be able to negotiate a reduction in price to compensate you for the inconvenience and loss of a guarantee. You can only claim compensation for breach of contract once the secured creditors have been paid in full. If the company is in liquidation, you can make a claim for compensation, but cannot insist that work be carried out. If the company is a member of a trade association, it may have a deposit

protection scheme that allows for the work to be completed by another of its members

- unsatisfactory goods or services. If the company is in administration and the goods are faulty, the administrator may arrange to have the goods repaired or the work remedied or completed. You should contact the administrator to see if this is possible, but cannot insist. If the administrator refuses, you will find it difficult to enforce your rights, as there are unlikely to be sufficient assets to pay compensation. If the company has been sold as a going concern, you will have to negotiate with the new owner, who will take over the company's assets but not its liabilities. You cannot enforce a guarantee or maintenance agreement, but the new owner may agree to honour the guarantee or agreement if it appears beneficial to do so
- goods held by the company. If your goods are being held by a company, for example awaiting a repair, you have a right to have them returned. You should write to the administrator or liquidator asking for their immediate return and for an undertaking that they will be kept safe until returned.

WHAT TO DO IF THERE ARE PROBLEMS WITH SERVICES YOU HAVE ORDERED

Services are everything from work done by professionals, such as solicitors, estate agents and accountants, to leaving a coat in a cloakroom, or using a parking space, in return for payment.

If the plumber's been but the tap still drips, you are entitled to have matters put right. It is the seller of the services who is responsible for sorting the problem out. Services must be performed with reasonable care and skill; they must be done within a reasonable time and you must be charged a reasonable price.

If you are unhappy with work that has been done for you, decide what it is that you want from the trader – do you want your money back, a repair, the service done again or the job finished? You may want to claim under a guarantee, or just pay less or not pay at all.

If things have gone seriously wrong, you may want to claim compensation from a trader for injury or damage, or even to see the trader prosecuted.

Problems can often be sorted out in the early stages and most negotiations end successfully, especially if you have prepared your case well.

You are entitled to inspect the service and examine any goods that are supplied with it, so check those new taps work before the plumber leaves your house. You must tell the service provider if you see any faults as soon as you discover them. If you want to stop the service, you should do so straight away, and discuss the problem with the trader.

The law does not say that you must allow the trader a chance to put things right. However, it would be reasonable of you to suggest it and you should not let someone else alter things or do repairs unless it is an emergency. If you want someone else to carry on with the work, you should get two or three estimates of the cost, and choose the cheapest one. You may be able to claim for extra expenses from the original trader, but they must always be reasonable.

Write to the trader first of all at their address, or e-mail the website if you contacted the trader over the internet.

Keep a copy of your letter or e-mail. If the trader has a head office address, send a copy of your letter there. If you bought the services on credit, send a copy of your letter to the credit company.

Your letter or e-mail should say:

- what was to be done, and what goods were to be used, if any
- how much you have paid so far, or were going to pay
- what the problems are – in detail – and when you first discovered them
- that you are stopping the service and you want a full refund, together with any compensation for extra expenses.

You should also give a trader a firm date by which to reply. The date that you give is usually seven or 14 days after you send the letter.

You may prefer to phone the trader, or go and talk to them. Even if you get nowhere with this, it is always a good idea to follow up a visit or a phone call with a letter or an e-mail. The letter or e-mail should follow the format suggested above.

Refunds for services

You are entitled by law to have a full refund only in certain circumstances. If the problem is serious, and the service is a total failure, you can get back any money that you have paid. If you are entitled to a full refund because something has gone seriously wrong with the service, you may also be able to claim additional compensation to cover the extra costs of putting things right. This could include, for example, site clearance before building or landscaping work starts again. If the trader has caused damage to property or personal injury to you or someone else, compensation may be awarded to cover the costs of damage.

You will not be entitled to a full refund if there is nothing seriously wrong with the service. However, you may be able to claim some money as compensation if there are minor faults, if you have been overcharged, or if the trader has taken an exceptionally long time to carry out the service. The trader may offer you a repair, or suggest that you can claim under a guarantee. These may be practical solutions, and you may want to accept them, but you are still entitled to ask for some money back. However, the amount of compensation you can get will probably be less than the value of a repair or replacement.

The trader may refuse to refund you, even if you have the legal right to ask for your money back. They may offer you alternatives such as repairs, or starting the service again. Some traders claim that the problem lies with the manufacturer of the goods they are using.

If you want a refund and the trader does not offer one, you can go to court, or use an alternative dispute resolution procedure to enforce your rights. Both these procedures can be straightforward and do not usually need a solicitor.

Goods bought with services

If you bought goods with services, you are entitled to examine the goods. If you find something wrong with them, you must tell the trader immediately. You can refuse to accept the goods, cancel the service and ask for your money back, but only if you do this within a very short time after the goods are delivered. If the trader does not agree that there is something wrong, it will be up to you to prove that there is.

If you are not entitled to a full refund or you do not want to cancel the service, you may be entitled to get some of your money back, or to a free repair or replacement instead. You will only have these options if you bought the goods from the same person who installed them. You do not have these options if you bought the goods from one person and had them installed by another.

> ### My favourite suede jacket has been comprehensively trashed at the dry-cleaners. What can I do about it?
>
> First, remember that dry-cleaning may not remove all stains and may highlight existing wear, like the weakening of curtains by

exposure to sunlight. If your jacket has been poorly cleaned, you can ask for a refund. The law says that a dry-cleaning service should be carried out with reasonable care and skill so you have a right to expect this. If the cleaner offers to re-clean the item, it is reasonable to let them do that. If that doesn't work, you may be entitled to compensation. You may also be entitled to compensation if the cleaner was negligent – for example, advised you that your jacket was safe to be dry-cleaned when it wasn't, and now it is in tatters.

If you cannot agree on what has caused the fault or who is to blame, find out whether the firm is a member of a trade association like the Textiles Services Association (020 8863 7755; www.tsa-uk.org). The TSA has an informal conciliation service that will attempt to resolve the matter. If this fails, they may suggest assessment by an independent test house. There will be a charge for this, and the fee will be paid by the losing party. If the dry-cleaner makes an alternative offer, be realistic about what you will accept. You may not get a better offer by going to court. Always keep dry-cleaning tickets, as you may have difficulty claiming your property without them.

Delays in starting and finishing services

Been waiting in all week for the builders to start work on the conservatory? If the trader has not started work in a reasonable time from the date of the order, or finished within a reasonable time from the date of starting, you can make 'time of the essence' of your agreement. Write to the trader, giving a firm but reasonable date by which to start or finish. What is 'reasonable' depends on the circumstances – for example, the conditions in the trade concerned and whether the delay was due to circumstances beyond the trader's control.

Once you have a proper date for the start or completion of the services, and these dates have been missed, you can claim compensation from the trader. They may offer you a fixed amount, but you can also claim for the real losses of waiting for the work to be done – for example, the costs of time off work, or of employing someone else to do the job. If you want to bring in someone else, you should get three estimates of what it will cost to do the work, and send them to the trader.

You could also cancel the agreement, and ask for your money back. However, you may have to go to court or use an alternative dispute resolution scheme to enforce your claim.

GUARANTEES, WARRANTIES AND MAINTENANCE CONTRACTS

You have no automatic legal right to a guarantee, warranty or maintenance agreement. In general, a guarantee is given to you free when you buy goods or services. You often pay for a warranty or a maintenance contract.

If there is a guarantee or warranty, it may give you rights in addition to your usual legal rights. Guarantees and warranties often have terms and conditions attached to them and set limits on what they offer you.

A trader may give you manufacturers' guarantees or warranties on goods that they installed as part of a service. These may be useful if the trader has gone out of business, so that you can no longer claim against them. But if you claim under a guarantee or warranty you may have to pay for someone else to come and do any necessary work – for example, to replace a double-glazed window if the seal has blown within the guarantee period.

COOLING-OFF PERIODS AND YOUR RIGHTS TO CANCEL

You may be legally entitled to a 'cooling-off' period. This is the right to cancel within a certain period of time, usually quite short. If you cancel within the agreed time, you will not have to pay anything.

If you buy goods from a trader without having face-to-face contact with them – for example, by telephone or over the internet (called distance selling) – you have a *seven-day* cooling-off period in which to cancel the agreement.

If you buy goods from someone face-to-face but away from trade premises (called doorstep selling), you have an automatic right to a *seven-day* cooling-off period in which to cancel the agreement. There are some exceptions to this general rule – for example, when a service includes new building works such as a conservatory. To be able to cancel, you must not have invited the sales person to your home.

There are different rules about cancelling if you signed a credit agreement at home. When you buy a service on credit in your own home after a face-to-face discussion with the seller, you are entitled to a cooling-off period, as long as the goods cost more than £35. This means you may be able to change your mind and cancel the order without having to pay anything. You have this right, regardless of whether or not you invited the salesperson to call.

After signing the agreement, you should be given a copy of the credit agreement clearly setting out your cancellation rights. You should also receive by post a second written notification of your cancellation rights. The cooling-off period begins on the day you sign the agreement and ends *five days* after you have received the second notification of your cancellation rights.

If you wish to cancel your credit agreement, send your letter or the notice by recorded delivery and keep a copy of your letter.

BUYING OVER THE INTERNET, BY TELEPHONE AND BY MAIL ORDER

Goods that are bought by the following means are all examples of 'distance sales':

- by telephone or fax
- by mail order
- electronically through the internet, e-mail or digital television (see p. 338 for the rules about internet auctions)
- through a shopping channel, or teletext
- from a catalogue
- through a newspaper or magazine advert order form.

If you buy goods in any of these ways from a UK-based trader, you have rights *in addition* to those you have when you buy goods in a shop. These include the right:

- to be given the name and address of the trader
- to be given the price of the goods, including taxes and delivery charges
- to be given a cooling-off period of seven working days and information about your right to cancel the order. You may not have this right to cancel if you agreed to the service starting within seven days of placing your order
- to receive the goods within 30 days.

If you use a credit card to buy goods in any of these ways, you also get special protection against the fraudulent use of your credit card details.

> ## I've had a personal letter telling me that I've won a prize in a lottery. How can I find out whether it's genuine or not?
>
> If you find that you have unexpectedly won an exciting prize in a prize draw, lottery or other form of promotion you should be suspicious. While some of these approaches are genuine, some are dishonest attempts to trap you into parting with your money. Many common scams take the form of prize draws or lotteries designed to trick the unwary. Scams are usually based outside the UK, although they may use UK Post Office boxes.
>
> You can find out about common scams on the Office of Fair Trading website (www.oft.gov.uk).

Buying over the internet

When you buy goods over the internet from a UK-based company, you have the same rights as if you bought them from a shop.

You also have additional rights when you buy over the internet, including the right to:

- clear information before you decide to buy, including the name of the seller and the price of the goods, including 'extras' like VAT or delivery charges. If you pay any money before the goods are delivered, the seller must also give you their full postal address, either in a letter, fax, e-mail or on the website
- cancel your order at any time up to seven working days after you received your goods and get your money back, although you might have to pay to return them. You cannot cancel if the goods were made to order, perishable, newspapers, or software, audio or video recordings which have been unsealed
- have the goods delivered within 30 days of ordering, unless you and the seller agreed otherwise. If the seller realizes later they cannot deliver within the time, they must give you the option of cancelling and getting a full refund
- protection from fraud if you pay by a credit, debit or store card. If someone uses your card fraudulently you can cancel the payment and the card issuer must refund all the money to your account.

These rights *do not* apply when buying:

- financial services, such as insurance or banking (although you may have other rights if you buy some types of financial services over the internet – for example, certain types of loans)

- timeshare agreements (although there are other laws that protect you when you buy a timeshare)
- services such as accommodation, catering or leisure services that you order for a certain date.

Also, these rights may not apply when buying goods at an online auction – see p. 338

If the goods are damaged when they are delivered or are substantially different from their description on the website, you are entitled to ask for a full refund, including the cost of all postage and packaging. Faulty goods are not subject to the return time limit, but you must contact the seller within a reasonable time.

More about e-commerce

In addition to the rights mentioned above, there may be other rules that apply to traders who sell using electronic commerce, or e-commerce, which includes selling by e-mail, on the internet, by interactive TV, or by sending and receiving written information on a mobile phone. Your rights will depend on the law of the country where the trader is based. All traders based in the UK or another EU country must follow certain rules, even if the customer is in a different EU country when buying the goods or services. See p. 501 for a list of EU countries. There are a few exceptions to these rules (for example, betting or lotteries) but generally all electronic promotional material must contain certain information and must be correctly presented. It must, for example, identify the trader who sent the message, and you must be given in a permanent, easily accessible way the name of the trader, a postal address and an e-mail address. The price of goods must state whether it includes tax and delivery costs. The trader usually has to provide a facility that allows you to identify and correct any errors that were made when inputting the order.

There is a voluntary membership scheme called Euro-label for traders in EU countries who use websites to sell goods and services. Its members must comply with a code of conduct and, if you have a dispute with a trader who is a member, you could use the Euro-label dispute resolution scheme. You can find them at www.euro-label.com.Internet

Internet auction sites

This information is about your rights when you *buy* goods from a website calling itself an internet auction site. It does not cover your rights if you are *selling* goods through one of these sites.

There are different types of sale available on internet auction sites. Some are auction-style sales involving bidding for items, while others, such as *Buy-it-now* on eBay, are not auction sales at all. Your rights will depend on the type of sale, who you buy from and where the site is based. Your rights also depend on whether any extra protection is available through the terms and conditions of the site, or through the method of payment you have used.

When you buy something from an internet auction site, you are usually buying from the seller, not the site, and it is the seller you will need to complain to if something goes wrong. The seller could be a private individual, or a business trader. As a general rule, you will have more rights if the seller is a business trader than if they are a private individual, although it may not always be possible to tell if the seller is a business trader. You may be buying from a business trader if, for example, there is a large number of similar items for sale or the items for sale are mostly new. Another example is if the items are being sold in a 'shop' within the site or have 'power-seller' status on eBay.

If the seller is a business trader, you have at least as many rights as if you had bought the goods in a shop – see p. 318.

As well as your normal consumer rights, you also have some extra rights when you buy goods online from a business trader. For example, you have the right to be given the name and address of the business trader before you place your order.

You may also have some additional rights because you have bought something from a trader without having face-to-face contact with them. You will get these additional rights when:

- the items are sold at a fixed price (for example, *Buy-it-now* on eBay)
- the items are being offered by auction, but you use an instant purchase option to buy
- you are the losing bidder for an item in an auction sale which has been re-offered to you after the winning bidder failed to pay
- it is a sham auction. It is likely to be a sham auction where the item is widely available elsewhere and where the opening bid amount is not much lower than what you would normally pay for the item.

The most important extra right you have when you buy online from a business trader in one of these ways is the right to a 'cooling off' period. This means you can cancel your order if you change your mind about wanting the goods. You can do this within seven working days after the day the goods are delivered. You can cancel your order within this period, even if there is nothing wrong with the goods, and get all your money back, including the original postage charge.

If you used your credit card to buy something from a business trader on an internet auction site, you may be able to make a claim against the credit card company instead of the trader if there is something wrong with the goods.

When you buy something on an internet auction site from a private individual, you have very few rights. You cannot complain if the goods are not of satisfactory quality or fit for the purpose you bought them. Also, you do not have the right to cancel your order, or any of the other extra rights you get when you buy on an internet auction site from a business trader without having face-to-face contact.

However, you do still have the right to complain to the seller if your goods do not match the description they have given on the website. This applies to second-hand as well as new goods. If the goods do not match the description, you may be entitled to compensation from the seller. But you might need to go to court to try and get this, and even if you win your case, the seller might not have enough money to pay you.

Options for solving your problem

Some internet sites have a protection scheme. These schemes can deal with problems such as non-delivery of goods or goods not matching their description. They can be useful if you want to avoid going to court, or the seller is from overseas, so it is worth checking if you can make a claim under one of these schemes.

However, you need to bear in mind the following:

- you may only have a very short period of time in which to make a claim
- there may be several types of problem which the scheme does not cover
- the amount of money you can claim on the scheme might be limited
- the number of claims you can make on the scheme may be limited
- you may have to try other options for solving your problem first – for example, making a claim through your credit card provider, if you paid by credit card.

To make a claim, you will also need to have followed the auction-site rules, policies or user agreement. This means that you will not be able to claim if you dealt with the seller directly through e-mail instead of through the site.

Some internet sites offer a dispute resolution service. This is a scheme which will help you and the seller try to reach an agreement. Some schemes involve the services of trained mediators and will charge a fee.

Many payments for things bought on internet auction sites are now made through special payment services, such as PayPal. Payment services will collect your money and do not release it to the seller until you have received your goods.

These services can be useful, but they do offer very different levels of protection for your money. Look carefully at the terms and conditions to find out what the scheme does or does not do. You may have to pay a fee to use a payment protection scheme, so it is important to shop around for the best one.

When you use an online payment service, you may find that your payments are not fully protected in some circumstances – for example, if you are dealing with sellers from overseas. You may also find that you are not protected if:

- fraud is involved
- you did not complain within the time limits, which are sometimes very short
- you entered into a deal with the seller outside the internet site.

Many card networks, including credit cards and charge cards, operate *chargeback* arrangements. This means that, in some circumstances, you may be able to get a payment reversed. Check with your credit or charge card provider whether they operate chargeback arrangements.

Chargeback time limits can be tight and the schemes may not cover all types of claim. However, where they do operate, they will apply to payments made to overseas as well as UK sellers.

If you have a problem with the seller and you cannot trace them, contact the website. The site may be able to give you the seller's details. There is nothing in law which prevents them from doing this. However, they do not have to give you the seller's details if they do not want to.

If the seller appears to operate their own website with their own domain name, it may be possible to find out how to contact them by searching on a 'Who is' search engine, such as www.samspade.org, www.truewhois.com or www.nominet.org.uk (UK domains only).

If you suspect that fraud is involved in an internet auction site, you should report it to Consumer Direct (0845 404 05 06). They can also give you advice about what you can do. You can also report the fraud to the police and to the auction site. There are a number of things the site can do about someone who is acting outside the rules of the site, including suspending their account.

Mail order goods which do not arrive

If mail order goods are not delivered by the agreed date or within 30 days, you have the right to cancel the order and get your money back.

If you paid for the goods in advance and the seller has gone out of business, you might get your money back if the seller is a member of the Safe Home Ordering Protection Scheme (SHOPS: 01628 641930; www.shops-uk.org.uk) or the Periodical Publishers Association (PPA: 020 7404 4166; www.ppa.co.uk). Check the advert to see if it has the logo of one of these associations. If it does, write to the advertising manager of the publication in which the advertisement appeared within three months of the date of the publication, giving the seller's name and address, the publication date of the newspaper or magazine, the date you placed the order, how much you paid and a summary of any action you have already taken.

Who can help?

Many large companies that sell through catalogues belong to the **Mail Order Traders' Association** (MOTA: 020 7735 3410; www.mota.org.uk) and its members have to comply with a code of practice. MOTA also runs an independent arbitration scheme which you can use if you cannot resolve the problem directly with the trader. There is a small charge for using the scheme, although this would be refunded if the arbitration finds in your favour.

Many of the companies that advertise through direct marketing, which includes book and music clubs, charities, motoring associations and companies that advertise through inserts placed in magazines or papers, belong to the **Direct Marketing Association** (DMA: 020 7291 3300; www.dma.org.uk). DMA runs an independent arbitration scheme which you can use if you cannot resolve the problem directly with the trader.

There is a small charge for using the scheme, although this would be refunded if the arbitration finds in your favour.

All mail order advertisements that appear in the UK must be legal, decent, honest and truthful. If you think a mail order advertisement describes goods or services in a misleading way in order to sell them, you should contact the **Advertising Standards Authority** (ASA: 020 7492 2222; www.asa.org.uk).

BUYING ON THE DOORSTEP

If you buy goods or services from a trader who visits your home – for example from a door-to-door salesperson or a double-glazing representative – or if you buy from a home party or party plan sale, you have the same rights as if you bought them from a shop. The goods must match their description (if a pair of sheets is described as fitted then they must be fitted) and must be of satisfactory quality. This means the goods meet the standards that any reasonable person would expect, taking into account the description, the price and all other relevant information. The goods must also be fit for their purpose. For example, if you tell a door-to-door salesperson you need a cleaning product that is suitable for cleaning your car, they should not sell you one that will scratch the paintwork.

If you make an agreement to have a service carried out – for example, you agree to have a patio laid – the work must be carried out with reasonable care and skill, finished in a 'reasonable' time, unless a specific time has been agreed, and provided at a reasonable cost, unless a specific cost has been agreed. All these elements form part of the contract between you and the seller. This contract exists even if nothing is written down.

Cancelling an agreement made in your own home

If you decide you do not want the goods or services, you have a right in certain circumstances to cancel the agreement as long as you do so within seven days. This is known as the cooling-off period. Some sellers may allow a longer cooling-off period. If you cancel during the cooling-off period, you are entitled to get your money back, although if some work has already been carried out you will have to pay for that part of the work. The trader may have committed an offence if they do not give you written cancellation rights when the contract is formed. You should contact Consumer Direct (0845 404 0506) if you were not given your cancellation rights in writing.

You do not have the right to cancel agreements made at home if:

- the goods or services you bought cost less than £35
- you contacted the seller and asked them to visit you
- the service included new building works, such as a conservatory. However, the right to cancel does include agreements for home repairs and improvements, such as fitting double glazing
- you bought food or other perishable goods
- you bought the goods from a home party sale.

There are different rules about the cooling-off period if you signed a credit agreement at home – see p. 334.

Who can help?

The **Direct Selling Association** (DSA: 020 7497 1234; www.dsa.org.uk) is concerned with all types of direct sales agreements made in the home. Under the DSA's Consumer Code, member firms must give customers a 14-day cooling-off period. This applies whether or not the customer asked the salesperson to call and regardless of the value of the sale. You can check whether a firm is a member of the DSA by looking at its website. If you have been unable to resolve the problem with the seller, the DSA has an independent complaints procedure. Although the decision is binding on the seller, it does not prevent you taking legal action.

BUYING GOODS FROM A TRADER OVERSEAS

If you buy goods from a trader overseas – for example, when you are on holiday – your rights usually depend on the laws of the country where you bought the goods. However, if you bought the goods in another European Union member state, your consumer rights will be similar to your rights in the UK. This is because consumer law in each EU country comes from EU law. See p. 501 for a list of EU countries.

You will have both UK rights and the rights of the country where the seller is based if:

- you signed a contract with a seller who advertised in the UK and you concluded the contract in the UK. For example, you bought shoes from a mail

order company in Italy which advertised in a UK magazine and you sent the order from the UK
- the seller received your order while in the UK
- you bought the goods or services in another EU member state during an excursion organized by the seller to encourage you to buy – for example, you bought wine in France while on a wine-tasting trip organized by the wine seller.

You will not usually be entitled to UK rights as well as those of the country where the seller is based if the contract involves:

- a service not usually provided in the UK
- transport (although there are some exceptions to this, including package travel contracts)
- insurance
- land or property – for example, buying or selling an apartment. However, there are specific, different rules about timeshare properties.

If you buy something from the internet site of a company based in another EU country, in most cases you have the same statutory rights as if the company were based in the UK.

You will not have to pay additional VAT or other tax when you buy goods in another EU country and bring them back to the UK, although it is a good idea to check before you buy, as special rules apply for some goods, including new and nearly new cars, motorbikes and boats.

If you bought goods and services by credit card and they cost between £100 and £30,000, the credit card company may be equally liable – for example if the goods are faulty. It may be easier to get redress from the credit card company than from a seller based abroad.

There is a network of European Consumer Centres (ECC) in many EU countries that provide information about consumer law and procedures for enforcing your rights. For more information, go to www.ukecc.net.

PRIVATE SALES AND CAR BOOT SALES

If you buy goods from a private individual – for example, through an advert in a newspaper or shop window, or at a car boot sale – you have very few legal rights that you can enforce as a consumer. However, if the goods are described, the description should be accurate. It is important to check goods before you buy, because generally goods bought from a private seller do not have to be free from faults, so you would be unlikely to get a refund on the basis of a discovered fault. However, if you were told by the seller that the goods were in good working order and they weren't, you might be able to take action on the grounds that the goods did not match their description. Sometimes people who sell goods as part of their business pose as private sellers because then the customer has fewer rights. This is a criminal offence and, if you think that a private seller is actually in business, you could inform Consumer Direct (0845 404 0506).

It is also an offence for a private seller to sell an unroadworthy car. Again, you should report suspected offences to Consumer Direct.

Remember: if the seller arranged credit to pay for the goods, or you paid by credit card and the goods cost more than £100 and less than £30,000, the credit company may be equally liable for any breach of contract.

It is unlikely that you would be able to claim against a guarantee that came with goods bought from a private seller, as usually guarantees are only valid for the person who first bought the goods.

You may be entitled to compensation if:

- the seller has described the goods wrongly, although this may be difficult to prove unless it was in a written advert or you have a witness
- someone has been injured by an unroadworthy vehicle
- the seller knowingly made a false statement about the goods in order to persuade you to buy them.

It is always worth taking legal advice before deciding whether to accept an offer of compensation for personal injury.

Second-hand goods

You have the same rights when buying second-hand goods as you do when buying new, but you must take into account the fact that they are second-hand and so won't necessarily be of the same quality as new. Even though you can still claim your money back for faulty goods, you won't be able to claim that the goods are faulty if the faults are down to reasonable wear and tear or were obvious when you bought them. So be sure to check the goods carefully before you buy.

AUCTIONS

Remember that these rules apply to genuine auctions only. The rules about buying things from an internet site which calls itself an internet auction site may be different – see p. 338.

If you buy *new* goods at an auction, you have the same legal rights that you have if you buy goods in a shop.

If you buy *second-hand* goods at an auction, you only have legal rights if you were not given the opportunity to attend – for example, at an internet auction, such as eBay. You'll also lose your rights if the auction house makes it clear that you do not have normal consumer protection or that the goods are sold 'as seen'. However, the auctioneer has to show that it is reasonable to exclude your normal consumer rights.

When you buy goods at an auction, you enter into a contract with the owner of the goods, not the auctioneer, so if there is a dispute you will have to take action against the owner and not the auction house. In addition, the auction house is not obliged to give you the owner's details, so tracing them may be difficult. However, the auction house must not make false statements about the goods. Contact the auction house as soon as possible if you have a problem. If you have paid an indemnity fee, check whether it covers your particular problem. For example, if you discover that the car you have bought at auction is recorded as a 'write-off' you may have a claim under the indemnity policy.

These rules apply to distance auctions in the UK and the EU. If you buy something via an internet auction from a firm based in another country, the law of that country will usually apply. If you have a dispute in these circumstances, it is a good idea to seek specialist advice.

Did you know ...

that if you buy goods for your business, the legal rights that you normally have as a private consumer may not apply?

KEEPING LOST, FOUND AND UNCOLLECTED GOODS

If you want to find out whether you can keep something you have found, you must first check whether the goods are:

- uncollected or abandoned
- stolen
- lost
- treasure
- goods found in the sea or on the seashore
- goods you have received but you did not order (unsolicited goods). You have the right to keep or dispose of these goods. If a seller demands payment for unsolicited goods, you do not have to pay for or return the goods.

Uncollected or abandoned goods

Someone may leave their goods with you and appear to have abandoned them. Examples might include scaffolding or other equipment left by builders on site, uncollected goods left by a tenant in a landlord's property or goods ordered and received but then rejected or not paid for.

If you have uncollected or abandoned goods, you have a duty to look after them but you are not allowed to use them or treat them as your own. You may be liable for any damage caused to the goods while they are in your care.

You are not allowed to abandon goods that are dangerous, such as a leaking fridge. If you do abandon dangerous goods, you can be prosecuted. Otherwise, if you are in possession of someone else's goods, you can sell or get rid of them if they remain uncollected. However, you first have to make reasonable attempts to get the owner to collect them and provide the opportunity for the owner to take the goods away. If you want to sell the goods, you must take reasonable steps to trace the original owner if they or their whereabouts are unknown. Money received from the sale has to be returned to the original owner or, if this is not possible, kept on account for them. The owner only loses their right to the money after six years.

Stolen goods

When goods are stolen, the original owner still retains their legal right of ownership over the goods. When stolen goods are found, a court can order the return of the goods or a compensation payment for the value of the article to be made to the original owner.

If you get stolen goods, even if you have paid a fair price and are unaware that the goods were stolen, the general rule is that you do not get a legal right of ownership. You must inform the owner and allow them to take the goods away, if you discover that they were stolen. If you buy something that you later find out was stolen, you could try to claim compensation from the seller.

Lost goods

If you find goods that appear to be lost, then you can keep the goods as long as:

- you did not find the goods dishonestly or while trespassing
- you did not find the goods on your employer's property
- the goods are actually lost, and not uncollected or abandoned, stolen or treasure
- you have taken reasonable steps to find the owner of the goods – for example, left them to be claimed at a police station for a reasonable length of time
- the goods were not found on premises or land where the occupier does not exercise much control – for example, an air terminal lounge, the public part of a shop, or a recreation ground. (Sometimes it can be the owner of the land rather than the finder who has the right to keep the goods.)

Goods handed in to the police

The usual police practice is that the finder can have the goods back and keep them if they are not claimed within six weeks. However, the police may want more time if there are special circumstances and they want to investigate – for example, if they suspect the goods are stolen or think that the owner can be traced. Once the property has been returned to the finder by the police, the original owner cannot usually then claim the goods.

Treasure

Treasure is the property of the Crown. Anyone who finds treasure should report this directly to the coroner for the district where the object was found within 14 days of the find (or of first having reason to believe the object may be treasure). A finder who fails to report a discovery without a reasonable excuse will be committing a criminal offence. The coroner may hold an inquest to determine whether the object is treasure and, if so, who the finder was. This process can take several months.

An object is normally only treasure if it is at least 300 years old and made of silver or gold.

When an object has been declared treasure it is dealt with in one of the following ways:

- if it is not required for any museum, it is returned to the finder, who can then sell the object (the finder must have had permission to be on the land where the treasure was found)
- if the find, or any part of it, is kept for a museum, the finder is paid a sum equal to the market value of what is kept.

It is to the finder's advantage to report the find at once. The finder will either get the find back or its market value as an ex gratia reward. A finder should generally receive a reward within twelve months of having delivered the find. If the find is not required by a museum, it will be returned to the finder within six months.

Goods found in the sea or on the seashore

Property found in the sea or on the seashore could be from a ship and is known technically as 'wreck'. All wreck must be reported to the Receiver of Wreck. This can be done by downloading a form from the Receiver's website (www.mcga.gov.uk) or by calling 02380 329474.

BUILDERS

Most of us need to employ builders at one time or another, so it's best to know what the deal is from the start.

When you have building work done, the law says the work must be performed with reasonable care and skill and done within a reasonable time, and you must be charged a reasonable price. Any goods or materials provided as part of the work must match their description and be of satisfactory quality. This covers the normal use associated with the goods or materials. For example, if you tell the builder that you want a block-paved drive that will withstand the weight of vehicles, it shouldn't crack when you drive on it.

Who is the contract with?

Before you deal with a building problem, you will need to work out who you have the contract with. It could be:

- a builder, if you made an agreement with a building firm who agreed to carry out the work, or agreed to subcontract part of the work to other builders
- an architect or structural engineer, who took responsibility for employing the builders
- an individual contractor, if you employed each worker yourself
- a subcontractor, if you have agreed for them to carry out additional work. For example, if you ask a plumber, who was contracted by your builder, to service your central heating system, then you have a contract with that subcontractor.

If you are unsure with whom you have a contract, any action you take should be against all the builders and subcontractors involved.

General tips on dealing with builders

- You cannot usually cancel the work because you have changed your mind or have found another builder who will do the work more cheaply.
- Only pay the final amount when the work has been completed to your reasonable satisfaction.
- Do not sign any document that says you are satisfied with the work until you have had sufficient time to test it.
- If you used your credit card or the trader arranged finance for you, and the cost of the work is over £100 and under £30,000, the credit company may be equally liable for any breach of contract – for example, if there was any damage to your house during fitting.

What to do if the work is shoddy or the goods supplied are unsatisfactory

So, the double-glazing has been installed, but the windows don't open properly. What can you do about it? First you will need to ascertain whether the windows themselves are faulty or the trader has installed them incorrectly.

If you buy goods from a trader who installs them for you, you can ask them to replace or repair the goods free of charge if they are faulty, or if they were installed without reasonable care or skill.

If it is impossible to replace or repair the goods, or it would be unreasonably costly for the trader when compared to alternative remedies, or if the trader fails to replace or repair within a reasonable timescale, or causes you significant inconvenience, you can ask for a partial or full refund, the amount of which would take into account any use you have had out of the goods.

You may be entitled to compensation:

- if the work was not carried out with reasonable care, or takes an unreasonable length of time to be completed

---

A builder I hired to build us a garden wall is taking a very long time to complete the job. Is there any way that I can make him finish it?

When you hire a builder to work for you, you are buying a service and are entitled to expect that it should be done with the care and skill you would expect from a tradesman. That means that any walls built should not crack or roofs be leaky.

You do not need to have agreed a timescale before the work is started but you can expect it to be carried out within a 'reasonable' time. There is no legal definition of 'reasonable' but it would not be reasonable to expect a builder to build a complete house in two weeks or for it to take three months to build a barbecue.

If you think that the builder is taking an unreasonable time, you could begin by keeping a diary of the times that the builder is doing your work and photographs of the stages of the work as it is going on. This could be used as a form of evidence if you decide to take legal action. If you talk to the builder about your concerns and this makes no difference, it would be a good idea to write to the builder (keeping a copy of the letter) setting out what you want. If this still makes no difference, then you may be able to take court action.

If you agreed with the builder that the work would start on a certain day, you've paid a deposit and the agreed date has passed, you may be entitled to a refund. This is because a condition of the contract has been breached.

- if the trader has been negligent – for example, if your new windows let in rain and you have to redecorate
- if the goods or services are unsafe and someone has suffered an injury. Always take legal advice before accepting compensation for personal injury
- if you have incurred additional expenses, such as the cost of employing someone else to rectify any faults.

If you think a criminal offence has been committed – for example, the trader has described the glass as safety glass, but you believe it is not – you should contact Consumer Direct (0845 404 0506) before allowing the trader to rectify the work. Strict rules apply to the construction of new buildings/extensions, and so you should discuss your concerns with your local Building Regulations department.

Steps to work through

1. Once you've decided where you stand, collect all the relevant documents together and contact the trader as soon as possible, either by telephone or by visiting their offices. Explain the problem calmly but firmly and ask for a refund, repair, replacement or compensation. Set a time limit. If you can't agree who is responsible for the problem, try to arrange for the trader to visit your home to examine the work.

2. If you are still dissatisfied and cannot reach a satisfactory agreement, try to find out whether the trader is a member of a trade association that might be able to arbitrate.

3. If the matter is still not resolved, or there is not a trade association who can help, write to the trader (and the credit company, if applicable) repeating your complaint and what steps you have taken to resolve the matter. Say you are giving them 14 days to resolve the problem, or you will ask another trader to carry out the work and that you intend to recover the charges from them. You can add that you will consider legal action. Send the letter by recorded delivery, with a copy to their head office, if applicable, and remember to keep a copy yourself.

4. If the trader then makes you an alternative offer, you can either accept or continue to negotiate. Be realistic in what you will accept – you may not get an improved offer by going to court.

Court – the last resort

If you do not receive a reply to your letters, or the trader refuses to do anything or makes you an unacceptable offer, you will have to consider going to court. Before going to court, you need to consider whether you have sufficient evidence. You will have to prove in court that the trader is responsible for the problem and you may have to provide expert evidence. You will also need to find out whether the trader is solvent, as there is no point suing a person or company who has no money. And if you have lost money on shoddy building work, don't waste any more on a case you can't win!

Who can help?

The Architects' Registration Board (020 7580 5861; www.arb.org.uk) deals with complaints against architects.

The **Royal Institute of British Architects** (0906 302 0400 – premium rate; www.riba.org) has an internal conciliation and arbitration scheme to deal with complaints against its members.

The **Federation of Master Builders** (FMB: 020 7242 7583; www.fmb.org. uk) has a complaints procedure to deal with disputes.

BUYING SECOND-HAND CARS

Getting a new motor? After buying a house, a new set of wheels is probably one of your biggest one-off purchases, so it's worth spending some time getting to know your rights.

When you buy a second-hand car, your rights will depend on whether you buy the car from a dealer, at an auction or from a private seller.

Buying from a dealer

If you buy a second-hand car from a dealer, it must:

- match the description given by the seller and this includes any written description in an advertisement or catalogue; *and*
- be of satisfactory quality – that is, be in reasonable condition, considering its age and make, its past history and the price paid.

It must also be fit for its purpose. For example, if you request a vehicle that is capable of towing a large caravan, it must be up to the job.

It must also be roadworthy. In fact, it is a criminal offence to sell an unroadworthy car. A car is not roadworthy if its brakes, tyres, steering, or construction make it unfit for the road.

You will not have these rights if:

- the dealer pointed out the full extent of any fault before you bought the car
- you examined the car and should have noticed the fault. This mainly applies to cosmetic defects if examined by a lay person. The dealer would not be able

to evade responsibility for mechanical defects if they were not apparent on your examination.

Vehicle checks

Before purchase, it is worth carrying out a check to discover whether the car has been the subject of an insurance write-off or stolen, or whether there is outstanding finance from a previous sale. Mileage checks may be available. For peace of mind, you may wish to get the vehicle inspected for mechanical faults by an expert. There is a charge for these services. For further information about organizations that can do vehicle checks, go to www. consumerdirect.gov.uk (follow the link to Advice on goods and services).

Criminal offences

A criminal offence will have been committed if the dealer:

- gives a false description (for example, states there has been one careful owner when the logbook shows four former keepers)
- sells an unroadworthy car
- alters the mileage reading or sells you a car with an altered mileage reading
- pretends to be a private seller.

If you think that any of these might apply to your situation, before taking any action against the seller you should report the matter to Consumer Direct (0845 404 0506) and, in the case of personal injury, take legal advice on your claim.

Changing your mind

Do not agree or sign anything unless you are absolutely sure that you wish to go ahead with the purchase, and beware of signing any document that states that you have examined the car and found it satisfactory in all respects.

- If you are paying for the car by cash, there is no cooling-off period. You would normally be legally bound from the moment you both agreed the deal.
- If the deal is subject to finance, but you have not signed a finance agreement, neither party is legally bound until the finance agreement has been signed by both parties.
- If you have signed a finance agreement but the finance company has not yet

approved it, you may be able to withdraw if you act very quickly. Telephone the finance company immediately and follow it up with a letter confirming withdrawal.

Guarantee or extended warranty

If the car was sold with a guarantee or an extended warranty, you may have additional rights. The guarantee or warranty cannot take away your statutory rights. You should check the small print on your warranty. Many have exclusions such as wear and tear. If you are buying a high-mileage car, you need to ask yourself if the warranty is likely to cover the problems most likely to occur and consider whether the warranty offers value for money.

Special rules if you paid by credit

If you used your credit card or the seller arranged the finance for you to pay for the car, and it cost more than £100 and less than £30,000, the credit company may be equally liable for any breach of contract. This means that, if the car is faulty, you may be able to claim a refund or the cost of repairs from the finance company, the dealer, or both jointly. The rules regarding hire purchase and conditional sale are different to other agreements in that it is the finance company that is solely responsible.

Your rights if the car is faulty

Refund

Whether you can return the car and demand your money back depends in part on how long you have had the car and how many miles it has travelled before you report the fault. If the fault is serious and you have not done many miles and return (reject) it very shortly after purchase, you may be entitled to a full refund. If, however, you keep the car for a longer time without returning it, you may lose this right, although you may still be entitled to ask for the fault to be rectified. If you are entitled to a refund, this will include both the money you paid for the faulty car and the return of any part-exchanged car. If the part-exchanged car has since been sold, you are entitled to the cash value as represented on your paperwork.

Replacement or repair

You can ask the seller to replace or repair the car free of charge if it is faulty. If you do this within six months of receiving the car, and it is reasonable to expect it to have lasted for the period of time you have had it, it will be assumed that the problem existed when you bought the car, unless the seller can show otherwise. However, you can still ask for a replacement or a repair for up to six years from the date that you bought the car, if it is reasonable for it to have lasted that long. In this case it will be up to you to show that the car was faulty at the time of sale. The longer you have had the car, the more difficult it is to prove that the fault was there at the time of sale. You can ask for a partial or full refund if:

- it is impossible to replace or repair the car
- replacement or repair would be unreasonably costly for the seller when compared with alternative remedies
- the seller fails to replace or repair the car within a reasonable time of having agreed to do so, or causes you significant inconvenience.

The amount of money you get back may be reduced to take account of any use that you have had out of the car.

Compensation

You may be entitled to compensation if:

- the contract has been broken (breach of contract) because the vehicle is not as described, of satisfactory quality or fit for its purpose
- the dealer has made a false statement about the car to make you buy it (for example, telling you it has had a new engine fitted when the engine is reconditioned)
- you have had an injury because the car is unroadworthy or unsafe (you should always take legal advice before deciding whether to accept an offer of compensation for personal injury)
- a fault with the car caused damage to something else
- you accept a repair which turns out to be unsatisfactory
- you have incurred additional expenses because of the dealer's breach of contract – for example, having to make telephone calls or pay for alternative transport.

How to solve your problem

Once you have decided what your rights are, contact the dealer. It is the dealer and/or the finance company and *not* the manufacturer who is responsible for dealing with your complaint.

Follow the steps below:

- Stop using the car.
- Collect all your documents together, including your sales invoice, guarantee or warranty and/or credit agreement.
- If someone has been injured or if you feel a criminal offence has been committed (for example, the car is unroadworthy), you should contact Consumer Direct (0845 404 0506) before going back to the trader.
- Contact the dealer and the finance company (if applicable) as soon as you discover the fault. Take the car back, and ask to speak to a manager or the owner. Alternatively, write to the manager or owner, enclosing a copy of your sales invoice. Keep a copy of your letter. Explain your problem calmly but firmly and ask for a full refund, a repair, a replacement, or compensation and set a time limit.
- If you are still dissatisfied, write to the dealer and/or the finance company repeating your complaint and the steps that have been taken. Say that you will give them 14 days to sort out the problem or you will consider legal action. Send your letter by recorded delivery with a copy to the head office. Be sure to keep copies of all letters.
- If the dealer makes an alternative offer (for example, a replacement car), you can either accept or continue to negotiate. Be realistic in what you will accept. You may not get a better offer by going to court.
- If the dealer doesn't reply to your letters, refuses to do anything, or makes a final offer that you are unwilling to accept, your only other choice is to go to court. If you are claiming the cost of repairs make sure you have obtained sufficient evidence to prove your claim – for example, expert reports, photographs, etc. – before you allow another garage to repair the car.

Remember, court is your last resort. You also need to find out if the dealer is solvent. It is not worth suing a person or a firm that has no money, and if you have lost money on a faulty car, don't waste more money on a case you cannot win.

Getting an expert opinion

If the cause of the problem is in dispute, it may be necessary to obtain an expert opinion. This could be obtained through a trade association or could be from anyone suitably qualified who is willing to put their findings in writing. Reports must usually be paid for, and you should reach agreement with the seller in advance on the choice of expert and that you will both be bound by the expert's findings. You should then be able to recover the cost if the complaint is upheld. If you go through a trade association, it may offer conciliation or arbitration. Arbitration is often legally binding. If you would like more information before you commit yourself, contact the trade association for further details.

Buying a car at an auction

If you buy a second-hand car at an auction that you have the opportunity to attend in person, your rights may be limited if the car turns out to be faulty. You should check the terms and conditions of business of the auction – for example, in the catalogue or on notices on display. If they state that your rights under the Sale of Goods Act 1979 are excluded, then you are buying the car *as seen*, and it is your responsibility to check the car before you bid for it.

Some auctions will offer insurance against the vehicle turning out to be stolen and some may offer you a cooling-off period (although this may often be very small – a matter of a few hours).

Buying a car from a private seller

If you buy a car from a private seller, you will only be able to take action against the seller if the car is not as described. Sellers will be liable for a false description even if they believed the description to be true. Be wary of a seller who wants to meet you away from his private address, whose name is not on the logbook, or who is evasive about answering your questions.

Who can help?

If you have a dispute regarding a warranty from a manufacturer or from a mechanical breakdown insurance company that is a member of the **Society of Motor Manufacturers and Traders** (0870 7518270; www.smmt.co.uk), you may be able to use the SMMT conciliation service.

The **Retail Motor Industry Federation** and the **Society of Motor Auctions** (01788 576 465; www.rmif.co.uk) are both part of the same organization and members must follow a code of practice. There is an internal conciliation service and an independent arbitration scheme run by the Chartered Institute of Arbitrators to deal with complaints against its members.

INSURANCE

You buy insurance in order to protect, or 'cover', yourself against unexpected financial loss that can result from, for example, personal injury, illness, or damage to your property or personal possessions. Some of the most common types of insurance cover are:

- motor insurance
- household contents insurance
- buildings insurance
- travel insurance
- private health insurance
- life insurance (often called life assurance).

You can buy insurance direct from an insurer, through an insurance agent (usually employed by one insurer), or through an insurance broker or independent intermediary. An insurance broker or intermediary is not usually tied to any one particular insurer, but will receive commission for selling you an insurance policy. It is sometimes quicker and easier to go to an intermediary than directly to an insurer, and they are useful if you want insurance for something special. You can also buy insurance through a bank, building society, solicitor, travel agent, mail order agent or accountant.

Companies and individuals who sell, arrange or give advice on the common types of insurance must be registered with the Financial Services Authority (FSA), and must comply with FSA rules.

When you apply to buy insurance, you must answer the insurer's questions, or those of the person selling you insurance, truthfully, as the insurer may refuse to pay out on a future claim if you withhold information. Your insurance policy will contain the terms of your contract with your insurer. This will include what is known as a 'schedule'. The schedule has your personal details on it, and the particulars of your specific policy. You have the right to a full copy of your policy. It is important to make sure that the information in your policy is correct, and you should check it very carefully as soon as you receive it.

Insurance firms and brokers selling most types of insurance must give you details about the service they are offering and a summary document which contains certain key facts about the insurance policy they want to sell you. The summary document should display a 'Keyfacts' logo, and must tell you, among other things, details of the insurer, the main features and benefits of the insurance, any significant or unusual exclusions in the policy, how long the cover will last and whether you have any cancellation rights. This information will make it easier to compare policies from a number of firms when you are choosing an insurance policy.

Traders selling travel insurance sold as part of a package holiday and those selling extended warranties for electrical items do not have to give you this information.

The amount you pay for an insurance policy is called a 'premium'. Premiums can either be paid to your insurer in one lump sum or in instalments.

A 'no-claims bonus' increases for every year that you make no claims on your policy, up to a maximum amount. Most insurers will let you transfer the discount, if you want to change your insurer. If you make a claim, you will also need to compare the amount by which your no-claims bonus would be reduced.

Discrimination

If you experience difficulty in getting insurance cover, it may be because of discrimination on the grounds of your race, sex, disability, sexuality or religion. If you think that you have been refused insurance cover because of discrimination on these grounds, you should consult an experienced adviser – for example, at a Citizens Advice Bureau.

Claiming on your insurance policy

If you want to make a claim on your insurance policy, do this without delay, and follow the procedure set out in your policy document.

You do not have to make a claim on your insurance policy, even if you are entitled to do so. However, you should think very carefully about this decision as costs that you have to pay yourself may turn out to be higher than you think. It is always advisable to make an insurance claim if someone has been injured. Personal injuries can be expensive, and they can have unexpected and long-term effects on your health.

Even if you don't wish to make a claim, you must always tell your insurer about an event. If you do not report it, you may find that this leads to problems later on when you do wish to make a claim.

An insurance policy may include an 'excess', which is the fixed amount of any claim, for example the first £50, that you must pay yourself.

If your claim is substantial, you may want to employ loss assessors to help you with your claim. Make sure that they are members of the Institute of Public Loss Assessors (0208 988 7581; www.lossassessors.org.uk). Get details of all fees and services offered, in writing, before any work is carried out. You may be able to claim the fees back.

Cancelling your insurance policy

You may want to cancel an insurance policy if you have just bought it and have changed your mind. You have a right to do this if you bought your policy over the phone, on the internet, or from someone who called at your home or place of work. You may also have a right to cancel your insurance policy if you paid for it by a credit agreement that you signed in your own home or anywhere other than the offices of the credit company, or if the insurance contract itself says that there is a right to cancel. Many general insurance policies give you an automatic right to cancel within 14 days of purchase, and many life insurance policies give you the right to cancel within 30 days. Your insurer is allowed to make a small charge for the administration costs of cancellation, but they are not allowed to make a profit from this charge.

How to resolve an insurance problem

If you have a problem with your insurance policy, or an insurance claim, write to your insurer, giving details of your complaint and how you would like it resolved. If you are not satisfied with your insurer's response, make a formal complaint, using their official complaints procedure. If you are still not satisfied with the outcome of the formal complaints procedure, consider taking the complaint further.

All insurance companies must be covered by the rules of the financial watchdog, the Financial Services Authority (FSA). This means that if you have a complaint about an insurer you can complain to the Financial

Ombudsman Service (FOS). There is a free service to policy-holders who have already followed their insurer's complaints procedure. The FOS will try to resolve the problem through mediation between yourself and the insurer. A decision made by the FOS is binding on your insurer, but if you do not agree with it, you can still take your insurer to court.

To find out whether the FOS can investigate your complaint, you can contact them on 0845 080 1800, or visit their website (www.financial-ombudsman.org.uk).

If your insurer is a member of Lloyd's, contact Lloyd's Complaints Department on 020 7327 5693. If you are not satisfied with the outcome of this complaint, you can then go on to complain to the FOS.

If you have tried all the options for resolving your complaint through the complaints procedures, but have not met with success, or if your insurer is based outside the UK, you may wish to consider taking legal action. However, you should only consider going to court as a last resort. This is because the amount of compensation a court may award you could be reduced if you have not tried other ways of resolving the problem before taking legal action.

If your insurer has disappeared

If you want to trace an insurer, intermediary or broker, contact the Financial Services Authority (FSA: 0845 606 1234; www.moneymadeclear.fsa.gov.uk).

If your claim has not been settled because your insurer has gone out of business, you may be able to get help from the Financial Services Compensation Scheme (020 7892 7300; www.fscs.org.uk). If your insurer is a member of Lloyd's, you should contact the complaints department at Lloyd's (020 7327 5693).

Motor insurance

(see *Motor insurance*, p. 412).

Household contents insurance

Household contents insurance (sometimes known as home contents insurance) covers most of your personal belongings and household possessions against loss or damage. This includes furniture, domestic equipment, electrical appliances, furnishing, clothing, food and drink, some valuables and cash up to a certain limit.

Household contents insurance covers the possessions belonging to you and to close family members who live with you. Your husband, wife or civil partner would be covered. Some insurance companies automatically include people who are cohabiting in their definition of 'family members', but you may want to check. A friend who lives with you or who is staying with you would not normally be covered, unless their name was included in your policy. There is no legal requirement for you to take out household contents insurance, but it is advisable for you to do so.

Your household insurance policy will only cover some forms of accidental damage. It will normally cover damage due to fire, floods and storms as well as accidental damage to mirrors and fixed glass in furniture. You can often extend your policy to cover accidental damage to all of the contents of your home. You will have to pay extra for this.

If you rent any of your possessions, for example a television set or a DVD/video recorder, it is advisable to take out insurance cover for these items. This is because you are legally responsible for any loss or damage that occurs to them.

If you rent your home and it has some contents belonging to your landlord, such as furniture or a television set, you may be responsible for any loss or damage to them and will need to arrange insurance cover. Check your tenancy agreement to see if this is the case.

Making a claim

Contact your insurer as soon as possible and request a claim form. Complete the claim form carefully and keep a copy.

If your claim is substantial, you may want to employ loss assessors to help you with your claim. Make sure that they are members of the Institute of Public Loss Assessors (020 8988 7581; www.lossassessors.org.uk). Get details of all fees and services offered, in writing, before any work is carried out. You may be able to claim these fees back.

Buildings insurance

Buildings insurance covers the cost of damage to the structure of your property. This includes the roof, walls, ceilings, floors, doors and windows. Outdoor structures such as garages and fences are also included.

Buildings insurance covers permanent fixtures and fittings, interior decoration and underground tanks, pipes, cables and drains for which you are responsible from your home to the mains supply. Buildings insurance commonly covers loss or damage that happens as a result of fire, storms, floods, theft or vandalism.

Your buildings insurance should cover the full cost of rebuilding the property. This should include costs such as demolition, clearing the site, and architects' fees. Make sure any special features such as a luxury fitted kitchen or a conservatory are also included. The Association of British Insurers (ABI: 020 7600 3333; www.abi.org.uk) produces yearly guidelines on rebuilding costs.

You can extend a buildings insurance policy to include cover for accidental damage to the inside of your home. This will cost extra. However, anything that is not clearly listed in the policy is not usually covered.

A buildings insurance policy will usually also cover the cost of alternative accommodation up to a certain limit, if you have to leave your home while repairs are carried out.

If you own the property, you can also be insured against legal responsibility if someone dies or is injured when they visit your property. You can also get cover for damage to someone else's goods or property when they visit you.

Who should have buildings insurance

If you are an owner-occupier with a mortgage, it will be a condition of the mortgage that your home is insured. Your mortgage lender will make sure that the amount of cover is sufficient to meet the outstanding amount of your mortgage. However, you should make sure that this is enough to cover the full rebuilding costs of your home.

Your mortgage lender should give you the choice of at least three insurers, or allow you to propose one you have chosen yourself. Your mortgage lender will usually accept your choice of insurer, as long as the policy provides adequate cover. They may make a small charge for this. Your mortgage lender does have the right to turn your choice of insurer down, but they cannot insist that you take out their own insurance policy unless you have agreed to a special mortgage package that includes insurance.

If you buy or sell a house, responsibility for the buildings insurance passes to the new owner when contracts are exchanged. It is therefore very important that, if you are buying a house, you insure the property from the day that contracts are exchanged. This is because if the house is damaged or destroyed, you will be expected to cover the loss. If you are selling your house, you have a legal responsibility to look after the property until the sale is completed, and you should therefore keep on your buildings insurance until then.

If your mortgage lender repossesses your home, you are still responsible for the insurance until it is sold. Your insurance policy may no longer cover you if you are not living in the property. You should explain the circumstances to your insurer so that they can change the terms of your policy. They may want assurances that someone, for example a neighbour, is watching over the property while it is empty.

If you are a freeholder without a mortgage, you do not have to take out buildings insurance, but it is advisable to do so.

If you are an owner-occupier who is a leaseholder, you may have a condition in your lease that says that you have to take out buildings insurance with a specified insurer. This may be the case even if you don't have a mortgage. However, in England, you might have the right to take out buildings insurance with an insurer of your choice as long as certain conditons are met.

Alternatively, the freeholder of your building may take out the insurance and charge you for the premium.

If you are a tenant, your landlord usually has responsibility for the buildings insurance. Check that your landlord has taken out buildings insurance. You may also have some responsibility for certain loss or damage to fixtures and fittings. Check your tenancy agreement for this. Your household contents insurance may cover some of these losses.

Making a claim

If your claim is substantial, you may want to employ loss assessors to help you with your claim. Make sure that they are members of the Institute of Public Loss Assessors (020 8988 7581; www.lossassessors.org.uk). Get details of all fees and services offered, in writing, before any work is carried out, and do not arrange for permanent repairs to be done without your insurer's permission. Your insurer may ask a claims inspector or loss adjuster to visit you, to investigate the circumstances of your claim. If your claim is accepted, your insurer will either arrange for a company to do the repairs, or ask you to get estimates for their approval before going ahead with any work.

Travel insurance

(see *Travel Insurance*, p. 422).

ALTERNATIVE DISPUTE RESOLUTION

If you have a dispute over the supply of goods or services that you have been unable to settle through negotiation, you may wish to consider using an alternative dispute resolution (ADR) scheme rather than taking court action.

These schemes use a third party such as an arbitrator or an ombudsman to help you and the supplier reach a solution. You will usually have to complete the supplier's internal complaints procedure beforehand and you may have to pay a fee for using the scheme. This is usually refunded if you are successful.

Some schemes are legally binding, which means you cannot take court action if you aren't satisfied with the decision, except to enforce an award. If your claim is over £5,000, you should discuss the possibility of ADR with your solicitor. If your claim is less than this amount, you should look at the pros and cons of ADR and small claims actions, and decide which would be the best course of action for you.

The main advantages of using an ADR are:

- you may resolve your problem
- you may be awarded compensation
- the procedure is less formal than going to court
- in some schemes, the decision may be binding on the trader but not on you, leaving you free to pursue the action through court if you wish
- it may cost you less than going to court
- the procedure is confidential.

You might want to think about these points:

- The costs involved. Compare the arbitrator's/mediator's fee with the costs involved in going to court.
- Would you prefer to have a hearing, where you can put your point across in person, or have the matter dealt with on paper, in a 'documents only' process?
- If the arbitrator's decision is legally binding, it will prevent you taking the matter through the courts.
- You may have to pay further costs to enforce the arbitrator's decision through the courts.

● Most schemes have a time limit within which you must start the complaint. This time limit may be shorter than those for taking court action.

Types of ADR scheme

The main types of ADR scheme that deal with consumer disputes are conciliation, arbitration and mediation and are usually provided by trade associations. If you wish to use one of these schemes, you should ask the suppliers whether they are members of a trade association and, if so, contact the trade association to find out whether it has a conciliation or arbitration service.

Conciliation

In consumer disputes, conciliation is usually the first stage in the arbitration process and the conciliator is usually a member of the trade association. Both you and the supplier will be asked to give written details of the complaint, including any evidence, and the conciliator will give an opinion on the best solution. Any decision is not binding and won't prevent you from taking court action. If you disagree with the opinion offered, you can then proceed to the arbitration stage or consider suing in court. There is usually no charge for conciliation.

Arbitration

Arbitration is a procedure for settling disputes in which both you and the supplier usually agree to accept the decision of the arbitrator as legally binding. This means you cannot take court action, except to enforce the award if the supplier doesn't pay. The arbitrator will usually be a member of the Chartered Institute of Arbitrators (020 7421 7444; www.arbitrators.org) and often acts independently of the trade association. The arbitrator will make a decision based on the written evidence presented by you and the supplier. The decision is confidential and cannot be made public without the supplier's agreement. You will have to pay a registration fee, which may be refunded if you are successful. Some contracts for services and delivery include an arbitration clause stating that you will refer any dispute to arbitration. Although this is binding once you have signed the agreement, if the total cost is below the small claims limit (£5,000), you cannot be forced to arbitrate unless you gave your agreement after the dispute arose.

Mediation

If you use a mediation scheme, the mediator will help you and the supplier to negotiate an acceptable agreement and will act as a go-between if you don't want to meet. If the supplier agrees to mediation, you will both be asked to give details of the dispute, including copies of any evidence, and will be asked to sign a mediation agreement giving a framework for the mediation. The mediator may arrange joint or separate meetings with you and the supplier and will help you to identify the strengths and weaknesses in your case. Any agreement reached will be legally binding unless you state otherwise and will prevent you from taking court action except to enforce any award. Mediation can be expensive but you may be able to get legal aid to help with the costs. Contact your local Citizens Advice Bureau for more help.

Ombudsman schemes

Many services have an ombudsman scheme that you can use, but you will only be able to refer the matter to the ombudsman after you have completed the supplier's internal complaints procedure. You will need to give written details of your complaint, together with copies of any of your evidence. The ombudsman will make a recommendation or a ruling, which is usually accepted by the supplier, but isn't legally binding. Hence you can still take court action if you aren't satisfied with the decision. However, the court will take the ombudsman's ruling into account when deciding your claim. All the ombudsman schemes are free.

Who can help?

If you are interested in ADR, you should find out whether the trader is a member of any trade association that offers such a service. If you have any difficulty contacting the trade association or finding out whether there is a relevant ombudsman scheme, or if the trader is falsely claiming membership of an association, you should contact **Consumer Direct** (0845 404 0506). You should enquire whether there is a charge for their services before you commit yourself. The Law Society has established a **Civil and Commercial Mediation Panel** (0870 606 3555, extension 3286) to help members of the public find qualified solicitor mediators.

STARTING COURT ACTION

If you have been negotiating with a trader to resolve a consumer complaint but have not been successful, you may want to consider going to court. Before taking legal action, you should make sure that you have tried all other options for resolving your dispute, such as alternative dispute resolution (ADR – see above).

Most consumer cases are heard in the county court. If the case is defended by the trader, the court will allocate the case to one of three tracks: the small claims track, which deals with claims of £5,000 or less; the fast track for most cases between £5,000 and £15,000; or the multi-track for cases above £15,000.

In a small claims case you won't be awarded costs to pay for a solicitor even if you win the case, so only the least complex cases are dealt with in this way.

You may decide to take court action rather than using an ADR if:

- the trader is not a member of a trade association with a conciliation or arbitration scheme
- the amount you are claiming is under £5,000 and will be dealt with as a small claim
- you have a reluctant witness – only a court can order a witness to attend
- there is no limit on the amount of compensation you can claim – for example, in a negligence claim. An ADR may have limits on the level of payments it can award.

Can the trader afford to pay?

You are unlikely to get your money if the trader is:

- unemployed or on a low income
- bankrupt, or the company has been wound up. You can find out whether an individual is bankrupt by telephoning the Insolvency Service (0845 602 9848) or by doing an on-line search (www.insolvency.gov.uk). You can find out if a company has gone into administration or liquidation by contacting the Companies Registration Office (0870 333 3636; www.companieshouse.gov.uk)
- in debt and cannot afford to pay. You can find out whether the trader has other unpaid county court judgments, High Court judgments or unpaid fines by contacting the Registry Trust (020 7380 0133; www.registry-trust.org.uk)
- has no money and owns nothing else of value.

You would be wasting your money taking court action against a bankrupt or a company in liquidation. If the trader has a very low income, you may get your money if you are prepared to accept very low payments (sometimes as little as £1 per month).

Do you need a solicitor?

If you are claiming over £5,000, or making a claim such as replacement or repair of faulty goods, or making a claim for negligence or personal injury, you should consult a solicitor before starting court action. These cases are more complex and you could find yourself paying the legal costs of the other side if you lose the case.

Is there a time limit?

There are time limits within which you can start court action. These are usually six years for consumer contract issues. The time starts from the date the problem arose. If you are unsure about whether you have missed the time limit, you should consult a solicitor.

Do you have the trader's details?

You will need the full address of the individual or firm you are suing. If you are suing:

- a limited company, you will need to claim against the company, not the owner(s). You should send the claim form to its registered office or to the address of the shop you have done business with. If you want details of the registered office, you can obtain this by telephoning Companies House (0870 333 3636; www.companieshouse.gov.uk)
- an individual (sole trader), you must name the individual you are suing and not just sue the trading name. The address for service can be either the trader's home address or their business address
- a partnership, each partner is fully liable for any debts. You should sue all the partners at the same time, as you cannot sue them one after the other. A business that does not trade under the names of the partners should display details of the owner or partners on its headed notepaper or at its premises or be willing to provide them if asked. If it fails to do so, it may have committed a criminal offence and should be reported to Consumer Direct (0845 404 0506) or to the police.

For more information, see *The small claims procedure*, p. 505.

GENERAL ORGANIZATIONS THAT HELP WITH CONSUMER COMPLAINTS

Organizations that help with complaints about communications and the media

The **Advertising Standards Authority** (020 7492 2222; www.asa.org.uk) supervises the British Codes of Advertising, Sales Promotion and Direct Marketing and deals with contraventions. It will take up complaints in writing about all forms of advertising.

The **Press Complaints Commission** (0845 600 2757; www.pcc.org.uk) is concerned with maintaining high professional and commercial standards in the British press. It will investigate any complaints about newspapers or magazines, except those involving advertising, where compensation is sought or where the complaint might result in a court case. Complaints should be sent in writing to the Director.

Organizations that help with complaints about travel and transport

The **Retail Motor Industry Federation** (01788 576465; www.rmif.co.uk) operates an internal conciliation service and an independently run arbitration scheme.

The **Society of Motor Manufacturers and Traders** (New Car Code Conciliation Service: 0870 7518270; www.smmt.co.uk). If you have a problem with a new car which is still under a manufacturer's guarantee or extended warranty, and have been unable to resolve it, contact the SMMT. The SMMT operates an impartial conciliation service and arbitration scheme.

The **Society of Motor Auctions** (01788 576465; www.rmif.co.uk) represents car auctioneers and has a code of practice, which members must comply with. The SMA has an internal conciliation and arbitration service.

The **British Vehicle Rental and Leasing Association** (01494 434747; www.bvrla.co.uk) represents firms that rent or lease vehicles. The BVRLA will investigate complaints made against its members.

The **Motor Cycle Industry Association** (024 76 408 000; www.mcia.co. uk) has an internal conciliation scheme and an independent arbitration scheme to deal with complaints against member firms.

The **Vehicle Builders and Repairers Association** (0113 253 8333; www.vbra.co.uk) has an internal conciliation scheme and an independent arbitration scheme to deal with complaints against VBRA members.

Organizations that help with complaints about property and building services

The **National Association of Estate Agents** (01926 496800; www.naea.co. uk) investigates complaints against members and helps with complaints against non-members. The Association operates an indemnity scheme to protect the public against loss of money held by the Association's members.

The **British Association of Removers** (01923 699 480; www.bar.co.uk) gives general advice on removals and produces a range of free leaflets. These include advice on choosing a removal firm, preparing to move and moving abroad. BAR has a conciliation scheme and also an independently run arbitration scheme.

The **National House-Building Council** (01494 735 363; www.nhbc.co.uk). The NHBC is an independent organization with over 25,000 builders on its register. Before being accepted on to the NHBC register, builders must be able to show that they are technically and financially competent, and agree to abide by the NHBC Rules and Standards. These cover technical requirements and guidance on practical design, suitable materials and quality of workmanship. The NHBC runs the Buildmark scheme, which covers homes built by NHBC-registered builders once the NHBC has certified them finished.

The **Federation of Master Builders** (020 7242 7583; www.fmb.org.uk) gives advice on how to choose a builder and details of member firms in the customer's area. It also has a complaints procedure to deal with disputes with its members, and an independently run arbitration scheme.

The **Confederation of Roofing Contractors** (01206 306600; www.corc.co. uk) has about 300 members. There is a free internal conciliation and arbitration scheme to deal with complaints against members and non-members.

The **National Federation of Roofing Contractors** (020 7436 0387; www.nfrc.co.uk) has an arbitration scheme to deal with disputes, for which a fee is payable.

The **Painting and Decorating Association** (02476 353776; www.paintingdecoratingassociation.co.uk) operates an internal complaints and arbitration scheme to deal with complaints against members.

The **National Inspection Council for Electrical Installation Contracting** (0870 013 0382; www.niceic.org.uk) is an independent consumer safety organization that publishes a Roll of Approved Electrical Installation Contractors of over 10,500 electrical contractors, who work to the technical standards set by the NICEIC. It operates an internal complaints procedure to resolve disputes over the technical standard of work carried out by members. The NICEIC will not investigate if the complaint is just about the cost of the work.

The **National Heating Consultancy** (020 7936 2710) investigates complaints about defective domestic heating or insulation work. Members of the NHC are qualified heating engineers who can act as independent experts. Telephone advice is given free.

The **Association of Plumbing and Heating Contractors** (024 7687 0626; www.aphc.co.uk) can provide details of member firms in your area, and operates internal conciliation and arbitration schemes to deal with complaints against members. There is a fee to use the arbitration scheme, which may be refunded if you win your case.

The **Institute of Plumbing and Heating Engineering** (01708 472791; www.iphe.org.uk) keeps a register of qualified plumbers and can provide details of its members in your area. The IoP runs a free internal arbitration scheme to deal with complaints against members. The IoP cannot award compensation or order that a member remedy faulty work, but it can remove a member from its register.

The **Glass and Glazing Federation** (0870 042 4255; www.ggf.org.uk) produces free leaflets giving advice on choosing new windows, doors and conservatories, a list of member firms and the Customer Charter. The GGF has an internal conciliation service, and an independently run arbitration scheme, to deal with complaints against its members.

The **Conservatory Association** (020 7207 5873; www.ggf.org.uk) produces Minimum Technical Specifications and a Recommended Code of Practice for conservatory construction and a list of member firms. The

Association has an internal arbitration scheme for disputes between customers and member companies.

The **British Pest Control Association** (0870 609 2687; www.bpca.org.uk) can give general advice on pest control and has an internal arbitration scheme to deal with complaints. It operates the BPCA Code of Practice.

Organizations that help with complaints about clothing and household goods

The **Independent Footwear Retailers Association** (0870 330 8620) represents shoe shops and wholesalers. Shoe shops that are not members can affiliate to the IFRA if they agree to abide by its code of practice.

The **Multiservice Association** (01536 760374; www.msauk.biz) represents some shoe repairers. Members must follow their Code of Practice for Shoe Repairers. Multiservice has a free internal arbitration scheme to resolve complaints against its members.

The **Textile Services Association** (general inquiries: 020 8863 7755; dry-cleaning information bureau: 020 8863 8658; www.tsa-uk.org) represents most dry-cleaners and launderers and has a conciliation service that can be used to resolve a dispute between a customer and a TSA member. The TSA can also give information on which TSA members specialize in cleaning particular items, for example antique fabrics.

The **National Association of the Launderette Industry** (020 8856 9798; www.nali.org.uk) has a code of practice that its members must follow and an internal conciliation scheme to deal with complaints against its members. NALI does not deal with dry-cleaners.

The **National Carpet Cleaners Association** (0116 271 9550; www.ncca.co.uk) represents carpet and upholstery cleaning firms and will give advice to customers on cleaning carpets, curtains and upholstery, including information on dealing with stains. The NCCA has an internal conciliation and arbitration scheme to resolve complaints against its members.

The **Association of Manufacturers of Domestic Appliances** (020 7405 0666; www.amdea.org.uk) represents British manufacturers of domestic appliances, but does not deal with radios, televisions or stereo equipment. Members of the AMDA must comply with the Principles for Domestic Appliance Servicing. If you have a complaint about the way in which an electrical appliance has been serviced by the manufacturer of the appliance, the AMDA has an internal conciliation scheme to resolve the problem. There is also an independent arbitration scheme. The AMDA cannot deal with complaints where someone other than the manufacturer has serviced the appliance, or where the manufacturer is not a member of the AMDA.

The **Domestic Appliance Service Association** (0870 224 0343; www.dasa. org.uk) represents firms that service and repair domestic electrical appliances. DASA members should provide service within three working days at reasonable cost and carry adequate stocks of spare parts to meet reasonable demands for repairs and to resolve customer complaints.

The **Radio, Electrical and Television Retailers Association** (01234 269110; www.retra.co.uk) represents shops selling domestic electrical appliances, including televisions, radios and stereo equipment. RETRA has a conciliation procedure for disputes involving its members.

The **Hampers Industry Trade Association Ltd** (01482 631410; www.hitauk.co.uk) represents the retailers of hampers, which are defined as 'collections of foodstuffs'. HITA will investigate, and attempt to resolve, complaints against members.

Organizations that help with complaints about door-to-door and distance selling

The **Direct Selling Association** (020 7497 1234; www.dsa.org.uk) represents traders who sell from door to door and those who sell at parties in the customer's home. The Association has an internal complaints procedure to deal with complaints against its members. A list of members is available through the Direct Selling Association website.

The **Direct Marketing Association** (020 7291 3300; www.dma.org.uk) manages the Mail Preference Service, the Telephone Preference Service and the Fax Preference Service. They will remove your name from lists so that you no longer receive advertising from companies. The Association also runs a conciliation service that deals with complaints against member companies.

The **Mail Order Traders' Association** (020 7735 3410; www.mota.org.uk) represents firms that sell through catalogues. It has an internal conciliation scheme, and an independent arbitration scheme, to deal with complaints against its members.

Organizations that help with complaints about financial services

The **British Bankers' Association** (020 7216 8800; www.bba.org.uk) is the main trade association for banks operating in the UK. It produces free information sheets called Bankfacts that cover most aspects of banking practice. They are available by telephoning the BBA Bankfacts orderline (020 7216 8801).The BBA will not give advice or take up an individual problem about a bank.

The **Banking Code Standards Board** (0845 230 9694; www.bankingcode. org.uk) is the body that makes sure that banks and building societies that subscribe to the Banking Code honour their commitments to it. If the BCSB receives a complaint that a bank or building society has failed to comply with the Banking Code, it will ask the bank or building society for an explanation and insist that it complies.

The BCSB cannot deal with claims for compensation, nor intervene in a dispute between you the customer and your bank or building society. However, the BCSB is interested in hearing about cases where a bank or building society appears to have breached the Banking Code.

The **Association of British Insurers** (020 7600 3333; www.abi.org.uk) is the trade association for most insurance companies and has codes of practice that its members must follow. It will take up complaints about its members. Although it does not operate an arbitration procedure and cannot insist that any of its members follow a particular line of action, it can exert pressure to resolve a dispute. If the problem is not resolved, or if an insurance company is not a member of the ABI, you should complain to the Financial Ombudsman Service.

The **Financial Services Authority** (FSA: 0845 606 1234; www.moneymadeclear.fsa.gov.uk) is an independent watchdog that regulates financial organizations and protects consumers in the UK. The FSA can provide basic information and guidance on financial services, including pensions, mortgages, insurance and Individual Savings Accounts (ISAs). The FSA does not deal with specific consumer complaints, recommend firms or give financial advice.

The **Financial Ombudsman Service** (0845 080 1800; www.financial-ombudsman.org.uk) can deal with consumer complaints about most personal financial matters including financial advice, banking services, insurance and personal pensions advice. The FOS can investigate complaints only if the problem has not been resolved after going through the company's formal complaints procedure.

The **Motor Insurers' Bureau** (01908 830001; www.mib.org.uk) can give compensation to someone who is involved in a motor accident caused by an uninsured driver or untraced driver. If the driver was uninsured, the MIB can pay compensation for personal injury or death and/or damage to property. If the driver has not been traced, the MIB can only pay compensation for personal injury or death.

4
Travel and Transport

CONTENTS

INTRODUCTION

Years ago, you were born, lived and died sometimes without leaving your village. From Shanks's pony to space travel, the world has got smaller since then, with some people thinking nothing of jetting to another continent for lunch. Tourist space travel is now on the agenda and an explosion of cheap flights is taking people to more places than ever before. But, for most of us, the trials (and pleasures) of travelling about by bus, train and car are enough to keep us busy. The first public bus service is thought to have been Mr Shillibeer's horse-drawn carriage, which started to charge passengers in 1829 for taking them from Paddington station to the City of London. The private railways were taken into public ownership after the Second World War and then, for the most part, privatized again in the 1990s. The first automobiles began to appear on the roads in the late nineteenth century, quickly followed by laws to regulate their use, like the one stating that self-propelled vehicles on public roads must be preceded by a man on foot waving a red flag and blowing a horn.

This section looks at passengers' rights and responsibilities in the world of modern travel and who to complain to if you run into trouble on the move.

PUBLIC TRANSPORT

Bus and coach travel

Bus services outside London are run by private operators or are services subsidized by a Passenger Transport Executive or a local authority. There are six Passenger Transport Authorities (PTAs) in England.

Local authorities may provide some bus services and they must provide bus services to meet the needs of elderly and disabled people. The local authority will normally have a public transport officer responsible for bus services.

Bus services in London are the responsibility of Transport for London (TFL), which gives contracts and licences to private bus operators.

All coach services in Britain are privately operated.

Concessionary bus fares

In England, all people aged 60 or over, and disabled people of any age, are entitled to free bus travel within the local authority area in which they live. There are often restrictions on the times when you can travel on the bus for free. Usually you can travel for free at off-peak times but the rules may be different in some areas. Your local authority will tell you what the time restrictions are.

You can get more information about what is included in your local authority area from your local authority. Some local authorities have joined together to offer county-wide or area-wide schemes or to offer specific concessions on journeys which cross from one authority to another.

In Wales, the following people can have a free bus pass:

- people aged 60 or over
- disabled people
- essential companions for disabled people. The bus pass shows whether a companion is essential.

The bus pass is available from your local authority. It can be used in all local authority areas in Wales, at any time.

Penalty fares on buses

In London only, you may be liable to pay a penalty fare if you travel without a ticket or valid pass. A penalty fare is not a fine but is a fare set at a higher rate than the normal fare.

If you do not pay the bus penalty fare when asked, you must give your name and address to the official representative of Transport for London (TFL). Refusal to supply these details is a criminal offence and you could be prosecuted. If you want to appeal against being charged a penalty fare, whether you have paid it or not, you have 21 days to do this. TFL then has to show why you should pay and, if you continue to refuse, will have to take proceedings in the county court. If you want to appeal, write to Revenue Protection Services at: London Bus Services, PO Box 3893, London SW1W 9TN.

If you feel you have been unfairly treated by being charged a bus penalty

fare you should complain in writing to Transport for London Buses
(0845 300 7000, www.tfl.gov.uk/buses).

Complaints about bus services

If you have a complaint about any bus service (for example, unsafe driving,
overcharging, late running, unacceptable staff behaviour), you should complain directly to the bus operator. The name and address of the operator
must be shown on the vehicle and will also usually be displayed inside.

In London, you can complain directly to Transport for London Buses
(0845 300 7000).

Many private operators and Passenger Transport Executives (see below
for contact details) have charters or codes of practice setting out how
complaints are dealt with and what a passenger can expect.

If you have complained about a bus service outside London and are not
satisfied with the way the operator has dealt with your complaint, you can
take it to:

- the Bus Appeals Body, whether the service is operated privately or subsidized
  (in England, 023 9281 4493; www.bususers.org or in Wales, 029 2022 1370)
- the Traffic Commissioner for the area, the local authority responsible for the
  service or the local Passenger Transport Executive (contact details listed
  below).

If you have complained about a London bus service and are not satisfied,
you should contact London TravelWatch (020 7505 9000; www.
londontravelwatch.org.uk).

If you are travelling outside London and have a general complaint about
bus services – for example, about the lack of a service in your area or where a
bus stop or shelter is situated – you should contact the local authority or, if
you are in an area covered by a Passenger Transport Authority, the Passenger Transport Executive (contact details below).

In London, you should contact Transport for London Buses Customer
Service Centre (0845 300 7000; www.tfl.gov.uk/buses).

Complaints about coach services

Anyone who has a complaint about the quality of a coach service should
address the complaint to the operator. If you are not satisfied with the way
in which the operator has dealt with the complaint you should complain to

the Bus Appeals Body (023 9281 4493; www.bususers.org in England or 029 2022 1370 in Wales).

Rail and Underground services

Penalty fares (rail services)

Railway operators can only impose a penalty fare on a passenger who travels without the correct ticket in some areas. This will be an on-the-spot penalty above the normal fare and is not a fine. If the fare you should have paid is less than £10.00, the penalty is £20.00. If the fare was over £10.00, the penalty fare is double the fare.

You may want to appeal against a penalty fare if:

- there was insufficient notice that you were travelling in a penalty fare area – because, for example, signs were inadequate
- English is not your first language, or you were unable to read the notices because you are visually impaired
- there was inadequate opportunity to buy a ticket to travel because, for example, there was a long queue at the ticket office and the ticket machine was not available, or you were unable to use a machine because of a physical disability.

An appeal should be made to the Independent Penalty Fares Appeal Service, PO Box 14697, London SE1 8ZJ (www.penaltyfares.co.uk).

It is a criminal offence to travel on a train with the intention of avoiding paying the fare.

Penalty fares (Underground services)

Penalty fares are only imposed on London Underground services and not Underground services outside London. Penalties are imposed for the same reason as on buses, and are dealt with in the same way.

If you want to appeal against a penalty fare, you should write to the London Underground Penalty Fares Appeals office at London Underground Limited, 55 Broadway, London, SW1H 0BD.

If you feel you have been unfairly treated by being given a penalty fare, you should complain in writing to the Customer Service Centre (0845 330 9880; www.tfl.gov.uk/tube).

Complaints about rail services

If you have a complaint about a train journey or a train delay or cancellation, you should address it to the train operator's customer services officer. You may be entitled to compensation for late or delayed services. You should check this with the train operator's customer services officer. If you are complaining about a station, you should find out whether the station is run by a train operating company or by Network Rail. You can do this by checking the logo displayed at the station. You should then address the complaint to the appropriate customer services officer.

Train operators must have a passengers' charter that has been approved by the Rail Regulator. As well as setting out service standards, the charter gives information on how to complain. If you want to make a complaint, you can get a complaint form at a station or you can complain by telephone. Notices at stations and on trains give complaint addresses and telephone details.

If a complaint is likely to involve more than one company, or you are not sure which company you should make your complaint to, complain to whoever seems most likely. This company should then deal with the complaint or forward it to the appropriate company or companies.

If you are travelling outside London and you are not satisfied with the way in which the train company or Network Rail has dealt with your complaint, you should complain to Passenger Focus (08453 022 022; www.passengerfocus.org.uk).

In London, you should contact London TravelWatch (020 7505 9000; www.londontravelwatch.org.uk).

If my train is late, what compensation can I get?

You are unlikely to get compensation for the full value of your original ticket. The national conditions of carriage for trains allow for a voucher of at least 10 per cent of the value of a return ticket (20 per cent of the value of a single ticket) if your train arrived more than an hour late. If you chose not to make the journey on discovering how late the train was, you can claim a full refund. If you had to get a taxi to complete your journey because of the delay, you can claim a refund of the taxi fare if you send in the receipt. But you should inform the Duty Officer that you are intending to take a taxi.

Complaints or requests for vouchers or refunds should be made to the customer services officer of your train's operator. You can get details from the ticket collector on your train or from the station where you bought your ticket. You will have to write and enclose your ticket or other proof that you bought it, for example a credit card receipt. There may be a time limit within which to make your claim.

The rules about season tickets are different.

It is always wise to check with the National Rail Enquiry Service (08457 484950) shortly before you travel to avoid having your travel plans disrupted. They should have up-to-date information about timetable alterations and engineering works. There is another complaints procedure if the information they give you is wrong, and they can give you details of this.

Complaints about the National Rail Enquiry Service

The National Rail Enquiry Service (08457 484950) gives telephone information on timetables, fares and tickets on any route. It also gives information about engineering works and the best or cheapest route to use. If you have been given incorrect information, complain to Passenger Focus (see above). You will need to give them the date and time you made the call to the National Rail Enquiry Service and your own telephone code for them to identify the call centre that handled your original enquiry.

Complaints about Underground Services

Outside London, there are Underground services in Merseyside, Tyne and Wear, and Glasgow. They are the responsibility of the Passenger Transport Executive for the area (contact details listed below). Underground services in London are the responsibility of Transport for London (0845 330 9880; www.tfl.gov.uk/tube).

If you have a complaint, contact the service operator. The operator's name and address must be displayed on the train and will also be displayed in the Underground station.

In London, if you are not satisfied with the outcome of your initial complaint to the line manager, you can complain to London Underground Customer Service Centre (0845 330 9880; www.tfl.gov.uk/tube).

If you are still not satisfied, you should complain to London TravelWatch (see above).

Taxis and minicabs

In all areas outside London, the local authority regulates taxis and minicabs and their drivers.

In London, taxis, minicabs and their drivers are licensed by the Metropolitan Police at the Public Carriage Office (0845 602 7000).

Complaints about taxis and minicabs

Taxis

If you have a complaint about, for example, a driver's behaviour, unsafe driving, the driver not taking the direct route, or the meter apparently being wrongly set, complain to the taxi operator. If you are not satisfied with the response and you are outside London, then complain to your local authority, quoting, where possible, the licence number. The licence number is usually displayed both inside and outside the taxi.

If you are complaining about a taxi service in London and are not satisfied with the response you have received, take the complaint to the Public Carriage Office (0845 602 7000), giving the driver's badge number and as much information as possible about the complaint.

Minicabs

You should first complain to the operator. If you are not satisfied with the result of a complaint to the minicab operator, contact your local authority or the Public Carriage Office (0845 602 7000) if you live in the London area.

Personal injury and damage to property

If you are injured or your property is damaged while you are travelling on public transport other than a train (if, for example, you have fallen downstairs on an escalator), you should report it to the operator. You may also want to consider whether you can get compensation for any injury or damage caused by the accident. You should get specialist legal advice before you consider making a legal claim for compensation.

If you are injured or your property is damaged on a train, complain to the train operator or Miller Rail Claims, Room A201, MacMillan House,

Paddington, London w2 1yj. If you suspect there has been a health and safety breach, you should report it to the Health and Safety Executive (020 7717 6533; www.hse.gov.uk).

Passenger Transport Executives (PTEs)

Greater Manchester PTE:	0161 242 6000
Merseyside PTE (Merseytravel):	0151 227 5181
South Yorkshire PTE:	0114 276 7575
Tyne and Wear PTE (Nexus):	0191 203 3333
West Midlands PTE (Centro):	0121 200 2787
West Yorkshire PTE:	0113 251 7272

Traffic Commissioners

Northern:	0113 254 3291
Eastern:	01792 454390
West Midlands and South Wales:	0121 609 6801
Western:	0117 900 8577
South Eastern and Metropolitan area:	01323 452400

Who can help?

Office of Rail Regulation (ORR: 020 7282 2000; www.rail-reg.gov.uk).

TRANSPORT OPTIONS FOR DISABLED PEOPLE

Driving

Buying or hiring a vehicle

If you are disabled and want to buy a vehicle, you may be able to get a discount. Contact car dealers and ask if they operate any disabled drivers discount schemes. Motability (0845 456 4566; www.motability.co.uk) can sell or hire new or second-hand cars to anyone receiving the higher-rate mobility component of Disability Living Allowance or war pensioners' mobility supplement.

If you are not entitled to either of the above allowances, contact car dealers and ask if they operate any disabled drivers discount schemes.

Some commercial hire companies offer discounts to disabled people when they hire a car or van. It is worth checking to see if a discount is available.

Adaptations to vehicles

A car may need to be adapted to suit the needs of a disabled person. The Forum of Mobility Centres (0800 559 3636; www.mobility-centres.org.uk) is made up of 17 centres that offer advice and information to disabled motorists, including information about adaptations.

Exemption from road tax

Any vehicle that is used only for a disabled person (whether they are the driver or the passenger) will be exempt from road tax. To get exemption, the disabled person must be either:

- receiving the higher-rate mobility component of Disability Living Allowance; *or*
- receiving war pensioners' mobility supplement.

The vehicle must be registered in the name of the disabled person or in the name of someone authorized to act on their behalf.

Parking concessions

The Blue Badge scheme allows certain groups of disabled people to park in parking-restricted areas on public roads. For example, the blue badge enables disabled people to park free of charge and without time limit at on-street parking meters. Some London boroughs, and some town centres, do not operate the Blue Badge scheme. There is an online service called the Blue Badge parking map which can help you find blue badge parking bays in 64 towns and cities across the UK. You can find the map at www.direct.gov.uk/bluebadgemap.

You are eligible to apply for a blue badge if you are a driver or passenger who:

- receives the higher-rate mobility component of the Disability Living Allowance or war pensioners' mobility supplement, or is registered blind;
- has a permanent and substantial disability that means you are unable to walk or can walk only with considerable difficulty;
- has very severe upper limb disabilities (drivers only).

To apply for a blue badge, contact your local authority social services department. There is a small fee.

If you have a blue badge you may be able to get parking concessions when travelling in another country that also recognizes the badge. However, each country continues to determine its own set of parking concessions for which the badge can be used. There is further information on the Department for Transport website (www.mobility-unit.dft.gov.uk).

Public transport for disabled people

Public transport operators have the same duties as any other service provider as far as disability discrimination is concerned. This means they must not treat you less favourably than they would treat a person who is not disabled, unless they can show that the treatment is justified. This applies to the vehicle itself as well as to other services provided by the operator, such as timetable information or facilities at a station. Ships are not covered by these rules but the other services provided by shipping companies are covered, such as services in ferry lounges.

It is against the law for an airline, travel agent or tour operator to refuse a booking because someone is disabled. It's also against the law for them to refuse to allow a disabled person to board an aircraft if they have a valid ticket and reservation. This applies to any flight leaving an airport in the European Union (EU) and to flights on European airlines arriving in the EU. This law covers people who wouldn't normally be covered by disability discrimination legislation, such as those with a temporary injury.

Rail services for disabled people

All station and train operators have a disabled persons protection policy that sets out what provision a station or train operator makes for disabled people using its services. Information on these services and a copy of the protection policy is available from the local train or station operator. Alternatively, most local authorities and Passenger Transport Executives publish guides for disabled travellers that are a useful source of information on the facilities at railway stations.

If you need assistance when travelling by train – for example, if you are a wheelchair user and need help getting on and off the train, or you are visually impaired and need to be guided to the train – contact the train operator and ask them to arrange assistance. Try to give the operator at least 48 hours' notice of when you intend to travel and the type of help you require. Most mainline stations have a staff member who deals with requests for assistance. That person will be able to make any arrangements needed with other operating companies.

Concessionary rail fares for disabled people

If you are disabled, you can buy a disabled person's railcard that entitles you and an accompanying adult to one third off the price of a rail ticket. Application forms are available from main stations, or from the Disabled Persons Railcard Office (0191 218 8103; www.disabledpersons-railcard.co. uk). Existing railcard users can renew their railcard by telephone.

Complaints about accessibility

If you are not satisfied with any arrangements made or any aspect of accessibility, complain to the train operator. If the operator has not kept to the terms of its disabled persons protection policy, a complaint should be made to the Office of Rail Regulation (020 7282 2000; www.rail-reg.gov.uk).

Buses and disabled people

Outside London, most Passenger Transport Authorities and local authorities with responsibility for public transport publish guides for disabled travellers. In London, if you have an enquiry about disability access to buses, you should contact Transport for London Access and Mobility (020 7222 1234; www.tfl.gov.uk).

In some areas there are dial-a-bus schemes providing door-to-door services for disabled people. You can get information from the local authority social services department or a local organization for disabled people.

There are regulations covering coaches and buses so that disabled people can get on and off in safety and reasonable comfort. These depend on when a bus was brought into service, but may include the need for ramps, steps and priority seating. A driver or conductor must help you get on or off the bus if you ask, unless there are health and safety concerns about doing so.

Concessionary bus fares for disabled people

In England, disabled people of any age are entitled to free bus travel within the local authority area in which they live. There are often restrictions on the times when you can travel on the bus for free. Usually you can travel for free at off-peak times but the rules may be different in some areas. Your local authority will tell you what the time restrictions are.

You can get more information about what is included in your local authority area from your local authority. Some local authorities have joined together to offer county-wide or area-wide schemes or to offer specific concessions on journeys which cross from one authority to another.

In Wales, the following people can have a free bus pass:

- disabled people
- essential companions for disabled people. The bus pass shows whether a companion is essential.

The bus pass is available from your local authority. It can be used in all local authority areas in Wales, at any time.

Complaints about accessibility of bus services

If you are dissatisfied with access to a bus service, complain to the bus operator. You may also want to draw the problem to the attention of the director of your local authority. The local authority may take up the complaint but will have no formal powers to make the operator respond.

Coaches and disabled people

There are similar provisions for disability access to coaches as for buses (see above). If you plan to travel by coach, you may want to contact the operator when arranging the journey to let the operator know what arrangements you need and to see whether the facilities exist to meet them.

Underground services and disabled people

There are similar provisions for disability access to Underground services as for coaches and buses – see above.

Disabled people may be entitled to concessionary fares on the Underground.

London Underground has an interactive online service. You can use it to search for accessibility information about every station on the network. The service shows wheelchair users, older people, travellers with heavy luggage and people with pushchairs the best routes through stations. It can also help you if you've got visual or hearing difficulties. To find out more, go to www.directenquiries.com or contact Transport for London's Access and Mobility for travel in London (020 7222 1234). Outside London, contact the Passenger Transport Executive.

For more information on how to complain about Underground services and addresses of Passenger Transport Executives, see *Public transport*, pp. 384, 386.

Taxis and minicabs and disabled people

Drivers of licensed taxis and minicabs are required to carry a guide dog and hearing dog, or an assistance dog accompanying a person with epilepsy or a physical disability, free of charge.

In London, all taxis must be able to carry a standard wheelchair. It may also be obligatory for taxis in other areas to be wheelchair-accessible.

Drivers of taxis which have been made accessible for disabled people are obliged to help them in and out of their taxis and help with luggage (unless they have a special exemption because they are disabled themselves).

Apart from the provision about dogs, mentioned earlier, there is no provision for disability access to minicabs.

In London, the Taxicard scheme subsidizes the cost of taxis for people with serious mobility problems who cannot use public transport. For more information, go to the Transport for London website (www.tfl.gov.uk).

Escort services

The Red Cross provides an escort service to enable disabled people make short or long journeys that they would otherwise find difficult. Escort services include providing a companion for a journey on public transport, a private car with a driver or a Red Cross ambulance. A charge is made.

The St John Patient Transport Service can provide non-emergency medical transport for people in Wales who have difficulty in using public transport or normal cars. They can provide specially adapted wheelchair-accessible vehicles and fully equipped ambulances. They also provide a hospital car service for able-bodied patients, driven by drivers trained in emergency aid and manual handling. A charge is made for all these services. For more information, visit the St John Cymru Wales website (www. stjohnwales.co.uk).

Who can help?

The **Disabled Drivers' Motor Club** (01832 734724; www.justmobility.co. uk) gives help and advice on motoring problems, vehicles and conversions.

The **Disabled Drivers' Association** (08707 703333; www.justmobility.co.
uk) provides advice and information to members on all aspects of
mobility.

CAR TRAVEL

Can I use my mobile phone in the car?

It is a criminal offence to use a hand-held mobile phone when driving. The ban also applies when you are waiting at traffic lights or in
a traffic jam. You can get a fixed penalty (a sort of fine) of £60 and
three penalty points on your licence if you break the law. Although
hands-free phones are not included in the ban and can be used
while driving, you can risk getting a fixed penalty of £60 and three
penalty points if you lose control of your car. If a case goes to court,
in addition to points, you could face disqualification and a maximum
fine of £1,000 (£2,500 for drivers of buses, coaches or goods
vehicles).

Driving tests

A driving test is made up of a theory test and a practical test. You cannot
normally take the practical test without first having passed the theory test.
You have to pay a fee for each part of the test.

Before you can apply for a test, you must have a valid Great Britain
provisional driving licence.

The theory test

The theory test is in two parts. The first is a computerized touch-screen test
in which you have to select the correct answer from a number of choices.
The second part is called the hazard perception test. You will be shown a set
of video clips of driving hazards and asked to click the mouse button as soon
as you spot a hazard. You have to pass both parts of the theory test at the
same sitting in order to pass.

If you have special needs, the Driving Standards Agency (0191 201 8161 (north) or 029 2058 1218 (south); www.dsa.gov.uk) can make special arrangements.

You do not have to take a theory test if you:

- want to upgrade your licence in the same category – for example, upgrade your car licence to be able to drive a car towing a large trailer
- have a licence to drive automatic cars and/or motorcycles and want to upgrade your licence to a manual gearbox for the same type of vehicle
- have passed a theory test and a practical moped test, and now want to upgrade to a motorcycle licence
- have full entitlement to drive certain motor vehicles – for example, motor tricycles, because you have a full motorcycle licence issued before 1 February 2001
- have a full licence for an invalid carriage.

You can apply for the test:

- in writing, by completing an application form available from theory test centres, driving instructors or the theory test booking line (0870 010 1372, or 0870 010 0372, if you want to apply in Welsh)
- by phone on 0870 010 1372 using a credit or debit card
- by fax on 0870 010 4372
- online (www.dsa.gov.uk).

You have to pay a fee for the test.

Candidates with special needs

If you have special needs – for example, you are dyslexic or deaf, or if you need special physical access to the centre or want to take the test in a language other than English – the Driving Standards Agency (0191 201 8161 (north) or 029 2058 1218 (south); www.dsa.gov.uk) can make arrangements. Indicate what your special needs are when you book the test.

If you are ill and have to cancel your theory test, you should normally send the DSA a doctor's certificate within ten days of the test day if you want to be given another date without having to pay the fee again. Otherwise, you must pay another fee. You must give three working days' notice to cancel for any other reason.

The practical test

You cannot take the practical test until you have passed the theory test unless you are exempt. The practical test will test your ability to exercise adequate control of your vehicle and normally lasts 40 minutes.

The practical test also includes two questions on vehicle safety, designed to make sure that you know how to check the safety of your vehicle.

You must have completed a course of compulsory basic training (CBT) before applying for a motorcycle test, and must show your CBT certificate when you take your practical test. Information on the CBT is available from the Driving Standards Agency (DSA: 0191 201 8161 (north) or 029 2058 1218 (south); www.dsa.gov.uk).

If you fail, or do not take the practical test within two years of having passed the theory test, you will have to take the theory test again and pass it before you can apply for a practical test.

Applying for a practical test

You will have to pay a fee for the test. There is no fee for a test to drive an invalid carriage. You can apply for the test by phone and pay by debit or credit card, or by post and pay by cheque or postal order.

You can choose to take the test at any test centre but often the choice is determined by the driving instructor and the availability of the instructor's car for the test.

Candidates with special needs

The DSA (0191 201 8161 (north) or 029 2058 1218 (south); www.dsa.gov.uk) can make provision for a candidate with special needs if you ask when you book the test. If you are deaf, you can ask for the test to be carried out in stages to enable sufficient time for the examiner to give instructions. A friend or family member can act as an interpreter or signer and the examiner can allow stopping at safe places on the route for the signer (who will sit in a rear seat) to communicate with you.

If you have a physical disability you may be asked to demonstrate any special controls on the vehicle in which you are being tested before the start of the test.

Practical test result

At the end of the practical test, the examiner will tell you whether you have passed or not.

If you fail the practical test, you can only appeal on the grounds that the test was not conducted in accordance with regulations.

When you have passed the practical test, if you have a photocard provisional licence and your personal details have not changed, you can hand it over to the examiner and a full licence will be issued to you automatically. Otherwise, you must apply to the Driver and Vehicle Licensing Agency (DVLA) for your full licence within two years of the test date. If you do not do this, you will have to take the practical test (and the theory test) again.

When you pass the car or motorcycle-only practical test, you will be subject to a probationary period.

Probationary period

When you pass your driving test for the first time you will be subject to a two-year probationary period. This applies to anyone driving on a licence issued by the DVLA. The two-year period begins on the day you pass the practical test.

If during the probationary period you are convicted of driving offences for which six or more penalty points are awarded, your driving licence will be revoked.

If your full driving licence is revoked, you will revert to learner status and be treated as if you had never passed a driving test. To continue driving, you will have to get a provisional driving licence and drive with learner's plates until you have passed both the theory and practical parts of the driving test. You cannot appeal against the revocation of your licence. However, if you appeal against the conviction or sentence that brought the number of penalty points up to six or more, you can apply to the DVLA to have your licence restored pending the result of the appeal. If the court notifies the DVLA that the sentence is under appeal, the full licence should be restored without a further test.

There is no minimum period for which the licence must be revoked. As soon as you have passed both the theory and practical parts of another driving test, you can apply for a new full licence. However, the penalty points will remain on the driving licence for four years from the date of your offence. After four years you can ask the DVLA to have them removed from your licence.

Disqualification/extended driving test

For some offences, a court can disqualify you or order that you be re-tested. If the offence is very serious the court can order that you are 'disqualified until test passed' and that you must take a double-practical driving test known as an 'extended driving test'. The fee to be paid for this test is higher than that for a normal test.

A motorcyclist who is disqualified by a court will have to retake compulsory basic training in order to ride as a learner and will have to retake the practical test.

Fees
You can find details of current driving test fees on the Driving Standards Agency website (www.dsa.gov.uk).

Complaints
Step one

If you want to complain about the way in which any part of your test was administered, you should contact either the Theory Test Operations or Practical Test Operations at the Driving Standards Agency (DSA). You can contact the offices by phone but in most cases you will have to put the complaint in writing.

If you want to complain about the *theory test,* contact the DSA Customer Service Unit (0870 600 0067; www.dsa.gov.uk).

If you want to complain about the *practical test,* you should complain to the Driving Standards Agency (0870 010 1372).

Step two

If you are not satisfied with the outcome of your complaint about any general administration of the test, you can write to the DSA chief executive at the DSA's headquarters. You can also ask one of the following to investigate your complaint:

- an independent complaints assessor. You would need to contact the DSA's chief executive at the DSA headquarters (0115 901 2500; www.dsa.gov.uk) about this
- the Parliamentary Ombudsman. You would need to ask your MP about this. See *Parliamentary Ombudsman*, p. 483.

Who else can help?
There is more information about the **Driving Standards Agency**, the **Driver Vehicle Licensing Agency** and the **Vehicle Inspectorate** at www.direct.gov.uk.

Driving licences

You need a licence to drive most vehicles on a public road. You do not need a licence to drive any vehicle on a private road. A private road is one to which the public does not have access, such as a road on a private estate.

However, there are some vehicles which do not require a licence, on either a public or a private road. The most common examples of these are bicycles and horse-drawn carts.

Ages at which you can drive

Age	Vehicle
14 years	• electrically assisted pedal cycles
16 years	• mopeds
	• cars. This applies to people receiving Disability Living Allowance at the higher level
	• small agricultural tractors
	• small mowing machines or any other small pedestrian-controlled vehicle
17 years	• motorbikes up to 125 cc
	• cars
	• large agricultural tractors
	• small road-rollers
18 years	• medium lorries
	• vans and lorries if you are a member of the young driver scheme
21 years	• large road-rollers
	• all other vehicles
70 years	• A provisional or full licence only lasts until your 70th birthday. Once you are 70, you must apply to renew your licence. The licence will normally be renewed for three years, after which you will need to apply to renew again.

The young driver scheme

The young driver scheme provides an opportunity for a young person to obtain a full licence for large vehicles at the age of 18 rather than 21. The scheme is run by Skills for Logistics (01908 313360; www.skillsforlogistics.org).

The type of vehicle the licence covers

These are the most common types of vehicle which you require a licence to drive. For full details of all of the categories of vehicles that need a licence contact the DVLA (0870 240 0009; www.dvla.gov.uk).

Vehicle	Category
Cars (including cars with a trailer weighing up to 750 kg)	B
Motorbikes	A
Mopeds	P
Vans and lorries weighing up to 3,500 kg (including vehicles with a trailer weighing up to 750 kg)	B
Vans and lorries weighing between 3,500 and 7,500 kg (including vehicles with a trailer weighing up to 750 kg)	C1
Buses with fewer than nine seats (including vehicles with a trailer weighing up to 750 kg)	B
Buses with more than eight but fewer than 17 seats (including vehicles with a trailer weighing up to 750 kg) provided they are not used for hire or reward	D1
Invalid cars	B1

Vans, lorries and passenger-carrying vehicles

These vehicles do not require a special licence but do require you to have additional entitlements – for example, to drive vans, lorries or passenger-carrying vehicles. If you are unsure what type of licence you need, you should consult the Driver Vehicle Licensing Agency (DVLA: 0870 240 0009; www.dvla.gov.uk).

Types of driving licence

A driving licence is either a 'provisional' licence or a 'full' licence.

Provisional driving licence

You must apply for a provisional licence if:

• you have never had a full driving licence

- you are unable to show you are entitled to a full driving licence.

If you want to drive a motorbike, and are applying for a provisional licence, you should indicate this on the application form. If you already have a full licence to drive a moped, car or certain vans and buses, you can use it automatically as a provisional licence for driving a motorbike.

A provisional licence has certain restrictions on its use. If you have a provisional licence to drive a car or other vehicle (except a motorbike):

- you must display 'L' plates on the front and back of the vehicle (or 'D' plates in Wales)
- you must not drive on a motorway
- if the vehicle has more than one seat, you must have someone with you whenever you are driving. The person supervising you must sit in the front passenger seat and be fit to drive the vehicle – for example, they must not have drunk more than a legal amount of alcohol. They must also be aged 21 or over and have had a full driving licence for at least three years.

However, if you have passed a driving test and are still waiting to receive a full licence, you are not subject to the above restrictions.

Full driving licence
You are entitled to apply for a full driving licence if you have passed a driving test in the UK within the previous two years.

If you have a full driving licence issued outside the UK, the Isle of Man and the Channel Islands, see *Driving abroad*, p. 403.

Restrictions on the use of a full licence
A full licence does not have any restrictions on its use other than those relating to:

- the age of the driver
- supervision of learner drivers
- the type of vehicle the licence covers
- the medical condition of the driver – for example, defective eyesight that cannot be corrected by glasses.

How to apply for a driving licence
You apply for a driving licence by filling in Form D1, which is available from the post office. This form is used for applying for either a provisional licence

or a full licence. You must send the fee with the completed application form and a recent colour photograph and:

- your valid passport (this is the preferred document and should speed up the application); *or*
- your birth/adoption certificate or other similar official document.

Unless you send a UK, EU or EEA passport with the application, you will also need to get your photograph verified by a doctor, lawyer, teacher, police officer, MP, magistrate, minister of religion or another similar professionally qualified person. (For a list of EU and EEA countries, see p. 501.) If you are a foreign national and you do not want to send your passport, and you do not know anyone who can verify your photograph, you may be able to take your application form, photograph and passport to your local vehicle registration office (details from DVLA: 0870 240 0009; www.dvla.gov.uk), as some VROs operate an over-the-counter identity checking service. Your application will be checked and your passport handed back to you.

You must tell the DVLA about any health condition that affects or may affect your ability to drive – for example, giddiness, heart attack or mental illness. If you have a disability, you will have to inform the DVLA of its nature. They may require you to undergo a medical examination.

If the DVLA refuses to give you a licence on medical grounds, you can appeal to a magistrates' court.

Licences are issued in two parts. One section is a credit card-sized photocard and contains details of the categories of vehicles that you are entitled to drive. The other section is a paper document setting out your licence entitlement history and any valid endorsements, including penalty points and disqualification periods. These licences are called photocard licences.

Paper licences issued before the introduction of photocard licences remain valid until they run out or the details on them need to be changed. Photocard licences must be renewed every ten years to ensure the photograph remains up to date.

When you can start driving

If you have applied for a first provisional licence, you must not start driving until you receive the licence. This will usually take at least three weeks. If you have a medical condition, you may have to wait longer because more information may be needed before the licence is issued.

If you have had a licence before (and you are still entitled to one) and you are not applying for your first provisional licence and there are no medical problems, you are allowed to drive as soon as the application form reaches DVLA. You do not have to wait until you receive the licence.

Compulsory basic training for motorcycles and mopeds

All learner moped- and motorcycle-riders (except for those listed below) must complete a compulsory basic training (CBT) course.

These people do not have to complete a CBT course:

- people who are learning to drive a motorbike and who have already obtained full moped entitlement as a result of passing a moped test on or after 1 December 1990
- people riding a moped with the full entitlement given automatically with a full car licence.

CBT courses are run by motorcycle training bodies approved by the Driving Standards Agency (0115 901 2500). They are listed under 'motorcycle training' in the Yellow Pages or 'motorcycling instruction' in Thomson directories.

Problems with sight

In order to get or keep a licence, a minimum eyesight standard must be met.

If you need glasses or contact lenses to meet the eyesight standard, you must always wear them when you drive. If you drive without wearing your lenses or glasses, you are committing an offence.

Disqualifications and endorsements

Disqualifications

If you have been disqualified from driving, you can have a licence again either:

- at the end of the disqualification period; *or*
- earlier if the disqualification is lifted.

If you intend to wait until the end of the disqualification period, you will usually receive a reminder from the DVLA to apply for a new licence eight weeks before the end of the disqualification period. If you do not receive a reminder, you should fill in form D1 available from the post office and send it to the DVLA. You can apply to the court that dealt with your case to have the disqualification lifted if you have been disqualified for a total of more than two years.

Endorsements

You may incur penalty point endorsements on your licence for being convicted of committing certain driving offences. After a certain time, you can apply to the DVLA on form D1 to have endorsements removed (for a small charge). The time you will have to wait to have endorsements removed from your licence will vary according to the type of driving offence committed.

Lost, stolen or defaced licences

If your licence is stolen or lost, you should tell the police as soon as possible. You should also apply for a duplicate licence using form D1. You can obtain this form from the post office and send it to the DVLA. There is a charge for obtaining a duplicate licence. Duplicate licences may also be obtained by phoning the DVLA.

If your licence is destroyed or defaced in some way so that the information on it is no longer clear, you have to apply for a duplicate licence. You do not have to tell the police in this situation.

Change of name or address

For both paper and photocard driving licences, documentary evidence of a change of name is required – for example, a birth certificate, passport or deed poll. You can continue to drive while you are waiting for the licence to be returned to you. The DVLA does not make a charge for changing the details of your name and address. You may be fined if you do not tell the DVLA about a change in your name or address.

Paper driving licences

If you hold a paper driving licence and you need to notify a change of name or address, you must complete a D1 application form, available from most post offices.

Photocard driving licences

If you hold a photocard driving licence and you need to notify a change of address, you should complete the 'changes' section on your paper counterpart licence and send it to the DVLA (0870 240 0009; www.dvla.gov.uk) together with your photocard licence. If you need to notify a change of name, you should use form D1.

Driving abroad

Driving in the EEA

If you have a full Great Britain (GB) driving licence, you can drive in any EEA country on this licence and an International Driving Permit is not required. For a list of EEA countries, see p. 502.

You can exchange your GB licence for one of the country in which you are living if you want to.

Driving outside the EEA

If you wish to drive outside the EEA as a visitor – for example, on holiday – you may need to apply for an International Driving Permit (IDP). For a list of EEA countries, see p. 502. If you need an IDP, you may apply by post to one of the motoring organizations or get one in person from a major post office. You do not have to be a member of the organization. You can only be issued with an IDP if you have a full GB licence.

If you go to live permanently in another country, you may be able to exchange your licence for a driving licence in that country. You should check with the driver licensing authority in the country in which you are going to live. The appropriate embassy may be able to provide this information.

Driving licences issued abroad

Licences issued in another EEA country

If you have a full and valid driving licence that has been issued in another EEA country (a 'Community licence'), you may be able to drive in the UK on this licence. For a list of EEA countries, see p. 502. You do not have to exchange your Community licence immediately for a GB licence. Provided the Community licence remains valid in the issuing country, and it is a licence to drive an ordinary car, you can use it to drive here until you are 70, or for three years after you become resident. If it is a 'vocational licence' – for example, a licence to drive a minibus or bus – the rules are different.

However, if you want to, you can exchange your Community licence for a full GB licence. You should complete form D1 available from post offices and send your own driving licence with the application form. A photocopy will not be accepted. A fee is payable.

Licences issued outside the EEA

If you have a full and valid driving licence that has been issued in a country other than an EEA country you can drive in the UK on this licence for twelve months. For a list of EEA countries, see p. 502.

If you intend to be resident in the UK beyond this period, you can exchange your licence for a full GB licence if it is a British Forces Germany licence or if it was issued in certain countries, including Australia, Barbados, Canada, Hong Kong, Japan, New Zealand and South Africa. For some other countries you must take a UK driving test to obtain a full GB licence if you intend to drive after the initial twelve-month period.

Traffic accidents

An accident is defined as a traffic accident if it occurs on a road or in a place to which the public have access. This can include footpaths and bridleways. A driver involved in a traffic accident should stop whether or not the accident was their fault if:

- anyone, other than themselves, is injured
- another vehicle, or someone else's property, is damaged
- an animal in another vehicle or running across the road is injured
- a bollard, street lamp or other item of street furniture is damaged.

If the driver has to stop, they must remain near the vehicle long enough for anyone who is involved directly or indirectly in the accident to ask for details. This could be, for example, the owner of an injured animal, a relative of someone who is injured, or the police. The driver must then give their name and address, the name and address of the owner of the vehicle (if the driver is not the owner), and the registration number of the vehicle.

The driver may also have to report the accident to a police officer or at a police station, in person, as soon as practicable and in any case within 24 hours. This duty arises whenever the driver has not given their name and address at the scene of the accident, whether or not they were asked to do so.

If any personal injury is caused to another person, the driver must also produce a valid insurance certificate if asked to do so by a police officer, an injured person, or anyone else directly or indirectly involved in the accident. If the insurance certificate is asked for, but not produced at the time, the accident must be reported to a police station as soon as practicable, or in any case within 24 hours, and the insurance certificate must be taken to a police station within seven days of the accident. However, if the driver is asked at the time of the accident to produce insurance details and does so, there is no further obligation to report the accident to the police, as long as they have complied with the duties described above.

In the case of a damage-only accident, the driver must give insurance details to anyone who may wish to make a claim against them. In all accidents, drivers should inform their own insurance company.

If you are involved in a road accident it's helpful if you can establish the following:

- full details of the accident – where and when it happened and who was involved (sketch plans and/or photographs would be useful)
- whether anyone was responsible for the accident
- whether there was any injury or damage
- whether there is any independent evidence about what happened – for example, witnesses or police reports
- whether any criminal proceedings have been started or threatened
- whether any civil proceedings have been started or threatened
- what type of insurance the people involved have
- whether free legal advice or assistance – for example, from a motoring organization or under an insurance policy – is available.

It is important to establish, as soon as possible after the accident, whether anyone was at fault. It may be obvious that someone caused the accident and there will be no dispute about liability. However, there will be cases where it is not obvious, or where the extent of liability is difficult to work out.

As a general rule, the driver of a vehicle that runs into the back of another vehicle will be held liable for the accident. This is the case even if the car in front has braked sharply or unexpectedly, because drivers are required to drive a safe distance behind other vehicles. However, there may be circumstances when this does not apply, and if liability is disputed, legal advice will be necessary unless the insurance company is dealing with it.

Independent evidence about what happened

It is important to establish whether there were any witnesses to the accident – for example, other people involved in the accident, other drivers, pedestrians or police who saw what happened. If there are no witnesses, it may be difficult to prove liability, especially if the other party denies responsibility.

> ## I have had an accident in my car but the other driver is refusing to give me his details. What can I do?
>
> A driver involved in an accident is required to give information. The keeper of a vehicle can also be required to provide the police with information on who was driving a vehicle at the time that an offence was committed. There is no legal requirement for anyone else to provide information. Drivers include motorcyclists but not cyclists.
>
> If a driver involved in a traffic accident refuses to give details, such as name and address, at the scene of the accident, this information can be obtained in other ways. If the registration number of the vehicle has been noted and the accident has been reported, the police can trace the owner (not necessarily the driver) of the vehicle and their insurance company. However, the police can refuse to pass on this information.
>
> The Driver and Vehicle Licensing Agency (DVLA: 0870 240 0009; www.dvla.gov.uk) can give the name and address of the person registered as the keeper of the vehicle to anyone who has a good reason for needing it. Someone who wants this information should write to the DVLA explaining why it is needed. A fee is payable. The registration number, make and model of the car and the date of the accident must be given. If the DVLA does not consider there are adequate reasons for providing the information, it will return the fee.

If a driver is driving illegally

If an accident happens involving a driver who is driving illegally, they will not be in a strong position to take any action, even if someone else caused the accident. Examples of illegal driving are driving:

- alone on a provisional licence
- without a driving licence, tax or insurance
- while disqualified from driving
- a stolen vehicle
- an unsafe vehicle
- without an MOT certificate
- while drunk or under the influence of drugs.

Accidents caused by sudden illness

If an accident occurs because a driver has become ill – for example, through a stroke or heart attack – they will not be prosecuted for the way they were driving. However, in some circumstances they could be liable to pay compensation. This may be covered by their insurance.

Payment for hospital treatment following an accident

Immediate treatment

The driver of a vehicle involved in a road accident may be charged for any emergency medical treatment provided by a doctor (other than one working in or called from a hospital), such as a hospital doctor who is off duty and happens to be passing by the accident. There is a standard charge plus, in certain circumstances, a mileage allowance. The driver will receive a bill from the doctor some time after the accident. This charge should be included as part of any claim for damages. The driver's insurance company will usually pay this charge without affecting their no-claims bonus.

Further hospital treatment

If anyone involved in the accident receives further hospital treatment in a non-NHS hospital, as an in-patient or an out-patient, the hospital may claim from the driver's insurance company up to a certain amount for the cost of treatment. The hospital will write to the patient, or their parents if a child was injured, asking for the driver's name and address, details of their insurance company, whether or not the patient is making a claim against the driver and if a solicitor is acting for the patient.

If someone has a road accident and receives further hospital treatment at an NHS hospital, the Department of Health can require the insurance company of the other driver to meet some of the costs. Where the driver who caused the accident is not insured or cannot be traced, the costs will be recovered from the Motor Insurers' Bureau (MIB: 01908 830001; www.mib. org.uk).

The Department of Health automatically recovers NHS charges from the insurance company on behalf of the hospital. There is no need for the injured person to be involved in routine cases. In cases where the person takes civil legal action against the other party, there is no need to include a claim for NHS charge recovery.

Failure to respond to claim letters

If someone does not reply to a claim letter holding them liable for damages following a road accident, you should take one of the following courses of action:

- If you have fully comprehensive insurance, let the insurance company pursue the claim. If the insurance company does not manage to recover damages from the other person you will lose your no-claims bonus, unless you can successfully sue the liable person.
- If you have no insurance, or have only third-party insurance, you will have to pursue the claim yourself. If the other person does not respond, you may have to take court action.
- If the police were involved, they can be contacted to ask whether they are following up the accident and whether they have heard from the other person.

Civil court proceedings

If you do not have an insurance company acting for you, because, for example, some losses are uninsured, you may have to sue the liable person. When this is the case, bear the following points in mind:

- If the claim is defended and is allocated to the small claims track at the county court (that is, most claims of £5,000 or less), you will not usually be entitled to claim solicitors' costs, and will therefore have to deal with the case yourself, or pay for a solicitor.
- If the claim is defended and allocated to either the fast track or the multi-track at the county court, you will need legal advice and representation. You might get legal aid to help with these costs.

If a claim form has been issued against you, you need to respond quickly, as time limits for entering a defence are quite short. You may admit you are liable for some or all of the damages claimed but you may have a good counterclaim to make and this must be done quickly.

Traffic accidents related to work

If you are an employee and have a traffic accident while travelling for work (or possibly on the way to work), you should bear in mind the following points:

- If the vehicle is insured by the employer, you will be covered by the employer's vehicle insurance, whether or not you were responsible for the accident.
- If you are an injured pedestrian or cyclist, the employer will normally be liable

in the same way as for any industrial injury, unless you clearly acted negligently.

- If you are a trade union member and are injured, you will usually get free legal help from the trade union.
- You may be able to claim benefits under the industrial injuries scheme.

Learner drivers

Learner drivers who are driving legally are in exactly the same position as any other driver in relation to a traffic accident. The supervisor of a learner driver must do all that is reasonable to prevent the driver from driving in a way likely to cause danger to others. It is the duty of the driver to report an accident and the liability and responsibility of the supervisor depends on the particular circumstances.

The police have the power to require the supervisor of a learner driver to produce their licence and certificate of insurance.

Bicycles

If you have been in an accident involving a bicycle, you should be aware that cyclists do not have to be insured for damage to the bicycle or any other vehicle or for personal injury. However, the cyclist may be covered under another insurance policy – for example, their home contents policy. If the accident happened on the way to or from work, or while at work, the person who had the accident may be covered by their employer's insurance or may be able to obtain advice and assistance from a trade union.

If the cyclist has inadequate insurance, it will probably be easier to claim on your own insurance and let the insurance company take action against anyone who is liable.

If none of these is possible, the cyclist could be sued in court for compensation.

Children

If you are involved in an accident caused by a child, you should check whether the child was accompanied by a responsible adult at the time of the accident. If it can be shown that the adult acted negligently, the adult may be liable for any accident caused by the child and could be sued in the civil court for damages caused by the child.

If the child was unaccompanied and it can be shown that an adult was negligent by failing to supervise the child adequately at the time of the accident, they may be liable for any accident caused by the child and could be sued in the civil court for damages.

Children can be held liable for their own negligence. However, it may be difficult to prove that a young child's behaviour is negligent. Even if negligence by the child can be proved, it may not be worth pursuing any legal action as the child is unlikely to have any money.

Stationary or fixed objects

If someone hits a stationary object, either on the road itself or alongside the road, they should consider the following:

- Was the object adequately marked or lit to enable the driver to see it clearly and in time to avoid it – for example an unlit car, skip or roadworks? If not, it will be necessary to find out who was responsible for failing to do so: for example, if the object was a parked car, the responsible person is the owner, or, in the case of roadworks, whoever is carrying out the roadworks is responsible. It will be necessary to find out whether this was the local authority or a gas, water or electricity company, or contractors doing the work on their behalf
- Had the object been left on the road either unlawfully or in an unsafe way – for example, a car parked on a blind corner? If so, the owner of the object or vehicle may be liable
- Have there been any similar accidents caused by the object? If so, this is evidence that the object has contributed to the accident.

The condition of the road surface

An accident may be caused by the condition of the road surface – for example, by pot holes, ice, mud or leaves. Adequate warning may not have been given of a problem with the road surface. For example:

- the local authority may have failed to respond reasonably to a problem with the road surface. If so, it may be liable for any accident caused
- individuals or firms, such as farmers or contractors, may have left mud or grease on the road surface for an unreasonable period of time without adequate warnings. If so, they may be liable for any accident caused.

Animals

If an accident is caused by or to an animal, the following points should be considered:

- If the animal is a cat or poultry, the incident does not count in law as an accident. This means that the driver is not required to stop. If there is injury to cattle or to a horse, ass, mule, pig, sheep, goat or dog, the driver must stop.

- If it can be shown that the owner of an animal has been negligent in allowing the animal on the road – for example, failing to maintain a fence they are responsible for maintaining, then the owner will be liable. Owners are not responsible for the actions of their cats or poultry.
- If a driver is responsible for an injury to an animal, other than cats or poultry, then they may be sued for damages.

Emergency vehicles

Emergency vehicles have no special exemption from liability for accidents that they are involved in or cause. The same rules apply as with any other accident.

Drivers from abroad

If an accident happens in the UK and the driver is from abroad, their obligations are the same as if they came from the UK.

However, it may be difficult to get compensation for any damage or injuries. You could:

- contact the Motor Insurers' Bureau (MIB: 01908 830001; www.mib.org.uk), which can obtain details of the driver and their insurance company if the vehicle's registration number can be provided and the driver comes from a country participating in the green card scheme. If the driver was not insured, or the insurance company does not have an agent in the United Kingdom, the Motor Insurers' Bureau will take up the case. If the insurance company does have an agent in the UK you will be advised to contact them
- seek advice from a motoring organization
- take action against the driver's insurance company if it has an agency agreement with another insurance company in the UK
- claim on your own insurance policy if you have comprehensive cover. This will affect any no-claims bonus.

If you cannot pursue the claim in the UK, you should consider carefully before proceeding with a claim against the driver in their own country. Claims heard abroad can be difficult, time-consuming and expensive, and a solicitor's help would be needed. A claim pursued through the UK courts could become very involved and expensive if the driver refused to attend court.

MOTOR INSURANCE

If you drive your vehicle on the road, or leave it parked in the street, the law says that you must have motor insurance. It is a criminal offence not to insure your motor vehicle.

Types of motor insurance

There are three main types of motor insurance:

Third-party insurance

This is the minimum amount of insurance cover that you must have by law for your vehicle. Third-party insurance only covers you for damage to someone else's vehicle or property, or injury to someone else in an accident that involves your car. This includes accidents caused by your passenger. If your vehicle is damaged in the accident, you will have to pay for the repairs yourself.

Third-party, fire and theft insurance

This includes third-party cover and, additionally, damage to or loss of your car by fire or theft.

Comprehensive insurance

This includes third-party, fire and theft insurance. In addition, it will also pay for repairs to your car. There is a range of extra cover that some policies provide, including cover for your own death or injury, or that of your partner or other member of your family, up to a limited amount, cover for your personal belongings if they are stolen from your vehicle, medical and legal expenses, and hire of a replacement vehicle.

Motor insurance policies normally run for a year. Your insurer does not have to send you a notice reminding you to renew but most companies do send out notices. When you take out or renew motor insurance, you will get a cover note at first. This will be valid for 30 days or until you get a copy of the full insurance certificate. It is a criminal offence to drive without a cover note or full insurance certificate, so do not rely only on a telephone conversation in which someone has told you that you are covered. The police can ask you to show them your insurance certificate or cover note. If you can't produce the right document, they will give you seven days to do so at a police station of your choice. If you are stopped under the 'fixed penalty system', they can specify the station.

How to make a claim

If your car has been stolen

If your car has been stolen, tell your insurer and the police immediately. Your insurer will wait a few weeks before settling your claim to allow time for the car to be found. Check your policy to see whether it covers the cost of hiring another car during this time. If you were paying your premium by instalments, you may have to carry on paying, even though you have no vehicle to insure.

If your car is found after your claim has been settled, it will belong to your insurer. If your car is not found, your insurer will offer to pay you the market value of the car, which is the amount you could have sold it for before it was stolen. This payment will bring your policy to an end, and you will not have the rest of your premium refunded, unless this is included in your policy. If you are not satisfied with the offer, try to get evidence that the car is worth more, by using car price guides or prices of similar vehicles in local papers.

If your car has been in an accident

If you have an accident:

- never admit that it was your fault at the scene of the accident, as this could make your policy invalid
- exchange names, addresses and insurance details with the drivers of the other vehicles involved, and get the details of any independent witnesses. If someone refuses to give you details about themselves or their insurance, your insurer may be able to trace them through the registration number of their car
- tell your insurer about the accident straight away, even if you do not intend to make a claim. If you do not make a claim for the accident, you will not risk losing your no-claims bonus.

Third-party and third-party, fire and theft policies

Third-party and third-party, fire and theft policies do not cover accidental damage to your car, but they may cover damage or personal injury to the other party, depending on who is to blame for the accident. Always make a claim against the other party first, and allow the insurer to decide who is responsible for the accident. If they decide that you are responsible, you will have to pay for the repairs yourself.

To make a claim from the other driver, write to them saying that you intend to make a claim from them. Say that you hold them responsible for the accident and ask them to tell their insurer. Tell your own insurer that you are claiming from the third party. The other driver must report the accident to their own insurer before the claim can be dealt with. The insurer can only act on the instructions of their own policyholder. You can find out if there is an insurance policy covering the other driver's vehicle by checking the Motor Insurance Database. You can access this by contacting the Motor Insurer's Information Centre (0845 165 2800; www.miic.org.uk).

If the driver was uninsured, or cannot be identified, the Motor Insurers Bureau (MIB: 01908 830001; www.mib.org.uk) may be able to settle your claim. In certain circumstances, an insurer may be able to deal with your claim, even when the driver is technically uninsured.

Comprehensive insurance policies

If you have a comprehensive insurance policy, it is usually best if you claim from your own insurer. Be aware that you may lose your no-claims bonus if your insurer is unable to recover the money from the other driver's insurer. You will still need to claim from the other driver's insurer for any injuries you have suffered or any losses that are not covered by your insurance policy.

To make a claim, get a claim form from your insurer, or write to the other driver or their insurer, giving full details of the accident and the driver's policy number. Tell the insurer about any independent witnesses, and send them any witness statements as soon as possible. If you used a broker or an agent to buy your insurance policy, they may help you to prepare your claim. Be sure to keep copies of all documents, including letters, claim forms and statements.

Don't arrange to have your car repaired without the insurer's permission, as you will be responsible for the cost. The insurer may ask an engineer or a motor claims assessor to inspect your car, and use an approved repair firm to carry out the work. Alternatively, you may be asked to get estimates yourself and send them to your insurer for approval before you can go ahead with the repairs. You may have to pay part of the repair costs yourself if your vehicle ends up in a better condition after it has been repaired than it was before.

Insurance when driving abroad

You will have third-party motor insurance to drive in any European Union (EU) country as long as your policy was bought from any EU-based insurer. This includes those based in the UK. For a list of EU countries, see p. 501. You should be aware that third-party cover is often inadequate and it is advisable to contact your insurer to arrange extra cover.

Your policy may also give you third-party cover to drive in some non-EU countries. Check with your insurer to see if the country you are travelling to is included in your policy. If it is not, you will need to take out extra cover. Your insurer can issue you with a green card to show that you have increased insurance cover. Some countries abroad require you to have a green card.

Motorcycle insurance

There are two different types of motorcycle insurance:

- specified cycle policy. This is the more common type of motorcycle insurance policy. It insures you to drive one specific motorcycle
- rider policy. This type of policy insures you to drive any motorcycle up to a certain cc rating, with the owner's permission.

Motorcycle insurance is usually limited to one person only. If you want someone else to drive your motorcycle, you must either name them on your policy, or make sure that they have their own motorcycle insurance. There is usually a compulsory excess on motorcycle insurance and you do not generally get a no-claims bonus.

TRAVEL AND HOLIDAYS

Package holidays

When you buy a package holiday your general consumer rights apply. The holiday must:

- match its description, so if the brochure says the hotel is within walking distance of the beach, it must be so; *and*
- be of a reasonable standard, bearing in mind the price paid and the location. For example, you would not expect a budget-priced holiday to be of the same

standard as a luxury holiday, but whatever the price, you would expect basic standards of hygiene to apply.

Once a holiday booking is confirmed, there is a binding contract between the holiday organizer and the person who booked the holiday. Problems with package holidays are usually a result of one or more terms of the contract having been broken. For example, if the brochure said that the hotel had certain facilities, such as a swimming pool, and there wasn't one, you may be entitled to compensation.

Remember: as with other purchases, if you used your credit card to pay for the holiday and the cost was more than £100 and less than £30,000, the credit card company may be equally liable for any breach of contract. This means that you could claim against the travel operator, the credit card company, or both of them jointly.

Prices

The law says that all holiday brochures must give the price legibly, comprehensibly and accurately. Once confirmed, the price of the holiday can be increased only if the booking conditions state that this is allowable, there are at least 30 days before your departure date and the increase is for one of the following reasons:

- an increase in transport costs – for example, for fuel
- to cover fees and taxes for services, such as landing fees
- variations in the exchange rate.

If the contract allows for an increase in price, the first 2 per cent must be absorbed by the tour operator. If the increase is significant, you should be given the opportunity to cancel the holiday. No price increase should be passed on in the period of 30 days before departure.

Refunds and compensation

Once a holiday booking is confirmed, you have a right to a refund without having to pay a cancellation fee if:

- the organizer cancels the holiday. If an alternative holiday is offered, you can choose whether to accept the alternative or the refund. The alternative holiday should be of at least the same standard as the one you booked or, if it is of a lesser standard, you should be refunded the difference in price between the original holiday and the alternative
- the organizer has made significant changes to the package holiday. An

example of this kind of change would be that the price of the holiday has been significantly increased or the departure date has been moved.

Also, once your holiday booking is confirmed, you may be entitled to compensation if:

- there is a breach of contract that, for example, results in the holiday being a complete disaster, or the departure date is altered significantly. You would not be able to claim compensation if circumstances were outside the operator's control – for example, if it rained continuously
- the tour operator has been negligent and as a result someone booked on the holiday suffers injury, illness or loss. Always take legal advice before deciding whether to accept compensation for personal injury
- your luggage has been lost. However, in practice it is usually quicker and easier to claim through any holiday insurance
- you have incurred additional expenses or suffered inconvenience because of a breach of contract or negligence – for example, if your flight was delayed for 24 hours and you had to take an extra day off work.

Dealing with the problem

Once you have decided what your rights are, contact the person who put together your package holiday. This is usually the tour operator but sometimes it is the travel agent. Whoever organized the holiday is responsible for dealing with most complaints. Even if the problem has been caused by the actions of a third party, such as staff at your hotel, the organizer may still be responsible if they were aware there was a potential problem but did nothing to rectify this.

Complain as soon as possible after the problem arises, if possible to a representative of the tour operator in the resort, and insist that they complete a report on the problem. Gather as much evidence as you can. Take photographs, and ask for witnesses' names and addresses. Back this up with a letter to the tour operator within 28 days of your return. Refer in your letter to any booking reference number, or send a copy of your invoice. Keep a copy of your letter and send it by recorded delivery.

If someone has been injured or you suspect that a criminal offence has been committed – if, for example, the tour operator claims that the hotel has a swimming pool or air conditioning but it does not – you should report the matter to Consumer Direct (0845 404 0506).

If you aren't happy with the response, write to the tour operator and the credit card company, if applicable. Repeat the complaint and request any compensation. Give them 14 days to resolve the matter or tell them you will consider taking legal action. If the operator has sent you a cheque for compensation, you can cash the cheque, but write back explaining why you feel the amount is inadequate and say you are accepting the money on account. But don't cash the cheque if the letter says 'encashment is deemed acceptance', because, by doing so, you are accepting the amount as a final settlement.

Not good enough ...

If you are still dissatisfied, find out if the tour operator or travel agent is a member of a trade association such as the Association of British Travel Agents (ABTA: 020 7637 2444; www.abta.com). ABTA represents travel agents and has a code of practice which its members must follow. If one of its members breaks the code, ABTA's legal department will investigate the matter internally but it doesn't take up cases on a customer's behalf. However, ABTA does operate an arbitration and conciliation service to resolve disputes, which can deal with claims up to £7,500 per booking, but doesn't deal with claims for compensation for illness or injury. There is a fee, but this will be refunded if the claim is successful. The deadline for applying to use the service is nine months from the end of the holiday.

You should try to use an arbitration and conciliation service, or alternative dispute resolution scheme (ADR), where available, before taking court action. This is because the amount of compensation a court may award you could be reduced if you have not tried other ways of resolving the problem before going to court.

If you choose not to use ABTA, and if the tour operator doesn't respond, simply refuses to do anything, or makes a final offer you are unwilling to accept, your only other choice is to go to court. But remember that court should be your last resort. Before starting court action you need to consider whether you have sufficient evidence. You also need to find out if the tour operator is solvent. It's not worth suing a person or company with no money. And you should consider whether, if you've lost money over a holiday, it is worth losing more on a court case you may not win.

Overbooking

Package holiday accommodation

> *Help! Our hotel room was double-booked and the holiday company sent us to a hotel on the other side of the island. It was perfectly pleasant but not really where we wanted to be. We're home now, but would like to know if we can claim compensation.*
>
> Generally speaking, if your holiday plans were changed as a result of an overbooking, it is likely that the agreement between you and the holiday company was broken. When a contract is broken in this way, you are entitled to claim compensation or a refund from the provider. In law, the contract is made up of things like the booking conditions printed on the back of a ticket, a letter confirming a booking and information given in the brochure or by a travel agent. If an overbooking problem is in connection with a package holiday, you should take action against the organizer, not the provider of the transport or accommodation. If you used your credit card to pay for the accommodation or travel and the cost was over £100, the credit card company may be equally liable for any breach of contract. This means you may be able to claim a refund from the credit card company, if you get no joy from the holiday company. In this case, unless you made it clear at the time you accepted the alternative accommodation that you were doing so 'under protest' and that the alternative accommodation was of a lower standard than the one you booked, it is unlikely that a claim for compensation will be successful.

If your holiday accommodation was overbooked and you could not stay there, the organizer should offer you:

- a full refund; *or*
- alternative accommodation of a similar standard to the one you booked; *or*
- if an alternative cannot be agreed, transport back to a place where you can return home and compensation.

How to solve your problem

Once you have decided what your rights are, contact the company, and the credit card company if applicable, as soon as possible. Keep copies of your letters. Explain your problem calmly but firmly and ask for what you want, a refund or compensation. Send proof of your booking, including the dates of your holiday, confirmation letter or tickets. Send photocopied evidence of any extra costs you incurred, such as hotel receipts, if you are claiming compensation. Send a copy of the letter to the travel agent, if the booking was made through one.

If you are not satisfied with the response and booked through a travel agent, find out if the agent is a member of the Association of British Travel Agents (ABTA: 020 7637 2444; www.abta.com) or Association of Independent Tour Operators (AITO: 020 8744 9280; www.aito.co.uk), both of whom operate a conciliation service to help resolve disputes. Conciliation is usually free. Arbitration is chargeable and any decision will be legally binding and likely to prevent you taking court action.

If you decide not to use conciliation or arbitration, write to the owner or manager of the company and the credit card company, if applicable, repeating your complaint and the steps you have taken so far. Say you are giving them 14 days to resolve the problem or you will consider taking legal action. Send the letter by recorded delivery with a copy to the head office of the company, if applicable. Keep copies of all your letters and a note of any phone conversations you have in connection with the problem.

If the company makes you an offer, be realistic in what you will accept. You may not get an improved offer by going to court. If the company doesn't respond, refuses to do anything, or makes a final offer you are unwilling to accept, your only other choice is to go to court.

Overbooking of flights

There are special rules covering compensation for overbooked flights from airports in the European Union (EU). These rules also apply to flights from airports outside the EU, but flying into an EU airport on an EU airline. The compensation is available if you are overbooked on a scheduled or charter flight.

You can get compensation for overbooking of your flight, as long as you meet certain conditions. You must have a valid ticket, which has been confirmed for the overbooked flight, and you must have checked in by the deadline given to you by the airline. As long as you meet all these conditions you will be able to get:

- a full refund of your ticket and a free return flight to your first point of departure, if you need it; *or*
- another flight as soon as possible or at a later date of your choice.

You will also be entitled to compensation in cash, or by cheque or bank transfer. The amount you can get depends on the length of flight and how late you are getting to your final destination. You can also get two free telephone calls, e-mails or faxes, and reasonable meals and refreshments if you have to wait for a later flight. Also you could get hotel accommodation if you are delayed overnight.

If your flight is overbooked, the airline should give you a form stating what compensation is available. (These overbooking rules only apply if you were not allowed to board the flight, not if you volunteered to take a different flight.)

If you are overbooked on a flight to which the EU rules do not apply, you may still be able to get compensation for overbooking. You will need to check with your airline whether any compensation is available for your particular circumstances.

For more information about overbooking on all flights, see the Air Travel Advice section on the Air Transport Users Council website (www.caa.co.uk).

Overbooking on other forms of transport

If you were booked on a specific ferry or similar sailing, and you could not travel because of overbooking, you may be able to claim compensation from the provider, on the grounds of breach of contract. You could claim an amount for any loss you suffered as a result of the overbooking, such as the cost of staying in a hotel until the next sailing. Also, check your travel insurance to see if it covers you for delays caused by overbooking. If it does, it will probably be easier to claim on your insurance than through the courts. You would not be entitled to compensation if you were travelling by coach or train unless you had tickets for a specified service, for example the 10:51 London to Edinburgh express.

If the transport was booked as part of a package holiday, you would need to claim from the organizer.

Travel insurance

Travel insurance can provide you with cover for:

- cancelling or cutting short your trip for specific reasons outside your control – for example, your unexpected illness or that of a close family member or a member of your travelling party
- missed transport or delayed departure for reasons outside your control
- medical and other emergency expenses
- personal injury and death
- lost, stolen or damaged personal property, including baggage
- accidental damage or injury you cause to someone else.

You can buy travel insurance to cover a single trip, or an annual policy covering several trips. If you are taking out a single-trip policy, take it out when you book your trip so that you are covered if you have to cancel. Some package holidays offer to include travel insurance, but you do not have to accept this. You are free to make your own arrangements. A travel agent must not charge you more for a package holiday because you do not buy their insurance. If a travel agent tries to do this, you should contact Consumer Direct (0845 404 0506).

Ask for quotes from several insurers, to help you get the best deal for your circumstances. Some policies exclude dangerous activities or high-risk sports such as skiing or scuba diving, and if you are going on a holiday involving one of these activities, you may have to pay more for your insurance.

It is worth checking your household contents insurance policy, as this may cover you for loss or damage to your personal belongings while you are abroad. You may decide that you only want to take out insurance for some of the other risks you can be covered for while you are abroad.

Your credit card company may provide you with some free insurance cover when you use it to pay for a holiday. Check carefully what is covered. In general, this should not be used as a substitute for your own insurance as it may not cover you for everything.

Remember to take a copy of your travel insurance policy away with you.

Making a claim

If you need to make a claim on your travel insurance policy, check that you are within the time limits for making a claim and that you are covered for the situation you are claiming for. There is usually a maximum amount that can be claimed under each section of the policy, and a limit on the amount you can claim for any single item. Contact your insurer as soon as possible to request a claim form. This may be once you have returned home. Your insurer may have an international helpline that you can use to get advice on the procedures you must follow.

Lost, stolen or damaged personal property or luggage

You will be expected to take reasonable care of your belongings, and to minimize any losses. Your insurer will want evidence of the loss or damage. This may mean making a report to the local police, which should be done within 24 hours, if possible.

If you have to replace any essential items that are lost, such as toiletries or clothing, make sure you ask for receipts as you will probably need to provide your insurer with copies. Ask for receipts for any essential services that you need to pay for as well.

Remember that unless you have a 'new for old' policy, the amount you get for an item may be less than the cost of replacing it. This is to take account of any use you have had out of the item.

Medical emergencies and personal injury

If you need medical treatment while you are away, contact your insurer by phone as soon as possible to get authorization for the treatment. If possible, you should try to contact them before agreeing to the cost of the treatment. Get receipts for treatment and medication.

Some insurance policies will not cover you for the treatment of a health problem that you knew about at the time the policy was taken out. You may also be excluded from claiming for the cost of medication that you usually need and may have to take while travelling.

In EEA countries and Switzerland, urgent medical treatment is available free of charge if you have a European Health Insurance Card (EHIC). For a list of EEA countries, see p. 502. You can apply for an EHIC online – go to www.dh.gov.uk.

Some countries in other parts of the world also have agreements with the UK that allow you to get free emergency treatment.

You can find out more by looking at the Health Advice for Travellers section at www.dh.gov.uk.

Travel insurance usually covers you if you are pregnant, as long as you are in normal health.

Cancelling or shortening your trip

Your insurer will only meet a claim for a cancelled or a shortened trip if you can show that you had good reason to cancel or shorten it. A list of reasons will be included in your policy.

Buying a timeshare property

When you buy a timeshare, you buy the right to use holiday accommodation for a set amount of time each year. The accommodation is usually a villa in a resort, but you can also get timeshares in caravans, cottages and flats. How you pay will vary, but usually you pay a one-off lump sum, and then annual maintenance charges.

Please note that this section covers your rights if you buy a timeshare from a company, but not if you buy it from a private individual.

When is a timeshare not a timeshare?

Holiday and vacation clubs are not timeshares because they do not give you the right to stay in a specific property. As a general rule, accommodation on boats is not covered by timeshare laws. However, it is not clear whether timeshares for canal boats in the UK are covered or not.

Factors to consider before buying

- Do you want this type of holiday every year?
- Is it value for money? Don't forget that the cost of transport to the resort is not included.
- Shop around.
- Ask for a brochure.
- Insist on full details in writing. Do not rely on verbal promises alone.
- Do not be tempted by free gifts offered as an incentive.

Before signing a timeshare agreement

When you buy a timeshare, you sign a binding agreement with a timeshare company. It can be difficult to cancel the agreement, so it is important to get as much information as possible before you sign, including details of:

- the full costs, including charges for things such as legal fees, gas, electricity and water, annual management and maintenance charges
- the duration of the agreement. If you are asked to sign a contract for less than three years, this is usually a deliberate attempt to avoid giving you legal rights
- what the resort is like. If it is still being built, check that planning permission has been granted, the extent of the development and the amount of work still to be completed
- the type of ownership you will have and whether you will own the title to the property and an interest in the land which, for example, you could sell or leave in a will (this is unusual)
- the terms and conditions of the agreement
- who is responsible for the day-to-day running of the resort and maintenance of the property
- whether there is an owners' committee or association and what powers it has – for example, whether it can dismiss the management company.

Cancelling a timeshare agreement

Once you have signed a timeshare agreement, the law gives you a cooling-off period, during which you can cancel the agreement and have your money back without having to pay a cancellation fee. You are entitled to a cooling-off period only if the timeshare lasts at least three years and is for a property or caravan in the European Economic Area (EEA). For a list of EEA countries, see p. 502. The rules about cancelling a timeshare agreement do not apply to timeshares bought before 1 May 2004 in countries which joined the European Union on this date – for example, Malta.

The length of the cooling-off period will be 14 days if you signed your timeshare agreement in the UK. If you signed the agreement in another EEA country, the cooling-off period is ten days.

In some EEA countries, a lawyer has to witness you signing the agreement. The timeshare seller does not have to refund the cost of this if you cancel the agreement.

Timeshare sellers in the UK and EEA must tell you about the cooling-off period when you sign the agreement. If they don't, the cooling-off period will be extended, usually by three months.

After the cooling-off period, you can cancel the agreement if the terms of the agreement allow for this. If you want to sell your timeshare, a timeshare resale company or the original timeshare company may be able to arrange this for you, although they will charge you commission. You may be asked to pay a fee upfront and you should be wary before you get involved with a company offering to sell your timeshare. In the past some owners have handed over money only to find that the company offering to sell on their behalf has disappeared.

Protection if you pay by credit card

If you want to cancel your timeshare agreement, and you paid for the timeshare with your credit card, your credit card company might agree to get the money back. In these circumstances, it is essential that you write to both the timeshare seller and the credit card company, notifying them that you wish to cancel the agreement, within ten days of signing the timeshare agreement. You should check whether your credit card company offers this type of protection.

What to do if there are problems

Your rights depend upon the terms of the agreement and the law that applies to it. That could be the law in the country where the agreement was signed, the law in the country where the timeshare company is based, or the law of a third country that the agreement says applies to it. You may need the help of a specialist solicitor to decide which law applies. The organizations below might be able to recommend a specialist.

Compensation

You may be entitled to compensation if:

- the terms of your agreement have been broken – for example, if the agreement says the resort has a well-maintained swimming pool and in fact the swimming pool has been out of action for two years
- repairs and maintenance aren't carried out in line with the agreement
- the seller invites you to attend a presentation, offering a reward in return and you don't get the reward, or it is not the same as what was offered.

If any of these apply, you could sue for breach of contract.

How to solve your problem

Once you have decided what your rights are, you will need to contact the timeshare seller. Contact the company as soon as possible. Write to the manager and keep a copy of your letter. Explain your problem firmly but calmly, and ask for what you want – to cancel the agreement or compensation.

If you are not satisfied with the response and the timeshare is in Europe, find out if the company is a member of the Organization for Timeshare in Europe (OTE). OTE operates a conciliation service to help resolve disputes. If you use these services, any decision will be legally binding and is likely to prevent you taking court action.

If you decide not to use conciliation, write to the owner or manager of the company and the credit card company (if applicable) repeating your complaint and the steps you have taken so far. Say you are giving them 14 days to resolve the problem, otherwise you will consider taking legal action. Send the letter by recorded delivery with a copy to the head office of the company, if there is one. Keep copies of all your letters and a note of any phone conversations you have in connection with the problem.

If the company makes you an offer, you can either accept or continue to negotiate. Be realistic in what you will accept. You may not get an improved offer by going to court.

If the company doesn't respond, refuses to do anything, or makes a final offer you are unwilling to accept, your only other choice is to go to court.

Who can help?

If you have bought a timeshare in a European Economic Area (EEA) country and you ask for a brochure and this is not provided, or if the seller takes money from you during the cooling-off period, or the seller makes false or misleading claims about the timeshare, a criminal offence may have been committed, and you should contact **Consumer Direct** (0845 404 0506). The **Organization for Timeshare in Europe** (Fax +32 2533 3061; www.ote-info.com) will be able to refer you to a specialist. The OTE gives general advice about timeshares to prospective purchasers, explains current legislation in the United Kingdom and Europe, and provides information sheets. It also offers a free conciliation service to those in dispute with its members.

The **Timeshare Consumers Association** (01909 591100; www.timeshare. org.uk) deals with complaints about timeshares and can provide help and specialist advice.

The **Association of British Travel Agents** (020 7637 2444; www.abta. com). ABTA is the regulatory body for British travel agents and tour operators. It has a code of practice which its members must keep to. If you book through an ABTA member, you get extra protection if things go wrong.

The **Association of Independent Tour Operators** (020 8744 9280; www.aito.co.uk), which represents independent tour operators, has a code of practice that all its members should follow. It also runs an independent mediation service that charges a non-refundable fee.

The **Advertising Standards Authority** (020 7492 2222; www.asa.org.uk). If the holiday is not as described in the brochure or advertisement, you can complain to the ASA. It cannot award compensation but can take action to have a brochure or advert withdrawn or changed so that it does not mislead others.

Natural England (formerly the Countryside Agency) (0845 600 3078; www.naturalengland.gov.uk) gives information about rights to access in the countryside.

5
Utilities

CONTENTS

INTRODUCTION

It is a truth universally acknowledged that not much in life comes for free and even keeping warm will cost you. Since peat started being used as domestic fuel at least 1,300 years ago, we've been searching for cheap sources of fuel. Along with supplies of clean water, fossil fuels like coal, oil and gas are the staples upon which our comfortable lives depend. With the re-privatization of those industries in recent years, it has fallen more and more to us, as consumers, to make sure that we are getting what we pay for. This section looks at your choices, what you can expect from the utility companies and what to do if their services don't come up to scratch.

GAS

There are many companies that can supply you with gas. You can find a list of the companies which supply gas in your area from the website of the gas and electricity consumer council, energywatch (www.energywatch.org.uk). All gas suppliers are licensed by the Office of Gas and Electricity Markets (Ofgem).

You have a right to a gas supply unless:

- your gas pipes are in a dangerous condition
- there is a debt, or disconnection
- the gas supplier wants financial security that is unavailable.

If you are refused a supply of gas for reasons other than those listed above, get advice from energywatch.

Gas safety

A gas supplier can authorize its officials to enter premises to inspect the gas installation and appliances. If a gas leak is reported, it will be made safe free of charge. This could often simply mean turning off the supply. If an appliance is faulty and has to be disconnected, you will be responsible for buying a replacement and getting it installed. National Grid (formerly Transco), the main public gas transporter, runs a 24-hour freephone national gas emergency service (0800 111 999).

Getting a gas supply or changing supplier

When you move to a new home, tell the gas supplier the date you want to take over the supply. If it has to be reconnected, the supplier may make a charge – energywatch can advise on whether a charge should be made and what is a reasonable amount. If the supply has not been disconnected, read the meter and inform the supplier of the reading. Keep a copy of the reading.

If you want to change your gas supplier, notify both the current and the new gas supplier. Both will want a final meter reading taken on the day you change suppliers. Some suppliers will send a meter reader; others will ask you to read the meter and send the reading to them. In either case, keep a note of the meter reading in case there is a dispute later.

Energywatch can provide advice on what to check if you want to change suppliers and you can check the most up-to-date prices on their website. You can also call energywatch for a price comparison fact sheet or use online price comparison websites which make it easy to compare and switch suppliers. You can find a list of these websites on the energywatch website.

If you have a gas debt, you may not be accepted by a new supplier. If you have owed money for less than 28 days – for example, you have not paid a recent bill – you will still be able to change supplier. The money you owe will be transferred to your new supplier.

You will also be allowed to change supplier if you use a prepayment meter and have a debt of up to £100. Your debt will be transferred to your new supplier.

Providing financial security

In some circumstances the gas supplier will refuse to connect the gas supply until you have provided suitable financial security. You may be asked to:

- join a regular payment plan; *or*
- agree to have a prepayment meter; *or*
- provide a guarantor; *or*
- make a cash deposit.

The gas supplier will normally only require security in certain circumstances – for example if you are a new customer and cannot provide proof of your identity or previous address or have a poor payment record at your present or last address.

Guarantors

If you name a guarantor, the gas supplier will check whether their record of gas payments is satisfactory. The guarantor will be legally responsible for paying your gas bills if you do not pay.

Deposits

The gas supplier must only request a 'reasonable' amount as a deposit and the maximum you can be charged is a sum based on the estimate of the highest six months' use in the year following the request for a deposit. The gas supplier will review the deposit after one year. If the bills have been paid in full, the deposit will be returned within two months of the end of the year.

Meters

A gas supplier must provide an appropriate meter to a customer who asks for one. There are two main types of meter:

- credit or quarterly meters, where you use the gas and pay for it later
- prepayment meters, where you pay in advance for your gas supply.

Most customers will have a *credit meter* and will receive bills four times a year. The gas supplier will call to read the meter at regular intervals or contact you and ask you to read the meter and pass it on to them. The meter must be read at least once every two years.

If you have difficulty paying for your gas, you can ask for a *prepayment meter*. If you are in arrears, you should be offered a prepayment meter as an alternative to disconnection. In most areas, electronic prepayment meters are the only available prepayment meter option. The gas supplier will give you a list of the places where you can get your card, token or key charged up.

Meter readings

Gas meters are usually read every six months. If the gas supplier has been unable to gain access to read the meter, it will leave a card for you to fill in with your own reading. If you are disabled, chronically sick or of pensionable age, you can ask the gas supplier to read your meter every three months. The gas supplier must inspect and test the meter at least once every two years.

If you are disabled, chronically sick or of pensionable age and find it difficult to read your meter because of its position, you can ask the gas supplier to move the meter, where reasonably practicable, free of charge.

Gas marketing

When a gas company sells you gas, it must keep to certain standards. Most suppliers have signed up to a code of practice produced by the Association of Energy Suppliers (AES). Sales agents must follow the guidelines in the code. The guidelines cover all methods of selling gas, including door-to-door sales (doorstep selling) and telephone sales (distance selling). For example, agents must only call at your home between 9 a.m. and 8 p.m., except at your request, and if they are visiting sheltered accommodation, they must first approach the warden. Sales agents must try to make sure that customers have understood any contract signed and their right to cancel.

If a gas sales agent has broken the code of practice, you may be entitled to compensation. In the first instance, take up your complaint with the company concerned. Ask them for a copy of the code of practice and use it to help you with your complaint. If you cannot reach agreement with the supplier, contact energywatch. If energywatch cannot resolve the complaint, they may refer it on to Ofgem.

Cancellation rights

If you sign a contract to buy gas from someone who has called at your home, you may have the right to cancel the contract if you change your mind. You will be able to cancel as long as:

- you cancel within seven days of signing; *and*
- you did not ask the sales agent to call at your home.

If you sign the contract to buy gas over the phone, you may also have the right to change your mind – see *Buying over the internet, by telephone and by mail order* (p. 335).

Dual fuel offers

Most gas and electricity suppliers are licensed by Ofgem to supply customers with both gas and electricity. Some gas suppliers supply both fuels under one contract, while others give one contract for gas and another for electricity.

Suppliers who make dual offers will often give a discount off the total bill. However, this does not necessarily mean that gas and electricity under a dual offer will be cheaper than that bought from separate suppliers.

Arrears and disconnections

If you have gas arrears, you risk being disconnected. However, it is very unusual to be disconnected if you fail to pay your gas bills.

A gas supplier cannot disconnect you until they have issued a disconnection notice and they cannot issue a disconnection notice until at least 28 days after issuing a bill. You must be given at least seven days' notice of disconnection. If you cannot pay your bill, contact your supplier immediately. You should be offered an arrangement to pay off your arrears at a rate you can afford. If you cannot afford to pay off the arrears in this way, they must offer to install a prepayment meter.

Some groups of customers may have extra protection from being disconnected. This may apply to you if you:

- are of pensionable age
- are very ill
- are disabled
- have severe financial problems.

You can find out more about the steps that a supplier has to take before disconnecting you on the energywatch website (www.energywatch.org.uk).

Buying and installing gas appliances

Anyone supplying a gas appliance must ensure that it is safe and that it meets European safety standards. Anyone installing or repairing a gas appliance or equipment must be registered with the Council for Registered Gas Installers (CORGI: 0800 915 0485; www.trustcorgi.com). They must carry an ID card listing the types of gas work that they are competent to carry out.

Complaints

If you have a complaint about your gas supplier, first raise it with the supplier; it must have a procedure for dealing with complaints. You may be entitled to compensation. If you are dissatisfied with the way the gas supplier dealt with a complaint, take it up with energywatch.

If your complaint is about a bill or changing supplier, and energywatch cannot resolve the problem, you may be able to complain to the Energy Supply Ombudsman – see below.

Who can help?

The Energy Supply Ombudsman. If you have a complaint about your gas bill or a problem when you change your supplier, you can make a complaint to the Energy Supply Ombudsman (0845 055 0760; www.energy-ombudsman.org.uk). You must have complained to your gas supplier first. Your supplier must be a member of the Energy Supply Ombudsman scheme. You can find a list of scheme members on the Energy Supply Ombudsman website.

energywatch (08459 060708; www.energywatch.org.uk), the gas and electricity consumer watchdog, is an independent organization that represents and protects the interests of gas consumers. It can help with complaints about the supply of gas.

Ofgem (Office of Gas and Electricity Markets) is an independent regulatory body, set up by the government to monitor and regulate the activities of gas suppliers. It has the power to make a gas supplier supply gas to a particular customer, or not disconnect a gas supply. Consumer complaints are dealt with by energywatch.

The **Council for Registered Gas Installers** (CORGI: 0800 915 0485; www.trustcorgi.com) is an independent organization that promotes gas safety. You can complain to them about a gas installer, or get details of CORGI-registered gas installers.

ELECTRICITY

There are many companies which can supply you with electricity. You can find a list of companies which supply electricity on the website of the gas and electricity consumer council, energywatch (www.energywatch.org.uk).

All electricity suppliers must have a licence from the Office of Gas and Electricity Markets (Ofgem). One of the licence conditions is that an electricity supplier must produce codes of practice on things like complaints procedures, payment of bills and dealing with arrears, as well as energy efficiency and services for older, disabled and chronically sick people.

Although the codes of practice are not legally enforceable, they will be useful when negotiating with an electricity supplier and any breach should be reported to energywatch.

Choosing an electricity supplier

If you are considering changing your electricity supplier you should be aware that the pricing structures, services offered and policies will differ between the different electricity suppliers. You should carefully check the information and contracts of the competing electricity suppliers, and compare these to your current terms, to make sure that you choose the best deal for your needs. You can check the most up-to-date fuel prices on the energywatch website (www.energywatch.org.uk). You can also call energywatch for a price comparison sheet or you can use online price comparison websites. You can find a list of online price comparison websites on the energywatch website.

Dual fuel offers

Dual fuel is the supply of gas and electricity by the same supplier. Most gas and electricity suppliers are licensed to supply customers with both fuels. Some electricity suppliers will supply both fuels under one contract, while others will give one contract for gas and another for electricity.

Suppliers who make dual offers will often give a discount off the total bill. However, this does not necessarily mean that the cost of gas and electricity under a dual offer will be cheaper than buying gas and electricity from separate suppliers.

Electricity marketing

When a company sells you electricity, it must keep to certain standards. Most suppliers have signed up to a code of practice produced by the Association of Energy Suppliers (AES). Sales agents must follow the guidelines in the code. The guidelines cover all methods of selling, including door-to-door sales (doorstep selling) and telephone sales (distance selling). Some of the guidelines are:

- sales agents must call at your home between 9 a.m. and 8 p.m., unless you have specifically asked them to call outside these times. If they are visiting sheltered accommodation, they must contact the warden first
- the sales agent must make sure you have understood the contract, including the right to cancel, before you sign
- you must be given a copy of the contract.

If the sales agent does not follow these guidelines, you may be entitled to compensation. If you have a complaint about the way you have been sold electricity, you should take this up first with the company concerned. Ask them for a copy of the code of practice and use the information in this to help you make your complaint. If you cannot reach an agreement with the electricity company, you can refer the complaint to energywatch. If energy-watch cannot resolve the problem, they will refer it to Ofgem (see p. 441).

How to get an electricity supply or change supplier

You have a legal right to a supply of electricity if it is 'reasonable' to provide a supply.

There is no duty to supply electricity where the wiring in your house is in a dangerous condition, where the supply has been disconnected and there is no obligation to reconnect, where security has been requested and not paid or where a prepayment meter has been refused. If you are refused a supply of electricity for reasons other than these, you should take the matter up with energywatch.

When you move to a new home, you should tell the new electricity supplier the date on which you wish to take over the supply. The electricity supplier may be your current electricity supplier, or you may wish to change to a different supplier when you move. You may have to change if your current electricity supplier does not supply electricity in the area to which you have moved.

If you want to cancel your contract with your current electicity supplier, you have to give them at least two days' notice. If you do not do this, they can continue to charge you for electricity, even if you have moved out of the property. Your electricity supplier can object to you changing to another supplier in other circumstances – for example, if you are in arrears.

Remember to cancel any standing orders or direct debits once you have paid the final bill to your current electricity supplier.

Your current and new electricity suppliers will want a final meter reading taken on the day you change electricity suppliers. Some electricity suppliers will send a meter reader and may make a charge for this, while others will ask you to read the meter and send the reading to them. In either case, you should keep a note of the meter reading yourself in case there is a dispute later.

You must give your new electricity supplier the supply number for the meter at your home. The supply number is an identification number for the meter and is shown on the bill relating to the meter. If you are moving home, you will have to ask the present occupiers for the supply number.

If the supply of electricity has to be reconnected, the electricity supplier may make a charge for reconnection. If you think the reconnection charge is unreasonable, you can refer the matter to energywatch.

Getting advice about changing to a new electricity supplier

For information and advice about changing to a new electricity supplier, contact energywatch (0845 906 0708; www.energywatch.org.uk). Energy-watch can provide advice on what to check if you want to change suppliers and you can get advice from them about the prices offered by different suppliers (see p. 435).

Changing suppliers when you have a debt

If you have an electricity debt, you may not be accepted by a new supplier. If you have owed money for less than 28 days – for example, you have not paid a recent bill – you will still be able to change supplier. The money you owe will be transferred to your new supplier. You will also be allowed to change suppliers if you use a prepayment meter and have a debt up to £100. Your debt will be transferred to your new supplier. For more information about changing suppliers when you have a debt, contact energywatch.

Providing security

Most customers will have a credit meter and receive regular bills, but if you are a new customer, cannot provide proof of your identity or have a poor payment record, the electricity supplier may refuse to supply until you have provided suitable security. The electricity supplier should first ask you to agree to a prepayment meter being fitted. Only if you refuse a prepayment meter should the electricity supplier ask for alternative security, but they will normally ask you to do one of the following:

- join a regular payment plan
- pay by direct debit
- provide a guarantor – the guarantor will be legally responsible for paying your electricity bills if you do not pay
- make a cash deposit – the electricity supplier can only request a reasonable amount, usually up to a maximum of one and a half times the average amount of a quarterly bill.

Meters

Most customers will have a *credit meter* and will receive bills four times a year – quarterly billing. The electricity supplier will call to read the meter at regular intervals or contact the customer and ask them to read the meter and pass on the reading. The meter must be read at least once a year, but it can be read by the customer rather than the electricity supplier.

If you have difficulty paying for your electricity, you can ask for a *prepayment meter* to be installed. If you are in arrears, you should be offered a prepayment meter as an alternative to disconnection. In most areas, electronic prepayment meters are the only available prepayment meter option.

The advantages of using a prepayment meter are

- it can be a useful way to budget if you are on a low income
- it can be used to pay off arrears as an alternative to disconnection.

There are several disadvantages to using a prepayment meter. These include:

- you will usually pay more for your electricity than if you have a credit meter
- if you cannot afford to buy tokens or recharge your card or key, you will have no electricity
- you will have to pay transport costs to get to the nearest charging point
- the meter can be set to collect arrears. This means you will have to pay for using electricity and for your arrears at the same time
- you will have to pay more towards the arrears when you are using more electricity.

Meter readings

A customer who is disabled, chronically sick or of pensionable age can ask the electricity supplier to read their meter every three months if neither they nor anyone else in the household can do so. However, the bill will be estimated if the electricity supplier cannot gain access.

A customer who is disabled, chronically sick or of pensionable age can get information and advice about:

- special controls or adaptors for prepayment meters or electricity appliances owned by the electricity supplier
- re-siting of the meter if it is owned by the electricity supplier and it is in a position which makes it difficult for the customer to read it.

Information and advice, and re-siting of the meter, must be provided free of charge. However, a charge can be made for any special controls or adaptors for the meter or appliances.

Tampering with a meter

The electricity supplier may disconnect your electricity supply by removing the meter if it has sufficient evidence that you have tampered with your meter. To prevent disconnection, you must convince the electricity supplier you did not tamper with the meter and took proper care of it.

Electricity bills

Electricity bills will be sent to you at regular intervals. If you are blind, or have impaired sight, the electricity supplier may make special provision, such as making regular quarterly telephone calls to keep you up to date with your account or offering a bill reading service. You can ask for your bills to be sent to someone else if you wish.

Standing charge

The standing charge is a fixed daily amount charged to electricity users, regardless of how much electricity is consumed. There are different charges for credit and prepayment meters. Your electricity supplier may offer you the option of not paying a standing charge, but paying a slightly higher rate for the electricity used instead. You would need to work out, from your bills, whether this option would be cheaper for you.

Arrears

If you have electricity arrears, you risk being disconnected. However, it is very unusual to be disconnected if you fail to pay your electricity bills.

An electricity supplier cannot disconnect you until they have issued a disconnection notice and they cannot issue a disconnection notice until at least 28 days after issuing a bill. You must be given at least seven days' notice of disconnection. If you cannot pay your bill, contact your supplier immediately. You should be offered an arrangement to pay off your arrears at a rate you can afford. If you cannot afford to pay off the arrears in this way, the supplier must offer to install a prepayment meter.

Some groups of customers may have extra protection from being disconnected. This may apply to you if you:

- are of pensionable age
- are very ill
- are disabled
- have severe financial problems.

You can find out more about the steps that a supplier has to take before disconnecting you on the energywatch website (www.energywatch.org.uk).

Complaints

If you have a complaint about your electricity supplier, you should first raise it with the electricity supplier. If you are dissatisfied with how the electricity company has dealt with your complaint, you can take it up with energy-watch and/or the Energy Supply Ombudsman.

Who can help?

energywatch (08459 060708; www.energywatch.org.uk), the gas and electricity consumer watchdog, is an independent organization that represents and protects the interests of electricity consumers. It can help with complaints about the supply of electricity.

Ofgem (Office of Gas and Electricity Markets) is an independent regulatory body, set up by the government to monitor and regulate the activities of electricity suppliers. It has the power to make an electricity supplier supply electricity to a particular customer, or not disconnect a supply. Consumer complaints are dealt with by energywatch.

The Energy Supply Ombudsman. If you have a complaint about your electricity bill or a problem when you change your supplier, you can make a complaint to the Energy Supply Ombudsman (0845 055 0760; www.energy-ombudsman.org.uk). You must have complained to your supplier first and the supplier must be a member of the Energy Supply Ombudsman scheme. You can find a list of scheme members on the Energy Supply Ombudsman website.

WATER

Water is supplied by a number of private water companies. As a domestic customer living in a property, you have the right to a water supply and there is no charge for taking over a water supply that is already connected.

The supply of water

A supply of water for domestic purposes must be:

- constant. If a company needs to interrupt a supply of water, it must give reasonable notice
- safe to drink. Fluoride may be added in some areas

- supplied at an adequate pressure
- sufficient for normal domestic use. If there is a serious shortage of water in the area, the company can impose a temporary hosepipe ban to restrict the watering of private gardens or the washing of private cars.

Calculating water charges

There are several different methods of calculating charges for water. The cost will be based on a standing charge and:

- an unmeasured charge based on the rateable value of the property, on a flat rate charge or on a banding system
- a measured charge (using a water meter) based on the amount of water used, usually per cubic metre, at a rate approved by the Director General of the Office of Water Services (OFWAT).

You may be able to choose which method is used. The choice will usually be between a water meter and another charging method.

Water meters

You may want to request that a meter is installed if you use very little water, the property has a high rateable value or you want more control of how much water you pay for.

However, disadvantages include the inconvenience of having it read, water lost through leakage after the meter is installed and which must be paid for, and the uncertainty of how much the annual bill will be.

All household customers can elect to have a water meter installed in their homes free of charge, unless it is not practical or would be unreasonably expensive to install. You may wish to do this to find out whether this will help to reduce your bills. You will normally be able to switch back to your old charging method, as long as you do so within twelve months of the start of metered charging.

Companies are entitled to install water meters in areas that have been declared areas of water scarcity, or where people use a high volume of water for non-essential purposes, for example:

- using a sprinkler system to water the garden
- using a system that replenishes a pond or swimming pool with a capacity in excess of 10,000 litres
- using a power shower

- filling a bath with a capacity of more than 230 litres.

Water bills

Your water bill may include the following:

- a standing charge
- a charge for water, based on a meter reading or another charging method
- a charge for sewerage. If your sewerage service is provided by a different company, you may receive a separate sewerage bill.

Bills are usually sent once or twice a year, depending on the company's practice. If the water charge is on an unmeasured basis, the bill will be for the forthcoming billing period. If the water charge is a measured charge, the bill will be for the preceding billing period.

Help with water bills
Some people may be able to get help with the costs of their water supply – for example, people with water meters who use a high volume of water because of certain medical conditions, or because they have three or more children under 16, and are receiving a qualifying benefit. They may benefit from a bill calculated as an average charge for domestic customers of that company rather than on their actual measured use of water.

All companies have provisions in place to help people who have difficulty paying their bills, such as budget schemes.

Who is liable to pay the bill
The occupier of the property is normally responsible for paying water charges. If someone shares accommodation, the liability is shared even if the bill is only in one name.

Arrears

Water companies cannot disconnect a domestic customer for water arrears. The company would have to take action in the county court for debt to recover money owing for water charges.

Arrangements to pay the arrears
You will have to pay for your current use of water as well as a reasonable amount towards the arrears. If you are receiving Income Support, income-

based Jobseeker's Allowance or Pension Credit, the Department for Work and Pensions (DWP) may be able to pay an amount each week from your benefit directly to the water company. This is called a third-party deduction.

Some water suppliers have set up independent charitable trusts which give grants to some of their customers to help them pay for water arrears. For more information, look at the Utility Trusts and Schemes booklet at www.britishgasenergytrust.org.uk.

Compensation

All water companies have certain standards of service covered by the statutory Guaranteed Standards Scheme with which they must comply. These standards cover:

- keeping appointments
- responding to account queries
- responding to complaints
- interruptions to supply
- water pressure
- installing meters
- sewer flooding.

If the company fails to meet a standard of service, you can claim £20 compensation. If your water pressure falls below a certain level twice in 28 days, you can claim £25. Usually, compensation will be automatically paid or credited by the company. If the complaint is about an interruption of supply, low pressure or sewer flooding, you must claim compensation in writing within three months of the incident.

As well as the standards of service and minimum compensation levels required of all companies, some companies may operate their own higher standards and/or compensation levels.

Who can help?

The **Consumer Council for Water** (CCWater: 0845 039 2837; www.ccwater.org.uk) is an independent organization which can investigate complaints about the water companies. If CCWater find your complaint to be justified, they will ask your water company to put the matter right. CCWater's office will keep you informed about the progress of the complaint and will write to let you know the outcome.

If CCWater cannot resolve the complaint, it will refer it to OFWAT. Alternatively, if you are not happy with the way CCWater has dealt with your complaint, you can complain to OFWAT yourself. OFWAT will only take the matter up if it is satisfied that CCWater has not dealt with your complaint properly.

The **Office of Water Services** (OFWAT: 0845 039 2837; www.ofwat.gov. uk) is the independent regulatory body set up by the government to monitor and regulate the activities of the water companies. If you have a problem with your water company, you should initially take up the complaint with the company. If you are not satisfied, you can take up the complaint with CCWater (see above). If the company does not accept CCWater's recommendation for resolving a complaint, the matter will be referred to OFWAT.

The **Drinking Water Inspectorate** (020 7082 8024; www.dwi.gov.uk) monitors the quality of water. If you are unhappy about the quality of your water, you can complain to CCWater or the Drinking Water Inspectorate.

Basic Rights

1

Civil Rights

CONTENTS

INTRODUCTION

'The nature and limits of the power which can be legitimately exercised by society over the individual.' That's how John Stuart Mill described civil rights in his essay *On Liberty* in 1869. The relationship between the citizen and the state is a subject that has been taxing hearts and minds since Greek and Roman times and long before in the great early civilizations. The rights and duties of the common person – what you can and cannot do in the privacy of your own home or in public, to yourself or to other people, what is expected of you and how you can contribute to the democratic process – are the stuff upon which modern politics is based. Today, ordinary people enjoy social and political rights that many did not have even a hundred years ago. Bodies like the United Nations, Amnesty International and Human Rights Watch have been founded to monitor and fight for the human and civil rights of people across the globe. Here the new Equality and Human Rights Commission has just been set up. Its purpose is to reduce inequality, eliminate discrimination, strengthen good relations between people and protect human rights. It deals with discrimination on the grounds of sex, race, religion, sexuality, age and disability.

This chapter looks at the basic voting system, some of the laws that govern us and how you can enforce your rights within them, including making complaints to the ombudsman responsible.

VOTING

The electoral register

There are two versions of the electoral register. One version is the full version which lists everyone in the constituency who is eligible to vote. This is available for public inspection all year round at council offices and selected other places. It is also available to political parties, some government agencies and credit reference agencies. The other version is an edited version of the electoral register. This is available for open sale and you have the right to opt out of this version of the register.

To be included on the electoral register you must:

- be aged 18 or over; *and*
- have one of the types of citizenship described below; *and*
- be resident in the constituency in which you wish to vote (if you are a British citizen living overseas, see below); *and*
- not be a person who is excluded from voting.

Age

If you are going to be 18 during the twelve-month period after the register is published, you should be entered on the register so that you will be able to vote as soon as you become 18.

Citizenship

If you are a British citizen, you can vote in European parliamentary elections, British parliamentary elections (this means general and by-elections) and local government elections. If you are resident in Wales, you can also vote in National Assembly for Wales elections. Some other citizens may be able to vote in these elections too – for example, citizens of the Republic of Ireland who are living in the UK and Commonwealth citizens who are living in the UK.

If you are a British citizen living overseas, you can register and vote in European and British parliamentary elections but not in local elections. If you have been living abroad for over 15 years, you might lose this right.

EU citizens

European Union (EU) citizens have the right to vote in European parliamentary and British local government elections. European nationals who are not EU citizens do not have this right. EU citizens cannot vote in British parliamentary elections. For a list of EU countries, see p. 501.

For European parliamentary elections, an EU citizen may vote in either their 'home' country or the EU country in which they are currently living. They cannot vote in both.

Residency

To register to vote, you must generally be resident in the constituency on the date on which you make the application to register. If you are temporarily away from home – for example, if you are studying away from home – you can still vote or declare a local connection in the constituency where you usually live.

There are some exceptions to the rules about residency – for example, people who live abroad, some homeless people and people in psychiatric hospitals.

Who cannot vote

Certain people are not eligible to vote. These include people aged under 18, sentenced prisoners, and people who have a severe mental illness and are unable to understand the voting procedure.

Getting on the electoral register

The electoral register is compiled annually. Each year, around August or September, all households in a constituency will receive an electoral registration form.

You should complete the form according to the instructions and include everyone in the household who is eligible to vote and who will be living in the household on 15 October. If someone is temporarily away from home, they should still be included on the form. Someone who will become 18 during the twelve-month period after the register is published (on 1 December that year) should also be included, so they can vote on becoming 18. It is against the law to give false information about voting on the electoral registration form, or on any other document.

You can apply to be added to the register or to have your details amended on the register at any time throughout the year, although, when an election is held, registration applications must be received two to four weeks before polling day, depending on the election timetable.

Can I register anonymously?

You can register anonymously if you feel at risk – for example, from an ex-partner. Otherwise failure to provide information to the registration staff or to complete the registration form, or giving false information, may result in your being prosecuted and fined.

If you have not been included in the register

If you consider you are eligible to register, but discover you have not been included in the register, you can obtain a form from the electoral registration officer on which to make an application for registration. Alternatively, the application can be made in the form of a letter containing all relevant information. This application can be made either by you or by someone else on your behalf.

> ### My father has been living abroad for ten years and has just asked me if he can still vote in UK elections.
>
> People who have been on a UK electoral register in the last 15 years can make an 'annual declaration', which lets them be included on the electoral register they were last on in the UK. British consulates abroad have the forms, which must be sent to the electoral registration office of their last constituency.

If you are eligible and you wish to register as an overseas elector, you must complete the necessary forms, normally available from British consulates and diplomatic posts. Or you can download them from the Electoral Commission's website (www.aboutmyvote.co.uk). You must return the completed forms to the electoral registration officer for the constituency in which you were last registered. You must do this annually. The first time the declaration is made, you must give details of your British citizenship, which is the only type of citizenship that counts to be an overseas voter. Once registered, you can vote at any parliamentary or European parliament election that occurs while you are on the register. You cannot vote in local government elections or in elections to devolved assemblies, such as the Welsh Assembly.

Special arrangements for specific groups when registering to vote

There are special arrangements for some groups of people when registering to vote. These groups include homeless people, patients in psychiatric hospitals, people remanded in custody and people resident in more than one constituency. For example, a *declaration of local connection* may be made by homeless people, remand prisoners and patients in psychiatric hospitals. This can be used if you are in one of these groups and do not fulfil the usual residence requirements but are otherwise entitled to register to vote. A Citizens Advice Bureau can help you draw up a declaration of local connection.

If you are remanded in custody, you can register at your address outside the prison. Alternatively, you can register at the address of the prison if the registration officer considers that you have been, or will be, on remand in the prison for a long enough period of time for it to be regarded as your place of residence.

If you do not wish to use your home address or the prison's address, you can make a declaration of local connection – see above.

Your position if you have more than one home is complex. Your rights to be included on the register and vote in a particular constituency depend on your circumstances. You will need to consult the electoral registration officer in this situation. It is illegal to vote twice in an election.

How to vote

Before polling day, everyone entitled to vote will be sent a polling card, unless a proxy or postal vote has previously been agreed. The card will give details of the polling station and the hours it is open. You do not need to take the polling card to the polling station when you go to vote, but it may be more convenient to do so.

If you do not want to, or cannot, attend the polling station in person, you can apply for a postal vote or a proxy vote if you meet the relevant criteria.

Help for disabled people

If you are disabled, you may be able to vote by post or by proxy.

If you are partially sighted and choose to vote in person, the polling station must display a large-print version of the ballot paper to assist you. If you are blind or partially sighted, the polling station must also provide a device to enable you to fill in your ballot papers without any need for help from anyone else.

If you are physically disabled or unable to read, you may take a companion to help you complete the ballot form and put it in the ballot box. Your companion must be aged 18 or over and be entitled to vote, and must make a written declaration to this effect. Your companion cannot help more than one disabled voter to vote at that election.

Alternatively, you can ask the presiding officer to mark the ballot paper on your behalf.

Postal votes

Once you are registered to vote, you can choose to vote by post at both parliamentary and local government elections for an indefinite period, a particular period or a particular election.

To make an application for a postal vote, you must complete the application form available from your electoral registration office or from the Electoral Commission's website (www.aboutmyvote.co.uk). Only one application form can be used for each person. Alternatively, you can apply in writing, although care must be taken to ensure that the letter contains all the necessary information. It is against the law to give false information about an application for a postal vote. It is also against the law to get the registration officer to send a postal vote application form to an address when the person entitled to vote has not agreed to this.

You will receive a ballot paper with a declaration of identity which you must sign in the presence of a witness who knows you. The witness must also sign and print their name, along with their address.

Proxy votes

Voting by proxy means that you appoint someone else to vote on your behalf. The person appointed as a proxy must be eligible to vote.

Once you are registered to vote by proxy, you will be able to do so at both parliamentary and local government elections for an indefinite period, a particular period or a particular election. Anyone can apply to vote by proxy for a particular election, but only certain people may be eligible to vote by proxy for a particular or indefinite period. These include people registered as members of the armed services, people registered as overseas electors and people who cannot reasonably be expected to vote in person because of the general nature of their occupation or that of their husband, wife or civil partner.

It is against the law to try to persuade someone to vote by proxy or to give false information about an application for a proxy vote. It is also against the law to get the registration officer to send a proxy vote application form to an address when the person entitled to vote has not agreed to this.

The registration officer has to receive your proxy vote application form at least six working days before the date of the poll. But if you become ill just before polling day, you can apply for an emergency proxy vote if you have medical evidence.

Appealing against refusal of a postal or a proxy vote

If the registration officer refuses an application for a postal or proxy vote, you will be notified of this decision and the reasons for it. You can appeal against this decision, but not if you applied to vote by post or proxy in a particular election only.

HUMAN RIGHTS

The United Kingdom first signed and ratified the European Convention on Human Rights (ECHR) in 1950. The Convention enshrines fundamental civil and political rights, but for many years it was not part of our own law. Using the Convention usually meant taking a case to the European Court of Human Rights in Strasbourg. This was often time-consuming and expensive.

Since coming into force on 2 October 2000, the Human Rights Act has made rights from the ECHR (the Convention rights) enforceable in our own courts. This is much quicker and simpler than the old arrangement.

The Human Rights Act means that it is unlawful for public authorities to act in a way that is incompatible with Convention rights. 'Absolute rights' under the Human Rights Act include the right to life and the prohibition of torture and degrading treatment. 'Qualified rights' have to strike a balance between individual rights and the general public interest. Examples include the right to respect for private and family life and freedom of expression. If one of your human rights has been breached, cases can be dealt with in a UK court or tribunal. You do not have to go to the European Court of Human Rights in Strasbourg. Human rights law has been used successfully to challenge a local authority which was not providing community care. In another case, failure to provide a prisoner with adequate psychiatric care, which may have prevented his suicide, was held to be a breach of human rights law.

Who can help?

The **Equality and Human Rights Commission** (EHRC: 0845 604 6610 in England; 0845 604 8810 in Wales; www.equalityhumanrights.com) can give you information about human rights law.

DISCRIMINATION

Race discrimination

It is generally unlawful to discriminate against someone because of their race, and public authorities have a legal duty to eliminate unlawful discrimination and actively to promote equality. Race discrimination can be 'direct' or 'indirect', or can take the form of harassment or victimization.

If you are taking action over race discrimination, you do not have to demonstrate that there was an intention to discriminate against you. It is only necessary to show that discrimination took place.

You do not have to demonstrate that racial grounds were the only reason for the discrimination you experienced. It is enough to show that racial grounds played a substantial part in the discrimination. For a definition of 'racial grounds', see below.

Direct race discrimination

It is direct race discrimination to treat a person less favourably on racial grounds than another person would be treated in the same circumstances. As well as words or acts of refusal, direct discrimination includes words or acts of discouragement.

A clear example of direct race discrimination in employment would be the refusal to appoint a person from a particular racial group because, according to the employer, 'they wouldn't fit in' or 'the customers would object'. Less obvious examples would be a person being turned down for a job because of a connection with someone of a particular racial group – for example, because their partner is Afro-Caribbean – or being dismissed for refusing to carry out instructions that would discriminate against people from that racial group.

Indirect race discrimination

It is indirect race discrimination to set conditions or requirements for a person to meet that may seem to apply to everyone but may place people of a particular racial, ethnic or national group at an unfair disadvantage.

There may have been indirect discrimination involved in such a requirement if:

- people of a particular racial, ethnic or national group are less likely to be able to meet it; *and*
- as a result, people who cannot meet it are placed at a disadvantage; *and*

- it cannot be justified by the person or institution setting it (see below).

There may be indirect discrimination if members of one or more racial, ethnic or national group are less likely to meet a requirement than others. An example would be if an employer insists that candidates for a job should speak faultless English when this is clearly not needed for the type of work. Further examples could be banning the wearing of the hijab or insisting on the wearing of skirts at work or school, or an employer insisting that a person have qualifications obtained only in the UK.

Victimization and harassment

You will have suffered victimization if you are treated less favourably because you have complained, brought proceedings or asserted your rights under race discrimination laws, or because you have helped or supported someone in doing this – for example, by giving evidence as a witness in a case of race discrimination. You will have suffered harassment if you have been intimidated or humiliated by another person because of your race.

What are 'racial grounds'?

'Racial grounds' include:

- colour
- race
- nationality
- ethnic or national origins. 'Ethnic origins' is a term that is hard to define. However, discrimination cases have clarified the position of certain groups of people. For example, Jews, Romany gypsies, members of the Irish traveller community and Sikhs were found to be ethnic groups, whereas Rastafarians were not. (However, it is against the law to discriminate against you on the grounds of religion if you are a Rastafarian.) Welsh and English people are covered on the grounds of 'national origins'.

You do not need actually to belong to one of these groups for discrimination to take place. Someone may act in a discriminatory way because they believe you belong to a different racial group.

Where race discrimination is unlawful

It is unlawful to discriminate on grounds of race in:

- employment and training
- education

- the provision of goods and services – for example, financial matters, entertainment and transport
- housing.

Employment and training

It is against the law for an employer to discriminate against someone on the grounds of race. This includes all employers, no matter how few workers they employ. Most workers, including employees, trainees and those who are self-employed, have legal protection from race discrimination in all aspects of employment, including recruitment, selection, promotion, training, pay and benefits, redundancy, dismissal, and terms and conditions of work.

Trade unions have a duty not to discriminate against their members or those wishing to become members.

I'm of Indian origin and was employed on a casual basis. Now all the casual workers have been asked to take a written test to decide whether we can stay in the job. I have problems with writing in English. We never have to write anything down in the job and my spoken English is fine. I complained to my boss but he just said I had to take the test or leave. Is there anything else I can do?

You may have a case for indirect race discrimination. Go to your CAB for further advice about what to do. They could help you negotiate with your employers. If this does not work, you may be able to go to the Employment Tribunal.

Education

It is against the law for any school or college to discriminate on grounds of race. This is the case whether or not it is maintained by the local education authority. A school must not discriminate in any of its policies and practices, including its admissions policies, its treatment of pupils, exclusions or decisions about a pupil's special educational needs.

A local education authority must not discriminate in any of the decisions it makes.

Goods, facilities and services

It is against the law for anyone providing goods, facilities or services in the UK to discriminate on grounds of race, either by refusing to provide goods, services or facilities, or by providing them on less favourable terms or conditions. This is the case regardless of whether the goods, services or facilities are provided for payment or free.

Housing

In most circumstances, it is against the law for a person or organization responsible for selling or letting a property to discriminate on grounds of race, either by refusing to sell or rent the premises or in the terms on which the premises are offered.

It is against the law for local authorities, housing associations or other registered social landlords to discriminate on grounds of race – for example, in the allocation of property to people on the local housing lists.

It is against the law for a landlord to discriminate against a tenant once a property is occupied.

When race discrimination is not against the law

The law on race discrimination says there are some situations where race discrimination is permitted.

Employment

If certain conditions or requirements in employment can be shown to be a 'genuine occupational qualification', they may not be discriminatory. For example, it may be justified for the owner of a Chinese or a Greek restaurant to ask for a Chinese or a Greek waiter because the restaurant setting requires this. It is justifiable for a hostel for Asian women who have suffered violence to specify that it wants only Asian women workers on the grounds that the women would find it easier to relate to and communicate with people of the same racial group.

Race discrimination is not against the law if the job involves working for a private household or working abroad for most of the time or when, with regard to certain jobs, the Crown is the employer.

Goods, facilities and services

Clubs, associations and charities set up especially for people of a parti-cular ethnic or national group are allowed to discriminate on the basis of nationality or ethnic or national origin but not on the grounds of colour.

Housing

Owner-occupiers who are selling their property can lawfully discriminate on the grounds of race, as long as they do not advertise or use an estate agent. So can people who are renting out small premises – if the landlord or a member of their family have to share facilities. This exemption does not apply if the landlord advertises the property or uses an estate agent to let it. Also, the landlord is not allowed to discriminate on the grounds of race, or ethnic or national origins.

Courses of action

If you think that you have suffered race discrimination there are a number of courses of action you can take. These include:

- negotiating with the person or body that discriminated against you
- using an established grievance or complaints procedure
- publicizing your case through the media
- taking legal action using race discrimination laws or other laws
- giving details of the problem to the Equality and Human Rights Commission (EHRC: 0845 604 6610 in England; 0845 604 8810 in Wales; www.equality humanrights.com) if you believe the problem is widespread.

The course of action you choose to take will depend partly on the outcome you wish to achieve – for example, financial compensation, justice or publicity – and the speed with which you wish to get a result.

If you are an employee and you think you have suffered race discrimination at work, you must raise a written grievance with your employer before you can make a claim to an employment tribunal. For more information, see pp. 267, 280.

Help with the costs of taking a case to court

If you are taking a case to court, you may face financial costs. Some help may be available. The Equality and Human Rights Commission (EHRC: 0845 604 6610 in England; 0845 604 8810 in Wales; www.equalityhumanrights. com) may be able to give help.

If you feel that you have been discriminated against in your job, your case will be heard at an employment tribunal (see *Employment tribunals*, p. 280). If you qualify for legal aid, you may be able to get advice and assistance from a solicitor to prepare your case for the employment tribunal, but a solicitor will not be able to represent you at the hearing. For more information and advice about legal aid, see *Help with legal costs*, p. 520.

Racially and religiously motivated attacks

Racially motivated attacks and religiously motivated attacks are attacks that are carried out because of someone's racial or ethnic origin, or their religion or lack of religion. They include the following:

- a physical attack on a person or family by another person or group of people
- an attack on a person's or family's home or property – for example, breaking a window, throwing an object through a letterbox or setting a car alight
- verbal abuse or threats
- written abuse, such as a letter, pamphlet, e-mail or telephone text message
- an abusive slogan painted on a wall or building.

Racial offences

If you have been harassed, distressed, insulted or attacked because of your racial origin, the person who carried out the attack can be prosecuted.

In addition, if someone stirs up hatred of a particular racial group – for example, by publishing or distributing insulting information – that person may be prosecuted for racial hatred. Information can include printed material such as leaflets or magazines. It can also include content on websites, e-mails and internet chat rooms. You can report internet content which stirs up racial hatred to the Internet Watch Foundation at www.iwf.org.uk.

Religious offences

If you have been harassed, distressed, insulted or attacked because of your religion, the person who carried out the attack can be prosecuted. Stirring up hatred of a religious group is against the law.

Racially and religiously aggravated criminal offences

If a criminal offence is racially or religiously aggravated, the court can impose a more severe sentence than if it was not racially or religiously aggravated. The offences that can be racially or religiously aggravated are:

- criminal damage
- actual bodily harm

- wounding
- grievous bodily harm
- common assault
- using threatening, abusive or insulting words or behaviour to cause harassment, alarm or distress
- displaying threatening, abusive or insulting writing or signs to cause harassment, alarm or distress
- disorderly behaviour to cause harassment, alarm or distress.

An offence is racially or religiously aggravated if, at the time it is committed, the offender is insulting about the victim's membership (or presumed membership) of a racial or religious group, or the offence is motivated by hostility towards members of a particular racial or religious group.

There may have been previous attacks in the area that could help to indicate that an attack was racially or religiously aggravated. There may also be a local organization, such as a community group or the Citizens Advice Bureau, that can confirm that there is a history of such attacks in the area. Evidence of a history of attacks in an area may help to prove to the police that an offence is racially or religiously aggravated.

Dealing with a racially or religiously motivated attack

If you have been the victim of an attack, it will help, when reporting it, if you can give the following information:

- how you were attacked
- if you know it, the identity of the attacker and where they live or, alternatively, what the attacker looked like and/or what they were wearing
- what, if anything, was said by the attacker, particularly anything insulting about your race or religion
- why else you regard the attack as having been racially or religiously aggravated
- if you have been attacked before, when and by whom
- where the attack was made
- when the attack was made (date and time of day or night)
- the nature of any injuries sustained (it might be helpful to obtain medical evidence)
- if anyone else was attacked
- the names and addresses of any witnesses.

Reporting the attack to the police

If you want help or support in contacting the police, you can approach a Citizens Advice Bureau (CAB). If you have been attacked by a member or members of the police, you should always obtain advice.

The government's own guidance defines a racist incident as 'any incident which is viewed as racist by the victim or any other person'. This means that if either the victim or any other person – for example, a witness or a police officer – perceives an attack to be racially motivated, the police should record it as such. The definition does not currently take into account religiously motivated attacks.

When you contact the police, you can ask to be interviewed at the police station, your home or a mutually agreed neutral location, such as the CAB (if they allow this). In any case, it is generally advisable for another person to attend with you – for example a solicitor experienced in this type of work, a CAB adviser or a friend.

If you have difficulty speaking or understanding English, you may find it helpful to have an interpreter with you. You can ask the police to provide an interpreter, ask a friend or relative, or approach a local organization, for example the CAB. If the police refuse to provide an interpreter, you can ask to see their policy on translators and interpreters and you may want to consider making a complaint.

Helpline

The Monitoring Group Freephone Emergency Helpline (0800 374 618) advises victims of racial harassment and abuse. It is available 24 hours a day and it is staffed by volunteers recruited from black and minority ethnic communities.

Discrimination because of your sexuality

It is against the law for you to be treated less favourably than other people because of your sexuality. The law protects you against discrimination whatever your sexuality – lesbian, gay, bisexual or heterosexual.

It is against the law to discriminate against you directly. An example of direct discrimination at work would be refusing to employ you or dismissing you because of your sexuality. It is also against the law for someone you work for to have rules, policies or practices which, though not aimed at you personally, put you at a disadvantage because of your sexuality. The law calls this indirect discrimination. An example would be a rule that restricts employment benefits for family members to opposite-sex partners only. Indirect discrimination can be justified if it can be shown to be an unavoidable business need.

It is against the law to discriminate against you because of your sexuality:

- at work
- when you are supplied with goods or services
- in education.

In certain circumstances, there are some exceptions to these rules which mean that discrimination is allowed. For example, adoption agencies which are run by religious organizations can refuse to accept gay couples as adopters.

Employment and training

Discrimination at work because of your sexuality could include:

- denying you opportunities at work for development, promotion, or other benefits such as pension and insurance schemes and cheap travel (unless the benefits depend on marital status)
- dismissing you because of your sexuality
- bullying at work because of your sexuality
- refusing to give you a reference, or giving you an unfair reference when you leave your job
- treating you differently – for example, if your employer expects workers to bring an opposite-sex partner to business meals but same-sex partners are not welcome.

If you have been discriminated against at work, you may be able to take a case to the employment tribunal. You must raise a written grievance with your employer before you can make a claim to an employment tribunal. For more information, see pp. 267, 280.

Goods and services

Some of the places where you are protected against discrimination include work, shops, clubs, restaurants, pubs, schools, estate agents, colleges and universities. For example, the children of lesbian or gay parents must not be treated unfairly at school and lesbian or gay pupils must not be bullied. You are also protected when you use healthcare services, council services and care homes, and when you buy financial products such as mortgages, pensions and insurance.

You are protected against discrimination regardless of whether you are buying something or getting it for free.

If you have been discriminated against in the supply of goods or services, you may be able to take a case to the county court.

Religious discrimination

> ### I think I'm being treated unfairly at work because of my religion. Is this legal?
>
> *I'm Jewish and need to take Friday afternoons off work in winter to get home before dark and prepare for the Sabbath. At the moment, my boss is happy to let me do this and make up the time during the rest of the week. However, he is thinking of introducing a new shift pattern which means I will not be able to do this any more. Can he do this?*
>
> It is unlawful to discriminate against any worker because of their religion or belief. So, if your employer is introducing a new shift pattern that will be difficult for you because of your religion, it may be that you are the victim of indirect discrimination on religious grounds. Your employer would have to show exactly why it is essential for you to work on Friday afternoons. If he is unable to show that there is no other reasonable way to reorganize your work, his behaviour towards you may count as discrimination on religious grounds.

It is against the law for you to be treated unfairly because you follow a religion or belief.

Having a religion or belief may mean:

- belonging to an organized religion such as Judaism or Islam
- having a profound belief that affects your way of life or world view
- belonging to a smaller religion or sect, such as Scientology or Rastafarianism
- taking part in collective worship
- having no religion – for example, you are an atheist.

It is against the law for you to be discriminated against directly. An example of direct discrimination at work would be refusing to employ you or dismissing you because of your religious belief. It is also against the law for someone you work for to have rules, policies or practices which, though not aimed at you personally, put you at a disadvantage because of your belief. The law calls this indirect discrimination. An example would be a rule that requires everyone to dress in a particular way, meaning you cannot wear an item of clothing you regard as part of your faith. Indirect discrimination can be justified if it can be shown to be an unavoidable business need.

It is against the law to discriminate against you because of your religion:

- at work
- when you are supplied with goods or services
- in education.

In certain circumstances, there are some exceptions to these rules which mean that discrimination is allowed. For example, faith schools can refuse to accept pupils of another religion.

Employment and training

Discrimination at work because of your religion or belief could include

- making you dress in a certain way or remove sacred items
- making you work at times that are against your religion
- bullying at work because of your religion.

If you have been discriminated against at work, you may be able to take a case to the employment tribunal. You must raise a written grievance with your employer before you can make a claim to an employment tribunal. For more information, see pp. 267, 280.

Goods and services

Some of the places where you are protected against discrimination include work, shops, clubs, restaurants, pubs, schools, estate agents, colleges and universities. For example, it may be unfair discrimination to refuse to allow a woman wearing a *hijab* to attend classes at college. You are also protected when you use healthcare services, council services and care homes and when you buy financial products such as mortgages, pensions and insurance.

You are protected against discrimination regardless of whether you are buying something or getting it for free.

If you have been discriminated against in the supply of goods or services, you may be able to take a case to the county court.

Age discrimination

It is against the law to discriminate against you at work because of your age – either because you are too young or too old. The law also covers adult education and training but does not cover other areas such as the supply of goods or services. For example, insurance companies are still allowed to treat you differently because of your age.

An employer cannot have rules or practices which put you at a disadvantage at work. For example, they are not allowed to say you must have twelve years' experience after you have qualified to apply for a job. This would put younger people at a disadvantage and be against the law.

There are some exceptions to the general rule. For example, an employer could argue that it does not make business sense to recruit people over 60 when there is a long and expensive training period in the job. The employment tribunal would decide whether a particular exception was justified and it is believed that not many employers will be able to justify discrimination.

Retirement age

The normal retirement age for both men and women is now 65, unless your employment contract says it is higher. Even if your contract says you have to retire at 60, it is unlikely that your employer will be able to force you to retire before 65 unless they have a very good reason for having a younger age limit. Your employer is allowed to force you to retire at the normal retirement age. They have to give you at least six months' written notice before retirement. You have the right to ask your employer to be allowed to stay on after the normal retirement age and your employer has to consider your request but does not have to agree.

Unfair dismissal

If you are sacked unfairly, you can make a claim for unfair dismissal, whatever your age. It is unfair to dismiss you just because of your age, although, if they follow the correct procedures, your employer can force you to retire at 65.

Courses of action

If you have been discriminated against at work, you may be able to take a case to the employment tribunal. You must raise a written grievance with your employer before you can make a claim to an employment tribunal. For more information, see pp. 267, 280.

Sex discrimination

It is against the law to discriminate against someone on the grounds of their sex, and public authorities have a legal duty to eliminate unlawful discrimination and actively to promote equality. The law covers both men and women and also transsexual people. Sex discrimination can be direct or indirect. It can also take the form of harassment. Although there are some exceptions to the general rules, it is usually against the law to discriminate:

- at work
- in the supply of goods and services
- in education and training.

It is direct sex discrimination to treat a person less favourably on the grounds of their sex than someone of the other sex would be treated in the same circumstances.

Examples of direct sex discrimination include:

- refusing credit to a married woman without her husband's signature, while a married man is not required to have his wife's signature
- refusing to accept a woman's salary as the basis for a mortgage because of her sex
- allowing women (or men) free entry to a club or cheap drinks when this concession is not given at the same time to men (or women)
- advertising a vacancy for a 'waiter', implying that the job is only open to men
- sexual harassment
- dismissing an employee because she is pregnant.

Indirect sex discrimination

It is indirect sex discrimination to set conditions or requirements which, while apparently applying to everyone, have a greater effect on one sex.

Examples of indirect sex discrimination include:

- a requirement that an employee should not have young children – women are more likely than men to have responsibility for young children and this is also unlikely to be a justifiable requirement for employment (regardless of sex)

- the dismissal of all part-time workers in a firm where all of the part-time workers are female – this may also be direct sex discrimination
- a mortgage provider insisting that only people who work full-time can be given a mortgage. This is more likely to have an adverse effect on women than men, as women are more likely to work part-time.

Victimization

Under the law, victimization occurs when you are treated less favourably as a result of complaining, bringing proceedings or asserting your rights under sex discrimination legislation. It is also victimization if you are treated less favourably because you have supported someone else taking action – for example, by acting as a witness in a sex discrimination case.

Employment and training

It is against the law for an employer to discriminate on the grounds of sex. Discrimination in employment also includes discrimination in recruitment and in vocational training.

The Equal Pay Act 1970 gives you the right to be treated equally in terms of pay in comparison to a member of the opposite sex. The people who are being compared must be working in the same place or working at different establishments for the same employer. A woman who believes she is being discriminated against would have to show that she is employed:

- in like work – that is, work that is the same as or broadly similar to a man's; or
- in work that has been rated as equivalent to a man's job under a job evaluation study; or
- in work that is of equal value to that of a man in terms of, for example, effort, skill and decision making.

Pregnancy and employment

It is direct sex discrimination to dismiss a woman because she is pregnant. As only a woman can become pregnant, dismissal on the grounds of pregnancy is automatically discrimination on grounds of sex.

A woman who is dismissed because she is pregnant can also claim that she has been unfairly dismissed, regardless of how long she has worked for her employer. There is a maximum limit on the compensation that can be awarded for unfair dismissal, but no limit on compensation for sex discrimination. Therefore, a woman dismissed for being pregnant should claim sex discrimination as well as unfair dismissal.

Transsexual people

It is unlawful to discriminate against someone who intends to undergo, is undergoing, or has already undergone gender reassignment. There are some exceptions to this general rule.

Married people and people in a civil partnership

In the case of employment, it is sex discrimination to discriminate against you for being married or for being in a civil partnership. This applies whether you are a woman or a man. There is no provision covering discrimination against a person for being single.

Education

It is against the law for a state or private educational establishment to discriminate in its admission policies, unless it is a single-sex establishment. For example, a mixed-sex school should not refuse admission to a student on the grounds of their sex, or attempt to maintain a gender balance in the school by admitting one sex and not another when places are limited.

A girl and boy must have the same access to the school curriculum – that is, they must be given exactly the same subject options and the same amount of subject teaching.

Goods, facilities and services

It is against the law for anyone providing goods, facilities or services to discriminate by refusing to provide the goods because of your sex, or to discriminate in the way in which they are provided. This is irrespective of whether the goods, services or facilities are provided for payment or for free and both direct and indirect discrimination are covered, as well as harassment.

Financial services

It is against the law for a financial services provider to discriminate by, for example, asking a married woman to provide a guarantor for a loan (unless a man in a similar position would also be asked to do this), insisting that a married woman seeking a loan must apply jointly with her husband (unless all married applicants are asked to apply jointly) or setting more stringent conditions when a woman asks for a business loan than when a man does. It may be lawful, however, to discriminate when providing insurance cover. There are rules which set out the circumstances under which insurance companies may charge different premiums to men and women.

Housing

It is unlawful for a person or organization responsible for selling or letting a property to discriminate on the grounds of sex in the terms on which the premises are offered. It is unlawful to discriminate in the treatment of people listed as needing accommodation – for example, in local authority housing lists. It is also unlawful to discriminate against a tenant once a property is occupied.

Advertisements

It is unlawful for someone to publish an advertisement that indicates an intention to discriminate on grounds of sex. For example, it is unlawful for a club open to the public to advertise free admission for women while making men pay, or for an employer to use expressions that have a gender connotation in advertisements, such as 'craftsman', 'manageress' or 'handyman'.

When sex discrimination is not against the law

There are a number of situations in which it is not against the law to discriminate on grounds of sex. For example, it is not against the law for a charity to provide benefits to people of one sex only, provided this is set out in the charity's constitution or rules.

It is not against the law to discriminate on the grounds of a person's sex when providing some types of communal accommodation, such as a women's refuge.

Also, it may not be against the law to discriminate on the grounds of sex when a landlord is letting a 'small dwelling' and the landlord or a close relative share accommodation with other people living there.

Taking action about sex discrimination

When taking action about sex discrimination, you do not have to demonstrate that there was an intention to discriminate against you. It is merely necessary to show that discrimination took place.

When taking action under legislation against sex discrimination, a comparison must normally be made between how a woman has been treated and how a man has been treated. However, if a woman cannot identify a man who is being treated, or has been treated, more favourably, she can still take legal action if she can show that a man would have been treated more favourably. If you think you have suffered sex discrimination, there are a number of actions you can take. These include:

- negotiating with the person or body that discriminated against you
- using an established grievance or complaints procedure
- taking legal action using sex discrimination laws or other laws
- giving details to the Equality and Human Rights Commission (EHRC: 0845 604 6610 in England; 0845 604 8810 in Wales; www.equalityhumanrights. com).

If you are an employee and you think you have suffered sex discrimination at work, you must raise a written grievance with your employer before you can make a claim to an employment tribunal. For more information, see pp. 267, 280.

Education cases

There are specific procedures for taking action about sex discrimination in education.

In general, the law against sex discrimination applies to both state and private schools. Before making a complaint against a state school, in England you must first notify the Department for Children, Schools and Families (DCSF) within six months of the date of the discriminatory act. In Wales, contact the Welsh Assembly Government. If the complaint is about a private school, you should first consult the Equality and Human Rights Commission (EHRC: 0845 604 6610 in England; 0845 604 8810 in Wales; www.equalityhumanrights.com).

Disability discrimination

It is against the law to discriminate against disabled people in various areas of their lives. For example, it is against the law to discriminate against disabled people at work and when providing goods, facilities and services. There is also limited protection against discrimination for disabled people who are renting or buying property, and in education.

There are rules about what the law counts as a disability when considering whether or not discrimination has taken place.

The law says that 'disability' means a physical or mental 'impairment', which has a substantial and long-term negative effect on your ability to carry out normal day-to-day activities. There are special rules for people with cancer, HIV and multiple sclerosis and for people who are blind or partially sighted – see below.

According to this definition, impairments can include sensory 'impairments', such as sight and hearing, or mental 'impairments', such as learning disabilities, dyslexia and mental illness. Some severe disfigurements count as a disability. Some conditions that can worsen over time, such as multiple sclerosis and HIV/AIDS, are regarded as a disability as soon as they are diagnosed, even before they start to affect your day-to-day activities.

To have a long-term disability means that the disability:

- has lasted for at least twelve months; *or*
- is expected to last for at least twelve months; *or*
- is likely to last for the rest of your life, if you are expected to live for less than twelve months.

An impairment will be treated as affecting your ability to carry out normal day-to-day activities if it affects at least one of the following:

- mobility
- ability to use hands – for example, for writing or cooking
- physical co-ordination
- continence (the ability to control your bladder or bowels)
- the ability to lift, carry or move ordinary objects
- speech, hearing or eyesight
- memory, or the ability to concentrate, learn or understand
- being able to recognize physical danger.

In some cases, even if medical aids or treatment are used to help control or remove a disability, it is still regarded as a disability. Examples of this include the use of an artificial limb or medication to control epilepsy. However, visual impairment corrected with glasses or contact lenses is not regarded as a disability.

Although a minor impairment may not, on its own, count as substantial, you could have a number of minor impairments which, taken together, might be seen as having a substantial effect. If an impairment stops having a substantial effect, it can still be regarded as an impairment if there is a reasonable likelihood of the condition recurring, as, for example, in the case of epilepsy.

People with cancer, HIV or multiple sclerosis

If you have cancer, HIV or multiple sclerosis, you are automatically counted as having a disability. This means that you do not have to show that you have an impairment that has a substantial, adverse, long-term effect on your ability to carry out normal day-to-day activities. You are counted as having a disability from the date you are diagnosed with the condition.

People who are blind or partially sighted

You are counted as having a disability if you are either:

- certified as blind or partially sighted by a consultant ophthalmologist; *or*
- registered as blind or partially sighted by a local authority.

What does not count as a disability?

The law does not currently count the following as disabilities:

- addiction to alcohol, nicotine or any other substance not prescribed by a doctor. However, damage to health caused by the addiction may be considered a disability
- hay fever
- certain personality disorders (for example, exhibitionism, voyeurism or a tendency to steal, set fires, or physically or sexually abuse other people)
- tattoos and body piercing.

Disability discrimination at work

It is against the law for an employer:

- to discriminate directly against you if you are disabled
- to treat you less favourably because of your disability – including in recruitment and selection, terms and conditions, dismissal and redundancy (but see below)
- not to make 'reasonable adjustments' to the workplace to enable you to work or to continue to work (see below)
- to harass you if you are disabled – for example, by making jokes about your disability
- to victimize you if you take legal action because of discrimination against you, or if you help someone else to take legal action because of discrimination.

Employers can treat disabled people less favourably only if they have a sufficiently justifiable reason for doing so, and only if the problem cannot be overcome by making 'reasonable adjustments'. For example, an employer would be justified in rejecting someone with severe back pain for a job as a carpet fitter, as they cannot carry out the essential requirements of the job.

Examples of the types of adjustments that an employer might make include:

- making physical adjustments to the premises
- supplying special equipment to help you do your job
- transferring you to a different post or workplace
- altering your hours of work or giving you extra time off.

When employers are deciding whether an adjustment is reasonable, they can take into account several things, including the cost of making an adjustment and the size of their business. If you are already in the job, your employer can also take into account your skills and experience and the length of time you have worked there.

Access to goods, facilities and services

It is against the law for a provider of goods, facilities and services to discriminate against a disabled person.

Examples of the types of goods and services covered include services provided by hotels, banks, building societies, solicitors, local authorities, advice agencies, pubs, theatres, shops, telesales, churches, doctors' surgeries and law courts. It does not matter whether the service is free or has to be paid for.

Providers of these goods and services must not treat you less favourably than they would treat a person who is not disabled (unless they can show that the treatment is justified). An example of less-favourable treatment is when a hotel refuses a booking from a person with a hearing impairment, saying that the hotel is not suitable for people with a hearing impairment.

Service providers must make 'reasonable adjustments' to allow a disabled person to use their services. If they do not do this, they must be able to show that their failure to do so is justified. Examples of making reasonable adjustments include providing information on audiotape as well as in writing, or installing a ramp to allow wheelchair access.

The government has produced a Code of Practice about disability discrimination. It is a statement of good practice which you can use when dealing with someone who provides goods, facilities or services. If you decide to take legal action because you have suffered disability discrimination, the court must consider the Code when it arrives at a decision. A copy of the Code is available from the website of the Equality and Human Rights Commission (EHRC: 0845 604 6610 in England; 0845 604 8810 in Wales; www.equalityhumanrights.com). There is also a guide to taking court action for disability discrimination. It is called 'How do I make a claim'.

Buying or renting land or property

Someone who rents or sells you property may be discriminating against you if:

- they refuse to sell or rent a property to you
- they offer you a property for sale or rent on worse terms than they would to a person who is not disabled
- they treat you less favourably on a housing waiting list than a person who is not disabled
- you are renting and they unreasonably prevent you from using benefits or facilities or do not allow you to use these facilities in the same way as other tenants do
- you are renting and they evict or harass you for a reason connected with your disability.

Landlords who rent out accommodation in their own homes are allowed to discriminate against people with disabilities.

Services such as estate agents must make their offices accessible, as long as it is reasonable to do so.

A landlord's duty to make alterations for disabled people

If you are disabled, you can ask your landlord (or future landlord) to make certain changes to the property, and to their policies, when this is necessary for you to be able to live in the property. These changes are known as reasonable adjustments. Landlords who refuse to make reasonable adjustments, and who cannot justify this, are discriminating against you and they are breaking the law.

Reasonable adjustments can include:

- providing aids and services, such as a copy of the tenancy agreement in Braille or a temporary ramp for a wheelchair user with a small step up to their flat
- changing practices, policies or procedures. An example of this would be to change the parking policy so that a disabled occupier who has difficulty walking can park in front of the building
- changing a term in the letting agreement. An example of this would be changing a term in the letting agreement which says that tenants cannot make

improvements so that a disabled person could make a disability-related improvement. Another example would be changing a term which bans pets for a disabled person who has an assistance dog.

What is reasonable will depend on the individual circumstances, including:

- the type and length of your letting
- how much difference the adjustment will make to you
- how much money your landlord has.

Your landlord does not have to take any steps that involve the removal or alteration of physical features, such as putting in a permanent, concrete ramp or undertaking major works which would involve serious damage to the property.

Your landlord must not discriminate against you by, for example, evicting you or increasing the rent because of the cost of the adjustment.

Education

Providers of education must not discriminate against disabled students or disabled people applying to be students. Providers of education include schools, and establishments for further education, higher education, and adult and community education.

Unless they can justify it, providers of education must not:

- refuse to offer a disabled student a place because they are disabled, or offer them a place on less favourable terms than a student who is not disabled
- treat a disabled student less favourably in any aspect of educational life, including trips, excursions and extra-curricular activities
- exclude a disabled student from school because of their disability.

For example, if a school refuses to take a child who suffers from epilepsy unless they stop having fits, this will count as discrimination.

However, in some cases, an education provider can treat a disabled student less favourably if it can justify this. A school can justify less-favourable treatment if it is because of a permitted form of selection. For example, a child with learning difficulties applies to a school that selects its intake on the basis of academic ability and fails the school's entrance exam. Under these circumstances, the school would be able to justify not offering the child a place.

Providers of education must not discriminate against disabled students or applicants by failing to make reasonable adjustments to allow for their disability. If this places a disabled student at a substantial disadvantage compared with students who are not disabled, this will be regarded as discrimination. For example, a deaf pupil who lip-reads is at a disadvantage if teachers continue to speak while facing away to write on a whiteboard.

Making reasonable adjustments includes providing special aids such as equipment and sign language interpreters.

Schools do not have to make reasonable adjustments to buildings and the physical environment of the school. However, all local education author-ities must have plans to make their schools more accessible to disabled pupils. Maintained schools, independent schools, and non-maintained spe-cial schools must produce their own accessibility plans. The plans must be in writing and publicly available.

Providers of further and higher education do have to make reasonable adjustments to their premises to allow better access for disabled students. However, issues such as cost can be taken into account when they decide whether an adjustment is reasonable.

Providing for children with special educational needs

All schools must comply with a statement of special educational needs when one has been issued for a child. For example, a school must recruit a learning support assistant or provide information in Braille or on audio tape if the student's statement provides for one. In some cases, colleges of further education must also comply with a statement of special educational needs.

For more information about special educational needs, see p. 200.

What action can you take about discrimination in education?

If you have a child who has special needs, you may be able to complain to the Special Educational Needs (and Disability) Tribunal (in Wales, The Special Educational Needs Tribunal for Wales).

Public transport

Access to public transport

If you are disabled, providers of public transport must not treat you less favourably than they would treat a person who is not disabled (unless they can show that the treatment is justified). They have the same duties as other providers of services – see Access to goods, facilities and services, p. 476. These rules apply to the transport service itself as well as to other related services, such as at a railway station.

There are exceptions to these rules – for example, ships are not covered by the rules although their related services are. So, if you are disabled, you must not be treated less favourably at the port.

Who can help?

The law provides protection for people who have been treated unfairly because of who they are. Get advice as soon as possible as there are strict time limits within which you can take legal action. Many organizations' employment and customer services policies provide additional protection against types of unfair treatment that are not covered by the law. Your local Citizens Advice Bureau can tell you whether the law covers your situation, find out if there is a relevant policy, and advise you about what you can do.

The **Equality and Human Rights Commission** (EHRC: 0845 604 6610 in England; 0845 604 8810 in Wales; www.equalityhumanrights.com) deals with all kinds of unlawful discrimination and human rights law.

If you have been the victim of a racially and/or religiously motivated attack, you should always seek advice. You can get this from a CAB. You could also get help from your local **Victim Support** scheme (Helplines: 0845 3030 900; www.victimsupport.org.uk) or another local organization. You could also contact the **Monitoring Group** freephone emergency helpline (0800 374 618), which advises victims of racial harassment and abuse. It is available 24 hours a day, and is staffed by volunteers recruited from black and ethnic minority communities, to ensure that they can communicate with the caller in the appropriate language.

There is also a Home Office support line for Muslims – **'Muslim Line'** (0208 840 4840) – which can give advice if you have been abused because of your religious beliefs.

If you have suffered a personal injury as the result of a racially or religiously motivated attack, you may be eligible for compensation under the **Criminal Injuries Compensation Scheme** (0800 358 3601; www.cica.gov.uk).

Stonewall (020 7593 1850; www.stonewall.org.uk) is a lobbying group which works with lesbians, gay men and bisexual people of all political parties to achieve equal rights. The information bank on their website contains much useful information.

Law Centres can offer free legal advice to people who want to take action about discrimination. If you are represented by a solicitor from a law centre, you may be entitled to legal aid. Details of the nearest law centres are available from the **Law Centres Federation** (020 7428 4400; www.lawcentres.org.uk).

Members of the **Discrimination Law Association** (020 8365 8744; www.discrimination-law.org.uk) work in the areas of race, disability and sex discrimination. The Association can provide names of member practitioners. You should remember that most members are likely to be solicitors in private practice and so charges will be made if legal aid is not available.

INVESTIGATING COMPLAINTS – THE OMBUDSMAN

An ombudsman is a person who has been appointed to investigate complaints about an organization. Using an ombudsman is a way of trying to resolve a complaint without going to court.

There are a number of ombudsmen:

- the Parliamentary Ombudsman, who investigates complaints about government departments and some other public bodies
- the Public Services Ombudsman for Wales
- the Local Government Ombudsman, who investigates complaints about local councils and some other local organizations
- the European Ombudsman
- the Health Service Ombudsman
- the Financial Ombudsman Service (FOS)
- the Legal Services Ombudsman
- the Ombudsman for Estate Agents
- the Housing Ombudsman (England only)
- the Prisons and Probation Ombudsman
- the Energy Supply Ombudsman – see p. 441.

An ombudsman should be a member of the British and Irish Ombudsman Association (BIOA). To check whether an ombudsman is a member of the BIOA, visit the BIOA website at www.bioa.org.uk.

Ombudsmen are independent, free of charge and impartial – that is, they do not take sides with either the person who is complaining or the organization being complained about.

In most cases, you must complain to the organization first, before you make a complaint to the ombudsman.

If you need to spend money making a complaint to an ombudsman, such as travel expenses to an ombudsman's office, you may be able to claim this back. You should check with the ombudsman first before you spend any money that you want to claim back.

If an ombudsman finds that your complaint is justified, they will recommend what the organization should do to put things right. An ombudsman cannot force an organization to go along with their recommendations but organizations almost always do.

Investigations by an ombudsman sometimes take a long time.

The ombudsman's job is to investigate cases of maladministration. This means the way in which an organization has dealt with a situation or reached a decision. Examples of maladministration include:

• an organization not following its own policies or procedures
• rudeness
• delay in taking action or failing to take action
• treating someone unfairly compared to others
• giving wrong or misleading information.

The ombudsman will only investigate a case where an individual (or in some cases a group of individuals) has suffered personal injustice, hardship or financial loss because of the action or lack of action of a particular organization. The complaint must be brought by the person who has suffered this injustice, hardship or loss.

In most cases, an ombudsman cannot look into a decision made by an organization just because you disagree with it.

You should complain to the ombudsman only if you have given the relevant organization an opportunity to comment on the complaint and resolve any problems.

The ombudsman will not investigate a case if it is about to go to court or if court action has been started. In some cases, the ombudsman will not look into cases which could be dealt with by a court or tribunal.

You can find out more about which types of complaints an ombudsman can take up and what you must do before complaining to the ombudsman in the information that follows.

How to complain to the ombudsman

The procedure for starting the investigation by the ombudsman differs slightly depending on which ombudsman the complaint is being made to. Most of the offices of the ombudsmen provide an application form for making a complaint. It is not, however, necessary to use an application form. You can send a letter containing the following information:

- name and address of the person making the complaint
- name and address of the organization the complaint is being made about
- details of what the complaint is about – that is, what the organization did wrong or failed to do
- date when you first identified the event you are complaining about
- what personal injustice, financial loss or hardship was suffered
- what the organization should do to put the situation right
- details of how the complaint has been followed up prior to contacting the ombudsman.

Copies of any correspondence relevant to the complaint should also be sent.

Parliamentary Ombudsman

The Parliamentary Ombudsman (0845 015 4033; www.ombudsman.org.uk) can take up complaints about the way an individual has been treated by a government department or other public body. The Parliamentary Ombudsman can deal with complaints about maladministration by a public body – for example, about how procedures are used.

The Ombudsman can only help if asked to do so by an MP. First, you should contact your MP, setting out the problem and asking them to refer the case to the Ombudsman. The MP should be sent all relevant correspondence. The MP may wish to look into the problem before referring it to the Ombudsman, and may decide not to pass on your complaint.

Examples of the type of complaint the Parliamentary Ombudsman could deal with are:

- slow and unsatisfactory responses to letters to government departments
- incorrect or misleading information and advice given by officials of government departments or refusal to give information
- rudeness, discrimination, unhelpfulness of staff of government departments or refusal to give information
- failure to follow reasonable rules in procedures and administration.

The Parliamentary Ombudsman cannot investigate the following types of complaint:

- complaints about nationalized industries

- problems that can usually be taken to court
- complaints about the way legal proceedings are conducted – for example, complaints about the administrative staff of courts, unless the staff acted on the authority of the judge, magistrate, etc.
- complaints about the police
- complaints about things that have not caused the complainant hardship or suffering
- complaints about government policies
- complaints reported to an MP more than twelve months after you became aware you had reason to complain.

Public Services Ombudsman for Wales

The Public Services Ombudsman for Wales (01656 641 150; www.ombudsman-wales.org.uk) can deal with complaints of maladministration in public services in Wales. These include services provided by the following organizations:

- local authorities
- joint boards of local authorities
- police and fire authorities (not complaints about individual police officers)
- the National Assembly for Wales
- local health boards
- NHS trusts
- GP services
- Community Health Councils
- housing provided by housing associations and by local authorities
- national park authorities
- the Environment Agency
- Education Appeal Panels
- school governing bodies (admission matters only).

The Ombudsman can also investigate complaints that a member of a local government body has broken the code of conduct of the body. This might be, for example, if a councillor has brought the council into disrepute or used their position to gain an advantage for themselves. The Ombudsman can consider a complaint about a person who is a member of:

- a county or county borough council
- a community council
- a fire, police or national park authority.

If you have a problem, complain first to the organization concerned. Write a letter to the department setting out the problem. If you do not get a satisfactory response or you do not get an answer within a reasonable time, ask the Ombudsman to look into the complaint. You can send your complaint directly to the Ombudsman or you can ask a local councillor to do this for you.

Local Government Ombudsman

The Local Government Ombudsman can deal with complaints of maladministration in the following organizations:

- local authorities (but not town or parish councils)
- joint boards of local authorities
- police and fire authorities (not complaints about individual police officers)
- English Partnerships (some housing and planning matters only)
- the Commission for the New Towns (housing matters only)
- housing action trusts
- national park authorities
- the Environment Agency (flood defence and land drainage matters only)
- the Greater London Authority
- the Norfolk and Suffolk Broads Authority
- education appeal panels
- school governing bodies (admission matters only).

The Local Government Ombudsman can only investigate complaints of maladministration that cause injustice, suffering or hardship. This means that they can only take up complaints about the way an organization has done something, or not done something it should have done. Examples of the type of complaint it can investigate are:

- delay or neglect in responding to enquiries or providing a service
- failure to follow the agreed policies, rules or procedures of the organization
- rudeness, discrimination or unhelpfulness of staff
- incorrect or misleading information and advice by officials, or failure to provide advice and information.

The Local Government Ombudsman cannot deal with:

- a complaint that could go, or has already gone, to a court or tribunal or in which a government minister is involved

- a complaint about something that affects all or most of the inhabitants in a local area – for example, a complaint that the council has wasted public money
- a complaint about court proceedings
- a complaint about the internal affairs of schools and colleges
- contracts for the supply of goods and services to the council
- personnel policies and practices.

Contact details of the Local Government Ombudsmen are listed here. You should contact the Ombudsman for your area.

London boroughs north of the Thames (including Richmond and excluding Harrow and Tower Hamlets), Berkshire, Buckinghamshire, Hertfordshire, Essex, Kent, East and West Sussex, Surrey, Suffolk and Coventry: 020 7217 4620.

London Borough of Tower Hamlets, Birmingham, Cheshire, Derbyshire, Nottinghamshire, Lincolnshire and the North of England (except the cities of York and Lancaster): 01904 380200.

London boroughs south of the Thames (excluding Richmond), Harrow, the cities of York and Lancaster and the rest of England not covered by London: 024 7682 0000.

More information is available from the national helpline on 0845 602 1983 or online (www.lgo.org.uk).

Wales: Contact the Public Services Ombudsman for Wales (01656 641 150; www.ombudsman-wales.org.uk).

European Ombudsman

Examples of the problems that can be investigated by the European Ombudsman (00 33 88 17 23 13; www.euro-ombudsman.eu.int) include administrative delay, refusal of information, discrimination and abuse of power.

Before you can make a complaint to the European Ombudsman, the European institution concerned should be given the opportunity to investigate and try to resolve the problem.

Health Service Ombudsman

The Health Service Ombudsman (England: 0845 015 4033; minicom: 020 7217 4066; www.ombudsman.org.uk; Wales: 02920 394621; www.ombudsman-wales.org.uk) can investigate complaints about NHS hospitals or community health services.

Some examples of the type of problems the Health Service Ombudsman can investigate are:

- poor service, such as a long wait for treatment or an operation
- failure to provide a disability aid
- dirty wards at a hospital
- unhelpful staff or inadequate staffing
- the care and treatment provided by a doctor, nurse or other trained professional
- complaints about GPs, dentists, opticians and pharmacists working for the NHS
- refusal to give you information to which you are entitled.

The Health Service Ombudsman cannot investigate the following types of problem:

- complaints that have gone or could go to court or a tribunal
- complaints relating to services in a non-NHS hospital or nursing home (unless paid for by the NHS)
- decisions an NHS authority or individual providing NHS services has a right to make, even if you do not agree with the decision
- a problem which you have complained about more than twelve months after you first became aware of it (however, there is some flexibility with this in certain situations).

The Health Service Ombudsman does not have to investigate a complaint, and the local community health council or the Health Service Ombudsman's office will be able to advise on whether or not the Ombudsman can take up a complaint. Before you make a complaint to the Ombudsman, the practice, hospital or trust concerned must be given an opportunity to investigate and, if possible, sort out the problem. The Health Service Ombudsman will only deal with complaints that have not been satisfactorily sorted out through Local Resolution, or by an Independent Review panel. You can get help with making your complaint from the Independent Complaints Advocacy Service (ICAS).

For more information on how to make a complaint about an NHS service and the procedures involved, see p. 105.

You should complain to the Health Service Ombudsman in writing, no later than a year from the date when you first became aware of the events that are the subject of the complaint.

Financial Ombudsman Service

The Financial Ombudsman Service can deal with consumer complaints about most personal financial matters, including:

- financial advice
- banking services
- endowment policies
- mortgages
- personal pension plans
- building society services
- insurance.

The Financial Ombudsman Service is impartial and is free of charge. It mainly deals with consumer complaints about companies which are authorized by the Financial Services Authority, although it can also deal with some unauthorized companies. You should contact the Financial Ombudsman Service consumer helpline directly to find out if it can deal with your complaint.

Before you complain to the Financial Ombudsman Service, you must complain to the company, using its formal complaints procedure. If you are not happy with the outcome, a complaint can be made to the Financial Ombudsman Service. There is a time limit for making the complaint. This is six months from when you get a final decision from the company about how it is going to deal with the matter. You can get a complaint form from the Financial Ombudsman Service website. You can contact the Financial Ombudsman Service directly for information on how to make a complaint (0845 080 1800: www.financial-ombudsman.org.uk).

Legal Services Ombudsman

The Legal Services Ombudsman can deal with complaints about solicitors, barristers, legal executives and licensed conveyancers.

The Legal Services Ombudsman will not deal with a complaint if:

- the internal complaints procedure of the lawyer's professional body has not yet been exhausted
- the complaint is being or has been dealt with by a court of law
- the complaint is about how a barrister handled a case in court
- the complaint is made more than three months after the lawyer's professional body has informed you of its decision, unless the Ombudsman decides there are special reasons.

You can contact the office of the Legal Services Ombudsman on 0845 601 0794 (local call rate), online (www.olso.org), or in writing, and get a complaints form to complete and return.

Ombudsman for Estate Agents

The Ombudsman for Estate Agents will investigate complaints about member companies if you have lost money or suffered inconvenience because a company has:

- infringed your legal rights
- treated you unfairly
- been guilty of maladministration (including inefficiency and delay).

The Ombudsman for Estate Agents will not deal with complaints if:

- the complaint is not against a member company
- the complaint is being or has been dealt with by a court
- the complaint relates to a dispute over a survey
- the claim is for more than a certain amount
- the complaint is sent more than six months after the company complained about has made its final offer.

You can write to the Ombudsman for Estate Agents (01722 333 306; www.oea.co.uk) giving full details of the complaint.

Housing Ombudsman (England only)

The Housing Ombudsman Service can deal with complaints about maladministration by any registered social landlord or other private landlord who has joined the scheme voluntarily. The Housing Ombudsman cannot deal with complaints about local authority landlords. You can make a complaint about a local authority landlord to the Local Government Ombudsman – see p. 485. Complaints that can be dealt with include:

- failure to make repairs in a reasonable time
- mistakenly accusing a tenant of rent arrears and not acknowledging the mistake
- charging you more than other tenants for the same service
- unreasonably refusing to provide a home or a transfer.

The Ombudsman will not normally deal with complaints which involve:

- the level of rent or service charges
- matters that have gone to court or which the Ombudsman decides are better dealt with by a court
- council tenants (complaints can be dealt with by the Local Government Ombudsman instead).

You should first go through your landlord's complaints procedure. There is a time limit for complaining to the Ombudsman. This is twelve months from the end of your landlord's complaints procedure. However, if the procedure is inadequate, the Ombudsman may accept complaints before the procedure is complete.

You can write to the Housing Ombudsman Service (0845 712 5973; www.ihos.org.uk) giving full details of your complaint.

Prisons and Probation Ombudsman

The Prisons and Probation Ombudsman can consider complaints about most aspects of a prisoner's treatment in prison, including disciplinary hearings. They also deal with complaints by people on probation. The Prisons and Probation Ombudsman can consider whether a decision taken by the Prison Service or National Probation Service was correct and whether the proper procedures were followed in making the decision. This includes action taken by prison staff employed by private companies and by people such as prison probation officers or members of the Independent Monitoring Board. The Ombudsman is also responsible for investigating the deaths of all prisoners and residents of probation hostels and immigration detention accommodation.

The Prisons and Probation Ombudsman cannot consider complaints about the actions of outside agencies, such as the police, courts or the Immigration Department.

Complaints can be made to the Prisons and Probation Ombudsman (0845 010 7938; www.ppo.gov.uk). Before you make a complaint to the Prisons and Probation Ombudsman, you must first have used the internal complaints procedures. If you are not satisfied with the reply or if the Prison Service Headquarters or Area Probation Board has not replied within six weeks, a complaint can be made to the Ombudsman.

GOVERNMENT IN WALES

The Government of Wales Act 2006 created a National Assembly for Wales and allows for a separate Welsh Assembly Government. Led by the First Minister, the Welsh Assembly Government is responsible for many issues, including health, education, economic development, culture, the environment and transport.

The relationship between the Welsh Assembly government and the National Assembly is similar to that of the UK government and Parliament. The National Assembly can debate the laws proposed by members of the Assembly government and hold government members to account. It can also approve certain laws itself, instead of waiting for the laws to go through the UK Parliamentary programme.

However, some laws will still need to be approved by the UK Parliament. For more information, see www.wales.gov.uk.

FREEDOM OF INFORMATION

Your right to information

Under freedom of information laws, anybody can request information from a public authority. This means you have the right:

- to be told whether or not a public authority holds information that you want; and if so
- to have access to the information.

You do not need to say why you want the information and, generally, there are no restrictions on how you can use the information once you have it.

Any information held by a public authority is eligible for release. However, information does not have to be provided if the authority decides there are good reasons for keeping it confidential – for example, if your request relates to someone else's personal details. You may have to pay a fee for the information.

Broadly, freedom of information applies to all public authorities within the following categories:

- central and local government
- the health sector
- the police and armed forces
- the education sector
- other public bodies.

The publication scheme

All public authorities have a publication scheme. This scheme lists the information that the public authority routinely makes available and states whether you have to pay for the information or not. Check the scheme to see if the information you want has already been published as this will save you time and money.

How do I ask for information?

All requests must be in writing, by letter, fax or e-mail. You must clearly state what you want and supply your name and address. You can ask for any recorded information, so the information could be in the form of e-mails, notebooks, videos or tapes as well as paper or electronic documents. In most cases, a public authority must respond to your request within 20 working days. If it cannot, it must explain why and let you know when you will get a reply.

The reply should confirm or deny whether or not the authority holds the information, and either provide the information you requested or explain why it cannot.

What if my request is refused?

If your request is refused, the public authority must give you details of how to apply for an internal review of its decision. If, after an internal review, the public authority still refuses your request, you may ask the Information Commissioner (0845 630 6060; www.ico.gov.uk) to review that decision.

PRIVACY AND DATA PROTECTION

Personal data is data about an identifiable living individual. Examples of personal data include:

- your health record
- an entry about you on the police national computer
- your credit reference file
- an e-mail about your conduct at work.

There are rules about what personal data can be accessed by others and the way in which data is processed. Data can only be processed for specific and limited purposes: for example, your local authority is not allowed to pass on the names and addresses of council tax payers to any commercial organization.

Data must be accurate and, where necessary, kept up to date. It must not be kept longer than necessary and must be secure. There is extra protection relating to 'sensitive' personal data – for example, information about your racial or ethnic origin, political opinions or sex life. This sort of data can be processed only if you give your express consent or if it is in connection with legal proceedings.

The Information Commissioner's Office is the UK independent supervisory authority that oversees and enforces data protection law. Contact the Data Protection helpline (0845 630 6060; www.ico.gov.uk) for more information.

2
The Legal System

CONTENTS

INTRODUCTION

Access to justice is a basic right in a fair society and we need to trust the laws that support us and those who administer them. The right to a fair trial and to appeal against a decision are cornerstones of the justice system, as high-profile miscarriages of justice cases have illustrated. Access to publicly funded legal services is also vital so that low income is no barrier to justice; consequently legal aid has developed as part of the welfare state – although increasingly this is under strain. The justice we demand and the laws we live by have developed over many centuries, but the rule of law and judges regulating the power of the state remain guiding principles.

The face of the legal system has changed in recent years, with the increased emphasis on human rights, changes to the role of the Lord Chancellor and the creation of a new Department of Justice, with responsibility for legal aid and services, the courts, prisons and probation, and criminal law. Approaches to crime have also changed, with significant increases in the prison population and new punishment measures from community sentences to ASBOs.

This chapter looks at the basic structures of our legal system, which courts do what, the prison system, police powers, how to use the small claims court and how to use a solicitor.

JARGON BUSTER

statutory charge	money or property you are awarded in a civil court case may have to be used to pay your solicitor's fees if you were getting legal aid
LSC	Legal Services Commission
CLS	Community Legal Services
criminal law	deals with illegal acts committed against individuals or society as a whole
civil law	involves disputes over property, commercial transactions or family matters like divorce and adoption
JPs	justices of the peace
summary offences	criminal offences, dealt with in the magistrates' court, where the defendant is not entitled to trial by jury
VOs	Visiting Orders

THE LEGAL STRUCTURE

The county court

The county court deals with civil (that is, not criminal) cases, which are dealt with by a judge or district judge. The claimant is the person who makes the claim and the defendant is the person against whom a claim is made. A case can be started in any county court but it may be transferred to the defendant's local court. If the case is defended and the claim is for a fixed amount of money, the case will be transferred automatically by the court to the defendant's local court (if the defendant is an individual not a company). In other cases the defendant can request its transfer.

All claims arising from regulated credit agreements must be started in the county court, whatever their value.

Examples of cases dealt with by the county court

County courts can deal with a wide range of cases, but the most common ones are:

- landlord and tenant disputes – for example, possession (eviction), rent arrears, repairs
- consumer disputes – for example, faulty goods or services
- personal injury claims (injuries caused by negligence), such as traffic accidents, falling into holes in the pavement and accidents at work
- undefended divorce cases and proceedings to end a registered civil partnership, but only in some county courts. In inner London the Principle Registry of the Family Division in the Strand deals with undefended divorces and proceedings to end registered civil partnerships
- some domestic violence cases, but these may also be heard in the magistrates' court
- cases of discrimination in the provision of goods and services
- debt problems – for example, a creditor seeking payment
- employment problems – for example, wages or salary owing or pay in lieu of notice.

Small claims cases

A case will, if defended, be dealt with in one of three ways. The court will decide which procedure will apply and then allocate the case to the corresponding 'track'. The three tracks are:

- the small claims track
- the fast track
- the multi-track.

The small claims track is the usual track for claims with a value of £5,000 or less. The procedure in the small claims track is simpler than in the other tracks and in most cases the losing party will not have to pay the other party's costs.

For more information on using the small claims track, see *Using the small claims procedure*, p. 507.

Magistrates' courts

Magistrates' courts deal with mainly criminal cases but some civil ones too. Cases are dealt with either by justices of the peace (JPs) or by district judges (magistrates' courts) who together are known as magistrates. (JPs are unqualified and are paid only expenses, while district judges are salaried.) Magistrates' courts usually deal only with cases that arise in their own area.

Criminal cases in the magistrates' court

All criminal cases start in the magistrates' court.

Some cases begin in the magistrates' court and then automatically go to the Crown Court for trial by jury.

Other cases are started and finished in the magistrates' court. These are where the defendant (the person accused of the criminal offence) is not entitled to trial by jury. They are known as summary offences. Summary offences involve a maximum penalty of six months' imprisonment and/or a fine of up to £5,000.

Magistrates also deal with offences where the defendant can choose trial by jury but decides to have their case heard in the magistrates' court. If the defendant chooses trial by jury, the case will be passed on to the Crown Court.

The youth court

The youth court deals with young people aged between ten and 17 who have committed criminal offences. The youth court is part of the magistrates' court and up to three specially trained magistrates hear the case. If a young person is charged with a very serious offence, which in the case of an adult is punishable with 14 years' imprisonment or more, the youth court can commit them for trial at the Crown Court.

Civil cases in the magistrates' court

Magistrates can deal with a limited number of civil cases as follows:

- some civil debts – for example, arrears of income tax, National Insurance contributions, council tax and VAT
- some matrimonial problems, such as maintenance and removing a spouse from the matrimonial home
- welfare of children, including local authority care or supervision orders, adoption proceedings and residence orders.

Crown Courts

The Crown Court deals with the following types of cases:

- serious criminal offences that will be tried by judge and jury

- appeals from the magistrates' court, which are dealt with by a judge and at least two magistrates
- convictions in the magistrates' court that are referred to the Crown Court for sentencing.

Imprisonment and fines in the Crown Court are more severe than in the magistrates' court.

The High Court

The High Court deals with civil cases, hears appeals in criminal cases, and also has the power to review the actions of individuals or organizations to make sure they have acted legally and justly. The High Court has three divisions, as follows:

The Family Division

The Family Division deals with complex defended divorce cases and dissolution of civil partnerships, wardship, adoption, domestic violence, and so on. It also deals with appeals from magistrates' and county courts in matrimonial cases.

The Queen's Bench Division

The Queen's Bench Division deals with large or complex claims for compensation. It also deals with a limited number of appeals from magistrates' courts or Crown Courts, and with libel and slander actions, as well as reviewing the actions of organizations to see whether they have acted legally.

The Chancery Division

The Chancery Division deals with trusts, contested wills, bankruptcy, winding up companies, mortgage foreclosures, charities and contested revenue (usually income tax) cases.

The Court of Appeal

The Court of Appeal deals with civil and criminal appeals. Civil appeals from the High Court and the county court, as well as from the Employment Appeal Tribunal and the Lands Tribunal, are dealt with. Criminal appeals include appeals against convictions in the Crown Court, and points of law referred by the Attorney General following acquittal in the Crown Court or where the sentence imposed was unduly lenient.

The House of Lords

The House of Lords deals mainly with appeals from the Court of Appeal, or direct from the High Court, where the case involves a point of law or general public importance. Appeals are mostly about civil cases, although the Lords do deal with some criminal appeals.

JURY SERVICE

I'm very busy at work. Do I have to do jury service?

Work commitments can be important and hard to break. Being busy at work isn't enough to excuse you from jury service altogether, but you can ask for your service to be postponed until a later date. Postponing for this kind of personal reason is known as deferral of jury service.

Your work commitments may prevent you from serving on a jury at the time that you are summoned but won't prevent you from serving at another date. If your service is deferred, you will be asked to confirm any other dates in the year when you won't be able to attend, so that you are given a new date that is convenient. Jury service can only be deferred once.

You apply to have your jury service deferred by completing the section in the summons form called 'Deferral and Excusal'. When this has been accepted you will get a letter confirming the deferral and giving you a new date for your jury service. You cannot defer twice and must attend on this second occasion.

You can find out more about jury service online (www.juror.cjsonline.org).

Jury service is an important civic duty. You do not need any knowledge of the legal system to be a juror and the experience and knowledge of each person on the jury will differ. Each individual juror will be asked to consider the evidence presented and then decide whether the defendant is guilty or not.

Jurors usually try the more serious criminal cases, such as assault, burglary, fraud or murder, that take place in the Crown Court. Jurors might also be needed to serve in a civil case such as libel, though this does not happen often. When it does, the trial will take place in the High Court or a county court. You might also be needed to serve in a coroner's court.

Jurors are chosen at random from the electoral roll to serve on a jury. If summoned, you are legally required to serve on a jury unless you are disqualified from jury service – for example, if you have been convicted of certain criminal offences.

The jury summons tells you which court you have been summoned to attend and the date and time on which your service will begin. You must reply to a jury summons within seven days of receipt.

If you have confirmed that you are able to serve at the time you have been summoned, you will receive details of how to get to the court and what to expect once you're there.

If you apply to have your jury service deferred or to be excused from jury service you will receive confirmation of whether your application has been granted. You should receive a reply within ten days of sending your letter.

If you are a juror, you are able to get travelling expenses, a subsistence allowance and an allowance for certain other financial losses that you may suffer while on jury service. The cost of childcare can also be reimbursed. If you have any queries about being summoned for jury service, you can contact the Jury Central Summoning Bureau (0845 803 8003; www.juror. cjsonline.org).

LAW-MAKING INSTITUTIONS OF THE EUROPEAN UNION (EU)

The member states of the European Union (EU) are:

- Austria
- Belgium
- Bulgaria
- Cyprus
- Czech Republic
- Denmark
- Estonia

- Finland
- France
- Germany
- Greece
- Hungary
- Ireland
- Italy
- Latvia
- Lithuania
- Luxembourg
- Malta
- Netherlands
- Poland
- Portugal
- Romania
- Slovakia
- Slovenia
- Spain
- Sweden
- United Kingdom.

(Note the European Economic Area (EEA) includes these EU member states plus Norway, Liechtenstein and Iceland.)

The European Union has four decision-making institutions:

- the Council of Ministers
- the European Commission
- the European Parliament
- the European Court of Justice.

The Council of Ministers

The Council of Ministers is made up of ministers who represent each of the EU member states. The Council of Ministers makes the final legal decisions on important issues based, mainly, on proposals from the European Commission.

The presidency of the EU rotates every six months, in alphabetical order of country. The country that holds the EU presidency also presides over the Council of Ministers for that period.

The European Commission

The European Commission is the institution that initiates new EU policies and laws. Members of the European Commission (commissioners) are nominated for a five-year term of office by each member state. The European Commission is based in Brussels. The duties of the European Commission include administering EU funds and investigating complaints of breaches of EU laws by member states.

The European Parliament

The European Parliament is composed of publicly elected members (MEPs) from each member state. Elections are held every five years.

The European Parliament can, in some circumstances, both recommend and decide on legislation in certain areas. The European Parliament is based in Strasbourg.

The European Court of Justice

The European Court of Justice (ECJ) is composed of judges and Advocates-General, who are appointed by member states' governments. Broadly, the ECJ oversees and enforces EU law. It is based in Luxembourg.

Individuals who want, for example, to challenge EU legislation or to force a member state to implement EU legislation cannot take a case directly to the ECJ. These types of cases must be taken through the domestic legal system of the member state concerned and the relevant domestic court will, if necessary, refer the case to the ECJ.

The European Ombudsman

The European Ombudsman can investigate maladministration in the activities of the European community institutions and bodies.

Examples of the problems that can be investigated by the European Ombudsman include administrative delay, refusal of information, discrimination and abuse of power. For contact details, see p. 486.

How EU law relates to UK law

Under UK law, Acts of Parliament are not challengeable unless they conflict with European law.

As well as treaties, European law is made by European Court of Justice case law and also regulations and directives.

A *regulation* takes precedence over any member state's domestic law that is inconsistent with it. A *directive* sets a goal that must be reached by a certain date.

Who can help?

The **Office of the European Commission**: in the UK: 020 7973 1992; in Wales: 029 2089 5020.

The **European Parliament Information Office** (020 7227 4300).

Europe Direct (freephone hotline: 00800 6789 1011; www.europa.eu.int/europedirect) provides information and advice about citizens' rights in the European Union – for example to work, live or study in another country of the EU. You can order guides and detailed fact sheets if you contact the hotline number above. They can also refer you to a 'Signpost' service which is staffed by a team of multilingual lawyers in Brussels. A member of the service will contact the enquirer within four working days.

There are 26 **Euro Info Centres** in the UK. They are sometimes called European Business Information Centres. They are usually based in existing organizations that have links with the business community. Their function is to provide EU information likely to be of value to small and medium-sized businesses.

The **European Documentation Centres** hold a substantial collection of the publicly available documentation of the EU. There are 44 European Documentation Centres in the UK, based mainly in university libraries. Some of them provide an information service and some will provide photocopies of, for example, relevant directives and regulations. They cannot offer legal advice. The joint website for all European Documentation Centres is www.library.law.uu.nl/edc-eu/.

There are **European Consumer Centres** throughout most of the EU member states. They can provide information and advice on EU consumer issues and help if you have purchased goods or services from another EU member state. For more information, go to www.ukecc.net.

THE SMALL CLAIMS PROCEDURE

You can start a civil legal action in the county court or in the High Court depending on the circumstances of the case. If the claim is for £15,000 or less, it must be started in the county court. If the case is a simple one, and it is defended, the county court will usually allocate the case to the 'small claims track'. This information is about a small claims case.

You can use the small claims procedure for claims of £5,000 or less (£1,000 or less for personal injury) against a person or company. It is an informal way of settling a dispute without using a solicitor and the level of costs that you will have to pay is limited.

The most common types of claim in the small claims track are:

- compensation for faulty services provided by, for example, builders, dry-cleaners or garages
- compensation for faulty goods, such as televisions or washing machines that go wrong
- disputes between landlords and tenants – for example, rent arrears or compensation for not doing repairs
- wages owed or money in lieu of notice.

If a case is complex, the judge may refer it to another track for a full hearing, even if it is below the financial limit of that track.

Can I claim money I am owed by taking a case to court?

If your case is a simple one and the amount owed to you is less than £5,000, then the court will probably allocate the claim to the small claims track if it is defended. The most common claims are for compensation for faulty services, compensation for faulty goods and disputes with employers for wages due or for money in lieu of notice. These are just examples and the small claims track can be used for other claims too.

Although you may be able to get help to prepare your case through the Legal Help scheme you will not be able to get Legal Help for representation. If the case is considered to be complex, the judge may decide to use a different procedure that means there can be a full hearing. You must have tried to settle your claim before taking court action – for example, by writing to the person who owes you money. You must have also given them time to respond. Keep a copy of all correspondence.

You can start a claim by filling in a claim form and taking two copies to the court. You keep a third copy for yourself. You also pay the court fee at this time – see below. Forms are available from local courts, or from Her Majesty's Courts Service website at www.hmcourts-service.gov.uk. Some claims for a fixed amount of money can be issued online (www.moneyclaim.gov.uk.). Court fees for online claims must be paid by credit or debit card.

There will not always be a hearing – for example, the person who owes you money may just agree they owe the money and pay up. But if the case is disputed, there may have to be a hearing. If so, the hearing will usually be informal. You and the other party will have a chance to give your reasons for starting the claim and why it is disputed. At the end of the hearing the judge will give the judgment. If you win, you get your court fees back. You can appeal against the judgment but you have only 14 days to do so.

Costs

If you are using the small claims procedure, the costs you may have to pay include:

- *court fees.* You have to pay a fee when starting your claim (the amount will depend on how much you are claiming), and further fees if the other person (the defendant) defends the case. The fee depends on the amount of money claimed. You can find out how much the fee is from Her Majesty's Courts Service website (www.hmcourts-service.gov.uk). If you win, these fees will be added to the amount the defendant has to pay. If you are in receipt of Income Support or some other benefits, or if you are on a low income, you can ask for that fee to be waived or reduced. If you do not meet these conditions, but would suffer financial hardship if you had to pay that fee, you can ask the court to waive or reduce that fee
- *witness costs.* If your case is defended and you use witnesses, you may have to pay their travelling expenses and a fixed amount towards the cost of any lost earnings
- *expert's fees and expenses* – if you need an expert's report to support your case; *and*
- *additional travel costs* – if the case is for a fixed amount of money, the

defendant is an individual who defends your claim and the case is transferred to their local court.

If you win, the court may order the defendant to pay all or part of these costs. You may also be able to claim some other costs, such as a limited amount of compensation to cover you for such things as time lost at work and the cost of telephone calls, but you are unlikely to recover all you have paid out.

You should try and take proof of any losses to the court with you. If you lose, you will have to pay the defendant's costs, including travelling expenses and an amount towards any lost earnings.

In most cases, the court will not order solicitors' costs to be paid by the losing party in a small claims case, and if you instruct a solicitor you will have to pay the costs yourself. For this reason most claimants deal with a small claim without the help of a solicitor. It is possible to have the help of a friend or 'lay representative' – for example, some Citizens Advice Bureaux can offer trained advisers to help people with small claims. It may be possible to get legal advice (not representation) from a solicitor under the Legal Help scheme. If your case is in the small claims track, you will usually be unable to claim any of your own solicitor's costs from the other side, except a fixed amount to cover the cost of issuing your claim, if you are successful. If you lose, you will not have to pay the defendant's solicitor's costs. If you are unsure about speaking in court and your case is defended, you can ask a relative, a friend or an advice worker to speak on your behalf as your lay representative.

Using the small claims procedure

How to start a small claim

Before you make a claim, you must write to the individual or company with whom you are in dispute, giving them a specific time, such as 14 days, to put the situation right and stating that, failing this, you will take court action. This is called a *letter before action* and should be sent by recorded delivery. If you do not try to settle the case first, the court may penalize you later.

Completing the claim form

You start a claim by filling in a claim form (N1 form). Claim forms are available from local courts, and from Her Majesty's Courts Service website (www.hmcourts-service.gov.uk). Some claims for a fixed amount of money can be issued online (www.moneyclaim.gov.uk). Court fees for online claims must be paid by credit or debit card. Usually claims will be issued, printed and sent to the defendant on the day the claim is submitted.

You will need to give the following information:

- your name and address
- the name(s) and address(es) of the other party you are suing. If you are suing a limited company, you will have to say whether you are giving its registered office address. If you are suing the owners or partners of a business you will need to add 'trading as' and give their business name after their names. If you are suing a firm you should add 'sued as a firm' after the name of the firm
- brief details of the claim such as 'return of money for faulty goods' or 'compensation for breach of contract'
- value, which is the amount you are claiming. The court fee you pay will be based on this amount. You can either put the exact figure you are claiming – for example, if you are claiming back the cost of a faulty item (a 'specified amount') – or you can leave it to the court to assess damages – for example, if you are claiming compensation for a disappointing holiday (an 'unspecified amount'). If you are leaving the court to decide the exact amount, you should state on the court form 'I expect to recover not more than £…'. This amount should not exceed £5,000 if you wish the matter to be allocated to the small claims track. The amount of interest you are claiming does not count towards the value of the claim – see below
- particulars of claim. This section explains what the problem is and the steps you have taken to try to solve the problem. You can either complete this section of the form or send your particulars of claim separately within 14 days of sending the form
- statement of truth. You will have to sign a statement of truth confirming that the facts in your claim are true.

Claiming interest

You should always claim for interest. You must say in your claim whether you are claiming interest under the terms of a contract or whether you are claiming statutory interest.

If the claim is for a specific sum of money, and you are claiming statutory interest, this is the way to calculate how much interest to claim:

- Step one: calculate the daily rate of interest. This is done by multiplying the amount of your claim by 0.00022
- Step two: multiply the daily rate of interest (that is, as calculated in step one) by the number of days since the money you are claiming became due to you.

You should include the following words in your claim:

'The claimant claims interest under Section 69 of the County Courts Act 1984 at the rate of eight per cent a year from (*date when the money became owed to you*) to (*date of issue of claim*) of £... (*that is, the figure in step two*) and also interest at the same rate up to the date of judgment or earlier payment at a daily rate of ... (*daily rate of interest, that is, the figure in step one*).'

If the claim is for an unspecified amount, you do not need to calculate the interest, but should include this wording after your particulars of claim: 'The claimant claims interest under section 69 of the County Courts Act 1984 at the rate of eight per cent per annum and continuing at the same rate up to the date of judgment or earlier payment.'

You may be able to get interest for the period after the order but you don't claim this on the particulars of claim, and if the defendant agrees to pay by instalments, no interest will be payable until an instalment is late.

If you need help in completing the claim form, your local CAB may be able to help. Or you could look on the website of Her Majesty's Courts Service (www.hmcourts-service.gov.uk). Look under 'Information about', then Claims. Although court officers can help you to complete your claim form, they cannot give you legal advice, such as whether you have a good claim or who you should be claiming from.

Serving the claim

You may find it easier to return your completed forms (including photocopies) to the court in person, as a court officer will go through the form and may point out any irregularities. You will be asked to pay a fee for starting proceedings. This will be based on the amount you are claiming and on your financial circumstances – you may be able to get a reduction or have the fees waived if you are on a low income. You can find out how much the fee is from the Her Majesty's Courts Service website (www.hmcourts-service.gov.uk). When you issue proceedings you will be given a notice of issue (N205), giving your case number, which you should use whenever you contact the court. The court will post the claim form to the defendant(s) – called 'serving the claim form' – and will inform you when it is served. If it is returned undelivered, you will be informed and must take responsibility for serving it.

510 | The Legal System

What happens next?

The defendant will have a limited time in which to reply to your claim. This is usually 14 days after the date the claim form was served (16 days after it was posted), but can be extended by a further 14 days if the defendant serves an acknowledgement of service stating that they intend to defend the case.

If the defendant doesn't reply

If the defendant fails to reply and you claimed a specific amount of money, you can complete form N225 asking the court for judgment by default. If you started your claim online, you can use an online request form for this at www.courtservice.gov.uk/mcol). Obtaining judgment by default means the court will order the defendant to pay you the full amount you have claimed because no reply has been received. You should do this as soon as the court will allow you to do so, as the court will accept the filing of a late defence if this is received before you file your request for judgment by default. You will have to complete a section stating how you want the defendant(s) to pay and will need to take their circumstances into account. You may have a better chance of being repaid if you accept payment by instalments rather than asking for the full amount immediately.

If the defendant fails to reply and you claimed an unspecified amount of money, you can complete the bottom of form N205B (which you were given when returning your claim form), asking the court to make an order that the defendant is liable (responsible) for your claim. This is called entering judgment for an amount to be decided by the court. Your claim will be referred to a judge, who will decide whether a court hearing is necessary and if any further evidence is required (giving directions). Both you and the defendant will be sent a copy of the judge's decision (order) and any other directions the judge has given. Your claim will either be allocated to the small claims track or given a disposal hearing. A disposal hearing is a court hearing where the judge gives more detailed instructions about the case or decides how much the defendant must pay.

If the defendant is not defending the case

If you are the defendant and you are not defending the case, you may accept that you owe the money claimed. If so, and you can pay the money immediately, you should send it to the claimant directly.

If you accept that you owe the money but you need time to pay, you can propose, for example, that you pay the money in instalments or all the money in one lump sum at a specified future date. If the claimant accepts this offer, they will have to return a form to court requesting 'judgment on admission'. As the defendant, if you do not keep to the arrangement, the claimant can take enforcement action.

As the claimant, if you do not accept the offer, you must give your reasons and a court official will decide what a reasonable arrangement should be. The court will send both parties an order for payment ('judgment for claimant after determination'). As the claimant, if you are not happy with the order, you should write to the court giving your reasons and you must send a copy of the letter to the defendant. A judge will then decide what is reasonable for the defendant to pay. If the defendant does not keep to the arrangement, the claimant can take enforcement action.

If the defendant is defending the case

If you are the defendant and you are defending the case, you have to respond to the claim form and the particulars of claim within 14 days of the date of service (this is the second day after posting). If the particulars of claim were served after the claim form, you must respond within 14 days of the date of service of the particulars of claim. You must respond by filling in the defence form that was sent to you with the claim form.

You can send your defence to the court. However, if you need more time to prepare a defence, you can send back an acknowledgement of service and then the defence within 14 days (the acknowledgement of service would be sent to you initially with the claim form).

When the defence is returned to the court, the court will send an allocation questionnaire to both the claimant and the defendant. This must be returned no later than the date specified on it. As the claimant, when you return the allocation questionnaire you have to pay a fee, although this may be waived on financial grounds. The court will use the information given on the allocation questionnaire to decide which track the case will be allocated to.

The notice of allocation

When the court has decided to allocate the case to the small claims track, the parties will be sent a notice of allocation. This form will tell the parties what they have to do to prepare for the final hearing. These instructions are called 'directions'. For example, the parties may be told to send copies of all the documents they intend to use to the court and to the other party at least 14 days before the hearing is due to take place.

There are standard directions for a number of common cases; for example, if the claim is to do with a holiday, there are standard directions about the documents that have to be sent to the other party. If the claimant wants to show a video as evidence in a holiday claim, they have to contact the court to make the arrangements for the video to be shown at the hearing.

The hearing date

The notice of allocation will usually specify the time, date and place where the hearing will take place and how much time has been allowed for it.

If you are the claimant and want to attend the hearing but cannot, you can write to the court and apply for a later date to be set. A fee is payable for this application and the court will agree only if there are good reasons.

If you are the claimant and do not wish to attend the court hearing – for example, because the travel costs of getting to the hearing are higher than your claim merits – you can write to the court to ask it to deal with the claim in your absence. The letter must arrive at court no later than seven days before the hearing date, and a copy must be sent to the defendant. The letter will ensure that the judge takes into account any written evidence that you have sent to the court and the defendant.

Sometimes the court will not set a final hearing date at the allocation stage. It could instead:

- propose that the claim is dealt with without a hearing. If the parties do not object, the case will be decided on the papers only. If the parties do not reply by the date given, the judge may treat the lack of reply as consent
- hold a preliminary hearing. This could happen if the claim requires special directions that the judge wants to explain to the parties personally, or where the judge feels that the claimant (or the defendant) has no real prospect of succeeding and wants to sort out the claim as soon as possible to save everyone time and expense, or if the papers do not show any reasonable grounds for bringing the claim. A preliminary hearing, therefore, could become a final hearing where the matter is decided once and for all.

Preparing the case

It is important to prepare the case carefully – the court has to be convinced. The following points are a general guide to what preparation should be made. But if you are not confident about how to present your case, you should consider taking someone else along to help, or getting specialist advice first. The main points are:

- if you have a low income you might be able to get legal aid to cover the cost of legal advice (but not representation) from a solicitor. This advice can include getting expert reports – for example on faulty goods (but a report may be used in court only with the permission of the court)
- notes about the case should be set out in date order. It is very useful to note down what your case is – for example, the points to make, the documents that are relevant, and what they prove. A list of all documents and other evidence is useful to make sure nothing is forgotten
- damaged or faulty goods should be taken as evidence, if possible – for instance, clothes ruined by a washing machine, shoes, etc. If this is not possible, photographs could be used instead
- evidence of expenses should be prepared and any receipts taken along
- all letters (and any other relevant documents, including photographs) about the case should be ready for the hearing
- in most cases the claimant and the defendant will be the only witnesses. If the court has agreed that other witnesses can attend, they must attend. If a witness has difficulty getting time off work, it may be helpful to serve a witness summons. The court can explain how to do this
- if you wish to use an expert witness, you must get the permission of the court first, and you must instruct the expert jointly with the other party in the case.

The final hearing

The final hearing is usually held in public but it could be held in private if the parties agree, or if the court believes it necessary in the interests of justice. Hearings in the small claims track are relatively informal and strict rules of evidence do not apply. The judge can adopt any method of dealing with the hearing that they consider to be fair, and they may ask questions of the witnesses before allowing anyone else to do so. The judge may limit the time that parties or witnesses have to give evidence.

A lay representative has the right to speak on behalf of a party at the final hearing, but only if that party attends the hearing.

If you do not speak English as your first language, you might find it helpful to have an interpreter help you to put your case. The court will not be able to assist in finding an interpreter. Your local Citizens Advice Bureau will often hold a list of interpreters, if you need help with finding one.

After the hearing, the judge will give the judgment. The judge has to give reasons for their judgment. The reasons must be given as simply and briefly as possible, and usually will be given orally to the parties present at the hearing. However, the judge may give them later either in writing or at a later hearing.

If you are the claimant and you win your case, you will get the court fees back as well as the amount of the claim, and you can ask for certain expenses also. If you lose, you will not get the court fees back. But it is unlikely that you will have to pay any other costs.

Appeals

You may appeal against a judgment in the small claims track only if the court made a mistake in law or there was a serious irregularity in the proceedings. If you want to appeal, you must file a notice of appeal within 14 days. A fee is payable, although this could be waived in cases of financial hardship.

If you want to appeal against a decision in the small claims track, you should consult a solicitor or an experienced adviser.

Enforcement of court orders

As the defendant, if you lose the case and you do not pay the claimant will have to go back to the same court to apply for an order to get the money. This is called enforcing the judgment. As the claimant, you will have to pay a fee to start enforcement proceedings.

SOLICITORS

It is worth remembering that solicitors are not the only people who can provide legal advice. Legal help may be available from:

- other professionals – for example, an accountant who can give advice on tax and company law
- advice centres, such as the Citizens Advice Bureaux, housing advice centres, money advice centres and law centres
- other organizations, such as trade unions and motoring organizations.

You may also act for yourself in court proceedings or, if you are acting for yourself, you may have a friend or lay representative to assist you in court. So before paying out for a solicitor – sometimes fees can be hefty – it is worth considering whether there is anyone else who can help.

Choosing a solicitor

If you decide that you do need a solicitor, you should choose one who has experience in the appropriate area of law.

A local advice agency, such as a law centre or Citizens Advice Bureau, should be able to recommend local solicitors who are experienced in the appropriate area of law or will be able to provide information on how to find a suitable solicitor. In some cases, a CAB can refer you to an organization that can offer free legal help. You can also find details of solicitors on the Law Society website (www.lawsociety.org.uk) or go to the Community Legal Services website (www.clsdirect.org.uk) for details of solicitors and advice agencies.

If you are at a police station, or have been charged with a serious offence, you can obtain free legal advice under the duty solicitors scheme. If you are at the police station, the police will contact the duty solicitor. If you are at the magistrates' or youth court, the arrangements for providing the solicitor will vary.

When you have chosen your solicitor, you will need to make an appointment. This will usually be within five working days. If the matter is urgent, the solicitor should try to arrange an earlier appointment.

You should take all relevant documents to the appointment and it may be helpful to prepare a list of questions for the solicitor in advance.

In some cases, a solicitor will need identification from you before they can act. This applies, for example, to transactions involving more than £10,000, such as a house purchase. Identification can include a current passport, driving licence or benefit book. A recent utilities bill will also have to be provided. If you do not have this sort of identification, you should check with the solicitor how best to prove your identity.

A solicitor must comply with certain rules and standards laid down by the Law Society. The solicitor must, for example, give you certain information at the first interview. The information should include:

- how the solicitor intends to deal with the problem
- what the solicitor's next step will be
- information about costs, which must be confirmed in writing as soon as possible after the interview
- whether you will be eligible for legal aid
- the expected timescale of the case
- whether the solicitor has a relationship with another company that could affect the steps taken in relation to your case.

The Law Society has also produced a document called 'The Client's Charter', which tells you what you can expect from your solicitor and what to do if you want to make a complaint.

You should make sure you understand what the solicitor has told you, and don't be afraid to ask questions.

During the case, the solicitor should keep you regularly informed of progress and costs, even if there are no significant developments. Remember that each contact you have with the solicitor will increase your costs.

Solicitors' costs and bills

At the beginning of the case, the solicitor must give you information about the likely cost of the case and how the charge is calculated – for example, a fixed fee, an hourly rate or a percentage fee.

In some cases, for example, personal injury cases, you may enter into a conditional fee agreement with the solicitor. This means that if you lose the case, you will have to pay the costs of the other side and you will normally be asked to take out insurance to cover this situation. If you win the case, your solicitor will normally try to get their fees paid by the other side, at a higher rate. Generally, only people who are not receiving legal aid can enter into a conditional fee agreement.

If you are considering entering into a conditional fee agreement, you must be clear what the terms of the agreement will entail and you should consult an experienced adviser – for example, at a Citizens Advice Bureau.

In all cases, the solicitor must discuss how the costs are to be met and whether you are eligible for legal aid. If the solicitor does not do legal aid work, they must still explain the advantages of legal aid to you if you are eligible, and give you the opportunity of going to a solicitor who does legal aid work.

The solicitor must keep you informed about the costs throughout the case.

If the solicitor is holding your money, it must be kept in a separate deposit account and you may be entitled to interest.

You should get your bill within a reasonable time after your solicitor has finished the work they have done for you, and it will be made up of three elements: disbursements, fees and VAT. Disbursements are the expenses the solicitor has had to pay out on your behalf – for example, fees paid to court and barristers' fees.

Fees cover the professional services carried out by the solicitor on your behalf. If the work was court work, the fees that the solicitor can charge are subject to court rules. There are no scales that regulate non-court work, but the charges must be fair and reasonable. VAT will be charged on the fees and some disbursements.

If you think the bill is too high
You can:

- ask the solicitor for a detailed account
- in some cases, ask your solicitor to apply for a remuneration certificate (that is, ask the Legal Complaints Service to look at the bill)
- ask a court to look at the bill.

An experienced adviser's help will usually be needed to assess whether you should challenge a solicitor's bill.

Getting a detailed bill from the solicitor
You can write to the solicitor asking for full details of how some or all of the charges on the bill were worked out. This letter should also include a request for a written reply. Items such as stamp duty for buying a house are fixed amounts and cannot be questioned.

Remuneration certificates
This procedure only applies to work which does not include court work. You can, within one month of receiving the bill, ask the solicitor to obtain a remuneration certificate which approves it or reduces the bill. There is no charge. You must pay half the bill and VAT and disbursements before asking the solicitor to apply for a remuneration certificate. Disbursements cannot be questioned. There is a time limit for applying for the remuneration certificate. It is usually one month but may be longer in some circumstances. The solicitor may also agree to waive the time limit. You should check the relevant time limits with the Legal Complaints Service (LCS: 0845 608 6565; www.legalcomplaints.org.uk).

Asking a court to examine the bill
This procedure can be used for any work done by a solicitor, including court work, and is known as assessment.

The court can examine the whole bill, and can either approve it or reduce it. If the reduction is more than one fifth, you will not pay the costs of assessment. Some publicly funded legal services may be available.

For non-court work, the court that assesses the bill is the High Court in London. Where court work is involved, the bill will be assessed by the court that dealt with the case. If you are receiving legal aid, bills may be assessed by the Legal Services Commission.

If you ask for assessment within one month of getting the bill, the court must assess it. Between one month and a year, the court decides whether to agree to assessment of the bill; after a year it is very unusual for the court to agree.

The court cannot agree to assess the bill if it has been paid and more than one year has gone by.

You can ask the court to examine the bill even if you have signed a conditional fee agreement.

If you have problems paying the bill

If you have problems paying a solicitor's bill, try and negotiate a payment plan with the solicitor – for example, paying in instalments. But the solicitor could insist on immediate payment. They could also, after a month, charge interest on bills for non-court work.

Complaints about solicitors

You may be dissatisfied with your solicitor for a number of reasons – for example you may have problems with legal aid or you may be dissatisfied with the outcome of the case. You cannot complain about these things to your solicitor. However, if you are dissatisfied with the way the case was handled by the solicitor – for example, delays, or losing documents or money – you can complain.

You should first try to resolve the complaint by discussing it with the solicitor. All solicitors' firms must have a written complaints procedure and the firm will tell you who to contact if you have a problem with the solicitor handling the case. The solicitor must give you a copy of the complaints procedure if you ask for it.

If this does not resolve the matter, you can contact the Legal Complaints Service (LCS: 0845 608 6565; www.legalcomplaints.org.uk). They can advise you about whether there are grounds for a complaint and, if so, how to proceed. You will need to contact the LCS within six months of the end of the work which your solicitor did for you, or within six months of your solicitor's final response to your complaint.

If you wish to proceed with the complaint, you should fill in a special form available from the LCS.

The LCS will consider the complaint and, if appropriate, pass it on to a different section of the Law Society that could discipline the solicitor and/or order the solicitor to:

- refund money that has been paid
- correct any mistakes or take any other necessary action at their own expense
- pay compensation to you up to £15,000.

I need a solicitor but I don't have much money. What can I do?

Solicitors are not the only people who can provide legal advice. Legal help may be available from other professionals, such as an accountant who can give advice on tax and company law. Legal help can be obtained from advice centres, such as Citizens Advice Bureaux, housing advice centres, money advice centres or law centres and from other organizations such as trade unions and motoring organizations. You can also represent yourself in court proceedings and you may have a friend or a representative who is not a solicitor to assist you in court. If you think that you need a solicitor, you should choose one who has experience in the appropriate area of law. For example, if you are seeking custody of children you should go to a family law specialist.

If you need help with legal costs you may be able to get legal aid. You could be entitled to free legal advice on any legal problems, writing letters, negotiation, getting a barrister's opinion and preparing a written case for tribunal. In some cases, you could get free legal representation.

If you think you qualify for legal aid, you will need to see a solicitor, or an organization with a contract to provide legal aid, such as a Citizens Advice Bureau or law centre. You will be asked to fill in an application form at the start of the interview to check whether you qualify.

There are other ways of obtaining legal help at a lower cost. These include fixed-fee interviews with solicitors. Trade unions sometimes provide free legal advice (not just about employment problems) and motoring organizations can help with many issues from buying a car to insurance.

If you are at a police station, or have been charged with an imprisonable offence, you can get free legal advice under the duty solicitors scheme.

If the solicitor has made a mistake that has caused you financial loss of more than £5,000, the LCS cannot deal with the case and you may need to take legal action against the solicitor. You will certainly need to obtain legal advice, and remember that legal aid may be available.

If you are not satisfied with the way that the LCS has handled your complaint, you may also be able to complain to the Legal Services Ombudsman (see *Civil Rights*, p. 488).

HELP WITH LEGAL COSTS

If you need help with legal costs, you may get legal aid. Legal aid is organized by the Legal Services Commission (LSC). It is provided in the following ways:

- Legal Help
- Help at Court
- Family Help
- Family Mediation
- Legal Representation
- Controlled Legal Representation
- Legal aid for criminal cases.

Legal Help

Legal Help allows people with a low income to get free legal advice and assistance from a solicitor or other organization. The solicitor or organization has to have a contract with the Legal Services Commission (LSC) to be able to provide Legal Help.

Legal Help covers all the help you might need from a solicitor or legal adviser in preparing a case to go to court. This may include getting general advice on any legal problems. It may also include your solicitor or adviser writing letters, negotiating, getting a barrister's opinion and preparing a written case for a tribunal. Legal Help could also cover the costs of mediation in non-family cases. Mediation is a way of negotiating, where the parties are helped by a neutral mediator to find a solution acceptable to them both.

Legal Help will not pay for the costs of starting or taking a court case. Also, it will not pay for a lawyer to represent you in court or at a tribunal (although other types of legal aid might).

Legal Help covers advice on general legal problems, including the following:

- housing law – for example, if you're in arrears and your landlord wants to evict you
- consumer law – for example, if you have bought faulty goods
- debt cases – for example, if someone is taking you to court because you owe them money
- family law such as financial support after marriage or disputes about children. You could also get advice about undefended divorce or dissolution of a civil partnership
- the buying and selling of your home, but only if this is needed to carry out a court order or if it is the result of a divorce, legal separation or dissolved civil partnership
- an adoption, but only if there is a dispute about adoption
- how to prepare for a tribunal hearing, such as an employment tribunal in an unfair dismissal case or a unified appeal tribunal in a benefits appeals case. Legal Help does not cover representation at the tribunal itself
- medical negligence cases
- personal injury cases, but only when the injury is the result of an assault or deliberate abuse.

You might be able to get advice about making a will, but only in certain circumstances – for example, if you're 70 or over, if you are disabled, or if you are a parent making provision for a disabled child.

To qualify for Legal Help, there are financial conditions. If you meet these financial conditions, you will normally get Legal Help for as long as the solicitor or adviser agrees there is 'sufficient benefit' in continuing with the case. 'Sufficient benefit' means that the case has to be one that has a chance of success. Also if it is a case where money is involved, there has to be a clear cost benefit to you. This is designed to weed out hopeless and non-legal matters. Once you have been granted Legal Help, your case will be regularly reviewed to make sure that these conditions continue to be met.

You may stop getting Legal Help if you become entitled to a different sort of legal aid. For example, if your case needs to go to court, you may qualify for Help at Court instead of Legal Help.

What are the financial conditions for the scheme?

If you are getting Income Support, income-based Jobseeker's Allowance or the guarantee credit part of Pension Credit, you will automatically qualify for Legal Help, regardless of the value of your home or of any other capital you have. Also, you will automatically qualify for Legal Help if you are an asylum seeker getting government asylum support.

Otherwise you have to meet both income and capital conditions. Capital includes the value of your home (if you own it). This depends on how much the property is worth and how much your mortgage is.

If you want more information about whether you qualify for Legal Help, there is an online calculator which helps you work out if you can get Legal Help. Go to www.clsdirect.org.uk.

What you may have to pay towards Legal Help

You may have to pay towards Legal Help if you win or keep money or property in:

- a family case
- a medical negligence case
- a personal injury case.

Your solicitor or adviser must use this money to pay their bill. You get what is left. For example, if you win £1,750 as a result of the case, and the solicitor's bill is £750, you will actually get £1,000. This deduction is called the *statutory charge*.

However, you do not have to pay the statutory charge if your solicitor believes:

- this would cause you serious hardship or distress
- it would be too difficult to get you to pay up.

If you do have to pay the statutory charge, you can postpone payment if:

- the property you won or kept is your home or the home of your dependants
- the money you won or kept is to be used to buy a home for yourself or your dependants.

Your solicitor or adviser must give you more information about the statutory charge before you decide to go ahead with your case.

How to apply

If you qualify for the Legal Help scheme, you will need to see a solicitor, or organization with a contract to provide Legal Help. The solicitor will ask you to fill in an application form at the start of the interview. The solicitor will then be able to decide whether you qualify.

Help at Court

In some cases, you can get help from the Legal Services Commission (LSC) to pay for a solicitor or adviser to speak for you in court. Examples of cases which you might get Help at Court for include:

- when you have agreed you owe money to someone but need to sort out when and how the debt is to be paid
- when you disagree about the amount of rent or mortgage arrears you owe and your lender or landlord has taken legal action to repossess the property.

You must meet certain financial conditions to get Help at Court. These conditions are the same as for the Legal Help scheme – see p. 520. There are also other conditions that must be met. You can get Help at Court only:

- if it can be shown that having someone to speak on your behalf is appropriate and of real benefit to you
- if it is reasonable for Help at Court to be provided
- if it is considered to be cost-effective to attend a hearing, rather than simply writing a letter on your behalf.

Family Help

If you have a serious family dispute, you may be entitled to Family Help. Family Help covers assistamce in resolving that dispute, through negotiation or otherwise. It covers all forms of Legal Help and Legal Representation but not representation at a defended final hearing or appeal.

It can also cover help with mediation in a family dispute – for example, help with drawing up an agreement you reached with the other party.

You must meet certain financial conditions to qualify for Family Help. These are the same as for Legal Help – see p. 520.

Family Mediation

If you are involved in a family dispute – for example, about contact with your children after your relationship has broken down – you might find it helpful to go to mediation. This is when an independent mediator helps you to reach an agreement without you needing to go to court. The mediator does not make any decisions for you but helps you and the other party to make your own decisions. If you decide to go to mediation, you may be able to get help under Family Mediation to pay for the mediator. You must meet certain financial conditions. These are the same as for Legal Help – see p. 520.

Legal Representation

Legal Representation helps with all the costs of taking certain types of non-criminal (civil) cases to court. It includes representation by a solicitor or barrister. To get Legal Representation, you must meet certain financial conditions. Your case also has to meet certain other conditions, for example, whether the Legal Services Commission (LSC) considers it reasonable to fund your case.

You might only get Legal Representation for as long as it takes a solicitor to look into your case. If the solicitor does not think your case is strong enough, Legal Representation might be stopped.

The types of case that you might be able to get help with under Legal Representation include:

- a housing case, including eviction, repairs and rent arrears
- a debt case
- consumer problems – for example, if you were claiming compensation for faulty goods or services
- an appeal to the Employment Appeal Tribunal (but not for representation at an Employment Tribunal)
- a judicial review case in the High Court
- a case at a mental Health Review Tribunal
- an immigration or asylum case before the Asylum and Immigration Tribunal and in some High Court cases
- the costs of mediation in non-family cases. For more information about Family Mediation, see p. 524.

Legal Representation will not usually pay for the costs of taking a personal injury case to court.

What are the financial conditions for Legal Representation

If you are getting Income Support, the guarantee credit part of Pension Credit or income-based Jobseeker's Allowance, you will qualify for Legal Representation. Otherwise, you have to meet both the capital and income conditions. Even if you meet the income conditions, you may have to pay a monthly contribution. This has to be paid for as long as you are getting Legal Representation. The amount of the contribution depends on your income.

Capital includes the value of your home (if you own it). This depends on how much your home is worth and how much your mortgage is. Even if you meet the capital conditions, you may have to pay a contribution towards the costs of your case. This contribution has to be paid immediately and it will be all of the capital you have over a certain limit.

There is an online calculator which can help you work out if you may be entitled to Legal Representation. Go to the Community Legal Services website (www.clsdirect.org.uk).

Extra costs you may have to pay towards Legal Representation

If you win your case

If you get money or property as a result of work carried out through Legal Representation, your solicitor will use this money to pay their bill and you will get what is left. This deduction is called the *statutory charge*.

In some cases, payment of the statutory charge can be postponed if:

- the property you won in the case is your home or the home of your dependants
- the money you won in the case is to be used to buy a home for yourself or your dependants.

Your solicitor or adviser has to give you full details about the effects of the statutory charge before you decide to go ahead with your case.

If you lose your case

If you lose your case, you may be ordered to pay the legal costs of the other side if the court considers this would be reasonable.

How to apply for Legal Representation

You should apply for Legal Representation through a solicitor or adviser who has a contract with the Legal Services Commission (LSC) to provide this type of legal aid. The solicitor or adviser will help you to fill out an application form along with a financial assessment form on which you must put details of your income and capital. The LSC will use these forms to decide whether you are entitled to Legal Representation.

Controlled Legal Representation

Controlled Legal Representation gives you free representation if you are:

- appearing before a Mental Health Review Tribunal
- appearing before an Asylum and Immigration Tribunal.

You must meet certain conditions to qualify for Controlled Legal Representation. These will depend on what sort of case it is. If you are appearing before a Mental Health Review Tribunal or receive government asylum support, you do not have to meet any financial conditions to qualify. In other asylum cases, you must meet the same financial conditions as for Legal Representation – see p. 525. In immigration cases, you must meet the same financial conditions as for Legal Representation, except that you must have capital of under a certain amount to qualify.

Legal aid for criminal cases

Legal aid in criminal cases is organized by the Criminal Defence Service (CDS). There are different types of help you might be able to get, depending on your circumstances. For example, if someone is at the police station, they have the right to free, independent legal advice from a duty solicitor. This does not depend on financial circumstances. You could also choose your own solicitor and do not have to pay for advice if they have a contract with the CDS.

You could get help with a criminal case even if you have not been charged with a criminal offence. For example, a solicitor could give general advice, write letters or get a barrister's opinion. This type of help is called Advice and Assistance.

You will get Advice and Assistance if you get Income Support, income-based Jobseeker's Allowance or the guarantee credit part of Pension Credit.

If you get Working Tax Credit, you might get Advice and Assistance depending on your income and personal circumstances.

If you are not getting one of these benefits or Working Tax Credit, you will only get Advice and Assistance if your income and savings are below a certain amount.

Help with representation at court

There are three ways you could be helped if you need to be represented in court for a criminal offence.

A Representation Order

A Representation Order covers representation by a solicitor and, if necessary, by a barrister in criminal cases.

To qualify for a Representation Order in the magistrates' court, you must meet certain financial conditions. You automatically meet these conditions if you are under 18. Also you automatically meet the conditions if you are getting Income Support, income-based Jobseeker's Allowance or the guarantee credit part of Pension Credit. Otherwise, the financial conditions depend on your income and how many dependent children you have.

If you do meet the financial conditions, you will usually get help with representation in a criminal case in the magistrates' court, as long as it is in the interests of justice that you are legally represented. This means, for example, if you are likely to go to prison or lose your job if you are convicted.

There are no financial conditions to get a Representation Order in the Crown Court. It must be in the interests of justice that you are legally represented in the Crown Court.

Representation Orders do not cover minor offences such as motoring offences.

To apply for a Representation Order, ask for an application form at the court dealing with your case.

Advocacy Assistance

Advocacy Assistance covers the costs of a solicitor preparing your case and initial representation in certain cases such as:

● anti-social behaviour orders

- non-payment of council tax
- some hearings in prison.

You do not have to meet any financial conditions to qualify for Advocacy Assistance, except if it is a prison hearing.

Free advice and representation at the magistrates' court

If you did not get legal advice before your case comes up at the magistrates' court, you can get free legal advice and representation by the court duty solicitor. This does not apply to less serious cases, such as minor driving offences, but it could cover cases of non-payment of council tax.

You do not have to meet any financial conditions to get free advice and representation at the magistrates' court.

The court staff will tell you how to find the duty solicitor.

Other sources of legal help

Depending on the nature of the matter, you may be able to get legal help from other sources. Some of these are listed below.

Fixed-fee interview

Some solicitors may give up to half an hour's legal advice for a fixed fee. Some schemes may offer free advice. This can be useful if you want to get an idea of whether you have a case that is worth defending or pursuing.

The fixed-fee interview scheme does not depend on your income or savings: the charge will be the same for everyone.

Your local CAB will refer you to solicitors who can offer this service.

Trade unions

Trade unions may provide free legal representation for a variety of problems, not just work-related issues. Free union representation may be more suitable than Legal Representation because you do not have to make a financial contribution towards legal help from your union.

Motoring organizations

Motoring organizations may offer a cheap or free legal advisory service if you are a member.

Legal expenses insurance

Some insurance companies offer policies that cover the expenses of certain legal matters – for example, consumer disputes, personal injuries, employment problems and motoring offences. It is important for you to consider carefully what the policy offers. Many policies will exclude certain kinds of legal expenses – for example, in matrimonial disputes – or may not meet the total cost of claims that are covered.

Other organizations, such as Which (01992 822800; www.which.net), offer a legal advisory service if you pay a subscription.

You may have an insurance policy or credit card which offers you legal advice as an extra. It is worth checking your insurance policies and credit card agreements if you have a legal problem.

Law centres

In some areas, there are law centres that give free legal advice. The cases that they tend to specialize in are housing, employment, immigration, juvenile crime and welfare benefits. A law centre may take up a case where legal aid is not available, although some may also provide legal aid.

You can get the address of your local law centre from the Law Centres Federation (020 7428 4400; www.lawcentres.org.uk).

Conditional fee agreements

In all civil non-family cases, you may enter into a conditional fee agreement with your solicitor. This means that if you lose the case, you will only have to pay the costs of the other side and, depending on the agreement, the solicitor's expenses, including any barristers' fees. If you win the case, you will pay your solicitor a higher fee. In certain cases, you can take out a special insurance policy that can cover your costs if you lose the case.

If you are considering entering into a conditional fee agreement, you must be clear what the terms of the agreement will entail and should consider consulting an experienced adviser to discuss the implications.

PERSONAL INJURY

A personal injury can include, for example, an injury at work or in a traffic accident, an injury received as a result of faulty goods or services, an injury sustained by tripping over paving stones, an injury caused by errors in hospital treatment or one sustained by a victim in the course of a crime. An injury can be physical, psychological or both.

If you have sustained a personal injury, you may want to make a complaint to the person or organization you believe was responsible for the injuries or claim for compensation to cover losses you have suffered as a result of the injury. You should consider whether there are any immediate financial problems arising because of the injury – for example, if you are unable to work. You may want to contact an organization that could offer support or counselling.

Whatever you are intending to do about your personal injury, you may want to:

- inform the police if, for example, the injury resulted from a road accident (if the injury was caused by the police, you will need to consult an experienced adviser)
- report it to your insurance company, if the injury resulted from a road accident (remember that the policy may be invalid if the accident is not reported)
- notify your employer if the injury resulted from an accident at work. The accident must be recorded in the accident book. Your employer has a legal responsibility to report the accident to the Health and Safety Executive or the local authority environmental department and can be prosecuted if they fail to do so
- report the injury to your doctor because it could become more serious. You should do this even if the injury seems minor. If you subsequently go to court to get compensation for the injury, the doctor will be asked to provide a medical report
- gather evidence about the accident and injuries. It may be useful to take photographs of the scene of an accident and of what caused the injury. You should also, if possible, write an account of the incident while details are still fresh in your mind. If there are witnesses, you should make a note of their names and addresses.

Making a complaint

If you have had an accident or suffered an injury, you might be able to get an explanation of what went wrong and receive an apology. In some cases, there may be an official complaints procedure you can use.

Complaints procedures are often time-consuming and the final result will be no more than an apology. If you have suffered a personal injury and you also want compensation, you should be aware that there are time limits for taking legal action and going through a complaints procedure may delay matters.

If you decide that making a complaint will provide a sufficient remedy, you can complain to whoever caused the injury, for example:

- a government department
- a local authority
- your employer
- the police
- your school or other educational institution
- your hospital or other National Health Service institution.

If you want more information about how to complain to these types of bodies you should seek specialist advice from an experienced adviser, like a CAB.

Compensation

There are four main ways of getting compensation for a personal injury:

- using a claims assessor
- taking legal action in a civil court
- making a claim to the Criminal Injuries Compensation Authority
- through a criminal compensation order.

Amount of compensation

If you have sustained a personal injury you may be able to claim two types of compensation: general damages and special damages.

General damages are paid as compensation for an injury – for example, a payment for pain and suffering or loss of future earnings. The court will decide on the amount to be paid.

Special damages are paid as compensation for actual financial loss caused by the accident up to the date of the hearing. These can include damage to clothing or other belongings, the costs of care, travel costs to hospital, medical expenses (including the cost of private treatment) and the cost of hiring or repairing a car if it has been damaged in the accident. If a court decides that you were partly to blame for the accident, it may reduce the amount of damages you receive. An example of this would be if you were not wearing a seat belt when you were involved in a traffic accident.

Deduction of social security benefits from compensation

If you have been receiving certain social security benefits because of an accident in which you sustained a personal injury, you may have to pay these back out of any compensation you get. The rules on this are complex and, if you think you may be affected, you might want to seek specialist advice.

Claims assessors

If you have sustained a personal injury you may be considering using the services of a claims assessor, sometimes known as a claims manager.

Claims assessors offer to take up cases on a 'no win, no fee' basis but there may be some disadvantages, including:

- a claims assessor will not usually be a solicitor and may not have a solicitor taking responsibility for the case. If this is so, the assessor will not be able to claim compensation through the courts and you may receive less compensation
- the claims assessor may ask you to pay a percentage of whatever compensation you receive to the assessor. You should be aware that while paying 50 per cent of £1,000 damages may be acceptable to you, paying 50 per cent of £10,000 may not.

All claims assessors must be authorized by the government to carry out business. They must keep to a strict set of rules which cover how they advertise, and take on business, deal with and represent clients.

Before you use a claims assessor, you should check that they are authorized. You can report a claims assessor who is not authorized to the Claims Management Regulation Monitoring and Compliance Unit (0845 450 6858, or by email at: info@claimsregulation.gov.uk). To find out more about the rules covering claims assessors and to check whether a claims assessor is authorized, go to www.claimsregulation.gov.uk.

If you are not happy with the service you get from a claims assessor, you can make a complaint. They must have an internal complaints procedure which they must tell you about.

If you are considering using a claims assessor, you should first seek advice from an experienced adviser.

Taking legal action in a civil court

If you want to take legal action to claim compensation for a personal injury, you will need to get advice from a solicitor specializing in these types of case. This must be done as soon as possible as there are strict time limits on taking legal action.

The most common claim in a personal injury case is negligence and the time limit for this is three years. This means that court proceedings must be issued within three years of your first being aware that you have suffered an injury.

Paying for legal action

Legal action for compensation for a personal injury can be expensive. You may be able to get help with legal costs – see *Help with legal costs*, p. 520.

Conditional fee agreements

Conditional fee agreements are common in personal injury cases – see p. 529.

Choosing a solicitor

If you want to take legal action over a personal injury you should consult a solicitor who is a member of the Law Society's personal injury panel or clinical negligence panel, depending on the nature of the injury. The Law Society (0870 606 2555; www.lawsociety.org.uk) can give details of solicitors on these panels.

Who can help?

The **Association of Personal Injury Lawyers** (0115 958 0585; www.apil.com) is an association of solicitors who are experienced in personal injuries work.

The **Motor Accident Solicitors Society** (0117 929 2560; www.mass.org.uk) is an association of solicitors experienced in dealing with personal injuries resulting from motor accidents. Participating solicitors provide a free initial consultation.

If you have sustained an injury as a result of a traffic accident and you are a member of a **motoring organization**, you may be able to get specialist legal advice through that organization.

If your injury resulted from an accident at work, you should contact your **trade union** if you are a member. The union may instruct solicitors to pursue a claim on your behalf and you will not have to pay for this.

Criminal Injuries Compensation Authority

If you have been injured as a result of a criminal act, you may be able to claim compensation through the Criminal Injuries Compensation Authority (0141 331 2726/0800 358 3601; www.cica.gov.uk). You may have been the direct victim of, for example, an assault or your injury may have been sustained when you were attempting to help the police after a crime had been committed. A close relative of a person who died because of injuries can also make a claim.

You must report the incident to the police at the earliest opportunity and an application must normally be made within two years of the incident. However, in exceptional circumstances, the authority may be willing to extend this limit. An example would be if you are making a claim for abuse you suffered as a child. The details of the crime and injuries that must be entered on the claim form are important, and if you are completing the form, you may want to consult an experienced adviser.

Criminal compensation orders

A person convicted of a criminal offence may be ordered by the court to pay compensation for injury, loss or damage they have caused to someone else by committing the offence. If you are the person who has sustained the injury or loss you cannot apply for this yourself, so it is important that you give the prosecution full and accurate information about the injuries and losses to put before the court.

The amount of compensation will depend on what the offender can afford to pay, but the maximum is £5,000. If a criminal compensation order is made, the court will be responsible for making sure the offender pays.

Financial problems

If you are having financial problems as a result of a personal injury you sustained in, for example, an accident or an incident of violent crime, you may need to consult a specialist money adviser for help with debt and benefits. You may need financial advice because a member of your family has been injured or killed in an accident or as the result of a crime. You may be able to claim compensation for the loss of financial support.

Support and counselling

There are a number of voluntary organizations and schemes that may be able to give support if you have been injured, or your partner, friend or relative has been injured or killed.

Action against Medical Accidents (0845 123 2352; www.avma.org.uk) can provide information, support and referral to solicitors if you are the victim of a medical accident. AvMA has a panel of medical experts prepared to give independent opinions.

The **Disabled Living Foundation** (0845 130 9177; www.dlf.org.uk) gives advice and information about equipment available for people with disabilities.

Disaster Action (01483 799066; www.disasteraction.org.uk) was set up by a group of people affected by major disasters. The group campaigns for changes in the law and for improved counselling and compensation, as well as giving support to people involved in disasters and their relatives and friends. It can also make referrals to specialists.

A number of **self-help groups** have been set up for people who have been injured by, for example, unsafe medicines. A list of groups of this kind can be found in the 'Voluntary Agencies Directory', a copy of which will be available in the local public reference library or a CAB.

Headway, the brain injury association (0808 800 2244; www.headway. org.uk), supports people with brain injuries and their carers. It also campaigns for improvements in health and social care services. It runs a helpline, and can provide a list of solicitors who specialize in brain injury cases.

The **Medical Foundation for the Care of Victims of Torture** (020 7697 7777; www.torturecare.org.uk) provides medical care, counselling and therapy to people who have suffered an injury as a result of torture. It sets up self-help groups and can examine patients – for example, to provide forensic evidence of torture injuries. The organization can be of use to people who are applying for asylum.

MIND (0845 766 0163; www.mind.org.uk) promotes the interests of people suffering from mental illness or distress and provides advice and advocacy services.

There are a number of **rape organizations** offering help and advice to people who have been raped. A list of groups of this kind can be found in the 'Voluntary Agencies Directory', a copy of which will be available in the local public reference library or a CAB.

Roadpeace (0845 450 0355; www.roadpeace.org.uk) provides support and advocacy for bereaved and injured victims of road accidents. It also promotes public awareness of road dangers, and campaigns for justice for victims.

Victim Support (0845 3030 900; www.victimsupport.org.uk) offers information and support to all victims of crime, except theft of, or from, cars and child abuse in the family. There are local schemes.

Women's Aid (0808 200 0247; www.womensaid.org.uk) provides advice, information and sometimes temporary refuge for women and their children who are threatened by mental, emotional or physical violence, harassment or sexual abuse.

POLICE POWERS

Most of the rules that cover police behaviour are set down in codes of practice. There are also other laws that give the police particular powers. If the police fail to act in accordance with police codes of practice or law, it may mean that they can be sued in the civil courts or convicted in a criminal court. Officers could also be disciplined, or a court might be unable to accept police evidence that had been obtained by the police acting beyond their powers. This information does not cover every situation, and if you have problems with the police, you should always take further advice. If you are cautioned or taken to a police station, you should always contact a solicitor.

Stop and search

The police can stop and search any person or vehicle for certain items. However, before they stop and search they must have reasonable grounds for suspecting that they will find any of the following:

- stolen goods
- an offensive weapon
- any article made or adapted for use in a burglary

- an article with a blade or point
- items that could damage or destroy property.

The police can also search a football coach going to or from a football match if they have reasonable grounds for suspecting there is alcohol on board or that someone is drunk on the coach.

In all of these situations where the police have a right to stop and search, they should not require you to take off any clothing other than an outer coat, jacket or gloves.

If you are arrested, the police can search you for anything you might use to help you escape or for evidence relating to the offence that has led to your arrest. Again you should not be required to take off any clothing in public except for an outer coat, jacket or gloves, but the police can search your mouth.

In some circumstances, a police officer of the rank of inspector or above can give the police permission to make stops and searches in an area for a certain amount of time. When this permission is in force, the police can search for offensive weapons or dangerous instruments whether or not they have grounds for suspecting that people are carrying these items. When this permission is in force, a police officer in uniform can also order you to remove any item if you are wearing it to hide your identity.

An officer with the rank of assistant chief constable or above can also give permission for searches in an area in order to prevent acts of terrorism.

Where can the police search you?

The police can search you in any place that is generally open to the public. This means they can search you anywhere other than your home and your garden, or the home or garden of someone who has given you permission to be there. If the police have reasonable grounds for believing that you are not, in fact, in your own home or that you are somewhere without the permission of the homeowner, they can search you.

The police can use reasonable force when they stop and search, but must make every effort to persuade you to co-operate. They should only use force as a last resort, and the force used must be reasonable.

Before searching, the police officer should tell you that you are being detained so you can be searched. They should also give you their name, the name of their police station, the purpose of the search and their grounds or authorization for making the search. If the search is connected to terrorism, or if the officers believe that giving their name would put them in danger, they can give their police number instead of their name. You should also be told that you have a right to a copy of the record of the search. If it is impractical to make a record of the search there and then, the police officer should tell you that you have the right to apply for a copy, as long as you apply within twelve months.

When can the police question you?

The police should not question you with a view to getting evidence until they have cautioned you. If you have been arrested, you must not be interviewed before being taken to the police station unless:

- delay could lead to interference with or harm to evidence connected with the offence
- delay could lead to physical harm to others
- delay would alert someone suspected of committing an offence who has not yet been arrested
- delay would hinder the recovery of property that is the subject of the offence.

If you are cautioned without having been arrested, you must be told you are free to leave whenever you want.

Powers of entry

Police can enter premises without a warrant in a number of different situations. These include entry to:

- deal with a breach of the peace or prevent it
- enforce an arrest warrant
- arrest a person in connection with certain offences
- recapture someone who has escaped from custody
- save life or prevent serious damage to property.

Apart from a situation where the police are preventing serious injury to life or property, they must have reasonable grounds for believing that the person they are looking for is on the premises.

If the police do arrest you, they can also enter and search any premises where you were during or immediately before the arrest. The police must have reasonable grounds for believing there is relevant evidence there relating to your suspected offence. They can also search any premises occupied by someone who is under arrest for certain serious offences. Again, the police officer who carries out the search must have reasonable grounds for suspecting that there is evidence on the premises relating to the offence or a similar offence.

If the police have a search warrant, they can enter the premises. The codes of practice state that in most cases they should enter property at a reasonable hour unless this would frustrate their search. When the occupier is present, the police must ask for permission to search the property – again, unless it would frustrate the search to do this.

When they are carrying out a search, police officers must:

- identify themselves and – if they are not in uniform – show their warrant card; *and*
- explain why they want to search, the rights of the occupier and whether the search is made with a search warrant or not.

If the police have a warrant they can use reasonable force to enter if:

- the occupier has refused entry; *or*
- it is impossible to communicate with the occupier; *or*
- the occupier is absent; *or*
- the premises are unoccupied; *or*
- they have reasonable grounds for believing that if they do not force entry it would hinder the search, or someone would be placed in danger.

Seizure of property

The police have wide powers to seize property. They are able to seize goods if they have reasonable grounds for believing that:

- they have been obtained illegally; *or*
- they are evidence in relation to an offence.

In either of these cases they must also have reasonable grounds for believing that it is necessary to seize the goods to prevent them being lost, stolen or destroyed.

Powers of arrest

Arresting someone means that the police deprive you of your freedom to go where you want. Police can arrest you if they have a valid arrest warrant. There are also some situations where they can arrest you without a warrant. Examples are when:

- you are in the act of committing certain offences
- they have reasonable grounds for suspecting you are committing certain offences
- they have reasonable grounds for suspecting you have committed certain offences
- you are about to commit certain offences
- they have reasonable grounds for suspecting you are about to commit certain offences.

The police can also arrest you if they have reasonable grounds for suspecting you have committed or attempted to commit any offence, or if you are committing or attempting to commit any offence, but it is impractical or inappropriate to serve a summons. However, they can only do this if one of the following conditions applies:

- they do not know, and cannot get, your name
- they think you have given a false name
- you have not given a satisfactory address – this means an address where the police can contact you
- they think you have given a false address
- the arrest is necessary to prevent you causing physical injury to yourself or others, suffering physical injury, causing loss or damage to property, committing an offence against public decency, or causing an unlawful obstruction of the highway
- they have reasonable grounds for believing that arrest is necessary to protect a child or other vulnerable person.

If they are arresting you because you have failed to give them a satisfactory address, they must explain that you may be arrested and give you the opportunity to provide the address.

What should happen on arrest

The police should only use reasonable force to make an arrest and they should inform you that you are under arrest as soon as possible. After the arrest they should explain why they have arrested you. The police must caution you unless it is impractical to do so or unless they cautioned you immediately before they arrested you.

If the police arrest you somewhere other than at a police station, they should take you to a police station as soon as possible. If they arrest you for theft, and you were seen taking property but did not have it after a chase, the police officer can retrace your tracks. This may allow them to recover the property. They should take you to the station once they have recovered the property.

At the police station

If you are under 17 years of age and are detained by the police, 'an appropriate adult' – usually your parent or guardian – should be informed as soon as possible. The police should not interview you until your parent is present, unless a delay would mean an immediate risk of harm to someone or serious loss of or damage to property.

People with learning difficulties

If the person arrested has learning difficulties, the police should only interview them when a responsible person is present, unless delay would result in a risk of injury or harm to property or people. The person with learning difficulties should be accompanied at interview by:

- a relative or other person responsible for their care; *or*
- a person who is not employed by the police, and who is experienced in dealing with people with learning difficulties; *or*
- some other responsible adult who is not employed by the police.

People from abroad

If the person arrested is not usually resident here the police may have the right to request help from their High Commission, embassy or consulate in tracing them. Certain countries have special agreements with the UK so that the High Commission, embassy or consulate is automatically informed if one of their nationals is arrested.

If your first language is not English

If you have difficulty understanding English and the interviewing officer cannot speak your language, you should be provided with an interpreter. The police must not interview you until the interpreter is present unless a delay would mean an immediate risk of harm to someone or serious loss of or damage to property.

Deaf people and people with hearing or speech difficulties

If you have hearing or speech difficulties the police should offer you an interpreter. They should not question you until the interpreter is present, unless a delay would mean an immediate risk of harm to someone or serious loss of or damage to property, or unless you agree in writing to be interviewed without one.

What should happen if you are detained

At the police station the police should inform you of:

- your right to let someone know of your arrest; *and*
- your right to talk to a solicitor in private and the fact that this is free of charge; *and*
- your right to look at the police codes of practice.

The police should also inform you that you do not need to use these rights immediately. You can exercise them at any time while you are detained. You should be given a written notice of these rights while you are at the police station, and of your right to a written copy of your custody record when you are released. The police will ask you to indicate on the custody record whether you wish to have legal advice and will also ask you to sign the record.

If you do ask for another person to be informed of your arrest, this should happen as soon as possible, unless you have been arrested for certain offences and an officer of the rank of superintendent (or above) allows a delay. In order to allow a delay, the officer should be satisfied that there are reasonable grounds for believing that informing someone of your arrest would:

- lead to interference with evidence
- affect the police's ability to recover property
- lead to other suspects being alerted
- prevent recovery of the proceeds resulting from drug offences.

If a delay is authorized, the police should tell you and write the reason on your custody record. The maximum delay is 36 hours unless you are detained in relation to a terrorist offence, in which case it is 48 hours. If someone asks about your whereabouts then, as long as you agree, they should be informed, unless an officer of the rank of superintendent (or above) decides that they should not.

How long can the police hold you?

The police should not detain you for more than 24 hours without charging you, unless an officer with the rank of superintendent (or above) or a magistrate gives permission.

A police officer with the rank of superintendent (or above) can authorize detention for a further twelve hours. Magistrates can authorize further detentions up to a maximum of 96 hours. Once charged, you should be brought before the magistrates the next day (but not on Christmas Day, Good Friday or any Sunday). Arrests in suspected terrorism cases have different detention rules.

Right to silence

Although you have a right to silence, courts can take your silence into account when deciding whether you are guilty or innocent.

Your right to legal advice

If you are arrested, charged or questioned by the police, there are several ways you can get legal advice. You can:

- ask the police to contact the duty solicitor call centre. A duty solicitor is available 24 hours a day. A duty solicitor will give you initial advice over the phone and decide whether they should come to see you at the police station.
- ask the police for a list of local solicitors. You do not have to pay if the solicitor you choose has a contract with the Legal Services Commission.
- ask the police to contact your own solicitor. You do not have to pay if your solicitor has a contract with the Legal Services Commission.

Once you have asked for legal advice, the police must not normally question you. You do not have to answer any questions until you have spoken to a solicitor.

In exceptional circumstances, a delay of up to 36 hours can be authorized before you have access to legal advice. This is longer in cases of suspected terrorism.

Complaints

If you feel the police have treated you unfairly and you want to complain, there are different courses of action you can take. The appropriate course of action will depend on the nature of your complaint. For example, if the police have obtained evidence by breaking code of practice rules, a court can refuse to accept police evidence in any case against you. Alternatively, you may wish to use the police complaints procedure to complain about an individual officer's behaviour or take civil court action.

Making a complaint

You can make a written complaint to the chief constable of the force or, in London, to the Commissioner of the Metropolitan Police. You should send the letter by recorded delivery and keep a copy. If you think you might also take court action, you should ask a solicitor to write the letter. The police station will record the complaint and you will be invited to an interview at the police station. You should take a friend or solicitor with you. If you have been injured you may also be asked to attend a medical examination, which can only be carried out with your consent. The police may ask you whether you want the complaint to be dealt with informally under a procedure called 'local resolution'. If you do not agree, then the matter will be investigated formally.

If after formal investigation the complaint is upheld:

- the police officer may be given an informal warning or words of advice; *or*
- the police officer may be formally disciplined; they may be dismissed or required to resign, suffer a reduction in rank or pay, be fined, given a warning or reprimanded; *or*
- the matter will be referred to the Crown Prosecution Service if there is an allegation of criminal offences by the police officer. (If the complaint is upheld, you may want to consider suing the police.)

The Independent Police Complaints Commission (08453 002 002; www.ipcc.gov.uk) oversees and investigates complaints against the police.

Suing the police

If your complaint is serious, you may wish to sue the police. You can sue the police in the same way that you can sue members of the public. If you want to sue the police you should talk to a specialist solicitor.

Who can help?

Liberty (08451 232307; www.liberty-human-rights.org.uk) campaigns on civil liberties issues, including police policies and powers, and can advise people who have problems with the police. However, they can only take on a few cases each year. They can also recommend solicitors with experience in police complaints.

Inquest (020 7263 1111; http://inquest.gn.apc.org) offers legal advice on any problems relating to a coroner's inquest.

Police monitoring groups are campaigning organizations that aim to increase public awareness of police work and improve police policies. Most police monitoring groups are in London. The groups offer free advice, may take up a complaint and will make referrals to a solicitor. To find out whether you have a local group, contact your local authority.

Law centres offer free advice and representation. The Law Centres Federation (020 7428 4400; www.lawcentres.org.uk) can provide details of your local law centre.

PRISONERS

Prisoners' rights

You have certain rights and privileges when you are in prison. The rules are written down and they are available in prison libraries. Ask to see the Prison Standing Orders (PSOs) and the Prison Service Instructions (PSIs). You can also see the rules on the Prison Service website (www.hmprisonservice.gov.uk).

The Prison Service and the Prison Reform Trust (PRT) have co-written a guide to prisoners' rights and a copy of this should be given to you when you arrive in prison. If you are disabled, you should also get a guide called 'Information for disabled prisoners' when you arrive in prison. You can also get copies of the guides from PRT (020 7251 5070; www.prisonreformtrust.org.uk).

If you want to know more about rights and privileges in prison, you should consult a specialist adviser.

Complaints about conditions in prison

If you have a problem with conditions in prison, there are rules about how you can try and sort the problem out. There are different ways to make a complaint. These are:

- the prison complaints procedure
- complaining to the Independent Monitoring Board
- contacting someone outside the prison system.

There are rules about discrimination in prison, so if you feel you were treated unfairly because of your race, sex, sexuality, disability or religion, make sure you mention this in any complaint you make.

The prisons complaints procedure

If you have a complaint, start off by talking to a prison officer. If this does not sort out the problem, think about making a written complaint. There is a deadline for this which is three months from the date when the problem happened.

Complaints forms are available on every wing. To make a complaint, fill out a form. Make sure you make a copy of what you have written, then post the form into a yellow complaints box. These can be found on most landings and in other communal parts of the prison. The complaint will be dealt with first of all by a prison officer. If you are not happy with the outcome, you can appeal to someone more senior and then to the governor. If you're still not satisfied, you may complain directly to the Prisons and Probation Ombudsman – see p. 547.

You can make a confidential complaint about things like ill-treatment in prison or the behaviour of staff on your wing. In these cases, fill in an ordinary complaint form and write on the envelope 'Confidential Access'. Seal the envelope and put it in a yellow complaints box. The complaint may not stay confidential as an investigation in the prison may take place.

Complaining to the Independent Monitoring Board

The Independent Monitoring Board is a group of independent people appointed by the government. They act as a 'watchdog' to make sure that the prison is being run properly and that prisoners are treated fairly. You can make a complaint to the Independent Monitoring Board at any time. But they will not usually look at a complaint unless you have already tried to sort out the problem by using the prison complaints procedure.

To make a complaint to the Independent Monitoring Board, you can ask to speak directly to a member of the Independent Monitoring Board or write to them. Make a copy of what you have written and put the letter in an envelope marked 'Confidential Access'. Address it to the Chair of the Independent Monitoring Board. Seal the envelope.

You can talk to members of the Independent Monitoring Board out of the sight and hearing of a prison officer if the Board agrees. They can pass on information to prison staff.

Contacting someone outside the prison system
The Prisons and Probation Ombudsman

The Prisons and Probation Ombudsman is independent of the Prison Service. They can investigate most complaints made by prisoners. You should use the prison complaints procedure before you contact the Prisons and Probation Ombudsman. If the Ombudsman agrees with your complaint, they will make a recommendation to put the problem right.

To make a complaint to the Ombudsman, write a letter. Put your prison number at the top of the letter. Make a copy of what you have written and put the letter in an envelope marked 'Confidential Access'. Seal the envelope. For the contact details of the Prisons and Probation Ombudsman, see p. 490.

Complaints to other people

There is usually no point in making a complaint to someone else unless you have already used the prison complaints procedure. If you have used the prison complaints procedure and you are still not satisfied, you could try writing to your MP. You can write to them at the House of Commons, London SW1A 0AA . Or write to your solicitor.

Property in prison

The amount of property you can have in your cell is limited to property which fits into two boxes. Every prison has its own rules about what you can keep in prison. The Prisoners' Information Book gives you details of what you might be allowed to keep – see p. 556. If you keep things in your cell, you do so at your own risk. The Prison Service does not accept responsibility for loss or damage to the things in your cell unless it can be shown that the loss or damage happened because they did not take proper care of your things. If this is the case, compensation can be made. Governors can deal with claims up to £3,000. If you want to apply for compensation, follow the normal complaints procedure – see p. 546.

Property that you are not allowed to keep with you in the cell is sent to a central property store outside the prison. It will be kept in a sealed container and listed. You should read the list carefully before you sign it.

If the governor believes that the amount of property you have in your cell may make it difficult to carry out searches, your things can be taken away.

This also applies if the governor believes your things may put health and safety at risk or if they are a risk to good order and discipline in the prison.

Your belongings can also be taken away as a punishment if you have broken prison rules. They can be taken for up to 42 days (21 days for young offenders).

Any money you take into prison with you will be taken away and put into a special prison account in your name (your private cash account).

Your family and friends may be able to send in money for you, as long as the governor agrees. If they are allowed to send you money, they should post postal orders or cheques. These should be payable to HM Prison Service.

You can send money out of prison, to help your family or friends. All the money in your prison accounts can be taken out with you when you leave prison.

Keeping in touch while you are in prison

If you are in prison, it is very important to try and keep in touch with friends and family. There are rules about letters, phone calls and visits while you are in prison.

Sending letters

If you are in prison, you can usually write letters to anyone you want. But you need to get permission from the prison governor to write to some people. For example, you need the governor's permission before you can write to the person you committed the offence against or their family. The governor can stop letters if they are considered to be a threat to security or if they are obscene or racist. If a letter is stopped, you will be told and given another chance to write it again without breaking the rules.

You must not seal up your letters before you give them to the post room. But you can seal them up if they are confidential letters (see below).

Some outgoing letters are read – for example, if you are in a maximum security prison or if you are a Category A prisoner. The governor can also order that your outgoing letters are read if it is thought that this will stop a crime happening or help detect a crime. Some letters are read at random. You can complain if you think your letters are being read without a good reason.

If you are on remand, you can send two letters a week, paid for by the prison. If you are a convicted prisoner, you can send one letter a week paid for by the prison. You may be able to send more than these letters if you pay for the postage yourself but this is a privilege that can sometimes be taken away.

Getting letters

Generally speaking, you can get letters from anyone. All letters arriving at the prison are opened to check that they do not contain anything forbidden. The only exception to this is a confidential letter which cannot be opened unless there are very special reasons. Some letters will be thoroughly read, like letters to Category A prisoners. Other letters will just be glanced at. If you're a Category A prisoner or in a high-security prison, the number of letters you can get may be limited. Otherwise, there is no limit.

Letters to and from legal advisers, courts and some other organizations, such as the Prisons and Probation Ombudsman's office, are confidential. Letters to Citizens Advice Bureaux are not confidential. You should write 'Prison Rule 39' on confidential letters to your legal adviser or the courts. You should write 'Confidential Access' on letters to the Prisons and Probation Ombudsman.

Confidential letters are not normally opened and read. But they can be opened and read if the governor believes:

- they contain something which is forbidden
- they contain something that could put prison security in danger.

Phone calls

You are not allowed to make phone calls to a prisoner in prison.

If you are in prison, you can make telephone calls using the PINphone system. In some prisons, you can only call certain numbers that you have already given to the prison staff and which have been approved by them. In other prisons, you can call any number except for numbers barred by the prison. You are never allowed to ring certain premium rate numbers, which may include chatlines or adult-only lines. The length of calls you can make may be limited.

All telephone calls made by prisoners are recorded and may be monitored at any time. This does not apply to calls to the following people:

- your legal advisers
- the Independent Monitoring Board

- the Criminal Cases Review Commission
- the Prisons and Probation Ombudsman's Office
- the Samaritans.

If you are a Category A prisoner, your calls are more strictly controlled.

There are rules about what can be said in a phone call. For example, you are not allowed to talk about things that are considered to be a threat to prison security or which are racist. If you break the rules, you may be cut off.

Some prisons allow a free short phone call home as soon as you arrive at prison from court. Other prisons allow you to make a short call and then take away the cost of your call from your PINphone account later on.

You have the right to make confidential telephone calls to your legal adviser. This means a solicitor, barrister or anyone working for them directly. You are **not** allowed to make confidential calls to Citizens Advice Bureaux.

Foreign national prisoners are allowed one free five-minute overseas call per month, instead of visits.

Visits

Up to three adults at the same time can visit someone in prison. Check with the prison whether there are special rules about visits by children.

If you are a prisoner, your legal adviser can visit you as often as necessary. 'Legal adviser' means your solicitor, barrister or someone who is directly supervised by them. Other professionals, such as a social worker or probation officer, can also visit you. These professional visits do not affect the number of visits by friends or family.

There are special rules if you want to visit someone who is a Category A prisoner. The police will get in touch with you and your criminal record will be checked.

If it is thought that a visitor is unsuitable, the prison can refuse the visit. If you think that a prison visit has been refused unfairly, you can make a complaint.

You can visit a prisoner on remand or a civil prisoner without making a formal request. Contact the prison to find out about visiting arrangements as most prisons have a booking system for these visits. Some prisons allow visits to unconvicted prisoners every day. These visits should total a minimum of one and a half hours per week. Most prisons allow visits three times a week and each visit can last for at least one hour. The governor may allow more than this minimum in exceptional circumstances. The rules about visits to civil prisoners are different to the rules about visits to unconvicted prisoners. Civil prisoners can have as many visits as they wish, subject to 'practical limitations'.

If you are a convicted prisoner, you have to fill in a Visiting Order (VO) to get a visit. You must name everyone who is planning to visit, then send the VO to one of the visitors. You get a VO when you first go into prison. After that, you get at least one VO every two weeks. Visits to convicted prisoners should normally last for a minimum of one hour. Many prisons may allow longer visits or more frequent visits.

You may be able to get financial help to visit a prisoner – for example, if you are a married partner, civil partner or close relative. To find out more about financial help for visits, contact the Assisted Prison Visits Unit (0845 300 1423).

If you want to take things into prison when you visit, check with the prison what you are allowed to bring. If the prisoner is on remand, you are usually allowed to take in clothing and toiletries but not food, drink or money.

When you visit a prison, you will need to hand in the VO at the gate if you are visiting a convicted prisoner. You will be asked for identification. You could be photographed and fingerprinted. Every visitor, including children, may be searched both before and after the visit. You could be asked to open your mouth and to remove items of clothing, such as shoes, hats and religious head-coverings.

During the actual visit, the following rules apply:

- visits will take place in the sight and hearing of a prison officer
- you normally have to stay sitting down if the visit takes place in a visiting room
- you can normally speak in any language you choose, whether or not the prison officer understands it
- hugging and kissing is normally allowed.

The visit can be cut short if a member of the prison staff in charge of visits suspects that any of these rules have been broken, or if the visitor is a threat to prison security or if the visit is upsetting other people.

Sometimes instead of cutting short a visit, the governor can order a closed visit. This is where no direct contact is allowed between visitor and prisoner. A closed visit could also be ordered if the prison is worried that there might be a risk to prison security or if illegal or unacceptable behaviour might take place, such as the passing of drugs.

Benefits and prisoners

You may have problems with benefits, either when you first go into prison or when you leave prison. In some cases, the rules for prisoners claiming benefits are different from those for other people. It is very important to get help with your benefit problem as soon as possible.

Housing and prisoners

If you are in prison, you might have a problem holding on to your home for when you come out. It is very important to seek specialist advice about keeping your home as soon as possible when you first go into prison.

Discrimination in prison

It is against the law for the prison to treat you less fairly because:

- of your race
- of your sex
- you have a disability
- of your religion
- of your sexuality.

This applies to both prisoners and their visitors. If you are not treated equally or fairly because of any of these things, this is called discrimination.

If you think that you are being treated unfairly because of your race, you could discuss the problem with the Race Relations Liaison Officer. Fill in a Racist Incident Reporting Form, which is available on all wings. Put it in a complaints box. The Race Relations Liaison Officer will come and talk to you about the complaint. If you are not happy with the result, a full investigation will be carried out.

If you think that you are being treated unfairly because of disability, you could discuss the problem with the Disability Liaison Officer or fill in a complaint form.

If you think that you, or other prisoners, are being treated unfairly for other reasons, you will have to make a complaint in the normal way – see p. 546.

You may be able to take court action against the prison for discrimination. You might get compensation. You need to speak to a specialist adviser about how to do this. Legal aid might be available.

Health in prison

If you are in prison, you should get the same health services as you would get from the NHS. This includes mental health services. If you need to see a doctor, ask the wing staff. You could be moved to a local NHS hospital but, if so, you are still under the control of the Prison Service.

If you become seriously ill, ask the governor to tell your family. Extra visits may be allowed. If you become so ill that you're not expected to get better, you may be released from prison on compassionate grounds.

You do not have to be tested for HIV when you go into prison. If you are asked if you want to be tested, you can refuse, but if you are worried that you are HIV positive, you can ask for an HIV test. The main risks of becoming infected by HIV in prison are from unprotected sex and sharing needles. There are no needle exchange schemes in prisons. Condoms are available in prisons if the doctor thinks there is a risk of infection. Condoms are also available if you are going to be temporarily released from prison.

If you had a drug or alcohol problem before you came into prison, ask the doctor for help as soon as possible. Methadone may be prescribed as detox for heroin addicts. Longer-term treatment for addiction is not generally available in prisons, but all prisons have special workers whose job is to give support to prisoners with drug problems.

Many prisoners suffer from mental health problems. In most prisons, there are special units which can give specialist treatment and all prisons have access to these units where necessary. In some cases, you could be sectioned. This is where you are sent to a psychiatric hospital without your agreement. Time spent inside a psychiatric hospital counts towards your sentence. You will not be released at the end of your sentence if you are still mentally ill.

If you are thought to be a suicide risk or at risk of self-harm, a support plan will be drawn up. You may be placed on a special wing or staff may come and talk to you more often to check on you. You and your family can contact the Samaritans if there are concerns about suicide. There might be a Buddy or Listener scheme in your prison that could help.

If a prisoner dies in prison, the prison governor must inform the next of kin immediately. In all cases where a death has occurred, the coroner will be called in to examine the body and the case will be investigated by the police and the Prisons and Probation Ombudsman. An inquest will be held to decide how the death happened.

If you have problems with your healthcare in prison, you can make a complaint using the NHS complaints procedure. There is a specialist organization called ICAS that can help prisoners in England complain about NHS services. The contact details are:

- 0845 456 4212 (east of England, London, West Midlands)
- 0845 045 0376 (East Midlands)
- 0845 122 8692 (North-East, Yorks and Humberside)
- 0845 122 8592 (North-West).

In Wales, the Community Health Council may be able to help you – see p. 106.

Early release from prison

If you were sentenced to more than twelve months in prison, you may be released early on licence. You will also have a licence if you are out of prison on a home detention curfew (on a tag). Being on licence means that you are still serving a prison sentence but you can live in the community instead of being in prison. While you are on licence, there are rules you must follow. If you break the rules, you'll have to go back to prison (be recalled).

You will be told what the rules are. They include:

- you must not commit any further offences or do anything that could put members of the public or your friends or family in danger
- you must keep in touch with your probation officer and do what they ask you to
- if your probation officer needs to visit you at home or somewhere else, you have to agree to this
- you have to live at an address that your probation officer has approved. Tell your probation officer in advance if you plan to leave that address or stay at another address, even if it is for just one night. Also, you have to tell your probation officer if you change your phone number
- you must not travel outside the UK without the permission of your probation officer

- if you are on home detention curfew, you have to keep to a curfew. This means at certain times of the day or evening, you have to stay in. The tagging company monitors you and tells the Home Office if you break the rules.

As well as these rules, your probation officer might have recommended extra conditions, such as not making contact with certain people or not living at the same address as children.

You will not be considered for early release until you have a suitable address. This could be with friends or family or at a hostel. You might get help from the council to pay for your accommodation. If you are serving a prison sentence in the community, you have the right to claim benefits. For example, you could claim Jobseeker's Allowance. You can get help to claim benefits.

You are not allowed to take a job unless your probation officer approves of it. There are rules about declaring your criminal record when you apply for a job. For some jobs, such as working with children, disabled people or other vulnerable people, you always have to declare all your criminal convictions.

You can be sent back to prison if you break the rules. First, your probation officer will look at your case, and in some cases they will ask the Home Office to order you to return to prison. This decision can be taken very quickly – in emergency cases, the decision can be taken within two hours. You will be arrested and taken straight to prison. This would usually be your local prison, not necessarily the one you were released from.

The decision to send you back to prison will be reviewed by the Parole Board once you are back in prison. You have the right to put your arguments in writing to the Parole Board. The Parole Board may decide you should be released, but if they decide you should be in prison, you may have the right to a hearing where you can put your case. If they still decide you have to stay in prison, the Parole Board will set a date in the future for your release or for another review.

If you are sent back to prison for breaking your conditions, you should get legal advice as soon as possible. You might get legal aid. If you are not sure why you have been taken back to prison or if you have any other problems, get specialist advice.

Getting further help

Citizens Advice Bureaux

Some Citizens Advice Bureaux run advice sessions in prison. If you are in prison, check if they run these sessions in your prison. If they do not run advice sessions, you could write to your local CAB and explain your problem. Ask a member of the prison staff for the address of your local CAB.

Specialist organizations

Action for Prisoners' Families (0800 808 2003; www.prisonersfamilies. org.uk) is an umbrella organization that encourages the development of groups that help prisoners' families. It gives information on local family support services.

The **Joint Council for the Welfare of Immigrants** (020 7251 8706; www.jcwi.org.uk) offers help, information and advice to prisoners with immigration problems, including the threat of deportation.

Liberty (0845 123 2307; www.liberty-human-rights.org.uk) campaigns to improve prisoners' rights. It can advise you on all aspects of the prison system, including treatment in prison.

The **Miscarriage of Justice Organization** (MOJO: 0121 789 8443; www.mojo.freehosting.net) provides free and impartial expert advice to individuals who are suffering because of a miscarriage of justice.

The **National Association for the Care and Resettlement of Offenders** (England: 020 7582 6500; www.nacro.org.uk; Wales: 01248 354 602) provides various services for ex-prisoners, including housing, resettlement and education. It also runs a number of employment training schemes. It has offices in different parts of the country.

The Prison Reform Trust (020 7251 5070; www.prisonreformtrust.org. uk) provides advice and information to prisoners on many aspects of imprisonment and complaints about treatment in prison. It cannot deal with cases of wrongful conviction. It produces a number of useful leaflets, which you can get from its head office, and co-produces (with the Prison Service) the *Prisoner's Information Book*, given to all prisoners on arrival at prison. The Prison Reform Trust also campaigns on issues relating to prison policy and practice.

The **Prisoners' Advice Service** (020 7253 3323; www.prisonersadvice.org. uk) provides advice and information to prisoners on their rights as prisoners. The service deals with prison rules, standing orders and circular instructions, such as parole, home leave and security categorization. PAS does not deal with miscarriages of justice or appeals against conviction or sentence.

Women in Prison (020 7226 5879; www.womeninprison.org.uk) is an organization that campaigns on aspects of women's imprisonment. They welcome contact from women prisoners about any aspect of imprisonment.

3
Nationality and Immigration

CONTENTS

INTRODUCTION

Britain is a nation of immigrants. From the Roman, Saxon and Viking invasions, the Protestant refugees from France and the Low Countries, the Africans brought to Britain via the slave trade and the waves of Jewish arrivals over the centuries to the Irish fleeing rural poverty and famine, incoming populations have always made a huge contribution to life in Britain. More recently, British citizens from the Commonwealth invited to come to Britain after the Second World War and the recent migrants from Eastern Europe and Africa escaping wars and persecution in their home countries have continued this history of immigration. Twenty-three per cent of Britain's doctors were born overseas, two thirds of independently owned shops are owned by people from minority ethnic communities and Britain's cultural and sporting life has been hugely enriched by a diverse range of cultural influences. Political life too has been informed by the experiences of new Britons, from Olaudah Equiano, who as a free man in Britain fought the slave trade that brought him here from West Africa, to Diane Abbot, who became the first black female MP in 1987. Newcomers have often had a hostile reception, whatever their reasons for coming, and, in recent years, have faced increasingly strict immigration controls. The increase in the number of European Union countries has resulted in a growth in migrant workers with sometimes complex issues to face. Immigration law is about how and why people from countries outside the UK are allowed to come to the UK and how long they can stay. It is also about what they are allowed to do when they are here – whether they can work, whether relatives can join them afterwards, and whether they can use the National Health Service or claim benefits.

Immigration law is made more complicated because it overlaps with nationality law – that is, the law about who is or is not a British citizen, and the rights of the different types of British citizen. Because these laws are so complicated, it would be misleading to give any general guidelines on them. Instead, this chapter gives some examples of the sorts of problems that may arise, and a list of organizations which may be able to help.

IMMIGRATION CONTROL AND NATIONALITY

The system of immigration control in the UK broadly establishes two distinct groups of people:

- those who have 'right of abode' in the UK and who can live, work and move in and out of the country as they wish
- those who require permission in order to enter and remain here. The technical term for this permission is 'leave' and people who do not have an automatic right to be in the UK are often described as people who 'need leave' to come and stay in the UK.

There are certain groups of people who do not fit easily into these two groups and who do not have to get leave to 'enter and remain', even though they do not have 'right of abode'. Included in this group are people who can benefit from European rights of free movement.

Where people do need leave to enter the UK, immigration rules (which are law) set out various ways in which it can be granted.

'Visitor', 'spouse', 'au pair' and 'student' are all examples of different immigration categories. In each category, the rules indicate different requirements that must be satisfied before a person will be granted leave to come and stay – for example, students must show that they will follow a full-time course of study. Most of the categories under the rules require that people coming to the UK will be able to support themselves without relying on public funds.

The immigration rules also spell out how long leave to remain in the UK should be granted. Leave can be either 'limited' or 'indefinite'. Limited leave is granted to those people who are coming here for 'temporary' purposes – for example as students. Other categories of applicant may be eligible for 'indefinite' leave with the possibility that the person may be able to apply for citizenship.

People in most 'temporary' categories, such as visitors, will also need to show that they intend to leave the country when the purpose of their stay is over.

Nationality law is a branch of law in its own right in the UK, but questions of nationality or citizenship are closely associated with immigration law because a person's nationality is central in determining what immigration rights they have. It is also important to remember that there are different 'kinds' of citizenship in UK law and not all British nationals have the 'right of abode' that allows them freely to enter and live in the UK.

People who require leave to enter the UK will usually need to get 'entry clearance' to show that they are entitled to enter the UK under the immigration rules. There are detailed rules about how to qualify for entry clearance within each category of applicant coming to the UK. Some groups, such as refugees and asylum seekers, do not require entry clearance, but most do.

Immigration laws are strictly enforced in the UK and the consequences of misunderstanding your right to be here can be very serious. They can include the risk of deportation. It is essential to consult a specialist adviser if you are unsure about your position or the position of family and friends.

For this reason you should seek specialist advice in the following situations:

- you want permission to stay in the UK longer than you originally intended

- you want permission to do something that you are not at present allowed to do, such as work
- you want to bring relatives into the country, such as your wife or children
- you are being threatened with deportation from the UK
- you are being held by the immigration authorities in a detention centre
- you want a passport and don't know whether you are entitled to a British passport or some other one
- you want to apply to become a British Citizen
- you are already living in the UK but want to travel abroad and are unsure whether you will be allowed back into the UK
- you are not sure whether you are entitled to use state services or claim benefits
- you are not sure whether you have the right to vote
- a relative or friend has been refused entry to the UK at an airport or port.

Who can help?

Registration of Immigration Advisers

All immigration advisers must be registered with the **Office of Immigration Services Commissioner** (OISC: 020 7211 1500; www.oisc. org.uk), or be an adviser with an organization, such as the Citizens Advice Bureaux, that is exempt from registration. Anyone who gives immigration advice and is neither registered nor exempt will be committing a criminal offence. Every registered or exempt advice agency should display a certificate issued by the OISC to show it meets the OISC standards.

A list of all registered and exempt advisers and advice organizations can be seen on the OISC website, which also includes details of how to make a complaint about an immigration adviser. The OISC does not deal with enquiries about immigration problems.

The **Immigration Advisory Service** (IAS: 020 7967 1200; www.iasuk.org) operates a number of regional offices – details are on their website. The **Refugee Legal Centre** (020 7780 3200; detention helpline – 0800 592 398 or 020 7780 3333; www.refugee-legal-centre.org.uk) can give advice and assistance to asylum seekers and refugees. This includes helping with applications, advising on temporary admissions, refusal of asylum, family reunion, and representing appeals in court. Appointments can be made by phoning the main advice line. The website has the telephone numbers of advice lines in other regions.

I'm a British citizen, and I want to marry my girlfriend, who is from abroad and in the UK on a student visa. Do we need to do anything special about her status in this country?

If you marry, your new wife should ask for permission to stay in the UK as your spouse. There are strict requirements that she will have to meet to satisfy the immigration authorities that your marriage is genuine and that she should be allowed to stay. She will also have to show that she did not intend to deceive the authorities when she entered the country as a student and that, as a couple, you can support yourselves without help from the state once you get married. Permission to stay as your wife will initially be given for two years. Towards the end of the two-year period she can apply to stay permanently.

Don't forget that UK immigration law is complex and getting it wrong has serious consequences, so it is always advisable to consult a specialist adviser.

The **Refugee Council** (020 7346 6777 – London advice line; www.refugeecouncil.org.uk) in England and Wales offers advice and support to all refugees and asylum seekers. As part of this it operates a one-stop service, providing advice and support to newly arrived refugees and asylum seekers on social security benefits, housing, immigration and education. No appointment is necessary, but people are seen on a first come, first served basis. The Refugee Council also offers training and work experience. You can find out the telephone numbers of advice lines in other regions from their website.

The **UK Lesbian and Gay Immigration Group** (UKLGIG: 020 7922 7811; www.uklgig.org.uk) is a national lobbying and campaigning organization working for legal equality for lesbians and gay men. UKLGIG is a support and campaign group for lesbians and gay couples with immigration problems that they would not face if they were heterosexual. The group works to change the immigration rules to ensure this discrimination is removed. It also arranges for exchanges of information, provides a support network, and advises on and supports applications to the Home Office.

UK Council for International Student Affairs (UKCISA: 020 7107 9922;

www.ukcosa.org.uk) campaigns on behalf of foreign students and produces a number of very useful booklets on students' problems. Individual foreign students looking for advice should consult their local NUS office (contactable through NUS headquarters). In an emergency, you may ring UKCISA on the public casework line (020 7109 9922).

I came to the UK on a visitor's visa and would like to stay here to do a degree. Will I be allowed to do this?

When you came to the UK, you were allowed to enter on the basis that you left the UK when your visitor's visa ran out. Under immigration rules, you will not be allowed to stay here to study. If you want to become a student, you will have to leave the UK and re-apply to return as a student at a future date.

If you stay on in the UK beyond the date of your visa, you will be in breach of your conditions of entry. This is a serious offence and you can be prosecuted and deported.

The **Joint Council for the Welfare of Immigrants** (JCWI: 020 7251 8706; www.jcwi.org.uk) is an independent voluntary organization financed by trusts and charity. It campaigns for changes in immigration law, both on its own and together with other organizations. It also provides advice and training to other advice agencies. It does not do casework.

The few **solicitors in private practice** who specialize in immigration work are generally based in larger urban areas. To find out whether there are any solicitors in private practice in your area who specialize in immigration work, you can contact the **Immigration Law Practitioners' Association** (020 7251 8383).

The **Community Legal Service** (CLS: www.clsdirect.org.uk) website contains a directory with contact details of solicitors, advice agencies and sources of specialist advice locally. Information is available in English, Welsh, Urdu, Bengali, Cantonese, Punjabi and Gujarati. You can consult a copy of the CLS Directory for English and Welsh regions in your local library or call the CLS Directory line (0845 345 4 345).

Law centres generally have fairly strict catchment areas, so it is important to check whether a law centre in the area will be able to take on a case. Sometimes, the catchment area will include people who either live or work in the area. If the law centre can offer advice and representation in immigration cases, it will be free. For more information, contact the **Law Centres' Federation** (020 7428 4400; www.lawcentres.org.uk).

> *My uncle lives in a country where there is a lot of political unrest and violence. He says he's getting afraid to leave the house, and wonders if he could come to the UK for a while until things calm down a bit.*
>
> The UK has signed a United Nations Convention on refugees, which means that it is committed to offering asylum to people who are at risk of persecution in their own country. The process of applying for asylum in the UK is extremely complex and you should seek specialist advice to find out whether your uncle might qualify for asylum at the present time. Only a small proportion of asylum applications are successful, so you should also consider whether your uncle could come to this country in another capacity. He may, for example, have family links with the UK that could give him rights to be here while things are unsettled in his home country.
>
> UK immigration law is complex and getting it wrong has serious consequences. It is always advisable to consult a specialist adviser.

Money

1
Tax

CONTENTS

INTRODUCTION

We've all been complaining about taxes since Robin Hood started redistributing wealth and Lady Godiva rode naked through the streets of Coventry to get her husband to reduce them. Income tax was introduced in 1799 as a way of funding the war against Napoleon – 10 per cent on all income over £60. It is still a 'temporary' tax, which expires each year on 5 April, and Parliament has to reapply it by an annual Finance Act.

Taxes can win and lose elections and have always been centre stage for politicians fighting for our votes. Whether the politicians are promising to cut taxes and put more money in our pockets or planning to 'tax and spend' to pay for public services, taxes are at the heart of the political agenda.

Like it or not, most of us have to pay them so the best you can do is make sure you know your way around the tax jungle. This chapter looks at income tax, tax relief, tax rebates, Self Assessment, PAYE and 'fringe benefits', like that company car. There is also a tax 'jargon buster' to help you understand the lingo.

JARGON BUSTER

deeds of covenant
a way of giving money regularly to charity that allows the charity to reclaim the income tax that was paid on the gift

filing date
the date by which completed tax returns must be received by HM Revenue and Customs. If a return is not received by this date, you may have to pay penalties. The filing date is the 31 January after the tax year to which the tax return relates

fringe benefits
non-cash benefits, such as company cars, given to employees. Most fringe benefits are taxable. HM Revenue and Customs now uses the term employment benefits

Gift Aid
a way of giving a one-off amount from taxed income to a charity. The charity may then claim the tax back

HM Revenue and Customs
the government department responsible for assessing and collecting tax, including VAT. It used to be called the Inland Revenue

inheritance tax
tax paid on a person's estate after death. It was formerly known as estate duty or capital transfer tax. Inheritance tax may also be payable on some gifts made during a person's lifetime,

ISA
stands for Individual Savings Account. ISAs allow money to be saved in several ways without tax having to be paid on any interest earned

PAYE
stands for Pay As You Earn and is the way that all employees, and some other people, pay income tax

payments on account
payments of income tax and Class 4 National Insurance contributions that must be paid by self-employed people, or by certain employees. The payments are made in advance of the taxpayer sending in a tax return for a particular tax year, and mean that tax will be paid in two instalments during the tax year

remission of tax arrears
a taxpayer with tax arrears may have some or all of them 'remitted', that is, the taxpayer

will not have to pay all of the arrears if certain conditions are met

Self Assessment Self Assessment taxpayers are responsible for assessing which parts of their income are taxable and filling in a tax return accordingly

stamp duty land tax a tax that is paid on documents that convey a sale of property or shares. The document is sent to the Stamp Office for stamping, and the tax is paid then

tax arrears a debt to HM Revenue and Customs for tax owed

tax assessment the amount of tax which someone must pay

tax-exempt income income on which income tax is never payable – for example, some income from National Savings certificates and winnings from gambling

tax-free income not the same as tax-exempt income. Tax-free income is the personal allowances and tax relief that reduce income on which tax would be payable. Once these have been deducted, what remains is called the taxable income

tax rebates payments from HM Revenue and Customs to an individual who has paid too much tax in any particular year. The payment will often not be made until the end of the tax year

tax return Form SA 100 on which taxpayers must list all income and certain expenses so that the amount of tax due can be calculated. You can do the calculation yourself, or can ask HM Revenue and Customs to calculate how much tax you should pay

tax years 6 April one year to 5 April the following year

taxable income the part of total income on which income tax is payable, that is, after tax-exempt income and tax-free income have been deducted

TESSA stands for Tax Exempt Special Savings Account and, as the name suggests, is a special savings account that allows interest to be paid tax-free. No new ones can be started, but any already in existence can continue until the end of their term

VAT stands for value added tax, which is a tax on

goods and services, and is payable at a certain percentage. It is administered and collected by HM Revenue and Customs

INCOME TAX

Income tax is a tax paid on income. It is paid by employees and people who are self-employed and may also be payable if you are not working but have an income, such as a retirement pension or an occupational pension. Not all types of income are taxable and it will seldom be the case that all of your income is taxed. There is no minimum age at which a person becomes liable to pay income tax. What matters is your income. If this is below a certain level, no tax is payable.

How it is calculated

There are five main steps in calculating income tax:

1. Add together all your yearly income, including social security benefits, income from renting out accommodation, wages, occupational pension and interest from bank and building society accounts.

2. Take off any income that is exempt from tax. Calculate whether you can claim tax relief on any of the money you have spent over the year (tax relief usually applies to people who are self-employed and have to buy items for the business). Deduct this tax relief. This leaves income on which tax may be payable (taxable income).

3. Work out which tax allowances you are entitled to. You will be entitled to a personal allowance (plus age-related additions if appropriate). These allowances are deducted at this stage in the calculation.

4. Multiply the taxable income by the correct tax rate. This gives the tax due to be paid that year (unless you are entitled to married couple's allowance – see p. 598).

5. If applicable, deduct the appropriate percentage rate of married couple's allowance.

Income that is taxable

Income that is taxable includes:

- some social security benefits and pensions, such as Retirement Pension, Jobseeker's Allowance and Statutory Maternity and Paternity Pay
- employment-related allowances and benefits
- earned income, such as wages and salaries and profits from self-employment
- other types of income – for example, profits from the sale of most goods and property or rental income from property you let out
- some fringe benefits, such as company cars
- some occupational pensions
- interest on some types of savings – for example, building society and bank accounts.

There is actually no single definition in tax law of income. Income tax law divides various types of income into schedules. If an item comes within a schedule, it counts as income and income tax must be paid on it. The way the tax must be paid will depend on which schedule it falls into. The most common schedules are Schedule E for employees and Schedule D for self-employed people.

The percentage rate of tax payable varies according to the amount of the taxable income. Further advice is available from HM Revenue and Customs. You can find the correct telephone number by looking on their website at www.hmrc.gov.uk.

Tax-exempt income

Some income is exempt from income tax, which means that tax is never paid on this income. You should check whether any income is exempt from tax before doing a tax calculation. Examples of income which is exempt from tax include premium bond prizes, Housing Benefit, Child Benefit and profit-related pay.

Tax allowances

Everyone is entitled to a basic personal tax allowance. In addition, you may be entitled to other allowances on top of the basic allowance. This means that some of your income, which would otherwise be taxable, will be tax-free.

Tax allowances are announced in the Budget each year. If you are an employee and so are taxed under Pay As You Earn (PAYE), your personal allowance(s) will be spread throughout the year, so that each week or month you will be left with a certain amount of tax-free income after the tax has been deducted. If you are self-employed or have an income but are not working, your personal allowance(s) will be taken into account when HM Revenue and Customs assesses your tax liability each year.

All taxpayers can claim at least one tax allowance and some taxpayers can claim more than one. The allowances are given to all taxpayers, whether they are employees or self-employed or do not work. If you are entitled to an allowance and are not getting it, you should claim it from your tax office. If you have not received allowances to which you are entitled, you can make a backdated claim for them for up to six years.

In practice, if you receive earnings or an occupational pension, this income is taxed through the Pay As You Earn (PAYE) system. This means your allowances are spread over the year and you pay your tax throughout the year, not just when your income reaches the amounts of your allowances. The following tax allowances can be given:

- personal allowances
- blind person's allowance
- married couple's allowance. This applies to someone living with a spouse or civil partner if either partner was born before 6 April 1935.

Personal allowances

Everyone automatically gets a personal tax allowance, whether they are male or female, married or single, and regardless of how young they are. This can be set against all types of income. There are three amounts of personal allowance:

- a standard amount for people aged under 65
- a higher amount for people aged 65–74
- the highest amount for people aged 75 or over.

Blind person's allowance

You can claim a blind person's allowance for the whole tax year if you are a registered blind person or become a registered blind person during the tax year. You can claim this in addition to your personal allowance.

If you are married or have a civil partner and cannot use all your blind person's allowance because you do not have enough income, you can ask your tax office to transfer the unused part of the allowance to your partner, whether or not the partner is blind. If both you and your partner are blind, you can each receive the allowance.

Married couple's allowance
See p. 598.

Tax relief (excluding self-employed people)

As a taxpayer, if you spend money on certain outgoings, the amount you spend can be deducted from your total taxable income and you will therefore pay less tax. Tax relief can be claimed in addition to any personal tax allowances that you are entitled to and can be backdated for up to six years. Some reliefs have to be claimed by writing to your tax inspector, although most are automatic. No action need be taken by you to claim automatic relief. Tax reliefs for employees are spread throughout the year in the same way as personal tax allowances. Tax relief for self-employed people and people who have an income but are not working is taken into account by HM Revenue and Customs when assessing tax each year, once it has received the taxpayer's tax return.

Types of tax relief
There are six main types of tax relief:

- tax relief available to self-employed people
- tax relief available to employees
- tax relief on training and education
- tax relief on property
- tax relief on some insurance premiums
- tax relief on payments to other people, such as maintenance payments and payments to charities.

Income tax rates

Tax is paid at different rates on your total taxable income. Income tax rates are reviewed annually and usually change in April. Contact HM Revenue and Customs (www.hmrc.gov.uk) for details of current tax rates.

Income on which tax has already been paid

When calculating the tax due, it is necessary to work out whether or not you have received any income on which tax has already been paid – for example, interest on savings in a building society or bank account, where the interest is paid to you after the bank/building society has taken the tax off it. Payments from an occupational pension will also have had tax taken off before the payment is made to you.

When working out the total tax due for the year, it is necessary to take into account the fact that tax has already been paid on this income. This income (which needs to have the tax deducted added back in) will also count towards taxable income on which personal tax allowances are allowed.

National Insurance contributions

When checking whether your tax has been correctly calculated, it may also be useful to calculate the National Insurance contributions that you have to pay, as this will give the figure for your take-home pay. National Insurance contributions are calculated on gross income. National Insurance contributions for employees are deducted at different rates depending on your pension arrangements and on your level of income.

Record-keeping

If you are a taxpayer, you must keep records of your income to enable you to complete a tax return. Personal or non-business records must be kept until 22 months after the end of the tax year that they relate to, and business records must be kept for five years after the fixed filing date.

How HM Revenue and Customs collects income tax

Deduction of tax at source

Only a minority of taxpayers pay tax directly to HM Revenue and Customs every year. The majority of taxpayers pay their tax through deductions that are made from their income before they receive it. This is called deduction at source.

Some of the most common examples of deduction at source are PAYE and deductions from bank and building society interest.

Pay As You Earn (PAYE)

By law, anyone making payments to employees or members of occupational pension schemes has to operate the PAYE system. This means they must deduct income tax and Class 1 National Insurance contributions from the payments that they make, and must send these sums to HM Revenue and Customs. You are entitled to receive written confirmation of deductions that have been made by:

- payslips, showing gross pay, deductions made and net pay if you are an employee
- a P60 certificate at the end of each tax year, confirming the amount of gross earnings, and the income tax and Class 1 National Insurance contributions deducted
- a P45 certificate whenever you change jobs, which shows the tax code operating on your earnings at the time you left and, in some cases, the earnings and income tax deducted in the tax year to date.

Bank and building society interest

Banks and building societies deduct income tax from the interest paid on most deposits made with them by individuals, and pay this over to HM Revenue and Customs. This is done before the interest is paid to the account holder.

Confirmation of the interest earned in each tax year and the income tax deducted must be provided by the bank or building society free of charge to you, the saver, if you ask for it. A number of banks and building societies send these details to all their investors each year as a matter of course.

If you do not need to pay any tax on this interest – for example, because your total income from all sources falls below your tax-free income for the tax year – you can arrange to receive your interest gross – that is, without deduction of any tax. This is called taxback. You should ask your branch of the bank or building society for a taxback form. This avoids the need to claim a tax refund.

Collection of tax by Self Assessment

See *Self Assessment*, p. 592.

Tax rebates

A tax rebate is a refund of tax that has been overpaid. There are a number of reasons why tax may have been overpaid, including when:

- you start a new job and are taxed under an emergency code for a while
- your circumstances change – for example, you marry or enter into a civil partnership, you reach retirement age or you become a single parent

- HM Revenue and Customs sends the wrong tax code to your employer
- HM Revenue and Customs made an assessment – for example, for a self-employed person – that was too high
- you are not a taxpayer, but have had tax deducted from your building society or bank interest.

Rebates under PAYE

If you pay tax through PAYE, you have your tax adjusted throughout the tax year by your employer. If too much tax has been deducted, the tax office will send your employer a new tax code, which will enable your employer to pay the rebate through your wages or salary.

Rebates for unemployed people

If you become unemployed and claim Jobseeker's Allowance, you will not immediately receive a tax rebate. A rebate will be paid either under PAYE if you go back to work, or at the end of the financial year, whichever is sooner. If you are on Income Support you will be treated in the same way.

Rebates following a death

An overpayment of income tax may arise following a death. HM Revenue and Customs should be informed of the death in writing as soon as possible and a copy of the death certificate should also be sent to the tax office. Special rules apply to the tax allowances if the person who has died was married or in a civil partnership. If a refund of tax is made, it is counted as part of the estate of the person who has died.

Rebates for strikers

If you are on strike, you will only be paid a rebate when you either leave the job or go back to work. The rebate will not be paid at the end of the financial year.

Leaving a job

If you leave work and do not claim social security benefits, you may be able to claim a rebate after four weeks of leaving work. Circumstances in which this may be possible include:

- leaving the country permanently
- giving up work to care for a sick or elderly relative
- leaving work to go into full-time education

- retirement
- leaving work to care for a child.

Time limits on claiming a tax rebate

A claim for a tax rebate can usually be made up to five years after 31 January following the end of the tax year in which tax was overpaid. However, this time limit can be extended in cases where overpayment of tax occurred because of an error by HM Revenue and Customs or another government department, and where there is no dispute or doubt as to the facts.

Interest on rebates

HM Revenue and Customs must pay interest on some tax rebates that have been delayed. For interest to be paid, the rebate must:

- have been delayed for more than twelve months after the end of the year of assessment (or the end of the year in which tax was paid, if it was paid late)
- be for a certain minimum amount
- be for a tax year when the taxpayer was resident in the United Kingdom.

PAYE

The Pay As You Earn (PAYE) system is a method of paying income tax. Your employer deducts tax from your wages or occupational pension before paying you your wages. Wages include sick pay and maternity pay. This means that you pay tax over the whole year, each time you are paid. Your employer is responsible for sending the tax on to HM Revenue and Customs.

If you pay tax on your wages or occupational pension under PAYE, the PAYE system can also be used to collect the income tax of any other taxable income you have. For example, if you pay tax under PAYE on an occupational pension, the tax due on your state retirement pension is collected through PAYE by deducting tax from your occupational pension.

Tax codes

The tax office will tell your employer how much tax to deduct from your wages/occupational pension, but will not give details about how your code has been decided. If the tax office does not have enough information to issue a full tax code, it will use an emergency tax code until more information is received and the tax can be adjusted.

If you are given a PAYE tax code it will be shown on:

- a notice of coding sent by the tax office; *or*
- your payslip; *or*
- your pension statement if you are getting an occupational pension.

Most PAYE codes are made up of a number followed by a letter:

- the letter relates to the type of allowance(s) you are getting
- the number shows the amount of income you have as allowances that may be set against tax.

The letter in the tax code

The letter in the tax code, which shows which tax allowances you are receiving, will be one of the following:

L	if you are aged under 65 and getting the personal allowance. You will be given this code if you are a single person or a person who is being taxed on the emergency code
P	if you are a single person, or a married woman, aged between 65 and 74 who is entitled to the full age-related allowance
V	is used if you are aged between 65 and 74, eligible for the full personal allowance and the full married couple's allowance (for those born before 6 April 1935 and aged under 75) and estimated to be liable at the basic rate of tax
T	may be allocated for a number of reasons – for example, if there are any things that HM Revenue & Customs needs to review in your tax code, or if you ask HM Revenue and Customs not to use any of the other tax code letters listed above
K	is used when your total allowances are less than your total 'deductions'
Y	if you are aged 75 or over and have the full personal allowance
NT	if you do not have to pay tax. This code does not include a number
BR	if you have not been given any allowances and tax will be deducted at the basic rate. This code may be given where you have more than one job
DO	if you have tax deducted at the higher rate.

The number in the tax code

If you multiply the number in your tax code by 10, you will get the total amount of income you can earn in a year before paying tax.

Emergency tax codes

The tax office may not be able to give your employer a tax code to allow deduction of the right amount of tax over the whole year. In this case, the tax office gives your employer an emergency code with which to tax you. An emergency code assumes that you are only entitled to the basic personal allowance and your PAYE tax code will include the letter L, which shows that you are only receiving this personal allowance. It does not take into account any other allowances and reliefs you may be entitled to.

You will stop being taxed on an emergency code:

- when the tax office sends your employer (and you) a PAYE tax code, and details of previous earnings and tax paid for that tax year. This enables your employer to deduct the correct tax in future and refund any tax overpaid as a result of the emergency code
- at the end of the tax year. Your employer will usually start deducting tax cumulatively – that is, when deducting tax your employer will take into account the amount of tax you have already paid. If, at the end of the tax year, you think you have paid too much tax because you have been taxed on an emergency code, you should claim a rebate by writing to the tax office.

Notice of coding

A notice of coding shows your tax code if you are going to pay through the PAYE system. The notice is usually sent out in January or February for the tax year beginning on the following 6 April. The code shown in the notice is given for that tax year only. The notes that come with the notice of coding explain how the code is worked out.

Not everyone gets a notice of coding each year. It depends on what allowances and relief you are claiming and whether these tend to change from year to year. It is important to check that the notice of coding gives the correct allowances and relief, because if it is wrong you will be paying the wrong amount of tax.

You should check carefully that you have been given all the allowances and relief that you are entitled to claim and that all your income has been taken into account. If help is needed, consult a local tax office or an experienced adviser.

There is also a HMRC leaflet called 'Understanding your tax code'. You

can access this from HM Revenue and Customs website (www.hmrc.gov.
uk).

PAYE and Self Assessment

Under the system of Self Assessment, you have to assess how much tax you
have to pay on any income which you receive that is not taxed through
PAYE, for example:

- income from renting out a room
- income from freelance work.

You must tell the local tax office if you receive taxable income in addition to
that on which you pay tax through PAYE. You will then have to complete a
tax return form and either ask HM Revenue and Customs to calculate how
much tax is due (Revenue calculation) or do the calculation yourself (taxpayer calculation). If you owe less than a certain amount in tax on sources of
income that are not taxed through PAYE, and you send your completed tax
return form back by the 30 September following the end of the tax year, you
can pay all your tax through PAYE. If you owe more than this amount, or if
you prefer, you can pay the tax due on the other sources of income directly
to HM Revenue and Customs. If you want to check that you are paying the
right amount of tax, or, for example, if you think you may have over- or
underpaid tax, you should contact your local tax office and ask if you can
complete a tax return form. Once you have completed the form you can
either ask HM Revenue and Customs to calculate the amount of tax due, or
do the calculation yourself.

Change in circumstances

If your circumstances change during the tax year – for example, if you
become entitled to a new allowance or incur a new outgoing – you must
inform HM Revenue and Customs as soon as possible.

You cannot rely only on telling an employer of a change in circumstances.
In fact, as an employer can do nothing until instructed by HM Revenue and
Customs, you do not have to inform your employer at all. You should write
to your tax office with the details of the change.

PAYE: Common problems

Starting a new job

When you start a new job your employer needs to know your tax code. If you have a form called a P45 from a previous job in the same tax year, your employer will use the information on this to deduct the right amount of tax. If you were unemployed and receiving Jobseeker's Allowance, you should give your new employer the P45U you were given by your Jobcentre Plus office.

No P45 or P45U

You may not have a P45 or P45U. This may be because you:

- are starting your first job
- were unemployed but not receiving Jobseeker's Allowance and therefore do not have a P45U
- have lost the P45 or P45U
- were not given a P45 by your last employer.

If you cannot give the employer a P45 or a P45U, your employer will give you a P46 form, which, when completed, allows your employer to deduct tax on an emergency code until the right amount of tax to be deducted is worked out. If you have lost your P45 or P45U, you will not be able to obtain a duplicate, as these are never issued. Your new employer, or the Jobcentre if you are claiming benefit, will ask you to complete a P46.

Fringe benefits (employment benefits)

Fringe benefits are any benefits which you receive from your employment that are not actually included in your salary cheque or wages. On the tax return form they are called employment benefits. They include such things as company cars, private medical insurance and cheap or free loans. Not all fringe benefits are taxable and some are only taxable if you are earning over a certain limit. See *Fringe benefits*, p. 586.

More than one job

If you have more than one job, you will get a separate PAYE code for each job in which your earnings are taxed under PAYE, and normally a separate notice of coding for each job. All the reliefs and allowances you are entitled to will normally be included in the tax code for your main job. This means that all your earnings from the second job may be taxed. If so, the tax code you are given for the second job will be:

BR   if you are being taxed at the basic rate of tax; *or*

DO   if you are being taxed at a higher rate of tax.

If the income earned from the second job takes you into the higher rate of tax, all the earnings from the second job will be taxed at the higher rate. If you are in this situation you may find that your tax bill will need adjusting at the end of the tax year.

Other taxable income

If you have other taxable income in addition to wages or an occupational pension, the tax due on this can be deducted from these payments by your employer. This is done by altering the amounts of the allowances given to you, in effect reducing the amount of income you can receive before you have to pay tax. The most common forms of other income that are taxed in this way are state retirement and widow's pensions.

Wage rises

When you get a wage rise you are liable to pay more tax and the adjustments for this will be done automatically by your employer.

Changes to income tax in the Budget

Changes to income tax are usually made by the government in the annual Budget – for example, the amount of the allowances is usually increased. The changes are announced during November and take effect from the following 6 April.

If the allowances go up in the Budget, this increases the amount of tax-free pay you can receive before you start paying tax. If your tax code includes the letters L, P or V, your employer can make the adjustments automatically. This will usually be done in January so that the new allowances can be implemented on 6 April.

If your PAYE tax code includes the letters T or K, the tax office has to send a new code to you and your employer before the adjustments can be made. The adjustments should be in place by 6 April, but if there is any delay you will receive a tax refund.

Change in circumstances

Your tax code will be affected if:

- your personal circumstances change, and you are entitled to different allowances
- your outgoings change and you can claim extra relief
- your taxable income changes – for example, you start receiving a taxable pension. This other income can also be deducted from your wages through PAYE.

If your tax position changes, your tax code may need amending. You should write to the tax office with full details of the changes and ask for the code to be amended. You should give your full name and National Insurance number and details of your employer's name, address and tax reference number. You can obtain these details from your P60 or by asking your employer. You should enclose your last notice of coding if you have one.

It is important to write as soon as possible because you may be paying the wrong amount of tax because your tax code is incorrect. This could result in either an overpayment or an underpayment of tax. If an underpayment arises the tax office will collect this and has the power to charge interest or impose a fine.

If the tax office needs further details before they can change the code, they will sometimes send a tax return for completion. This should be returned within 30 days. If there is any delay in its return, this will result in a change to the tax code being delayed.

Sick or on maternity leave

If you are sick or on maternity, paternity or adoption leave, you will have the tax on your pay collected under PAYE.

If you do not receive any pay, you will be entitled to a rebate. This is because you did not use your tax allowance during the period when you were unpaid.

The rebate can either be paid when you return to work or while you are off work. If you are not getting any pay, you might prefer to have the rebate as soon as possible rather than wait until you are next paid. You should ask your employer to arrange this or confirm when the rebate will be paid.

Unemployment, short-time working or on strike

If you are unemployed, on short-time working or on strike, you may be entitled to a rebate of tax at the end of the tax year. This is because the amount of tax you have paid may be too high for the amount of earnings you are now likely to receive over the tax year. However, if you get Job-seeker's Allowance, which may be taxed, the rebate may be cancelled out.

If you are temporarily on short-time working, your employer should make whatever tax rebate you are entitled to on your normal paydays.

If you are on strike or involved in a trade dispute, you will not be able to claim a tax rebate while on strike. Instead, you will have to wait for a rebate under PAYE – in other words, when you either leave the job or return to work. If you are still on strike at the end of the tax year, you will not get a rebate until you leave the job or return to work. However, your employer will give you your P60, which will show the rebate that is due as if it had been paid. Your employer must also give you an additional note saying how much tax rebate under PAYE is being withheld until you leave or return to work.

The employer or tax office makes a mistake

Your employer or tax office may make a mistake – for example, if the tax office gives your employer the wrong PAYE code or your employer wrongly calculates your tax and deducts too much or too little tax. In these circumstances the amount of tax that you have over- or underpaid will be rebated or reclaimed by adjusting your PAYE tax code for the following tax year. In a limited number of circumstances you may not have to pay all the tax arrears that you owe.

If you think that a mistake has been made in the amount of income tax you have been paying, you should inform the tax office as soon as possible.

Leaving a job

If you leave your job – whether voluntarily, through dismissal or redundancy, or because you retire – your employer should give you a Form P45. The P45 gives details of your employer's tax office, your employer's tax reference number, your tax code and the total amount of pay and tax deducted during the current tax year. If tax has been deducted on the emergency code, the P45 will have an X in the box marked week 1 or month 1 and there will not be any details of pay or tax. You should keep the P45 in case you start work again.

If your employer fails to give you a P45 after being asked to do so, you should contact your tax office as they may encourage your employer to issue a P45. If your employer cannot be persuaded, a new employer will ask you to complete a P46 form, which allows your new employer to deduct tax on an emergency code until the right amount of tax to be deducted is worked out.

If you claim Jobseeker's Allowance, you will have to give the P45 to your Jobcentre Plus office. If you start work again before the end of the tax year, the Jobcentre will give you a P45U, which includes details of the taxable benefit you have received as well as the normal P45 details.

If you leave at the very end of the tax year, you should be given a P60 and a P45.

Students

If you are a student who is working during vacations, you will usually pay tax in the same way as other employees. However, you and your employer can fill in a form P38S, which your employer can obtain from the tax office or local tax enquiry centre, which means tax will not be deducted under PAYE. The form must show that all the student's earnings, plus any other income for the tax year, will not exceed the total allowances and reliefs that can be claimed.

Dealing with a PAYE problem

If you have a problem about your income tax, you may be able to resolve it by talking to your employer. Your employer will have guidance from the tax office on how to operate the PAYE tax system and deal with problems.

If the problem cannot be resolved by talking to your employer, you can contact:

- a tax enquiry centre
- the tax office that holds your records.

FRINGE BENEFITS

Fringe benefits are benefits that employees or directors receive from their employment but which are not included in their salary cheque or wages. On the tax return form they are called 'employment benefits'. They include such things as company cars, private medical insurance paid for by the employer, and cheap or free loans. Some fringe benefits will not be taxed, some will, and some will be taxed only for employees who are directors or higher paid.

Tax-free fringe benefits

Some fringe benefits are tax-free and do not need to be entered on your tax return. These include:

- contributions paid by your employer into an approved occupational or personal pension scheme for the employee
- cheap or free canteen meals, if these are provided for all employees
- in-house sports facilities
- counselling services to redundant employees
- childcare for children aged under 18
- works buses, or subsidies to public bus services, to get employees to and from work
- bicycles and cycling safety equipment provided for employees to get to and from work, and workplace parking for bicycles and motorcycles
- the loan by the employer of computer equipment up to a certain value
- reasonable removal expenses if you have to move to take up a new job
- genuine personal gifts given for reasons unconnected with the job, for example retirement gifts or wedding gifts
- gifts, other than cash, that you receive from someone other than your employer – for example, seats at sporting or cultural events, providing they are not worth more than a certain amount
- if you are disabled, equipment and facilities provided for you to carry out your job.

Taxable fringe benefits

For fringe benefits that are taxable, tax is paid on the taxable value of the benefit. The way the taxable value is worked out depends on whether or not you are a higher-paid employee or a director.

If you get taxable fringe benefits, you must enter the value on your tax return for the relevant year, even if you have already paid tax on the benefit under PAYE and whether or not you count as higher-paid.

Common fringe benefits

The following paragraphs list some of the more common fringe benefits.

Accommodation

Generally, where any employee, whether higher-paid or not, is provided with accommodation, either rent-free or for a very low rent, the difference between the rent paid, if any, and the annual value of the property is taxable. There are three exceptions to this rule. No tax will have to be paid on the accommodation if:

- it is necessary for you to live in the accommodation to perform your duties properly
- it is provided so that you can perform your duties better than you could without it
- the job involves a special security risk and special accommodation is provided for your safety.

Hotels and temporary accommodation

The cost of hotels and temporary accommodation while travelling for business purposes is not taxed. However, if you are given an overall cash allowance to cover these costs, this will be taxed, but anything you spend on accommodation for the purpose of your job can be deducted from your taxable income as a tax relief.

Company cars and vans

Free private use of a car provided by your employer mainly for business use is normally only taxable for higher-paid employees and directors. Cars that are used only for business, and are not available for private use, are not taxable. In nearly all cases, travel between home and work by higher-paid employees and directors is considered by HM Revenue and Customs to be private use of a vehicle, not business use, and therefore is a taxable benefit.

Childcare expenses

If you pay childcare costs yourself, you cannot claim these costs as relief against tax. Neither can you claim travel expenses to and from work for childcare reasons.

If you are getting childcare support from your employer under the Employer Supported Childcare Vouchers scheme, you do not have to pay tax or National Insurance contributions on the first £55. This only applies if you are getting vouchers from your employer for childcare and not if you are getting a cash benefit.

Accepting childcare vouchers from your employer will mean a cut in pay.

This could reduce your salary to a sum below a certain limit which may affect your right to some benefits.

Clothing

Work and safety clothes provided by your employer, such as overalls and protective helmets or shoes, are not liable to tax. However, any normal clothing provided by your employer is taxable.

Council tax

If your employer pays your council tax, you will have to pay tax on it. But you will not have to pay tax if it is necessary for you to live in the accommodation to do your job. You may be entitled to Council Tax Benefit.

Credit cards and charge cards

If you use your employer's credit card to buy goods or services for yourself, you will have to pay tax on the cost to the employer of allowing you access to the employer's credit facility. You will not have to pay tax if you buy goods or services for yourself that are necessary for your job.

Fuel

Fuel given by an employer to a higher-paid employee or director for private use is taxable.

Holidays

If you are a higher-paid employee or director and receive a free holiday, you will have to pay tax on its value. Other employees do not have to pay tax on a free holiday as long as the holiday has no resale value – for example, if payment is made direct to a hotel. A payment to a travel agent for a holiday abroad would be taxable.

Job-related benefits

Job-related benefits are benefits to employees provided from within the employer's business. They include cheap airline seats for airline staff, cheap rail travel for railway employees, and goods or services provided by a business that are offered free or at a discounted price to employees. They are taxable only for higher-paid employees and directors. They do not include company cars and fuel, loans, accommodation or mobile phones, as there are special rules for these items.

Cash allowances given in lieu of job-related benefits are taxable for all employees.

Loans

Interest-free and cheap loans are taxable for higher-paid employees and directors.

Meals

Meals provided in a staff canteen that is available to all staff are not taxable and you do not need to list them on your tax return. In addition, if you get free or subsidized meals at work, and the meals are available to all employees, they will also not be taxable and do not need to be listed on your tax return. This extends to tickets or vouchers given by employers for free and subsidized meals if the meals are not provided by the employer.

Medical insurance

If your employer provides private medical insurance this is taxable for higher-paid employees and directors.

Mileage allowances

If you get a mileage allowance for using your own car for business purposes, you will be taxed on any profit you make from the allowance. This is the amount by which the total mileage allowance paid exceeds the costs incurred in running the car for business. These costs include running costs such as petrol, oil, servicing and tyres, as well as fixed costs such as road tax, insurance and depreciation.

HM Revenue and Customs operates a 'Fixed Profit Car Scheme', which sets out tax-free rates of mileage allowances. If you are paid less than the tax-free rates, you will not be liable for tax. If your employer pays more than the tax-free rates, you will be taxed on the difference between what the employer pays and the tax-free rate.

Employers do not have to use the 'Fixed Profit Car Scheme', and if you believe your costs are more than the tax-free rate, you can still make an individual claim for tax relief.

Relocation expenses

If your employer pays your removal expenses up to a certain amount, this amount is tax-free. This limit applies to each move.

Shares

In most cases, the value of shares transferred to an employee or director at a discount is liable to tax.

Training

If you are on a full-time or sandwich course at university or college that lasts one year or more with an average of at least 20 weeks' full-time attendance, you can get up to £7,000 pay tax-free while you are still on the course.

If your employer pays for your training course in order to retrain you for another job, the value of the payment made by the employer is not taxable.

If your employer pays for an external training course that is not intended to train you for another job with the same employer, you will not be liable to pay tax on this payment if:

- the course is for general education and you are aged under 21 when the course starts; *or*
- the course is related to your job and you are going to be away from work on the course for less than twelve months.

If you pay for an external course that you attend while still being paid your usual wages, you may be able to claim tax relief.

Travelling expenses

If your employer reimburses you for the costs of travelling to and from work or pays these direct – for example, by buying a season ticket for you – the value of this benefit is generally taxable. However, you can claim tax relief on any travelling expenses paid by your employer to cover the cost of journeys made by you as a necessary part of your job, excluding journeys to and from work.

Vouchers

If you get vouchers, including luncheon vouchers, of more than 15p a day and cheque vouchers that are exchangeable for goods and services, you will be taxed on the cost to your employer of providing the voucher and these goods and services. Cash vouchers such as Holiday Stamp schemes used in the building industry are subject to tax in all cases. If the voucher can be exchanged for cash, the tax will generally be paid through PAYE as if it were a payment of cash.

Overnight expenses

If you stay away from home overnight on business and incur personal expenses – for example, for newspapers, telephone calls home or laundry – you can have these expenses reimbursed by your employer without the payment being taxable. The limit for non-taxable reimbursement is £5 per night for stays in the United Kingdom or £10 per night for stays elsewhere.

How tax is declared and paid on fringe benefits

If you get any taxable fringe benefits, you must enter their value on your tax return for the relevant year, even if tax has already been paid on them under PAYE. Your employer also has to make a return to the tax office with details of any fringe benefits given to you. Your employer makes the return on the form P11D, which lists the benefits and expenses for the relevant tax year. You should get a copy of this form by 6 July following the end of the tax year.

Fringe benefits may be taxed under PAYE by being offset against personal tax allowances in your PAYE code. Otherwise, tax will be collected after the end of the tax year by the issue of an assessment on the fringe benefits.

SELF ASSESSMENT

Tax may have to be paid to HM Revenue and Customs direct by Self Assessment if the full liability was not, or cannot be, met by deduction at source. This may occur with, for example:

- earnings from self-employment (you work for yourself or in a partnership)
- rental income from property
- interest received gross – for example, on National Savings investment accounts
- income from overseas
- fringe benefits received by employees and earnings of employees if an insufficient amount has been paid under PAYE.

When tax needs to be collected by Self Assessment – for example, because you are self-employed – a tax return form must be completed. You can fill in the tax return form online. You can then either ask HM Revenue and Customs to calculate the tax due based on the figures in the tax return, or calculate the amount of tax due yourself.

If you have completed a tax return, you will usually be sent a statement of account, which is like a tax bill, when the tax is due. If you asked HM Revenue and Customs to do the tax calculation, the statement of account will show the result of the calculation and how much tax is due. If you did the tax calculation yourself, you will need to enter the amount that you are due to pay on the statement of account. There are set dates in each tax year for tax due to be paid.

Who should complete a tax return

Not all taxpayers are required to fill in tax returns and they are not usually issued to people who have salaries and pensions taxed under Pay As You Earn (PAYE), since it is usually assumed that the correct amount of tax is being deducted at source.

Returns are routinely issued to taxpayers whom HM Revenue and Customs believes have:

- income from self-employment
- rental income from property
- other income that is received gross – that is, which tax has not already been deducted from, such as interest on National Savings investment accounts
- complex tax affairs – for example, higher-rate taxpayers or company directors.

Even though returns are not normally issued if you pay tax under PAYE, HM Revenue and Customs may send one to you as a way of checking that your tax affairs are in order. This is quite common after you have changed jobs, or moved from a salary to an occupational pension.

If you know that you have not paid the correct amount of tax on your income for a particular tax year, you should not wait for HM Revenue and Customs to send a tax return but should contact your local tax office. Otherwise, you may incur penalties or pay more tax than is necessary.

If you have received income on which tax is payable, and no tax return has been issued, it is your obligation to notify your tax office of the income received. This should be done in writing, and by no later than 6 October following the end of the tax year in which the income was received. If you fail to notify HM Revenue and Customs of your income, this can lead to penalties and interest on the outstanding tax. If you write to notify HM Revenue and Customs of untaxed income, you will be sent a tax return form, so it is often simpler to telephone HM Revenue and Customs for a tax return form and use this to report the income concerned.

If you believe that you have paid too much tax, you should not rely on HM Revenue and Customs to find out about this automatically. You should contact your tax office for an appropriate form to claim a refund.

HM Revenue and Customs has a legal right to demand completion of a tax return from anyone, and if a return form has been issued, the tax office will normally insist upon its completion.

Completing a tax return form

The tax return consists of a main form, which everyone who receives a tax return has to complete, and extra pages, which you have to fill in only if you have certain types of income. There is also an accompanying booklet that gives further guidance on how to fill it in.

If you do not provide all the information required on the form, this will be regarded by HM Revenue and Customs as the tax return not being completed. This would leave you liable to pay interest and possibly penalties.

You have a duty to keep records of your income and, each year, you should receive documents from your employer or pension administrator that give details of the income you have received, including any fringe benefits. You will need these records and documents to be able to complete a tax return.

Self-employed or rental income

If you have been self-employed, or are receiving rental income from property that is not within the Rent a Room scheme, details of this income will need to be reported in the appropriate supplementary pages of the tax return.

You will normally have to give details of expenses incurred in the course of running a business, or renting out property that is not within the Rent a Room scheme.

Deadline for sending back a tax return

You must send your tax return back to the local tax office by the 31 January following the end of the tax year. The tax year ends on 6 April. If you do not do so, you will automatically incur penalties. However, if you want HM Revenue and Customs to do the tax calculation, you must send the completed return back to the local tax office by the 30 September following the end of the tax year.

Errors on tax returns

If you or the tax office finds a minor error on a tax return, this can often be remedied quite simply by correspondence.

If your income was overstated, resulting in you paying more tax than is actually due, HM Revenue and Customs will repay the amount of the overpayment with the appropriate amount of interest.

If, however, there is a significant error – for example, if income was under-declared – the tax office may consider this to be grounds for opening an enquiry into the tax return.

Who can help?

HM Revenue and Customs produces a useful leaflet called 'Self Assessment – Your guide' which is available from www.hmrc.gov.uk or from the HMRC Orderline (0845 9000 404).

For general enquiries on Self Assessment, telephone your local tax office or call the Self Assessment Helpline (0845 9000 444).

INCOME TAX AND THE OVER 65s

If you are 65 or over, you are liable to pay tax in the same way as any other taxpayer but you may be able to claim higher tax allowances than a younger person.

You may have income from a number of sources that may be either taxable or tax-free:

- earnings – taxable
- an occupational pension – taxable
- a personal pension – taxable
- social security benefits (for example, Retirement Pension), Pension Credit – some benefits are taxable and some are tax-free
- savings or investments. The income from savings and investments is usually taxable. Only a few types of investment income are tax-free.

How much tax must you pay?

You have to pay income tax only on your taxable income. This is worked out for the tax year, which runs from 6 April one year to 5 April the following year. To work out your taxable income, add together your total income from all sources for the tax year concerned. Taxable income is this total less:

- any tax allowances you are entitled to
- any tax reliefs you are entitled to
- any income you have that is tax-free.

The amount left is known as taxable income and is taxed at the appropriate percentage rate.

When the tax office has assessed your tax, it will tell you how much tax you have to pay. It will do this by giving you either:

- a PAYE tax code, if you pay tax under the PAYE tax system; *or*
- a notice of assessment, if you pay tax by direct collection assessment.

Types of income and how they are taxed

The following outlines the types of income that people aged 65 or over are most likely to have and how they are taxed.

People whose only taxable income is state retirement pension

State Retirement Pension is taxable (although increases for dependent children are not) but tax on this is never deducted directly from pension payments. If your only taxable income is the basic rate State Retirement Pension (excluding graduated or additional pension), you will not pay any tax, because your allowance(s) will be more than the basic pension.

If you get basic State Retirement Pension plus graduated and/or additional pension (SERPS), but do not get any income from earnings or an occupational pension, you will pay tax directly to HM Revenue and Customs by Self Assessment, and must complete a tax return form.

People with income from Pension Credit

Pension Credit is not a taxable benefit and no tax is therefore payable on your income from Pension Credit.

People with income from an occupational or personal pension

Occupational pensions are taxable. Any tax will be deducted by your former employer under the PAYE scheme before the pension is paid. If you have other taxable income, the tax on this is also collected through the PAYE system. For example, the tax due on your state pension is collected by deducting extra tax from your occupational pension.

Personal pensions are taxable. Any tax due is deducted by the company providing the pension before the pension payment is made. If you have other taxable income, the tax due on this other income is paid directly to HM Revenue and Customs by Self Assessment. However, if you have an occupational pension or earnings from employment, the tax due on your income (other than on your personal pension) will be collected through the PAYE system.

People with earnings from employment

If you work for an employer, your earnings are taxed under the PAYE system. The tax due on your other taxable income, such as state retirement pension, is also deducted from your earnings under the PAYE system.

If you are working and getting an occupational pension, your total allowances and reliefs will be set against your occupational pension and, unless the occupational pension is too low to use up all the allowances and reliefs, no allowances will be given against your earnings. The tax code given on your notice of coding will relate to your occupational pension only. Your payslip will show a special PAYE code that is a standard second job code. This code means that you pay tax on all your earnings without any tax allowances or reliefs.

If you are working and getting an occupational pension, and also have another source of taxable income – for example, rent from a tenant or lodger – the tax due on this source of income is usually deducted from your occupational pension unless the pension is too small, in which case the tax is collected by reducing your PAYE code.

How income from savings and investments is taxed

The way that income from savings and investments is taxed and paid depends on the type of investment. You can find information on how your savings and investments are taxed earlier in this chapter.

Getting a tax rebate on retirement

When you retire, you may be entitled to a tax rebate if your income drops. If you get an occupational pension or have income from employment, there is no need to apply to the tax office for a tax rebate, as any overpaid tax will be automatically rebated through the PAYE system. If not, you can apply for a rebate. To do this, you can either:

- contact your local PAYE Enquiry Office and ask for a form on which to apply for a rebate
- write to your tax office claiming a rebate. Your former employer will be able to give you the address.

Tax allowances and relief you can claim

Tax allowances

Tax allowances are a type of tax-free income – fixed amounts of income that you can receive before you have to pay tax. Everyone is automatically given a personal allowance but, at 65, you may be entitled to a higher allowance depending on your income.

You may also be able to claim a married couple's allowance. The amount you get depends on your ages (either partner needs to have been born before 6 April 1935) and:

- for couples who married before 5 December 2005, the husband's total income; *or*
- for people who got married or became civil partners on or after 5 December 2005, the total income of the spouse or civil partner with the higher income.

A blind person can also claim a blind person's allowance.

Married couple's allowance

To claim married couple's allowance, you must be married (or in a civil partnership) and living together. Also, at least one of you must have been born before 6 April 1935. You will be treated as living together unless you are separated by a court order or separation deed, or have separated in such circumstances that the separation is likely to be permanent.

Tax relief

Tax relief is given on certain outgoings – for example, on property that is let out. In practice this means that you will not pay tax on the amount of income you spend on these items.

WHO CAN HELP?

If you have a tax problem and are an employee, you may be able to resolve it by talking to your employer. Your employer will have guidance on how to operate the PAYE tax system and deal with problems.

If the problem cannot be resolved by talking to your employer, or you are not working, you should first contact:

- a tax enquiry centre
- the tax office that holds your records.

If the problem remains unresolved, you may wish to:

- challenge or negotiate with HM Revenue and Customs – see p. 600
- complain to the Adjudicator's Office – see p. 600
- complain to the Parliamentary Ombudsman – see p. 601
- contact TaxAid or TaxHelp for Older People for help – see p. 601.

Tax enquiry centres

Tax enquiry centres are local tax offices that can help with income tax problems. The centres can help with general enquiries – for example, whether you can claim certain allowances or reliefs – and with specific problems relating to your tax records. Most tax enquiry centres are open to the public and deal with written or telephone enquiries.

Tax enquiry centres are either listed in the local telephone directory under 'HM Revenue and Customs', or details of them will be available from local Inspectors of Taxes' offices or on the HMRC website (www.hmrc.gov.uk).

Tax offices

Each employer has a tax office that holds the tax records for everyone who works for that employer. The tax office may be some distance from where you work.

Your empoloyer must give you the name and address of your tax office, your tax reference number and your National Insurance number if you ask for these details. They should also be on your P45 and P60.

When you contact the tax office, you must quote your National Insurance number and your tax reference number.

Most tax offices only deal with written or telephone enquiries and are not open to the public.

CHALLENGING AND NEGOTIATING WITH HM REVENUE AND CUSTOMS

You may wish to challenge a decision or negotiate with HM Revenue and Customs. The procedure to follow, and the office concerned, will differ according to the type of challenge or dispute.

Some of the main procedures are:

- appealing – for example, against a calculation of tax liability or a PAYE code
- seeking a waiver, because of HM Revenue and Customs delays
- negotiating tax debts
- complaining about HM Revenue and Customs conduct.

The Adjudicator's Office

The Adjudicator considers complaints of HM Revenue and Customs maladministration, for example:

- excessive delay
- errors
- discourtesy.

The Adjudicator will not consider:

- legal disputes
- complaints that have already been investigated by the Parliamentary Ombudsman – see below
- appeals against property valuations, including appeals against council tax bandings – these should be referred to valuation tribunals
- matters relating to a criminal prosecution during the course of legal proceedings.

A complaint should not usually be referred to the Adjudicator until you have given HM Revenue and Customs a chance to remedy matters. However, in urgent cases the Adjudicator may offer immediate help without you approaching HM Revenue and Customs first – for example, if there is a risk that any delay might cause irreparable damage. If you do contact the Adjudicator's Office directly (020 7930 2292; www.adjudicatorsoffice.gov.uk), you will be guided through the necessary procedures.

The Parliamentary Ombudsman

The Parliamentary Ombudsman may be able to help with complaints against HM Revenue and Customs if, for example, there has been avoidable delay, failure to give appropriate advice or failure to follow proper procedures. The Ombudsman cannot investigate complaints about government policy or about tax legislation.

If you want to complain to the Parliamentary Ombudsman, you must first contact your MP and ask for the matter to be referred. For more details, see p. 483.

TaxAid

TaxAid (0845 120 3779; www.taxaid.org.uk) provides a free and independent tax service offering advice, assistance and advocacy to people needing help with tax. It covers subjects such as tax allowances, PAYE codes, tax arrears, self-employment, tax returns and HM Revenue and Customs administration and complaints. The service is intended for people who cannot afford to employ an accountant. Advice can be given over the telephone and interviews may be arranged.

TaxHelp for Older People

If you are over 60 and on a low income and you have a tax query, you can contact TaxHelp for Older People (0845 601 3321; www.litrg.org.uk).

COUNCIL TAX

Council tax is a system of local taxation collected by local authorities. It is a tax on domestic property. Generally, the bigger the property is, the more tax will be charged. Some property will be exempt from council tax.

Valuation bands

Each local authority keeps a list of all the domestic property in its area. This is called the valuation list. Each property is valued and put into a valuation band. A different amount of council tax is then charged on each band. The valuation bands are:

In England

Valuation band	Range of values
A	Up to £40,000
B	Over £40,000 and up to £52,000
C	Over £52,000 and up to £68,000
D	Over £68,000 and up to £88,000
E	Over £88,000 and up to £120,000
F	Over £120,000 and up to £160,000
G	Over £160,000 and up to £320,000
H	Over £320,000

In Wales

Valuation band	Range of values
A	Up to £44,000
B	Over £44,000 and up to £65,000
C	Over £65,000 and up to £91,000
D	Over £91,000 and up to £123,000
E	Over £123,000 and up to £162,000
F	Over £162,000 and up to £223,000
G	Over £223,000 and up to £324,000
H	Over £324,000 and up to £424,000
I	Over £424,000

To find out what band a dwelling is in you can:

- inspect a copy of the valuation list
- look at the council tax banding lists published on the internet by the Valuation Office Agency (www.voa.gov.uk)
- check with your local authority before you get a council tax bill
- if you are the liable person, you can also find the valuation band from the council tax bill or from an alteration to the valuation list by the listing officer.

A copy of the valuation list is kept at the local authority's main offices and is available for public inspection. Local authorities may also make the list available in other offices, including libraries. You can look at and make copies of the valuation list at the local authority's office or at the local valuation office. There may be a small charge.

If an alteration is made to the valuation list, including adding a new dwelling to the list, the listing officer will inform the liable person.

Properties exempt from council tax

Some property is exempt from council tax altogether. It may be exempt for only a short period, for example six months, or indefinitely.

Properties that may be exempt are:

- empty property. It has to be unoccupied and substantially unfurnished. The exemption applies for a maximum of six months and the property has to be vacant for the whole of this period (although up to six weeks of occupation during the period is allowed)
- property which is vacant because it needs major repairs or alterations to make it habitable. The exemption applies for a maximum of 12 months whether the work is actually finished or not by then
- condemned property
- property that has been repossessed by a mortgage lender
- property unoccupied because the person who lived there now lives elsewhere because they need to be cared for – for example, in hospital, in a care home or with relatives
- property that is unoccupied because the person who lived there has gone to care for someone else
- any property that only students live in – this may be a hall of residence or a house
- a caravan or boat which is used as a main residence but which is unoccupied.

This exemption lasts for up to six months. A holiday caravan or boat is exempt if it is on a property where council tax is paid
- a property where all the people who live in it are aged under 18
- a property where all the people who live in it are either severely mentally impaired or are students or where there is a mixture of both
- a self-contained 'granny flat' where the person who lives in it is a dependent relative of the owner of the main property.

Who has to pay?

Usually one person, called the liable person, is liable to pay council tax. Nobody under the age of 18 can be a liable person. A couple living together will both be liable, even if there is only one name on the bill. This applies whether they are married, civil partners or cohabiting.

Usually, the person living in a property will be the liable person, but sometimes it will be the owner of the property who will be liable to pay.

The owner will always be liable if:

- the property is in multiple occupation – for example, a house shared by a number of different households who all pay rent separately; *or*
- the people who live in the property are all under the age of 18; *or*
- the people who live in the property are all asylum seekers who are not entitled to claim benefits, including Council Tax Benefit; *or*
- the people who are staying in the property have their main homes somewhere else; *or*
- the property is a care home, hospital, hostel or women's refuge.

If only one person lives in a property, they will be the liable person. If more than one person lives there, a system called the hierarchy of liability is used to work out who is the liable person. The person at the top, or nearest to the top, of the hierarchy is the liable person. Two people at the same point of the hierarchy will both be liable.

The hierarchy of liability in England and Wales is:
1. a resident owner-occupier who owns either the leasehold or freehold of all or part of the property
2. a resident tenant
3. a resident who lives in the property and who is a licensee. This means that they are not a tenant, but have permission to stay there
4. any resident living in the property, for example, a squatter
5. an owner of the property where no one is resident.

How much is it?

Each year, every local authority will set a rate of council tax for each valuation band. Not everyone will have to pay the full amount of council tax. There are three ways in which your council tax bill may be reduced. These are:

- the reduction scheme for disabled people
- discounts
- Council Tax Benefit (CTB) and second adult rebate.

Reduction scheme for people with disabilities

If there is someone (adult or child) living in a household who is substantially and permanently disabled, the council tax bill for the property may be reduced. The reduction is made by charging council tax on a lower valuation band than the one the property is in. For example, if the property is in band D, the council tax bill will be worked out as if it were in band C. There is also a reduction if the property is in band A.

To claim a reduction, you must show that a disabled person lives in the property and also that the property has at least one of the following:

- an extra kitchen or bathroom to meet the needs of a disabled person
- any other room (except a toilet) which is mainly used by a disabled person to meet their needs
- enough indoor space for a disabled person to use their wheelchair.

An application for this reduction must be made in writing to the local authority. Many local authorities will have a special application form. Some will ask for supporting evidence, such as a doctor's letter.

Discounts

If only one person lives in a property, they will get a 25 per cent discount on the council tax bill. When working out how many people live in a property, some people are not counted. These are called disregarded people. If everyone who lives in the property is disregarded, there will still be a council tax bill, but there will be a 50 per cent discount. Examples of people who are disregarded are:

- children aged under 16

- people aged 17 or under
- young people aged 16–20 (and occasionally over) if Child Benefit is payable for them
- people living in the property temporarily and for whom this is not their normal home
- prisoners or people in detention awaiting deportation or under mental health legislation
- people who are severely mentally impaired
- full-time students on a qualifying course of education, including student nurses
- a spouse, civil partner or a dependant of a student who is a non-British citizen and who is not allowed under immigration rules either to work in the UK or to claim benefit
- young people on government training schemes and some apprentices
- long-term hospital patients and care home residents
- someone living in a hostel which provides care or treatment because of a person's old age, physical or mental disability, past or present alcohol or drug dependence, or past or present mental illness or in a bail or probation hostel
- care workers and some live-in carers
- someone staying in a hostel or night shelter – for example, in a Salvation Army or Church Army hostel
- members of a religious community
- members of visiting armed forces and their dependants.

A local authority may automatically send a council tax bill that includes a discount. The discount will be shown on the bill.

If you believe that you are entitled to a discount and your bill does not show that you have had one, you should apply to the local authority for a discount as soon as possible.

If the bill shows that the local authority has applied a discount and you do not think that you should have one, you must tell the local authority within 21 days. If you do not do this, the local authority may later impose a penalty.

Holiday homes

Second or holiday homes in England will be liable for council tax but will have a 10–50 per cent discount because no one lives there. In Wales, local authorities can reduce or end the discount in a second home.

Council Tax Benefit and second adult rebate

A person who is liable to pay council tax may be able to claim Council Tax Benefit. The amount of benefit they may get will depend on their income and capital.

If you have someone living with you who is not liable to pay council tax on your property, you may be able to claim a benefit called a 'second adult rebate'. You will not be able to claim a second adult rebate as well as Council Tax Benefit. If you are entitled to both, you will receive whichever is the higher.

How to pay

Council tax bills should be sent out in April. You have the right to pay by ten instalments. Local authorities may accept weekly or fortnightly payments. Some may also offer a reduction in the total bill if it is paid all at once, at the beginning of the year.

Arrears

In England, when you have not paid an instalment of council tax on the date it is due, your local authority must issue a reminder, asking for payment within seven days. If you fail to pay within this period, you lose the right to pay by instalments and a full year's council tax becomes payable. If you do not pay this within the next seven days, your local authority can ask the magistrates to issue a liability order.

If your local authority issues you with three reminders for late payment of instalments within the same financial year, you will also lose the right to pay by instalments. A full year's council tax becomes payable when the third reminder is issued. However, in practice, your local authority may continue to accept payment by instalments, as long as they are paid on time.

In Wales, if you do not pay an instalment of council tax within 28 days of the date it is due, and have been late with two instalments previously, you lose the right to pay by instalments and become liable to pay the full amount immediately. In practice, most local authorities will still accept payments by instalments.

When you have not paid an instalment of council tax within 28 days of the date it is due, the local authority may ask a magistrates' court to issue a court summons for the arrears. If these are not paid by the date of the court summons, the local authority can ask the magistrates to issue a liability order.

A liability order allows a local authority to make arrangements for the arrears to be paid by deductions from your Income Support, Jobseeker's Allowance or wages, or for bailiffs to seize your goods to the value of the amount owed. Alternatively, you could be sent to prison by the magistrates' court if you do not pay.

Appeals

Appeals can be made about a range of issues concerning council tax. An appeal must be made to either the valuation office or the local authority, depending on what it is about.

Appeals can be made to the valuation office about:

- whether or not the property should be on the valuation list
- which valuation band the property is in
- in a property which is partly domestic and partly business, what proportion of the property is domestic.

Appeals can be made to the local authority about:

- whether or not someone is a liable person – this includes someone who is jointly liable because there are two or more people on the same level of the hierarchy or because they are one of a couple
- whether or not the property is exempt
- whether or not a discount applies and how much it is
- whether or not the reduction scheme for people with disabilities applies.

Appeals cannot be made about the level of council tax set or the valuation bands for the area.

You can appeal against a decision of the valuation office if you are:

- the owner of the property
- the liable person, including a person who is jointly liable – there are special rules about when a liable person can appeal about the valuation band of a dwelling
- the person who would be liable if the property was not exempt
- the local authority.

The following people can appeal against a decision of the local authority:

- a liable person, including a person who is jointly liable

- an aggrieved person. This is a person who is directly affected by the decision, for example the administrator of the estate of a liable person who has died.

People who wish to appeal must have moved into the property less than six months before the date of their appeal, or be in a new property that has recently been added to the valuation list.

Appeals to alter the valuation band of a dwelling

The valuation list may be altered to place a dwelling in a different valuation band if:

- there was an error when the list was compiled
- the dwelling was valued incorrectly – for example, because the valuation officer did not know about internal features of the dwelling that reduced its value
- in a dwelling that is partly domestic and partly business, the domestic proportion has increased or decreased, or the dwelling has become wholly domestic or wholly business
- there have been changes to the dwelling that have reduced its value
- there have been changes to the dwelling that have increased its value and the dwelling has subsequently been sold.

There are special rules about when a liable person can appeal regarding the valuation band a dwelling has been put in – see below.

If the person liable for a dwelling changes, the new liable person(s) will have six months from the date they become liable to make a proposal to change the valuation band. So, for example, if you become the liable person on 13 July 2008, you will have six months from 13 July 2008 to make a proposal to change the list. This is provided that your grounds for the proposal have not already been considered and rejected by a valuation tribunal or the High Court.

If a dwelling has recently been added to the valuation list, the liable person has six months from the date they become the liable person to make a proposal to change the list. In practice this means six months from the date the dwelling goes on to the valuation list.

Appealing to the valuation office

In order to appeal you must first make a proposal to the valuation office saying what you think should be changed and why. If the valuation office does not agree to the changes, the proposal automatically becomes an appeal and is heard by a valuation tribunal.

Properties can only be put in a different band under certain circumstances – for example, if something has happened to reduce the value of the property significantly.

Appealing to the local authority

The first stage of an appeal to the local authority involves making a written complaint about the problem to the local authority. If the local authority does not resolve the problem, an appeal can then be made to the valuation tribunal.

The valuation tribunal

In all cases the valuation tribunal will consider all the information about the particular case and will decide what should happen. They may decide on the basis of written representations or may call everyone involved to a meeting to hear their evidence.

Particular circumstances

There are particular points to remember in the following circumstances:

- if you live permanently in a hotel, you will not be liable for council tax on the property although the hotel charges would probably include an amount towards any council tax payable
- if you have more than one home, you will probably pay a reduced council tax on your second home (if no one lives there) and a full council tax on your main home
- if you live permanently in a caravan or mobile home, you will have to pay council tax. If you have a holiday caravan which you let out as a business, you will have to pay business rates, not council tax. You do not have to pay council tax for a movable caravan kept for holidays
- if you are a full-time student in advanced education, you will have to pay council tax if you are the liable person for a property. However, if all the people living in the property are students, no council tax will be payable, and if some of the residents are students, the council tax may be reduced.

2

Credit and Debt

CONTENTS

INTRODUCTION

Years ago, the motto was 'never a borrower or a lender be' and debt was shrouded in shame. Debtors' prisons, like the Marshalsea in South London where Charles Dickens's father was imprisoned in 1824, may no longer exist, but unmanageable debt is still an invisible prison for those unable to escape from it. Low rates of unemployment, low interest rates and soaring house prices in recent years have resulted in a substantial increase in mortgage and consumer credit lending, now standing at over £1.1 trillion.

The credit landscape has undergone dramatic changes in the last 30 years and there are now more than 31 million credit and charge card holders, an increase of over 14 million in the last ten years.

Credit is available at every turn. Offers of loans and credit cards drop unsolicited on to our doormats and opportunities to buy more stuff 'on credit' are offered to us in most high street stores. But, according to the Financial Services Authority, two in three people feel that financial matters are too complicated for them and the underside of the credit boom is the rise in the number of people sliding from handling credit into tackling debt. Citizens Advice Bureaux gave advice on 1.7 million debt problems in 2006/07 to over half a million people – an increase of 27 per cent in just four years. All in all, it has never been a better time to get your head around your money matters and a grip on your finances.

In this chapter, we cover what to look out for when taking out credit, what to do if you are getting into debt and who can help.

JARGON BUSTER

AER   stands for Annual Equivalent Rate. This shows what the interest rate would be if the interest on savings were paid and added to savings at the end of each year. The higher the AER the better the return is on your savings

APR the Annual Percentage Rate of the total charge for credit. This tells you the cost of a loan, taking into account the interest you pay, any other charges, and when the payments fall due. A loan with an APR of 15 per cent is more expensive than one with an APR of 11 per cent

basic bank account a type of bank or building society account for people who may have difficulty in opening a standard current account, or who have a current account that is overdrawn. There is no risk of going overdrawn and running up overdraft charges

CCJ stands for County Court Judgment. This is an order made by a county court judge to deal with debt. CCJs are usually registered and credit reference agencies will note them on someone's credit file

compound interest this is the type of interest usually paid on a savings account. It is calculated by adding together the amount you have paid into your account (the capital) with the interest paid on it. This is also the type of interest you pay on money you borrow – so the amount you owe can increase quite dramatically over quite a short period of time

consolidation loan a loan that combines (consolidates) all your outstanding credit cards, housing arrears, loan repayments and household bills into one monthly payment

credit reference agency (CRA) allows creditors to share credit-related information, such as electoral roll entries, to help them lend responsibly

credit repair companies companies offering, for a charge, to advise on how, for example, to erase bad credit from your credit record. Credit repair companies have no special powers to do anything that you couldn't do yourself

credit report the information stored about you with a credit reference agency. It will include electoral roll information for your address, how you have handled credit in the last six years and a record

	of credit checks made about you with that agency
debt management plan (DMP)	a debt management plan is a way of deciding how to repay all your non-priority creditors after giving consideration to your priority payments such as mortgage and fuel bills
financial adviser	an individual or firm that can assess your financial needs, recommend suitable products, and arrange for you to buy or invest in these products
hire purchase agreement	a form of credit agreement which allows you to pay for goods in instalments
interest rate	the percentage that is paid on savings or loans. A savings account that was offering 8 per cent would give you a better return than one which was offering 5 per cent. Similarly, borrowing money at 22.5 per cent is going to cost more than borrowing at 18 per cent
investment	financial products that typically involve some risk of losing your original money but give you the opportunity of better returns than you can get from savings – for example, stock market-based investments, such as bonds, shares, trusts and so on
ISA	means Individual Savings Account. You do not have to pay tax on the gains or income from an ISA
non-priority debts	non-priority debts are those where non-payment will not result in the loss of the debtor's home, liberty, essential goods or services
priority debts	these are debts that carry the strongest penalties if payment is not made – for example, eviction from your home, disconnection of gas or electricity, or imprisonment for non-payment of court fines or council tax
re-financing	negotiating a new loan to pay off an existing loan or loans
risk	refers to the risk of losing money through savings or investments. Generally, the higher the potential rate of return on your investment or savings, the greater the risk
secured loan	money borrowed from a lender, using your

	property as an extra guarantee of repayment. If the amount is not paid in full, the lender may repossess and sell the property
stakeholder	a type of pension scheme designed to be good value for money by having low charges and flexible payments
sub-prime lenders (non-status or impaired credit lending)	lenders willing to make loans to people who are unable to obtain credit from mainstream lenders, such as high street banks or building societies, because of a poor credit record. Interest rates may be higher than if you get a loan from a mainstream lender
tax credits	means-tested allowances administered by HM Revenue and Customs
unsecured loan	money borrowed from, for example a bank that is not secured against your home. The lender may only sue for payment if you default on the loan.

CREDIT

'Annual income twenty pounds, annual expenditure nineteen nineteen six, result happiness. Annual income twenty pounds, annual expenditure twenty pounds nought and six, result misery.' Mr Micawber, *David Copperfield*.

If your account is in credit, you have money available to spend. If you obtain goods or services 'on credit', it means that someone, such as a bank or credit institution, has given you the money to make a purchase. The money has been credited to you on a temporary basis, and you must pay it back.

What the law says

Anyone who offers credit must be licensed by the Office of Fair Trading.

There are laws which give you consumer protection if you take out a credit agreement for £25,000 or less. These agreements are called regulated agreements. The rules will change in April 2008 – after that, the financial limit of £25,000 will be removed and all new consumer credit agreements will be regulated, unless they fall into the list of exemptions. The most common exemption will be mortgages, which are regulated by the Financial Services Authority.

If you have a regulated agreement, you are entitled to:

- have specific information included in your agreement, such as the amount you are borrowing, the length of the agreement, interest rates, any charges, the amount and frequency of payments, and your cancellation rights. It must also include the total charge for credit and the Annual Percentage Rate (APR), which is the annual cost of credit after interest and all other charges have been added together. If this information is not included, the agreement may be unenforceable
- be given a copy of the agreement, which is not binding until signed by both you and the creditor
- be sent a statement or copy of other documents on request. You may have to pay a small amount
- be informed of the procedures that the creditor must follow – for example, they must send you a default notice before taking court action.

Your agreement will state under its heading whether it is a regulated agreement. If you want to check whether your loan is regulated, you could also contact an experienced debt adviser.

Buying on credit

Before applying for credit, you should work out your regular outgoings to be sure you can afford the extra payments each month.

The following steps will help you find the best deal:

- shop around, to see whether you can buy the goods or service cheaper elsewhere, as this will reduce the amount you have to borrow
- compare the cost of different types of credit by looking at both the APR and the length of the agreement. A fixed-interest loan that you arrange yourself may be cheaper than arranging a loan through the supplier. If you are using your credit card, try to estimate how long it will take you to repay the money, taking the monthly interest charges into account
- you may be tempted by interest-free or other special deals. Look at the total cost of the deal – you may be able to buy the goods cheaper elsewhere. If interest-free credit is offered for a limited period, make sure you check what happens if you don't finish paying during this period. Often there is a high rate of interest payable from the beginning of the agreement
- ask for a written quotation before you sign anything and read it thoroughly at home
- if you are offered insurance to cover your payments in certain circumstances, check the cover is right for you and that you do not fall into one of the

excluded groups. Some policies exclude, for example, self-employed people or pregnant women. Ask yourself whether you can find cheaper or more inclusive cover elsewhere

- do not take out a loan secured on your home without considering the consequences. If your circumstances change and you are unable to keep up your monthly instalments, you could lose your home.

Equal liability

If you use your credit card, or if the seller arranged finance for you, the finance company in a regulated agreement is equally liable for the supplier's breach of contract, providing the purchase price was over £100 and under £30,000. This means that you may claim against the credit company, the supplier, or both jointly. If you arrange your own credit, such as a bank loan, the bank will not be liable for problems with the goods or services. The principle of equal liability is especially useful if the supplier has gone out of business. The Court of Appeal has ruled that credit card companies have equal liability for purchases made abroad. If your credit card company denies liability, Consumer Direct (0845 404 0506) may be able to help.

Cancellation of a regulated credit agreement

Cancellation by you

In certain circumstances, you have the right to cancel a credit agreement if:

- you have signed the credit agreement recently; *and*
- you have talked to the seller about the deal face to face (rather than only on the telephone); *and*
- you did not sign the agreement on the seller's business premises; *and*
- the goods have been delivered and it is still possible to return them to the seller in their original state. You will not be able to cancel if the goods are perishable. If you have allowed the seller to install goods (for example, double glazing), you would be able to cancel the credit, but would still be liable to pay the cash price.

In such circumstances, it is essential that you act quickly and notify the creditor immediately in writing that you wish to cancel. When you sign an agreement, you must be given a copy containing cancellation rights and details of how you would exercise these rights. These rights will only last a short length of time.

The *cooling-off period* runs from the date you signed the agreement and ends five days after you received the notice of your cancellation rights. If you have not been given notice of your cancellation rights, the agreement is unenforceable. Keep copies of any correspondence you send and proof of postage.

Even if the above rules do not apply, you may still have the right to withdraw from the deal if the creditor has not yet signed their part of the agreement. In these circumstances, you should telephone the creditor immediately to establish whether they have signed their agreement and, if not, inform them you wish to cancel. Make a note of what is said and the name of the person you speak to. You should then confirm this in a letter. Make a copy of your letter and send it by recorded delivery.

Once you have signed a credit agreement and any cooling-off period has ended, any rights you may have to cancel your agreement will be included in your contract and will depend on the type of credit you took out:

- credit card agreements can be cancelled by writing to the creditor, enclosing the card(s) cut in pieces and making arrangements to repay any money you owe. If there is a second card on your account held by someone else, this should also be returned
- hire purchase or conditional sale agreements can be terminated at any time by giving notice that you wish to return the goods and cancel the agreement. This may be an expensive option, as you will be liable for half the total amount payable under the agreement as well as any arrears outstanding and compensation if any damage has been caused to the item. Once you have paid a third of the total amount payable under the agreement, the credit company cannot repossess the goods without a court order. Repossession without a court order in these circumstances cancels the agreement, so you can recover all the payments you have made.

Cancellation by the credit company

If you are in breach of your credit agreement (for example, if you are behind in your payments), the creditor must send you a *default notice* before they can take certain types of action against you. This notice must specify the breach, tell you how to remedy it, what action will be taken if you don't and give you a time limit to put the matter right. If you fail to act on this notice, the creditor may be entitled to terminate the agreement, demand early payment of the sum owing, or repossess goods.

Being refused credit

You cannot insist on being given credit. Most creditors use credit reference agencies and credit scoring to decide whether to give credit. Creditors do not have to give reasons for refusing to give you credit, although the codes of practice they follow suggest you should be given the main reason for any refusal.

If your application for credit has been refused and there is a dispute about an entry on your credit reference file, you can complain to the Office of the Information Commissioner (www.ico.gov.uk).

Credit reference agencies

There are three credit reference agencies, Callcredit (0870 060 1414; www.callcredit.co.uk.), Equifax (0870 010 0583; www.equifax.co.uk) and Experian (0870 241 6212; www.experian.co.uk). They collect and store information on everyone's financial situation. Agency records are not a 'black-list'. Credit reference agencies provide factual information to lenders, for example banks, building societies, finance houses and major retailers. The lender uses the information provided by the credit reference agency, together with the information given by you on an application for credit, to decide whether or not to grant credit. Information held includes details of county court and High Court judgments, bankruptcy, any property repossessed, any other credit accounts you have and a record of everyone who has requested a credit check on your file. The agencies do not hold detailed information about your bank and building society accounts. No details are held about magistrates' court nor about liability orders for council tax arrears. Credit information is usually held for six years.

You can check the information held by the credit reference companies by writing to them asking for a copy. Alternatively, you may be able to apply online via the website. A small fee is payable. You can ask that incorrect information be corrected, but cannot ask that correct information be removed.

Credit repair agencies
Beware of companies that promise to repair your credit record for a fee. They have no special powers to do anything you could not do yourself.

Credit scoring

Credit scoring is a system used by most lenders to decide whether credit should be offered. Points are awarded for such things as your age, occupation, marital status and whether you own your own home. If you have been refused credit, you can ask the lender to review the decision and you could provide any additional information you think would be relevant.

BASIC DO-IT-YOURSELF DEBT ADVICE

Many people fall into debt at some point in their lives, often through no fault of their own. The information and suggestions given in this section will help you to deal with your debts and remove the pressures of being in debt. The following steps will help you regain control of your finances:

Step One – make a list of your debts
Step Two – work out your budget
Step Three – sort out your priority debts
Step Four – sort out your non-priority debts.

Step One – make a list of your debts

Before you can tackle a debt problem, you need to collect together information about your money affairs. Make a list of all the people and companies you owe money to (your *creditors*). You will need the following information for each debt:

- the name and address of the creditor
- the account or reference number
- the amount you owe.

It is a good idea to keep the latest letter or statement for each debt together in one place so that you can easily find them if you need them. If you have received any court papers or letters giving you notice of court action, you may need to act quickly. If you are not sure from the papers what you should do next, get advice immediately from an experienced adviser.

Once you have made a list of all your creditors, you need to work out which ones to deal with first. You need to deal with some debts first before others because the consequences of not paying these debts can be more serious than for other debts. The debts you deal with first are called *priority debts.* The debts you deal with after your priority debts are called *non-priority debts.*

Priority debts

Priority debts include:

- mortgage or rent arrears. If you do not pay these, you could lose your home
- fuel arrears. If you do not pay these, you could have your fuel supply disconnected
- council tax arrears. If you don't pay these, a court can use bailiffs to take your goods away. If, after this, you still have arrears unpaid, you can be sent to prison
- court fines such as magistrates' court fines for traffic offences. If you do not pay these, the court can use bailiffs to take your goods. If, after this, you still have arrears unpaid, you can be sent to prison
- arrears of maintenance payable to an ex-partner or children. This includes Child Support you owe to the Child Support Agency. If you do not pay these, a court can use bailiffs to take your goods. If, after this, you still have arrears unpaid, you can be sent to prison
- income tax or VAT arrears. You can be sent to prison for non-payment of income tax or VAT.

Non-priority debts

Non-priority debts include:

- benefits overpayments
- credit debts such as overdrafts, loans, hire purchase, credit card accounts and catalogues
- student loans
- money borrowed from friends or family.

You cannot be sent to prison for not paying non-priority debts. But if you do not make any offers to pay, without explaining why, your creditors may take you to court. If you still fail to pay when the court has ordered it, your creditors can take further action. For example, they could get another court order which allows them to send bailiffs round to take your property away. This will be sold to cover your debts.

Step Two – work out your budget

List all the income and expenses for your household. Be honest and make sure that the amounts are realistic. You can use the budget sheet on p. 631 to help you make this list.

Under income, include:

- wages or salaries for your partner and yourself. Put in your net earnings – that is, after deductions. This should be the amount you regularly receive
- any benefits you are paid, including Child Benefit and tax credits
- maintenance from an ex-partner for you or your children. Include any Child Support from the Child Support Agency
- contributions from other members of your family and any lodgers.

Think about the ways in which you might earn extra money or increase your income. You may be able to claim benefits or tax credits.

Under expenses, include:

- housekeeping. Include realistic amounts for what you spend on things like food, toiletries, cleaning materials and cigarettes
- housing costs. This should include mortgage or rent, a second mortgage or secured loan, buildings and contents insurance, service charges, and life or endowment insurance cover attached to your mortgage
- council tax
- fuel and water charges
- telephone charges
- travel expenses. Include both public transport and the costs of running a car, such as road tax, insurance and maintenance
- insurance that is not part of your housing costs (see above)
- childcare costs
- TV licence and any TV rental costs
- clothes
- any other essential expenses, such as medical and dental expenses or support for an elderly relative
- money you should set aside for unexpected events and contingencies. This includes saving for things such as the replacement of essential household goods when they break down.

When you have added up all the figures, you will see if you have any money left over to pay your debts. You may even be able to see if you can make some savings. An advice agency can help you draw up a budget and help you increase your income if this is possible.

Step Three – sort out your priority debts

Do not ignore letters or phone calls from your priority creditors. Get in touch with them as early as possible and explain to them why you are in debt. If you phone, you should follow up the call with a letter, confirming what you said on the phone. Keep copies of any letters you write to them.

If your priority creditors are threatening to take court action or have started to take court action against you and you need a little time to sort out your finances, send them a holding letter explaining your problems. Say that you will contact them again within two or three weeks. Ask them not to take any further action during this time.

When you have worked out how much you have left over after paying your expenses, contact each of your priority creditors and try to make an arrangement to pay back what you owe. For example, you may be able to pay an extra bit each month until the arrears are cleared. Or you may not have any extra money at the moment but know you will have a lump sum in three months' time which will clear the debt completely.

If you cannot afford to pay anything to your priority creditors and your situation is not likely to get better, the outcome may be very serious. Get advice straight away.

Step Four – sort out your non-priority debts

After dealing with your priority debts, you will need to work out how to deal with your non-priority debts. This will depend on whether you have any money left over from dealing with your priority debts and paying for essential household expenses.

If you have money to spare

If you have money to spare, you may have several options for dealing with your non-priority debts.

You should weigh up the advantages and disadvantages of each of these options carefully. Get as much information as you can before making a decision and do not sign anything until you are sure it is the best option for you. If you have any questions, get advice.

You may have the option of:

- making offers to creditors yourself
- asking a debt management company to make offers for you

- applying for a court order that allows you to pay only a proportion of the debt. This is called an administration order
- arranging a legal agreement with your creditors. This is called an Individual Voluntary Arrangement (IVA)
- putting all your debts into one loan. This is called *loan consolidation.*

If you have no money to spare

If you have little or no money left after you have done your budget, you have nothing of value to sell and you think your circumstances are unlikely to get better soon, you will have limited options for dealing with your non-priority debts. The options you will have are:

- asking your creditors to write off your debt
- applying for bankruptcy.

Making offers to creditors yourself

Any money you have left over after paying your expenses and your priority creditors is called your *available income.* You can use this to pay off your non-priority creditors.

You should share out your available income fairly between all your non-priority creditors. This means you should offer each creditor a percentage of your available income, based on the amount you owe them. These offers are called pro-rata offers.

To work out your pro-rata offers, first of all multiply each individual debt by your available income. Then divide this sum by the total amount you owe to all of your non-priority creditors.

Example:
You have total debts of £15,000. You have available income of £200 a month. You owe £10,000 to credit card company A and £5,000 to credit card company B.

Credit company A

Multiply £10,000 (debt to company A) by £200 (your available income). This equals £2,000,000.

Divide this by £15,000 (your total debt). This gives you the sum of £133 per month to offer to company A.

Credit company B

Multiply £5,000 (debt to company B) by £200 (your available income). This equals £1,000,000.

Divide this by £15,000 (your total debt). This gives you the sum of £66 per month to offer company B.

This is the system used by the courts for working out what you can reasonably afford to pay and it is accepted by most creditors.

You will need to write to each creditor. Send them a copy of your personal budget and a list of your other creditors to show them how you have worked out your offers. Make sure you keep a copy of everything you send to your creditors.

Creditors do not have to accept your offers but usually they will accept them if the amount you offer is fair. Creditors often want to look at your offer again after a fixed time – for example, six months – to see if your situation has improved.

If creditors do not agree to your offer and you cannot persuade them, they may take further action.

Debt management plans

If you have enough money left over after paying your priority creditors and essential expenses, you may be able to arrange a debt management plan.

A debt management plan is an arrangement with your creditors to pay back the debt by regular instalments. Instead of you speaking to your creditors yourself to arrange the plan, a debt management company (DMC) does it for you. Usually you have to pay for this service, although there are some DMCs who will do this for free.

The advantages of using a DMC are that:

- you make only one payment direct to the DMC. They divide the payment fairly between all your creditors
- you do not have to contact your creditors yourself, the DMC will do this for you.

However, there are also disadvantages to using a DMC:

- most DMCs charge an upfront fee which can be quite high and most DMCs also charge an administration fee to the customer each month. This leaves you with less money to pay off your debts

- DMCs only deal with non-priority debts and you will have to deal with the more important priority debts yourself
- most DMCs do not give benefits advice or financial advice so you may lose out on important information about your finances.

If you do use a DMC, check the agreement carefully before signing anything. Check:

- whether you can cancel at any time if you are not happy with the service
- what the fees are
- whether you will get your fee back if you cancel
- which creditors the DMC will deal with and which creditors you still need to deal with.

Administration orders

If you have enough money left over after paying your priority creditors and essential expenses, you may be able to apply to the county court to have all your non-priority debts put together into one affordable monthly payment. This is called an administration order.

You can apply for an administration order if your total debts are less than £5,000 and you have a county court judgment (CCJ) against you. The court decides what is a fair amount, depending on your income. The court can agree that you write off part of the total debt. This is called a composition order.

Once the order is agreed by the court, you make one regular payment to the court and your creditors cannot take any further action to get the money back, as long as you keep to the payments.

You can get an administration order application form from your local county court. You don't have to pay a fee to apply for an administration order. The court will take off an administration fee every time you make a payment.

Individual Voluntary Arrangements (IVAs)

If you have enough money left over after paying your priority creditors and essential expenses, you may be able to arrange an Individual Voluntary Arrangement (IVA). An IVA is a legal agreement with creditors (usually non-priority creditors) to repay your debts. This could be either in part or in full. The arrangement is negotiated, written up and checked regularly by an independent solicitor or accountant called an insolvency practitioner. Not all the creditors have to agree to an IVA as long as the creditors to whom you owe 75 per cent of your debt agree.

Putting all your debts into one loan – consolidation

If you have enough money left over after paying your priority creditors and your essential expenses, you could think about taking out a loan to pay off your non-priority debts. This is called a *consolidation loan*. You can use a consolidation loan to pay off things like credit card debts and loans.

It is usually not a good idea to borrow more money to repay your existing debts as this can make things worse and cost more in the long run. Many creditors ask for the new loan to be secured against your home. This means you could lose your home if you do not keep up the payments.

However, if you can afford the repayments, have stable finances and are good at controlling your spending, this could be an option for you.

If you are thinking of borrowing to pay off your debts:

- make sure you have enough money left in your budget to afford the repayments
- check you can afford the repayments for the whole life of the loan
- shop around for the best deals
- do not borrow more than you need
- if you get a consolidation loan to pay off your credit card loan, make sure you close the credit card account and do not use your card any more.

If you do take out a consolidation loan, be careful you do not end up with more debt than you started with.

Always get advice from an independent financial adviser before signing a new loan agreement. Make sure that the financial adviser is regulated by the Financial Services Authority (FSA). You can check this by looking on the FSA website (www.moneymadeclear.fsa.gov.uk).

Asking to write off your debt

In exceptional circumstances, your creditors may agree to write off your debt or stop action altogether. This is most likely to happen if you have a low income and your situation is particularly difficult and unlikely to get better – for example, if you have long-term serious health problems or are elderly.

You will usually need to show proof of your situation, such as medical evidence, before creditors will agree. If creditors do agree, ask them to put this in writing.

Bankruptcy

If you have no money left over in your budget, or you have so little that it will take many years for you to repay your debts, you may want to look at bankruptcy as an option. Going bankrupt can take the pressure of creditors away from you. You are allowed to keep certain things, like household goods and a reasonable amount to live on. When the bankruptcy order is over, you can make a fresh start and the money you owe is usually written off. In many cases, this can be after only one year. Creditors have to stop most types of court action to get their money back following a bankruptcy order (but in some cases the bailiffs may still be able to take your belongings away).

However, there are disadvantages to going bankrupt. For example:

- it will cost you money to go bankrupt
- if you own your own home, it will usually have to be sold
- some of your possessions might have to be sold – for example, you will usually lose your car and any luxury items you own
- if you own a business, it is more than likely that your business will be closed down and your employees sacked
- you cannot keep your bankruptcy private. A list of bankrupt people is published on the internet and your case could also be published in your local newspaper
- even when you are no longer bankrupt, you could have another order, called a *bankruptcy restrictions order,* made against you. These orders can be made if, for example, you took on debts knowing that you had no hope of paying them back. A bankruptcy restrictions order can last for 15 years and will make your financial affairs very restricted
- even when you are no longer bankrupt, there are some debts such as court fines and student loans that will never be written off.

Negotiating with creditors

You are allowed to negotiate with your creditors and most creditors will consider any reasonable request or offer of repayment that you make. Sometimes, you need to contact creditors several times before they will agree to what you are asking. What you ask your creditors for will depend on:

- what debts you have
- whether you have money left over to offer
- whether you have belongings worth selling to pay some or all of the debt off
- whether or not your situation is likely to get better.

It is important that creditors can see that what you are asking for is reasonable in the circumstances. So make sure you:

- are clear about what you are asking for
- always ask to freeze interest. Unless they freeze interest, your debt will carry on growing even if you are making regular payments
- tell them what the regular payment interval you are able to offer is – that is, whether you can pay monthly or weekly
- explain your situation fully. If you have priority debts, explain to non-priority creditors that you have to pay off priority debts first and say what you are offering to each of your priority creditors
- show evidence to support your request or offer of payment – for example, medical evidence if you cannot pay your debts because of illness
- mention any changes that you know are going to happen and which will affect your ability to pay or the amount you are offering.

Be prepared to contact your creditors more than once. Keep copies of all your letters to creditors and their replies and a note of any phone calls with them, in case you need them later. Do not be tempted to offer more than you have if creditors are difficult. If you cannot get the creditors to agree after a few tries, get help from an adviser.

Even if you believe that you have sent all the information to your creditors that they need, you will sometimes find that creditors will not accept your offers at first. Creditors may try to find reasons to pressurize you into paying more than you can afford. Or one creditor may ask you to pay more than you are paying other creditors. If you find this is happening, you should get advice.

If you are not confident about negotiating with your creditors, or you are finding it difficult to negotiate with them, you should get advice.

If creditors do not reply to your offers, start paying them what you can afford anyway, and get advice.

If a creditor is using a debt collector to collect money, there is Office of Fair Trading (OFT) guidance that they must follow. If debt collectors do not follow this guidance – for example, if they are intimidating or pretend to have more legal powers than they really have – the OFT (www.oft.gov.uk) can take action against them. If you are being harassed by your creditors, get advice about what to do.

How debt affects your credit record

You need to be aware that some of the options to deal with your debts will affect your credit record. This will mean that it will be more difficult for you to get credit in the future, including a mortgage or even getting a new mobile phone contract.

This is because information about your financial situation is collected and stored on file by credit reference agencies. They give this information to lenders such as banks, building societies, finance houses and major retailers. The lender uses this information to help them decide whether or not to give you credit.

Information held by credit reference agencies includes:

- your credit agreements, including balances and payment histories
- failure to pay your mortgage
- whether you have had your home taken back (repossessed)
- county court money judgments (CCJs) and High Court judgments
- bankruptcy orders
- Individual Voluntary Arrangements (IVAs)
- previous credit searches
- administration orders.

You can check your credit file to make sure it is correct – see p. 619.

Further help

If you are having difficulties in dealing with debt problems, you should get specialist advice. Before seeing an adviser about debt, gather together all your financial papers. These should include:

- court papers and letters
- bills
- credit agreements
- your budget and your partner's budget.

If you have to wait for an appointment with an adviser, it may be useful to tell creditors that you have contacted an adviser for help. Most creditors welcome the involvement of a specialist adviser. They may be willing to hold off action so that an agreement can be reached.

Budget sheet

Use this budget sheet to help you sort out your debts. You can use it to list all the income and expenses for your household. When you've added up all the figures, you will see if you have any money left over to pay your debts.

You can show the budget sheet to the people you owe money to, to help you come to an arrangement to pay back what you owe.

Budget sheet

Name ....

Address ....

Number of people in my household ....

Income (weekly/monthly)

Wages/salary	£_____
Wages/salary (partner)	£_____
Benefits	£_____
Money from other people	£_____
Other	£_____
	£_____
Total income	£_____

Outgoings (weekly/monthly)

Mortgage/rent	£_____
Second mortgage/secured loan	£_____
Ground rent/service charges	£_____
Buildings/contents insurance	£_____
Life insurance/endowment	£_____
Council tax	£_____
Gas	£_____

Electricity	£	_____
Water	£	_____
Food/housekeeping	£	_____
Travel	£	_____
Telephone	£	_____
TV licence/rental	£	_____
Clothing/emergencies	£	_____
Prescriptions/health costs	£	_____
Other	£	_____
Total outgoings	£	_____

My total income is £ ....

My total outgoings are £ ....

This leaves me an available income of £ .... for my creditors.

Priority debts

Type of debt	Money owed	Payments negotiated to pay off debts (weekly/monthly)
Rent arrears	£ _____	£ _____
Mortgage/second mortgage arrears	£ _____	£ _____
Council tax arrears	£ _____	£ _____
Gas arrears	£ _____	£ _____
Electricity arrears	£ _____	£ _____
Fines	£ _____	£ _____
Maintenance arrears	£ _____	£ _____
Other	£ _____	£ _____
Total	£ _____	£ _____

Total payments to priority creditors are £ .... per month/week.
When I have made payments to my priority creditors, I have £ ....
for my non-priority creditors.

Non-priority debts

Debt (fill in name of creditor)	Money owed	Offer (weekly/ monthly)
Debt	£_____	£_____
Debt	£_____	£_____
Debt	£_____	£_____
Debt	£_____	£_____
Debt	£_____	£_____
Debt	£_____	£_____
Total	£_____	£_____

This is a true record of my financial situation on .... (date)

Signed ....

Sample debt letters

You should amend these letters to suit your individual circumstances.

Holding letter
Send this letter to creditors if you aren't able to make an offer immediately.

[Name of creditor
Address/postcode
Date]

Dear Sir/Madam
Re: Account No. ....

I regret that I am unable to maintain my current monthly payments because .... [*explain your reasons*].

I am writing to all my creditors requesting details of the balance outstanding on my accounts and would be grateful if you would let me know how much I owe you. Once I have obtained this information, I will contact you again with a pro rata offer for repaying the above debt.

[*or*]

I have applied for .... benefit and will contact you again as soon as I start to receive it.

[*or*]

I have been sick/unemployed since .... and am due to start/return to work on [*date*] and will contact you again once I have started/returned to work. Meanwhile I request that you hold action on my account for two months and suspend interest and other charges to prevent my indebtedness from increasing.

Yours faithfully,

....

Offer letter to non-priority creditors
Send this letter to non-priority creditors when you have drawn up a financial statement and are able to make an offer.

[Name of creditor
Address/postcode
Date]

Dear Sir/Madam
Re: Account No. ....

Further to my letter dated [*date*], I am now able to make an offer to repay the above debt. [*or*]

I regret that I am unable to maintain my monthly payments at their current level because .... [*explain your reasons*].

I am enclosing a copy of my financial statement, which gives details of my income and expenses and makes pro rata offers to all my creditors. You will see from this information that I am able to offer you £ .... per month. I propose to make my first payment on .... I trust you will accept my offer as realistic given my circumstances and agree to suspend interest and other charges on my account provided regular payments are made. I shall of course keep you informed of any changes in my circumstances.

I thank you for your co-operation and look forward to hearing from you.

Yours faithfully,

....

No offer letter

[Name of creditor
Address/postcode
Date]

Dear Sir/Madam
Re: Account No. ....

I regret that I am unable to pay my current monthly payments because .... [*explain your reasons*].

I am enclosing a copy of my financial statement, which gives details of my income and expenses. You will see from this information that I am unable to make you an offer of payment at this time as I am on a low income/dependent on Income Support/Jobseeker's Allowance/Working Tax Credit/Pension Credit, which is a subsistence benefit only intended to cover my/my family's basic needs.

I request that you hold action on my account for six months and suspend interest to prevent my debt from increasing.

I am making every effort to increase my income/find work, and will contact you again as soon as my financial circumstances improve.

I thank you for your co-operation and look forward to hearing from you.

Yours faithfully,

....

Free advice agencies

Citizens Advice Bureaux are able to deal with money advice and debt problems. If it is a very complicated case, they will usually be able to refer you to a money advice specialist. This may be a solicitor or insolvency practitioner. You can find your local Citizens Advice Bureau in the telephone directory or by going online (www.adviceguide.org.uk). Help is also available through **Money Advice Centres** or **Law Centres**. The addresses and telephone numbers of Money Advice Centres and Law Centres can be found in the telephone directory.

The **National Debt Line** (0808 808 4000; www.nationaldebtline.co.uk) can give free information. It also provides an information pack on dealing with debt.

Business Debtline (0800 197 6026; www.bdl.org.uk) is a dedicated advice service for small businesses.

Advice UK (020 7407 4070; www.adviceuk.org.uk) is a large network of advice-providing organizations.

BAILIFFS AND DEBT

Bailiffs recover money that people owe the bailiff's clients. In most cases the person who is owed money has to get a court order before being able to instruct a bailiff to recover a debt from you. Bailiffs will ask for a secure method of payment – cash, or debit or credit card. If a bailiff visits your home, you will also have to pay a fee, which is set at different rates depending on the type of debt owed and the court that has authorized the bailiff to recover the debt from you. If you cannot repay the debt, they may be able to take your belongings and sell them at auction to pay off your debt.

In many cases, you do not have to let the bailiffs in and they are not allowed to force their way into your property. However, they are allowed into your property without your permission if they can enter without breaking in. This is called *gaining peaceful entry* and includes getting in through an unlocked door or open window.

Sometimes, bailiffs *are* allowed to break in to your property. For example, if you have got unpaid criminal fines, bailiffs working for the magistrates' court can, in some circumstances, use reasonable force to get into your home to seize goods. Also, in some circumstances, bailiffs can, with the court's permission, force their way into commercial property if there is no living accommodation attached.

However, it is unlikely that a bailiff would be allowed to break into your property in other circumstances. If this happens, you should get urgent legal advice.

The law on bailiffs is very complicated and the rules depend on the type of debt you owe and who it is owed to. If you are having problems paying a fine or other debt, it is always important to try to negotiate and to get specialist advice. At most stages of the debt recovery process there are opportunities to sort the problem out before a court or bailiff gets involved.

BANKS AND BUILDING SOCIETIES

When you open an account, the law says that, like other service providers, the bank or building society must carry out its business:

- with reasonable care and skill. This means, for example, that the bank or building society must act responsibly and keep accurate records of your finances
- in a reasonable time, unless a specific time has been agreed – what is reasonable would depend on the service the bank was carrying out (for example, it should give a decision on a loan within a couple of days)
- at a reasonable cost, unless a definite price has been agreed.

Some of the bank's or building society's services, such as loans and overdrafts, are covered by the Consumer Credit Act 1974. When you use any of the bank's or building society's services, you will be entering into a contract.

General tips

- You don't have to be given an account or a loan. The bank or building society will want proof of your identity, including your full name, date of birth and address before giving you one. However, you cannot be refused a loan on account of your race, sex, sexuality, religion or disability.
- Your bank or building society can transfer money without your permission from your personal account into your joint account to cover a debt in the joint account but cannot transfer money from your joint account to your individual account without the permission of all the joint account holders (unless the terms and conditions of your contract with the bank say that this can happen).

- Even if your account is overdrawn, you can choose how any further money you pay into the account is used (for example, to pay your mortgage or rent). This is called *first right of appropriation*. You will need to write to the bank or building society to tell them this before the money is paid in. You'll have to write to them with new instructions each time you make a deposit.

The Banking Code

The Banking Code sets out minimum standards of service for banks, building societies and credit card companies providing personal banking services to their customers. A bank, building society or credit card company does not have to sign up to the Code, but if it does, it must follow the Code's standards of service.

A bank, building society or credit card company which has signed up to the Banking Code must act fairly and reasonably in all its dealings with customers. This includes how it should deal with a customer in financial difficulties. If it breaches the Code, you can complain using the bank or building societies' own complaints procedure, and if you are still not satisfied, you can complain to the Financial Services Ombudsman (FOS) – see below.

Your rights if the service is unsatisfactory

You may be entitled to compensation if:

- the contract has been broken (breach of contract), for example if the bank or building society fails to honour a cheque or pay a standing order or direct debit when you have sufficient money in your account to cover it; *or*
- the bank or building society has been negligent in the way it has handled your account. As it is very difficult to prove negligence, you may find it easier to claim breach of contract – for example, that it has not handled your affairs with reasonable care and skill.

You will have to show that you have suffered a loss before you can claim compensation and the amount you can claim will usually be limited to the amount you have actually lost.

Bank charges

Banks and building societies are allowed to charge for their services. These charges must be set out in the bank's or building society's terms and conditions.

Bank charges can include *default charges*. These are charges for things such as going over your agreed overdraft limit. However, the bank or building society is only allowed to charge you what it costs to cover their administrative charges. If they charge you more than this, you may have a legal right to get back the difference. If you think you have paid a default charge which is unreasonably high, you should ask the bank or building society to refund it. You can find out more about how to do this from the website of Which? at www.which.net/campaigns.

How to solve your problem

Once you have decided what your rights are, you will need to contact the bank or building society as quickly as possible. The following steps should solve your problem:

- check that the problem has been caused by the bank or building society – for example, the bank or building society will not be responsible if you give someone else your bank card and pin number and they use these to withdraw money without your consent
- collect all your documents together, including your contract, bank statements and cheque stubs
- contact the bank or building society as soon as you discover the problem. If you visit, take a copy of all your documents and ask to speak to the person responsible for dealing with your account or the branch manager. Alternatively, write to the branch manager, enclosing copies of your documents, and keep a copy of your letter. Explain your problem calmly but firmly and request the action or compensation that you require
- if you are dissatisfied with the branch manager's response, you should ask for details of the bank's or building society's complaints procedure. Find out whether the bank or building society subscribes to the Banking Code of Practice. You can obtain a copy from your bank or building society or from the British Bankers' Association (BBA: 020 7216 8800; www.bba.org.uk). You should follow each stage of the complaints procedure by writing to the relevant manager, giving full details of your case, including any breaches of the Banking Code of Practice and stating what action you require. When you

have completed the internal complaints procedure, you will be sent a letter of deadlock if your complaint has not been settled

- if you cannot reach an agreement with the bank or building society, find out if it is a member of the Financial Ombudsman Service (FOS: 0845 080 1800; www.financialombudsman.org.uk). The Ombudsman can investigate the majority of banking complaints, but there are some exceptions such as when you are questioning the bank's commercial judgement. You must have followed your bank's or building society's complaints procedure, and have made your complaint to the Ombudsman within six months of receiving its final decision. You cannot use an ombudsman scheme after taking court action
- if the Ombudsman cannot resolve your complaint, your only other option is to consider going to court. It is extremely rare for a bank or building society to be sued. If you are thinking about doing this, you should see a solicitor.

The Financial Ombudsman Service (FOS)

Your complaint must be brought to the Ombudsman within six months of the deadlock letter. The Ombudsman will try to deal with your complaint informally, but if this fails, the Ombudsman will make a preliminary decision. You and the bank or building society can make comments on the decision, which the Ombudsman will consider before making a recommendation or a ruling. The bank or building society must comply with the ruling, but if you are not satisfied, you can take court action. However, if you do so, the court would take the Ombudsman's ruling into account when deciding your case.

Changing to another bank or building society

If your bank or building society subscribes to the Banking Code, it must co-operate with your new bank or building society to help the transfer of your account to take place as smoothly as possible. It must give information about regular payments from your account within three working days. You should not have to pay bank charges incurred as a result of mistakes or delays in the transfer process.

3
Benefits

CONTENTS

INTRODUCTION

It's over 65 years since the British Government asked Sir William Beveridge to write a report on the best ways of helping people on low incomes. His report suggested weekly contributions paid by all people of working age that would help fund the payment of benefits to people who were sick, unemployed, retired or widowed. The system would provide a minimum standard of living 'below which no one should be allowed to fall'. 'Social provision against rainy days' is how the 1945 Labour manifesto put it and, soon after the election victory, that government began the process of implementing the proposals that provided the basis of our modern welfare state.

The benefits and tax credits system that we know today is larger, more all-encompassing and far more complex than Beveridge could ever have envisaged, but one fact remains the same. The number of people entitled to benefits but not claiming them is very high and this is particularly true of people over 75. It may be the stigma of claiming for a generation brought up to 'make do or mend', or long, complicated forms and a confusing claims process, but not claiming can mean scraping by on an unnecessarily low income, struggling to afford the basics.

This chapter looks at the basic benefits and tax credits, what you may be entitled to, how to claim and how to appeal if you think the powers that be have got it wrong.

BENEFITS AND TAX CREDITS

Benefits and tax credits are payments you can get if you:

- are on a low income for the number and ages of people in your family. Your income can be compared to figures set by the Department for Work and Pensions (DWP) to see if you are entitled to any financial help. This is called means-testing. *Or*
- have certain costs to meet because of your situation. Your income may not affect your right to get some payments.

The DWP pays most benefits. However, the local authority where you live helps with council tax and rent (Council Tax Benefit and Housing Benefit). HM Revenue and Customs administers Working Tax Credit and Child Tax Credit. You have to meet a set of conditions for each benefit or tax credit that you want to claim. In order to get the payment, you must meet these conditions and usually have to make an application and provide all the necessary information.

You may be entitled to more than one benefit or tax credit – for example, a combination of means-tested payments and payments for extra costs because of your situation. However, some benefits cannot be paid together.

Benefits and tax credits are usually paid directly into your bank or building society account. However, some benefits can be paid by cheque payable at a post office if you do not have, or would find it difficult to manage, an account.

If you have dependent children

If you have a child under 16, you are entitled to *Child Benefit*. Child Benefit is also payable for some other young people, usually under the age of 20 if they are still in full-time education up to A-level or equivalent or on certain approved training courses, or if they have been accepted on such a course. Child Benefit does not depend on having paid any National Insurance contributions or on your income. However, Child Benefit may be restricted if you come from outside the UK and you or the child sometimes live abroad. If you get Child Benefit for a child born after September 2002, they will also qualify for a Child Trust Fund account. This is a savings account to which the state makes a contribution (you can find out more at www.childtrustfund.gov.uk). You may also be entitled to *Guardian's Allowance* if you get Child Benefit for a child whose parents are dead or if one parent is dead and the other is unable to take care of the child.

If you are responsible for a child under 16, you may also be entitled to *Child Tax Credit*. Child Tax Credit is also payable if the young person is still in full-time education up to A-level or equivalent, or if they have been accepted on such a course. Child Tax Credit depends on your income but not on National Insurance contributions. You can get extra amounts for a child with a disability.

If you are on a low income

If you are on a low income, your savings are below a set limit, and you are working fewer than 16 hours a week or not working, you may be able to get either *Income Support* or *income-based Jobseeker's Allowance*. If you can look for work, you should usually claim Jobseeker's Allowance. You will only be able to claim Income Support if you are a person who does not have to be available for work according to rules for getting benefit – if you are a lone parent with dependent children, you are sick or disabled or you are caring for a disabled person. If you are in this situation you may be entitled to Income Support.

If you are on a low income, are not working (or working fewer than 16 hours a week), and are not entitled to Income Support, you may be able to get *income-based Jobseeker's Allowance* (if you are looking for work) or *Pension Credit* if you are 60 or over.

If your income is not low enough, or your savings are too high, but you have been paying National Insurance contributions in the last two years and are now looking for work, you may be entitled to *contribution-based Jobseeker's Allowance* for a limited period instead.

You may be able to choose between claiming Income Support and income-based Jobseeker's Allowance if you are under 60 and are able to look for work, but do not have to be available for work under the rules for getting benefit.

If you are working 16 hours a week or more

If you or your partner works 16 hours or more a week, you may be entitled to *Working Tax Credit*, or *Pension Credit* if you are 60 or over.

Help with rent

If you are on a low income and have savings below a set limit (whether or not you are working) and are paying rent on your home, you may be entitled to *Housing Benefit*. Housing Benefit may help pay all or part of your rent.

Help with council tax

If you are on a low income and have savings below a set limit (whether or not you are working) and are liable for council tax on your home, you may be entitled to *Council Tax Benefit*, which may help pay all or part of your council tax. If you live with someone else who does not pay council tax and you are on a low income, you may be entitled to second adult rebate as well. You may also be able to reduce your council tax bill if you are eligible for reductions or discounts.

If you are sick or disabled

If you are unable to work or look for work because of sickness or disability

If you are unable to work because you are sick or disabled, you may be entitled to *Statutory Sick Pay* (paid by your employer) if you usually work as an employee, earn more than a certain amount and have not been sick for more than 28 weeks. If you do not meet these conditions, you may get *Incapacity Benefit* instead. Depending on your circumstances, you may have to meet National Insurance contribution conditions to get Incapacity Benefit. If you are not working, and you are not entitled to Incapacity Benefit, but you are on a low income, you may be entitled to *Income Support* or *Pension Credit*. You can also get Income Support to top up Statutory Sick Pay or Incapacity Benefit. You should claim it at the same time. Whether or not you can claim any of these benefits, you may also be entitled to benefits for your care needs or mobility problems.

If you are disabled and work 16 hours or more a week

If you are disabled and work 16 hours or more a week, you may be entitled to *Working Tax Credit* with an extra amount for your disability. This may apply to anyone who is or has been getting a benefit for sickness and disability.

Other help for sick or disabled people

If you are disabled you may also be able to get *Income Support* or *Pension Credit*. You may be able to get *Housing Benefit* or *Council Tax Benefit* as well. The means-testing for these benefits is more generous for disabled people. This means that you are entitled to a higher combined income of benefits and other money.

If you have care needs or mobility problems

If you have care needs or mobility problems and you are under 65, you may be entitled to *Disability Living Allowance* (DLA). You do not have to be getting help with your care to get DLA. You may get DLA because you cannot prepare a cooked main meal by yourself, or because you need attention for some or all of the time in connection with your bodily functions, or you need supervision to avoid danger to yourself or others. You may get DLA for mobility problems if you have difficulty walking, you cannot walk, or you need guidance and supervision to walk out of doors. You can get DLA whether or not you work.

If you have care needs and you are 65 or over, you may be entitled to *Attendance Allowance.* You cannot get Attendance Allowance for difficulties with mobility, but you can get it if you need attention in connection with your bodily functions, or supervision to avoid danger, throughout the day or for significant periods during the night. You can get Attendance Allowance whether or not you work.

If you are caring for a disabled person

If you care for someone for at least 35 hours a week who has care or mobility problems and is entitled to Disability Living Allowance or Attendance Allowance, you may be entitled to *Carer's Allowance.* To get this you must not be earning more than a set amount. You should be aware that if you get Carer's Allowance, it can affect the amount of any Income Support, Pension Credit, Housing Benefit or Council Tax Benefit the person you care for gets.

If you are 60 or over

If you are a woman aged 60 or over, or a man aged 65 or over, you may be entitled to a *State Retirement Pension,* depending on your National Insurance contribution record and your married or civil partner's contribution record. If you are getting State Retirement Pension, *Income Support* or *Pension Credit* you are also entitled to a one-off payment just before Christmas (the *Christmas bonus*). If you are aged 60 or over, you are also entitled to a *Winter Fuel Payment,* which is a one-off annual payment intended to help with fuel costs. It does not matter how you use the money. Winter Fuel Payments do not depend on how cold the weather gets. There are other payments called Cold Weather Payments which are only paid when the weather reaches a certain temperature.

If you are 60 or over, you may also be able to get Pension Credit and *Housing Benefit* or *Council Tax Benefit.* The means-testing for Housing Benefit and Council Tax Benefit is more generous for people of pension age. You are entitled to a higher combined income of benefits and other money, and your savings can be higher before they affect these benefits.

> ### My neighbour has just come out of hospital. He's retired and seems to be finding it difficult to cope. Is there any help available for him?
>
> Depending on how long your neighbour has been ill and the type of help he needs, he may be able to claim Disability Living Allowance if he is under 65, or Attendance Allowance if he is aged 65 or over. Neither of these benefits is means-tested so any capital he has will not be taken into account if he makes a claim. Your neighbour may also be eligible to claim Pension Credit. Pension Credit is a means-tested benefit, so capital such as savings is taken into account in the assessment. If he pays rent for his accommodation, he can claim Housing Benefit and Council Tax Benefit. Your local social services department can make an assessment of your neighbour's needs. It may be able to arrange help in a number of ways – for example, having rails or lifting equipment fitted to the bathroom, or having someone come to visit on a regular basis.
>
> Your neighbour may also be entitled to help with health costs and visits to hospital.

If you were injured at work or have an industrial disease

If you were injured at work or contracted a disease due to your working conditions, you may be entitled to *Industrial Injuries Benefit*. You must have been working as an employed earner (not have been self-employed). Only certain diseases in certain types of work qualify as industrial diseases, and you must show that you are disabled as a result of the accident or disease.

If you are pregnant or have recently had a baby

If you are pregnant or have recently had a baby, are off work and usually work as an employee earning more than a certain amount, you may be entitled to *Statutory Maternity Pay*, paid by your employer. If you are not entitled to Statutory Maternity Pay – because, for example, you are self-employed or gave up work before you became pregnant – but you were earning more than a certain amount, you may be entitled to *Maternity Allowance*. If you get Statutory Maternity Pay or Maternity Allowance, you may also be entitled to Income Support. If you usually work 16 hours or more each week, you may be entitled to *Working Tax Credit*.

If you are not earning enough to qualify for Statutory Maternity Pay or Maternity Allowance, you may be entitled to *Incapacity Benefit* and/or *Income Support*. (This is because you are treated as incapable of work for the period around the birth, and any other day when working would mean a serious risk to your or your baby's health.) You may also be entitled to a one-off *Maternity Grant* if you or your partner are receiving certain means-tested benefits or tax credits at the time of the claim. If you are responsible for a child, you may be entitled to *Child Tax Credit* and you can get an extra amount if you have a child under the age of one.

I've recently had a baby and have heard that the Government has set up trust funds for children. What are they, and how do I claim?

The Child Trust Fund is a savings and investment account for children. The Government makes payments to children through this account and your family and friends will also be able to contribute. When your child is 18, they will have access to the account and will be able to spend the money however they like. If you are currently getting Child Benefit, your child will be eligible for a Child Trust Fund account (CTF).

The Government makes an initial payment of at least £250, followed by another payment on your child's seventh birthday. You do not have to claim or register for the scheme as payments are made automatically.

For more information on Child Trust Funds, call the CTF helpline (0845 302 1470) or go to their website (www.childtrustfund.gov.uk).

If your husband, wife or civil partner dies

If your husband, wife or civil partner dies, you may be able to claim a *Bereavement Payment*, *Widowed Parent's Allowance* or *Bereavement Allowance*, depending on your partner's National Insurance contributions, their age, and whether you have dependent children. If your partner died of an industrial injury or disease, the National Insurance contributions may be waived.

If you have one-off expenses that you cannot afford

If you have one-off essential expenses that you cannot afford, you may be entitled to help from the *Social Fund*. You can get *Budgeting Loans*, *Crisis Loans*, *Community Care Grants*, *funeral payments*, *Cold Weather Payments* and *Maternity Grants* from the Social Fund. If you get a loan, you have to pay it back. You can usually only get help if you are on certain means-tested benefits or tax credits. However, Crisis Loans, which can help with expenses in an emergency or disaster, do not depend on you being on any benefit, as long as you do not have enough resources from anywhere else. You may be able to get a Budgeting Loan for help with essential items such as furniture if you are on income-based Jobseeker's Allowance, Income Support or Pension Credit.

You may be able to get a Community Care Grant if you are on Income Support, income-based Jobseeker's Allowance or Pension Credit and are leaving institutional or residential care, and need help to establish yourself in the community. You may also be able to get a grant if it will help you avoid being taken into care. Community Care Grants can also be paid to help families under exceptional pressure, to help care for prisoners or young offenders who are temporarily released, and to help people who have been homeless and are setting up home. You can get a funeral payment to help with the cost of a funeral if you get Income Support, income-based Jobseeker's Allowance, Housing Benefit, Council Tax Benefit or Pension Credit. You may get a payment if you are on Working Tax Credit or Child Tax Credit. You will only get a funeral payment if it is reasonable for you to take responsibility for the funeral and there is no one else who can pay.

In cold weather, if you are on Income Support, income-based Jobseeker's Allowance or Pension Credit, you may be entitled to automatic Cold Weather Payments if the temperature drops below a certain level.

If you have expenses or costs for school-age children

If you are on Income Support, income-based Jobseeker's Allowance or Pension Credit, or you are otherwise on a low income, you may be entitled to help with health expenses such as dental treatment and travel costs to hospital. In England, you could also get help with the cost of prescriptions (in Wales, prescriptions are free). You may also be entitled to help with legal costs. If you are getting Income Support, income-based Jobseeker's Allowance or Pension Credit, you are entitled to free school meals for your children if they are under 19. You may also get help with the costs of school clothing, or payments to help children who are 16 and over to continue their education.

How to claim

There are different ways to make a claim for benefits. Sometimes you have to fill in a claim form, or you may be able to claim by phone or online. The government website (www.direct.gov.uk) has a lot of useful information about claiming benefits. If you want more information or help to fill in a claim form, you may want to speak to an experienced adviser – for example, at a Citizens Advice Bureau.

Appealing against a benefits decision

Appealing against a benefit decision that you think is wrong can be complicated. If you wish to ask for a decision to be reconsidered, or if you wish to appeal, you should consult an experienced adviser – for example, at a CAB.

WORKING TAX CREDIT AND CHILD TAX CREDIT

Working Tax Credit (WTC) and Child Tax Credit (CTC) are benefits that are administered by HM Revenue and Customs (HMRC). Tax credits are awarded for a complete tax year. A tax year runs from 6 April to 5 April the following year. If you claim after 6 April, your award will run from the date you claim to the end of the tax year.

CTC is available to people responsible for a child or young person and who have income below a certain amount. All households with an annual income of £50,000 or less will qualify for some CTC. The amount you get will depend on how many children you have, and whether they have any disabilities. CTC is available whether or not you are in work and is paid to the main carer in a household, usually straight into a nominated bank account.

WTC is a payment to top up earnings of people working on low incomes, including those who do not have children. Extra amounts are payable if you have a disability, if you work 30 hours or more a week, and if you have childcare costs. WTC is paid directly into a nominated bank account.

If you are a member of a couple who live together, you must make a joint claim. You claim both tax credits on the same form. Claims can only be backdated three months, so you should claim as soon as you can.

Renewing a claim

At the end of each tax year, HMRC will look at your circumstances again. They will then send you a notice asking you to give them certain information. This is so that your award for the previous tax year can be finalized and your award for this tax year can be calculated. In the meantime, you will carry on getting money at the same rate.

The deadline for responding may be different each year, so make sure you check the date when you get the notice from HMRC and make sure you send back the information they require.

If you do not supply the information asked for, your payments will stop and you may be asked to pay back earlier payments.

I am on Income Support and would like to go back to work. The job I am considering is not that well paid and I am worried I will be worse off if I give up my benefits. Is there any help for me?

If you work for 16 or more hours a week, you may be able to claim Working Tax Credit (WTC) to top up your earnings. If you have children, you may be able to get Child Tax Credit (CTC).

Depending on how much you earn, you might still be able to claim Housing Benefit and Council Tax Benefit with your WTC or CTC, although the tax credits will be taken into account as income when the amount of your Housing Benefit and Council Tax Benefit are worked out. If you stop working during that period, or work fewer than 16 hours each week, you may be able to get Jobseeker's Allowance or Income Support to top up your income.

Appealing against a tax credit decision

If you think you have been wrongly refused Working Tax Credit or Child Tax Credit, or you think the amount you have been awarded is wrong, you can ask HM Revenue and Customs (HMRC) to explain their decision. If you are not satisfied with their reply, you can ask for the decision to be looked at again. You must do this within 30 days of receiving a decision from HMRC.

If your claim is reconsidered and you are still not satisfied, you can appeal to an independent unified appeal tribunal. Appealing against a decision can be complicated and time limits apply. If you want to appeal, you should consult an experienced adviser immediately.

Overpayments

HM Revenue and Customs (HMRC) might decide that they have paid you too much money and ask you to pay it back. This could be, for example, because you took too long to tell them about a change in your income or personal circumstances.

If you do not agree you have been overpaid, ask the Tax Credits Helpline to explain the overpayment. Keep a record of your telephone call, including the date and time of the call. If there is not an obvious explanation for the overpayment, the query should be referred to the Overpayments Dispute Team. The Team should give you an explanation of the overpayment in writing. If you do not agree with the explanation, you can fill in form TC846 and ask HMRC to reconsider whether they have overpaid you. You can get the form from HMRC's website (www.hmrc.gov.uk) or from the Helpline.

You can ask for the decision to be reconsidered a second time, but this will be final. You do not have the right to appeal against an overpayment decision. You may be able to take legal action, but you'll need to get expert advice first and act quickly because strict time limits apply.

You can ask HMRC for more time to pay back an overpayment. You can call them on 0845 302 1429 and ask either to pay back the money in instalments, or to wait a while before they start to collect the overpayment.

In exceptional circumstances, HMRC can write off all or part of an overpayment if it would cause you or your family hardship to pay it back.

Who can help?

HM Revenue and Customs Tax Credits Helpline (0845 300 3900; textphone 0845 300 3909; www.hmrc.gov.uk).

PENSION CREDIT

Pension Credit is a means-tested benefit for people aged 60 or over. It has two parts – a guarantee credit and a savings credit. Guarantee credit tops up your weekly income to a guaranteed level and savings credit is for people who have a small amount of income or savings. You may be able to claim either part of the Pension Credit separately or both together, depending on your circumstances.

You can claim Pension Credit whether or not you are working and do not need to have paid National Insurance contributions to get the benefit. Arrangements for claiming and paying pension credit are made by the Pension Service. The Pension Service does not have its own offices for people to visit, but you can contact them by telephone, through their locally based services, or through other organizations such as your local Jobcentre Plus office.

Who can help?

Pension Service (helpline: 0845 60 60 265; textphone 0845 60 60 285; www.thepensionservice.gov.uk).

FRAUD

To find out whether you are entitled to a benefit, the DWP can carry out certain checks to make sure that the information you have given on the claim form or during an interview is correct. One of the ways in which the DWP can make these checks is to compare what you have said or written on the claim form with records about you held by another government agency. This means that the DWP could ask HM Revenue and Customs (HMRC) if its records show that you are paying tax, in order to check whether you are working.

Local authorities, who administer Housing Benefit and Council Tax

Benefit, can also carry out checks on these benefit claims. HMRC can carry out checks on tax credit claims.

Checks on a claim can be made at any time, not just when you first make the claim. Sometimes checks will be made on everyone receiving a certain benefit or on certain groups, such as lone parents.

Authorized fraud officers can request information about you and members of your family from a range of private and public organizations including:

- banks, building societies and credit providers, including credit card companies, money transmission companies
- insurance companies
- credit reference agencies
- education providers
- water, gas and electricity providers
- telecoms companies, including mobile phone companies
- the Student Loans Company
- overseas authorities.

If you are dishonest in some way with the DWP, HMRC or local authority, you may be committing fraud – for example if you did not tell them about a change in your circumstances that affected your entitlement to a benefit. Even if you are not committing fraud, failure to report a fact or change of circumstances could result in an overpayment of benefit, which you may have to repay.

If the DWP, HMRC or the local authority suspects you of claiming benefit or tax credit fraudulently, it will carry out an investigation into your circumstances. Benefit fraud is a criminal offence. If the DWP, HMRC or the local authority has evidence that you are committing fraud, you can be prosecuted or be asked to pay a penalty as an alternative to prosecution.

MAKING A COMPLAINT

Everybody has the right to expect a reasonable standard of service from a public sector agency. This includes people who claim benefit, tax credits and Pension Credit or who make National Insurance enquiries or have a child support maintenance assessment. If you have received poor service or have been disadvantaged because of errors or a slow response, you should consider complaining.

You can complain whether or not you have claimed a benefit or tax credit. However, a complaint is not a way of challenging a decision. If you think that a decision is wrong, you should ask for it to be reconsidered or appeal. You can make a complaint as well as asking for a decision to be reconsidered or appealing.

Types of complaint

Poor service

You should consider complaining about poor service if you have experienced any of the following:

- rudeness
- unwillingness to treat you as somebody with rights
- refusal to answer reasonable requests
- not being informed on request of your rights or entitlements
- advice that is misleading or inadequate
- bias or partiality, for example because of race, sex, sexuality, religion or disability. You should make a complaint if you think there has been discrimination on these grounds, which is against the law
- not being told about your right to dispute a decision and/or to appeal.

Delay

You should consider complaining if you have had to wait too long for a claim to be decided, or for an explanation to be given. Offices that administer benefits or tax credits usually have target times for deciding a claim. These may be on display in the local office, or you can ask to see them.

Inefficiency

You should consider complaining if there has been inefficiency – for example, if the office administering benefit or tax credit loses case papers or stops payment by mistake.

Inadequate information

If you are not satisfied with advice or information you have been given by a government office, you should consider complaining. For example, you may not have been told about a benefit you could have applied for, or you may have been given incorrect information about your National Insurance record.

Difficulty in contacting the office

You should consider complaining if it has been very difficult to contact the office concerned, or they have not responded to letters or telephone calls.

Over- and underpayments

If there has been an over- or underpayment of benefit, you should consider complaining. Even if you are repaid the correct balance of an underpayment, you may have been disadvantaged by not receiving the correct money for a period of time. Overpayments that have to be repaid can also cause unexpected distress.

Interpretation facilities

If your first language is not English, and the office does not provide adequate interpretation facilities, you should consider complaining. You have a right to help with claim forms, letters and understanding your entitlement if you do not speak English as a first language.

Outcomes of making a complaint

Following a complaint, you may achieve, for example:

- an apology for what has happened
- an explanation of how the problem occurred
- an assurance that the problem will be put right, if this is possible
- a change in procedure
- financial compensation, in certain circumstances.

Compensation

In certain circumstances – for example, excessive delay, wrong advice or financial loss – you may be able to obtain compensation. However, these payments are discretionary, so there is no enforceable right to compensation.

Where to make a complaint

You should complain to the office that administered your benefit or tax credit or dealt with your Pension Credit, National Insurance record or child support assessment. Most organizations have their own internal complaints procedure, which should be available on request. There will usually be a customer service manager or equivalent who acts as a point of contact for complaints. There will then be further formal stages for dealing with the complaint.

You should make your complaint about:

- Housing Benefit and Council Tax Benefit to your local authority
- benefits and Social Fund payments to the DWP
- Pension Credit to the Pension Service
- child support issues to the Child Support Agency
- treatment at the Jobcentre Plus office to the Jobcentre Plus office
- National Insurance contributions to HM Revenue and Customs National Insurance Contributions Office
- tax credits to HM Revenue and Customs Tax Credit Office.

You may be able to complain informally by talking to a manager at the relevant local office. If this does not resolve the problem, it may be necessary to put the complaint in writing. The complaints procedure may be explained in a leaflet that will list the different stages of making a complaint and may contain a complaints form which you can fill in.

Taking the complaint further

You may find that an internal complaints procedure takes a long time and does not produce a satisfactory result. There are external, independent procedures for complaining about public services. You are usually expected to have tried any internal complaints procedure first.

Complaints about Housing Benefit and Council Tax Benefit can be investigated by the Local Government Ombudsman.

Complaints about other benefits and child support can be investigated by the Parliamentary Ombudsman. In many cases, you can complain to the Independent Case Examiner (0845 606 0777; www.ind-case-exam.org.uk).

Complaints about National Insurance and tax credits can be investigated by the Adjudicator's Office (020 7930 2292; www.adjudicatorsoffice.gov.uk).

For more information about using an ombudsman, see *Civil rights*, p. 481.

Using an MP or local councillor

You can contact your Member of Parliament for help at any stage in an external or internal complaints procedure. For complaints about Housing Benefit or Council Tax Benefit, a local councillor may also be able to help.

The MP or councillor may be able to get the complaint resolved more quickly and/or ensure that practices are changed so that the problem does not occur again.

NATIONAL INSURANCE

People in work have to pay National Insurance contributions if they have earnings over a certain amount of money. This amount is called the lower earnings limit. It changes every year, usually in April.

Anyone who pays National Insurance contributions builds up a contribution record. Whether or not you can claim certain benefits will depend on this contribution record.

There are four types of contributions. These are called 'classes'. Credits are contributions that are added to your contribution record either when you are unemployed or unable to work because of illness, or when you have a gap in contributions and apply for credits to fill the gap. The person who gets the credits does not have to pay for them.

Credits are also given to men aged 60–65 who are either getting benefits or who are not paying contributions out of earnings.

Credits do not cover all benefits, and problems with credits are usually quite complex and should be dealt with by an experienced adviser, such as a CAB.

How to get a National Insurance number

A National Insurance number (NINO) is used to identify your contribution and benefit record. The same NINO is used throughout your working life. The number consists of two letters, six numbers and one letter – for example, AB 123456 C.

Most young people whose parents receive child benefit for them are automatically sent a plastic card showing a NINO just before they reach the age of 16.

If you have lost your number – for example, because you haven't worked for some time or have forgotten it – you should ask your local Jobcentre Plus office for a record of your number. You will be issued with a new card.

If you do not have a number and you need one, you should telephone the National Employment NINO application number on 0845 600 0643 to arrange an interview (textphone: 0845 600 0644). You will have to go to an office for this interview. The interview will seek to establish your identity and you will need to prove who you are. You can do this by taking along documents such as a birth certificate, driving licence, identity cards or letters from the Home Office.

You will be asked questions about where you have lived and what jobs you have done. You will also be expected to provide evidence to prove you have a right to work in the UK.

If you do not have the right to work in the UK, you are not entitled to a NINO.

You will not be issued with a number until the office is satisfied that you have proved your identity.

If you are an asylum seeker, you can apply for a NINO in the usual way. If you have applied for asylum and your claim has been successful, a NINO will usually be allocated automatically.

I have two jobs. Should I be paying National Insurance contributions on both?

If you have more than one job with different employers you must pay Class 1 contributions on each employment where the earnings from that job are above a certain limit.

If you have more than one low-paid job, you may not be paying National Insurance contributions at all. This is because the earnings from each employment are treated separately, and if they are each below the limit, no National Insurance contributions are paid.

Paying late contributions

If you are an employee who has not paid contributions when you have had earnings above the lower earnings limit, you can be required to pay and may face a penalty or prosecution.

If you have an incomplete contribution record – for example, because you have been studying – you may wish to pay late voluntary contributions. There are a number of issues you will need to consider – for example, whether the late contributions would enable you to qualify for additional benefits.

660 |Benefits

Married women and widows

Until April 1977 some married women and widows could choose to pay reduced Class 1 contributions. Some women may still be paying the reduced-rate contribution. However, this means they cannot get contributory benefits and may get less pension when they retire. If you are in this situation, you can choose to start paying contributions at the full rate. Some women on low earnings who give up the reduced rate can be treated as paying full-rate contributions without paying anything. Get in touch with your local Jobcentre Plus office or HMRC (NI contributions) office to find out more.

Women employees aged 60 and men employees aged 65

As an employee, once you reach 60 (women) or 65 (men), you will not have to pay contributions. You should automatically receive a certificate of age exemption. This form must be given to your employer so that contributions are not paid. If you do not receive your certificate, you should contact your local Jobcentre Plus office.

Index